TRAINING & REFERENCE

murach's
CICS
for the COBOL
programmer

Raul Menendez

Doug Lowe

MIKE MURACH & ASSOCIATES, INC.

2560 West Shaw Lane, Suite 101 • Fresno, CA 93711-2765

Writers:	Anne Prince
	Raul Menendez
Editor:	Judy Taylor
Cover design:	Zylka Design
Production:	Tom Murach

Other books for COBOL programmers

The CICS Programmer's Desk Reference by Doug Lowe

Murach's Structured COBOL by Mike Murach, Anne Prince, and Raul Menendez

DB2 for the COBOL Programmer, Parts 1 & 2 by Curtis Garvin and Anne Prince

MVS JCL by Doug Lowe

MVS TSO, Parts 1 & 2 by Doug Lowe

Printed in the United States of America

10 9 8 7 6 5 4 3 2
ISBN: 1-890774-09-X

Library of Congress Cataloging-in-Publication Data

Menendez, Raul.
    Murach's CICS for the COBOL programmer / Raul Menendez, Doug Lowe.
        p. cm.
    Includes index.
    ISBN 1-890774-09-X
    1. COBOL (Computer program language) 2. CICS (Computer system) I. Lowe, Doug.
II. Title.

QA76.73.C25 M455 2001
005.2'22--dc21

2001030589

Contents

Expanded contents

Section 2 How to design, code, and test a CICS program

Section 3 Other CICS programming essentials

Section 4 A complete CICS application

Section 5 CICS for file and database processing

Introduction

CICS is the world-class transaction processor that's used on IBM mainframe computers. In fact, CICS systems are used to handle billions (yes, billions) of online transactions every day for banks, airlines, insurance companies, hospitals, e-business sites…even the Olympics. So when you withdraw money from an ATM, place an airline reservation, or order a product over the Internet, chances are that CICS has been used to process your transaction.

The vast majority of the CICS code for those applications is in the form of CICS commands that are embedded within COBOL programs, which is why this book is called "CICS for the COBOL Programmer." Today, there are close to a million CICS programmers, and they are among the highest paid programmers. These programmers not only maintain the billions of lines of CICS code that is currently in operation, but they also develop new CICS applications. In fact, CICS can now be used as the transaction processor for applications that have user interfaces written in languages like Java and Visual Basic or that run in a Web browser. In short, CICS programming is a valuable skill today, and CICS is going to continue to be the transaction processor for enterprise applications of the future.

The intent of this book is to teach people with COBOL experience how to become CICS programmers. By the time you complete the first four sections of this book, you'll have the skills of an entry-level CICS programmer in industry. And you'll add to those skills as you read the chapters in the last two sections of the book.

4 ways this book helps you learn faster and better

- If you're new to CICS, this book gets you started fast. In chapter 2, you'll learn how a complete CICS program works. And by the end of section 2 (just 6 chapters), you'll be able to design, code, and test CICS programs on your own.

- Once you complete the first two sections of the book, you can read most of the chapters in sections 3, 5, and 6 in whatever sequence you prefer. That's because the chapters in those sections are designed as independent modules. We refer to this as "modular organization," and it helps you get the training you need when you need it.

- 12 programs and dozens of coding segments illustrate the design and coding practices that are used in the best CICS shops. Whether you're a beginner or a professional, you'll boost your productivity by using these as models when you code your own programs.

- All of the information in this book is presented in "paired pages" with the essential syntax, guidelines, and coding examples on the right and the perspective and extra explanation on the left. This lets you learn faster by reading less…and it's an important feature of all our recent books.

What this book does

The overall goal of this book is to teach you how to develop CICS programs as quickly and easily as possible. To get you started right, chapter 1 presents the CICS concepts and terms you have to understand, and chapter 2 shows you how all the pieces of a CICS program work together. Then, chapter 3 shows you how to design a CICS program using pseudo-conversational design; chapter 4 shows you how to create the BMS mapset that defines the screens your program will display; chapter 5 teaches you the CICS commands you'll use in every program; and chapter 6 shows you how to test a CICS program.

At that point, you'll be able to develop CICS programs on your own, and you'll have a solid understanding of what you have to do to become a proficient CICS programmer. Then, the three chapters in section 3 present some additional CICS commands and techniques that you'll use regularly. And section 4 presents a complete CICS application that consists of four programs. Once you understand the design, BMS mapsets, and COBOL code for these programs, you'll have the skills of an entry-level CICS programmer in industry.

To complete your mastery of CICS, the chapters in the last two sections of this book present commands and skills that you can learn in whatever sequence you prefer. Specifically, the chapters in section 5 present the CICS commands and techniques you need for file and database processing. And the chapters in section 6 present advanced CICS features and skills. For instance, because maintenance programming is a reality in every CICS shop, chapter 22 presents the type of code that you may come across as you maintain older programs.

Of particular interest are chapters 20 and 21 in section 6 because they give you a view of where CICS is headed. In chapter 20, you'll learn how to design, code, and test CICS programs in which the "presentation logic" (all the functions related to sending data to and receiving data from the terminal) is separated from the "business logic" (the functions that process the data). This makes it possible for CICS to be used for the transaction processing on the mainframe while languages like Java or Visual Basic are used for the user interface. In chapter 21, you'll see that this approach can also be used for Web applications, making CICS a more flexible transaction processor for the enterprise applications of the future.

What the prerequisites for this book are

The only prerequisite for this book is that you know how to develop COBOL programs that process indexed files. If there's any doubt about that or if you have trouble following any of the COBOL code in this book, please get a copy of *Murach's Structured COBOL*. It's a fast-paced training course, an efficient COBOL reference, and the ideal companion for this CICS book.

A word about CICS versions

At this time, IBM supports four versions of CICS for the OS/390 environment: CICS Transaction Server 1.1, 1.2, and 1.3, and CICS MVS/ESA 4.1 (due to be discontinued December 31, 2002). For the VSE environment, IBM offers CICS VSE/ESA 1.1.1. IBM also just recently announced the availability of CICS Transaction Server 2.1, which runs under the z/OS operating system. Unless specifically noted, the CICS elements presented in this book will work for any of the current versions of CICS.

With each new CICS release, IBM adds new application programming features. However, these new features are usually minor and have little effect on the way you code your programs. Even in the last major overhaul of CICS (CICS Transaction Server), the application programming interface changed very little. So if you're using a version of CICS that comes out after this book is published, everything in this book should still work for you.

In fact, the most significant enhancement in recent versions of CICS lies in its Web interface capabilities. These capabilities were introduced in earlier versions of CICS, but they took a major step forward in terms of ease-of-use and stability in CICS TS 1.3. Although CICS Web programming is a book in itself, you'll get an introduction to what it involves in chapter 21.

Incidentally, we used Micro Focus Mainframe Express to develop the programs in this book. Mainframe Express, a product of the Merant company, lets you code and test CICS programs on a PC. After we compiled and tested the programs with Mainframe Express, we uploaded them to a mainframe and compiled and tested them using CICS TS 1.3 and CICS MVS/ESA 4.1. Using Mainframe Express is a highly-productive way to develop CICS programs, and we thank Merant for letting us experiment with it.

Downloadable model programs

As we mentioned earlier, the 12 programs used in this book can be time-saving models for your own programs. That's why we make them available to you as downloadable items from our web site. To download them, go to our web site at www.murach.com, click on the "Downloads button," and proceed from there. As you'll see, you can download the source programs, copy members, mapsets, and data as individual files or as a single Mainframe Express project.

Support materials for trainers and instructors

If you're a trainer or instructor who would like to use this book as the basis for a course, we offer an Instructor's Guide with a complete set of instructional materials for it on CD ROM. These include PowerPoint slides for classroom presentations, objectives, tests and test answers, and student projects with data and solutions. To find out more from our web site, please go to www.murach.com and click on the "Instructor Info" button. Or, if you prefer, you can e-mail us at murachbooks@murach.com or call us at 1-800-221-5528. Just ask about the Instructor's Guide for *Murach's CICS for the COBOL Programmer*.

Please let us know how this book works for you

Since the first edition of our CICS book came out in 1984, more than 150,000 COBOL programmers have learned CICS from it. Now, we think the improvements to this latest edition are going to make training and reference easier than ever before.

If you have any comments about this book, we would enjoy hearing from you. We would especially like to know if this book has lived up to your expectations. To reply, you can e-mail us at murachbooks@murach.com or send your comments to our street address.

Thanks for buying this book. Thanks for reading it. And good luck with your CICS programming.

Raul Menendez
Author

Mike Murach
Publisher

Section 1

Introduction to CICS

Before you can start learning the details of coding CICS programs, you need to understand some basic CICS concepts and terms. So in chapter 1, you'll learn about CICS and the services it provides for application programs. Then, in chapter 2, you'll learn how CICS programs work and how you access CICS services from within a COBOL program. This chapter includes a complete interactive application so you can see from the start what's involved in developing CICS programs. When you complete these two chapters, you'll have a good foundation for learning the details of CICS programming that are presented in the remainder of this book.

CICS concepts and terms

This chapter presents the concepts and terms that you need to know when you develop CICS programs. After you're introduced to CICS and its environment, you'll learn how CICS can handle hundreds of users at the same time. Then, you'll learn about the CICS services that you use as you develop COBOL programs that issue CICS commands.

An introduction to CICS

The CICS environment has evolved over the years since it was first introduced in 1968. At that time, it ran only on IBM mainframes and in a limited capacity. Today, CICS can be used on a variety of platforms and with several different programming languages. And with the introduction of IBM's CICS Transaction Server 1.3, CICS became the premier server for Internet applications.

What is CICS?

CICS, which stands for *Customer Information Control System*, is a world-class transaction processing system. As such, it can process the transactions from hundreds of users at the same time as they run a variety of application programs. CICS loads those programs, coordinates their execution, manages the data transmissions between programs and terminals, controls the access to data, and maintains the integrity of that data. Because CICS is a transaction processing system, it can be called *online transaction processing* (*OLTP*) software.

As you can see in the first drawing in figure 1-1, CICS acts as an interface between the application programs and the operating system's services. So when the application program wants to access a terminal or a disk device, it doesn't communicate directly with the device. Instead, it issues commands to communicate with CICS, which communicates with one of the operating system's access methods. Then, the access method communicates with the device. This shelters your application programs from specific device and operating system details.

CICS is needed with operating systems like OS/390 and VSE/ESA because these operating systems were designed to run batch programs, not online programs. As a result, these operating systems work best when a small number of jobs are running at the same time and when each of these jobs has exclusive use of the data files or other resources it requires. In contrast, an online program may need to provide for hundreds of concurrent users who need to share the same files and resources.

To a large extent, then, CICS is an operating system in itself because it provides many of the functions normally associated with an operating system. For example, CICS manages its own processor storage, provides its own file management functions, and includes a task manager that handles the concurrent execution of multiple programs. So when CICS runs under OS/390 or VSE/ESA, you can think of CICS as an operating system within an operating system.

The second drawing in this figure shows that CICS actually runs as a batch job within the OS/390 operating system. As a result, two or more CICS systems, also called *regions*, can run at the same time. In this example, OS/390 has assigned address spaces to two different CICS regions that are running at the same time. Then, the CICS production region can handle all CICS production programs, while the CICS test region can be used to test new or modified CICS programs. This is a common setup that protects production programs from failures caused by programs that are still being tested.

A CICS interface

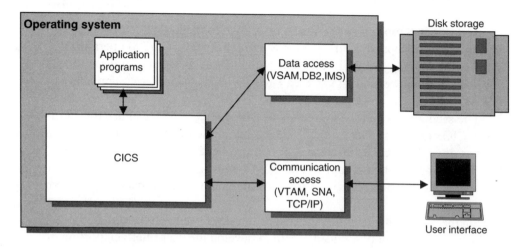

CICS in an OS/390 address space

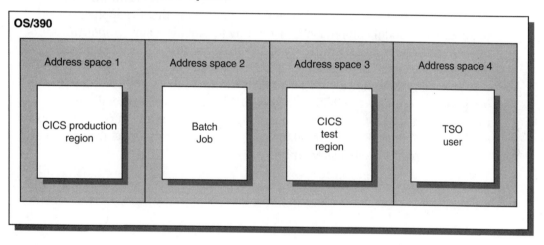

Description

* The *Customer Information Control System*, or *CICS*, is designed to control information in a modern online environment by providing database and data communication functions.

* CICS provides an interface between application programs and operating system services, such as data access and communication access.

* On a mainframe, CICS runs under an operating system like OS/390 or VSE/ESA. Although CICS runs as a batch job, it can handle hundreds of interactive users that are using a variety of applications.

* More than one CICS system (or *region*) can run on the same computer at the same time. Because each region runs in its own address space, programs running in one region won't interfere with programs running in another region.

Figure 1-1   What is CICS?

CICS platforms and programming languages

Today, CICS can run on the platforms shown in the first table of figure 1-2. By far, the most popular of these is the S/390 running the OS/390 operating system. On a large system like that, CICS can handle millions of transactions per hour. Note, however, that CICS can also be used on smaller systems like AS/400s, RS/6000s, and even PC servers.

The second table in this figure lists the six languages you can use for developing CICS programs. Of these, COBOL is by far the most popular with billions of lines of COBOL code currently in operation. Because COBOL provides a structured language that is easy to understand and maintain, COBOL is likely to remain the most popular language for developing CICS programs for many years to come.

On the other hand, now that languages like Java can be used for CICS applications, some shops are using them to develop the user interface portion of new applications (they can be used to develop entire CICS applications, but in practice, that rarely happens). In that case, though, COBOL is still the language that's most likely to be used for the business processing that the application requires. This modular approach is also a way to provide a new *graphical user interface* (*GUI*) for an existing CICS/COBOL application. You'll learn more about this in chapter 20.

Although CICS can be used on all the platforms shown in this figure, this book focuses on the way CICS is used on IBM mainframes, especially those running under the OS/390 or MVS operating system. That, of course, is the most used platform today. Keep in mind, though, that CICS itself works the same way on all of the platforms that support it.

CICS transaction server platforms

Hardware	Operating system
IBM zSeries 900	z/OS
IBM S/390	OS/390, MVS, VSE
IBM AS/400	OS/400
IBM RS/6000	AIX (UNIX)
PC server	Windows NT, OS/2

CICS programming languages

Language	Description
COBOL	The most used programming language for both batch and online applications in a mainframe environment. Today, an overwhelming majority of CICS programs are in COBOL.
Assembler language	Assembler language was fairly popular in the 70s and early 80s before COBOL became the dominant business language. Today, assembler language is still used for special-purpose devices like ATM machines.
PL/I	In the 70s and 80s, PL/I was an alternative to COBOL that was used by a small percentage of CICS shops. Today, you probably won't find any new program development being done in PL/I.
C and C++	Traditionally used in engineering and math environments, C and C++ can now be used to access CICS services. With C++, an object-oriented language, you can develop object-oriented classes that access CICS services.
Java	The newest language for writing CICS applications, Java can also be used for developing object-oriented classes that access CICS services.

Description

- Although CICS runs on several computing platforms, the most used platform today is the S/390 mainframe running the OS/390 or MVS operating system.

- Although CICS programs can be written in several languages, the vast majority of CICS programs today are written in COBOL.

Figure 1-2   CICS platforms and programming languages

The 3270 information display system

The *3270 display station* (or *terminal*) has been the standard workstation for CICS systems since 1971. The 3270 information display system includes terminals (display stations), printers, and controllers. As figure 1-3 shows, the terminals access the mainframe through IBM 3x74 controllers, which can provide for anywhere from 32 to 64 terminals. So a large system consists of many of these controllers.

Although 3270 terminals were common in the 1980s and early 1990s, you won't find too many mainframe shops using them any more. Today, *3270 emulation* software makes it possible for personal computers (PCs) to be used as 3270 terminals. That way, you not only have access to CICS applications but also to PC applications like word processing and spreadsheet software.

In this figure, you can see two ways to connect PCs with 3270 emulation software to CICS. One way is through a *Local Area Network* (*LAN*) or a *Wide Area Network* (*WAN*). The other way is through the Internet or an intranet. Either way, the 3270 emulation software interprets data streams sent from CICS and constructs a 3270 screen display on a PC's monitor, usually in a window. IBM includes 3270 emulation software as part of its CICS software package, but you can also purchase 3270 emulators from other companies. To test the examples in this book, I used an emulator called *EXTRA! for Windows 98* that accessed CICS at a remote site over the Internet.

The 3270 information display system

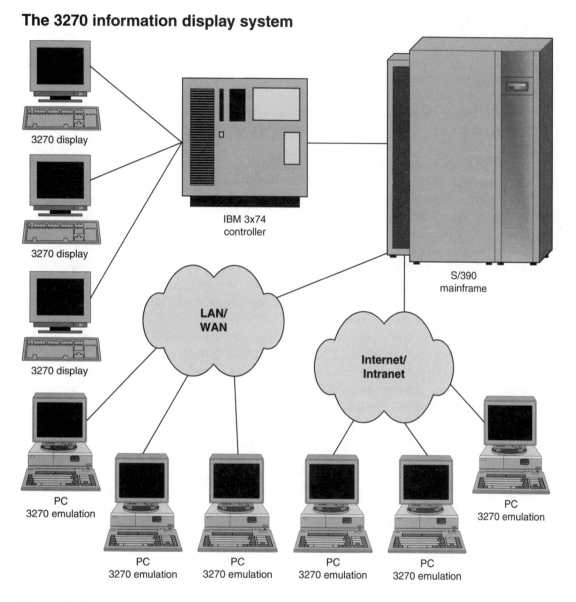

Description

- The 3270 family of terminal devices has been the standard for IBM mainframe computers since 1971. They can be connected to a mainframe directly or remotely via a 3x74 controller.

- Today, the typical user connects to CICS via a PC running some form of *3270 emulation* software. This software interprets 3270 data streams sent through a network and constructs a 3270 display screen, usually in a window on the PC's desktop.

- When you use 3270 emulation on a PC, the PC can connect to CICS through a *Local Area Network* (*LAN*) or a *Wide Area Network* (*WAN*) or through the Internet or an intranet.

Figure 1-3   The 3270 information display system

Alternate user interfaces

Today, the vast majority of CICS applications are written for 3270 display terminals or PCs that are emulating 3270 terminals. But as figure 1-4 shows, CICS can also be used with *front-end programs* that are written in other languages. In this case, the front-end program provides the user interface, or *presentation logic*, while the *back-end program* (the CICS application) provides the *business logic*.

As this figure shows, if you use 3270 terminals or 3270 emulation, the CICS application provides both the presentation logic and the business logic. In this case, the user interface is text only, not graphical. Also, all of the processing is done by the CICS application because 3270 terminals are "dumb" terminals, which means they can't do any processing.

If you want to provide a graphical user interface for an application or if you want the front-end program to do some of the processing, you can use one of the three alternate user interfaces shown in this figure. In this case, the front-end program provides the GUI and perhaps some processing, while the CICS application provides the business logic.

If you write the front-end for an application in a language like Visual Basic or Java, the front-end can use the CICS *External Call Interface*, or *ECI calls,* to send data to and from CICS. If you want to pass data to and from a program on another platform, you can use IBM's *MQSeries*, which allows disparate systems to exchange information through *message queuing*. If you want to access a CICS application from a Web application (an application that runs in a Web browser), you can do that in several different ways, including using standard *HTTP* (the *Hypertext Transfer Protocol*).

Note in all three cases that CICS is used for the business logic of the application. This insures that the same business rules are applied to the user requests for data no matter how the user accesses the system. In chapter 20, you'll learn how to write CICS programs with separate presentation and business logic so you can take advantage of these alternatives. And in chapter 21, you'll learn how CICS can be used for developing Web applications.

Alternate user interfaces

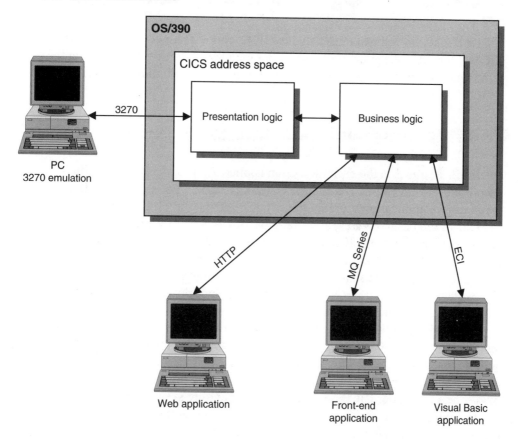

PC
3270 emulation

Web application

Front-end
application

Visual Basic
application

Description

- When you use 3270 terminals or PCs running 3270 emulation software, the CICS application provides the *presentation logic* for the terminals or PCs. That means that CICS determines what screens will be displayed and how they will work. In this case, CICS also provides the *business logic* that determines how the user requests will be processed.

- CICS can also be used with other types of user interfaces. In this case, the *front-end program* provides the presentation logic, but the CICS application is still the *back-end program* that provides the business logic.

- Visual Basic is one product that can be used to develop a front-end program with a graphical user interface (GUI) that accesses a back-end program written in CICS. To access CICS programs, the Visual Basic program issues *ECI calls*.

- A front-end program written for another platform can retrieve data managed by CICS by issuing message requests through an IBM product called *MQSeries*. This *message queuing* product lets you send data between two disparate computer platforms.

- Web applications run in a Web browser and can access CICS programs and services through an Internet protocol like *HTTP*.

Figure 1-4   Alternate user interfaces

How CICS manages multiple users

Now that you've been introduced to CICS, you're ready to understand how CICS is able to manage the processing for hundreds or thousands of users at the same time. To do that efficiently, CICS uses features called multitasking and multithreading.

How multitasking and multithreading work

In CICS, a *task* is the execution of an application program for a specific user. For every execution of a program, a task is started. For example, if User 1 is running an application program under CICS, then User 1 has created a task.

One of the basic features, and strengths, of CICS is its ability to multitask. *Multitasking* means that CICS allows more than one task to be executed at the same time, which is essential in an environment where hundreds of users can be logged into CICS at the same time. In figure 1-5, for example, you can see a CICS address space that has five tasks running, one for each of the five users currently logged on to the system.

Although all of the operating systems that support CICS are capable of multitasking on their own, CICS provides for multitasking within the single address space provided by the operating system. In other words, it ignores the multitasking capabilities of the operating system. As a result, multitasking works the same under CICS no matter which operating system you use.

In contrast to multitasking, *multithreading* allows all the users in a CICS region to use the same copy of a program at the same time. In this figure, for example, you can see that both User 1 and User 5 are running the order entry program. In this case, if both users had their own copies of the program, valuable internal storage space would be used unnecessarily. With multithreading, though, only one copy of a program is loaded and shared by all.

For multithreading to work, the program must be *reentrant*. A program that's completely reentrant doesn't change itself in any way. In other words, a truly reentrant program cannot modify data in working storage. Obviously, though, COBOL programs that can't use working storage would be difficult to write. So CICS provides a separate copy of working storage for each user running a program. As you can see in this figure, the users share the same copy of the program's executable code, but each is given a separate working storage area. Once the program finishes executing, the working storage for that user is released and the virtual memory that was used is free to be allocated to another user.

CICS uses its address space to support multitasking

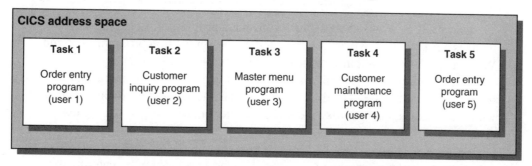

Multithreading provides a separate copy of working storage for each user

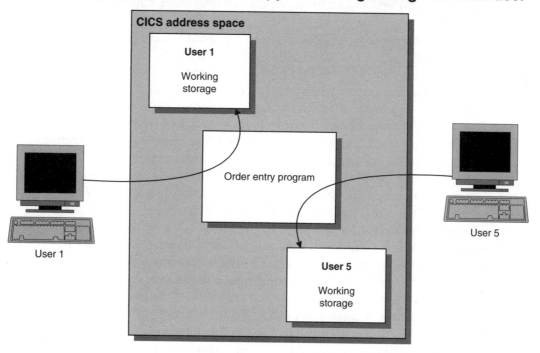

Description

- A *task* is the execution of an application program for a specific user. Within CICS, two or more tasks can execute at the same time using a CICS feature called *multitasking*.

- Although all of the operating systems that support CICS provide multitasking of their own, CICS handles multitasking internally. This provides for a stable system that works the same way under any operating system.

- CICS also provides a feature called *multithreading*. With multithreading, two or more users can access the same copy of a program at the same time. CICS accomplishes this by providing a separate copy of working storage for each user running the program.

Figure 1-5   How multitasking and multithreading work

How transactions work

Under CICS, a user cannot directly invoke a program. Instead, the user invokes a *transaction*, which in turn specifies the application program to be run. When a user invokes a transaction, CICS locates the application program associated with the transaction, loads it into storage (if it isn't in storage already), and starts a task. The difference between a task and a transaction is that while several users may invoke the same transaction, each is given a separate task.

Each transaction is identified by a unique four-character code called a *transaction identifier*, or *trans-id*. A user initiates a transaction by entering the transaction identifier at the terminal. If, for example, the user keys in the characters ORD1 and presses the Enter key, the transaction named ORD1 is invoked.

Every transaction must be defined in a special CICS table called the *Program Control Table*, or *PCT*. Basically, the PCT is a list of valid transaction identifiers. Each trans-id in the PCT is paired with the name of the program CICS will load and execute when the transaction is invoked.

Another CICS table called the *Processing Program Table*, or *PPT*, contains a list of all valid program names. This table keeps track of which programs are located in storage. CICS uses it to determine whether a new copy of a program needs to be loaded into storage when a transaction is invoked.

CICS creates these internal control tables based on *resource definitions* created by systems programmers. To create these definitions, a systems programmer can use a batch program for that purpose or an interactive program called *Resource Definition Online* (*RDO*). Because RDO lets the systems programmer define resources such as transactions and programs from a CICS terminal, it is the preferred way to create resource definitions. (Because the trans-id for RDO is CEDA, RDO is sometimes referred to as *CEDA*.)

To review the way transactions work, please refer to figure 1-6, which shows how a task is initiated under CICS. Here, a user enters the trans-id ORD1. Then, CICS searches the Program Control Table to find the program to be executed. As you can see, the program for transaction ORD1 is ORDPGM1. Next, CICS searches the Processing Program Table to determine if the program is currently in main storage. In this case, it isn't, so CICS locates the program on disk, loads it into storage, updates the PPT, and initiates a new task.

How CICS invokes an application program

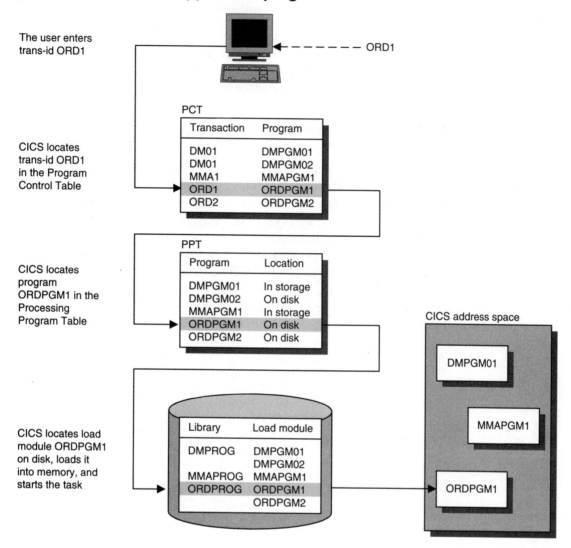

The user enters
trans-id ORD1

ORD1

PCT

Transaction	Program
DM01	DMPGM01
DM01	DMPGM02
MMA1	MMAPGM1
ORD1	ORDPGM1
ORD2	ORDPGM2

CICS locates
trans-id ORD1
in the Program
Control Table

PPT

Program	Location
DMPGM01	In storage
DMPGM02	On disk
MMAPGM1	In storage
ORDPGM1	On disk
ORDPGM2	On disk

CICS locates
program
ORDPGM1 in the
Processing
Program Table

CICS address space

DMPGM01

MMAPGM1

Library	Load module
DMPROG	DMPGM01
	DMPGM02
MMAPROG	MMAPGM1
ORDPROG	ORDPGM1
	ORDPGM2

CICS locates load
module ORDPGM1
on disk, loads it
into memory, and
starts the task

ORDPGM1

Description

- Each *transaction* is identified by a unique, four-character identifier called a *transaction identifier*, or *trans-id*. To start a transaction, the user enters its transaction identifier at a terminal.

- Transactions are defined in a CICS table called the *Program Control Table* (*PCT*). Each trans-id in the PCT identifies the program CICS should execute when the transaction is invoked.

- Programs are defined in the *Processing Program Table* (*PPT*). This table keeps track of which programs are already loaded into storage. If a program has not been loaded into storage, it's loaded when its associated transaction is invoked.

Figure 1-6   How transactions work

CICS services

To help the programmer develop application programs, CICS provides many services that are available to application programs. These services let a program communicate with terminals, access data files, use operating system features, and so on. The next four topics introduce you to these services.

The Application Programming Interface

To access CICS services from an application program, you use the CICS *Application Programming Interface*, or *API*. This is illustrated in figure 1-7. Here, an application program communicates with the API, which in turn communicates with the individual CICS services. In this way, the API insures that all of the CICS services are invoked in a consistent manner.

The primary focus of this book is to teach you how to code CICS commands within application programs to access CICS services through the API. Because CICS programs are written predominantly in COBOL, this book presents the CICS commands in the context of COBOL programs. Keep in mind, though, that you can use these commands in programs written in other languages, too.

How an application program accesses CICS services

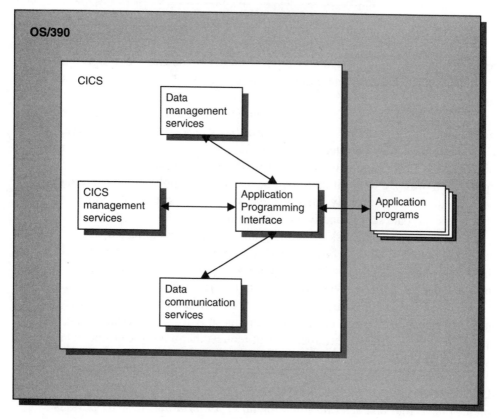

Description

- CICS provides many services that are available to an application program through its *Application Programming Interface*, or *API*. This API insures that all the services are invoked in a consistent manner.
- The data communication services allow users to communicate with programs through their terminals.
- The data management services let programs access data stored in files or databases.
- The CICS management services provide a variety of services for managing the execution of application programs.

Figure 1-7   The Application Programming Interface

Data communication services

CICS's *data communication services* let a CICS application program communicate with terminal devices. Typically, these services send information to a terminal screen or retrieve user input from it. As you can see in figure 1-8, terminal control and basic mapping support are the two CICS services in this group.

Terminal control is CICS's interface with the operating system's telecommunication access method. Terminal control lets you send text to or receive text from the terminal that initiated the task. Although terminal control handles most of the details of working with the access method, it is still difficult for your application program to use it directly. For instance, an application program that uses terminal control directly must process complicated strings of control characters and data sent to and received from the terminal.

To relieve you of the task of building and decoding complicated strings of control characters and data, *basic mapping support*, or *BMS*, was developed. As this figure shows, BMS is an interface between application programs and terminal control. BMS lets you create a *map* that specifies the format of data as it appears on the terminal display. To receive data from or send data to a terminal, an application program issues a BMS request. After BMS retrieves the specified map, it creates a terminal control request that will process the data according to the format specified by the map.

A special CICS table called the *Terminal Control Table*, or *TCT*, is used to define each terminal to the CICS system. In the TCT, each terminal is given a unique one to four-character *terminal identifier*, or *term-id*. These definitions make it possible for CICS to direct program output to the correct terminal and any input from the terminal to the correct program. Here again, creating and maintaining the TCT is the responsibility of CICS systems programmers.

How an application program communicates with terminal devices

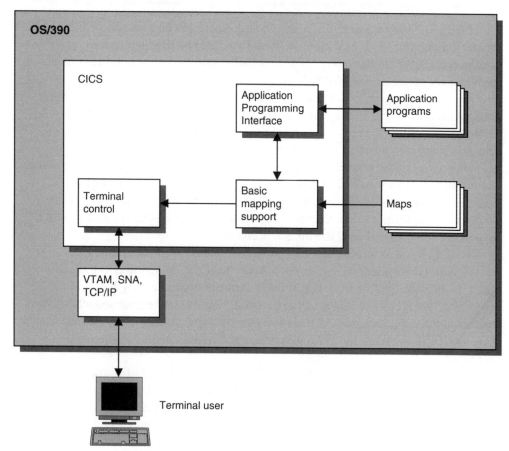

Description

- *Terminal control* provides the interface between CICS and the operating system's telecommunication access method. It lets you send text or receive text from the terminal that initiated the task.

- The most common telecommunication access methods are *VTAM* (the *Virtual Tele-communication Access Method*), *SNA* (*Systems Network Architecture*), and *TCP/IP* (*Transmission Control Protocol/Internet Protocol*). Some of these access methods can also be used in combination with each other.

- *Basic mapping support* (*BMS*) provides the interface between application programs and terminal control. It lets you create *maps* that specify the position and the characteristics of the individual display elements on the terminal screen. As a result, you can create interfaces that are easy for users to work with.

- Each terminal in the CICS system must be defined in the *Terminal Control Table* (*TCT*). Each terminal in this table is assigned a unique one- to four-character *terminal identifier*, or *term-id*.

Figure 1-8   Data communication services

Data management services

Figure 1-9 shows that CICS's *data management services* consist of file control, SQL, and DL/I. SQL and DL/I are interfaces to IBM's relational and hierarchical database managers (DB2 and IMS respectively), while file control provides the interface for VSAM files.

The data management service you'll use the most will probably be the *file control* service. As you can see in this figure, when an application program issues a file control request, file control passes it on to VSAM, which manages the data stored on direct access devices.

One of the major responsibilities of the file control service is to manage shared access to files so two or more users can't update the same record at the same time and thus corrupt the data. To provide for this, the file control service locks a record when a user accesses it for updating. As a result, other users can't access the same record until the update is complete.

To keep track of which files are available to application programs, CICS maintains a table called the *File Control Table*, or *FCT*. In addition to the name and type of each file, the FCT lists the file control operations that are valid for each file. Specifically, it lists whether existing records can be read sequentially, read randomly, deleted, or modified, and whether new records can be added. Like the TCT, entries in the FCT are created and maintained by systems programmers.

As you will see in the next chapter, CICS file control simplifies the file processing code in your COBOL programs. Because the FCT keeps track of each file's characteristics, you don't use Select and FD statements to identify the files. And instead of COBOL I/O statements like the Open, Read, and Write statements, you issue CICS commands to the API.

In contrast to the file control service, CICS's *SQL* service is used to access data in a *DB2* database. SQL, which stands for *Structured Query Language*, is a standard language that's used to access the data within a database. If you have DB2 experience, chapter 17 will teach you how to use SQL statements within CICS programs to get the data that your programs need. (If you don't have DB2 experience, you can gain the background you need in our book, *DB2 for the COBOL Programmer, Part 1.*)

The third data management service in this figure is the *DL/I* service. It is used to access data in an *IMS* database. Because DL/I isn't used much any more, it isn't presented in this book. If you need to learn how to use it, though, we recommend a book that we published a number of years ago but that is still useful today, *IMS for the COBOL Programmer, Part 1.*

Three ways an application program can access data from disk storage

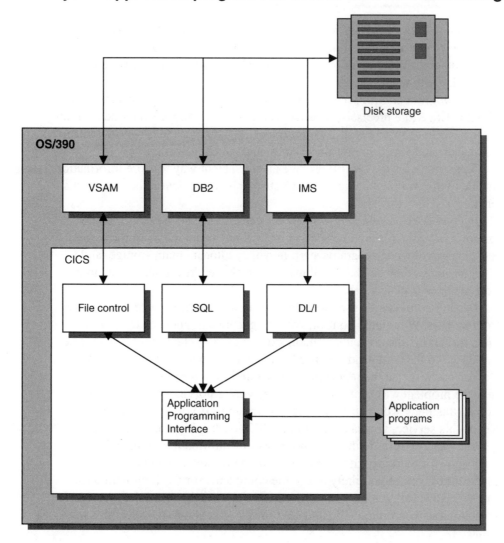

Description

- CICS provides three services to manage data: file control, SQL, and DL/I.
- *File control* passes data requests made by a program to VSAM. VSAM, in turn, manages the data stored in files on direct access devices.
- Each file accessed by CICS must be defined in the *File Control Table*, or *FCT*. The FCT specifies the file name, along with other information such as the file type and the operations that can be performed on the file.
- *SQL* passes data requests made by a program to IBM's relational database system, *DB2*.
- *DL/I* passes data requests made by a program to IBM's hierarchical database system, *IMS*.

Figure 1-9   Data management services

CICS management services

Figure 1-10 summarizes the nine *CICS management services*. These services allow your application program to take full advantage of the features of CICS. Although you may never need some of these services, you should at least be familiar with them.

The *program control* service manages the programs that are executing within CICS. More precisely, it manages the flow of control from one program to the next. In chapter 2, you'll be introduced to some of the program control commands, and you'll master these commands in chapter 5.

Temporary storage control provides a convenient way to store information outside of the working storage area. In chapter 7, you'll learn how to use this service.

Interval control, task control, and *storage control* are services used to control how programs are executed in a CICS environment. With these services, you can control when programs start, how they allocate main storage, and what CICS resources they can have exclusive control over. You'll learn how to use these services in chapter 18.

Dump control can be used to help determine what the problem is when a program fails. With dump control, you can generate a report called a *transaction dump* that shows the contents of main storage used by the program. You'll be introduced to the command you use to create a transaction dump in chapter 2.

You can also use the report that's generated by *trace control* to help determine the problem with a program. Because you're not likely to use this report, though, this book won't show you how to create it. If you want more information on this service, you can refer to the CICS desk reference we publish.

You can also refer to the desk reference for information on the CICS commands for working with *transient data control* and *journal control*. Like trace control, you're not likely to use the commands for working with these services. However, you may use the features of journal control that provide for the automatic recording of file updates. You'll learn about these features in chapter 18.

CICS services that help manage application programs

Management service	Description
Program control	Manages the programs executing within a task. With this service, programs can call or transfer control to other programs.
Temporary storage control	Provides a simple way to store data outside the working storage area of a program. The data is stored in simple files called *temporary storage queues*. Because they're temporary, any data they contain is lost if CICS is shut down.
Interval control	Provides time-related services, including services for getting the current date and time and scheduling tasks for execution.
Storage control	Provides for allocating main storage space outside of the working storage area of an application program.
Task control	Can be used to control the execution of a task. Provides for temporarily suspending a task that is monopolizing CICS resources or gaining exclusive control of a CICS resource.
Dump control	Produces a *transaction dump* when a fatal error is encountered during the execution of an application program. The dump can then be used to help debug the program.
Trace control	Maintains a trace table that indicates the sequence of CICS operations performed. This table can be used to help debug a program.
Journal control	Creates a record or *journal* that can be used to restore files in the event of a task or system failure.
Transient data control	Provides a convenient way to use sequential files called *destinations* to store data. Records written to a destination are added to the end of the destination. Records are read sequentially from a destination and then deleted.

Notes

- Although you may never use some of the CICS management services, you should be familiar with the features they provide so you can use them if you ever need to.

- The CICS commands for working with all of these services except for trace control, journal control, and transient data control are presented in this book.

Figure 1-10   CICS management services

Perspective

Now that you've completed this chapter, you should be familiar with the concepts and terms that you need to know as you develop CICS programs. The concepts will help you understand what is actually happening as you test your programs. The terms will help you converse with your colleagues.

That doesn't mean that you should remember exactly how every concept presented in this chapter works and what every term means. But you should at least be familiar with the concepts and terms so you can refer back to this chapter whenever necessary.

Terms you should be familiar with

CICS (Customer Information Control System)
online transaction processing (OLTP)
region
graphical user interface (GUI)
3270 display station
terminal
3270 emulation
Local Area Network (LAN)
Wide Area Network (WAN)
front-end program
presentation logic
back-end program
business logic
External Call Interface
ECI call
MQSeries
message queuing
HTTP
task
multitasking
multithreading
reentrant program
transaction
transaction identifier
trans-id
Program Control Table (PCT)
Processing Program Table (PPT)
resource definition
Resource Definition Online (RDO)
CEDA

Application Programming Interface (API)
data communication services
terminal control
VTAM
SNA (Systems Network Architecture)
TCP/IP
basic mapping support (BMS)
map
Terminal Control Table (TCT)
terminal identifier
term-id
data management services
file control
File Control Table (FCT)
Structured Query Language (SQL)
DB2
DL/I
IMS
CICS management services
program control
temporary storage control
temporary storage queue
interval control
task control
storage control
dump control
transaction dump
trace control
transient data control
destination
journal control

2

Introduction to CICS programming

Now that you understand the critical concepts and terms related to CICS, you're ready to learn how to develop CICS programs. To get you started, this chapter presents a simple but complete CICS program, including the BMS mapset that defines the user interface. When you complete this chapter, you should have a good understanding of how a CICS program works and what you have to do to develop one.

How a CICS program works

To understand how a CICS program works, this topic starts by presenting a sample terminal session for a program that displays customer information. That will give you an idea of what the user sees as a CICS program executes. What the user *doesn't* see, though, is that each time a new screen is displayed, the program actually ends. This is the basic idea of pseudo-conversational programming, and it's the key to understanding how CICS programs work.

The operation of the customer inquiry program

Figure 2-1 presents four screens from the customer inquiry program. To start this program, the user can enter the trans-id INQ1 or select the program from a menu that specifies that trans-id. In either case, CICS searches the Program Control Table to determine what program is associated with that trans-id. Then, CICS starts that program and displays the first screen shown in this figure.

On the first line of this screen, you can see the name of the map that's used to display this screen and the trans-id that's used to start the program. In addition, you can see the name of the program, Customer Inquiry. This information helps the user identify the map and the program that displays it.

Below the trans-id and program name are instructions for the user. In this case, the instructions tell the user to type a customer number and press the Enter key. In the second screen shown in this figure, you can see that the user has entered a customer number. Then, when the user presses the Enter key, the third screen shown in part 2 of this figure is displayed.

Screen 1

When the program first starts, it displays the customer inquiry map.

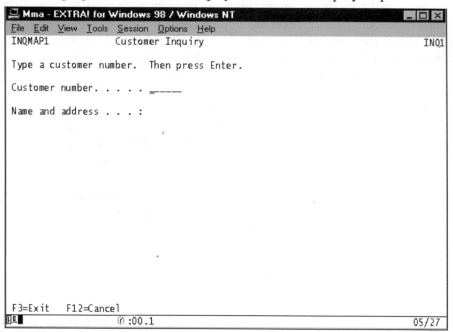

Screen 2

The user can then enter a customer number and press the Enter key.

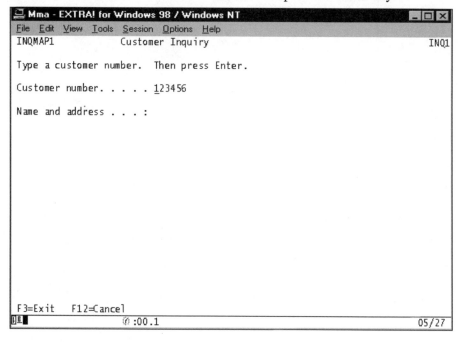

Figure 2-1   The operation of the customer inquiry program (part 1 of 2)

As you can see in screen 3, the program has retrieved the record for the requested customer and displayed the data for that customer on the screen. At this point, the user can do one of two things. First, the user can enter another customer number and then press the Enter key to display the information for that customer. Second, the user can press the PF3 or PF12 key to exit from the program. Although both keys cause the program to end in this example, they may perform different functions in more complex programs.

In screen 4, you can see that the user entered another customer number and pressed the Enter key. This time, though, no record was found for that customer number. Because of that, the program has displayed an error message near the bottom of the screen. At this point, the user can either enter another customer number and press the Enter key or press PF3 or PF12 to end the program.

Incidentally, the screens in figure 2-1 show the mainframe output as it appears in a PC window when using a program called EXTRA! for Windows 98. As you learned in chapter 1, this is one of many third-party programs that make it possible to emulate a 3270 terminal on a PC.

Screen 3

If the customer number is valid, the program retrieves the customer record
and displays the data for that customer on the screen.

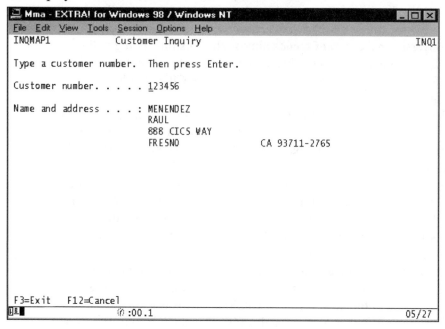

Screen 4

To display the data for another customer, the user can type over the current
customer number and then press the Enter key. If the customer number is
invalid, an error message is displayed.

Figure 2-1   The operation of the customer inquiry program (part 2 of 2)

How conversational programming works

In the screens in figure 2-1, the customer inquiry program appears to be sitting idle, waiting for the user to enter data. An online program that does sit idle while it waits for data is called a *conversational program*. As you can imagine, a conversational program spends almost all of its time doing nothing but waiting. On a single user system, this isn't a problem because there's nothing else for the computer to do. But in a system like CICS that has many users, it is a problem.

Figure 2-2 illustrates how a conversational program works. After it sends its initial map to the terminal, it waits for the user's input. Then, it retrieves the input, processes it, and sends output back to the terminal. This continues until the user ends the program.

Although CICS is free to dispatch other programs for execution while the conversational program is waiting for input, the execution of the conversational program itself (the task) must remain in main storage. That includes the working storage for the program and all of the CICS control blocks that are required to keep track of the program's execution.

Clearly, then, conversational programs are inefficient when it comes to the use of virtual storage...and virtual storage is one of the most critical CICS resources. In fact, one of the most common CICS problems is a condition known as *Short On Storage*, or, appropriately, *SOS*. When CICS goes short on storage, it suspends all work and begins terminating tasks in an effort to free up storage. As you can imagine, the result of an SOS condition can be disruptive as CICS grinds to a halt. And conversational programs are often a major cause of SOS conditions.

Conversational processing

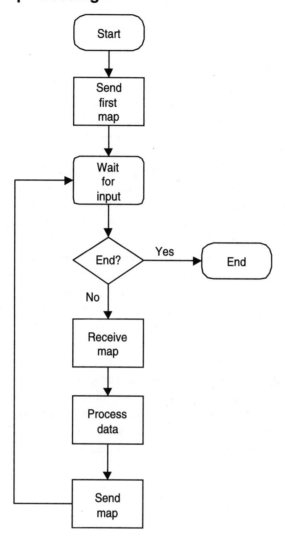

Description

- A *conversational program* is an online program that sits idle while it waits for user input.

- When a conversational program first starts, it sends its initial map to the terminal. Then, it enters into a loop where it waits for input, retrieves the input data from the terminal, processes the data, sends its output to the terminal, and waits again.

- While a conversational program waits for user input, the task associated with that program remains in storage. Because of that, conversational programs are inefficient in terms of virtual storage usage.

- Conversational programs are often the cause of a CICS condition known as *Short on Storage*, or *SOS*.

Figure 2-2   How conversational programming works

How pseudo-conversational programming works

The solution to the inefficiencies of conversational programs is to remove the task associated with a program from storage while the program is waiting for terminal input. And that's just what happens with a *pseudo-conversational program*. For example, while the map for the customer inquiry program in figure 2-1 is displayed, the inquiry program itself has terminated and its task is no longer in storage. When the user enters another customer number and presses the Enter key, the inquiry program is restarted. The result is that the task is in storage only when it needs to be: when the program is processing data. Because pseudo-conversational programs use main storage and other CICS resources far more efficiently than conversational programs, almost all CICS installations require that programs be pseudo-conversational.

Figure 2-3 illustrates how a pseudo-conversational program works. Like a conversational program, it starts by sending its initial map to the terminal. Unlike a conversational program, though, a pseudo-conversational program ends after it sends the map. Then, when the user presses one of the terminal's *attention identifier (AID) keys*—the Enter key, a PF key, a PA key, or the Clear key—it signals CICS to restart the program. At that point, the task is loaded back into storage, the data is retrieved from the terminal and processed, output is sent back to the terminal, and the program ends again. This continues until the user indicates that the program should end.

Unfortunately, pseudo-conversational programming is more difficult than conversational programming because each program must be coded so it can figure out what processing it should do each time it's started. This requires a different type of design and logic than you've seen before. You'll see how this works in the customer inquiry program later in this chapter.

Pseudo-conversational processing

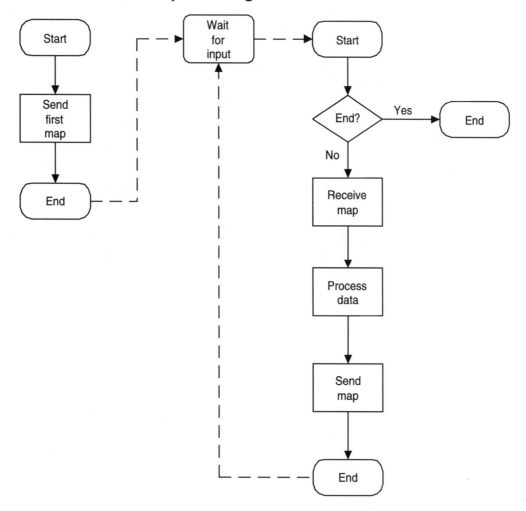

Description

- With *pseudo-conversational programming*, a program ends after it sends data to a terminal. This releases some of the resources that are used by the program. Then, CICS restarts the program when the user completes an entry and presses one of the terminal's *attention identifier (AID) keys*.

- A pseudo-conversational program requires a different type of design and logic than a conversational program because it must be able to figure out what to do each time it's restarted.

Figure 2-3   How pseudo-conversational programming works

How to code CICS commands

When you code a CICS program, you request CICS services by issuing CICS commands. To do that, you use the syntax shown at the top of figure 2-4. As you can see, you start each command with EXEC CICS, and you end each command with END-EXEC. Within these statements, you code the command and any options it requires. In this figure, you can see a list of some of the most common CICS commands for screen interactions, for passing control from one program to another, and for processing VSAM files.

In the example in this figure, you can see how the RECEIVE MAP command is coded. In accordance with standard CICS command syntax, the words outside the parentheses (MAP, MAPSET, and INTO) are all options of the command, while the values inside the parentheses are supplied by the programmer. As a result, this command tells CICS to receive data from a terminal using a mapset named INQSET1 that defines a map named INQMAP1. The data in that mapset should be returned to a group item in working storage named INQMAP1I. As you'll see in a moment, the MAP, MAPSET, and INTO values are all related to the BMS mapset that defines the maps for the program.

The general syntax of a CICS command

```
EXEC CICS
    command option(value)...
END-EXEC.
```

CICS commands for doing BMS-controlled screen interactions

RECEIVE MAP	Retrieves input data from the terminal.
SEND MAP	Sends information to the terminal for display.

CICS commands for passing control from one program to another

ABEND	Transfers control to an abend routine or returns control to CICS.
LINK	Invokes a program at a lower level.
RETURN	Returns control to CICS or the invoking program.
XCTL	Transfers control to another program.

CICS commands for processing VSAM files

DELETE	Deletes a record from a file.
READ	Retrieves a specified record from a file.
REWRITE	Updates a record in a file.
SYNCPOINT	Commits or reverses updates made to one or more files.
WRITE	Adds a record to a file.

A CICS command that receives data from the terminal

```
EXEC CICS
    RECEIVE MAP('INQMAP1')
            MAPSET('INQSET1')
            INTO(INQMAP1I)
END-EXEC.
```

Description

- Within a COBOL program, each CICS command must begin with the words EXEC CICS and end with the words END-EXEC.

- The command specifies the operation to be performed, and the options, or *parameters*, provide information CICS needs to perform the operation.

- When a command requires more than one option, you use spaces to separate them.

- To make your programs easier to read, we recommend that you code each option of a CICS command on a separate line. No special coding is required to continue a command from one line to the next.

Figure 2-4   How to code CICS commands

COBOL statements that aren't supported under CICS

Before I show you the code for the customer inquiry program, you should know about the COBOL statements that you can't use in a CICS program. These statements are summarized in figure 2-5. For the most part, CICS provides services that perform the functions of these statements. The exception is the Merge statement, whose function is not provided by CICS.

Although you can't code a Merge statement in a CICS program, you can code Sort, Release, and Return statements. Because of the restrictions for using these statements in a CICS program, however, you'll rarely use them. Instead, if you need to retrieve records in a particular sequence, you'll define that sequence through the primary key for the file or through an alternate index.

COBOL statements not allowed in CICS programs

Operator communication statements

Accept
Display

File I/O statements

Open
Close
Read
Write
Rewrite
Delete
Start

Other statements

Accept Date/Day/Day-Of-Week/Time
Merge

Description

- Under CICS, all terminal I/O is handled by the terminal control module, whose services are typically requested by issuing SEND MAP and RECEIVE MAP commands. Because of that, COBOL Accept and Display statements aren't allowed in CICS programs.

- Under CICS, all file I/O is handled by the file control module, whose services are requested by issuing CICS file control commands like READ, WRITE, REWRITE, and DELETE. Because of that, the COBOL statements for file I/O aren't allowed. In addition, Environment Division and File Section statements that pertain to data management should not be coded.

- COBOL statements that invoke operating system functions, like Accept Date and Accept Time, are not allowed.

- Although the COBOL statements for sorting (Sort, Release, and Return) are allowed, their functionality is severely restricted. Because of that, you'll probably never use them. Merge statements are never allowed.

Figure 2-5   COBOL statements that aren't supported under CICS

The specifications and BMS mapset for an inquiry program

Before you can code a CICS program, you need to create a *BMS mapset* to define the screens that are going to be used by the program. This mapset includes all the fields that are going to be displayed on the screens as well as the fields that need to be entered by the user. Before you can create a mapset, though, you need to know what the program will do and what its screens will look like. Although you saw the general operation of the customer inquiry program earlier in this chapter, the topics that follow will present the complete specifications for that program, including the program overview and screen layout. Then, you'll see the BMS mapset that's based on those specifications.

The program overview

Figure 2-6 presents the program overview for the customer inquiry program that you saw illustrated in figure 2-1. This overview begins with a brief description of the program's function. Then, it lists the I/O requirements for the program. Last, it presents a detailed list of processing specifications. These specifications state what the program is to do in response to various input actions. For example, if the user presses PF3 or PF12, the program is to return to the menu that invoked it.

The screen layout

Figure 2-6 also presents the screen layout for the one screen used by this program. This layout shows the positions of headings, captions, and data on the screen. For example, you can see that the caption "Customer number" begins in column 2 of line 5; that the user will enter the customer number in the entry field at column 27 on line 5; and that the program will display the customer's name and address in the fields on lines 7, 8, 9, and 10.

The program overview for the customer inquiry program

Program	CUSTINQ1: Customer inquiry
Trans-id	INQ1
Overview	Display customer information from the customer master file based on customer numbers entered by the user.
Input/output specifications	CUSTMAS Customer master file INQMAP1 Customer inquiry map
Processing specifications	1. Control is transferred to this program via XCTL from the menu program INVMENU with no communication area. The user can also start the program by entering the trans-id INQ1. In either case, the program should respond by displaying the customer inquiry map. 2. If the user enters a customer number, read the customer record from CUSTMAS and display it. If the record doesn't exist, display an error message. 3. If the user presses the Clear key, redisplay the customer inquiry map without any data. 4. If the user presses PF3 or PF12, return to the menu program INVMENU by issuing an XCTL command.

The screen layout for the customer inquiry program

Map name _____ INQMAP1 _____   Date _____ 2/13/2001 _____

Program name _____ CUSTINQ1 _____   Designer _____ Doug Lowe _____

```
 1  INQMAP1                Customer Inquiry                                                      XXXX
 2
 3  Type a customer number.      Then press Enter.
 4
 5  Customer number.  .  .  .  .  XXXXXX
 6
 7  Name and address  .  .  .  :  XXXXXXXXXXXXXXXXXXXXXXXXXXXXXXX
 8                                XXXXXXXXXXXXXXXXXXXXX
 9                                XXXXXXXXXXXXXXXXXXXXXXXXXXXX
10                                XXXXXXXXXXXXXXXXXX  XX  XXXXXXXXXX
11
...
23  XXXXXXXXXXXXXXXXXXXXXXXXXXXXXXXXXXXXXXXXXXXXXXXXXXXXXXXXXXXXXXXXXXXXXXXXXXXXXXXXXX
24  F3=Exit      F12=Cancel
```

Figure 2-6   The specifications for the customer inquiry program

The BMS mapset

The two parts of figure 2-7 present the BMS mapset for the customer inquiry screen. This is a special type of assembler language program that defines the format of each map that's used by a program. After you code the mapset, you run a program called an *assembler* that compiles (or assembles) the code into a physical mapset and a symbolic mapset. The *physical mapset* is used by CICS to determine the location, appearance, and operation of the data on the screen when the program that uses the mapset is run. The *symbolic mapset* is a copy member that can be copied into the COBOL program that uses the mapset. You use the fields in the symbolic mapset to work with the data on the screen.

When you code a mapset, you use three *macros*: DFHMSD to start the mapset; DFHMDI to start each map; and DFHMDF to define each field within a map. To end a mapset, you code another DFHMSD, as you can see on the second page of this mapset.

In this mapset, the first DFHMSD macro defines a mapset named INQSET1. Its parameters specify that the symbolic map that BMS generates from this mapset should be in COBOL (LANG=COBOL), that the symbolic map should include fields for both input and output (MODE=INOUT), and that the mapset should work with a standard 3270-type display station (TERM=3270-2). Although this macro includes other parameters, you don't need to worry about them now. You'll learn all the details in chapter 4.

Next, the DFHMDI macro defines a map named INQMAP1 that represents the one screen (map) that this program requires. This macro specifies that the size of the screen display is 24 lines of 80 characters each and that the map should be displayed starting in column 1 of line 1.

The other macros in this mapset except the last are the DFHMDF macros that define the fields on the screen. For example, the sixth DFHMDF macro defines a customer number field named CUSTNO. It says that this field should be positioned at column 26 in the fifth line. Actually, the POS parameter determines the location of the *attribute byte* for each field. This byte, which precedes each field, determines the characteristics of the field. As a result, the customer number field will actually start in column 27 of line 5.

The other parameters for a field give the length, attributes, color, and initial value for the field. Of these, the only entries that you may not understand are those for the ATTRB parameter. You'll learn more about these attributes in the chapter 4. For now, just realize that the PROT attribute indicates that the field is protected so it can't be changed, and UNPROT means that the field can be changed; NORM means that the field is displayed with normal intensity, and BRT means it's displayed with high intensity; and IC means that the cursor will be positioned on the field when the screen is displayed.

In addition to the parameters that are specified for each field, you should notice that most of the DFHMDF macros include a label, such as CUSTNO or LNAME, that gives a name to the field being defined. These labels will be used to generate the fields that are included in the symbolic mapset that's created from the BMS mapset. Since the only way to refer to a field in the BMS mapset

The code for the BMS mapset   **Page 1**

```
        PRINT NOGEN
INQSET1 DFHMSD TYPE=&SYSPARM,                                        X
               LANG=COBOL,                                          X
               MODE=INOUT,                                          X
               TERM=3270-2,                                         X
               CTRL=FREEKB,                                         X
               STORAGE=AUTO,                                        X
               TIOAPFX=YES
****************************************************************************
INQMAP1 DFHMDI SIZE=(24,80),                                        X
               LINE=1,                                              X
               COLUMN=1
****************************************************************************
        DFHMDF POS=(1,1),                                           X
               LENGTH=7,                                            X
               ATTRB=(NORM,PROT),                                   X
               COLOR=BLUE,                                          X
               INITIAL='INQMAP1'
        DFHMDF POS=(1,20),                                          X
               LENGTH=16,                                           X
               ATTRB=(NORM,PROT),                                   X
               COLOR=GREEN,                                         X
               INITIAL='Customer Inquiry'
TRANID  DFHMDF POS=(1,76),                                          X
               LENGTH=4,                                            X
               ATTRB=(NORM,PROT),                                   X
               COLOR=BLUE,                                          X
               INITIAL='XXXX'
****************************************************************************
        DFHMDF POS=(3,1),                                           X
               LENGTH=42,                                           X
               ATTRB=(NORM,PROT),                                   X
               COLOR=NEUTRAL,                                       X
               INITIAL='Type a customer number.   Then press Enter.'
        DFHMDF POS=(5,1),                                           X
               LENGTH=24,                                           X
               ATTRB=(NORM,PROT),                                   X
               COLOR=GREEN,                                         X
               INITIAL='Customer number. . . . .'
CUSTNO  DFHMDF POS=(5,26),                                          X
               LENGTH=6,                                            X
               ATTRB=(NORM,UNPROT,IC),                              X
               COLOR=TURQUOISE,                                     X
               INITIAL='_____'
        DFHMDF POS=(5,33),                                          X
               LENGTH=1,                                            X
               ATTRB=ASKIP
****************************************************************************
```

Description

- A BMS mapset is an assembler language program that defines the format of the maps that are used by a program. After you code a mapset, you *assemble* it to produce a *physical mapset* and a *symbolic mapset*.

- The physical mapset is used by CICS to determine the location, appearance, and operation of data that's displayed on a screen. The symbolic mapset is a COBOL copy member that allows you to manipulate the screen data in your COBOL program.

Figure 2-7   The BMS mapset for the customer inquiry program (part 1 of 2)

from a COBOL program is through the symbolic mapset, you need to include a label on the DFHMDF macro for any field you'll need to refer to in the code.

With that as background, you should be able to understand how each field in the inquiry screen is defined. For instance, CUSTNO will be unprotected, it will be displayed in turquoise with normal intensity, and it will have an initial display of underscores; LNAME will be protected and will be displayed in turquoise with normal intensity; and MESSAGE will be protected and will be displayed in yellow with high intensity. All of these definitions follow IBM's *CUA (Common User Access)* standards, which are designed to insure that programs interact with users in consistent ways. You'll learn more about these standards in chapter 4.

The last macro in the mapset is a DFHMSD macro. On this macro, you code a single parameter to mark the end of the mapset: TYPE=FINAL.

In addition to the macros for defining the mapset, maps, and fields, PRINT NOGEN can be coded at the beginning of a mapset. This is a command that tells the assembler not to print the statements that are generated as a result of assembling the macros. And at the end of a mapset, you need to code END. This command tells the assembler that there are no more source statements.

To enter the code for a BMS mapset, you use an editor like the ISPF editor. Another alternative, though, is to use a program called a *screen painter*. This lets you design the screen layout at your terminal interactively. Then, the screen painter generates the assembler language code that you need for the mapset. Even though the code is generated for you, you still you need to understand it because you may need to refer to it later on.

The code for the BMS mapset

```
           DFHMDF POS=(7,1),                                          X
                  LENGTH=24,                                          X
                  ATTRB=(NORM,PROT),                                  X
                  COLOR=GREEN,                                        X
                  INITIAL='Name and address . . . :'
LNAME      DFHMDF POS=(7,26),                                         X
                  LENGTH=30,                                          X
                  ATTRB=(NORM,PROT),                                  X
                  COLOR=TURQUOISE
FNAME      DFHMDF POS=(8,26),                                         X
                  LENGTH=20,                                          X
                  ATTRB=(NORM,PROT),                                  X
                  COLOR=TURQUOISE
ADDR       DFHMDF POS=(9,26),                                         X
                  LENGTH=30,                                          X
                  ATTRB=(NORM,PROT),                                  X
                  COLOR=TURQUOISE
CITY       DFHMDF POS=(10,26),                                        X
                  LENGTH=20,                                          X
                  ATTRB=(NORM,PROT),                                  X
                  COLOR=TURQUOISE
STATE      DFHMDF POS=(10,47),                                        X
                  LENGTH=2,                                           X
                  ATTRB=(NORM,PROT),                                  X
                  COLOR=TURQUOISE
ZIPCODE    DFHMDF POS=(10,50),                                        X
                  LENGTH=10,                                          X
                  ATTRB=(NORM,PROT),                                  X
                  COLOR=TURQUOISE
**********************************************************************
MESSAGE    DFHMDF POS=(23,1),                                         X
                  LENGTH=79,                                          X
                  ATTRB=(BRT,PROT),                                   X
                  COLOR=YELLOW
           DFHMDF POS=(24,1),                                         X
                  LENGTH=20,                                          X
                  ATTRB=(NORM,PROT),                                  X
                  COLOR=BLUE,                                         X
                  INITIAL='F3=Exit    F12=Cancel'
DUMMY      DFHMDF POS=(24,79),                                        X
                  LENGTH=1,                                           X
                  ATTRB=(DRK,PROT,FSET),                              X
                  INITIAL=' '
**********************************************************************
           DFHMSD TYPE=FINAL
           END
```

Description

- To code a BMS mapset, you use two assembler commands (PRINT NOGEN and END) and three *macros* (DFHMSD, DFHMDI, and DFHMDF).

- A DFHMSD macro marks the start and end of each mapset. A DFHMDI macro marks the beginning of each map in the mapset. And a DFHMDF macro defines each field in a mapset. Each field definition can include, among other things, the field's starting position on the screen, its length, its display attributes, its color, and its initial value.

Figure 2-7   The BMS mapset for the customer inquiry program (part 2 of 2)

The symbolic map

Figure 2-8 presents the symbolic mapset that the assembler produces from the BMS mapset in figure 2-7. This is a copy member that can be copied into your COBOL program. Because this symbolic mapset contains just one map, you can also refer to it as a *symbolic map*. Similarly, if a symbolic mapset contains more than one map, you can refer to each map as a symbolic map.

If you look at both pages of the symbolic map for the inquiry program, you can see that the group item named INQMAP1I is redefined by a group item named INQMAP1O. The fields in the INQMAP1I group item are intended for use with input operations, and the fields in the INQMAP1O group item are intended for use with output operations. As a result, different pictures can be used for input and output. This is most useful when you work with numeric fields. Then, the output fields can be defined as numeric edited so they're displayed properly, and the input fields can be defined as numeric or alphanumeric. Because the fields in the inquiry program are all alphanumeric, all of their pictures are the same for input and output.

For each screen field that's named in the mapset, the symbolic map contains a data field, a length field, an attribute field, and a field that indicates if the value of the field has changed. The names for these fields are created by adding a one-character suffix to the label that was coded on the DFHMDF macro in the mapset. So the name of the input field for the field labeled CUSTNO is CUSTNOI, the name of the length field is CUSTNOL, the name of the attribute field is CUSTNOA, and the name of the field that indicates a change is CUSTNOF.

The code for the symbolic map   **Page 1**

```
01 INQMAP1I.
    03 FILLER                          PIC X(12).
    03 TRANIDL                         PIC S9(4) COMP.
    03 TRANIDF                         PIC X.
    03 FILLER REDEFINES TRANIDF.
        05 TRANIDA                     PIC X.
    03 TRANIDI                         PIC X(4).
    03 CUSTNOL                         PIC S9(4) COMP.
    03 CUSTNOF                         PIC X.
    03 FILLER REDEFINES CUSTNOF.
        05 CUSTNOA                     PIC X.
    03 CUSTNOI                         PIC X(6).
    03 LNAMEL                          PIC S9(4) COMP.
    03 LNAMEF                          PIC X.
    03 FILLER REDEFINES LNAMEF.
        05 LNAMEA                      PIC X.
    03 LNAMEI                          PIC X(30).
    03 FNAMEL                          PIC S9(4) COMP.
    03 FNAMEF                          PIC X.
    03 FILLER REDEFINES FNAMEF.
        05 FNAMEA                      PIC X.
    03 FNAMEI                          PIC X(20).
    03 ADDRL                           PIC S9(4) COMP.
    03 ADDRF                           PIC X.
    03 FILLER REDEFINES ADDRF.
        05 ADDRA                       PIC X.
    03 ADDRI                           PIC X(30).
    03 CITYL                           PIC S9(4) COMP.
    03 CITYF                           PIC X.
    03 FILLER REDEFINES CITYF.
        05 CITYA                       PIC X.
    03 CITYI                           PIC X(20).
    03 STATEL                          PIC S9(4) COMP.
    03 STATEF                          PIC X.
    03 FILLER REDEFINES STATEF.
        05 STATEA                      PIC X.
    03 STATEI                          PIC X(2).
```

Description

- A *symbolic map* is a COBOL copy member that's created when you assemble a mapset. The fields in a symbolic map represent the data that's sent to and received from a terminal by a COBOL program.

- You use a Copy statement to copy the symbolic map into the Working-Storage Section of your program.

- A symbolic map includes two 01-level items: one for input and one for output. Because the second item contains a Redefines clause (see the next page), it occupies the same storage space as the first item. That way, different Picture clauses can be used for input to a field and output from it.

- For each input field in the mapset (I), the symbolic map contains a field that indicates the length of the data in the field (L), a field that indicates if the user made changes to the field (F), and a field that contains the display attributes (A).

Figure 2-8   The symbolic map for the customer inquiry program (part 1 of 2)

In the redefined area for the output fields, you'll notice that only the data fields are named, like CUSTNOO and LNAMEO. The length, attribute, and change indicator fields are coded as FILLER. To change the value of any of these fields for an output operation, then, you have to refer to the fields in the input area.

As you work with a symbolic map, you don't need to be concerned with the details of how the fields it contains are defined in the BMS mapset. You just need to know the names of the fields that you're going to use in your COBOL programs. The fields you'll use the most are the length fields (with data names ending in *L*) and the fields that contain the data (with data names ending in *I* for input fields and *O* for output fields). Next, you'll see how these fields are used by the customer inquiry program.

The code for the symbolic map   **Page 2**

```
03 ZIPCODEL                    PIC S9(4) COMP.
03 ZIPCODEF                    PIC X.
03 FILLER REDEFINES ZIPCODEF.
   05 ZIPCODEA                   PIC X.
03 ZIPCODEI                    PIC X(10).
03 MESSAGEL                    PIC S9(4) COMP.
03 MESSAGEF                    PIC X.
03 FILLER REDEFINES MESSAGEF.
   05 MESSAGEA                   PIC X.
03 MESSAGEI                    PIC X(79).
03 DUMMYL                      PIC S9(4) COMP.
03 DUMMYF                      PIC X.
03 FILLER REDEFINES DUMMYF.
   05 DUMMYA                     PIC X.
03 DUMMYI                      PIC X(1).

01 INQMAP1O REDEFINES INQMAP1I.
03 FILLER                      PIC X(12).
03 FILLER                      PIC X(3).
03 TRANIDO                     PIC X(4).
03 FILLER                      PIC X(3).
03 CUSTNOO                     PIC X(6).
03 FILLER                      PIC X(3).
03 LNAMEO                      PIC X(30).
03 FILLER                      PIC X(3).
03 FNAMEO                      PIC X(20).
03 FILLER                      PIC X(3).
03 ADDRO                       PIC X(30).
03 FILLER                      PIC X(3).
03 CITYO                       PIC X(20).
03 FILLER                      PIC X(3).
03 STATEO                      PIC X(2).
03 FILLER                      PIC X(3).
03 ZIPCODEO                    PIC X(10).
03 FILLER                      PIC X(3).
03 MESSAGEO                    PIC X(79).
03 FILLER                      PIC X(3).
03 DUMMYO                      PIC X(1).
```

Description

- The definitions of the input fields are redefined by the definitions of the output fields. For each output field (O), the symbolic map contains a Picture for the output data.

- Because all of the fields in the output area except for the output field are defined as Filler, you can't refer to these fields from the output area. Instead, you have to use the field names in the input area.

Figure 2-8   The symbolic map for the customer inquiry program (part 2 of 2)

The design and COBOL code for the inquiry program

Before you code a CICS program, you should take the time to develop an event/response chart and a structure chart for the program. These design tools let you create a program that's easier to code, test, and debug. The charts for the inquiry program are presented next, followed by the COBOL code for the program.

The event/response chart

A pseudo-conversational CICS program must be written so it responds appropriately to each type of user action that can occur. Because this is so important, it's worth taking the time to summarize all of the possible actions (*events*) and the appropriate responses before you start coding. The best way to do that is to prepare an *event/response chart* like the one in figure 2-9.

As you can see, this chart goes beyond what's in the program overview to clarify the processing that must be done to retrieve and display a customer record. As a result, it provides for several input actions that weren't included in the overview. When you develop a chart like this, you do your best to include every possible user action so your program can provide for it.

The structure chart

To plan the overall structure of a program, we recommend the techniques of *top-down design*. The basic idea of top-down design is to design a program by dividing it into its major functional modules, then dividing those modules into their functional components, and so forth until each module can be coded in a single COBOL paragraph. To develop and document this design, you can use a *structure chart* like the one in figure 2-9.

Once the design is complete, the structure chart becomes your guide to coding the Procedure Division of the CICS program. There, each module is implemented as a single COBOL paragraph, and the paragraph name consists of the module number followed by the module name. For instance, module number 1000 in the chart in this figure will be implemented by a COBOL paragraph named 1000-PROCESS-CUSTOMER-MAP.

In chapter 3, you'll learn the details of how to design a CICS program with a structure chart because we think that's a critical step in the development process. You'll also learn more about creating event/response charts because you can't design a CICS program without first knowing what events the program has to respond to.

An event/response chart for the customer inquiry program

Event	Response
Start the program	Display the customer map.
Enter key	Receive the customer map. Edit the customer number. If valid read the record. If the record exists display it. If the number isn't valid or the record doesn't exist display an error message.
PF3 or PF12	Return to the menu program.
Clear key	Redisplay the customer map without any data.
Any PA key	Ignore the key.
Any other key	Display an error message.

The structure chart for the customer inquiry program

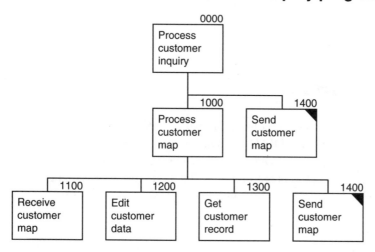

Description

- A pseudo-conversational program must be designed to respond appropriately to each type of user action that might occur.

- The best way to identify the user actions and responses is to create an *event/response chart*. This chart summarizes each user action (*event*) and the program's response to that event.

- The program *structure chart* specifies the overall program structure. For a pseudo-conversational program, the top-level module must determine what processing is to be done each time it's executed. Those processing options are identified by the modules in the second level of the chart.

Figure 2-9   The design for the customer inquiry program

The Execute Interface Block

When you prepare a CICS program for execution, CICS inserts code that's needed for the program to operate properly under CICS. One of these blocks of code is called the *Execute Interface Block*, or *EIB*. The EIB is inserted into the Linkage Section of a program, and its fields provide information about the current task.

In figure 2-10, you can see the start of this block of fields. Note that this block doesn't appear in the source listing of your COBOL program. As a result, you have to get the names of the fields that you want to use from other documentation.

The two EIB fields you'll use most often are EIBAID and EIBCALEN. The EIBCALEN field contains the length of the data that is passed to the program through its *communication area*. A program can use this area to store the data that it will need the next time it's executed. That's necessary because the contents of the working-storage fields are lost when a pseudo-conversational program ends. If the length of this area is zero, it means that no data was passed to the program. In other words, the program is being executed for the first time in a pseudo-conversational session.

In contrast, the EIBAID field gives the value of the last AID key that was pressed. You can use it to determine the processing the user has requested.

The DFHAID copy member

To make it easy to write the code that tests the values in the EIBAID field, IBM supplies a copy member named DFHAID. The first part of this member is shown in figure 2-10. It gives a name to each of the values that represents an AID key. For instance, DFHENTER is the name for the value that represents the Enter key, and DFHPF3 is the name for the value that represents the PF3 key. As a result, you can code

```
IF EIBAID = DFHPF3
```

when you want to see if the AID key that was pressed was the PF3 key, instead of coding

```
IF EIBAID = '3'
```

Once you get used to the names in this copy member, you'll have no trouble using them.

Two of the fields in the Execute Interface Block

```
01      DFHEIBLK.
        .
        .
        02   EIBCALEN     PIC S9(4) COMP.
        02   EIBAID       PIC X(1).
        .
        .
```

The DFHAID copy member

```
01      DFHAID.
        02   DFHNULL    PIC  X  VALUE IS ' '.
        02   DFHENTER   PIC  X  VALUE IS ''''.
        02   DFHCLEAR   PIC  X  VALUE IS '_'.
        02   DFHCLRP    PIC  X  VALUE IS '('.
        02   DFHPEN     PIC  X  VALUE IS '='.
        02   DFHOPID    PIC  X  VALUE IS 'W'.
        02   DFHMSRE    PIC  X  VALUE IS 'X'.
        02   DFHSTRF    PIC  X  VALUE IS 'h'.
        02   DFHTRIG    PIC  X  VALUE IS '''.
        02   DFHPA1     PIC  X  VALUE IS '%'.
        02   DFHPA2     PIC  X  VALUE IS ''.
        02   DFHPA3     PIC  X  VALUE IS ','.
        02   DFHPF1     PIC  X  VALUE IS '1'.
        02   DFHPF2     PIC  X  VALUE IS '2'.
        02   DFHPF3     PIC  X  VALUE IS '3'.
        02   DFHPF4     PIC  X  VALUE IS '4'.
        02   DFHPF5     PIC  X  VALUE IS '5'.
        02   DFHPF6     PIC  X  VALUE IS '6'.
        02   DFHPF7     PIC  X  VALUE IS '7'.
        02   DFHPF8     PIC  X  VALUE IS '8'.
        02   DFHPF9     PIC  X  VALUE IS '9'.
        02   DFHPF10    PIC  X  VALUE IS ':'.
        02   DFHPF11    PIC  X  VALUE IS '#'.
        02   DFHPF12    PIC  X  VALUE IS '@'.
        .
        .
```

Description

- The *Execute Interface Block* (*EIB*) is a CICS area that contains information related to the current task, such as the date and time the task was started and the transaction-id that was used to start it. The definition of this area is inserted into the Linkage Section of the program when the program is prepared for execution.

- The EIBCALEN field contains the length of the data passed to the program through its *communication area* (DFHCOMMAREA). A length of zero indicates that no data was passed to the program, which means that it's the first execution of the program.

- When the user presses an AID key, CICS passes a one-byte value to the program through the EIBAID field in the Execute Interface Block. You can use the value of this field to determine the processing the user has requested.

- The DFHAID copy member contains literal values that correspond to the AID keys that the user can press to communicate with the system.

Figure 2-10   The Execute Interface Block and the DFHAID copy member

The COBOL code

Figure 2-11 presents the source code for the customer inquiry program. The first thing you should notice is that the Environment Division doesn't include any entries, and the Data Division doesn't include a File Section. That's because the customer master file is defined in the CICS File Control Table (FCT). Because the FCT keeps track of the characteristics of the file, you don't have to code Select or FD statements for it.

In the Working-Storage Section, you can see the one switch and the one flag used by this program. The three conditions that are defined for the flag will be used to determine which options are coded in the SEND MAP command when the customer map is sent to the screen.

The next field is for data related to the communication area. As you'll recall, this area can be used to store the data that's passed to and from the program. To use the communication area, you need to provide two definitions for it in your program: one in the Working-Storage Section and one in the Linkage Section. The working-storage definition in this program is named COMMUNICATION-AREA, and the Linkage Section definition is named DFHCOMMAREA. Although you can use any name for the working-storage field, you must use the name DFHCOMMAREA for the Linkage Section field.

When a CICS program starts, the data in the CICS communication area is available through the DFHCOMMAREA field. The program can then use this information to determine the processing to be done. Then, when the program ends, it can specify that the data in the working-storage communication area be stored in the CICS communication area so it's available for the next program execution. In the inquiry program, the communication area is a one-byte field, but a more complicated program may require many fields.

The next working-storage entry is RESPONSE-CODE. This field is used to test the completion status of the CICS READ command that retrieves records from the customer master file.

After the response-code field, you can see the record description for the customer master records that are read by this program. Normally, a record description like this is copied into a CICS program, but we've included it here to make the program easier to follow.

This description is followed by two Copy statements. The first one copies the symbolic map for the mapset named INQSET1, while the second one copies the DFHAID member that is supplied by IBM.

Before I go on, I want to point out that each time a program is executed, a fresh copy of working storage is obtained. As a result, changes you make to the contents of working-storage fields aren't saved between executions of a pseudo-conversational program, and any initial values established by Value clauses are restored. If you need to preserve data from one program execution to the next, you can store it in the communication area.

The customer inquiry program   **Page 1**

```
      IDENTIFICATION DIVISION.
*
      PROGRAM-ID.  CUSTINQ1.
*
      ENVIRONMENT DIVISION.
*
      DATA DIVISION.
*
      WORKING-STORAGE SECTION.
*
      01  SWITCHES.
*
          05  VALID-DATA-SW             PIC X      VALUE 'Y'.
              88 VALID-DATA                        VALUE 'Y'.
*
      01  FLAGS.
*
          05  SEND-FLAG                 PIC X.
              88  SEND-ERASE                       VALUE '1'.
              88  SEND-DATAONLY                    VALUE '2'.
              88  SEND-DATAONLY-ALARM              VALUE '3'.
*
      01  COMMUNICATION-AREA            PIC X.
*
      01  RESPONSE-CODE                 PIC S9(8)  COMP.
*
      01  CUSTOMER-MASTER-RECORD.
*
          05  CM-CUSTOMER-NUMBER        PIC X(6).
          05  CM-FIRST-NAME             PIC X(20).
          05  CM-LAST-NAME              PIC X(30).
          05  CM-ADDRESS                PIC X(30).
          05  CM-CITY                   PIC X(20).
          05  CM-STATE                  PIC X(2).
          05  CM-ZIP-CODE               PIC X(10).
*
      COPY INQSET1.
*
      COPY DFHAID.
*
      LINKAGE SECTION.
*
      01  DFHCOMMAREA                   PIC X.
*
```

Figure 2-11   The COBOL code for the customer inquiry program (part 1 of 4)

Page 2 of the COBOL listing presents the top-level procedure for this program. It contains the logic required to implement the pseudo-conversational design. This logic is coded as an Evaluate statement that specifies the actions that are required for the conditions the program may encounter when it's started.

The first When clause in this statement tests the value of EIBCALEN, which is the EIB field that contains the length of the data passed to the program through its communication area. If the length is zero, it means that no data was passed to the program, which indicates that there was no previous execution of the program. As a result, procedure 1400 is performed to send the customer map to the screen. But first, the program initializes the map by moving Low-Value to the output area, it sets the TRANIDO field in the symbolic map to INQ1 so the correct trans-id is displayed, and it sets Send-Erase to True so procedure 1400 will know to clear the screen before displaying the map.

The next four When clauses test for values in the EIBAID field, which gives the value of the AID key that the user pressed to start this execution of the program. Each of these conditions uses a data name from the DFHAID copy member. The program checks the EIBAID field so it can avoid retrieving data from the terminal if the function it's about to perform doesn't call for it. That reduces network use and improves overall system performance.

If the user pressed the Clear key (DFHCLEAR), the program initializes the map, sets the TRANIDO field to INQ1, sets Send-Erase to True, and performs procedure 1400 to restart with a fresh screen. If the user pressed one of the program attention (PA) keys (DFHPA1 OR DFHPA2 OR DFHPA3), no special action is taken. Then, the Continue statement causes program execution to continue with the first statement after the Evaluate statement.

If the user pressed the PF3 or PF12 key (DFHPF3 OR DFHPF12), the program issues a CICS XCTL command to end the program and transfer control to the program named INVMENU. As you'll learn in chapter 10, this program displays a simple menu that you can use to start the inquiry program as well as other programs. Finally, if the user pressed the Enter key (DFHENTER), the program performs procedure 1000 to receive and process the customer map.

If none of these conditions are true, the When Other clause performs procedure 1400 to display an error message that indicates that an invalid key was pressed. This time, Send-Dataonly-Alarm is set to True so procedure 1400 will use the form of the SEND MAP command that sounds the alarm.

Unless the XCTL command was executed in response to PF3 or PF12, the program continues with the RETURN command that follows the Evaluate statement. This command causes CICS to invoke the same trans-id (INQ1) the next time the user presses one of the AID keys. It also says that the data in COMMUNICATION-AREA should be passed to the next execution of the program through the CICS communication area. Be aware that you can put a value in this field if it's required by the program specifications. In this case, though, that's not necessary because the program never checks the value of this field, only its length.

The customer inquiry program

```
PROCEDURE DIVISION.
*
0000-PROCESS-CUSTOMER-INQUIRY.
*
    EVALUATE TRUE
*
        WHEN EIBCALEN = ZERO
            MOVE LOW-VALUE TO INQMAP1O
            MOVE 'INQ1'    TO TRANIDO
            SET SEND-ERASE TO TRUE
            PERFORM 1400-SEND-CUSTOMER-MAP
*
        WHEN EIBAID = DFHCLEAR
            MOVE LOW-VALUE TO INQMAP1O
            MOVE 'INQ1'    TO TRANIDO
            SET SEND-ERASE TO TRUE
            PERFORM 1400-SEND-CUSTOMER-MAP
*
        WHEN EIBAID = DFHPA1 OR DFHPA2 OR DFHPA3
            CONTINUE
*
        WHEN EIBAID = DFHPF3 OR DFHPF12
            EXEC CICS
                XCTL PROGRAM('INVMENU')
            END-EXEC
*
        WHEN EIBAID = DFHENTER
            PERFORM 1000-PROCESS-CUSTOMER-MAP
*
        WHEN OTHER
            MOVE LOW-VALUE TO INQMAP1O
            MOVE 'Invalid key pressed.' TO MESSAGEO
            SET SEND-DATAONLY-ALARM TO TRUE
            PERFORM 1400-SEND-CUSTOMER-MAP
*
    END-EVALUATE.
*
    EXEC CICS
        RETURN TRANSID('INQ1')
                COMMAREA(COMMUNICATION-AREA)
    END-EXEC.
*
```

Figure 2-11   The COBOL code for the customer inquiry program (part 2 of 4)

If the user pressed the Enter key, procedure 1000 is performed. This procedure performs procedure 1100 to get the customer number the user entered on the screen and procedure 1200 to edit the number. If the number is valid, procedure 1000 performs procedure 1300 to retrieve the requested record from the customer master file. Then, if the record is retrieved (indicating that the customer number is still valid), the program displays the customer data by performing procedure 1400 with Send-Dataonly set to True. Otherwise, procedure 1000 performs procedure 1400 with Send-Dataonly-Alarm set to True to alert the user that the customer number isn't valid.

To get the user entry, procedure 1100 contains a single CICS RECEIVE MAP command. This command receives data from the terminal using the INQMAP1 map in the INQSET1 mapset. That data is then stored in the input area of the symbolic map (INQMAP1I).

The only editing requirement for this program is that the user must enter a customer number. Procedure 1200 does this editing by checking the length and input fields of the customer number in the symbolic map. If the length is zero, it means that the user didn't enter anything or pressed the Erase-EOF key. In either case, no data is transmitted back to CICS so the CUSTNOI field will contain low-values. Since low-values and spaces aren't the same, this routine also checks to see whether the input field contains spaces. If either of these error conditions is true, procedure 1200 turns the valid-data switch off so procedure 1000 can determine what processing it should do next. Procedure 1200 also moves an error message to the output MESSAGE field (MESSAGEO) in the symbolic map.

If procedure 1200 didn't turn the valid-data switch off, procedure 1000 performs procedure 1300 to retrieve the requested record from the customer file. This procedure starts by issuing a CICS READ command that tells CICS to read a record from the file named CUSTMAS into the working-storage field named CUSTOMER-MASTER-RECORD. The RIDFLD option specifies that the key value for the record is in CUSTNOI, which is the field in the symbolic map where the customer number entered by the user was stored by the RECEIVE MAP command. And the RESP option specifies that the response code that indicates whether the operation was successful should be placed in the working-storage field named RESPONSE-CODE.

The code that follows the READ command tests the value of the response-code field. To do that, it uses the special keyword DFHRESP followed by the condition to be tested. Here, the program tests for a NORMAL response and the not-found condition (NOTFND). If the command completed normally, the program moves data from the customer record to the corresponding fields in the output map. But if the NOTFND condition occurred, the program sets the valid-data switch to N, moves an appropriate error message to MESSAGEO, and clears the output fields in the symbolic map as shown on the next page of this listing.

The customer inquiry program   **Page 3**

```
1000-PROCESS-CUSTOMER-MAP.
*
    PERFORM 1100-RECEIVE-CUSTOMER-MAP.
    PERFORM 1200-EDIT-CUSTOMER-DATA.
    IF VALID-DATA
        PERFORM 1300-GET-CUSTOMER-RECORD
    END-IF.
    IF VALID-DATA
        SET SEND-DATAONLY TO TRUE
        PERFORM 1400-SEND-CUSTOMER-MAP
    ELSE
        SET SEND-DATAONLY-ALARM TO TRUE
        PERFORM 1400-SEND-CUSTOMER-MAP
    END-IF.
*
 1100-RECEIVE-CUSTOMER-MAP.
*
    EXEC CICS
        RECEIVE MAP('INQMAP1')
                MAPSET('INQSET1')
                INTO(INQMAP1I)
    END-EXEC.
*
 1200-EDIT-CUSTOMER-DATA.
*
    IF      CUSTNOL = ZERO
        OR CUSTNOI = SPACE
        MOVE 'N' TO VALID-DATA-SW
        MOVE 'You must enter a customer number.' TO MESSAGEO
    END-IF.
*
 1300-GET-CUSTOMER-RECORD.
*
    EXEC CICS
        READ FILE('CUSTMAS')
             INTO(CUSTOMER-MASTER-RECORD)
             RIDFLD(CUSTNOI)
             RESP(RESPONSE-CODE)
    END-EXEC.
*
    EVALUATE RESPONSE-CODE
        WHEN DFHRESP(NORMAL)
            MOVE SPACE          TO MESSAGEO
            MOVE CM-LAST-NAME   TO LNAMEO
            MOVE CM-FIRST-NAME  TO FNAMEO
            MOVE CM-ADDRESS     TO ADDRO
            MOVE CM-CITY        TO CITYO
            MOVE CM-STATE       TO STATEO
            MOVE CM-ZIP-CODE    TO ZIPCODEO
```

Figure 2-11   The COBOL code for the customer inquiry program (part 3 of 4)

If RESPONSE-CODE indicates any other condition, it means that a serious error occurred when the READ command was executed. In that case, the program handles the error by issuing a CICS ABEND command to terminate the program abnormally.

Unless procedure 1300 terminates the program, procedure 1000 continues by performing procedure 1400 to issue the appropriate SEND MAP command. In this procedure, one of three SEND MAP commands is issued depending on the setting of the Send-Flag field. Notice that all three commands specify the same mapset, map, and source of the data to be sent to the screen (the output area of the symbolic map). It's the other parameters that vary.

The first SEND MAP command is issued if the Send-Erase setting is turned on. That happens when the program is started for the first time or when the user presses the Clear key. This command includes the ERASE option, which causes the screen to be erased before the map is displayed. As a result, the screen will look like the first one in figure 2-1.

The second SEND MAP command is issued if the Send-Dataonly setting is turned on. That happens when the user enters a valid customer number. Then, the SEND MAP command includes the DATAONLY option. That means that only the data in the symbolic map is sent to the terminal, because the literals that make up the headings, captions, and instructions are already there from the previous execution of the program. This improves the performance of the program.

The third SEND MAP command is issued if the Send-Dataonly-Alarm setting is turned on. That happens when the user presses an invalid key or enters an invalid customer number. Then, the SEND MAP command includes the DATAONLY and ALARM options. The ALARM option causes an audio beep at the terminal to call the user's attention to the error.

The customer inquiry program   **Page 4**

```
            WHEN DFHRESP(NOTFND)
                MOVE 'N' TO VALID-DATA-SW
                MOVE 'That customer does not exist.' TO MESSAGEO
                MOVE SPACE TO LNAMEO
                              FNAMEO
                              ADDRO
                              CITYO
                              STATEO
                              ZIPCODEO
            WHEN OTHER
                EXEC CICS
                    ABEND
                END-EXEC
        END-EVALUATE.
*
    1400-SEND-CUSTOMER-MAP.
*
        EVALUATE TRUE
            WHEN SEND-ERASE
                EXEC CICS
                    SEND MAP('INQMAP1')
                        MAPSET('INQSET1')
                        FROM(INQMAP1O)
                        ERASE
                END-EXEC
            WHEN SEND-DATAONLY
                EXEC CICS
                    SEND MAP('INQMAP1')
                        MAPSET('INQSET1')
                        FROM(INQMAP1O)
                        DATAONLY
                END-EXEC
            WHEN SEND-DATAONLY-ALARM
                EXEC CICS
                    SEND MAP('INQMAP1')
                        MAPSET('INQSET1')
                        FROM(INQMAP1O)
                        DATAONLY
                        ALARM
                END-EXEC
        END-EVALUATE.
```

Figure 2-11   The COBOL code for the customer inquiry program (part 4 of 4)

The CICS commands used in the program

If you look back over the COBOL code in figure 2-11, you can see that the program used just six CICS commands. To make sure that you have a good grasp of what these commands do and how you should code them, the next three figures summarize them. To get you started, these figures show only the basic options for each command, but you'll learn how to use other options in chapter 5.

The SEND MAP and RECEIVE MAP commands

Figure 2-12 summarizes the two commands that work with maps. As you have seen in the inquiry program, the SEND MAP command sends the data from a map within a mapset to a terminal. As a result, you need to identify the mapset and map on the command. You also need to use the FROM option to specify the name of the data area in the symbolic map that contains the data to be sent to the terminal.

If you code just those options, the data in the symbolic map is combined with the data in the physical map, and both are sent to the screen. To limit the amount of data that's sent, however, you can code the MAPONLY or the DATAONLY option. In the first case, only the data in the physical map is sent, so you don't have to code the FROM option. In the second case, only the data in the symbolic map is sent.

Usually, you'll omit the MAPONLY and DATAONLY options the first time a map is displayed. You'll also code the ERASE option on this command to erase the previous contents of the screen before the new screen is displayed. Then, you'll code the DATAONLY option on subsequent SEND MAP commands so the headings aren't sent again, and you'll omit the ERASE option so the current headings aren't erased.

When you code the RECEIVE MAP command, you also code the mapset and map name. But this time, you use the INTO option to provide the name of the data area in the symbolic map that will receive the data.

The syntax of the SEND MAP command

```
EXEC CICS
    SEND  MAP(map-name)
          [MAPSET(mapset-name)]
          [FROM(data-name)]
          [MAPONLY | DATAONLY]
          [ERASE]
          [ALARM]]
END-EXEC
```

Option	Description
MAP	Specifies the one- to seven-character name of the map for the output data.
MAPSET	Specifies the one- to seven-character name of the mapset that contains the map.
FROM	Specifies the name of the area in the symbolic map that contains the data to be mapped.
MAPONLY/ DATAONLY	MAPONLY sends only constant data from the physical map, so no FROM area is used. DATAONLY sends only data from the FROM area, so no constant data from the physical map is sent. If neither option is specified, both the constant data in the physical map and the data in the FROM area are sent.
ERASE	Causes the contents of the screen to be erased before data is displayed.
ALARM	Causes the alarm to sound when the map is displayed.

A SEND MAP command that sends only the data from the symbolic map

```
EXEC CICS
    SEND MAP('INQMAP1')
         MAPSET('INQSET1')
         FROM(INQMAP1O)
         DATAONLY
END-EXEC.
```

The syntax of the RECEIVE MAP command

```
EXEC CICS
    RECEIVE  MAP(map-name)
             [MAPSET(mapset-name)]
             INTO(data-name)
END-EXEC
```

Option	Description
MAP	Specifies the one- to seven-character name of the map for the input data.
MAPSET	Specifies the one- to seven-character name of the mapset that contains the map.
INTO	Specifies the name of the data area where the mapped data should be placed.

A typical RECEIVE MAP command

```
EXEC CICS
    RECEIVE MAP('INQMAP1')
            MAPSET('INQSET1')
            INTO(INQMAP1I)
END-EXEC.
```

Figure 2-12   The basic formats of the SEND MAP and RECEIVE MAP commands

The READ command

Figure 2-13 summarizes the use of the READ command. This command can be used to read data from all three types of VSAM files: key-sequenced (indexed), entry-sequenced (sequential), and relative record files. Most of the time, though, this command is used to read key-sequenced files on a random basis. So that's what this summary emphasizes.

If you're familiar with the COBOL commands for working with indexed files, you shouldn't have any trouble using the CICS READ command. The three options that it requires provide the name of the file, the name of the data area where the data should be placed when a record is read, and the name of the field that contains the key of the record to be read.

To determine whether the read operation is successful, you can also code the RESP option with this command. Then, after a read operation is attempted, CICS puts a *response code* in the field that's named in the RESP option. You can then test this code to see whether the read operation was successful or whether an *exceptional condition* occurred. If, for example, the file doesn't contain a record with the key that the command has specified, a "not found" condition occurs.

As you have already seen, you can use the DFHRESP keyword to check the response code. To test for the not-found condition, for example, you code NOTFND in the parentheses after DFHRESP. And to test for a successful read operation, you code NORMAL in the parentheses. In chapter 5, you'll learn all of the common codes for exceptional I/O conditions.

As you might guess, the RESP option is used most often in file I/O commands, which is why we've only included it in the syntax of the READ command in this chapter. Be aware, though, that you can code the RESP option on any CICS command. The response codes that CICS returns will vary according to the function of the command. So throughout this book, you'll learn about new response codes whenever they apply to the functions presented in a chapter.

The syntax of the READ command

```
EXEC CICS
    READ  FILE(filename)
          INTO(data-name)
          RIDFLD(data-name)
         [RESP(response-code)]
END-EXEC
```

Option	Description
FILE	Specifies the name of the file that contains the record to be read.
INTO	Specifies the name of the data area where the input record is placed.
RIDFLD	For a key-sequenced file, specifies the name of the field that contains the key of the record to be read.
RESP	Specifies the name of the field where CICS stores the response code from the read operation.

A READ command that reads a record from a key-sequenced file

```
EXEC CICS
    READ FILE('CUSTMAS')
         INTO(CUSTOMER-MASTER-RECORD)
         RIDFLD(CUSTNOI)
         RESP(RESPONSE-CODE)
END-EXEC.
```

An If statement that tests the response code after a read operation

```
IF RESPONSE-CODE = DFHRESP(NORMAL)
      .
      .
      .
```

Description

- The READ command retrieves a record from a VSAM file. Although this command is usually used with key-sequenced (indexed) files, it can also be used with entry-sequenced (sequential) and relative record files.

- The RESP option can be used with any CICS command. The *response code* it returns indicates whether the operation was successful or whether an *exceptional condition* occurred.

- To test the response code that CICS places in the response-code field, you can use the DFHRESP keyword as shown above. Within the parentheses, you code the name of the condition that you want to test.

- If a READ command successfully reads a record, the NORMAL condition occurs. If the specified record can't be found, however, a NOTFND condition occurs.

Figure 2-13   The basic format of the READ command

The RETURN, XCTL, and ABEND commands

Figure 2-14 summarizes three of the commands that control the execution of the programs in a CICS application. The first of these, the RETURN command, is used to return control to CICS and set up the next execution of the program in a pseudo-conversational session. When you use it for that purpose, you include the TRANSID option to specify the trans-id of the program. You also include the COMMAREA option to name the area of working storage that will be stored in the CICS communication area between program executions.

When the RETURN command is issued in this form, the program associated with the trans-id will be started the next time the user presses an attention key. (This should be the same program that issued the RETURN command.) In addition, the data that was placed in the CICS communication area by the RETURN command is passed to that program in the DFHCOMMAREA field. In chapter 5, you'll see other uses of this command, but this use is common to all pseudo-conversational programs.

Unlike the RETURN command, the XCTL command is commonly used to transfer control from one program to another. In the example in this figure, control is transferred to a menu program named INVMENU. A command like this is often used when the user presses an AID key to exit from a program.

The last command in this figure is the ABEND command. This command ends the program abnormally (called an *abend*) and displays a message at the terminal. Then, before starting another transaction, the user must press the Clear key to clear the screen. By default, this command also causes a storage dump to be produced, but you can eliminate that by coding the NODUMP option.

The syntax of the RETURN command

```
EXEC CICS
    RETURN [TRANSID(trans-id)]
           [COMMAREA(data-name)]
END-EXEC
```

Option	Description
TRANSID	Specifies the one-to four-character name of the transaction to be invoked when the user presses an attention key.
COMMAREA	Specifies the name of a data area that's stored in the CICS communication area between program executions so it can be passed to the next execution of a pseudo-conversational program. The next program execution accesses the communication area via its DFHCOMMAREA field.

A RETURN command that sets up the next execution of a program

```
EXEC CICS
    RETURN TRANSID(INQ1)
           COMMAREA(COMMUNICATION-AREA)
END-EXEC.
```

The syntax of the XCTL command

```
EXEC CICS
    XCTL  PROGRAM(program-name)
END-EXEC
```

Option	Description
PROGRAM	Specifies the one- to eight-character name of the program to be invoked.

An XCTL command that invokes a program named INVMENU

```
EXEC CICS
    XCTL PROGRAM('INVMENU')
END-EXEC
```

The syntax of the ABEND command

```
EXEC CICS
    ABEND [NODUMP]
END-EXEC
```

Option	Description
NODUMP	Specifies that a storage dump should *not* be produced.

An ABEND command that doesn't produce a storage dump

```
EXEC CICS
    ABEND NODUMP
END-EXEC.
```

Description

- These commands let you control CICS program execution. The RETURN command ends the program, but if you specify the TRANSID option, CICS invokes that trans-id the next time the user presses an AID key. The XCTL command passes control to another CICS program. And the ABEND command terminates the program abnormally.

Figure 2-14   The basic formats of the RETURN, XCTL, and ABEND commands

How to develop a CICS program

The focus of this chapter so far has been on understanding the concepts of CICS programming and the code required to write a CICS program. But there's more to developing CICS programs than that. In the rest of this chapter, then, you'll learn more about the procedures for developing a CICS program.

A procedure for developing a CICS program

To develop a CICS program, you need to complete the eight steps outlined in figure 2-15. In step 1, you get the specifications for the program. This just means that you get the complete details about what the program is supposed to do. Then, in step 2, you design the program by developing an event/response chart and a structure chart. In chapter 3, you'll learn everything you need to know about developing these charts and designing a program.

When you complete the two steps of the analysis and design phase, you can continue with the implementation phase. In this phase, you start by preparing the BMS mapset for the maps that will be used by the program (step 3). You'll learn how to do that in chapter 4. Then, you code the program (step 4). The main purpose of this book, of course, is to teach you how to do that.

When the program is ready to test, you prepare it for execution by translating, compiling, and link-editing it (step 5). You'll learn more about that in the next figure.

After you prepare the program, but before you execute it, you must make sure that all of the CICS table entries required to support the program are in place (step 6). For most programs, this means that entries need to be made in three tables: the Program Control Table (PCT), the Processing Program Table (PPT), and the File Control Table (FCT). In the PCT, an entry is required to define the trans-id that's used to start the program. In the PPT, two entries are required: one for the program, the other for the program's mapset. If the program uses any files, appropriate entries are required in the FCT. If the program uses other CICS facilities, additional table entries may be required. Although the systems programmer is usually responsible for making these entries, you should at least know what's required so you can give the administrator the appropriate information.

Once the table entries are in place, you're ready to execute and test the program (step 7). In this step, you make sure that the program performs according to the program specifications.

Although our eight-step procedure for developing CICS programs separates coding and testing into two distinct steps, we recommend that you code and test in phases. That way, you reduce the amount of code that's tested in each phase, which makes it easier to isolate the cause of an error. You'll learn more about this technique, called *top-down coding and testing*, in chapter 6.

An eight-step procedure for developing a CICS program

Analysis and design

1. Develop a complete set of program specifications.
2. Design the program using an event/response chart and a structure chart.

Implementation

3. Prepare the BMS mapset.
4. Code the program.
5. Prepare the program for execution.
6. Create the necessary CICS table entries.
7. Test the program under CICS.

Documentation

8. Document the program.

Description

- The program specifications should include all the information you need to implement the program. That may include a program overview that describes the processing to be done by the program and the required input and output. It may also include screen layouts for maps used by the program and information on any related copy members or subprograms.

- To design a CICS program, we recommend you develop an event/response chart that identifies each event the program must provide for along with the program's response to that event. We also recommend that you create a structure chart that represents the overall structure of the program.

- To define the format of the BMS maps that will be displayed by a program, you code a mapset. Then, you assemble the mapset to produce a physical map and a symbolic map.

- To prepare a program for execution, you translate, compile, and link-edit it. If errors occur during this process, you must correct them and then translate, compile, and link-edit the program again.

- The CICS table entries that are required for most programs include an entry in the Program Control Table (PCT) for the trans-id, two entries in the Processing Program Table (PPT) for the program and the mapset, and an entry in the File Control Table (FCT) for each file used by the program.

- When you test a program, you make sure it performs according to its specifications. Although coding and testing are shown as separate steps in this procedure, we recommend you use a technique called *top-down coding and testing*, or just *top-down testing*. When you use top-down testing, you code and test in phases.

- The documentation for a program varies from shop to shop.

Figure 2-15   A complete procedure for developing a CICS program

The last step in this development procedure is to document the program. This just means that you organize the program specifications, structure chart, BMS code, COBOL code, test run data, and other documentation for the program. Later, this documentation is used by the person who has to maintain the program. Since this step varies from one COBOL shop to another, this book will say no more about it. When you're on the job, you need to find out what's required in your shop and then put the required documents together.

How to prepare a program for execution

Figure 2-16 presents the procedure for preparing a CICS program for execution. As you can see, you must compile and link-edit the program just as you do any COBOL program. Before you compile a CICS program, however, you must translate it using the *CICS command-level translator*. The translator converts each CICS command into appropriate COBOL statements that invoke the CICS services specified by the command. The translated program can then be used as input to the COBOL compiler.

In this figure, you can see the translated code for a RECEIVE MAP command. Notice that the original command is still included in the COBOL code, but it's commented out so it will be ignored by the compiler. After the original command is a series of Move statements followed by a Call statement. The Move statements assign values to the fields that are used as arguments of the Call statement. The Call statement invokes the command-level interface to invoke the required CICS services.

In addition to translating CICS commands, the translator also inserts other code into your program. You already know about one such block of code: the Execute Interface Block. The other code that's inserted is usually of little interest to you.

In chapter 6, you'll be introduced to the JCL for running the OS/390 procedure that translates, compiles, and link edits a CICS program. There, you can see how the DD statements identify the files that are used for each step of the procedure.

A CICS program preparation procedure

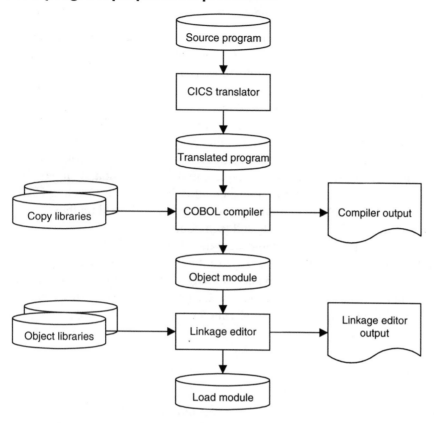

Translated code for a CICS READ command

```
*       EXEC CICS
*           RECEIVE MAP('INQMAP1')
*                   MAPSET('INQSET1')
*                   INTO(INQMAP1I)
*       END-EXEC.
            MOVE '..}............00109    ' TO DFHEIV0
            MOVE 'INQMAP1' TO DFHC0070
            MOVE 'INQSET1' TO DFHC0071
            CALL 'DFHEI1' USING DFHEIV0   DFHC0070 INQMAP1I DFHDUMMY
            DFHC0071.
```

Description

- Before you compile a CICS program, you must translate it. The *CICS translator* converts the CICS commands in the program to Move and Call statements that can be compiled by the COBOL compiler.

- The translator also inserts code into your program, like the Execute Interface Block, that it needs to operate under CICS.

- After you translate the program, you compile and link-edit it just as you would any other COBOL program.

Figure 2-16   How to prepare a CICS program for execution

Perspective

The goal of this chapter has been to introduce you to CICS programming. So at this point, you should understand how pseudo-conversational programs work. You should be familiar with the basic CICS commands. You should be familiar with the code you use to develop BMS mapsets. And you should have a basic understanding of the steps required for developing CICS programs.

If you're an experienced COBOL programmer, you could probably develop a simple CICS program like the one presented in this chapter with just the information presented here. However, there's a lot more that you need to know to become proficient at developing CICS programs. In the chapters in the next section, then, you'll learn the details for designing CICS programs, creating BMS mapsets, coding CICS programs, and testing them. After that, the rest of this book will build on those skills by presenting additional CICS commands and techniques.

Incidentally, if you had any trouble understanding the COBOL that's used in this chapter (not the CICS-specific code), you may want to refresh or enhance your CO-BOL skills. The best way to do that is to get our COBOL book, *Murach's Structured COBOL*. It will not only teach you all of the new COBOL coding skills that you may need, but it's a terrific reference and an excellent companion for this book.

Terms

conversational program	symbolic map
Short on Storage (SOS)	event/response chart
psuedo-conversational program	event
attention identifier (AID) key	top-down design
parameter	structure chart
BMS mapset	Execute Interface Block (EIB)
assembler	communication area
physical mapset	response code
symbolic mapset	exceptional condition
macro	abend
attribute byte	top-down coding and testing
Common User Access (CUA)	top-down testing
standards	CICS command-level translator
screen painter	CICS translator

Section 2

How to design, code, and test a CICS program

Now that you have been introduced to CICS programming, you're ready to learn the specific skills that you need to develop a complete CICS program on your own. So that's what you'll learn in this section of the book.

In chapter 3, you'll learn how to use an event/response chart and a structure chart to design a CICS program. In chapter 4, you'll learn how to create the BMS mapset you need for a program. In chapter 5, you'll learn the basic CICS commands and skills you need to code any program. And in chapter 6, you'll learn how to test a program to insure that it works as it's supposed to.

3

How to design a CICS program

In chapter 2, you were introduced to the two documents that we recommend for the design of pseudo-conversational programs: the event/response chart and the structure chart. Now, in this chapter, you'll learn the details of developing these design documents.

As you read this chapter, keep in mind that it teaches you how to design a traditional CICS program. In other words, both the presentation logic (that is, all the functions related to sending data to and receiving data from the terminal) and the business logic (the functions that process the data) are contained in a single program module. We feel that this is the best approach for teaching the basics of CICS. Later, in chapter 20, you'll learn how to design, code, and test a program whose presentation and business logic are coded in separate modules.

The customer maintenance program

To illustrate the techniques for designing a CICS program, this chapter shows how to design a program that lets the user maintain records in a customer master file. Before you can understand the design of this program, though, you need to understand how it should work.

The program specifications for the customer maintenance program

Figure 3-1 presents the program overview for the customer maintenance program, along with the copy member for the customer master file used by this program. This is the same file that was used in the inquiry program in chapter 2. While the inquiry program simply displayed records from this file, the maintenance program lets the user add new records to the file, change existing records in the file, and delete existing records from the file. To accomplish that, it uses two maps: a key map and a data map.

The key map lets the user enter a customer number and an action code that indicates the operation to be performed on that customer. If a valid combination of customer number and action code is entered, the data map is then displayed. For an add operation, this map displays a blank record so the user can enter the data for the new customer. For a change operation, this map displays the data for the selected customer so the user can change it. The data for the selected customer is also displayed for a delete operation, but the data is protected so it can't be changed. You'll see the layouts of these maps in a moment.

Like most CICS programs, the user can exit from this program by pressing PF3 or cancel the current operation by pressing PF12. Note, however, that the function of the PF12 key depends on which map is displayed when the user presses it. If the user presses it from the key map, the program ends just as it does if the user presses the PF3 key. If the user presses it from the data map, however, the current operation is canceled and the program displays the key map. You'll see how this affects the design of the program later in this chapter.

By the way, normally a program like this would edit the data for an add or change operation before updating the file. In fact, sometimes the editing requirements can be quite complex, as you'll see in later examples in this book. But for now, the program specifications have been simplified so you can focus more easily on the design considerations.

The program overview for the customer maintenance program

Program	CUSTMNT1: Customer maintenance
Trans-id	MNT1
Overview	Maintain customer information in the customer master file by allowing the user to enter new customers, change existing customers, or delete existing customers.
Input/output specifications	CUSTMAS Customer master file MNTMAP1 Customer maintenance key map MNTMAP2 Customer maintenance data map
Processing specifications	1. Control is transferred to this program via XCTL from the menu program INVMENU with no communication area. The user can also start the program by entering the trans-id MNT1. In either case, the program should respond by displaying the key map. 2. On the key map, the user enters a customer number and selects a processing action (Add, Change, or Delete). Both the action field and the customer number field must be entered. If the user selects Add, the customer number entered must not exist in the file. For Change or Delete, the customer number must exist in the file. If a valid combination isn't entered, an error message should be displayed. 3. If the user enters a valid combination of action and customer number, the program displays the customer maintenance data map. For an add operation, the user can then enter the customer information. For a change operation, the user can change any of the existing information. For a delete operation, all fields should be set to protected so the user can't enter changes. To complete any of these operations, the user must press the Enter key. 4. If the user presses PF3 from either the key map or the data map, return to the menu program INVMENU by issuing an XCTL command. If the user presses PF12 from the key map, return to the menu program. However, if the user presses PF12 from the data map, redisplay the key map without completing the current operation.

The copy member for the customer master record (CUSTMAS)

```
01  CUSTOMER-MASTER-RECORD.
*
    05  CM-CUSTOMER-NUMBER          PIC X(6).
    05  CM-FIRST-NAME               PIC X(20).
    05  CM-LAST-NAME                PIC X(30).
    05  CM-ADDRESS                  PIC X(30).
    05  CM-CITY                     PIC X(20).
    05  CM-STATE                    PIC X(2).
    05  CM-ZIP-CODE                 PIC X(10).
*
```

Figure 3-1   The program specifications for the customer maintenance program

The screen layouts for the customer maintenance program

Figure 3-2 presents the screen layouts for the customer maintenance program. On the key map (MNTMAP1), you can see the fields where the user will enter the customer number and action code, along with a list of the three possible actions. Then, the data map (MNTMAP2) displays the information for the selected customer. Notice that each customer field is displayed on a separate line in this map. That makes it easy for the user to enter information for new or changed records.

On both maps, line 1 is used to identify the map, the program function, and the trans-id that started the program (the trans-id will be supplied by the program in the last 4 columns). In both maps, too, line 3 contains instructions for the user. However, on the data map, the instructions will vary depending on whether the action code indicated an add, change, or delete operation. Finally, at the bottom of the screen, line 23 is used for displaying error messages, while line 24 lists the PF keys the user can press to exit from the program (PF3) or cancel the current operation (PF12).

The screen layout for the key map

Map name	MNTMAP1	Date	02/20/2001
Program name	CUSTMNT1	Designer	Doug Lowe

```
MNTMAP1                  Customer Maintenance                                                    XXXX

Type a customer number.  Then select an action and press Enter.

Customer number. . . . .  XXXXXX

Action . . . . . . . . .  X  1.  Add a new customer
                             2.  Change an existing customer
                             3.  Delete an existing customer












XXXXXXXXXXXXXXXXXXXXXXXXXXXXXXXXXXXXXXXXXXXXXXXXXXXXXXXXXXXXXXXXXXXXXXXXXXXXXXXXX
PF3=Exit      F12=Cancel                                                                            X
```

The screen layout for the data map

Map name	MNTMAP2	Date	02/20/2001
Program name	CUSTMNT1	Designer	Doug Lowe

```
MNTMAP2                  Customer Maintenance                                                    XXXX

XXXXXXXXXXXXXXXXXXXXXXXXXXXXXXXXXXXXXXXXXXXXXXXXXXXXXXXXXXXXXXXXXXXXXXXXXXXXXXXXXXX

Customer number. . . . . :  XXXXXX

Last name. . . . . . . .    XXXXXXXXXXXXXXXXXXXXXXXXXXXXXX
First name . . . . . . .    XXXXXXXXXXXXXXXXXXXX
Address. . . . . . . . .    XXXXXXXXXXXXXXXXXXXXXXXXXXXXXX
City . . . . . . . . . .    XXXXXXXXXXXXXXXXXXXX
State. . . . . . . . . .    XX
Zip Code . . . . . . . .    XXXXXXXXXX










XXXXXXXXXXXXXXXXXXXXXXXXXXXXXXXXXXXXXXXXXXXXXXXXXXXXXXXXXXXXXXXXXXXXXXXXXXXXXXXXXXX
F3=Exit       F12=Cancel                                                                            X
```

Figure 3-2   The screen layouts for the customer maintenance program

How to create an event/response chart

When you design a pseudo-conversational program, you need to think in terms of the user actions, or *events*, that can trigger the execution of the program. That makes sense if you realize that the user controls the path of execution through a pseudo-conversational program. The program simply responds to the user actions. When you design a pseudo-conversational program, then, you need to identify the events and define the program's response to those events. In some cases, you'll also need to consider the contexts in which an event can occur to determine how the program should respond.

How to identify user input events

The first step in *event-driven design* is to identify the events. To do that, you begin by listing all of the potential user actions that can cause the program to be invoked along with a brief description of the program's appropriate response to each event. The beginning event/response chart in figure 3-3 presents this information for the customer maintenance program.

The first event in any event/response chart should be something like "Start the program." This event occurs when the user initiates the program for the first time. Most programs respond to this event by displaying the initial map and then returning control to CICS.

The other events in an event/response chart are triggered by the use of attention keys. As you can see in this chart, if the program's response to two or more keys is the same, you can group those keys under a single event. For example, the PA1, PA2, and PA3 keys are grouped together because the program's response to each is to ignore the key. This chart also groups all the keys that are considered invalid since the program displays the same error message in response to each.

Notice that the program's response to the PF12 and Enter keys depends on the map that's displayed at the time the key is pressed. In other words, the program's response to these events depends on the event's *context*. The next step in designing an event-driven program, then, is to identify these contexts.

How to identify the context of input events

The context of an event is determined by a combination of factors, such as the map that's currently displayed and the selections the user has made. For example, the customer maintenance program's response to the Enter key depends on the map that's displayed when the event occurs. In addition, if the data map is displayed, it also depends on the action the user requested on the key map: Add, Change, or Delete.

To identify the event contexts for a program, you can start by listing one context for each map that's used by the program. For the customer maintenance program, those contexts would be something like "Get key" and "Get data."

A beginning event/response chart for the customer maintenance program

Event	Response
Start the program	Display the key map.
PF3	Transfer control to the menu program.

PF12	If the key map is displayed
	    transfer control to the menu program.
	If the data map is displayed
	    cancel the operation and display the key map.

Enter	If the key map is displayed
	    prepare the data map according to the requested action and display it.
	If the data map is displayed
	    add, change, or delete the customer as appropriate.

Clear	Redisplay the current map without any data.
PA1, PA2, or PA3	Ignore the key.
Any other key	Display an appropriate error message.

Event contexts for the customer maintenance program

Context	Explanation
Get key	The key map is displayed, awaiting input of a valid combination of action code and customer number.
Add customer	The data map is displayed in response to a request to add a customer.
Change customer	The data map is displayed in response to a request to change a customer.
Delete customer	The data map is displayed in response to a request to delete a customer.

Description

- To design an event-driven program, you start by identifying the *events* that can cause the program to be started. Then, you identify in general terms how the program should respond to each of those events.

- An event/response chart should always include a response to the user action that causes the program to be started for the first time. We call this event "Start the program." A program typically responds to this event by displaying the first map and then ending.

- If the final step in a response is to return control to CICS, you can omit this step from the event/response chart and it will be assumed.

- The *context* of an event can depend on the map that's displayed, previous selections made by the user, and previous processing done by the program.

- If the program's response to an event depends on the context in which it occurs, you should identify and describe each context before you finalize the event/response chart.

Figure 3-3   How to identify user input events and contexts

Next, you need to consider the conditions that can affect the context of each map. For the customer maintenance program, you know that the data map can be displayed for an add, a change, or a delete operation. So you want to replace the single "Get data" context with these three more specific contexts. The result is shown in the second table in figure 3-3. Notice that this table includes a brief description of each context so you know when it occurs.

By the way, CICS doesn't provide you with information about which map is currently displayed or what information the user entered on a previous map. So it's up to you to manage the event context. In most cases, you'll do that by storing the context information in the communication area between program executions. You'll see an example of that in chapter 5.

How to design the program's response to each event

Once you've identified all the user input events and contexts, you're ready to refine the program's response to each event in its context. To do that, you can expand your event/response chart so it looks like the one in figure 3-4. As you can see, this chart specifies the response to each event and context with a substantial amount of detail.

In addition to a column that indicates the event context, this event/response chart also includes a column that indicates the new context after the response processing is complete. If the user presses PF12 when the context is "Add customer," for example, the program will set the context for the next program execution to "Get key."

The most complicated processing occurs when the user presses the Enter key. In that case, the response is different for each of the four contexts. For example, if the user presses the Enter key when the context is "Get key," the program starts by editing the input data. If it's valid, the program displays the data map and changes the context to "Add customer," "Change customer," or "Delete customer" depending on the operation the user requested. If the input data is invalid, though, the program will display an error message and the context will remain unchanged.

If the user presses the Enter key when the context is "Add customer," "Change customer," or "Delete customer," the program adds, changes, or deletes the customer and then displays the key map. Note that the key map is displayed regardless of whether the add, change, or delete operation is successful. The difference is that if it's successful, a completion message is displayed. If it's not, an error message is displayed.

As you create an event/response chart, keep in mind that it is a planning tool, so it can be as detailed or as general as you need it to be. As you gain experience developing CICS programs, you may find it unnecessary to include the amount of detail shown here. In some shops, though, the event/response chart is included as part of the final documentation for a program. In that case, you'll need to include enough detail to properly document the program. And you'll need to keep the chart up-to-date when the program changes.

The final event/response chart for the customer maintenance program

Event	Context	Response	New context
Start the program	n/a	Display the key map.	Get key
PF3	All	Transfer control to the menu program.	n/a
PF12	Get key	Transfer control to the menu program.	n/a
	Add customer Change customer Delete customer	Cancel the operation and display the key map.	Get key
Enter	Get key	Edit input data. If valid display data map else display an error message.	Add customer, Change customer, or Delete customer Get key
	Add customer	Add the customer record. If not duplicate record display the key map with a completion message else display the key map with an error message.	Get key Get key
	Change customer	Change the customer record. If record found display the key map with a completion message else display the key map with an error message.	Get key Get key
	Delete customer	Delete the customer record. If record found display the key map with a completion message else display the key map with an error message.	Get key Get key
Clear	Get key	Redisplay the key map.	Unchanged
	Add, Change, or Delete customer	Redisplay the data map with unprotected data erased.	Unchanged
PA1, PA2, or PA3	All	Ignore the key.	Unchanged
Any other key	All	Display an appropriate error message.	Unchanged

Description

- To complete the event/response chart, you add the appropriate contexts for each event and expand the response processing.
- If the response to an event causes a change in the context, the event/response chart should indicate the new context.

Figure 3-4   How to design the program's response to each event

How to create a structure chart

Once you've planned the event processing for your program, you can use it as the basis for a program structure chart. The structure chart, in turn, will serve as the basis for your program code.

How to design the first two levels of a structure chart

To create a structure chart, you start by drawing a box for the top-level module. This module represents the entire program, and it will contain the code that manages the event processing for the program. As a result, it should be given a name that represents the overall function of the program.

Next, you decide which portions of the event processing summary should be implemented as separate modules, and you draw a box subordinate to the top-level module for each one. For example, figure 3-5 shows the first two levels of the structure chart for the maintenance program. In this case, because most of the program's processing is done in response to the user pressing the Enter key, it seemed reasonable to include one module for each of the contexts of the Enter key. Because the processing required to respond to the other program events is trivial, it wasn't necessary to include separate modules for them.

This figure also gives some guidelines you can follow to determine what modules make up the second level of a structure chart. In general, you should add modules that represent the major functions of the program. In most cases, those functions require receiving data from the terminal, processing it, and sending data back to the terminal. But even if a function doesn't include receiving and processing data, you should create a separate module for it if it requires more than a few lines of code. You may also add modules at the second level to simplify the coding in the top-level module if it requires extensive code.

The design that will result from following these guidelines will vary from program to program. For some programs, such as the customer maintenance program, you'll end up with one second-level module for each context. For other programs, you'll end up with second-level modules associated with particular function keys. Still other programs will have a combination of the two. Each of these approaches can be useful in certain circumstances as long as there's a clear relationship between the structure chart and the events and their contexts.

The second structure chart in this figure shows another possible design for the customer maintenance program. In this case, the chart includes only two second-level modules: one to process the key map, and one to process the data map. Then, the module that processes the data map has three subordinate modules to process add, change, and delete functions. Although this structure will work, we prefer the first one because it places all the event context logic in the top-level module. In contrast, the logic for the event context in the alternate design will be split between the top-level module and the module that processes the data map.

The first two levels of the structure chart for the customer maintenance program

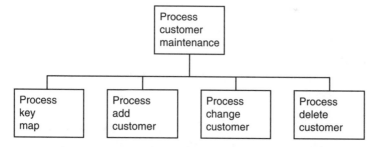

An alternative design for the customer maintenance program

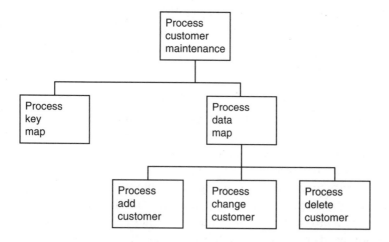

A general procedure for designing the first two levels of a structure chart

1. Draw the top-level module and give it a name that represents the entire program.
2. Decide what event processing should be implemented as separate modules, and draw a box subordinate to the top-level module for each one.

How to determine what modules should make up the second level of a structure chart

- If the program's response to an event includes receiving data from the terminal, processing it, and sending data back to the terminal, you should create a separate module for the event.
- If the program's response to an event doesn't include receiving data from the terminal, you should consider creating a separate module only if the response requires more than a few COBOL statements to implement.
- If the COBOL statements for implementing the top-level module require more than a page or two, you should consider creating additional second-level modules to simplify the coding in the top-level module.

Figure 3-5   How to design the first two levels of a structure chart

How to design the legs of a structure chart

When you've decided which modules to place at the second level of the structure chart, you can start dividing each of them into their component functions. For example, figure 3-6 presents the process-key-map *leg* of the customer maintenance program, which includes the process-key-map module (the *calling module* or *control module*) and all of its subordinate modules (the *called modules*). The idea is to create one subordinate module for each function that a higher-level module needs to do.

To process the key map, for example, you need to receive the key map and then edit the data in that map. Then, if the data is valid, you need to send the data map to the terminal. And if the data isn't valid, you need to send the key map back to the terminal with an error message.

After you create the subordinate modules for one calling module, you continue the process for the next level of the chart. To edit the key map, for example, the edit-key-data module must read the customer record to be sure that it exists for a change or delete operation and that it doesn't exist for an add operation.

If necessary, you continue this process for subsequent levels of the chart. You stop when the lowest-level functions require no other subordinate functions. When you're done, each module should represent one and only one function, and the code in each module should be manageable.

At this point, you may be wondering why a separate module is added for the read function. Although this function could be incorporated into the code for the edit-key-data module, we recommend you code a separate module for each I/O statement that's required by a program. That way, these modules can be called whenever an I/O operation needs to be performed. By isolating the I/O statements in this way, you end up with a more efficient program and one that's easier to debug.

We also recommend that you create a single, general-purpose send module for each map your program processes. This send module will contain one or more SEND MAP commands with various options. For example, one command might include the ERASE option to erase the screen when it's first displayed or when the user presses the Clear key, and another might include the ALARM option to sound the alarm when an error message is displayed. To determine which form of the command is issued, the calling module can set a flag that's evaluated by the send module.

This approach has several advantages. First, it simplifies your structure charts by avoiding the need for separate modules with names like "Send customer map erase" and "Send customer map dataonly." Second, the send module will be nearly identical from one program to the next. The main differences will be the names you specify in the MAP, MAPSET, and FROM options. Finally, the program will be easier to maintain if a change is made to a map since all of the SEND MAP commands for that map will be in the same module.

The process-key-map leg of the customer maintenance program

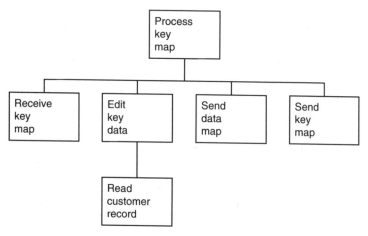

A general procedure for designing one leg of a structure chart

1. Draw one subordinate module for each function that the *control module* at the top of the *leg* needs to do. To process the key map, for example, the process-key-map module needs to receive the key map, edit the data in the map, send the data map if the entry is valid, and resend the key map if the entry is invalid.

2. Use the same thought process for the next level of modules. If any of them require more than one function, draw one subordinate module for each function. To edit the key map data, for example, the program must read the customer record.

3. If necessary, continue this process until each of the lowest-level modules consists of just one function.

Guidelines for designing the legs of a structure chart

- Each module should represent one and only one function.

- The function of a *called module* must be logically contained in the function of its *calling module*.

- The code in each module should be manageable.

- Use a generalized send module for each map. Each module will contain one or more SEND MAP commands with various options, such as ERASE, DATAONLY, and ALARM. The send module can decide which form of the SEND MAP command to use by evaluating a flag that's set by the calling module.

- Include a separate module for each file I/O statement so the statements are easy to locate and modify.

Figure 3-6   How to design the legs of a structure chart

How to complete a structure chart

Figure 3-7 presents the complete structure chart for the customer maintenance program. As you can see, the process-add-customer module calls modules that receive the data map, write the new customer record, and send the key map back to the terminal. The process-change-customer module is similar. Its subordinate modules receive the data map, read the appropriate customer record so it can be updated, rewrite the changed record, and then send the key map. In contrast, a delete operation doesn't require the user to enter data into the data map. So the process-delete-customer module doesn't need to receive the map. Instead, it just reads the appropriate customer record, deletes it, and redisplays the key map.

You should also notice that the send modules for both of the maps have been included as subordinates to the program's top-level module. That's because the top-level module will need to send the key map when the program first starts. And it will need to send the key map or the data map if the user presses the Clear key when one of those maps is displayed. So you'll want to be sure to add these modules to complete your structure chart.

A complete structure chart should also identify any other programs the program executes using the CICS LINK command (which you'll learn about in chapter 5) or the COBOL Call statement. To do that, you should add one module to the structure chart for each *linked* or *called program* that gives the program's name and function.

A structure chart should also identify any *common modules*. A common module is a module that's called by more than one calling module, so it's shown in more than one place on the structure chart. To indicate that a module is used in more than one place, you can place a black triangle in the upper right corner of the box as shown in the structure chart in this figure. Other graphic conventions like an asterisk after the module number can serve the same purpose.

Finally, when the structure chart contains all of the necessary modules, you should number the modules. When you code the program, you combine these numbers with the module names to form the paragraph names. Then, you code the paragraphs in numeric sequence in your program.

Although you can use complicated numbering schemes, we recommend the one that's illustrated in this figure. With this scheme, you start by numbering the top-level module with 000 or 0000. Then, you number the second level across in large increments (in this case, we used multiples of 1000), and you number down the legs from the third level on. As you number, be sure to leave gaps so you can add modules to the program later on without renumbering. For example, notice the gap between modules 2100 and 2300 in the process-add-customer leg. Later on, when we modify this program to edit the data for a new or changed customer, it will be easy to add an editing module numbered 2200 to the structure chart.

The final structure chart for the customer maintenance program

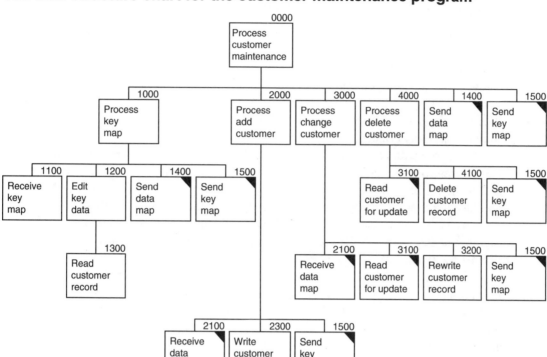

How to identify common modules and linked or called programs

* To identify a *common module* (a module that appears more than once in a structure chart), shade its upper right corner. If a common module has subordinate modules, you need to include them only once on the chart.

* To identify a *linked program* (a program that's executed using the LINK command), add a module to the structure chart. Include a stripe at the top of the module that gives the program name. You can use the same technique to identify a *called program* (a program that's executed using the COBOL Call statement).

How to number the modules in a structure chart

* Use 000 or 0000 for the top-level module.

* Number the modules in the second level from left to right leaving large enough gaps for subordinate modules.

* After the first two levels, number the modules down each leg in appropriate increments.

* When you code the COBOL paragraph for each module later on, the paragraph name will be the module number followed by the module name.

Figure 3-7   How to complete a structure chart

Alternatives to the structure chart

Although we've used the structure chart to illustrate the design process, you should be aware that there are other graphical alternatives. These include tree charts, Warnier-Orr diagrams, and Nassi-Schneiderman diagrams. No matter what you use, though, you must design from the top down with one function in each module if you want to develop an effective program that's substantially easier to code, debug, and maintain. In other words, the graphical differences shouldn't have any effect on the design and naming principles.

The trouble with all design documents including the structure chart is that it takes so long to create and modify them. That's true whether you draw them by hand or use PC software to create them. That's why most programmers today don't take the time to design their programs. Instead, they "compose" their programs as they enter the COBOL code, which means they're designing their programs as they code. As we see it, that's a major mistake that seriously degrades the quality of a COBOL program.

With that in mind, we suggest the simple alternative to the structure chart that's presented in figure 3-8. This is an outline called a *structure listing* that can be created in just a few minutes by using the outline feature of any modern word processor. Once created, you can easily make changes to the structure; you can analyze the structure with one or more of the lower levels hidden; and you no longer have an excuse for skipping the design phase of programming.

Then, when you finish a program, you can easily update the structure listing so it corresponds to the COBOL code and include it as part of the documentation for the program. An even better alternative, though, is to generate a structure listing from the COBOL code. That way, you're sure that the structure listing corresponds to the COBOL code.

In our shop, we developed a COBOL program called LISTMODS that generates a structure listing from another COBOL program. This program works as long as you adhere to the coding standards that are presented in this book. Then, the final documentation for a program is the COBOL code and the structure listing generated from the code.

A structure listing for the customer maintenance program

```
0000-PROCESS-CUSTOMER-MAINT
    1000-PROCESS-KEY-MAP
        1100-RECEIVE-KEY-MAP
        1200-EDIT-KEY-MAP
            1300-READ-CUSTOMER-RECORD
        1400-SEND-DATA-MAP (C)
        1500-SEND-KEY-MAP (C)
    2000-PROCESS-ADD-CUSTOMER
        2100-RECEIVE-DATA-MAP (C)
        2300-WRITE-CUSTOMER-RECORD
        1500-SEND-KEY-MAP (C)
    3000-PROCESS-CHANGE-CUSTOMER
        2100-RECEIVE-DATA-MAP (C)
        3100-READ-CUSTOMER-FOR-UPDATE (C)
        3200-REWRITE-CUSTOMER-RECORD
        1500-SEND-KEY-MAP (C)
    4000-PROCESS-DELETE-CUSTOMER
        3100-READ-CUSTOMER-FOR-UPDATE (C)
        4100-DELETE-CUSTOMER-RECORD
        1500-SEND-KEY-MAP (C)
```

Description

- A *structure listing* is an outline that uses indentation to show the levels of the modules. The letter C in parentheses can be used to identify common modules.

- A structure listing can be used to plan the modules of a program, and it also can be used as documentation when the program is finished.

How to create a structure listing

- When you're designing a program, you can use the outline feature of any modern word processor to prepare a structure listing. This feature lets you hide the lower levels of the outline so you can analyze the structure of the higher levels. This feature also makes it easy to reorganize the listing.

- When a program is finished, you can use a structure listing program to generate a structure listing from the COBOL code for the finished program. That way, you can be sure that the structure listing is accurate.

Figure 3-8   A simple alternative to the structure chart

Perspective

Before you begin coding a program, you should design it using techniques like the ones presented in this chapter. At the least, you should identify the events and event contexts that the program must handle, and you should plan the program's response to each one. In addition, you should plan the modules of the program so you know how it will be structured. If you take the time to do that, you'll find that your programs will be easier to code, and they'll contain fewer errors.

At this point, though, you may be unsure about your ability to design CICS programs on your own. Don't worry. As you go through this book, you'll see several more examples of event/response charts and structure charts that will help you make your own design decisions. You'll also have a better idea of how these design documents help you code a program when you see the code for the customer maintenance program in chapter 5.

Terms

event
event-driven design
context
leg of a chart
calling module
control module
called module
linked program
called program
common module
structure listing

4

How to create a BMS mapset

Before you can code a CICS program, you need a complete set of program specifications that includes a screen layout for each screen the program displays. If the specs you're given don't include the screen layouts, you have to develop them yourself. Then, as you saw in chapter 2, you have to define each screen using basic mapping support (BMS). In this chapter, you'll learn how to use BMS to create screens that are easy to use. Even if you use a screen painter to generate the BMS code for you, you'll need this knowledge to understand and modify the generated code.

How to design user-friendly screens

Because the users of interactive programs have a variety of skill and experience levels, CICS programs must be designed and implemented with ease of use in mind. One of the best ways to achieve that is to adopt a consistent approach to the way programs interact with users. Ideally, all of the applications within an installation should follow the same guidelines so that typical screen elements are handled in predictable ways. At the least, though, all of the programs in a particular application should have a consistent user interface.

Typical fields on a display screen

The 3270 screen is a *field-oriented display.* In other words, the screen is logically divided into a number of programmer-defined *fields* that contain specific types of information. Figure 4-1, for example, shows the screen fields in the customer inquiry screen that was presented in chapter 2. This screen includes a single *data entry field* that lets the user enter a customer number for the customer to be displayed. All the other fields are *display-only fields* that the user can't change.

In line 1, the map name identifies the screen. Because a map can be used by more than one program, though, it's also a good idea to include the trans-id to identify the program that displayed the map. Then, the screen title names the screen.

Lines 23 and 24 (the last two lines on the screen) are also informational. Line 23 is reserved for warning messages—alerting the user to an entry error, for example. And line 24 tells the user what function keys can be used. The last position on the screen is a field that's included in every BMS map. It's defined so that its contents will always be sent to the program (you'll learn more about this field in the next chapter).

Between lines 1 and 23, the contents of the screen vary depending on the requirements of the program. Typically, there will be fields that give the user instructions on what to do. There will be data entry fields that the user has to fill in. There will be fields for data that's displayed by the program in response to the user entries. And there will be fields with captions that identify the information on the screen.

As you can see in the figure, the customer inquiry screen includes all these types of fields. However, not all of the fields appear each time the screen is displayed. For example, remember that when the user first invokes the inquiry program, only the first 5 lines and line 24 are displayed. The user has to enter a customer number before lines 7 through 10 are displayed. And if the application doesn't detect any errors, it may never display any messages in line 23.

Likewise, the look of certain fields may change. For example, when the screen is first displayed, the customer number field will be underlined to alert the user that a value needs to be entered there. Once the user enters data, that data will be displayed instead.

The screen layout for the customer inquiry program

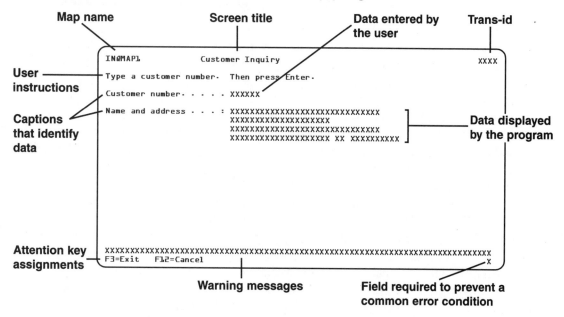

Map name

Screen title

Data entered by the user

Trans-id

User instructions

Captions that identify data

Data displayed by the program

Attention key assignments

Warning messages

Field required to prevent a common error condition

```
INQMAP1              Customer Inquiry                                    XXXX
Type a customer number.  Then press Enter.
Customer number. . . . . XXXXXX
Name and address . . . : XXXXXXXXXXXXXXXXXXXXXXXXXXXXXX
                         XXXXXXXXXXXXXXXXXX
                         XXXXXXXXXXXXXXXXXXXXXXXXXXXX
                         XXXXXXXXXXXXXXXXXX XX XXXXXXXXXX




XXXXXXXXXXXXXXXXXXXXXXXXXXXXXXXXXXXXXXXXXXXXXXXXXXXXXXXXXXXXXXXXXXXXXXXXXXXX
F3=Exit   F12=Cancel                                                      X
```

Description

- In a CICS program, the display screen is divided into user-defined *fields.* Each screen field is a specified area that contains a particular category of information.

- *Display-only fields* are used to display messages, captions, and data that can't be changed by the user.

- *Data entry fields* allow the user to enter data into the screen.

- Each screen should end with a single-byte field that ensures that at least one byte of data is sent to the program when the user presses an attention key. This helps prevent a common error condition that you'll learn about in chapter 5.

Figure 4-1   Typical fields on a display screen

Recommendations for formatting screen displays

IBM promotes a user interface standard called *CUA*, which stands for *Common User Access*. CUA provides three distinct user interface models. All of the programs in this book follow CUA's *Entry Model*, which is designed specifically for non-programmable terminals like the ones most often used for CICS applications. The most advanced CUA standard, called the *Graphical Model*, is designed for programmable workstations such as PCs. It includes features such as pull-down menus, pop-up dialog boxes, and scroll bars. The intermediate model, called the *Text Subset of the Graphical Model*, provides a standard way of implementing these elements of the Graphical Model using non-programmable terminals.

Figure 4-2 summarizes the CUA Entry Model standards that are widely used in IBM installations. The top part of the figure shows you standard locations, colors, and other attributes for various types of screen fields. As you can see, different colors are used for display-only fields depending on their function: blue for the screen ID and function key assignments, neutral (white) for user instructions, green for information like the screen title and captions that identify fields, turquoise for fields that contain variable data that's displayed by the program, and yellow for warning messages. Like fields that contain variable data, data entry fields are also displayed in turquoise. However, the captions that identify data entry fields end with a period, while those that identify variable fields end with a colon. In addition, data entry fields are underlined, while variable fields are not. Finally, warning messages are displayed with bright intensity so they stand out on the screen.

The CUA standards also give specific recommendations for using three lines of the screen: line 1 to identify the screen and its function, line 23 to display error messages, and line 24 to display the function key assignments. The other lines will vary depending on the program requirements.

The bottom part of this figure gives you standard assignments for the function keys. You'll find these implemented in IBM's software, including its interactive editor, TSO. Although some of the assignments may vary from one installation to another, F3, F7, and F8 almost always have the functions listed here.

In addition to the function key assignments, the standards for screen design in your installation may include additions or variations to the ones shown here. So be sure to find out what standards to use. Ultimately, your goal is to create interfaces that are consistent with the other applications in your shop so that users can do their work more easily.

Guidelines for the color and position of screen fields

Field	Design
Screen ID (often the trans-id, map name, or both)	Line 1; Blue
Screen titles	Line 1; Green
Instructions and emphasized text	Neutral (white)
Captions that identify fields	Green; Those that precede display-only fields end with a colon, while those that precede data entry fields end with a period
Variable data that the user enters (data entry fields)	Turquoise; Underline fields so users can see them easily
Variable data displayed by the program that can change as the program executes (display-only fields)	Turquoise
User entry errors	Reverse video
Warning messages	Line 23; Yellow with bright intensity
Function key assignments	Line 24; Blue

Guidelines for function key assignments

Key	Assignment
F1	Help: Provide online help for the program
F3	Exit: Exit from the program
F7	Backward: Display the previous screen or record, or scroll up when there's more information than will fit on a screen
F8	Forward: Display the next screen or record, or scroll down when there's more information than will fit on a screen
F12	Cancel: Return to previous screen or exit from the program if it's the first screen
Clear	Clear: Erase any data from the unprotected fields on the screen
F2, F4, F5, F6, F9, F10, F11	Unassigned: Use these keys for program-specific needs

Description

- The *CUA Entry Model* provides guidelines for standardizing screen displays so they're easy for users to work with.

- When designing screens for monochrome terminals, substitute the bright intensity attribute for all colors other than blue and green.

- Function key assignment is critical to the application and screen design. Whenever possible, adhere to the function key guidelines listed above.

Figure 4-2   Recommendations for formatting screen displays

How attributes control the look and operation of a field

Although you can't see them in figure 4-1, each field on a screen is preceded by an *attribute byte* that controls the appearance and operation of the field. In fact, you actually define a screen field by defining an attribute byte for it. In the topics that follow, you'll learn about attribute bytes and the types of attributes they can define.

Attribute bytes and the standard attributes

The shaded boxes in figure 4-3 mark the attribute bytes for the fields in the customer inquiry screen. Although each attribute byte is displayed as a space, it takes up a position on the screen, so you can't use that position to display data.

As you can see, every field is preceded by an attribute byte. In addition, a data entry field is followed by an attribute byte. That's necessary because a field doesn't end until there's another attribute byte. The customer number field in this figure, for example, would continue until the beginning of the name and address caption without the closing attribute byte. Note that if a data entry field is followed immediately by another field, the attribute byte for that field ends the entry field. If that's not the case, though, you'll need to include an attribute byte to explicitly end the entry field. In the screen layout, it's common to darken the position at the end of each data entry field that requires a closing attribute byte so you won't forget to define it in your BMS mapset.

The *attributes* that are set in an attribute byte determine a field's characteristics. The three *standard attributes* shown in this figure—protection, shift, and intensity—are available on any type of terminal. If your program will run on an enhanced terminal, however, you may be able to use attributes other than those shown here. You'll learn about those attributes in just a minute.

The *protection attribute* determines whether or not the user can key data into the field. Data entry fields are *unprotected fields* that allow for user entry, while display-only fields are *protected fields*. A *skip field*, defined with the *auto-skip* option, is similar to a protected field because the user can't enter data into it. When the cursor moves to a skip field, though, it automatically skips to the next unprotected field on the screen. In contrast, when the cursor moves to a protected field, it stops, even though the user can't enter data there. Then, the user has to press the Tab key to move to the next data entry field. The attribute byte at the end of an entry field is usually defined as a skip field so that when the user fills the entry field, the cursor automatically moves to the next entry field.

The *shift attribute* determines whether the keyboard is in *alphanumeric shift*, meaning that any character can be entered into the field, or *numeric shift*, which turns on the Num Lock feature so that only numerals, signs, and decimal points can be entered. Be aware, though, that even with numeric shift, the user

The attribute bytes on a screen

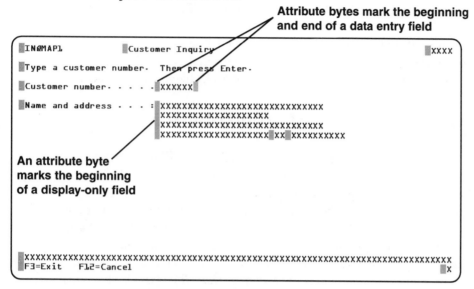

Attribute bytes mark the beginning and end of a data entry field

An attribute byte marks the beginning of a display-only field

Standard field attributes

Protection	Shift	Intensity
Unprotected	Alphanumeric	Normal
Protected	Numeric	Bright
Auto-skip		Dark (No-display)

Description

- The location and characteristics of screen fields are determined by special characters called *attribute bytes*, marked by the shaded boxes in the screen shown above. An attribute byte takes up one position on the screen, but it's displayed as a space.

- A field starts at the position immediately following its attribute byte and ends at the position immediately before the next field's attribute byte. If there's no subsequent attribute byte, the field continues to the end of the screen.

- A data entry field requires two attribute bytes: one to mark the beginning of the field, and the other to mark the end. To remind themselves to define the second attribute byte, many programmers darken the space that follows each data entry field in their screen layout.

- The standard *attributes* that control a field's look and operation are the protection, shift, and intensity attributes.

- Users can key data into an *unprotected field*, but not into a *protected field*. In contrast, a *skip field*, defined with the auto-skip protection option, is skipped over and causes the cursor to automatically advance to the next unprotected field.

- The numeric option turns on the numeric lock feature (Num Lock) on the terminal so that the user can enter only numerals, signs, and decimal points.

- A dark, or no-display, field displays only spaces, no matter what characters the field contains.

Figure 4-3   Standard attribute bytes

can still enter invalid numeric data, such as two decimal points or two minus signs. So your programs must still edit all numeric entry fields to be sure they're valid.

The *intensity attribute* controls how the data in the field is displayed. Normal and bright do just what they say. Dark means that even if the field contains data, it's not displayed on the screen so it looks like the field is blank.

The format and contents of an attribute byte

A field's attributes are determined by the bit settings in its attribute byte, as figure 4-4 shows. Here, you can see the bit settings that are used for the standard attributes in bits 2 through 5. Although you don't need to memorize the meaning of each bit position or the standard settings, you do need to understand in general terms how the attribute byte functions. Then, in chapter 8, you'll see how to change the value of an attribute byte in your COBOL code when you want to change the look or operation of a field during the course of a program.

The last bit in the attribute byte is the *Modified Data Tag (MDT)*. This bit is used to indicate whether the data in a field has been changed. It's turned on (set to a value of 1) whenever a user keys any data into the field. Then, for efficiency's sake, only fields with the MDT turned on are sent to your program. Unmodified fields are not transmitted.

The bit positions in an attribute byte

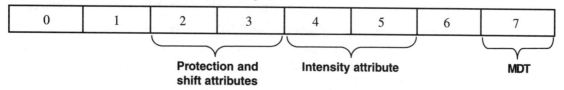

| 0 | 1 | 2 | 3 | 4 | 5 | 6 | 7 |

Protection and shift attributes   Intensity attribute   MDT

The contents of an attribute byte

Bit positions	Functions	Bit settings
0-1		Depends on the contents of bits 2-7
2-3	Protection and shift	00 = Unprotected alphanumeric 01 = Unprotected numeric 10 = Protected 11 = Protected skip
4-5	Intensity	00 = Normal 01 = Normal 10 = Bright 11 = Dark (No-display)
6		Must be 0
7	MDT	0 = Field has not been modified 1 = Field has been modified

Description

- The settings of bits 2-5 in a field's attribute byte control the standard attributes for the field. (The bit positions within a byte are always numbered from zero.)

- The settings in an attribute byte are initially based on the values you code for the field in the BMS mapset. However, you can change these settings from within the COBOL program.

- The last bit in the attribute byte, the *MDT (Modified Data Tag)*, indicates whether the user has modified the data in the field. To save transmission time, the terminal sends a field to the CICS program only if its MDT is on.

Figure 4-4   The format and contents of an attribute byte

Extended attributes

In addition to the standard attributes, some 3270 terminal models provide additional features that are controlled with *extended attributes*. Extended attributes are similar to standard attributes with one important exception: An extended attribute doesn't take up a position on the screen.

Figure 4-5 lists some of the optional features that are controlled by extended attributes. The ones you'll use most often are extended color and highlighting. The validation options are available on only a limited number of terminals, and the programmed symbols options are needed only when you're working with applications that require specialized character sets.

The *extended color* options are self-explanatory. They simply let you control the color of a field. Typically, you use extended color to draw attention to specific fields and to provide consistent user interfaces from one application to another. As you saw in figure 4-2, the CUA Entry Model has a number of recommendations on using color in your screens.

Extended highlighting lets you draw attention to a field by underlining it, causing it to blink, or displaying it in *reverse video*. For example, the CUA Entry Model specifies that when a user enters incorrect data, the program should highlight the error using reverse video. Likewise, CUA specifies that data entry fields should be underlined.

Be aware, though, that when a program is run on a terminal that doesn't support extended attributes, the extended attributes are ignored. That means your program might have to do extra processing to format fields properly. For example, your program might have to make sure that data entry fields are filled with underscores. In fact, because of this complication, most of the programs in this book define data entry fields with a starting value of underscores instead of using the underline option.

By the way, there are other types of extended attributes besides the ones shown. They aren't covered here because many terminals don't support them. But check your shop standards to see if you should use any of them in your screen designs.

Extended attributes

Type of attribute	Options			
Extended color	Blue	Red	Pink	Green
	Turquoise	Yellow	Neutral	
Extended highlighting	Blinking	Causes the field to flash on the screen.		
	Reverse video	Displays the field in dark characters against a light background—the opposite of the usual display.		
	Underline	Underlines the field.		
Validation	Must enter	The user must enter at least one character of data into the field.		
	Must fill	The user must enter data into each character position of the field.		
	Trigger	The terminal transmits the field's contents as soon as the user moves the cursor out of the field.		
Programmed symbols	Up to 6 alternate user-definable character sets.			

Description

- Many terminals allow for *extended attributes* that give more control over the look and operation of a field than the standard attributes. If extended attributes are specified but the terminal doesn't support them, they're ignored.

- Unlike the standard attributes, an extended attribute does *not* take up a position on the screen.

- Many of the extended color and highlighting options are used in the CUA guidelines for formatting easy-to-use screens.

- The validation options are not available on a wide variety of terminals, and the programmed symbols options are used only for applications that need specialized character sets (like engineering applications). So you may never need these options.

Figure 4-5   Extended attributes

How to code BMS macros

The programming required to operate a 3270 terminal is more complicated than you might guess from the information presented so far. Fortunately, *basic mapping support (BMS)* handles most of it for you. In this section, you'll learn how to code a BMS *mapset* to define the format of each screen (*map*) your programs display. Although you typically group all of the maps used by a single transaction or group of transactions in a single mapset, many mapsets contain a single map definition. Because of that, the terms *map* and *mapset* are often used to mean the same thing.

To code a mapset, you use the two assembler commands and three BMS *macros* shown in figure 4-6. (A *macro*, or *macro instruction*, is a single instruction that's replaced by two or more other instructions.) The PRINT and END commands are so simple there's no need to say any more about them. Instead, we'll concentrate on the coding details for the DFHMSD, DFHMDI, and DFHMDF macros.

How to code assembler language statements

An assembler language statement consists of three parts: a label, an op-code, and parameters. The *label* supplies a symbolic name for the statement. A standard assembler language label can be eight characters long, but for a BMS macro, the limit is seven characters. That's because CICS adds a one-character suffix to some of the labels you code. The exception to this rule is the label for a DFHMDF macro, which can be up to 29 characters long. That lets you use longer fields names, which is common in COBOL programs. In this book, though, we use shorter names for consistency within the mapsets.

The *op-code* specifies the instruction to be executed. For a BMS macro, the op-code is DFHMSD, DFHMDI, or DFHMDF.

The *parameters* provide the command with the specific information it needs. For example, the DFHMDF macro shown in this figure defines a field that will be displayed starting in column 27 of line 5. (Remember, the attribute byte occupies column 26.) It also indicates that the field will be six characters long, it will be unprotected so the user can enter data into it, it will be displayed in turquoise, and it will have an initial value of underscores. This macro also illustrates how you code parameters that include one or more options.

Note that if a parameter value contains special characters or spaces, you must enclose it in single quotes. Also, if a parameter value includes an apostrophe, you must code two consecutive apostrophes. So if the value is "Customer's name," you code:

```
INITIAL='Customer''s name'
```

To make your mapsets easier to read, you can code each parameter on its own line by using *continuation lines*. You can also improve readability by using *comment lines* to group related macros, as you'll see later in this chapter.

The assembler commands and macros used in BMS mapsets

Command or macro	Usage
PRINT NOGEN	Coded once at the beginning of the mapset; tells the assembler not to print the statements generated as a result of expanding the BMS macros that follow.
END	Must be the last statement in the input stream; tells the assembler that there are no more source statements.
DFHMSD	Coded once; supplies values that apply to the entire mapset.
DFHMDI	Coded once for each map within the mapset; supplies values that apply to a single map.
DFHMDF	Coded once for each field (or attribute byte) within the map; specifies the position, length, and attributes of a screen field.
DFHMSD TYPE=FINAL	Coded after the last map in the mapset; tells BMS that the mapset is complete.

The general syntax of an assembler language statement

```
label     op-code parameters...
```

A DFHMDF macro that defines a data entry field

```
CUSTNO   DFHMDF POS=(5,26),                                          X
                LENGTH=6,                                            X
                ATTRB=(NORM,UNPROT,IC),                              X
                COLOR=TURQUOISE,                                     X
                INITIAL='_____'
```

Description

- The *label*, when required, begins in column 1 and supplies a symbolic name for the statement. For a BMS macro, the label must begin with a letter and can be up to 7 characters long. An exception is the label for a DFHMDF macro, which can be up to 29 characters long.

- The *op-code* specifies the instruction to be executed and begins in column 10.

- The *parameters* (or *operands*) provide the information the instruction requires to work properly. They're separated from one another by commas with no intervening spaces and can be coded in any order. The first parameter should follow the op-code after one space.

- To specify a parameter's value, use an equals sign. If more than one value is required, separate the values with commas and enclose them in parentheses. If a value contains special characters or spaces, enclose it in single quotes. And to include an apostrophe in a value, code two consecutive apostrophes where you want the single apostrophe to appear.

- To make your mapset easier to read, we recommend you code only one parameter per line. Then, to continue the statement on the next line, code a comma after the parameter, place any non-blank character in column 72 (we use an X), and code the next parameter starting in column 16 of the following line (called a *continuation line*).

- You can also use *comment lines* to improve the readability of your mapsets. A comment line is any line with an asterisk in column 1 and a blank in column 72.

- With the exception of comment lines and values in the INITIAL parameter, you must code assembler statements using uppercase characters.

Figure 4-6   How to code assembler language statements

How to use the DFHMSD macro to define a mapset

The syntax of the DFHMSD macro is shown in figure 4-7. As you can see, you code this macro in one of two formats. You use format 1 at the beginning of a mapset and format 2 at the end. Format 2 is always coded just as it's shown. And format 1 is usually coded as it's shown in the example in part 2 of the figure. But you'll want to keep a few things in mind as you review this format.

First, you must specify the name of the mapset in the label field. In the example in this figure, the mapset name is INQSET1. This name will appear in the Processing Program Table (PPT) and in the Copy statement for the symbolic map in your COBOL program. Since mapset names must be unique within a CICS system, most installations have naming standards for them that you need to follow.

Second, note that the default values for the TYPE, LANG, MODE, and TIOAPFX parameters are *not* what you usually need for COBOL programs. So you'll almost always code these parameters just as they're shown in the example.

TYPE=&SYSPARM means that both a physical map and a symbolic map should be generated when the BMS mapset is assembled. Then, you can process the mapset using a JCL procedure that has two steps. In the first step, the procedure substitutes MAP for &SYSPARM, assembles the mapset, and saves the physical map in a load library. In the second step, it substitutes DSECT for &SYSPARM, generates the symbolic map, and saves it in a copy library. Later in this chapter, you'll see sample JCL for executing this type of procedure.

As you'd expect, you specify COBOL in the LANG parameter. This generates the symbolic map as an 01-level group item that can be copied into a COBOL program. The MODE parameter is generally coded as MODE=INOUT so that the symbolic map will include both an input and an output area. And you *must* specify TIOAPFX=YES for a COBOL map. This generates a 12-byte FILLER item at the beginning of the symbolic map. The system uses those 12 bytes to maintain required control information.

Look next at the TERM parameter. As you can see, it specifies what type of terminal the map can be used with. Then, when the mapset is assembled, CICS creates a name for the physical map by adding a one-character suffix to the mapset name that indicates the terminal type. For example, the DFHMSD macro shown in part 2 of this figure generates a symbolic map named INQSET1 and a physical map named INQSET1M, since M is the suffix for 3270 model 2 terminals.

This naming convention lets you use several different physical maps with a single symbolic map. For example, if you want to use this same mapset on a 3270 model 1 terminal, all you need to do is change the TERM parameter to 3270-1 and reassemble the map. Then, BMS generates a physical mapset named INQSET1L, since L is the suffix for 3270 model 1 terminals.

The syntax of the DFHMSD macro

Format 1

```
name      DFHMSD    TYPE={&SYSPARM | DSECT | MAP},
                    LANG={COBOL | COBOL2 | ASM | PLI | C},
                    MODE={IN | OUT | INOUT},
                    TERM=terminal-type,
                    CTRL=(option,option...),
                    STORAGE=AUTO,
                    MAPATTS=(COLOR,HILIGHT),
                    DSATTS=(COLOR,HILIGHT),
                    TIOAPFX={YES | NO}
```

Format 2

```
          DFHMSD    TYPE=FINAL
```

Explanation

name	The one- to seven-character name of the mapset. The mapset name must be unique within a CICS system.
TYPE	For format 1, specifies whether a physical map (MAP), symbolic map (DSECT), or both (&SYSPARM) will be generated. TYPE=&SYSPARM is usually coded. For format 2, marks the end of a mapset (TYPE=FINAL).
LANG	Specifies the programming language: COBOL, COBOL2, ASM (assembler), PLI (PL/I), or C. LANG=COBOL is usually coded.
MODE	Specifies whether the mapset is used for input (IN), output (OUT), or both (INOUT). MODE=INOUT is usually coded.
TERM	Specifies the type of terminal that will be supported by the physical map generated by this mapset. Common values are: ALL or 3270 Support for any terminal. 3270-1 Support for a 3270 model 1 terminal (40-character lines). 3270-2 Support for a 3270 model 2 terminal (80-character lines). The IBM manual documents other values you can code for more obscure terminal types. Usually, you'll code TERM=3270-2.
CTRL	Specifies a list of control options in effect for each map in the mapset. Two common options are: FREEKB Free the keyboard after each output operation. ALARM Sound the audio alarm during each output operation.
STORAGE	If STORAGE=AUTO is coded, the symbolic maps for the maps in the mapset will occupy separate storage locations. Otherwise, they'll occupy the same storage location. We recommend you always code STORAGE=AUTO.
MAPATTS	Specifies which extended attributes should be supported by the physical map. COLOR and HILIGHT are the most common and are usually coded together.
DSATTS	Specifies which extended attributes should be supported by the symbolic map. COLOR and HILIGHT are the most common and are usually coded together.
TIOAPFX	YES generates a 12-byte FILLER item at the beginning of the symbolic map that the system uses to maintain control information. YES should *always* be specified for COBOL maps (NO is the default).

Figure 4-7   How to use the DFHMSD macro to define a mapset (part 1 of 2)

When you refer to the mapset in an application program, you use the seven-character name without the suffix. CICS automatically retrieves the physical map that's appropriate for the terminal the program is running on. If CICS can't locate the appropriate physical map, it looks for one that has the same name as the mapset, but without a suffix. An unsuffixed name is generated when you code TERM=ALL or TERM=3270, so the map can be used on any terminal. To accommodate any terminal type, however, CICS requires considerable run-time overhead. So it's more efficient to specify the exact terminal type if you know it.

Next, the CTRL parameter specifies the *control options* used by the maps in a mapset. You can also specify the control options individually for each map on the DFHMDI macro, as you'll see in a moment. But since the same options usually apply to all the maps in the mapset, it's easier to code the CTRL parameter on the DFHMSD macro.

The most common control option is FREEKB. It unlocks the keyboard whenever a map is sent to the terminal. If you don't specify it, the keyboard is locked and the user has to press the Reset key to enter data—*not* a user-friendly approach!

The ALARM control option causes the audio alarm to sound whenever a map is sent to the terminal. Although some shops use the audio alarm to warn the user of an error condition, you generally don't want it to sound on *every* output operation. So rather than coding the ALARM option in the mapset, you usually code it on the SEND MAP command as you saw in chapter 2.

Finally, note that the MAPATTS and DSATTS parameters work together. They tell BMS what type of extended attributes should be supported in the physical map (MAPATTS) and the symbolic map (DSATTS). As you'll see in a moment, you can define fields with extended attributes without coding these parameters. But if you want to *change* a field's extended attributes within your COBOL program (for example, to highlight an error), you must include both parameters with the same set of options. You'll see examples of that in the programs throughout this book, so don't worry if it's confusing to you right now. And by the way, you can specify other options besides COLOR and HILIGHT, but these are the two you'll use most often.

The starting DFHMSD macro in the BMS mapset for the inquiry program

```
INQSET1  DFHMSD TYPE=&SYSPARM,                       X
                LANG=COBOL,                           X
                MODE=INOUT,                           X
                TERM=3270-2,                          X
                CTRL=FREEKB,                          X
                STORAGE=AUTO,                         X
                TIOAPFX=YES
```

Description

* You use Format 1 of the DFHMSD macro at the beginning of a mapset to define the mapset. You use Format 2 just before the END command at the end of a mapset.

* When you specify COBOL for the LANG parameter, the symbolic map will be an 01-level group item that can be copied into a COBOL program.

* For the TERM parameter, it's more efficient to specify the exact terminal type if you know it. Otherwise, you can code ALL or 3270.

* If the CTRL options apply to all the maps in the mapset, you should code them on the DFHMSD macro. Otherwise, you can code the appropriate options on the DFHMDI macro for each map.

* You should always code the FREEKB option of the CTRL parameter; otherwise, the keyboard is locked each time a map is sent to the terminal and the user has to press the Reset key to enter data.

* If you want to change a field's color or extended highlighting within your COBOL program, you must include the DSATTS parameter. And whenever you code DSATTS, you need to code MAPATTS with the same set of options.

Figure 4-7   How to use the DFHMSD macro to define a mapset (part 2 of 2)

How to use the DFHMDI macro to define a map in a mapset

To define a map within a mapset, you use the DFHMDI macro. The basic format of this macro is shown in figure 4-8. Although you can specify many options besides the ones shown, they're seldom used, and you'll usually code the parameters just as shown in the example.

The label on the DFHMDI macro is the name of the map. In the macro shown in this figure, for example, the map name is INQMAP1. You'll use this name, along with the mapset name you specified on the DFHMSD macro, in your COBOL program. A map name must be unique within a mapset, so if your installation has naming standards, be sure to follow them.

The other parameters are easy to understand. The SIZE parameter specifies the number of lines and columns in the map (*not* the screen, although the two are usually the same size). And the LINE and COLUMN parameters specify the starting position of the map on the screen.

If you didn't code the CTRL parameter for the entire mapset on the DFHMSD macro, you can code it on the DFHMDI macro for an individual map. If you want the control options to apply to all maps in a mapset, though, you'll code CTRL on the DFHMSD macro instead.

The syntax of the DFHMDI macro

```
name     DFHMDI  SIZE=(lines,columns),
                 LINE=line-number,
                 COLUMN=column-number,
                 CTRL=(option,option...)
```

Explanation

name	The one- to seven-character name of the map. Each map within a mapset must have a unique name.
SIZE	Specifies the size of the map in lines and columns. Usually coded SIZE=(24,80) for a 24x80 screen, but it can be smaller than the screen.
LINE	Specifies the line number on the screen where the map starts. Usually coded LINE=1.
COLUMN	Specifies the column number on the screen where the map starts. Usually coded COLUMN=1.
CTRL	Specifies a list of control options in effect for the map. Two common options are:
	FREEKB Free the keyboard after each output operation.
	ALARM Sound the audio alarm during each output operation.

The DFHMDI macro in the BMS mapset for the inquiry program

```
INQMAP1  DFHMDI SIZE=(24,80),                                    X
                LINE=1,                                          X
                COLUMN=1
```

Description

- You use the DFHMDI macro to define a map within a mapset.
- The label on the DFHMDI macro is the name you'll use to refer to the map in your COBOL code.
- If you don't code the CTRL parameter on the DFHMSD macro for the entire mapset, you can code it on the DFHMDI macro for an individual map.

Figure 4-8   How to use the DFHMDI macro to define a map in a mapset

How to use the DFHMDF macro to define a field in a map

Figure 4-9 gives the format of the DFHMDF macro, which you use to define a field on a screen. Actually, the DFHMDF macro defines an attribute byte. So you'll code one DFHMDF macro for each display-only field and two for most data entry fields—one to mark the beginning of the field and one to mark the end.

If you're going to work with a screen field in your COBOL program, you want to code a label on its DFHMDF macro. That causes items to be generated in the symbolic map that let you handle the field in your COBOL code, as you saw in chapter 2. In practice, that means you'll code labels for data entry fields and for display-only fields that contain variable data; you don't need labels for constant fields or skip fields. In the example in part 2 of this figure, the first DFHMDF macro is for a data entry field, so it has a label of CUSTNO.

Most of the other coding details you need to know are given in the figure. But here are a few points to keep in mind as you code DFHMDF macros on your own.

First, note that the POS parameter specifies the line and column position of the field's attribute byte. Remember that the field follows the attribute byte. So if you want a field to display starting in column 5 of line 10, you code POS=(10,4). Then, the LENGTH parameter specifies the length of the data field, *not* including the attribute byte. As a result, if you specify LENGTH=5, you actually define six screen positions: five for the field itself and one for its attribute byte.

The next parameter, ATTRB, specifies the settings of the attribute byte. Note that if you omit the ATTRB parameter, the defaults for the intensity and protection attributes are NORM and ASKIP. However, if you code *any* of the ATTRB options, the defaults change to NORM and UNPROT. As for the shift attribute, the default is alphanumeric. You have to code the NUM option if you want to facilitate numeric data entry by turning on the numeric lock feature.

The IC (initial cursor) option in the ATTRB parameter indicates that the cursor should be positioned at the beginning of the field when the screen is displayed. This option was used in the customer inquiry map in chapter 2 to position the cursor at the customer number field. However, it doesn't work well when there's more than one data entry field on a map. So in chapters 5 and 8, you'll learn more flexible ways to control the cursor position from your COBOL programs.

The last ATTRB option, FSET, causes the MDT bit in the attribute byte to be turned on. That way, the contents of the field will be transmitted back to the program, whether or not the user enters data in it. Usually, you don't specify the FSET option, since the MDT bit is set automatically when a user keys data into an unprotected field. In a minute, though, you'll see how to use this option for the last field in your mapset: the DUMMY field, which is a protected field.

The COLOR and HILIGHT parameters let you apply extended color and highlight attributes to a field. Note that if a map with these attributes is displayed on a terminal that doesn't support extended attributes, the attributes are ignored.

The syntax of the DFHMDF macro

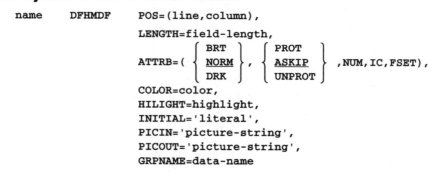

Explanation

name	The 1- to 29-character name for the field. If omitted, the field is not included in the symbolic map.
POS	Specifies the line and column position of the attribute byte.
LENGTH	Specifies the length of the field, *not* including the attribute byte.
ATTRB	Specifies one or more attribute byte settings for the field. If omitted, the default is NORM, ASKIP. If one or more options are specified, the default becomes NORM,UNPROT.
	BRT The field is displayed with high intensity.
	NORM The field is displayed with regular intensity.
	DRK The field is *not* displayed on the screen (it's darkened).
	PROT The field is protected; data may not be keyed into it.
	ASKIP The field is protected, and the cursor will automatically skip over it.
	UNPROT The field is unprotected; data may be keyed into it.
	NUM Turns on the numeric lock feature so only numeric characters can be entered; the field is right justified and zero filled. If omitted, the field is assumed to be alphanumeric and is left justified and space filled.
	IC Specifies that the cursor should be located at the start of the field.
	FSET Specifies that the MDT bit in the attribute byte should be turned on before the map is sent to the terminal.
COLOR	Specifies the field's color. You may specify DEFAULT for the terminal's default color, or you may specify BLUE, RED, PINK, GREEN, TURQUOISE, YELLOW, or NEUTRAL. If omitted, DEFAULT is assumed.
HILIGHT	Specifies the field's extended highlighting. Valid highlighting options are BLINK, REVERSE, UNDERLINE, and OFF. If omitted, the default is OFF.
INITIAL	Specifies the starting value of the field. If omitted, the default is hexadecimal zeros (Low-Value).
PICIN	Specifies a COBOL picture string that defines the format of the data on input, like PICIN='999V99'.
PICOUT	Specifies a COBOL picture string that defines the format of the data on output, like PICOUT='ZZZ,ZZ9.99'.
GRPNAME	Specifies that the field should be grouped in the symbolic map with other fields with the same GRPNAME. All fields within a group must be coded in sequence in the mapset and must have labels.

Figure 4-9   How to use the DFHMDF macro to define a field in a map (part 1 of 2)

Although you might think that you have to code the DSATTS and MAPATTS parameters of the DFHMSD macro to use extended attributes, you don't. You need to code these parameters only if you want to *change* any extended attributes in your COBOL code. You can use the COLOR and HILIGHT parameters on their own if you want the field to *always* display in the same color or with the same extended highlighting (underlined, for example). You'll see that illustrated in the BMS mapset that's shown later in this chapter.

You can use the PICIN and PICOUT parameters to specify COBOL pictures for input and output fields in the symbolic map. If you omit them, BMS assigns a default alphanumeric picture, so you'll seldom code them for alphanumeric fields. You'll seldom code the PICIN clause for numeric input fields either. Instead, if you let BMS generate an alphanumeric picture, your program can call a specialized numeric editing routine that determines whether the user has entered a valid number and formats the number using proper decimal alignment. In contrast, you'll often use the PICOUT parameter for numeric output fields so they're displayed properly.

The last parameter, GRPNAME, lets you group related fields under a single data name in the symbolic map. For a 9-digit zip code with a hyphen separating the first 5 digits from the last 4, for example, you could define three fields—ZIP5, ZIPH, and ZIPEXT—using a single GRPNAME like ZIPCODE. Then, you could refer to the individual fields or the group field in your COBOL code. Because the grouped items would be treated as a single, 10-character field on the screen, though, you'd want to be sure to indicate the format of the field on the screen so the user knows what's required.

The DFHMDF macros that define a data entry field in the inquiry program

```
CUSTNO     DFHMDF POS=(5,26),                                    X
                  LENGTH=6,                                      X
                  ATTRB=(NORM,UNPROT,IC),                        X
                  COLOR=TURQUOISE,                               X
                  INITIAL='_____'
           DFHMDF POS=(5,33),                                    X
                  LENGTH=1,                                      X
                  ATTRB=ASKIP
```

Description

- The DFHMDF macro defines an attribute byte for a screen field.

- If you want to work with a screen field in your COBOL program, you must code a name for it. Then, data items for the field are generated in the symbolic map.

- If there's more than one field on the same line of the screen, you can figure the starting column for the POS parameter of the second or subsequent field using this formula:

  `Previous-field-column` + `Previous-field-length` + 1 (for the attribute byte)

- The IC option of the ATTRB parameter should be coded only for the first data entry field on the screen. If it's coded on more than one field, the cursor will be positioned in the last field with this option. We recommend you use this option only for maps that have a single entry field.

- The FSET option of the ATTRB parameter causes the MDT bit to be turned on so that the field contents are transmitted back to the program, regardless of whether they're changed. The exception is if the field contains hexadecimal zeros (Low-Value), in which case the field is never transmitted. You'll sometimes use this option for protected fields.

- PICIN and PICOUT describe the Picture clauses that will be generated in the symbolic map for input and output fields. The picture string must be a valid COBOL Picture clause, and its implied length must agree with the LENGTH parameter. If omitted, $X(n)$ will be the assumed picture, where n is the LENGTH value.

- GRPNAME lets you combine multiple fields under a single group name in the symbolic map, so you can refer to the fields at either the group or elementary level in your COBOL code. In the screen display, though, the grouped fields are treated as a single field.

- The last DFHMDF macro in a map should define a field named DUMMY that's one byte long, has an initial value of space, and has these attributes: DRK, PROT, and FSET. This causes at least one byte of data to be sent to the program whenever the user presses an attention key. This avoids an error condition that can occur otherwise.

Figure 4-9   How to use the DFHMDF macro to define a field in a map (part 2 of 2)

Model BMS field definitions

Although you need to understand the functions of the DFHMDF parameters, you can base most of your coding on the model field definitions shown in figure 4-10. Here, example 1 is for a constant field. As a result, it's defined as a protected field, and its value is given in the INITIAL parameter. In the CUA guidelines, the color of a constant depends on its function. This constant is a user instruction, so it's displayed in white (NEUTRAL).

In contrast, the constant in the first DFHMDF macro in example 2 is a caption, so it's displayed in green. It's the first of three DFHMDF macros used to display an alphanumeric entry field. The second DFHMDF macro defines the entry field itself. Since you want this field to appear in the symbolic map, a label is assigned to it (CUSTNO). The field is unprotected to allow for data entry; it's displayed in turquoise; and it's filled with underscores to help the user recognize it as an entry field. (You can use the UNDERLINE option instead of underscores, but remember that underlining isn't available on all terminals.) The last DFHMDF macro defines a skip field. This marks the end of the entry field and causes the cursor to skip to the next unprotected field when the CUSTNO field is filled.

The third example, for a numeric entry field, is so similar that I've omitted the caption field. The only real difference is that the ATTR parameter specifies NUM, but not UNPROT. Usually, it's a good idea to include UNPROT even though it's the default when the ATTR parameter is coded. But since NUM is almost always used with unprotected fields, the intent should be clear.

Example 4 shows the coding for a numeric variable field and its caption. Notice that the caption field ends with a colon rather than a period to help distinguish it from an entry field. The data to be displayed in the BALDUE field is supplied by a COBOL program, so it's protected from any user entry. And the field is defined with a PICOUT parameter, so the data will display with zero-suppression and comma and decimal point insertion.

Example 5 shows three DFHMDF macros that define lines 23 and 24 of the screen as recommended in the CUA standards. Line 23 includes a field named MESSAGE that displays error messages in bright yellow. The actual messages that will appear in this area will be formatted and sent by the COBOL program, and they'll change during the course of the interactive session. In contrast, the function key assignments that are defined on line 24 are coded as a constant. Although that's usually the case, sometimes the function keys that are available can change depending on the operation that's being performed. Then, the initial value can be omitted, and the PF key display can be set by the program.

The last DFHMDF macro defines a field named DUMMY in the last position of the screen. This field is one byte long; it's dark and protected so it can't be seen or modified by the user; and it's always transmitted to the program because the FSET option turns on the MDT bit, and the INITIAL parameter gives it a value of space. (The initial value is needed; otherwise, the field would be given a value of Low-Value, and a field with a value of Low-Value is never transmitted to the program.) In chapter 5, I'll explain the purpose of this field in more detail. For now, just include a field like this in all your maps.

Example 1: A constant field (user instructions)

```
          DFHMDF POS=(3,1),                                       X
                 LENGTH=42,                                       X
                 ATTRB=(NORM,PROT),                               X
                 COLOR=NEUTRAL,                                   X
                 INITIAL='Type a customer number.  Then press Enter.'
```

Example 2: An alphanumeric data entry field and its caption

```
          DFHMDF POS=(5,1),                                       X
                 LENGTH=24,                                       X
                 ATTRB=(NORM,PROT),                               X
                 COLOR=GREEN,                                     X
                 INITIAL='Customer number. . . . .'
CUSTNO    DFHMDF POS=(5,26),                                      X
                 LENGTH=6,                                        X
                 ATTRB=(NORM,UNPROT),                             X
                 COLOR=TURQUOISE,                                 X
                 INITIAL='_____'
          DFHMDF POS=(5,33),                                      X
                 LENGTH=1,                                        X
                 ATTRB=ASKIP
```

Example 3: A numeric data entry field

```
QTY       DFHMDF POS=(6,26),                                      X
                 LENGTH=3,                                        X
                 ATTRB=(NORM,NUM),                                X
                 COLOR=TURQUOISE,                                 X
                 INITIAL='___'
          DFHMDF POS=(6,30),                                      X
                 LENGTH=1,                                        X
                 ATTRB=ASKIP
```

Example 4: A display-only field with numeric variable data and its caption

```
          DFHMDF POS=(7,1),                                       X
                 LENGTH=24,                                       X
                 ATTRB=(NORM,PROT),                               X
                 COLOR=GREEN,                                     X
                 INITIAL='Balance due. . . . . . :'
BALDUE    DFHMDF POS=(7,26),                                      X
                 LENGTH=13,                                       X
                 ATTRB=(NORM,PROT),                               X
                 COLOR=TURQUOISE,                                 X
                 PICOUT='ZZ,ZZZ,ZZ9.99'
```

Example 5: A message area, function key area, and FSET field

```
MESSAGE   DFHMDF POS=(23,1),                                      X
                 LENGTH=79,                                       X
                 ATTRB=(BRT,PROT),                                X
                 COLOR=YELLOW
          DFHMDF POS=(24,1),                                      X
                 LENGTH=20,                                       X
                 ATTRB=(NORM,PROT),                               X
                 COLOR=BLUE,                                      X
                 INITIAL='F3=Exit    F12=Cancel'
DUMMY     DFHMDF POS=(24,79),                                     X
                 LENGTH=1,                                        X
                 ATTRB=(DRK,PROT,FSET),                           X
                 INITIAL=' '
```

Figure 4-10   Model BMS field definitions

The BMS mapset and symbolic map for the customer maintenance program

Now that you've seen how BMS macros are coded, you should be able to understand all the code in the BMS mapset for the customer inquiry program that was presented in chapter 2. But to reinforce what you've learned, it will help you to see another complete BMS mapset and the screen layouts it's based on. So in the topics that follow, you'll look at the BMS mapset for the customer maintenance program that was designed in chapter 3.

The screen layouts

Figure 4-11 shows the screen layouts for the customer maintenance program. To refresh your memory, this program uses two maps. The key map has the user enter a customer number along with an action code that indicates whether the program should add, change, or delete the master record for the specified customer. Then, the data map displays the appropriate user instructions (in line 3) and customer data depending on what action was specified. Notice that lines 1, 23, and 24 are used for screen ID, error messages, and function key assignments, in accordance with the CUA guidelines presented earlier.

Also notice on the key map that the box immediately following the entry field for the customer number is filled in. That's a reminder that you need to code an attribute byte for a skip field there to mark the end of the entry field. Similarly, on the data map, all the customer data fields will be followed by skip fields in the BMS mapset. That's because these fields are entry fields for an add or change operation.

In contrast, in the key map, the box following the action code entry field is blank because you don't need to code a separate skip field there. Instead, the attribute byte for the constant field that follows will serve as the skip field.

The screen layout for the key map

Map name MNTMAP1 **Date** 02/20/2001

Program name CUSTMNT1 **Designer** Doug Lowe

```
MNTMAP1               Customer Maintenance                              XXX

Type a customer number.  Then select an action and press Enter.

Customer number. . . . . XXXXXX

Action  . . . . . . . . X 1.   Add a new customer
                          2.   Change an existing customer
                          3.   Delete an existing customer










XXXXXXXXXXXXXXXXXXXXXXXXXXXXXXXXXXXXXXXXXXXXXXXXXXXXXXXXXXXXXXXXXXXXXXXXXXXXXXXX
PF3=Exit      F12=Cancel                                                      X
```

The screen layout for the data map

Map name MNTMAP2 **Date** 02/20/2001

Program name CUSTMNT1 **Designer** Doug Lowe

```
MNTMAP2               Customer Maintenance                              XXX

XXXXXXXXXXXXXXXXXXXXXXXXXXXXXXXXXXXXXXXXXXXXXXXXXXXXXXXXXXXXXXXXXXXXXXXXXXXXXXXX

Customer number. . . . : XXXXXX

Last name. . . . . .     XXXXXXXXXXXXXXXXXXXXXXXXXXX
First name . . . . .     XXXXXXXXXXXXXXXXXXX
Address. . . . . . .     XXXXXXXXXXXXXXXXXXXXXXXXXXXX
City . . . . . . . .     XXXXXXXXXXXXXXXXXXXX
State. . . . . . . .     XX
Zip Code . . . . . .     XXXXXXXXXX










XXXXXXXXXXXXXXXXXXXXXXXXXXXXXXXXXXXXXXXXXXXXXXXXXXXXXXXXXXXXXXXXXXXXXXXXXXXXXXXX
F3=Exit       F12=Cancel                                                      X
```

Figure 4-11   The screen layouts for the customer maintenance program

The BMS mapset

Figure 4-12 shows the BMS mapset for the customer maintenance program. After the PRINT NOGEN command, the DFHMSD macro defines the mapset, naming it MNTSET1. Both physical and symbolic maps will be created for all the maps in this mapset (TYPE=&SYSPARM). Each physical map will be for a 3270 model 2 terminal (TERM=3270-2). Each symbolic map will be a COBOL copy member (LANG=COBOL) that begins with a 12-byte FILLER area (TIOAPFX=YES). It will include both input and output areas (MODE=INOUT), and it will have its own location in storage instead of sharing storage with other symbolic maps (STORAGE=AUTO). Each time a map in this mapset is sent to the terminal, the keyboard will be unlocked for ease-of-use (CTRL=FREEKB).

In contrast to the inquiry mapset in chapter 2, this mapset contains two DFHMDI macros. The first one defines the key map, MNTMAP1, and the second one (on page 2 of the listing) defines the data map, MNTMAP2. Aside from the map names, these macros are identical.

You should be able to understand the DFHMDF macros that define the fields without much trouble. If you compare these macros to the screen layouts in figure 4-11, you'll see that the POS parameters locate the attribute bytes for each field on each screen. Likewise, the LENGTH parameters match up with the lengths of the fields, not counting the attribute bytes.

The unlabelled DFHMDF macros define the constant fields on the screen, and their initial values reflect what will be displayed. The fields with labels will have fields generated for them in the symbolic map. Note that whenever a mapset contains more than one map, you must be sure to use unique names for all fields within the mapset. Since both maps have a customer number field, for example, the fields are named CUSTNO1 and CUSTNO2 to avoid confusion.

Note, too, that the customer number field in the key map (CUSTNO1) isn't defined with the IC attribute as it was in the mapset for the inquiry program in chapter 2. That's because this map contains more than one entry field. So the program will control the position of the cursor using the CURSOR option of the SEND MAP command, as you'll see in the next chapter.

Now, take a look at the definition of the second entry field in the key map, ACTION. Because the valid entries for this field are numeric, it's defined with the NUM attribute. The UNPROT option is omitted since it's the default and the NUM option makes it clear that this is an entry field.

The code for the BMS mapset

Page 1

```
                PRINT NOGEN
MNTSET1  DFHMSD TYPE=&SYSPARM,                                         X
                LANG=COBOL,                                           X
                MODE=INOUT,                                           X
                TERM=3270-2,                                          X
                CTRL=FREEKB,                                          X
                STORAGE=AUTO,                                         X
                TIOAPFX=YES
***********************************************************************
MNTMAP1  DFHMDI SIZE=(24,80),                                         X
                LINE=1,                                               X
                COLUMN=1
***********************************************************************
         DFHMDF POS=(1,1),                                            X
                LENGTH=7,                                             X
                ATTRB=(NORM,PROT),                                    X
                COLOR=BLUE,                                           X
                INITIAL='MNTMAP1'
         DFHMDF POS=(1,20),                                           X
                LENGTH=20,                                            X
                ATTRB=(NORM,PROT),                                    X
                COLOR=GREEN,                                          X
                INITIAL='Customer Maintenance'
TRANID1  DFHMDF POS=(1,76),                                           X
                LENGTH=4,                                             X
                ATTRB=(NORM,PROT),                                    X
                COLOR=BLUE,                                           X
                INITIAL='XXXX'
***********************************************************************
         DFHMDF POS=(3,1),                                            X
                LENGTH=63,                                            X
                ATTRB=(NORM,PROT),                                    X
                COLOR=NEUTRAL,                                        X
                INITIAL='Type a customer number.  Then select an action X
                and press Enter.'
         DFHMDF POS=(5,1),                                            X
                LENGTH=24,                                            X
                ATTRB=(NORM,PROT),                                    X
                COLOR=GREEN,                                          X
                INITIAL='Customer number. . . . .'
CUSTNO1  DFHMDF POS=(5,26),                                           X
                LENGTH=6,                                             X
                ATTRB=(NORM,UNPROT,FSET),                             X
                COLOR=TURQUOISE,                                      X
                HILIGHT=UNDERLINE
         DFHMDF POS=(5,33),                                           X
                LENGTH=1,                                             X
                ATTRB=ASKIP
         DFHMDF POS=(7,1),                                            X
                LENGTH=24,                                            X
                ATTRB=(NORM,PROT),                                    X
                COLOR=GREEN,                                          X
                INITIAL='Action . . . . . . . . .'
ACTION   DFHMDF POS=(7,26),                                           X
                LENGTH=1,                                             X
                ATTRB=(NORM,NUM,FSET),                                X
                COLOR=TURQUOISE,                                      X
                HILIGHT=UNDERLINE
```

Figure 4-12   The BMS mapset for the customer maintenance program (part 1 of 4)

The constant field that follows the ACTION entry field is defined with the ASKIP option. As I mentioned earlier, a separate field isn't used to end the entry field in this instance. Instead, the constant field that follows it ends the field and causes the cursor to move to the next entry field. Because NORM,ASKIP is the default when the ATTR parameter is omitted, this parameter could have been omitted entirely. But including it makes it easy to see how the field works.

Next, notice that all the input fields in both maps specify the HILIGHT=UNDERLINE parameter. Using underlines instead of underscores will make the COBOL code for this program somewhat simpler. But as you know, this code will only work on terminals that support extended highlighting. On other terminals, you'll need to fill the fields with underscores instead. You'll learn how to handle the coding implications of using underscores in chapter 8.

Notice, too, that the input fields all specify the FSET attribute. That way, they will always be transmitted to the program, whether or not the user enters data into them. This is not the most efficient way to handle screen transmission for this program, but it is the most straightforward. You'll learn what's involved in optimizing data transmission in chapter 8.

Now, look at the field in MNTMAP2 that displays the user instructions on the data map (at the top of page 3). Unlike the other user instruction fields you've seen so far, it's not defined as a constant. Instead, it's a 79-byte field named INSTR2 that the program can change. This is necessary because the instructions that appear on the data map depend on whether the user is entering data for a new customer, changing data for an existing customer, or deleting a customer.

The values of the TRANID1 and TRANID2 fields should also be set by the program. But programmers often give the trans-id field an initial value to remind them to assign a value in the program. In this case, these fields have been assigned an initial value of "XXXX."

Once all the screen fields have been defined, the second DFHMSD macro (on page 4 of the listing) tells BMS that the mapset is complete. Then, the END command signals to the assembler that there are no more source statements.

Although assembler statements are cryptic, there are techniques you can use to make the BMS code as readable as possible. First, you can use continuation lines as shown to put every parameter on a separate line. Although this makes the listing longer, it's much easier to find and modify parameters as needed. You can also use comment lines filled with asterisks to group related macros, again to improve the clarity of the code. If your installation has additional guidelines for coding readable mapsets, be sure to follow them. They'll save you time and confusion in the long run.

The code for the BMS mapset   **Page 2**

```
              DFHMDF POS=(7,28),                                    X
                     LENGTH=21,                                     X
                     ATTRB=(NORM,ASKIP),                            X
                     COLOR=NEUTRAL,                                 X
                     INITIAL='1. Add a new customer'
              DFHMDF POS=(8,28),                                    X
                     LENGTH=30,                                     X
                     ATTRB=(NORM,ASKIP),                            X
                     COLOR=NEUTRAL,                                 X
                     INITIAL='2. Change an existing customer'
              DFHMDF POS=(9,28),                                    X
                     LENGTH=21,                                     X
                     ATTRB=(NORM,ASKIP),                            X
                     COLOR=NEUTRAL,                                 X
                     INITIAL='3. Delete an existing customer'
MSG1          DFHMDF POS=(23,1),                                    X
                     LENGTH=79,                                     X
                     ATTRB=(BRT,PROT),                              X
                     COLOR=YELLOW
              DFHMDF POS=(24,1),                                    X
                     LENGTH=20,                                     X
                     ATTRB=(NORM,PROT),                             X
                     COLOR=BLUE,                                    X
                     INITIAL='F3=Exit    F12=Cancel'
DUMMY1        DFHMDF POS=(24,79),                                   X
                     LENGTH=1,                                      X
                     ATTRB=(DRK,PROT,FSET),                         X
                     INITIAL=' '
*********************************************************************
MNTMAP2  DFHMDI SIZE=(24,80),                                       X
                LINE=1,                                             X
                COLUMN=1
*********************************************************************
              DFHMDF POS=(1,1),                                     X
                     LENGTH=7,                                      X
                     ATTRB=(NORM,PROT),                             X
                     COLOR=BLUE,                                    X
                     INITIAL='MNTMAP2'
              DFHMDF POS=(1,20),                                    X
                     LENGTH=20,                                     X
                     ATTRB=(NORM,PROT),                             X
                     COLOR=GREEN,                                   X
                     INITIAL='Customer Maintenance'
TRANID2       DFHMDF POS=(1,76),                                    X
                     LENGTH=4,                                      X
                     ATTRB=(NORM,PROT),                             X
                     COLOR=BLUE,                                    X
                     INITIAL='XXXX'
*********************************************************************
```

Figure 4-12   The BMS mapset for the customer maintenance program (part 2 of 4)

The code for the BMS mapset   Page 3

```
INSTR2     DFHMDF POS=(3,1),                                      X
                  LENGTH=79,                                      X
                  ATTRB=(NORM,PROT),                              X
                  COLOR=NEUTRAL
           DFHMDF POS=(5,1),                                      X
                  LENGTH=24,                                      X
                  ATTRB=(NORM,PROT),                              X
                  COLOR=GREEN,                                    X
                  INITIAL='Customer number. . . . :'
CUSTNO2    DFHMDF POS=(5,26),                                     X
                  LENGTH=6,                                       X
                  ATTRB=(NORM,PROT,FSET),                         X
                  COLOR=TURQUOISE
********************************************************************
           DFHMDF POS=(7,1),                                      X
                  LENGTH=24,                                      X
                  ATTRB=(NORM,PROT),                              X
                  COLOR=GREEN,                                    X
                  INITIAL='Last name. . . . . . .'
LNAME      DFHMDF POS=(7,26),                                     X
                  LENGTH=30,                                      X
                  ATTRB=(NORM,UNPROT,FSET),                       X
                  COLOR=TURQUOISE,                                X
                  HILIGHT=UNDERLINE
           DFHMDF POS=(7,57),                                     X
                  LENGTH=1,                                       X
                  ATTRB=ASKIP
********************************************************************
           DFHMDF POS=(8,1),                                      X
                  LENGTH=24,                                      X
                  ATTRB=(NORM,PROT),                              X
                  COLOR=GREEN,                                    X
                  INITIAL='First name . . . . . . .'
FNAME      DFHMDF POS=(8,26),                                     X
                  LENGTH=20,                                      X
                  ATTRB=(NORM,UNPROT,FSET),                       X
                  COLOR=TURQUOISE,                                X
                  HILIGHT=UNDERLINE
           DFHMDF POS=(8,47),                                     X
                  LENGTH=1,                                       X
                  ATTRB=ASKIP
********************************************************************
           DFHMDF POS=(9,1),                                      X
                  LENGTH=24,                                      X
                  ATTRB=(NORM,PROT),                              X
                  COLOR=GREEN,                                    X
                  INITIAL='Address. . . . . . . . .'
ADDR       DFHMDF POS=(9,26),                                     X
                  LENGTH=30,                                      X
                  ATTRB=(NORM,UNPROT,FSET),                       X
                  COLOR=TURQUOISE,                                X
                  HILIGHT=UNDERLINE
           DFHMDF POS=(9,57),                                     X
                  LENGTH=1,                                       X
                  ATTRB=ASKIP
********************************************************************
```

Figure 4-12   The BMS mapset for the customer maintenance program (part 3 of 4)

The code for the BMS mapset   **Page 4**

```
            DFHMDF POS=(10,1),                                    X
                   LENGTH=24,                                     X
                   ATTRB=(NORM,PROT),                             X
                   COLOR=GREEN,                                   X
                   INITIAL='City . . . . . . . . . .'
CITY        DFHMDF POS=(10,26),                                   X
                   LENGTH=20,                                     X
                   ATTRB=(NORM,UNPROT,FSET),                      X
                   COLOR=TURQUOISE,                               X
                   HILIGHT=UNDERLINE
            DFHMDF POS=(10,47),                                   X
                   LENGTH=1,                                      X
                   ATTRB=ASKIP
*************************************************************************
            DFHMDF POS=(11,1),                                    X
                   LENGTH=24,                                     X
                   ATTRB=(NORM,PROT),                             X
                   COLOR=GREEN,                                   X
                   INITIAL='State. . . . . . . . .'
STATE       DFHMDF POS=(11,26),                                   X
                   LENGTH=2,                                      X
                   ATTRB=(NORM,UNPROT,FSET),                      X
                   COLOR=TURQUOISE,                               X
                   HILIGHT=UNDERLINE
            DFHMDF POS=(11,29),                                   X
                   LENGTH=1,                                      X
                   ATTRB=ASKIP
*************************************************************************
            DFHMDF POS=(12,1),                                    X
                   LENGTH=24,                                     X
                   ATTRB=(NORM,PROT),                             X
                   COLOR=GREEN,                                   X
                   INITIAL='Zip Code . . . . . . . .'
ZIPCODE     DFHMDF POS=(12,26),                                   X
                   LENGTH=10,                                     X
                   ATTRB=(NORM,UNPROT,FSET),                      X
                   COLOR=TURQUOISE,                               X
                   HILIGHT=UNDERLINE
            DFHMDF POS=(12,37),                                   X
                   LENGTH=1,                                      X
                   ATTRB=ASKIP
*************************************************************************
MSG2        DFHMDF POS=(23,1),                                    X
                   LENGTH=79,                                     X
                   ATTRB=(BRT,PROT),                              X
                   COLOR=YELLOW
            DFHMDF POS=(24,1),                                    X
                   LENGTH=20,                                     X
                   ATTRB=(NORM,PROT),                             X
                   COLOR=BLUE,                                    X
                   INITIAL='F3=Exit    F12=Cancel'
DUMMY2      DFHMDF POS=(24,79),                                   X
                   LENGTH=1,                                      X
                   ATTRB=(DRK,PROT,FSET),                         X
                   INITIAL=' '
*************************************************************************
            DFHMSD TYPE=FINAL
            END
```

Figure 4-12   The BMS mapset for the customer maintenance program (part 4 of 4)

The symbolic map

As you saw in chapter 2, once you've completed a BMS mapset, you assemble it to create a physical map and a symbolic map. The *symbolic map*, as you know, is the copy member you use in your COBOL program that lets you process data for the fields that were named in the BMS mapset. The *physical map* is a load module that contains a table BMS uses to determine the screen locations of data transmitted to and from the terminal. For example, a physical map might indicate that a particular field is displayed on the screen at column 16 of line 4. A physical map also indicates the initial attributes for each field. When an application program requests that a map be sent to a terminal, BMS takes data from the symbolic map, formats (or *maps*) it according to physical map, and transmits it to the terminal. Likewise, when an application program requests that data be retrieved from a terminal, BMS uses the physical map to map the data from the screen into the symbolic map.

Later in this chapter, you'll see the JCL you code to assemble a mapset. But first, we'll look at the symbolic map for the customer maintenance program so you can see how it relates to the BMS mapset. It's shown in figure 4-13.

Frankly, the symbolic maps that BMS generates are difficult to read. They follow no consistent rules of abbreviation or indentation, and they include data names that aren't needed. (The data names generated for this map are also less than adequate for COBOL programs, but you can improve them by using longer names in the DFHMDF macros as described in figure 4-9.) However, understanding the structure of the symbolic map BMS creates is critical to learning how to develop CICS programs. So you'll have to study it carefully.

If you code MODE=INOUT on the DFHMSD macro for the mapset, the symbolic map will have two 01-level items for each map in the mapset: one for input operations and one for output. On page 1 of the listing, you can see that these items for the key map are named MNTMAP1I and MNTMAP1O. Since the second 01-level item contains a Redefines clause, these items overlay each other.

Each 01-level item in this symbolic map starts with a 12-byte FILLER item, generated because TIOAPFX=YES was specified in the mapset. Then, five fields were created for each DFHMDF macro coded with a label. The data names for these fields consist of the DFHMDF label followed by a one-character suffix (the names generated for the data entry field labeled CUSTNO1 are highlighted in the figure). Although you were briefly introduced to these fields in chapter 2, the next topic describes their functions in more detail.

The code for the symbolic map   **Page 1**

```
01 MNTMAP1I.
   03 FILLER                          PIC X(12).
   03 TRANID1L                        PIC S9(4) COMP.
   03 TRANID1F                        PIC X.
   03 FILLER REDEFINES TRANID1F.
      05 TRANID1A                      PIC X.
   03 TRANID1I                        PIC X(4).
   03 CUSTNO1L                        PIC S9(4) COMP.
   03 CUSTNO1F                        PIC X.
   03 FILLER REDEFINES CUSTNO1F.
      05 CUSTNO1A                      PIC X.
   03 CUSTNO1I                        PIC X(6).
   03 ACTIONL                         PIC S9(4) COMP.
   03 ACTIONF                         PIC X.
   03 FILLER REDEFINES ACTIONF.
      05 ACTIONA                       PIC X.
   03 ACTIONI                         PIC X(1).
   03 MSG1L                           PIC S9(4) COMP.
   03 MSG1F                           PIC X.
   03 FILLER REDEFINES MSG1F.
      05 MSG1A                         PIC X.
   03 MSG1I                           PIC X(79).
   03 DUMMY1L                         PIC S9(4) COMP.
   03 DUMMY1F                         PIC X.
   03 FILLER REDEFINES DUMMY1F.
      05 DUMMY1A                       PIC X.
   03 DUMMY1I                         PIC X(1).
01 MNTMAP1O REDEFINES MNTMAP1I.
   03 FILLER                          PIC X(12).
   03 FILLER                          PIC X(3).
   03 TRANID1O                        PIC X(4).
   03 FILLER                          PIC X(3).
   03 CUSTNO1O                        PIC X(6).
   03 FILLER                          PIC X(3).
   03 ACTIONO                         PIC X(1).
   03 FILLER                          PIC X(3).
   03 MSG1O                           PIC X(79).
   03 FILLER                          PIC X(3).
   03 DUMMY1O                         PIC X(1).
```

Figure 4-13   The symbolic map for the customer maintenance program (part 1 of 3)

The code for the symbolic map

```
01 MNTMAP2I.
    03 FILLER                            PIC X(12).
    03 TRANID2L                          PIC S9(4) COMP.
    03 TRANID2F                          PIC X.
    03 FILLER REDEFINES TRANID2F.
        05 TRANID2A                       PIC X.
    03 TRANID2I                          PIC X(4).
    03 INSTR2L                           PIC S9(4) COMP.
    03 INSTR2F                           PIC X.
    03 FILLER REDEFINES INSTR2F.
        05 INSTR2A                        PIC X.
    03 INSTR2I                           PIC X(79).
    03 CUSTNO2L                          PIC S9(4) COMP.
    03 CUSTNO2F                          PIC X.
    03 FILLER REDEFINES CUSTNO2F.
        05 CUSTNO2A                       PIC X.
    03 CUSTNO2I                          PIC X(6).
    03 LNAMEL                            PIC S9(4) COMP.
    03 LNAMEF                            PIC X.
    03 FILLER REDEFINES LNAMEF.
        05 LNAMEA                         PIC X.
    03 LNAMEI                            PIC X(30).
    03 FNAMEL                            PIC S9(4) COMP.
    03 FNAMEF                            PIC X.
    03 FILLER REDEFINES FNAMEF.
        05 FNAMEA                         PIC X.
    03 FNAMEI                            PIC X(20).
    03 ADDRL                             PIC S9(4) COMP.
    03 ADDRF                             PIC X.
    03 FILLER REDEFINES ADDRF.
        05 ADDRA                          PIC X.
    03 ADDRI                             PIC X(30).
    03 CITYL                             PIC S9(4) COMP.
    03 CITYF                             PIC X.
    03 FILLER REDEFINES CITYF.
        05 CITYA                          PIC X.
    03 CITYI                             PIC X(20).
    03 STATEL                            PIC S9(4) COMP.
    03 STATEF                            PIC X.
    03 FILLER REDEFINES STATEF.
        05 STATEA                         PIC X.
    03 STATEI                            PIC X(2).
    03 ZIPCODEL                          PIC S9(4) COMP.
    03 ZIPCODEF                          PIC X.
    03 FILLER REDEFINES ZIPCODEF.
        05 ZIPCODEA                       PIC X.
    03 ZIPCODEI                          PIC X(10).
    03 MSG2L                             PIC S9(4) COMP.
    03 MSG2F                             PIC X.
    03 FILLER REDEFINES MSG2F.
        05 MSG2A                          PIC X.
    03 MSG2I                             PIC X(79).
```

Figure 4-13   The symbolic map for the customer maintenance program (part 2 of 3)

The code for the symbolic map   **Page 3**

```
03 DUMMY2L                        PIC S9(4) COMP.
03 DUMMY2F                        PIC X.
03 FILLER REDEFINES DUMMY2F.
   05 DUMMY2A                        PIC X.
03 DUMMY2I                        PIC X(1).
01 MNTMAP2O REDEFINES MNTMAP2I.
   03 FILLER                      PIC X(12).
   03 FILLER                      PIC X(3).
   03 TRANID2O                    PIC X(4).
   03 FILLER                      PIC X(3).
   03 INSTR2O                     PIC X(79).
   03 FILLER                      PIC X(3).
   03 CUSTNO2O                    PIC X(6).
   03 FILLER                      PIC X(3).
   03 LNAMEO                      PIC X(30).
   03 FILLER                      PIC X(3).
   03 FNAMEO                      PIC X(20).
   03 FILLER                      PIC X(3).
   03 ADDRO                       PIC X(30).
   03 FILLER                      PIC X(3).
   03 CITYO                       PIC X(20).
   03 FILLER                      PIC X(3).
   03 STATEO                      PIC X(2).
   03 FILLER                      PIC X(3).
   03 ZIPCODEO                    PIC X(10).
   03 FILLER                      PIC X(3).
   03 MSG2O                       PIC X(79).
   03 FILLER                      PIC X(3).
   03 DUMMY2O                     PIC X(1).
```

Figure 4-13   The symbolic map for the customer maintenance program (part 3 of 3)

The fields in a symbolic map

Figure 4-14 summarizes the fields that are generated in the symbolic map for each DFHMDF macro that contains a label. The first data name, with the suffix L, is for a field that contains the length of the data sent to the program. The value of this field is the actual number of characters sent, not the length of the field specified in the LENGTH parameter.

To illustrate, suppose the user enters ABCD into a field defined with LENGTH=20. The value of the length field will be 4 since the user entered four characters. Embedded spaces are included in the count, so if the user entered JOHN SMITH, the length would be 10.

If the user doesn't enter any data, the field's length value is set to zero. As a result, you can test the length field for a value of zero to see whether or not the user entered any data. You've already seen an example of this common programming technique in the customer inquiry program in chapter 2.

The next two fields in the symbolic map, with suffixes F and A, are redefinitions of a single byte of storage. After an input operation, the flag field (suffix F) contains a *flag byte* that indicates whether the user modified the field without entering data into it. If so, the value of the flag field is hexadecimal 80; otherwise, it's Low-Value.

The attribute field (suffix A) contains a value that records a screen field's standard attributes. If you set this field to a new value in your COBOL code, the attributes you specify override the attributes defined in the physical map when the field is sent to the screen. You'll learn how to modify field attributes in chapter 8.

If you specify extended attributes with the DSATTS option in the BMS mapset, fields for those attributes will be generated in the symbolic map following the flag and attribute fields. For example, if the DFHMSD macro in the inquiry mapset had included DSATTS=(COLOR,HILIGHT), one-byte fields with the suffixes C and H would appear immediately after each attribute field.

Two data names are generated in the symbolic map for the actual data field: one for the input that's sent from the terminal to the program, and one for the output that's sent from the program to the terminal. For example, the data items named CUSTNO1I and CUSTNO1O in figure 4-13 were generated for the CUSTNO1 field. If you look carefully at the definitions of the input and output areas of this map, you'll see that these two data items occupy the same storage location. Different names are provided for input and output so that different pictures can be given to each if a field's DFHMDF macro includes the PICIN or PICOUT parameter.

Data name suffixes

Suffix	Usage	Example
L	A binary halfword (PIC S9(4) COMP) that contains the length of the data returned in the input field.	CUSTNO1L LNAMEL
F	A single-character field (PIC X) that contains hexadecimal 80 if the user made a change to the field, but no data was transmitted; otherwise, it contains Low-Value.	CUSTNO1F LNAMEF
A	A single-character field that contains the attribute byte for output operations. Occupies the same storage location as the F field.	CUSTNO1A LNAMEA
C	A single-character field that contains the attribute for extended color. Generated only if DSATTS=COLOR is specified for the mapset.	CUSTNO1C LNAMEC
H	A single-character field that contains the attribute for extended highlighting. Generated only if DSATTS=HILIGHT is specified for the mapset.	CUSTNO1H LNAMEH
I	The input data field.	CUSTNO1I LNAMEI
O	The output data field. Occupies the same storage location as the input field.	CUSTNO1O LNAMEO

Description

- The length field (suffix L) takes up two bytes of storage and records the length of the data sent from the screen field to the program. This may be different from the length of the field specified in the LENGTH parameter, depending on how many characters the user actually entered into the field. If the user doesn't enter any data, the length field is set to zero.

- The flag field (suffix F) contains a *flag byte* that is normally set to Low-Value. But if the user modifies the input field without entering data into it—for example, by using the Delete key to erase the data in the field—the flag byte is set to hexadecimal 80.

- The attribute field (suffix A) redefines the flag field. It's used for output operations to override the field attributes defined in the physical map. You'll learn how to use this field in chapter 8.

- If you specify extended attributes with the DSATTS option in the mapset, fields for those attributes will appear in the symbolic map following the flag and attribute fields. The two most common attributes are color (suffix C) and highlighting (suffix H).

- The input field (suffix I) and output field (suffix O) are generated for the data field itself. As the names imply, one is used for input operations, the other for output operations. Both fields occupy the same storage location, but the two data names allow the Picture clauses to differ according to the PICIN and PICOUT parameters on the DFHMDF macro.

Figure 4-14   The fields in a symbolic map

A programmer-generated symbolic map

Although I don't usually recommend it, sometimes you'll find it necessary to discard the symbolic map generated by BMS in favor of one you create yourself. The most likely reason for this is if the map contains two or more lines of repeated fields. BMS doesn't take advantage of the COBOL Occurs clause to make this type of map easier to process. You'll see an example of this in the source code for an order entry program in chapter 13. The map for that program has ten lines of line item data, each with six fields. By creating my own symbolic map, I was able to process these line item fields as a simple table.

Figure 4-15 shows a programmer-generated symbolic map for the key map of the maintenance program. As you can see, only three fields are defined for each screen field instead of five: one to record the length of the data entry (suffix L), one to control the field attributes (suffix A), and one to contain the data itself (suffix D). If you need different pictures for input and output, you can code two fields instead of one to contain the data, like this:

```
05   MNT1-I-CUSTNO1                          PIC X(6).
05   MNT1-O-CUSTNO1 REDEFINES MNT1-I-CUSTNO1  PIC 9(6).
```

As you can see, the output field (suffix O) redefines the input field (suffix I), so they share the same six bytes of storage.

To create a symbolic map like the one shown, you can work from the mapset definition using the procedure summarized in the figure. If you follow these guidelines, the resulting symbolic map will be easy to read and understand.

Whenever you substitute your own symbolic map for the one generated by BMS, be aware of the possibility of error. When you use the BMS-generated symbolic map, you can make a change to the mapset, reassemble it, and then recompile your program with confidence that the physical map and the symbolic map agree. When you create your own symbolic map, though, it's up to you to make sure that any changes to the mapset are reflected in your symbolic map. That's why, in general, I don't recommend that you create your own symbolic maps.

A programmer-generated symbolic map

```
01  MNTMAP1.
*
    05  FILLER                  PIC X(12).
*
    05  MNT1-L-TRANID1          PIC S9(4) COMP.
    05  MNT1-A-TRANID1          PIC X.
    05  MNT1-D-TRANID1          PIC X(4).
*
    05  MNT1-L-CUSTNO1          PIC S9(4) COMP.
    05  MNT1-A-CUSTNO1          PIC X.
    05  MNT1-D-CUSTNO1          PIC X(6).
*
    05  MNT1-L-ACTION           PIC S9(4) COMP.
    05  MNT1-A-ACTION           PIC X.
    05  MNT1-D-ACTION           PIC X.
*
    05  MNT1-L-MSG1             PIC S9(4) COMP.
    05  MNT1-A-MSG1             PIC X.
    05  MNT1-D-MSG1             PIC X(79).
*
    05  MNT1-L-DUMMY1           PIC S9(4) COMP.
    05  MNT1-A-DUMMY1           PIC X.
    05  MNT1-D-DUMMY1           PIC X.
```

Guidelines for creating your own symbolic map

1. Code only one 01-level item rather than separate 01-level items that redefine one another for input and output purposes.
2. Code a 12-byte FILLER item for TIOAPFX at the beginning of the map.
3. For each labeled map field, code a group of 05-level items, following these rules to create the data names:
   a. Start each name with a two- to four-character prefix that relates the data name to the 01-level item.
   b. Include one character to identify the field's function: L for the length field, A for the attribute field, and D for the data field.
   c. If you need different pictures for input and output, create a fourth data name that redefines the data field. Then, identify the input and output data fields with the characters I and O.
   d. If you specified extended attributes with the DSATTS parameter, insert fields for them between the attribute field and the data field. Use the characters C and H to identify extended color and extended highlighting attributes.
4. Separate each set of data names with a blank comment line.
5. Align the elements of the symbolic map so it's easy to read.

Description

- When you create your own symbolic map, it's up to you to make sure that any changes to the mapset are reflected in your symbolic map. This can be a problem as an application is maintained over time. So check whether your installation allows you to create your own symbolic maps before you get started.

Figure 4-15   How to create your own symbolic map

How to assemble a BMS mapset

To create a physical map and a symbolic map from a BMS mapset, you use a JCL procedure like the one shown in figure 4-16. Most shops will have a procedure like this that you can use, so you won't have to create it from scratch. Instead, you can just replace the names in the EXEC and DD statements with names that are appropriate for the mapset you want to assemble.

As you can see, this JCL executes a cataloged procedure named DFHMAPS that contains the JCL for assembling a mapset. On the EXEC statement for this procedure, you usually include the name of the libraries where the physical map (MAPLIB) and the symbolic map (DSCTLIB) will be stored, along with the name you want to use for those maps (MAPNAME). However, if the cataloged procedure is already set up so it stores the physical and symbolic maps in the appropriate libraries, you can omit the MAPLIB and DSCTLIB parameters. But the MAPNAME parameter is required and should be the same as the name of the member that contains the source code for the mapset. This member is identified on the SYSUT1 DD statement, which is used in the COPY step of the DFHMAPS procedure.

An OS/390 procedure for preparing a mapset

```
//MM01MAPS JOB 36512,'R.MENENDEZ',MSGCLASS=X,CLASS=C,
//          REGION=4M,NOTIFY=MM01
//MAPASM    EXEC DFHMAPS,
//  MAPLIB='MM01CICS.CICSTS13.LOADLIB',      TARGET LOADLIB FOR MAP
//  DSCTLIB='MM01.CICS.COPYLIB',             TARGET COPYLIB FOR DSECT
//  MAPNAME=ORDSET1                          NAME OF MAPSET (REQUIRED)
//COPY.SYSUT1 DD DSN=MM01.CICS.SOURCE(ORDSET1),DISP=SHR   MAPSET SOURCE
/*
```

Description

- The JCL for preparing a mapset executes a cataloged procedure named DFHMAPS. This procedure includes a step that creates a physical map and a step that creates a symbolic map (sometimes called a *DSECT*).

- The MAPLIB parameter of the EXEC statement identifies the load library where the physical map will be stored. (This map must be identified in the Processing Program Table.) If you omit this parameter, the physical map is stored in the default load library specified in the DFHMAPS procedure.

- The DSCTLIB parameter of the EXEC statement identifies the copy library where the symbolic map will be stored. If you omit this parameter, the symbolic map is stored in the default copy library coded in the DFHMAPS procedure.

- The MAPNAME parameter of the EXEC statement specifies the name that will be given to the physical and symbolic maps. This parameter is required.

- The SYSUT1 DD statement identifies the library and member that contains the source code for the mapset you want to assemble. This DD statement is used as input to the COPY step of the DFHMAPS procedure.

Figure 4-16   How to assemble a BMS mapset

Perspective

Right now, you're probably thinking that the process of defining a BMS map is overly complicated. You're right! That's why many shops use map generators or screen painters to ease the burden of creating mapsets. When you use a screen painter, you create an image of the screen on a terminal using special codes for unprotected fields, numeric fields, and so forth. Next, you assign names to the fields that you want in the symbolic map. Then, the screen painter analyzes the screen image and creates a BMS mapset you can assemble in the usual way. At the same time, many screen painters produce screen documentation that's more useful than a BMS assembler listing. The screen painter may also let you save your screen image so you can recall it later to make modifications without having to reenter it. Obviously, a screen painter can be a tremendous time-saver. So if one is available, by all means use it.

Still, it's important to know how to create BMS mapsets. Since screen painters can't handle all situations, you may need to create your own mapsets for complicated screen layouts. Also, you may need to modify the output produced by the screen painter.

Terms

field-oriented display
field
data entry field
display-only field
Common User Access (CUA)
CUA Entry Model
CUA Graphical Model
Text Subset of the Graphical Model
attribute byte
attribute
standard attribute
protection attribute
protected field
unprotected field
auto-skip attribute
skip field
shift attribute
alphanumeric shift
numeric shift
intensity attribute
Modified Data Tag (MDT)

extended attribute
extended color
extended highlighting
reverse video
basic mapping support (BMS)
mapset
map
macro
macro instruction
label
op-code
parameter
operand
continuation line
comment line
control option
physical map
symbolic map
flag byte
DSECT

5

How to code a CICS program

In this chapter, you'll learn more about the commands that were introduced in chapter 2, and you'll learn about some other commands that you'll use regularly as you code CICS programs. You'll also learn some techniques related to coding CICS programs. And you'll see a complete program that uses many of these commands and techniques. When you complete this chapter, you'll have the basic skills you'll need to code a variety of CICS applications.

How to control the execution of the programs within a task

When CICS initiates a task, it loads a program and transfers control to that program. That program, in turn, can invoke other programs. In some cases, those programs will return control to the invoking program when their processing is complete. In other cases, those programs will return control to the program at the next higher logical level. And the initial program, of course, can return control to CICS and set up the next execution of that program. In the topics that follow, you'll learn about the commands and statements you can use to perform these functions.

The operation of the program control commands

The programs within a task can execute at different *logical levels*. When a program is invoked by CICS, for example, that program operates at the logical level below CICS. Then, that program can invoke another program using the XCTL command you learned about in chapter 2 or the LINK command you'll learn about later in this chapter. If the program is invoked with a LINK command, it operates at the logical level below the invoking program. If the program is invoked with an XCTL command, though, the invoked program operates at the same logical level as the invoking program.

These logical levels and the effect of the program control commands are illustrated in figure 5-1. Notice that CICS is at the highest logical level (level 0). When CICS invokes Program A, that program runs at the next lower level, level 1. When Program A issues a RETURN command, control returns to CICS at level 0. Notice that this RETURN command may or may not include a trans-id. You'll learn more about when to use a trans-id with the RETURN command later in this chapter.

Similarly, when Program A invokes Program B using a LINK command, Program B runs at the level below Program A (level 2 in this example). And when Program B issues a RETURN command (without a trans-id), control is passed back up to Program A.

In contrast, when Program B invokes Program C using an XCTL command, Program C operates at the *same* logical level as Program B. Then, when Program C issues a RETURN command (without a trans-id), control returns not to Program B, but to the program that invoked Program B, in this case, Program A.

In addition to the CICS commands shown in this figure, you can also invoke a program under CICS using a COBOL Call statement. And you can return control to an invoking program using a COBOL Goback statement. Frankly, you're not likely to use the Goback statement in place of the RETURN command. But you may use the Call statement instead of the LINK command to invoke subprograms that are used more than once within the same execution of a program. You'll learn more about that later in this chapter.

How control is passed from one program to another under CICS

Logical level

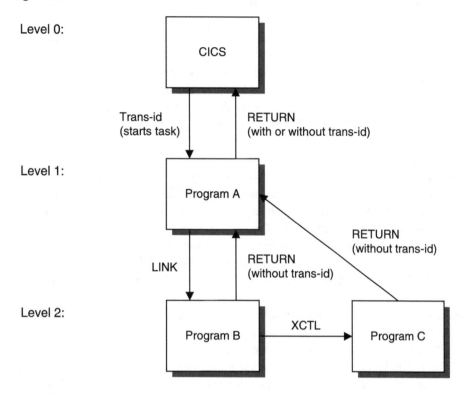

Description

- When a program is invoked by entering a trans-id from CICS like Program A above, the invoked program executes at the logical level below CICS. Then, when the program ends by issuing a RETURN command, control returns to CICS.

- When a program is invoked by executing a LINK command from another program like Program B above, the invoked program executes at the logical level below the program that invoked it. Then, when the invoked program ends by issuing a RE-TURN command, control returns to the program that invoked it.

- When a program is invoked by executing a XCTL command from another program like Program C above, the invoked program executes at the same logical level as the program that invoked it. Then, when the invoked program ends by issuing a RETURN command, control returns to the program at the next higher level, not to the program that invoked it.

Note

- You can use the COBOL Goback statement in place of the RETURN command for a program that's invoked by an XCTL or LINK command, but you won't usually do that.

Figure 5-1   The operation of the program control commands

How to code the RETURN command

Figure 5-2 presents the syntax of the RETURN command. You can use this command to return control to CICS and set up the next execution of the program in a pseudo-conversational session. When you use it for that purpose, you include the TRANSID option to specify the trans-id of the program. You also include the COMMAREA option to name the area of working storage that will be stored in the CICS communication area between program executions. In fact, this is the only case in which you can specify the TRANSID and COMMAREA options. If you use them in any other situation, an error will occur and the program will terminate abnormally.

The diagram shown in this figure illustrates how this works. When the RETURN command in the first execution of Program A is issued, the data in the working-storage field named CA-AREA is stored in CICS's temporary communication area. Then, the next time the user presses an attention key, Program A is started again because its trans-id, PRGA, was named on the RETURN command. In addition, the data in the temporary communication area is passed to the program and is accessible through the DFHCOMMAREA field that's defined in the Linkage Section. Note that although you can name the working-storage area you pass to the temporary communication area anything you want, the area in the Linkage Section must be named DFHCOMMAREA. If you want to, you can define data items subordinate to DFHCOMMAREA, but you usually don't need to do that. In any case, both the working-storage area and DFHCOMMAREA must be defined with the same length.

It's important to realize that the working-storage and Linkage Section fields define two distinct areas of storage. The working-storage area represents storage that's freshly allocated each time your program starts. In contrast, the Linkage Section area (DFHCOMMAREA) represents storage that's saved from the previous execution of the program. (That's true for each execution except the first, in which case the Linkage Section area receives null values.) Each time your program ends, the storage held by DFHCOMMAREA is released, and the contents of the working-storage area are saved in the temporary communication area. Then, the next time the program is executed, the contents of the temporary communication area are made available through DFHCOMMAREA. To access the data in DFHCOMMAREA, you typically move it to the newly allocated storage defined in the Working-Storage Section.

You can also use the RETURN command to return control to the invoking program or the program at the next higher level. To do that, you use a RETURN command without any options as illustrated by the command shown in this figure. If the program was invoked by a LINK command, control is returned to the invoking program. If the program was invoked by an XCTL command, control is returned to the program at the next higher level. And if the program was invoked directly from CICS, control is returned to CICS.

The syntax of the RETURN command

```
EXEC CICS
    RETURN [TRANSID(trans-id)]
           [COMMAREA(data-name)]
END-EXEC
```

Option	Description
TRANSID	Specifies the one- to four-character name of the transaction to be invoked when the user presses an attention key. The trans-id must be defined in the Program Control Table (PCT).
COMMAREA	Specifies the name of a data area that's passed to the next execution of a pseudo-conversational program. The next program execution accesses the communication area via its DFHCOMMAREA field.

How to use the RETURN command to pass the communication area to the next execution of the program

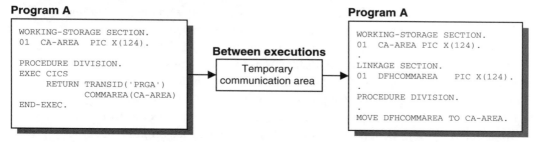

A RETURN command that returns control to the program that invoked it

```
EXEC CICS
    RETURN
END-EXEC.
```

Description

- The RETURN command ends the execution of a program. To end one interaction of a pseudo-conversational program and set up the next execution to process the next user input event, you code the RETURN command with the TRANSID and COMMAREA options.

- When you include the COMMAREA option, the data in the working-storage area it names is saved in the temporary communication area. Then, when the program is restarted, that data is passed to the program through the DFHCOMMAREA field defined in the program's Linkage Section.

- If a program is invoked directly from CICS by entering a trans-id, you can code the RETURN command without any options to end the task and return control to CICS.

- If a program is invoked by a LINK command, you can use a RETURN command without any options to return control to the program that issued the LINK command.

- If a program is invoked by an XCTL command, you can use a RETURN command without any options to return control to the program at the next higher logical level.

Figure 5-2   How to code the RETURN command

How to code the XCTL command

Figure 5-3 presents the syntax of the XCTL command. You use this command to transfer control to another program. The PROGRAM option names the program to be invoked, and the COMMAREA option names an area in working storage whose contents are passed to that program. That data is then available through the DFHCOMMAREA field that's defined in the Linkage Section of the invoked program, as you can see in the illustration in this figure.

Also notice in this illustration that the XCTL command passes a *copy* of the data in the working-storage area it names to the invoked program. Because of that, changes you make to this data aren't reflected in the invoking program. That makes sense because when the invoked program ends by issuing a RETURN command, control is returned to the program at the next higher level, *not* to the program that invoked it. In fact, the invoking program ends and its memory allocations are released after it issues the XCTL command, so control can't be returned to it.

The XCTL command is particularly useful when used with menu programs. In that case, the menu program can issue an XCTL command to invoke the program the user selects. That program can then use the RETURN command with the TRANSID and COMMAREA options to return control to CICS and set it up to restart the program when the user presses an attention key. Then, to end the program for the last time, the program can issue an XCTL command to return control to the menu program. You saw this code in the customer inquiry program, and you'll see it again in the customer maintenance program that's presented later in this chapter.

By the way, when you invoke a program using an XCTL command without the COMMAREA option, the invoked program can detect that it's being executed for the first time just as if it had been invoked directly from CICS. In other words, it can check the length of the data passed through the communication area using the EIBCALEN field.

Later in this chapter, you'll learn about the most common exceptional conditions that can occur when you issue a CICS command and how to handle them. One of those conditions is PGMIDERR, which can occur when the program identified on an XCTL command can't be found. In most cases, you won't test for this condition. Instead, you'll just let the program terminate if any condition other than NORMAL is returned.

The syntax of the XCTL command

```
EXEC CICS
    XCTL    PROGRAM(program-name)
            [COMMAREA(data-name)]
END-EXEC
```

Option	Description
PROGRAM	Specifies the one- to eight-character name of the program to be invoked. The name must be defined in the Processing Program Table (PPT).
COMMAREA	Specifies the name of a data area that's passed to the invoked program as a communication area.

How to use the XCTL command to pass data to another program

Description

- The XCTL command invokes another program at the same logical level. If you include the COMMAREA option on this command, a copy of the data in the area it names is passed to the invoked program and stored in its DFHCOMMAREA field.

- Because the invoked program receives a copy of the data sent to it from the invoking program, changes made to the data by the invoked program aren't reflected in the invoking program.

- If the program you specify doesn't exist, a PGMIDERR exceptional condition occurs. In most cases, you don't need to test for this condition.

- When you use the XCTL command to invoke a program, the invoking program ends and its memory allocations are released since control will not return to it. That makes it more efficient than the LINK command, since the memory allocation for a program that issues a LINK command must be maintained.

- You typically use XCTL without the COMMAREA option to invoke a program from a menu program. The invoked program can then detect the first-time condition by evaluating the length of the communication area using the EIBCALEN field just as if it had been invoked directly from CICS. When it's done, the invoked program can issue an XCTL command to return control to the menu program.

Figure 5-3   How to code the XCTL command

How to code the LINK command

Because the memory allocated to a program is released when it issues an XCTL command, using XCTL is an efficient way to transfer control to another program. If you need to return control to the invoking program, though, you'll want to use the LINK command shown in figure 5-4.

As you can see, the syntax of the LINK command is similar to the syntax of the XCTL command. When you use the LINK command, though, the program you specify on the PROGRAM option is executed at the next lower logical level. In addition, if you pass data to the linked program using the COMMAREA option, the linked program receives a pointer to that data rather than a copy of the data itself. In other words, both programs refer to the same area of storage for the data. That means that any changes you make to the data through the DFHCOMMAREA field in the invoked program will be reflected in the working-storage definition of the data in the invoking program. If you want to work with the data in the linked program without affecting the data in the invoking program, though, you can move that data from DFHCOMMAREA to a working-storage area. Later, you can move the working-storage area back to DFHCOMMAREA if you want the changes reflected in the invoking program.

The LINK command also has one option that's not available with the XCTL command. This option, DATALENGTH, lets you pass just a portion of the data area you name in the COMMAREA option. On this option, you specify the length of the data you want to pass. Then, the program will pass the data with the length you specify starting at the beginning of the area named in the COMMAREA option. In most cases, you'll omit the DATALENGTH option and pass all of the data area you specify. If the linked program doesn't need all of this data, though, it's more efficient to pass just the portion it needs.

The syntax of the LINK command

```
EXEC CICS
    LINK  PROGRAM(program-name)
         [COMMAREA(data-name)]
         [DATALENGTH(data-name | literal)]
END-EXEC
```

Option	Description
PROGRAM	Specifies the one- to eight-character name of the program to be invoked. The name must be defined in the Processing Program Table (PPT).
COMMAREA	Specifies the name of the data area that's passed to the invoked program as a communication area.
DATALENGTH	Specifies a binary halfword (PIC S9(4) COMP) or numeric literal that indicates the length of the data to be sent from the area specified in the COMMAREA option. The value may be less than the total length of this area.

How to use the LINK command to pass data to another program

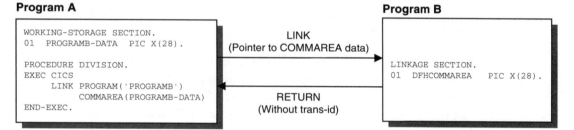

Description

- The LINK command invokes a program at the next logical level. If you include the COMMAREA option on this command, a pointer to the data area it names is passed to the invoked program. That program can then work with the data through its DFHCOMMAREA field.

- Because the DFHCOMMAREA field in the invoked program points to the same area of storage used by the invoking program, any changes made to the data by the invoked program are reflected in the invoking program.

- When you use the LINK command to invoke a program, the invoking program waits for control to be passed back to it when the invoked program ends. The invoked program can then use a RETURN command without a trans-id to return control to the invoking program.

- The program that's invoked by a LINK command can reside on the local system or on a remote system (see chapter 19).

- If the program you specify doesn't exist, a PGMIDERR exception condition occurs. In most cases, you don't need to test for this condition.

- Each time a LINK command is issued, a fresh copy of the invoked program is loaded into memory and its working storage is initialized. Because this can cause system degradation, you may want to use the COBOL Call statement to invoke programs that are called more than once during a single execution of a task.

Figure 5-4   How to code the LINK command

How to code the COBOL Call statement

Under older releases of CICS, Call statements were rarely used because called programs couldn't issue any CICS commands. Because of that, the use of LINK commands became the norm in many COBOL shops. Even though this restriction has been lifted, many shops continue to use LINK commands. One reason for this is that you can use the LINK command to invoke a program on either a local or a remote system. (See chapter 19 for information on invoking a program on a remote system.) A Call statement can only invoke a program on a local system.

If you don't need to invoke programs on remote systems, though, the Call statement can be more efficient than the LINK command in some situations. In particular, the Call statement is more efficient if it invokes the same program more than once within a single execution of the invoking program. If you use the LINK command, memory is allocated to the linked program and its working storage is initialized each time the command is issued. In contrast, memory is allocated to a called program and its working storage is initialized only the first time it's called.

Figure 5-5 presents the syntax of the COBOL Call statement. If you're an experienced COBOL programmer, you probably already know how to use this statement. You just name the program you want to invoke (or a field that contains the name of the program if it's invoked dynamically), and you specify the names of the fields you want to pass to that program on the USING clause as illustrated in the first two examples in this figure. Notice in the third example, though, that if the called program contains CICS commands, you must also pass the Execute Interface Block and the communication area since these fields are included in the called program by the CICS translator.

The syntax of the COBOL Call statement

```
CALL {'subprogram-name' | data-area} [USING identifier-1 ...]
```

A static Call statement that invokes a program that doesn't use CICS

```
CALL 'NUMEDIT' USING UNEDITED-NUMBER
                     EDITED-NUMBER
                     VALID-NUMBER-SW.
```

A dynamic Call statement that invokes a program that doesn't use CICS

```
MOVE 'NUMEDIT' TO PROGRAM-NAME.
CALL PROGRAM-NAME USING UNEDITED-NUMBER
                        EDITED-NUMBER
                        VALID-NUMBER-SW.
```

A static Call statement that invokes a program that uses CICS

```
MOVE COMMUNICATION-AREA TO DFHCOMMAREA.
CALL 'GETINV' USING DFHEIBLK
                    DFHCOMMAREA
                    INV-INVOICE-NUMBER.
```

Description

- The Call statement invokes a program at the same logical level. If the called program issues a Goback statement, control returns to the calling program. However, if it issues a RETURN command, control returns to the program at the next higher level.

- A program that's invoked with a static Call statement must be link-edited with the calling program to form a single load module. That means that each calling program maintains a separate copy of the called program. If the called program is modified, each program that calls it must be link-edited again.

- A program that's invoked by a dynamic Call statement is link-edited into a load module that's separate from the programs that call it. Because of that, two or more calling programs can share the same copy of the called program. In addition, only the called program needs to be link-edited again if it's modified.

- If the called program issues CICS commands, the Call statement must pass DFHEIBLK and DFHCOMMAREA as the first two parameters of the Using clause. The CICS translator automatically adds these areas to the Linkage Section of the called program and includes them in the Using clause of the Procedure Division statement.

- The program that's invoked by a Call statement must reside on the local system. To invoke a program on a remote system, you must use the LINK command.

- The first time a Call statement is issued within a task, the called program is loaded into memory and its working storage is initialized. Subsequent calls to the program do not cause it to be refreshed or its working storage to be reinitialized. Because of that, it can be more efficient to use than the LINK command for programs that are invoked more than once within a single execution of a task.

Figure 5-5   How to code the COBOL Call statement

How to code the ABEND command

The last command for controlling program execution is the ABEND command. Its syntax is shown in figure 5-6. This command terminates your program abnormally and displays a message at the terminal. Before starting another transaction, the user must press the Clear key to clear the screen.

By default, the ABEND command also causes a storage dump to be produced. To identify the dump, you can code the ABCODE option with the abend code you want included on the dump. If you don't need a storage dump, you can code the NODUMP option.

The syntax of the ABEND command

```
EXEC CICS
    ABEND [ABCODE(abend-code)]
          [NODUMP]
END-EXEC
```

Option	Description
ABCODE	Specifies that a storage dump should be produced, and the one- to four-character value supplied should be used as the abend code.
NODUMP	Indicates that a storage dump should not be produced.

An ABEND command that produces a storage dump

```
EXEC CICS
    ABEND ABCODE(RM17)
END-EXEC.
```

Description

- The ABEND command causes your program to terminate abnormally and, optionally, produces a storage dump.
- The ABEND command is typically used to terminate a program when a serious error occurs that the program can't handle.
- The abend code you specify must not start with the letter A, since it's reserved for CICS codes.
- If you omit both the ABCODE and NODUMP options, a storage dump is produced, but the abend code is set to question marks (????).
- When the ABEND command is executed and the program is terminated, a message is displayed at the terminal. Then, the user must press the Clear key to clear the screen before entering another trans-id.

Figure 5-6   How to code the ABEND command

How to work with mapsets

To work with BMS mapsets, you use the SEND MAP and RECEIVE MAP commands. You saw the basic formats of these commands in chapter 2. Now, you'll learn the details of using these commands.

How to code the SEND MAP command

Figure 5-7 presents the syntax of the SEND MAP command. As you know, this command sends data from your program to the terminal. You'll almost always code the MAP and MAPSET options on this command to identify the map to be sent and the mapset that contains it. If the map and mapset have the same name, however, you can omit the MAPSET option.

If you want to send the data in the symbolic map to the screen, you need to code the FROM option to identify the area in the symbolic map that contains that data. In addition, if you want to send just the data in the symbolic map, you can code the DATAONLY option. If you code the MAPONLY option, only the data in the physical map—in other words, the constant values—are sent to the screen. In that case, you can omit the FROM option. If you omit both MAPONLY and DATAONLY, the data in the symbolic map is combined with the data in the physical map, and both are sent to the screen.

Usually, you'll omit the MAPONLY and DATAONLY options the first time a map is displayed during a terminal session and each time a different map is displayed. That way, both the constants and the initial data are sent to the screen. You'll also code the ERASE option on these SEND MAP commands so that the previous contents of the screen are erased. In contrast, you'll code the DATAONLY option on subsequent SEND MAP commands so the headings aren't transmitted again, and you'll omit the ERASE option so that the current headings aren't erased from the screen.

The ERASEAUP option is similar to the ERASE option. The difference is that ERASEAUP causes only unprotected fields to be erased, while ERASE completely clears the screen. In most cases, you'll move Low-Values to the symbolic map and then issue the SEND MAP command with the ERASEAUP and DATAONLY options so that no data will be sent to the terminal. (Remember, CICS doesn't transmit Low-Values.) If you want to erase some of the protected fields as well, though, you can move Space to them.

The last SEND MAP option, CURSOR, is used for cursor positioning. You'll learn more about positioning the cursor in chapter 8. For now, just realize that if you code this option without a value, the cursor is positioned at the first field on the screen whose length field in the symbolic map is set to -1.

The syntax of the SEND MAP command

```
EXEC CICS
    SEND  MAP(map-name)
          [MAPSET(mapset-name)]
          [FROM(data-name)]
          [MAPONLY | DATAONLY]
          [ERASE | ERASEAUP]
          [ALARM]
          [CURSOR [(data-value)]]
    END-EXEC
```

Option	Description
MAP	Specifies the one- to seven-character name of the map to be used to map the output data.
MAPSET	Specifies the one- to seven-character name of the mapset that contains the map. If omitted, the map name is used. This name must be defined in the Processing Program Table (PPT).
FROM	Specifies the name of the data area in the symbolic map that contains the data to be mapped. If omitted, the map name with an O suffix is used.
MAPONLY	Causes only constant data from the BMS physical map to be sent; no FROM area is used.
DATAONLY	Causes only data from the FROM area to be mapped; constant data from the physical map is not sent.
ERASE	Causes the contents of the screen to be erased before data is displayed.
ERASEAUP	Causes all unprotected fields on the screen to be erased.
ALARM	Causes the alarm to sound when the map is displayed.
CURSOR	Specifies the position of the cursor. If a data value is specified, it indicates the position as a displacement from the beginning of the screen. If the data value is omitted, the cursor is positioned at the first field whose length in the symbolic map is set to -1.

A SEND MAP command that displays the data in a symbolic map, sounds the alarm, and positions the cursor

```
EXEC CICS
    SEND MAP('MNTMAP1')
         MAPSET('MNTSET1')
         FROM(MNTMAP1O)
         DATAONLY
         ALARM
         CURSOR
    END-EXEC.
```

Description

*   The SEND MAP command sends data from your program to the screen.
*   If you omit both the MAPONLY and DATAONLY options, the data in the symbolic map is combined with the data in the physical map, and both are sent to the screen.

Figure 5-7   How to code the SEND MAP command

How to code the RECEIVE MAP command

The RECEIVE MAP command, shown in figure 5-8, receives input data from the terminal. The MAP and MAPSET options indicate the map to be received and the MAPSET that contains it. Like the SEND MAP command, you can omit the MAPSET option if the mapset has the same name as the map. The INTO option names the area in the symbolic map where the data that's received will be placed.

When the operator enters data at the terminal and presses an attention key, the data is transferred to a CICS buffer. Then, when your program executes a RECEIVE MAP command, the data in the buffer is mapped into the symbolic map. Because of that, your program must not issue a RECEIVE MAP command before the operator has sent data from the terminal. Since a pseudo-conversational program isn't executed until the operators presses an attention key, though, this is only a problem in conversational programs.

The syntax of the RECEIVE MAP command

```
EXEC CICS
    RECEIVE  MAP(map-name)
             [MAPSET(mapset-name)]
             [INTO(data-name)]
END-EXEC
```

Option	Description
MAP	Specifies the one- to seven-character name of the map to be used to map the input data.
MAPSET	Specifies the one- to seven-character name of the mapset that contains the map. If omitted, the map name is used. This name must be defined in the Processing Program Table (PPT).
INTO	Specifies the name of the data area where the mapped data should be placed. If omitted, the map name with an I suffix is used.

A typical RECEIVE MAP command

```
EXEC CICS
    RECEIVE MAP('MNTMAP1')
            MAPSET('MNTSET1')
            INTO(MNTMAP1I)
END-EXEC.
```

Description

- The RECEIVE MAP command receives data from a CICS buffer. This data is placed in the buffer when the user enters the data at the terminal and presses an attention key.

Figure 5-8   How to code the RECEIVE MAP command

How to work with files

CICS provides file handling commands for performing all basic file manipulation operations, including random and sequential read, write, rewrite, and delete. You can use these commands on key-sequenced, relative record, or entry-sequenced VSAM files. (VSAM files are also called *data sets*, and you'll often see the abbreviations KSDS, RRDS, and ESDS for key-sequenced, relative record, and entry-sequenced data sets.) If you've used the COBOL statements for file handling before, you won't have any trouble using these commands.

How to code the READ command

Figure 5-9 presents the syntax of the READ command. You saw an example of this command in the customer inquiry program in chapter 2. In that case, the READ command retrieved a record randomly from a key-sequenced file based on the customer number entered by the user. To do that, it specified the name of the file on the FILE option, it named the working-storage area where the retrieved record would be placed on the INTO option, and it named the field that contained the key of the record to be retrieved on the RIDFLD option. In that program, the RIDFLD field was defined as part of the record description. Although that's usually the case, this field can be defined anywhere in working storage.

Unless you specify otherwise, CICS assumes that the value in the RIDFLD field is a key value, and the record to be read is in a key-sequenced file. If you want to retrieve a record from a relative record file, then, you have to include the RRN option on the READ command. If you do, CICS will interpret the value in the RIDFLD as a *relative record number*. A relative record number indicates the position of a record in the file. So, for example, if the RIDFLD value is 1, the first record in the file is read; if it's 2, the second record is read; and so on.

You can also read a record from a key-sequenced file or an entry-sequenced file by specifying the record's *relative byte address*, or *RBA*. The RBA is an indication of how far, in bytes, a record is displaced from the beginning of a file. If you include the RBA option on the READ command, CICS will interpret the RIDFLD value as an RBA. Frankly, though, you're not likely to read a record in a key-sequenced file by its RBA because it's much easier to use its key value. And you're not likely to use the READ command at all for an entry-sequenced file since these files are usually processed sequentially. Instead, you'll use the CICS browse commands, which you'll learn about in chapter 14.

If you intend to update the record a READ command returns, you must also specify the UPDATE option as illustrated in the example in this figure. This option causes the record to be reserved by your task until you issue a REWRITE, DELETE, or UNLOCK command or until your task ends. That means that no other task can modify the record while your task is updating it. You'll see in a moment how the REWRITE, DELETE, and UNLOCK commands are used.

The syntax of the READ command

```
EXEC CICS
    READ  FILE(filename)
          INTO(data-name)
          RIDFLD(data-name)
          [RRN |RBA]
          [UPDATE]
END-EXEC
```

Option	Description
FILE	Specifies the name of the file that contains the record to be read. This name must be defined in the File Control Table (FCT).
INTO	Specifies the name of the data area where the input record is placed.
RIDFLD	For a key-sequenced file, specifies the name of the field that contains the key of the record to be read. If RRN or RBA is specified, this field is interpreted as a relative record number or a relative byte address.
RRN	Indicates that the file is a relative record file, and the RIDFLD option should be interpreted as a relative record number.
RBA	Indicates that the RIDFLD option should be interpreted as a relative byte address for an entry-sequenced or key-sequenced file.
UPDATE	Indicates that you intend to update the record with a subsequent REWRITE or DELETE command.

A READ command that reads a record from a key-sequenced file for update

```
EXEC CICS
    READ FILE('CUSTMAS')
         INTO(CUSTOMER-MASTER-RECORD)
         RIDFLD(CM-CUSTOMER-NUMBER)
         UPDATE
         RESP(RESPONSE-CODE)
END-EXEC.
```

Description

- The READ command retrieves a record from a VSAM file. It's used most often with key-sequenced files, but can also be used with relative record and entry-sequenced files.

- A record in a relative record file is identified by its *relative record number*, or *RRN*. The field that contains the relative record number must be defined as a binary fullword (PIC S9(8) COMP).

- A record in an entry-sequenced file is identified by its *relative byte address*, or *RBA*. Because entry-sequenced files are usually read sequentially, you'll probably never use the READ command with these files.

- You can also identify a record in a key-sequenced file by its relative byte address, but you're not likely to do that.

- If the specified record doesn't exist, a NOTFND exceptional condition occurs.

Figure 5-9   How to code the READ command

You'll also notice that the READ command in this figure includes the RESP option. As you saw in chapter 2, this option lets you check for any exceptional conditions that may have occurred when a CICS command is executed. Because it can be used on *any* CICS command and its format is always the same, we've omitted it from the syntax for the commands in this book. But later in this chapter, you'll see its format and get more details on using it.

How to code the WRITE command

The WRITE command, whose syntax is shown in figure 5-10, adds a record to a file. As you can see, this command is similar in format to the READ command. The FILE option specifies the name of the file that contains the record to be read, the FROM option names the program area that contains the record to be written, and the RIDFLD option specifies the record's key value. Again, the RIDFLD data area can be a part of the record or a separate field defined in working storage.

To add a record to a relative record file, you must specify the RRN option. Then, the RIDFLD field must contain the record number of the record to be written. To add a record to an entry-sequenced file, you specify the RBA option. In that case, the initial value of the RIDFLD field has no effect. Instead, the record is added to the end of the file and the RBA of the new record is stored in the RIDFLD field. Here again, though, you'll rarely have to worry about these options. Most of the time, you'll be working with key-sequenced files.

The syntax of the WRITE command

```
EXEC CICS
    WRITE  FILE(filename)
           FROM(data-name)
           RIDFLD(data-name)
           [RRN | RBA]
END-EXEC
```

Option	Description
FILE	Specifies the name of the file where the record will be written. This name must be defined in the File Control Table (FCT).
FROM	Specifies the name of the data area that contains the record to be written.
RIDFLD	For a key-sequenced file, specifies the name of the field that contains the key of the record to be written. If RRN or RBA is specified, this field is interpreted as a relative record number or a relative byte address.
RRN	Indicates that the file is a relative record file, and the RIDFLD option should be interpreted as a relative record number.
RBA	Indicates that the file is an entry-sequenced file. The record will be written to the end of the file without regard to the contents of the RIDFLD field. When the command completes, the RIDFLD field will be set to the RBA of the new record.

A WRITE command that writes a record to a key-sequenced file

```
EXEC CICS
    WRITE FILE('CUSTMAS')
          FROM(CUSTOMER-MASTER-RECORD)
          RIDFLD(CM-CUSTOMER-NUMBER)
          RESP(RESPONSE-CODE)
END-EXEC.
```

Description

- The WRITE command writes a record to a VSAM key-sequenced, entry-sequenced, or relative record file.

- If the WRITE command tries to write a record with a key value that's already in the file, a DUPREC exceptional condition occurs. You'll want to test for this condition if you're writing to a key-sequenced or relative record file.

Figure 5-10   How to code the WRITE command

How to code the REWRITE command

Figure 5-11 presents the syntax of the REWRITE command. You use this command to update a record in a file. Before you issue a REWRITE command, you must first issue a READ command with the UPDATE option to retrieve and hold the record to be updated. Then, the REWRITE command just names the file (FILE option) and the area that contains the record to be rewritten (FROM option). The command shown in this figure, for example, could be used to rewrite the record read by the command in figure 5-9.

Because most CICS programs are pseudo-conversational, you don't usually read a record for update, change it, and rewrite it within a single execution of the program. Instead, after the user enters the key of the record to be updated, the program issues a READ command without the UPDATE option, displays the record on the screen so the user can change it, and then ends. After the user enters the changes and presses the Enter key to restart the program, the program issues another READ command with the UPDATE option followed by a REWRITE command. You'll see an example of this in the customer maintenance program that's presented later in this chapter.

By the way, when a READ command with the UPDATE option is followed immediately by a REWRITE command, you may want to code both commands in the same paragraph. Although that goes against our recommendation of placing each I/O statement in its own paragraph, we feel this is a reasonable exception. That's because in this case, you can consider the READ for UPDATE and REWRITE commands as a single function: updating a record.

The syntax of the REWRITE command

```
EXEC CICS
    REWRITE  FILE(filename)
             FROM(data-name)
END-EXEC
```

Option	Description
FILE	Specifies the name of the file that contains the record to be updated. This name must be defined in the File Control Table (FCT).
FROM	Specifies the name of the data area that contains the record to be rewritten.

A REWRITE command that updates the record read in figure 5-9

```
EXEC CICS
    REWRITE FILE('CUSTMAS')
            FROM(CUSTOMER-MASTER-RECORD)
            RESP(RESPONSE-CODE)
END-EXEC.
```

Description

- The REWRITE command updates a record in a file. Before you issue a REWRITE command, you must first issue a READ command with the UPDATE option.

- You can't change the value of the primary key of a record using the REWRITE command. If you try to do that, CICS will assume that you're trying to rewrite a record that has not previously been read, and an INVREQ exceptional condition will occur.

- If an error occurs during the execution of a REWRITE command, you'll typically terminate the program.

Figure 5-11   How to code the REWRITE command

How to code the DELETE command

Figure 5-12 presents the syntax of the DELETE command. You can use this command to delete a record from a KSDS or an RRDS, but not from an ESDS.

The examples in this figure illustrate the two ways you can use the DELETE command. First, you can delete a record that's retrieved by a READ command with the UPDATE option by including just the FILE option. Then, the DELETE command deletes the retrieved record. This works just as it does for the REWRITE command.

Second, you can delete a record that wasn't retrieved by a READ command. For a KSDS, you do that by naming a field that contains the key of the record to be deleted on the RIDFLD option. For an RRDS, you must include the RRN option, and you must place the relative record number of the record to be deleted in the RIDFLD field.

The syntax of the DELETE command

```
EXEC CICS
    DELETE  FILE(filename)
            [RIDFLD(data-name)]
            [RRN | RBA]
END-EXEC
```

Option	Description
FILE	Specifies the name of the file that contains the record to be deleted. This name must be defined in the File Control Table (FCT).
RIDFLD	For a key-sequenced file, specifies the name of the field that contains the key of the record to be deleted. If RRN or RBA is specified, this field is interpreted as a relative record number or a relative byte address.
RRN	Indicates that the file is a relative record file, and the RIDFLD option should be interpreted as a relative record number.
RBA	Indicates that the RIDFLD option should be interpreted as a relative byte address for a key-sequenced file.

A DELETE command that deletes a record previously read for update

```
EXEC CICS
    DELETE FILE('CUSTMAS')
           RESP(RESPONSE-CODE)
END-EXEC.
```

A DELETE command that deletes a record that was not previously read for update

```
EXEC CICS
    DELETE FILE('CUSTMAS')
           RIDFLD(CM-CUSTOMER-NUMBER)
           RESP(RESPONSE-CODE)
END-EXEC.
```

Description

* The DELETE command deletes a record from a key-sequenced or relative record file. It cannot be used to delete a record from an entry-sequenced file.

* If the record to be deleted has already been read for update, you can omit the RIDFLD option from the DELETE command and the current record will be deleted. If an error occurs during the execution of the command, you'll typically terminate the program.

* If the record to be deleted has not been read for update, you must include the RIDFLD option to indicate the record you want to delete. If the record doesn't exist, the NOTFND exceptional condition occurs.

Figure 5-12   How to code the DELETE command

How to code the UNLOCK command

If you issue a READ command with the UPDATE option and then discover that the record doesn't need to be updated or deleted, you can release the record by issuing an UNLOCK command. The syntax of this command is presented in figure 5-13. As you can see, you simply name the file that contains the record you want to release on the FILE option of this command.

In practice, you'll probably never use the UNLOCK command for two reasons. First, a record held by a READ command with the UPDATE option is released when your task is terminated. Since a pseudo-conversational update program terminates shortly after reading the record anyway, there's little point in issuing an UNLOCK command. Second, the UNLOCK command has no effect for files that are defined in the File Control Table as recoverable. And any file you intend to update is likely to be defined that way. So we included it here just for completeness.

The syntax of the UNLOCK command

```
EXEC CICS
    UNLOCK FILE(filename)
END-EXEC
```

Option	Description
FILE	Specifies the name of the file that contains the record to be released. This name must be defined in the File Control Table (FCT).

A typical UNLOCK command

```
EXEC CICS
    UNLOCK FILE('CUSTMAS')
END-EXEC.
```

Description

- The UNLOCK command releases a record that has been previously held by a READ command with the UPDATE option.
- A record that is held for update is released automatically when the task is terminated. Because of that, you won't usually need to use the UNLOCK command in a pseudo-conversational program.
- The UNLOCK command has no effect on files that are defined in the File Control Table as recoverable, and most files that are intended to be updated are defined as recoverable.

Figure 5-13   How to code the UNLOCK command

How to avoid problems when updating files

When you're developing a program that updates VSAM files, there are two potential problems you should be aware of. Both are summarized in figure 5-14.

The first problem occurs because the UPDATE option of the READ command reserves a record only for the duration of a task; it doesn't hold a record across executions of a pseudo-conversational program. That means that while a record is displayed on the screen at one terminal, a user at another terminal may modify or delete the record before the first user's task is restarted.

Although it's difficult to prevent this problem, the figure presents a standard approach to detecting and handling it. With this technique, each pseudo-conversational program that rewrites or deletes a record saves an image of the record between program executions, either in the communication area or in temporary storage. Then, when the program issues a READ command with the UPDATE option, it compares the newly read record with the one that was saved. If the records are different, it means that another program has changed the record, so the rewrite or delete attempt is canceled. Of course, if another program has deleted the record, it will be detected when the record is read for update. In that case, the program must cancel the update or delete request. You'll see these techniques illustrated in the customer maintenance program later in this chapter.

The second problem can arise when your program must update records from more than one file. If you're not careful, it's possible to encounter a situation known as *deadlock*. Deadlock occurs when two or more tasks are each waiting for a resource that the other is holding.

For example, suppose one program attempts to update record 100 in one file and record 200 in another file, and at the same time, another program tries to update the same records, but in reverse order. The first program reads and holds record 100, and the second program reads and holds record 200. Then, the first program tries to read record 200, but can't because the second program is holding it for update. At the same time, the second program tries to read record 100, but can't because the first program is holding it. Each program is waiting for the other, and neither program can progress until CICS intervenes.

A simple way to avoid this problem is to establish a standard order for file updates. Most shops simply say that all files should be updated in alphabetical order and, within the same file, records should be accessed in ascending key sequence. This simple technique prevents most deadlock situations.

Problem 1: One program changes or deletes a record while another is trying to update it

What happens

- The UPDATE option of the READ command reserves a record only for the duration of a task. While a record is displayed at the terminal waiting for the user to enter changes, then, another program may modify or delete the record.

How to handle it

- Each pseudo-conversational program that rewrites or deletes a record can save an image of the record between task executions, either in the communication area or in temporary storage. Then, when the program reads the record for update, it can compare the record just read with the saved record. If the records differ, it means that another program has changed the record, and the rewrite or delete is canceled.

- If another program deletes the record, the NOTFND condition occurs when the record is read for update. Then, the rewrite or delete is canceled.

Problem 2: Deadlock

What happens

- *Deadlock* occurs when two tasks are each waiting for a resource that the other is holding. This often happens when two programs are both attempting to update the same two records in two different files, but in a different order. In that case, each program could be holding a record that the other program needs to read for update.

How to handle it

- The easiest way to avoid deadlock is to establish a standard order for updating files. For example, the files could be updated in alphabetical order, and the records in each file could be updated in key sequence.

Figure 5-14   How to avoid problems when updating files

Other coding essentials

Before you see the complete code for the customer maintenance program, you should know about three other techniques for coding CICS programs. First, when you use CICS commands, you need to know how to handle the exceptional conditions that occur. You also need to decide what information will be stored in the communication area between program executions. And you need to know how to manage the event context of the program.

Common exceptional conditions

As you know, when CICS encounters an error situation it can't recover from, it raises an exceptional condition. Each exceptional condition has a name. For example, NOTFND is the name of the condition that's raised if you attempt to read a record that doesn't exist, and PGMIDERR is the name of the condition that's raised if the program name you specify in an XCTL or LINK command isn't found in the Processing Program Table. Figure 5-15 lists some of the most common exceptional conditions and the commands that can cause them to occur.

Most of the conditions listed in this figure should be self-explanatory. The condition that causes the most confusion is MAPFAIL. This condition is raised whenever you issue a RECEIVE MAP command and there is no data to be mapped. This can happen for two reasons: (1) the user presses the Enter key or a PF key without entering any data and there are no fields on the screen with the Modified Data Tag (MDT) set; or (2) the user presses the Clear key or one of the PA keys. The best way to deal with the MAPFAIL condition is to prevent it from occurring. You can do that by (1) not issuing a RECEIVE MAP command if EIBAID indicates that the Clear key or a PA key was pressed and (2) always including a one-byte DUMMY field in the mapset with FSET specified so that at least one byte of data is sent to the program when the user presses the Enter key or a PF key.

You might also wonder how the DUPREC condition can occur on a RE-WRITE command. After all, the record must already exist if you're going to rewrite it, and you can't change the record's primary key. However, you can change one or more of its alternate indexes. You'll learn how to work with alternate indexes in chapter 15. For now, just realize that if an alternate index doesn't allow duplicate values and you change the index to a value that already exists in the file, a DUPREC condition will occur.

Some exceptional conditions, such as NOTFND, represent conditions from which your program should be able to recover. Most exceptional conditions, however, do not. For example, there's nothing your program can do to correct a PGMIDERR condition.

CICS's default action for most of the exceptional conditions is to terminate your task abnormally. That's true even for the conditions that represent recoverable errors, such as NOTFND. As a result, your program must deal with these exceptional conditions explicitly to prevent CICS from abending your task.

Exceptional conditions

Condition name	Commands affected	Explanation
DISABLED	READ, WRITE, REWRITE, DELETE, UNLOCK	The file has been disabled by a master terminal operator.
DUPREC	WRITE, REWRITE	A record with the specified key already exists in the file.
FILENOTFOUND	READ, WRITE, REWRITE, DELETE, UNLOCK	The file isn't defined in the FCT.
ILLOGIC	READ, WRITE, REWRITE, DELETE, UNLOCK	A VSAM error has occurred.
INVREQ	READ, WRITE, REWRITE, DELETE	The request is invalid.
IOERR	READ, WRITE, REWRITE, DELETE, UNLOCK	An I/O error has occurred.
LENGERR	READ, WRITE, REWRITE	The length of the record exceeds the maximum length allowed for the file (WRITE or REWRITE) or the length of the INTO area (READ).
MAPFAIL	RECEIVE MAP	No data was entered by the user.
NOSPACE	WRITE, REWRITE	The file doesn't have enough space to hold the record.
NOTAUTH	READ, WRITE, REWRITE, DELETE, UNLOCK	The user is not authorized to access the file.
NOTFND	READ, REWRITE, DELETE	The record does not exist.
NOTOPEN	READ, WRITE, REWRITE, DELETE, UNLOCK	The file is not open.
PGMIDERR	LINK, XCTL	The requested program is not defined in the PPT.

Description

- When CICS encounters an error situation from which it cannot recover, it raises an exceptional condition. For most of these conditions, CICS's default action is to terminate the task abnormally.

- Of the more than 70 exceptional conditions listed in the IBM manual, only a handful represent conditions from which your program should be able to recover. For these, you write program code that overrides CICS's default error handling.

- The two conditions you're most likely to test for in your programs are DUPREC and NOTFND. For most of the other conditions, you'll want to terminate the program abnormally.

- You can prevent the MAPFAIL condition by 1) not issuing a RECEIVE MAP command when the user presses the Clear key or a PA key and 2) always including a one-byte dummy field with the FSET option specified on its ATTRB parameter.

Figure 5-15   Common exceptional conditions

How to use response code checking

To handle exceptional conditions, you use *response code checking*, as you saw in the inquiry program in chapter 2. To do that, you start by defining a binary fullword field (PIC S9(8) COMP) in working storage. Then, you name this field in the RESP option on the CICS command that can cause the condition you want your program to handle. CICS will then ignore any exceptional conditions that are raised by that command and will place a numeric value that represents the condition status of the command in the response code field. Your program can then check this field to determine if the command executed properly.

To check the response code field, you use the DFHRESP keyword. Figure 5-16 illustrates how this works. Here, a READ command is issued with a RESP option that specifies a field named RESPONSE-CODE. Following this command is an Evaluate statement that checks this field. The first When clause checks to see if the command executed normally (DFHRESP(NORMAL)). Then, the second When clause checks whether the NOTFND condition occurred (DFHRESP(NOTFND)). If so, it sets a switch, moves an appropriate error message to the message field, and does some additional processing. If any other error occurred, the program issues an ABEND command to end the program.

Notice that when you use DFHRESP, you specify the condition names shown in figure 5-15. When you translate the program, the CICS translator converts the DFHRESP specifications to numeric constants that correspond to the conditions you specify. Then, your program can compare those values against the value in the response code field.

When you use response code checking for a command, your program is responsible for handling all CICS exceptional conditions that might result. So whenever you use the RESP option, you have to add extra code to deal with exceptional conditions your program can't handle. In this example, the program simply issues the ABEND command for these exceptional conditions. However, most shops have other ways of dealing with these errors, often in the form of code you can copy into your Procedure Division or a standardized error handling program you can invoke with a LINK or XCTL command. You'll see an example of a generalized error handling program in chapter 8.

CICS also provides a second response code option, RESP2, which may provide additional information. To use it, you define another fullword field, and you name that field on the RESP2 option. Then, you can test the value of that field to determine if an error occurred. Unlike the RESP option, though, you have to know the constant values for the RESP2 conditions; RESP2 has no equivalent to the DFHRESP keyword.

Although you can specify RESP2 for any CICS command, only a few commands actually place a value in this field. So unless your error handling needs are specialized, you probably won't need to use RESP2. However, you may use it to determine the cause of an error as you test a program. After you correct the error, though, you can usually remove the RESP2 option.

The syntax of the RESP and RESP2 options

```
[RESP(data-name) [RESP2(data-name)]]
```

Response code checking in a read module

```
EXEC CICS
    READ FILE('CUSTMAS')
         INTO(CUSTOMER-MASTER-RECORD)
         RIDFLD(CUSTNOI)
         RESP(RESPONSE-CODE)
END-EXEC.
EVALUATE RESPONSE-CODE
    WHEN DFHRESP(NORMAL)
        MOVE SPACE          TO MESSAGEO
        MOVE CM-LAST-NAME    TO LNAMEO
        MOVE CM-FIRST-NAME   TO FNAMEO
        MOVE CM-ADDRESS      TO ADDRO
        MOVE CM-CITY         TO CITYO
        MOVE CM-STATE        TO STATEO
        MOVE CM-ZIP-CODE     TO ZIPCODEO
    WHEN DFHRESP(NOTFND)
        MOVE 'N' TO VALID-DATA-SW
        MOVE 'That customer does not exist.' TO MESSAGEO
        MOVE SPACE TO LNAMEO
          .
          .
    WHEN OTHER
        EXEC CICS
            ABEND
        END-EXEC
END-EVALUATE.
```

Description

- The RESP and RESP2 options can be coded on any CICS command. Then, if an exceptional condition occurs during the processing of the command, condition codes are placed in the fields specified by these options. Both of these fields must be defined as binary fullwords (PIC S9(8) COMP).

- With response code checking, CICS never takes its default action for exceptional conditions. You have to handle *all* possible responses to the commands that are coded with the RESP option in your program.

- You can use the DFHRESP keyword to check the RESP condition code. With this keyword, you can use the symbolic condition names shown in figure 5-15 instead of the actual condition codes. To test if a command completed normally, you can use the NORMAL condition.

- The RESP2 option can be used to provide additional error information. If you include this option, you must check its value directly. In most cases, though, the response code that's returned by the RESP option will be all you need.

- The response codes returned by RESP and RESP2 are also available in the Execute Interface Block as EIBRESP and EIBRESP2.

Figure 5-16   How to use response code checking

How to define the communication area

In the customer inquiry program in chapter 2, you saw how to evaluate the length of DFHCOMMAREA to identify the first execution of a program in a pseudo-conversational session. In that program, the communication area wasn't used to pass data between executions of the program. It just passed a one-byte dummy field so the length of the communication area would not be zero.

In many cases, however, you need to keep data between program executions. The customer maintenance program described in chapter 3, for example, can use the communication area to keep track of the context of the user input events. You also learned earlier in this chapter that when a program updates a record in a file, it can save a copy of that record in the communication area to make sure it isn't changed between pseudo-conversational interactions. Depending on the application program's requirements, other data may need to be saved between executions as well. For example, a program that accumulates control totals, such as the count of the number of transactions entered, must pass the totals forward from one execution to the next.

Figure 5-17 presents the definition of the communication area for the customer maintenance program. As you can see, it consists of two fields. The first one, CA-CONTEXT-FLAG, is a one-byte field that's used to manage the program's event context. The second field, CA-CUSTOMER-RECORD, is a 118-byte area that's used to hold an image of a record from the customer master file. You'll see how these fields are used when you see the COBOL listing for the customer maintenance program.

The communication area for the customer maintenance program

```
01  COMMUNICATION-AREA.
*
    05  CA-CONTEXT-FLAG                 PIC X.
        88  PROCESS-KEY-MAP             VALUE '1'.
        88  PROCESS-ADD-CUSTOMER        VALUE '2'.
        88  PROCESS-CHANGE-CUSTOMER     VALUE '3'.
        88  PROCESS-DELETE-CUSTOMER     VALUE '4'.
    05  CA-CUSTOMER-RECORD.
        10  CA-CUSTOMER-NUMBER          PIC X(6).
        10  FILLER                      PIC X(112).
```

Description

- The communication area must contain any data that needs to be saved between executions of the program.

- If the user events can occur in one or more context, the communication area should include a flag that indicates the current context. Then, you can use 88-level items to identify each context.

- If the program updates the records in a file and a procedure for preventing other programs from changing those records between program executions hasn't been established, the communication area should include a data area to hold the contents of the current record. Then, before that record is updated, the program can check to be sure that it hasn't been changed.

- If the program accumulates control totals, the fields that contain these totals must be included in the communication area.

- Even if you don't need to save data between program executions, you should code a one-byte communication area in working storage and a one-byte DFHCOMMAREA in the Linkage Section. Then, you can check the length of the communication area using the EIBCALEN field in the EIB to detect the first execution of the program in a pseudo-conversational session. If you don't define a DFHCOMMAREA field, the CICS translator will add a one-byte field for you.

Figure 5-17   How to define the communication area

How to manage the event context of a program

If you take the time to create an event/response chart for a program as recommended in chapter 3 and you include a context flag in the definition of the communication area as recommended in the previous topic, coding the program logic for managing the event contexts will be easy. The code in figure 5-18 illustrates how this logic works.

In most cases, the events and contexts can be managed using a single Evaluate statement that's coded in the top-level procedure. Then, a When clause can be used to respond to each possible input event. The first When clause typically tests for the first execution of the program. To do that, it tests to see if the length of the communication area is zero (EIBCALEN = ZERO). Then, the When clauses that follow test for all possible attention keys that the user may have pressed.

You should notice three things here. First, you can combine the processing of two or more keys if the response to each is the same. That's the case with the PA1, PA2, and PA3 keys in this example. Second, if an event can occur in two or more contexts, you can use an If statement or another Evaluate statement within the When clause for that event to respond to each context. In this example, an If statement is used to check for the context of the PF12 and Clear keys, and an Evaluate statement is used to check for the context of the Enter key. Finally, the last When clause typically tests for all other events not specifically handled by the previous When clauses. These events correspond to the keys that are considered invalid by the program. In most cases, an error message is displayed when the user presses one of these keys.

The general logic for managing the event context of the customer maintenance program

```
000-PROCESS-CUSTOMER-MAINT.
    .
    .

    EVALUATE TRUE
        WHEN EIBCALEN = ZERO ———— Check for the first execution
            .
        WHEN EIBAID = DFHPF3
            .
        WHEN EIBAID = DFHPF12
            IF PROCESS-KEY-MAP
                .
            ELSE
                .
            END-IF
        WHEN EIBAID = DFHCLEAR
            IF PROCESS-KEY-MAP
                .
            ELSE
                .
            END-IF
        WHEN EIBAID = DFHPA1 OR DFHPA2 OR DFHPA3
            CONTINUE
        WHEN EIBAID = DFHENTER
            EVALUATE TRUE
                WHEN PROCESS-KEY-MAP
                    .
                WHEN PROCESS-ADD-CUSTOMER
                    .
                WHEN PROCESS-CHANGE-CUSTOMER
                    .
                WHEN PROCESS-DELETE-CUSTOMER
                    .
            END-EVALUATE
        WHEN OTHER
            IF PROCESS-KEY-MAP
                .
            ELSE
                .
            END-IF
    END-EVALUATE.
```

Check for all contexts of all valid attention keys (except Enter)

Check for all contexts of the Enter key

Check for all invalid attention keys

Description

- The easiest way to manage the event contexts of a program is to code an Evaluate statement as shown above. This statement must test for each possible input event and, when appropriate, for each possible context in which that event can occur.

- The Evaluate statement should correspond closely to the event/response chart for the program. Specifically, each When clause should represent the program's response to one input event. Within each When clause, you can use an If statement or another Evaluate statement to process different contexts.

Figure 5-18 How to manage the event context of a program

The customer maintenance program

In chapter 3, you saw the specifications and design of the customer mainte-nance program. To review, this program lets the user maintain the customer master file by adding, changing, and deleting records. To accomplish that, the program uses two maps. The first map lets the user enter a customer number and an action code. Then, the second map lets the user perform the selected opera-tion. The BMS mapset and the resulting symbolic map were shown in chapter 4. Now, you're ready to see the COBOL code for this program. But first, I'll review the program's structure chart so you can see how it's used as a basis for the code.

The structure chart for the customer maintenance program

Figure 5-19 shows the structure chart for the customer maintenance pro-gram. As you'll recall, this structure is based on the four contexts that are possible when the user presses the Enter key: "Get key," "Add customer," "Change customer," and "Delete customer." The "Get key" context is current when the key map is displayed. If the user presses the Enter key from this map, the program checks the values the user entered for validity, then sends the data map with the appropriate instructions and customer fields.

Depending on the action code the user entered in the key map, the data map is displayed in one of the other three contexts. If the user presses the Enter key when the context of the data map is "Add customer," the program writes a new customer record with the data the user entered and then sends a new key map. If the context is "Change customer," the program reads the existing customer record for update and then rewrites it before sending a new key map. And if the context is "Delete customer," the program reads the existing record for update, then deletes it and sends a new key map.

The structure chart

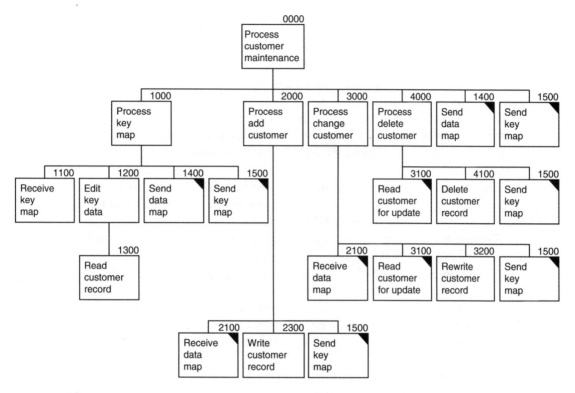

Description

- The four main modules in the second level of the structure chart provide the processing for the four contexts of the program: "Get key," "Add customer," "Change customer," and "Delete customer." The "Get key" context is current when the key map is displayed on the screen. One of the other contexts is current when the data map is displayed on the screen, depending on the action requested by the user.

- When the user presses the Enter key from the key map, module 1000 receives the map, edits the data (including reading the customer record), and displays the data map for the selected operation.

- When the user presses the Enter key from the data map and the "Add customer" context is current, module 2000 receives the map, writes a new record for the customer, and then displays a new key map.

- When the user presses the Enter key from the data map and the "Change customer" context is current, module 3000 receives the map, reads the customer record for update, rewrites the record with the changes entered by the user, and then displays a new key map.

- When the user presses the Enter key from the data map and the "Delete customer" context is current, module 4000 reads the customer record for update, deletes the record, and then displays a new key map.

Figure 5-19   The structure chart for the customer maintenance program

The COBOL code for the customer maintenance program

Figure 5-20 presents the COBOL code for the customer maintenance program. If you'd like to look at the BMS mapset or the symbolic map as you go through this program, please turn back to figures 4-12 and 4-13.

On page 1 of this listing, you can see that the program uses one switch (VALID-DATA-SW) and one flag (SEND-FLAG). The switch is used to determine if the entries made by the user are valid, and the flag is used to determine the options that are included on the SEND MAP command when a map is sent to the terminal.

This program also uses one work field, RESPONSE-CODE. This field will be used to store the value of any exceptional conditions that are returned by CICS commands that include the RESP parameter.

Because the instructions on the data map vary depending on the operation that's being performed, this program also defines the three possible instructions in working storage. Then, before the data map is sent to the terminal, the appropriate instruction is moved to the instruction field in the symbolic map.

Following the instruction fields is the definition of the communication area. This area contains a flag that indicates the current event context, and a field that contains the current customer record. You'll see how these fields are used in a moment.

The rest of the Working-Storage Section consists of four Copy statements. The first three are for the customer master record, the symbolic map used by the program, and the DFHAID copy member the program uses to detect which AID key the user presses. The last Copy statement is for a copy member that includes the definitions of some common attribute bytes. You'll learn more about this copy member and how to use it in chapter 8. For now, just realize that because the fields on the data map must be protected for a delete operation, this program must change the attribute bytes of the data entry fields in that map. And to do that, it uses the protected attribute that's defined in the ATTR copy member.

The Linkage Section for this program consists of a single field named DFHCOMMAREA. This field is the same length as the communication area that's defined in working storage. Because DFHCOMMAREA will be moved to the working-storage field each time the program is started, it's not necessary to define each field it contains in the Linkage Section.

The customer maintenance program   **Page 1**

```
        IDENTIFICATION DIVISION.
        *
        PROGRAM-ID.  CUSTMNT1.
        *
        ENVIRONMENT DIVISION.
        *
        DATA DIVISION.
        *
        WORKING-STORAGE SECTION.
        *
        01   SWITCHES.
            05   VALID-DATA-SW              PIC X   VALUE 'Y'.
                88   VALID-DATA                    VALUE 'Y'.
        *
        01   FLAGS.
            05   SEND-FLAG                  PIC X.
                88   SEND-ERASE                    VALUE '1'.
                88   SEND-ERASE-ALARM              VALUE '2'.
                88   SEND-DATAONLY                 VALUE '3'.
                88   SEND-DATAONLY-ALARM           VALUE '4'.
        *
        01   WORK-FIELDS.
            05   RESPONSE-CODE             PIC S9(8) COMP.
        *
        01   USER-INSTRUCTIONS.
            05   ADD-INSTRUCTION           PIC X(79) VALUE
                'Type information for new customer.  Then Press Enter.'.
            05   CHANGE-INSTRUCTION        PIC X(79) VALUE
                'Type changes.  Then press Enter.'.
            05   DELETE-INSTRUCTION        PIC X(79) VALUE
                'Press Enter to delete this customer or press F12 to canc
    -           'el.'.
        *
        01   COMMUNICATION-AREA.
            05   CA-CONTEXT-FLAG           PIC X.
                88   PROCESS-KEY-MAP               VALUE '1'.
                88   PROCESS-ADD-CUSTOMER          VALUE '2'.
                88   PROCESS-CHANGE-CUSTOMER       VALUE '3'.
                88   PROCESS-DELETE-CUSTOMER       VALUE '4'.
            05   CA-CUSTOMER-RECORD.
                10   CA-CUSTOMER-NUMBER       PIC X(6).
                10   FILLER                   PIC X(112).
        *
        COPY CUSTMAS.
        *
        COPY MNTSET1.
        *
        COPY DFHAID.
        *
        COPY ATTR.
        *
        LINKAGE SECTION.
        *
        01   DFHCOMMAREA                   PIC X(119).
        *
```

Figure 5-20   The COBOL code for the customer maintenance program (part 1 of 8)

The remaining pages show the Procedure Division code for this program. To start, this program moves the data in DFHCOMMAREA to the communication area that's defined in working storage if the length of the data passed to DFHCOMMAREA is greater than zero (in other words, if it's not the first execution of the program). Because DFHCOMMAREA contains the data that was stored in the temporary communication area by the previous execution of the program, this data is now available to the current execution.

The Move statement is followed by an Evaluate statement that manages the input events and contexts for the program. The key to understanding how this program works is understanding this code.

The first When clause in this Evaluate statement checks to see if the length of the communication area is zero (EIBCALEN = ZERO). If it is, it indicates that this is the first execution of the program in a pseudo-conversational session. In that case, the output fields in the key map are set to Low-Value so they're not sent to the screen, the Send-Erase condition is set to True so the screen will be erased, the length of the customer number field is set to -1 so the cursor will be positioned on that field when the map is displayed, and procedure 1500 is performed to display the key map. Then, the Process-Key-Map condition is set to True indicating that the key map is being processed.

The second When clause checks if the user pressed the PF3 key to exit from the program. If so, the program issues an XCTL command to transfer control to a menu program named INVMENU.

The third When clause checks if the user pressed the PF12 key to cancel the current operation. Because the function of this key depends on the map that's currently displayed, this clause includes an If statement that starts by checking if the key map is displayed. If it is, the program issues an XCTL command to transfer control to the INVMENU program just as if the user had pressed the PF3 key. If the key map isn't displayed, though, that means that the user is in the process of adding, changing, or deleting a customer. In that case, the program performs module 1500 to display the key map without completing the current operation and then sets the Process-Key-Map condition to True.

The fourth When clause checks if the user pressed the Clear key. Again, the response to this event depends on the map that's currently displayed, so this clause includes an If statement that checks the current context. If the key map is displayed, the program performs module 1500 to clear the screen and redisplay that map. If the data map is displayed, though, the program must perform some additional processing.

First, after it moves Low-Value to the output fields to clear them, it sets the customer number field in that map to the customer number for the current customer. That number can be found in the communication area. Second, it sets the value of the instruction field in that map depending on the current context. (That's why the instruction field in this map was defined as a variable field.) Finally, the program moves -1 to the length of the last name field so the cursor is positioned on that field, sets the Send-Erase condition to True so the data currently on the screen will be erased, and performs procedure 1400 to display the map.

The customer maintenance program

```
      PROCEDURE DIVISION.
*
      0000-PROCESS-CUSTOMER-MAINT.
*
          IF EIBCALEN > ZERO
              MOVE DFHCOMMAREA TO COMMUNICATION-AREA
          END-IF.
*
          EVALUATE TRUE
*
              WHEN EIBCALEN = ZERO
                  MOVE LOW-VALUE TO MNTMAP1O
                  SET SEND-ERASE TO TRUE
                  MOVE -1 TO CUSTNO1L
                  PERFORM 1500-SEND-KEY-MAP
                  SET PROCESS-KEY-MAP TO TRUE
*
              WHEN EIBAID = DFHPF3
                  EXEC CICS
                      XCTL PROGRAM('INVMENU')
                  END-EXEC
*
              WHEN EIBAID = DFHPF12
                  IF PROCESS-KEY-MAP
                      EXEC CICS
                          XCTL PROGRAM('INVMENU')
                      END-EXEC
                  ELSE
                      MOVE LOW-VALUE TO MNTMAP1O
                      MOVE -1 TO CUSTNO1L
                      SET SEND-ERASE TO TRUE
                      PERFORM 1500-SEND-KEY-MAP
                      SET PROCESS-KEY-MAP TO TRUE
                  END-IF
*
              WHEN EIBAID = DFHCLEAR
                  IF PROCESS-KEY-MAP
                      MOVE LOW-VALUE TO MNTMAP1O
                      MOVE -1 TO CUSTNO1L
                      SET SEND-ERASE TO TRUE
                      PERFORM 1500-SEND-KEY-MAP
                  ELSE
                      MOVE LOW-VALUE TO MNTMAP2O
                      MOVE CA-CUSTOMER-NUMBER TO CUSTNO2O
                      EVALUATE TRUE
                          WHEN PROCESS-ADD-CUSTOMER
                              MOVE ADD-INSTRUCTION    TO INSTR2O
                          WHEN PROCESS-CHANGE-CUSTOMER
                              MOVE CHANGE-INSTRUCTION TO INSTR2O
                          WHEN PROCESS-DELETE-CUSTOMER
                              MOVE DELETE-INSTRUCTION TO INSTR2O
                      END-EVALUATE
                      MOVE -1 TO LNAMEL
                      SET SEND-ERASE TO TRUE
                      PERFORM 1400-SEND-DATA-MAP
                  END-IF
*
```

Figure 5-20   The COBOL code for the customer maintenance program (part 2 of 8)

The fifth When clause, shown on page 3 of this listing, checks if the user pressed one of the PA keys. If so, the program issues a Continue statement so the key is ignored.

The sixth When clause checks if the user pressed the Enter key. This clause contains the main processing for the program. It consists of an Evaluate statement that determines the current context and performs the appropriate procedure in response to each. You'll learn more about these procedures in a moment.

The last When clause checks if the user pressed any other key. Because all other keys are considered invalid by the program, the program's response is to move an error message to the message field in the appropriate map and then send that map. Because the Send-Dataonly-Alarm condition is set to True, the SEND MAP command causes the alarm to sound when the map is displayed.

Following the Evaluate statement is a RETURN command that ends this execution of the pseudo-conversational program and returns control to CICS. Because the key map or the data map will have been sent to the terminal before this command is issued, the user will then be able to make the appropriate entries for that map. The RETURN command also sets up the next execution of the program by specifying the trans-id for the program and by passing the program's communication area to temporary storage. So when the user presses an attention key, the program will be restarted and the data in the communication area will be passed to that execution of the program.

Procedure 1000 processes the data from the key map using the typical receive-edit-send processing cycle. First, it performs procedure 1100 to receive the key map. Then, it performs procedure1200 to edit the data in that map. If it's valid, the data in the customer record that's retrieved is moved to the data map, and procedure 1400 is performed to display that map. Otherwise, procedure 1500 is performed to send the key map back to the terminal with an error message.

The customer maintenance program

```
            WHEN EIBAID = DFHPA1 OR DFHPA2 OR DFHPA3
                CONTINUE
*
            WHEN EIBAID = DFHENTER
                EVALUATE TRUE
                    WHEN PROCESS-KEY-MAP
                        PERFORM 1000-PROCESS-KEY-MAP
                    WHEN PROCESS-ADD-CUSTOMER
                        PERFORM 2000-PROCESS-ADD-CUSTOMER
                    WHEN PROCESS-CHANGE-CUSTOMER
                        PERFORM 3000-PROCESS-CHANGE-CUSTOMER
                    WHEN PROCESS-DELETE-CUSTOMER
                        PERFORM 4000-PROCESS-DELETE-CUSTOMER
                END-EVALUATE
*
            WHEN OTHER
                IF PROCESS-KEY-MAP
                    MOVE LOW-VALUE TO MNTMAP1O
                    MOVE 'That key is unassigned.' TO MSG1O
                    MOVE -1 TO CUSTNO1L
                    SET SEND-DATAONLY-ALARM TO TRUE
                    PERFORM 1500-SEND-KEY-MAP
                ELSE
                    MOVE LOW-VALUE TO MNTMAP2O
                    MOVE -1 TO LNAMEL
                    MOVE 'That key is unassigned.' TO MSG2O
                    SET SEND-DATAONLY-ALARM TO TRUE
                    PERFORM 1400-SEND-DATA-MAP
                END-IF
*
        END-EVALUATE.
*
        EXEC CICS
            RETURN TRANSID('MNT1')
                   COMMAREA(COMMUNICATION-AREA)
        END-EXEC.
*
     1000-PROCESS-KEY-MAP.
*
        PERFORM 1100-RECEIVE-KEY-MAP.
        PERFORM 1200-EDIT-KEY-DATA.
        IF VALID-DATA
            MOVE CUSTNO1I       TO CUSTNO2O
            MOVE CM-LAST-NAME   TO LNAMEO
            MOVE CM-FIRST-NAME  TO FNAMEO
            MOVE CM-ADDRESS     TO ADDRO
            MOVE CM-CITY        TO CITYO
            MOVE CM-STATE       TO STATEO
            MOVE CM-ZIP-CODE    TO ZIPCODEO
            MOVE -1             TO LNAMEL
            SET SEND-ERASE TO TRUE
            PERFORM 1400-SEND-DATA-MAP
        ELSE
            MOVE LOW-VALUE TO CUSTNO1O
                              ACTIONO
            SET SEND-DATAONLY-ALARM TO TRUE
            PERFORM 1500-SEND-KEY-MAP
        END-IF.
```

Figure 5-20   The COBOL code for the customer maintenance program (part 3 of 8)

Procedure 1200 begins by checking that the user entered a valid action code. If not, -1 is moved to the length of the action field, an error message is moved to the message field, and the valid-data switch is set to N. Similarly, if a customer number isn't entered, -1 is moved to the length of the customer-number field, an error message is moved to the message field, and the valid-data switch is set to N.

If the action code and customer number are valid, the procedure continues by moving Low-Value to the output area of the data map. The map is initialized at this point because the code that follows sets the value of the instruction field depending on the action code. Otherwise, it could have been initialized in procedure 1000 before the customer data was moved to the map.

Next, procedure 1200 issues an Evaluate statement to perform the edits specific to each action code. If the action code is 1 (add), the specified customer must not already exist in the customer file. So procedure 1200 performs procedure 1300 to read the customer file, expecting the result to be a NOTFND condition. If NOTFND does not occur, an error message is moved to the message field and the valid-data switch is set to N. Similarly, if the action code is 2 or 3 (change or delete), the specified customer must already exist in the customer file. So procedure 1200 performs procedure 1300, this time expecting the result to be NORMAL. If it is, the record that was retrieved is moved to the communication area so it's saved between program executions. Subsequent executions of the program can then read the customer record and compare it with the record stored in the communication area to determine if the record has changed since it was originally read.

Notice how each When clause in this Evaluate statement sets CA-CONTEXT-FLAG to reflect the program's new context. If the user selects action 1 and the record does not already exist, the Process-Add-Customer condition is set to True. If the user selects action 2 and the record exists, Process-Change-Customer is set to True. And if the user selects action 3 and the record exists, Process-Delete-Customer is set to True. In any other case, CA-CONTEXT-FLAG is left at its original setting of Process-Key-Map. Each When clause also moves the appropriate instruction to the instruction field in the map, and the When clause for an add operation moves space to the customer master record so the user can enter the data for the new record.

The customer maintenance program   **Page 4**

```
    1100-RECEIVE-KEY-MAP.
*
        EXEC CICS
            RECEIVE MAP('MNTMAP1')
                    MAPSET('MNTSET1')
                    INTO(MNTMAP1I)
        END-EXEC.
*
    1200-EDIT-KEY-DATA.
*
        IF ACTIONI NOT = '1' AND '2' AND '3'
            MOVE -1 TO ACTIONL
            MOVE 'Action must be 1, 2, or 3.' TO MSG1O
            MOVE 'N' TO VALID-DATA-SW
        END-IF.
*
        IF        CUSTNO1L = ZERO
            OR CUSTNO1I = SPACE
            MOVE -1 TO CUSTNO1L
            MOVE 'You must enter a customer number.' TO MSG1O
            MOVE 'N' TO VALID-DATA-SW
        END-IF.
*
        IF VALID-DATA
            MOVE LOW-VALUE TO MNTMAP2O
            EVALUATE ACTIONI
                WHEN '1'
                    PERFORM 1300-READ-CUSTOMER-RECORD
                    IF RESPONSE-CODE = DFHRESP(NOTFND)
                        MOVE ADD-INSTRUCTION TO INSTR2O
                        SET PROCESS-ADD-CUSTOMER TO TRUE
                        MOVE SPACE TO CUSTOMER-MASTER-RECORD
                    ELSE
                        IF RESPONSE-CODE = DFHRESP(NORMAL)
                            MOVE 'That customer already exists.'
                                TO MSG1O
                            MOVE 'N' TO VALID-DATA-SW
                        END-IF
                    END-IF
                WHEN '2'
                    PERFORM 1300-READ-CUSTOMER-RECORD
                    IF RESPONSE-CODE = DFHRESP(NORMAL)
                        MOVE CUSTOMER-MASTER-RECORD TO
                            CA-CUSTOMER-RECORD
                        MOVE CHANGE-INSTRUCTION TO INSTR2O
                        SET PROCESS-CHANGE-CUSTOMER TO TRUE
                    ELSE
                        IF RESPONSE-CODE = DFHRESP(NOTFND)
                            MOVE 'That customer does not exist.'
                                TO MSG1O
                            MOVE 'N' TO VALID-DATA-SW
                        END-IF
                    END-IF
```

Figure 5-20   The COBOL code for the customer maintenance program (part 4 of 8)

You should also notice that when the action is 3 and the record to be deleted does exist, the program moves ATTR-PROT to the attribute bytes of each unprotected field on the map. ATTR-PROT is one of the attributes that's defined in the ATTR copy member, which you'll learn more about in chapter 8. For now, just realize that its value specifies the protection attribute. That way, when the program displays the customer data, the user won't be able to change it. Instead, the user can examine the data to make sure that the correct record is going to be deleted.

Procedure 1300 reads a record from the customer file. Because the READ command includes the RESP option, it's followed by an If statement that checks the Response-Code field. If the response code is not NORMAL or NOTFND, procedure 1300 performs procedure 9999 to terminate the program. This procedure simply issues the ABEND command.

Procedures 1400 and 1500 issue the SEND MAP commands to display the data map and the key map. Both of these procedures use an Evaluate statement to test the value of the send flag to determine which form of the SEND MAP command is issued. Notice that these procedures start by moving the trans-id for the program, MNT1, to the appropriate field in the map.

The customer maintenance program

```
                    WHEN '3'
                        PERFORM 1300-READ-CUSTOMER-RECORD
                        IF RESPONSE-CODE = DFHRESP(NORMAL)
                            MOVE CUSTOMER-MASTER-RECORD TO
                                CA-CUSTOMER-RECORD
                            MOVE DELETE-INSTRUCTION TO INSTR2O
                            SET PROCESS-DELETE-CUSTOMER TO TRUE
                            MOVE ATTR-PROT TO LNAMEA
                                            FNAMEA
                                            ADDRA
                                            CITYA
                                            STATEA
                                            ZIPCODEA
                        ELSE
                            IF RESPONSE-CODE = DFHRESP(NOTFND)
                                MOVE 'That customer does not exist.'
                                    TO MSG1O
                                MOVE 'N' TO VALID-DATA-SW
                            END-IF
                        END-IF
            END-EVALUATE.
*
    1300-READ-CUSTOMER-RECORD.
*
        EXEC CICS
            READ FILE('CUSTMAS')
                INTO(CUSTOMER-MASTER-RECORD)
                RIDFLD(CUSTNO1I)
                RESP(RESPONSE-CODE)
        END-EXEC.
        IF      RESPONSE-CODE NOT = DFHRESP(NORMAL)
            AND RESPONSE-CODE NOT = DFHRESP(NOTFND)
            PERFORM 9999-TERMINATE-PROGRAM
        END-IF.
*
    1400-SEND-DATA-MAP.
*
        MOVE 'MNT1' TO TRANID2O.
*
        EVALUATE TRUE
            WHEN SEND-ERASE
                EXEC CICS
                    SEND MAP('MNTMAP2')
                        MAPSET('MNTSET1')
                        FROM(MNTMAP2O)
                        ERASE
                        CURSOR
                END-EXEC
            WHEN SEND-DATAONLY-ALARM
                EXEC CICS
                    SEND MAP('MNTMAP2')
                        MAPSET('MNTSET1')
                        FROM(MNTMAP2O)
                        DATAONLY
                        ALARM
                        CURSOR
                END-EXEC
        END-EVALUATE.
```

Figure 5-20   The COBOL code for the customer maintenance program (part 5 of 8)

Procedure 2000 is invoked to add a customer to the customer file. It starts by performing procedure 2100 to receive the data map. Then, it performs procedure 2300 to write the new record. This procedure moves the customer data from the data map to the customer record and then issues a WRITE command to add the record to the file. If the response code from the WRITE command is anything other than NORMAL or DUPREC, this procedure performs procedure 9999 to terminate the program.

Notice that the customer data isn't edited before the record is written. Although that's not typical, we omitted the editing from this program to keep it simple. In chapter 12, though, you'll see an enhanced version of the customer maintenance program that includes an edit procedure.

Next, procedure 2000 checks the response code from the WRITE command to determine if the record already exists (DUPREC). If not (NORMAL), a message is moved to the message field to indicate that the record was added and the Send-Erase condition is set to True. If the record does exist, though, it indicates that another user has already added a customer with the same number. In that case, an error message is moved to the message field in the key map and the Send-Erase-Alarm condition is set to True. Finally, procedure 2000 performs procedure 1500 to send the key map to the terminal and sets the Process-Key-Map condition to True.

Like procedure 2000, procedure 3000 starts by performing procedure 2100 to receive the data map. Then, it moves the customer number field in the symbolic map to the customer number field in the customer master record, and it performs procedure 3100 to read the customer record for update. Next, it checks the response code to determine if the record was found (NORMAL). If it was, the program continues by comparing that record with the record that was read previously and saved in the communication area. If the records are the same, procedure 2000 performs procedure 3200 to move the new data for the customer to the customer master record and rewrite the record. Otherwise, an error message is moved to the message field in the key map. An error message is also moved to the message field if the NOTFND condition occurs, indicating that the record was deleted by another user between program executions. Procedure 3000 ends by setting the length of the customer number field to -1 to position the cursor on that field, performing procedure 1500 to display the key map, and setting the Process-Key-Map condition to True.

Procedure 4000 processes the delete function. Unlike the add and change procedures, the delete procedure doesn't receive data from the terminal. So it doesn't perform procedure 2100. Instead, it moves the customer number that was saved in the communication area to the customer number field in the customer master record. Then, it performs procedure 3100 to read the record for update. If the record exists and it's identical to the record stored in the communication area, procedure 4100 is then called to delete the record. Otherwise, an error message is moved to the message field in the key map. Procedure 4000 ends by moving -1 to the length of the customer number field, performing procedure 1500 to display the key map, and setting the Process-Key-Map condition to True.

The customer maintenance program

```
    1500-SEND-KEY-MAP.
*
    MOVE 'MNT1' TO TRANID1O.
*
    EVALUATE TRUE
        WHEN SEND-ERASE
            EXEC CICS
                SEND MAP('MNTMAP1')
                    MAPSET('MNTSET1')
                    FROM(MNTMAP1O)
                    ERASE
                    CURSOR
            END-EXEC
        WHEN SEND-ERASE-ALARM
            EXEC CICS
                SEND MAP('MNTMAP1')
                    MAPSET('MNTSET1')
                    FROM(MNTMAP1O)
                    ERASE
                    ALARM
                    CURSOR
            END-EXEC
        WHEN SEND-DATAONLY-ALARM
            EXEC CICS
                SEND MAP('MNTMAP1')
                    MAPSET('MNTSET1')
                    FROM(MNTMAP1O)
                    DATAONLY
                    ALARM
                    CURSOR
            END-EXEC
    END-EVALUATE.
*
2000-PROCESS-ADD-CUSTOMER.
*
    PERFORM 2100-RECEIVE-DATA-MAP.
    PERFORM 2300-WRITE-CUSTOMER-RECORD.
    IF RESPONSE-CODE = DFHRESP(NORMAL)
        MOVE 'Customer record added.' TO MSG1O
        SET SEND-ERASE TO TRUE
    ELSE
        IF RESPONSE-CODE = DFHRESP(DUPREC)
            MOVE 'Another user has added a record with that custo
-           'mer number.' TO MSG1O
            SET SEND-ERASE-ALARM TO TRUE
        END-IF
    END-IF.
    MOVE -1 TO CUSTNO1L.
    PERFORM 1500-SEND-KEY-MAP.
    SET PROCESS-KEY-MAP TO TRUE.
*
2100-RECEIVE-DATA-MAP.
*
    EXEC CICS
        RECEIVE MAP('MNTMAP2')
                MAPSET('MNTSET1')
                INTO(MNTMAP2I)
    END-EXEC.
```

Figure 5-20   The COBOL code for the customer maintenance program (part 6 of 8)

The customer maintenance program

```
    2300-WRITE-CUSTOMER-RECORD.
*
    MOVE CUSTNO2I TO CM-CUSTOMER-NUMBER.
    MOVE LNAMEI   TO CM-LAST-NAME.
    MOVE FNAMEI   TO CM-FIRST-NAME.
    MOVE ADDRI    TO CM-ADDRESS.
    MOVE CITYI    TO CM-CITY.
    MOVE STATEI   TO CM-STATE.
    MOVE ZIPCODEI TO CM-ZIP-CODE.
    EXEC CICS
        WRITE FILE('CUSTMAS')
              FROM(CUSTOMER-MASTER-RECORD)
              RIDFLD(CM-CUSTOMER-NUMBER)
              RESP(RESPONSE-CODE)
    END-EXEC.
    IF      RESPONSE-CODE NOT = DFHRESP(NORMAL)
        AND RESPONSE-CODE NOT = DFHRESP(DUPREC)
        PERFORM 9999-TERMINATE-PROGRAM
    END-IF.
*
    3000-PROCESS-CHANGE-CUSTOMER.
*
    PERFORM 2100-RECEIVE-DATA-MAP.
    MOVE CUSTNO2I TO CM-CUSTOMER-NUMBER.
    PERFORM 3100-READ-CUSTOMER-FOR-UPDATE.
    IF RESPONSE-CODE = DFHRESP(NORMAL)
        IF CUSTOMER-MASTER-RECORD = CA-CUSTOMER-RECORD
            PERFORM 3200-REWRITE-CUSTOMER-RECORD
            MOVE 'Customer record updated.' TO MSG1O
            SET SEND-ERASE TO TRUE
        ELSE
            MOVE 'Another user has updated the record.  Try again
                '.' TO MSG1O
            SET SEND-ERASE-ALARM TO TRUE
        END-IF
    ELSE
        IF RESPONSE-CODE = DFHRESP(NOTFND)
            MOVE 'Another user has deleted the record.'
                TO MSG1O
            SET SEND-ERASE-ALARM TO TRUE
        END-IF
    END-IF.
    MOVE -1 TO CUSTNO1L.
    PERFORM 1500-SEND-KEY-MAP.
    SET PROCESS-KEY-MAP TO TRUE.
*
    3100-READ-CUSTOMER-FOR-UPDATE.
*
    EXEC CICS
        READ FILE('CUSTMAS')
             INTO(CUSTOMER-MASTER-RECORD)
             RIDFLD(CM-CUSTOMER-NUMBER)
             UPDATE
             RESP(RESPONSE-CODE)
    END-EXEC.
    IF      RESPONSE-CODE NOT = DFHRESP(NORMAL)
        AND RESPONSE-CODE NOT = DFHRESP(NOTFND)
        PERFORM 9999-TERMINATE-PROGRAM
    END-IF.
```

Figure 5-20   The COBOL code for the customer maintenance program (part 7 of 8)

The customer maintenance program   **Page 8**

```
 3200-REWRITE-CUSTOMER-RECORD.
*
     MOVE LNAMEI    TO CM-LAST-NAME.
     MOVE FNAMEI    TO CM-FIRST-NAME.
     MOVE ADDRI     TO CM-ADDRESS.
     MOVE CITYI     TO CM-CITY.
     MOVE STATEI    TO CM-STATE.
     MOVE ZIPCODEI TO CM-ZIP-CODE.
     EXEC CICS
         REWRITE FILE('CUSTMAS')
                 FROM(CUSTOMER-MASTER-RECORD)
                 RESP(RESPONSE-CODE)
     END-EXEC.
     IF RESPONSE-CODE NOT = DFHRESP(NORMAL)
         PERFORM 9999-TERMINATE-PROGRAM
     END-IF.
*
 4000-PROCESS-DELETE-CUSTOMER.
*
     MOVE CA-CUSTOMER-NUMBER TO CM-CUSTOMER-NUMBER.
     PERFORM 3100-READ-CUSTOMER-FOR-UPDATE.
     IF RESPONSE-CODE = DFHRESP(NORMAL)
         IF CUSTOMER-MASTER-RECORD = CA-CUSTOMER-RECORD
             PERFORM 4100-DELETE-CUSTOMER-RECORD
             MOVE 'Customer deleted.' TO MSG1O
             SET SEND-ERASE TO TRUE
         ELSE
             MOVE 'Another user has updated the record.  Try again
-                '.' TO MSG1O
             SET SEND-ERASE-ALARM TO TRUE
         END-IF
     ELSE
         IF RESPONSE-CODE = DFHRESP(NOTFND)
             MOVE 'Another user has deleted the record.'
                  TO MSG1O
             SET SEND-ERASE-ALARM TO TRUE
         END-IF
     END-IF.
     MOVE -1 TO CUSTNO1L.
     PERFORM 1500-SEND-KEY-MAP.
     SET PROCESS-KEY-MAP TO TRUE.
*
 4100-DELETE-CUSTOMER-RECORD.
*
     EXEC CICS
         DELETE FILE('CUSTMAS')
                RESP(RESPONSE-CODE)
     END-EXEC.
     IF  RESPONSE-CODE NOT = DFHRESP(NORMAL)
         PERFORM 9999-TERMINATE-PROGRAM
     END-IF.
*
 9999-TERMINATE-PROGRAM.
*
     EXEC CICS
         ABEND
     END-EXEC.
```

Figure 5-20   The COBOL code for the customer maintenance program (part 8 of 8)

Perspective

The commands and coding techniques presented in this chapter are the ones you'll use in most of the CICS programs you develop. If you understand these commands and techniques, then, you'll be able to use them to code a variety of CICS applications. However, there are some additional techniques you'll want to know about for storing data between executions of a pseudo-conversational program, for working with the terminal and the data that's entered at the terminal, for handling unrecoverable errors, for accessing data using the Linkage Section, and for formatting the date and time. You'll learn about these techniques in chapters 7 and 8. But first, chapter 6 will show you how to test CICS programs.

Terms

logical levels
relative record number (RRN)
relative byte address (RBA)
deadlock
response code checking

6

How to test a CICS program

One of the major pitfalls of program development is inadequate testing. All too often, a program is put into production without being tested on enough combinations of input data to be sure all of its routines work. Then, when it produces inaccurate results or simply fails, a crisis can occur.

As a programmer, it's your responsibility to develop programs that work properly. So this chapter presents some techniques and facilities you can use to test your CICS programs thoroughly.

Introduction to CICS program testing

Before you learn how to test a CICS program, you need to know about the different types of testing that are typically required and about the testing environment you'll be using. You also need to know how to prepare a COBOL program so you can execute it. That's what you'll learn in the topics that follow.

Types of testing

Figure 6-1 summarizes the four types of tests that are commonly done before CICS programs are put into production. To start, the program is tested on its own in a *unit test*. During the unit test, you make sure that the program works according to the program specifications. Although you'll usually do this test yourself, the other tests may be done by a separate quality assurance group.

A *concurrency test* is done for programs that will be run by two or more users at the same time, which is the case for most CICS programs. This test insures that two or more simultaneous executions of the program don't interfere with one another. For example, the maintenance program you saw in the last chapter holds a copy of a record being updated from one execution to the next so it can check that the record hasn't changed before it's updated or deleted. A concurrency test would insure that this mechanism works.

In an *integration test*, the program is tested in combination with other programs to make sure the program works as a part of a complete system. Many programming errors aren't detected until the program is allowed to interact with other programs. In addition, the integration test often reveals inconsistencies in the application design.

The last test is done whenever a program is modified. In that case, the entire program should be retested...not just the portion of the program that was modified. That's the purpose of a *regression test*. In a regression test, the testing that was originally done on the program before it was approved for production is repeated to make sure the results are the same. Because 70% or more of all program development work is maintaining and enhancing existing systems, the need for solid regression testing is clear. Unfortunately, regression testing is often overlooked because it is time-consuming.

Four common types of testing

Test	Description
Unit test	The program is tested on its own to insure that it works according to the program specifications.
Concurrency test	The program is tested simultaneously at several terminals to make sure that multiple executions of the same program don't interfere with one another.
Integration test	The program is tested in context with other programs in the application.
Regression test	Testing that was originally done against the program is repeated when the program undergoes maintenance.

Description

- The *unit test* is typically done by the programmer who develops the program. The other tests may be done by a separate quality assurance group.

- During the unit test, the programmer makes sure that the screens are displayed properly, all field edits work as planned, files are updated correctly, and so on.

- If a program will be run by two or more users at the same time, a *concurrency test* is typically required.

- The *integration test* insures that a program works as part of a complete system. The integration test can also reveal inconsistencies in program design.

- When a program is modified, the entire program should be retested, not just the portion of the program that was modified. That's the purpose of a *regression test*.

Figure 6-1   Types of testing for CICS programs

CICS testing environments

In most cases, you test your programs within a CICS testing environment, or *test region*, that's separate from the production environment. That way, you can thoroughly test your programs without fear of affecting the production system. The testing environment consists of a CICS system that's dedicated to testing and test versions of production files.

Some installations maintain several CICS testing environments for various levels of testing. For example, an installation might use one CICS system to let application programmers do unit testing and concurrency testing. When those tests are complete, the programmer promotes the program to another CICS system, where integration and regression tests are performed by a separate quality assurance group. Only then is the program promoted to the production system.

When you're working in a CICS system dedicated to testing, there are a few things you need to find out. The most important of these are listed in figure 6-2. To start, it's not uncommon for each programmer to be assigned one or more generic transaction identifiers and program names. That way, new resources don't need to be defined for each new program. If that's the case, you'll use these generic names as you test the program, and you'll replace them with actual names before you move the program to production.

You'll also need to know what files exist for testing purposes. Usually, test versions of production files will be available. These test versions may contain small amounts of data extracted from the production files, or they may contain representative data created by a test data generator. Either way, you need to know what test files are available, and you need to know how to create test files of your own when necessary.

In addition, you'll want to find out what testing and debugging aids are available. At the least, you should have access to the CEMT, CECI, and CEDF transactions. (You'll learn how to use CEMT and CECI later in this chapter, and you'll learn how to use CEDF in chapter 9.) But you may also have access to more sophisticated tools. If so, you'll want to find out what they are and how to use them.

Finally, most installations have policies for how program testing is managed. Some shops just have a simple set of manual procedures for moving programs from the test environment to the production environment. But most large shops use some sort of change management software to automate the process. Change management software keeps track of the status and location of each program within an application, and it helps insure that two programmers don't modify a program at the same time. It also manages multiple versions of programs, so that if a problem is discovered with the current version of a program, a previous version can be temporarily installed in production until the current version can be corrected. In either case, you need to learn the change management procedures in place at your installation.

What you need to know about the testing environment

- Is there a testing environment separate from the production environment? If so, find out what testing is done in what environment.

- Do you need to use generic transaction identifiers and program names within the testing environment? If so, find out what they are.

- Are there test versions of the files you need to test your program? If so, find out what files are available. If not, find out how to create test versions of the files.

- Are testing and debugging aids like the CEMT, CECI, and CEDF transactions available? Are any third-party tools for testing and debugging available? If so, find out how to use them.

- Does your shop have a procedure for managing program testing and program versions? If so, find out what it is and follow it.

Description

- Most installations create one or more CICS testing environments that are separate from the production environment. That way, programs can be tested without affecting the production system.

- Generic transaction identifiers and program names are often used so the systems programmer doesn't have to define resources for every program that's under development.

- Test systems often provide access to CICS testing and debugging aids, which are usually off-limits to users of production systems.

- Most installations have policies for how program testing is managed. Those policies may consist of a simple set of manual procedures for moving programs from test to production, or they may require the use of change management software.

Figure 6-2   CICS testing environments

How to prepare a CICS program for execution

Before you can test a CICS program, you must prepare it for execution. That involves translating the source program so it can be interpreted by the COBOL compiler, compiling the translated source program into an object module, and then link-editing the object module with required system modules. To do that, you typically use a JCL procedure like the one shown in figure 6-3.

As you can see, the procedure in this figure executes a cataloged procedure named DFHYITVL. The first step of this procedure (TRN) translates the source program you identify on the SYSIN DD statement for this step. Then, the compile step (COB) compiles the translated program. The SYSLIB DD statement for this step identifies one or more libraries that contain copy members used by the program. Notice that the first DD statement is left blank so the copy library specified in the cataloged procedure isn't overridden. Instead, the libraries you specify are concatenated with this library.

The last step (LKED) link-edits the object module created by the compile step into a load module. The load module is given the name you specify on the SYSIN DD statement, and it's stored in the library you specify on the PROGLIB parameter of the EXEC statement. Note that if the DFHYITVL procedure has been modified so it names the appropriate load library, you can omit the PROGLIB parameter. You can also omit the PARM.COB parameter if you want to use the compiler options specified in the procedure.

If your program calls static subprograms, you can also include a SYSLIB DD statement for the LKED step to identify the object library that contains those programs. Like the SYSLIB DD statement for the copy library, you'll want to concatenate this library to the libraries that are specified in the cataloged procedure as shown in this figure. In this case, the cataloged procedure names two object libraries, so two blank DD statements are coded.

Note that the JCL shown here is for an OS/390 system running CICS TS 1.3 and COBOL for OS/390. If you're using other versions of CICS or COBOL, the JCL you use to translate, compile, and link-edit a program may be different.

An OS/390 procedure for preparing a CICS program

```
//MM01CMPL JOB 36512,'R.MENENDEZ',MSGCLASS=X,CLASS=C,
//           REGION=4M,NOTIFY=MM01
//CICSCMP  EXEC DFHYITVL,
// PARM.COB='OFFSET,MAP',
// PROGLIB='MM.MM01CICS.CICSTS13.LOADLIB'
//TRN.SYSIN  DD DSN=MM01.CICS.SOURCE(CUSTMNT1),DISP=SHR
//COB.SYSLIB DD
//           DD DSN=MM01.CICS.COPYLIB,DISP=SHR
//LKED.SYSIN DD *
   NAME CUSTMNT1(R)
/*
```

Description

- The JCL for preparing a CICS program executes a cataloged procedure named DFHYITVL. This procedure contains steps to translate (TRN), compile (COB), and link-edit (LKED) the program.

- The PARM.COB parameter of the EXEC statement specifies the compiler options to be used. These options override the options specified in the DFHYITVL procedure.

- The PROGLIB parameter of the EXEC statement specifies the load library where the load module that's created by the link-edit step will be stored.

- The input to the translate step is the source program, which must be identified on the SYSIN DD statement. The translated program that's created by this step is then used as input to the compile step.

- The compile step compiles the translated program to create an object module. If the program contains any Copy statements, the library that contains the members to be copied must be specified on the SYSLIB DD statement for this step as shown above.

- The link-edit step link-edits the object module with any required system modules to create a load module. The SYSIN DD statement for this step specifies the name that's given to the load module and indicates that if a module already exists with that name, it should be replaced.

- If your program calls one or more static subprograms, you'll need to include a SYSLIB DD statement on the link-edit step that identifies the object library that contains the subprograms like this:

```
//LKED.SYSLIB   DD
//              DD
//              DD DSN=MMA2.CICS.OBJLIB,DISP=SHR
```

Figure 6-3   How to prepare a CICS program for execution

How to test a program from the top down

When you design a program using the techniques presented in chapter 3, you can then code and test the program from the top down. This is called *top-down coding and testing*, or just *top-down testing*.

When you use top-down testing, you start by coding and testing the top module of the program along with a few subordinate modules. Once these modules work correctly, you code and test a few more modules. When these modules plus the earlier modules work correctly, you code and test a few more modules, and you continue like this until all of the modules are coded and tested.

Two obvious benefits of top-down testing are (1) that it's relatively easy to find and correct bugs when you test only a few modules at a time and (2) that it's easier to make sure that you test all of the conditions in each module. This translates into improved productivity and fewer bugs in the programs that are put into production. The alternative is to code the entire program and then try to find and correct the dozens of bugs that a large program is likely to contain...a potential nightmare!

How to plan the coding and testing sequence

To plan the coding and testing sequence you're going to use, we recommend that you develop a *test plan* using the guidelines presented in figure 6-4. This figure also presents an acceptable test plan for the customer maintenance program. As you review this plan, keep in mind that other test plans may work just as well. The key is to break the development down into manageable phases and to test the critical modules first. Note that the module numbers in this test plan correspond to the numbers in the structure chart for this program that was presented in figure 5-19.

Phase 1 of this test plan tests that the key map is displayed properly and that the logic in module 0000 works for all possible attention keys that the user might press from this map. In particular, it tests to be sure that an error message is displayed if an invalid key is pressed. Then, phase 2 tests that the data the user enters into the key map is received and edited properly. Notice that no data is actually retrieved from the customer file and the data map is not displayed in this phase. That's done in phase 3. This phase tests that the data map is displayed when it should be, that all attention keys work properly from this map, and that invalid customer numbers are handled properly when they aren't found in the customer master file. No actual processing of the customer records is done in this phase, however.

The next three phases test that the add, change, and delete functions work properly. Notice that only valid entries are used in these phases. That's because this version of the maintenance program doesn't edit the data that's entered by the user, so all entries are valid. In a production program, though, you'd want to include invalid customer data to be sure that it is edited properly.

Guidelines for preparing a top-down test plan

- Test just a few modules at a time, but test all of the processing in each module.
- Test the critical modules of the program early in the plan, and test the remaining modules in whatever sequence you prefer.
- Keep the test data to a minimum in the early test phases.

A top-down test plan for the customer maintenance program

Phase	Modules	Test
1	0000 (Process customer maintenance) 1500 (Send key map)	Enter all valid and invalid attention keys from the key map to be sure that they're processed properly and that the key map is displayed properly
2	1000 (Process key map) 1100 (Receive key map) 1200 (Edit key data)	Enter valid and invalid customer numbers and action codes to be sure they're received and edited properly
3	1300 (Read customer record) 1400 (Send data map)	Enter valid key map entries and all valid and invalid attention keys from the data map to be sure that they're processed properly and that the data map is displayed properly; enter invalid customer numbers to be sure they're handled properly
4	2000 (Process add customer) 2100 (Receive data map) 2300 (Write customer record)	Enter valid key map and data map entries for an add operation to be sure that the record is written properly
5	3000 (Process change customer) 3100 (Read customer for update) 3200 (Rewrite customer record)	Enter valid key map and data map entries for a change operation to be sure that the record is rewritten properly
6	4000 (Process delete customer) 4100 (Delete customer record)	Enter valid key map and data map entries for a delete operation to be sure that the record is deleted

Note

- Before you begin coding and testing a CICS program, you should code, prepare, and test the maps used by the program to be sure that they display properly. The easiest way to test a map is to use the CECI transaction as described in figure 6-10. (See chapter 4 for information on preparing a map.)

Figure 6-4   How to plan the coding and testing sequence

How to code the new modules for each phase of testing

Figure 6-5 presents some basic guidelines for coding the new modules for each phase of testing. In particular, you should note that you don't have to code the complete Data Division before you start testing the program. Instead, you need to code only the entries that are required by the Procedure Division modules that are going to be tested.

When you add a module to the Procedure Division, it's usually best to code it in its entirety. Then, if you want to exclude the processing of one or more lines, you can add an asterisk to column 7 of the line so it's treated as a comment. Later on, when you're ready for a commented line to be tested, you can remove the asterisk. Another way to handle this is to code a program stub for each paragraph that isn't going to be coded and tested until a later testing phase.

How to code program stubs

Figure 6-5 also presents the guidelines for coding the *program stubs* (or *dummy modules*) required for a test run. These are the modules that are called by other modules, but aren't fully coded yet. In conversation, the process of writing a program stub for a module is often referred to as "stubbing off" a module.

If a program stub doesn't have to do anything for the test run to work properly, the stub can consist of just the paragraph name. This is illustrated by the first example in this figure. Then, when the paragraph is performed, nothing is done and the program continues.

For a program stub that represents an input module, it sometimes makes sense to simulate the reading of a record in the file. This is illustrated by the second example in this figure. Here, literal values are simply moved into the fields of a record.

Sometimes, a program stub doesn't need to do any processing, but you want to know that it's been executed. Unfortunately, there's no easy way to do that. One technique you may want to try, though, involves creating a string that includes the numbers of all the modules that are executed, in the order that they're executed. Then, before the next SEND MAP command is issued, you can move the string to the message area of that map so it's displayed on the screen.

As you create your program stubs, the goal is to get the testing done right with a minimum of extra work. In most cases, you can do that with simple stubs that cause little extra work but improve the results you get from top-down testing. When a program stub starts getting too elaborate, though, you're usually better off coding the entire module and adding it to that test phase.

Guidelines for coding and testing from the top down

- To start, code the Identification Division and as much of the Data Division as is needed for the first phase of testing. Then, code the Procedure Division modules that are going to be tested.

- When you add new modules to the Procedure Division for the next phase of testing, add any code in the Data Division that's required to support those modules.

- If you include a Perform statement for a module that isn't implemented yet, you can comment out the Perform statement or code a program stub for it. You can also comment out other statements you don't want executed.

Guidelines for coding a program stub

- If a program stub doesn't have to do anything for the successful completion of a test run, the module can consist of the paragraph name only.

- If necessary, a program stub can simulate the function that will be done by that module. For example, an input stub can simulate the reading of one or more records.

A processing stub that consists of only the paragraph name

```
    1300-GET-CUSTOMER-RECORD.
*
```

An input stub that simulates the reading of a record

```
    1100-READ-CUSTOMER-RECORD.
*
        MOVE 'JOHN'              TO CM-FIRST-NAME.
        MOVE 'DOE'               TO CM-LAST-NAME.
        MOVE '100 MAIN STREET'   TO CM-ADDRESS.
        MOVE 'ANYWHERE'          TO CM-CITY.
        MOVE 'CA'                TO CM-STATE.
        MOVE '99999'             TO CM-ZIP-CODE.
*
```

Note

- If you want to find out what modules of a program (including program stubs) are executed, you can add code to each module that creates a string of the module numbers that are executed. Then, you can move that string to the message area so it's displayed on the map.

Figure 6-5   How to code the new modules and program stubs

A checklist for program testing

Figure 6-6 presents a checklist you can use as you test your programs. To start, you want to be sure that all the fields are displayed properly and that the cursor works as intended. You can check the basic format of a map when you test it using CECI as described later in this chapter. As you test the program, though, you'll want to be sure that the maps are processed properly. That includes making sure that the right screen is displayed at the right time, that all the attention keys work properly, that the correct user messages and error messages are displayed at the right time, that work fields are cleared when appropriate, and that fields are displayed with the correct attributes.

Because most CICS programs are interactive, you can check most of the logic of the program by watching what happens on the screen. However, you can't rely on the appearance of the screen alone. If the program updates one or more files, you also need to be sure that the updates work properly. You'll learn how to do that in the next topic.

What to check for on the screen

*   Are all the headings and captions placed correctly?
*   Are the user instructions displayed properly?
*   Is there any garbage on the screen?
*   Are all words spelled correctly?
*   Do all the fields have the correct attributes?
*   Is the cursor in the correct initial location?
*   Does the cursor move correctly from field to field?

What to check for as you enter valid data

*   Are all the program screens displayed in the correct sequence?
*   Do all the attention keys work correctly?
*   Are the user messages always correct?
*   Are the functions of all attention keys indicated?
*   Does the program properly acknowledge the receipt of valid data?
*   Are work fields properly cleared after each valid transaction?
*   Are control totals accumulated properly?
*   Are files updated properly?

What to check for as you enter invalid data

*   Does each case of invalid data for each field yield an appropriate error message?
*   Do look-up routines work properly?
*   Is the field in error highlighted?
*   Is the cursor positioned at the field in error?
*   When you correct the error, do the error message and highlighting go away?
*   Does the program post transactions even though errors are detected?
*   Does the program detect all possible cross-validation errors?
*   Does the program properly detect and highlight multiple entry errors?

Figure 6-6   A checklist for program testing

How to view program results

If a program updates records in a VSAM file, you'll want to look at the file before and after the program is run to be sure it was updated properly. One way to do that is to print the contents of the file using the VSAM utility program called *IDCAMS* (or *AMS*). If you've written any COBOL programs that do file processing, you're probably already familiar with this program. Be aware, though, that before you use IDCAMS to print the contents of a file from CICS, you must close the file. To do that, you use the CEMT transaction as described later in this chapter.

Although you can get the information you need about a file from the print output IDCAMS produces, it's often quicker and easier to just display the file at your terminal. To do that, you can use an interactive utility program called *DITTO*. Figure 6-7 shows you what the DITTO display looks like for the customer master file. Notice that because all of the data in this file is alphanumeric, it's displayed in character format. If a file contains packed-decimal data, though, you can display the data in hexadecimal format by entering HEX for the Format option in the upper right corner of the display.

Of course, there are other non-IBM utility programs you can use to display and print the contents of files. So you'll want to be sure to find out what programs are available at your installation.

The customer master file as displayed by DITTO

```
Mma - EXTRA! for Windows 98 / Windows NT                    _ □ ×
 File  Edit  View  Tools  Session  Options  Help
  Process   View   Options   Help
─────────────────────────────────────────────────────────────
 DITTO/ESA for MVS              VB - VSAM Browse

 RBA 0          Key 040001                    Col 1      Format CHAR
 VOLSER LIB312  Type KSDS   DSNAME MM01.CUSTMAST

 RBA       Len    <==5>..10....5...20....5...30....5...40....5...50....5...60
 0         118    040001KEITH          MCDONALD                    4501
 118       118    040002WARREN         ANELLI                      40 F
 236       118    040003SUSAN          HOWARD                      1107
 354       118    040004CAROL ANN      EVANS                       74 S
 472       118    040005ELAINE         ROBERTS                     1291
 590       118    040006SPAT           HONG                        73 H
 708       118    040007PHIL           ROACH                       2568
 826       118    040008TIM            JOHNSON                     145
 944       118    040011WILLIAM C      FERGUSON                    BOX
 1062      118    040012ENRIQUE        OTHON                       BOX
 1180      118    040013S D            HOEHN                       PO B
 1298      118    040014DAVID R        KEITH                       PO B

 Command ==>                                              Scroll PAGE
 F1=Help  F2=Zoom  F3=Exit  F4=Left  F5=Right  F6=RFind  F7=Bkwd  F8=Fwd
 F9=Swap  F10=Actions  F11=CRetrieve  F12=Cancel
                      :01.0                                22/15
```

Description

- To make sure that a program that updates records in a file works correctly, you need to compare the data in the file before the program is run with the data in the file after the program is run.

- To display the contents of a file on the screen, you can use a utility program called *DITTO*. In addition to displaying the contents of a file, you can use DITTO to modify, print, and copy data in both VSAM and non-VSAM files.

- To print the contents of a file, you can use a VSAM utility program called *IDCAMS*. Before you can use this utility to print a file, though, you must use the CEMT transaction to close the file as described in figure 6-9.

Figure 6-7   How to view program results

How to use the CICS service transactions for testing

CICS provides four service transactions that you'll use as you test your programs. You use the first two, CESN and CESF, to sign on and off of CICS. You use the third one, CEMT, to manage the status of CICS resources. And you use the fourth one, CECI, to execute CICS commands interactively.

CESN: The sign on transaction

Sometimes, CICS is set up so you're signed on automatically when you connect to it. If that's not the case, though, you'll need to use the *sign on transaction*, *CESN*, to sign on. Figure 6-8 presents the syntax of the CESN command that starts this transaction.

As you can see, you can enter both a user name and a password on this command. If you omit one or both of these parameters, CICS displays a screen that lets you enter them. Because the password is displayed as blanks on this screen, you may want to use this technique for security purposes.

CESF: The sign off transaction

If you use the CESN transaction to sign on to CICS, you'll need to use the *sign off transaction*, *CESF*, to sign off. The syntax of the CESF command is also shown in figure 6-8. If you enter this command without any parameters, you're simply logged off of CICS. If you include the LOGOFF or GOODNIGHT parameter, though, you're signed off and the terminal is disconnected from CICS. Then, before you can sign back on, you have to reconnect to CICS.

The syntax of the CESN command

```
CESN [USER=username]
     [PS=password]
```

The syntax of the CESF command

```
CESF [LOGOFF | GOODNIGHT]
```

A CESN command that includes a user-id and password

```
CESN USER=RAUL,PS=MMA2000
```

A typical CESF command

```
CESF LOGOFF
```

Description

- The CESN command signs you on to CICS. Depending on how CICS is set up, you may or may not need to use this command to sign on to CICS before you test your programs.

- You can include the USER and PS parameters on the CESN command to supply your user-id and password. If you omit these parameters, CICS will display a sign-on screen where you can enter them.

- When you enter your password on the sign-on screen, it's displayed as blanks so that no one else can see it. Because of that, we recommend you use this technique if security in your shop is critical.

- If you use the CESN command to sign on to CICS, you should use the CESF command to sign off when you're done working with CICS.

- If you want to disconnect your terminal from the CICS region it's connected to when you log off, you can include the LOGOFF or GOODNIGHT parameter on the CESF command.

Figure 6-8   How to use CESN and CESF: The sign on and sign off transactions

CEMT: The master terminal transaction

The *master terminal transaction*, more commonly know as *CEMT*, lets you control a variety of CICS functions. To do that, you start CEMT and then enter CEMT commands. Figure 6-9 presents the CEMT commands you're most likely to use as you test your programs. When you enter one of these commands, the result is displayed on a full-screen panel. From this panel, you can enter additional CEMT commands. You can also display this panel by entering the CEMT trans-id without a CEMT command.

The underlining in the syntax indicates the minimum abbreviations you can use for each keyword in each command. Notice that these vary from one command to another. For example, the abbreviation for DISABLED is DI in the SET PROGRAM command but just D in the SET TRANSACTION command.

The first command in this figure, SET PROGRAM NEWCOPY, causes CICS to read a fresh copy of a program from disk. You should issue this command whenever you recompile a program while CICS is running. Otherwise, CICS may continue to use the previous version of the program. The first example in this figure shows how you can use this command to refresh the customer maintenance program.

You use the next command, SET FILE, when you need to print the contents of a file while CICS is running. Before you print the file, you use the SET FILE command with the CLOSE keyword as illustrated in the second example in this figure. This command closes and disables the file so it can be accessed by a batch job. After you finish printing the file, you use this command with the OPEN keyword to open it again.

The next two commands let you enable or disable a program or transaction. They're particularly useful when a programming error forces a program into a pseudo-conversational loop that doesn't provide for the final exit from the program. A loop like this can tie up a terminal indefinitely, restarting the same program over and over again every time you press an attention key.

To break this type of loop, you can use CEMT to disable either the program or the transaction that's causing the loop. To do that, you enter a command like the one in the third example in this figure at another terminal. Then, when you've corrected the problem, you can use the same command with the EN-ABLED keyword to enable the transaction or program again.

You can also use CEMT to disable a program that's stuck in a simple programming loop, like a Perform Until loop whose condition never becomes true. If you don't do that, though, CICS will eventually detect the problem and cancel the task.

The last command in this figure, INQUIRE, lets you display status information for files, programs, and transactions. If you enter the name of a specific file, program, or transaction, its status is displayed on the screen. However, you can also display the status of all files, programs, or transactions that match a pattern you specify. To do that, you include an asterisk (*) wildcard in the name. This is illustrated in the last example in this figure. This command will display the status of all files that start with the letter C.

The syntax of the CEMT commands commonly used for testing

To force a new copy of a program

```
CEMT SET PROGRAM(name) NEWCOPY
```

To open or close a file

```
CEMT SET FILE(name) {OPEN | CLOSE}
```

To disable or enable a program or transaction

```
CEMT SET PROGRAM(name) {DISABLED | ENABLED}
CEMT SET TRANSACTION(name) {DISABLED | ENABLED}
```

To check on the status of a file, program, or transaction

```
CEMT INQUIRE {FILE(name) | PROGRAM(name) | TRANSACTION(name)}
```

Command examples

A command that refreshes CICS's copy of the CUSTMNT1 program

```
CEMT SET PROGRAM(CUSTMNT1) NEWCOPY
```

A command that closes the customer master file

```
CEMT S FI(CUSTMST) CL
```

A command that disables the MNT1 transaction

```
CEMT S TRA(MNT1) D
```

A command that displays the status of all files that start with the letter C

```
CEMT I FI(C*)
```

Description

*   To use the *master terminal transaction*, type the CEMT trans-id followed by a CEMT command. The results are displayed on a full-screen panel. You can also enter CEMT without a command and CEMT will help you construct the command.

*   The underlined characters shown above are the minimum abbreviations CEMT allows.

*   After you modify and recompile a program, you should issue the SET PROGRAM NEWCOPY command so CICS will refresh its copy of the program from disk.

*   Before you can print a copy of a file while CICS is running, you must close and disable the file. To do that, you issue the CEMT SET FILE CLOSE command. Before you can use the file again, you must issue the CEMT SET FILE OPEN command to reopen it.

*   To end a program that's stuck in a pseudo-conversational loop, you can use the CEMT SET PROGRAM DISABLED or CEMT SET TRANSACTION DISABLED command. These commands must be entered from a terminal other than the one where the task is running.

*   To check on the status of a file, program, or transaction, you can use the CEMT IN-QUIRE command. You can use the asterisk (*) wildcard as shown above to check on the status of all files, programs, or transactions whose names match a specified pattern.

Figure 6-9   How to use CEMT: The master terminal transaction

CECI: The command-level interpreter

Another CICS service transaction that's useful for program development is *CECI*, the *command-level interpreter*. You can use it to issue CICS commands from outside a program. For example, you might want to use it to issue a SEND MAP command to test a map before you've written the program that will process it. You might also use it to update the contents of a file so you don't have to write a special-purpose program to do that.

Figure 6-10 presents the syntax of the CECI command and shows the start-up panel that's displayed when you enter the CECI trans-id without a CICS command. As you can see, this panel lists the CICS commands you can execute. To execute one of these commands, you just type it in at the top of the panel and then press the Enter key. For example, you can see a SEND MAP command at the top of the panel in this figure. If the syntax of the command is correct, CICS displays another panel that lets you know it's about to execute the command. Then, you can press the Enter key again to execute the command and display the results.

This figure also shows a CECI command that executes a CICS READ command. Notice that the key of the record to be read is specified in the RIDFLD option as a literal. Also notice that the INTO option has been omitted, since the results will simply be displayed on the screen.

You should also notice that neither of the CICS commands shown in this figure is bracketed with EXEC CICS and END-EXEC. That's not required in CECI. In addition, literal values, such as the map and mapset name in the SEND MAP command, don't need to be enclosed in apostrophes.

In some shops, only certain users are allowed to use CECI to execute CICS commands. Even if you can't use CECI to execute commands, though, you may still be able to use it to verify the syntax of those commands. To do that, you enter the CECS trans-id as shown in the command syntax. This also starts the command-level interpreter, but it restricts its functionality so that you can't actually execute the commands you enter.

The syntax of the CECI and CECS commands

```
{CECI | CECS} [CICS-command]
```

The CECI start-up panel

```
Mma - EXTRA! for Windows 98 / Windows NT          _ □ ✕
File  Edit  View  Tools  Session  Options  Help
 SEND MAP(INQMAP1) MAPSET(INQSET1) ERASE_
 STATUS:   ENTER ONE OF THE FOLLOWING

 ABend        DEQ          INquire      RECeive      STARTBr
 ACquire      DISAble      ISsue        RELease      SUspend
 ADdress      DISCard      Journal      RESEtbr      SYncpoint
 ALlocate     DUmp         LInk         RESYnc       Trace
 ASKtime      ENAble       LOad         RETRieve     Unlock
 ASSign       ENDbr        Monitor      RETUrn       Verify
 BIf          ENQ          PErform      REWrite      WAIT
 BUild        ENTer        POInt        ROute        WAITCics
 CAncel       EXtract      POP          SENd         WRITE
 CHange       FEpi         POSt         SET          WRITEQ
 COLlect      FOrmattime   PURge        SIGNOFf      Xctl
 CONNect      FREE         PUSh         SIGNON
 CONVerse     FREEMain     Query        SPOOLClose
 CReate       GDs          READ         SPOOLOpen
 DELAy        GEtmain      READNext     SPOOLRead
 DELETE       Handle       READPrev     SPOOLWrite
 DELETEQ      IGnore       READQ        START

 PF 1 HELP 2 HEX 3 END 4 EIB 5 VAR 6 USER          9 MSG
                    (0:00.2                              01/42
```

A CECI command that reads a record from the customer master file

```
CECI READ FILE(CUSTMAS) RIDFLD(123456)
```

Description

- To invoke the *command-level interpreter*, enter the CECI trans-id followed by the CICS command you want to execute. If you enter CECI without a CICS command, the command-level interpreter displays a start-up panel listing the commands you can issue.

- CECI checks the syntax of the command you specify and then displays a panel telling you it's about to execute the command. When you press the Enter key, CECI executes the command and displays the results.

- You can also start CECI by entering the CECS trans-id with or without a CICS command. This transaction restricts the functionality of CECI so that it only checks the syntax of the command you specify. It doesn't execute the command.

- When you issue a command from CECI, you don't have to bracket the command with EXEC CICS and END-EXEC, and you don't have to use apostrophes to identify literals.

- You can use the function keys listed at the bottom of the CECI panel to perform functions like displaying help information (PF1), displaying data in hex (PF2), displaying the values of the fields in the Execute Interface Block (PF4), and defining variables for use in the commands you issue (PF5).

Figure 6-10   How to use CECI: The command-level interpreter

A CECI session that reads and rewrites a record in the customer master file

To help you understand how CECI works, figure 6-11 presents a sample session that updates the contents of a record in the customer master file. Two commands are required to do that: a READ for UPDATE command that retrieves the current record, and a REWRITE command that updates the record. In addition, a variable will be defined to hold the record that's retrieved by the READ command. Then, that same variable can be used to rewrite the updated record. Without this variable, you'd have to reenter all the data for the record, even if it didn't need to be changed. This will make more sense as you proceed through this sample session.

Although it's not necessary for this particular example, a second variable will be defined to hold the key value of the record to be retrieved. That way, I can illustrate how you set the initial value of a variable. As the sample session illustrates, the ability to use variables is one of CECI's most powerful features.

In screen 1 of this session, you can see the Variables panel that's displayed when you press PF5 from the start-up panel. This panel lets you define variables and set their starting values. The first three variables listed on this panel are pre-defined by CECI. Notice that each variable name begins with an ampersand (&). To the right of each variable name is its length, followed by its current contents.

To define variables of your own, you simply add them to the list. In this screen, for example, you can see the definition of two user-defined variables: &REC and &KEY. &REC is a 118-byte variable that will hold the customer record, and &KEY is a 6-byte variable that will hold the record key.

After you enter the variable names and lengths and press the Enter key, CECI confirms the definitions. Then, you can enter initial values for the variables as shown in screen 2. Here, a value of 123456 has been entered for the &KEY variable, which will be used to read the customer record with that number. In contrast, the &REC variable doesn't require an initial value because the record that's read will be placed in it.

Screen 1

To add variables for use within CECI, press PF5 from the start-up panel to display the Variables panel. Then, enter a name (starting with an ampersand (&)) and length for each variable below the pre-defined variables and press the Enter key.

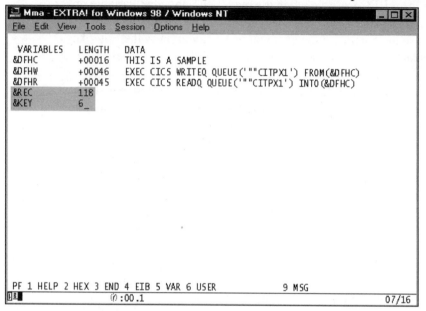

Screen 2

CECI confirms that the variables have been defined. Then, you can enter initial values for the variables and press the Enter key to return to the start-up screen.

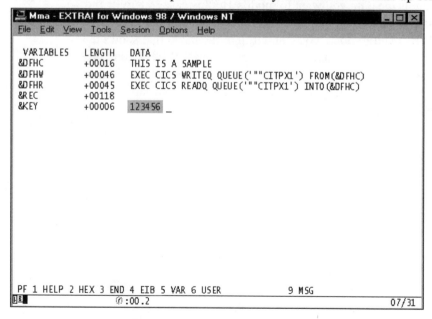

Figure 6-11   A CECI session that reads and rewrites a record in the customer master file (part 1 of 4)

When you press the Enter key from screen 2, you're returned to the start-up panel. Then, you can enter a READ command to retrieve the record for the customer that's identified by the &KEY variable. To do that, you name this variable on the RIDFLD option as shown in screen 3. And, to place the contents of that record in the &REC variable when it's read, you name that variable on the INTO option.

When you have the command the way you want it, you press the Enter key. Then, CECI checks the syntax of the command and displays the values of all of the command options as shown in screen 4. To execute the command, press the Enter key. The results of this command are shown in screen 5. Notice that the INTO option shows as much of the customer record as will fit on a single line, followed by an ellipsis (…) to indicate that not all of the data is displayed. Since the &REC variable was named on this option, the INTO area is 118 bytes long.

To change the data in the customer record so it can be updated, you can use one of two techniques. First, if the data you want to change appears in the INTO option of the READ command, you can start by replacing the READ command with a REWRITE command as shown in screen 6. Notice that the &REC variable is named on the FROM option of this command, so the record will be written from the contents of that variable. Then, when you press the Enter key, all of the options and values used by this command are displayed as shown in screen 7. At this point, you can change the value of the FROM option so it contains the updated data. In this example, the first name has been changed. When you press the Enter key again, the record is rewritten and the results are displayed as shown in screen 8.

If the data you want to change doesn't appear on the screen, you can press PF5 to display the Variables panel. Then, you can place the cursor under the variable that contains the data you want to modify (in this case, &REC), and press the Enter key. When you do, the data is displayed in another panel where you can edit it. When you're done, you can return to the panel that shows the results of the READ command, change the command to REWRITE, and press the Enter key. Then, a panel like the one in screen 6 is displayed. In this case, though, since you've already changed the value of the &REC variable, the FROM option will display the new data. So you can just press the Enter key to update the record.

Screen 3

Enter the READ command you want to execute and then press the Enter key. (If a syntax error is detected, CECI will notify you and you can press PF9 to display the error message. Then, you can correct the command and issue it again.)

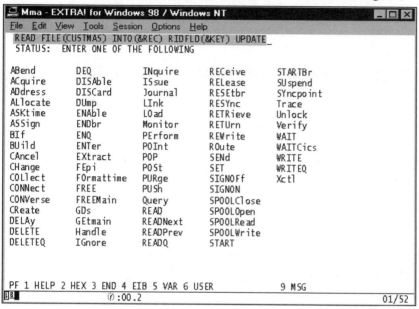

Screen 4

Before it executes the command, CECI verifies the option values. To execute the command, press the Enter key.

```
Mma - EXTRA! for Windows 98 / Windows NT                         _ □ ×
File  Edit  View  Tools  Session  Options  Help
READ FILE(CUSTMAS) INTO(&REC) RIDFLD(&KEY) UPDATE _
STATUS:   ABOUT TO EXECUTE COMMAND                      NAME=
EXEC CICS  READ
  File( 'CUSTMAS ' )
  < SYsid() >
  ( SEt() | Into() )
  < Length() >
  RIdfld( '123456' )
  < Keylength() < GEneric > >
  < RBa | RRn | DEBRec | DEBKey >
  < GTeq | Equal >
  < Update < Token() > >




PF 1 HELP 2 HEX 3 END 4 EIB 5 VAR 6 USER 7 SBH 8 SFH 9 MSG 10 SB 11 SF
▊▊                  (:00.1                                          01/53
```

Figure 6-11   A CECI session that reads and rewrites a record in the customer master file
                (part 2 of 4)

Screen 5

CECI executes the READ command and displays the result.

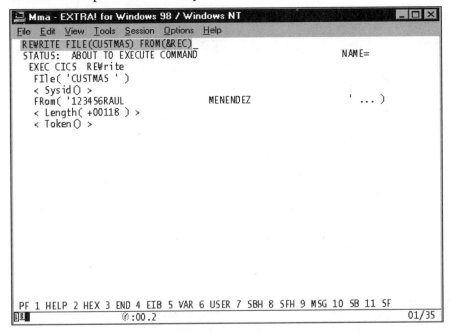

Screen 6

To update the record just read, type a REWRITE command over the READ command and press the Enter key.

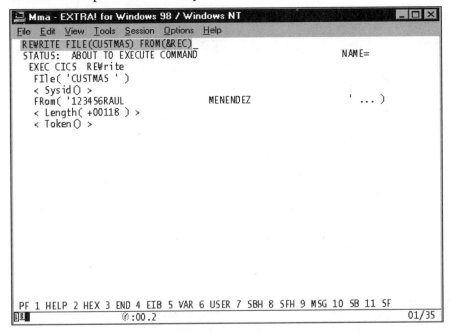

Figure 6-11   A CECI session that reads and rewrites a record in the customer master file (part 3 of 4)

Screen 7

When CECI confirms the command, change the data to be rewritten and press the
Enter key. CECI confirms the command again. Press the Enter key to execute the
command.

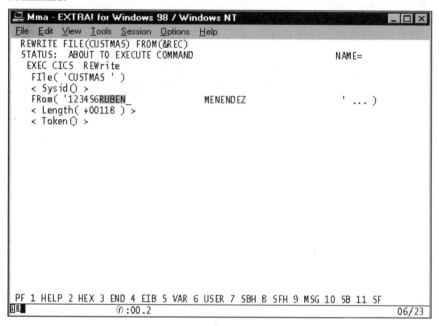

Screen 8

CECI executes the REWRITE command and displays the results. To end CECI,
press PF3.

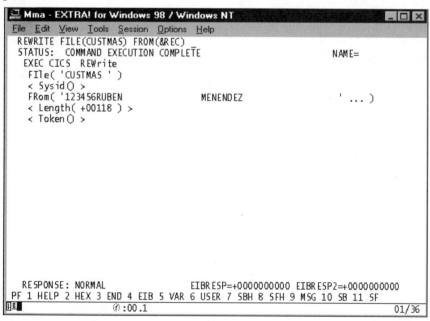

Figure 6-11   A CECI session that reads and rewrites a record in the customer master file
(part 4 of 4)

Perspective

The main purpose of this chapter has been to introduce you to the basic techniques for testing CICS programs. In particular, I hope this chapter has convinced you that the best and most efficient way to test a program is from the top down. To do that, you need to start by planning the coding and testing sequence. If you do, I think you'll find that testing is more manageable and that, most importantly, your programs will contain fewer bugs. Keep in mind, though, that testing procedures and techniques vary greatly from one installation to another. So you'll want to be sure to find out what's required at your installation.

Terms

unit test
concurrency test
integration test
regression test
CICS test region
top-down coding and testing
top-down testing
test plan
program stub
dummy module
IDCAMS (AMS)
DITTO
sign on transaction (CESN)
sign off transaction (CESF)
master terminal transaction (CEMT)
command-level interpreter (CECI)

Section 3

Other CICS programming essentials

The chapters in this section expand on the CICS concepts, commands, and techniques you learned in the first two sections of this book. In chapter 7, you'll learn how to use the services provided by temporary storage control to store data between executions of a pseudo-conversational program. In chapter 8, you'll learn about some additional CICS commands and programming techniques that you'll use in many of the programs you develop. And in chapter 9, you'll learn how to debug a CICS abend. Because these chapters are independent of each other, you can read them in any sequence you like.

7

How to use temporary storage control

In the maintenance program in chapter 5, you saw how to use the communication area to save data between executions of a pseudo-conversational program. Another way to save data between program executions is to store it in a temporary storage queue using temporary storage control services. That's what you'll learn to do in this chapter.

Temporary storage queue concepts

CICS provides an area called *temporary storage* that programs can use to store data temporarily. Temporary storage is divided into one or more *temporary storage queues*, or just *TS queues*. Each TS queue contains one or more *records*, as illustrated by the two queues shown in figure 7-1. As you can see, each record, or *item*, is assigned an *item number*. You can use these item numbers to retrieve and update specific records.

Although TS queues contain records, you shouldn't think of those records in file processing terms. Usually, a TS queue consists of just one record as illustrated by the first queue in this figure. Later in this chapter, you'll see how a queue like this can be used in the customer maintenance program.

Occasionally, you may need to use a queue that holds more than one record like the second one shown in this figure. This queue consists of four records, each of which contains information for a customer invoice. In chapter 17, you'll learn how you might use a queue like this to hold data from a DB2 table between program executions.

Each temporary storage queue is identified by a unique *queue name* (sometimes called a *data-id*). To ensure that TS queue names are unique, you can use the value in the terminal identification field of the EIB, EIBTRMID, as part of the queue name. Since each terminal-id within a CICS system is unique, queue names based on EIBTRMID are also unique. However, if your shop has other standards for creating queue names, by all means follow them.

Although CICS provides a *Temporary Storage Table* (*TST*) where you can define TS queues, you usually don't need to do that. Instead, you can let CICS create queues dynamically. Then, when an application program tries to write a record using a queue name that doesn't exist, temporary storage control creates a new TS queue. The only time you need to define a queue in the TST is if you want it to be recoverable, which is unusual.

An application program can retrieve records from a temporary storage queue either sequentially or randomly. Because most applications need only one record, you'll typically use random retrieval, specifying item 1. An application program can also rewrite a record in a TS queue. That's a common requirement for pseudo-conversational programs.

By default, TS queues are maintained in a single VSAM entry-sequenced file called the *temporary storage file*, or *DFHTEMP*. That's an efficient way to store data between executions of a pseudo-conversational program because it doesn't tie up system resources like the communication area does. In cases where you want to store and retrieve a temporary storage record within a single task execution, however, the additional overhead of disk processing can be a drawback. In that case, you can store a TS queue in main storage. Because main storage is a critical resource in a CICS system, however, you'll want to use it only when absolutely necessary.

A temporary storage queue that holds a single customer record

Item no.	Record
1	123456RAUL MENENDEZ 888 CICS WAY ...

A temporary storage queue that holds data for multiple customer invoices

Item no.	Record
1	118736493847349211/07/2000000026731
2	119203493847370512/28/2000000008973
3	119531493847398301/23/2001000011250
4	120082493847403102/07/2001000038289

Description

- CICS *temporary storage* is divided into one or more *temporary storage queues*, or just *TS queues*. Each TS queue contains one or more *records*, or *items*, that contain data stored by application programs.

- A temporary storage queue is identified by a unique one- to eight-character *queue name*, or *data-id*. To make sure that a queue name is unique, you can use the terminal-id as part of the name. This information can be found in the EIBTRMID field of the EIB.

- You don't have to define TS queue names in a CICS table. Instead, queues are created dynamically.

- Each record within a TS queue is assigned an *item number*. The first record written to a queue is item 1, the second is item 2, and so on. This item number is not part of the record it's associated with.

- It's uncommon to store more than one record in a TS queue. In most applications, you'll usually store a single record that the next execution of your pseudo-conversational program can retrieve.

- Since CICS automatically assigns an item number to each record you add to a queue, you only need to specify an item number when you retrieve or update a record.

- An application program can retrieve records from a TS queue sequentially or randomly. For sequential retrieval, records are retrieved in item number sequence. For random retrieval, you specify the item number of the record you want to retrieve.

- Normally, temporary storage control maintains TS queues in a single VSAM sequential file called the *temporary storage file*, or *DFHTEMP*. However, a TS queue can also be saved in main storage.

Figure 7-1   Temporary storage queue concepts

How to work with temporary storage queues

You use three CICS commands to work with temporary storage queues. To add or update a record in a queue, you use the WRITEQ TS command. To retrieve a record from a queue, you use the READQ TS command. And to delete a queue, you use the DELETEQ TS command.

How to code the WRITEQ TS command

Figure 7-2 gives the format of the WRITEQ TS command. As you can see, the only two required options are the one that provides the queue name (QUEUE or QNAME) and the one that names the area that the record will be written from (FROM). If you code just these options, a new record is added to the end of the queue and given the next item number in sequence. If the queue that's named doesn't exist, though, CICS creates it first and assigns item number 1 to the new record.

The first example in this figure shows a WRITEQ TS command that adds a record to a queue. Here, the record will be added to the queue whose name is stored in the TS-QUEUE-NAME field. The record itself is written from the field named TS-QUEUE-RECORD.

You can also code the NUMITEMS option when you add a record to a file. Then, CICS will return the number of records in the queue, including the new record, in the field you specify. The program can then use this field when it reads records from the queue to determine how many records are read. Since the queues you use will usually contain a single record, though, you won't use this option often.

To update an existing record in a queue, you include the ITEM option as illustrated in the second example in this figure. The ITEM option gives the item number of the record to be updated. In this case, the item number is stored in a field named TS-ITEM-NUMBER. When you use the ITEM option to update a record, you must also include the REWRITE keyword to indicate that the record is to be rewritten.

When you update a temporary storage record, one of two exceptional conditions can be raised. If you specify a queue that doesn't exist, the QIDERR condition is raised. And if you specify an item number that doesn't exist within the queue, the ITEMERR condition is raised. Note that if you're updating item number 1, the ITEMERR condition is never raised. That's because if item 1 doesn't exist, the queue doesn't exist. So the QIDERR condition is raised instead. You'll usually want to provide for these errors by including the RESP option as shown in this figure. Because there aren't any exceptional conditions that are likely to occur when you issue a WRITEQ TS command to add a record, though, you usually don't include the RESP option on that command.

The syntax of the WRITEQ TS command

```
EXEC CICS
    WRITEQ TS  {QUEUE | QNAME}(queue-name)
                FROM(data-name)
               [ITEM(data-name) REWRITE]
               [NUMITEMS(data-name)]
               [MAIN | AUXILIARY]
END-EXEC
```

Option	Description
QUEUE/ QNAME	Specifies the name of the temporary storage queue where data is written. With QUEUE, the name can be 1 to 8 characters. With QNAME, it can be 1 to 16 characters. QNAME is supported by CICS TS version 1.3 and higher.
FROM	Specifies the name of the data area that contains the record to be written.
ITEM	Specifies the item number of the record to be updated. Must be a binary halfword.
REWRITE	Indicates that an existing record in the temporary storage queue should be updated.
NUMITEMS	Specifies the name of a data area where CICS will place the number of records in the temporary storage queue after a new record is added. Must be a binary halfword.
MAIN	Indicates that the temporary storage queue will reside in main storage.
AUXILIARY	Indicates that the temporary storage queue will reside on disk in the temporary storage file (DFHTEMP).

A WRITEQ TS command that adds a record to a temporary storage queue

```
EXEC CICS
    WRITEQ TS QUEUE(TS-QUEUE-NAME)
              FROM(TS-QUEUE-RECORD)
END-EXEC.
```

A WRITEQ TS command that updates an existing record in a temporary storage queue

```
EXEC CICS
    WRITEQ TS QUEUE(TS-QUEUE-NAME)
              FROM(TS-QUEUE-RECORD)
              ITEM(TS-ITEM-NUMBER) REWRITE
              RESP(RESPONSE-CODE)
END-EXEC.
```

Description

- The WRITEQ TS command adds a record to a temporary storage queue or updates an existing record in a temporary storage queue.
- To add a record, you code just the QUEUE or QNAME and FROM options on the WRITEQ TS command. If a queue with the name you specify already exists, the data in the field you name on the FROM option is written in a new record at the end of that queue. Otherwise, CICS creates the queue and adds the data as its first record.
- To update a record, you include the ITEM option with the REWRITE keyword. Then, if the record with the number you specify exists, it's updated with the data in the field you name on the FROM option. If the item number doesn't exist, the ITEMERR exceptional condition is raised. If the queue itself doesn't exist, the QIDERR condition is raised.

Figure 7-2   How to code the WRITEQ TS command

The last option you can code is the one that indicates whether the queue is stored in main storage or on disk. The default is AUXILIARY, which indicates that the queue will be stored on disk. If you want to store the queue in main storage, you specify the MAIN option. Note that you need to code this option only when you write the first record to the queue. In other words, you code it on the command that creates the queue. You don't need to code it for queues that already exist.

How to code the READQ TS command

Figure 7-3 presents the READQ TS command. You use this command to retrieve a record from a temporary storage queue. The command in this figure, for example, will retrieve the record whose item number is stored in the TS-ITEM-NUMBER field. After it retrieves the record, it will store it in the TS-QUEUE-RECORD field as specified by the INTO option. Notice that the RESP option is also included on this command. That's because, like the WRITEQ TS command, both the ITEMERR and the QIDERR conditions can occur if the item number or the queue doesn't exist.

Because this command includes the ITEM option, the record is retrieved from the queue on a random basis. If a queue contains more than one record, however, you may want to retrieve them sequentially. To do that, you use the NEXT option instead of the ITEM option as illustrated by the second example in this figure.

You may also want to use the NUMITEMS option with sequential retrieval to determine how many records the queue contains. If you do that, though, keep in mind that you won't know how many records there are until after you issue the first READQ TS command. Because of that, you may want to code the NUMITEMS option on the WRITEQ TS command instead. Then, if you save the record count between program executions, the program can use it to determine how many records to read.

If you read records from a queue sequentially, you should realize that *any* task in a CICS system can affect the positioning of a READQ TS command. So if your task is reading queue records sequentially while another task is retrieving records from the same queue, your program won't work properly. Normally, this isn't a problem because a typical queue has a unique name that's used only by a single task.

If your application requires that two or more tasks have access to a common TS queue, you'll need to use two other CICS commands: ENQ and DEQ. You use the ENQ command to reserve a queue for exclusive use so that other tasks can't access it at the same time. And you use the DEQ command to release the queue when you're done so other tasks can access it. Because it's not common for several tasks to share access to a TS queue, I won't say any more about the ENQ and DEQ commands here. For additional information on these commands, see chapter 18.

The syntax of the READQ TS command

```
EXEC CICS
    READQ TS  {QUEUE | QNAME}(queue-name)
               INTO(data-name)
              [ITEM(data-name | literal) | NEXT]
              [NUMITEMS(data-name)]
END-EXEC
```

Option	Description
QUEUE/ QNAME	Specifies the name of the temporary storage queue that contains the data to be read. With QUEUE, the name can be 1 to 8 characters. With QNAME, it can be 1 to 16 characters. QNAME is supported by CICS TS version 1.3 and higher.
INTO	Specifies the name of the data area where the record will be placed.
ITEM	Specifies the item number of the record to be read. Must be numeric. If you use a data name, it must be a binary halfword.
NEXT	Indicates that the next record in sequence should be read.
NUMITEMS	Specifies the name of a data area where CICS will place the number of records in the temporary storage queue. Must be a binary halfword.

A READQ TS command that reads a record randomly

```
EXEC CICS
    READQ TS QUEUE(TS-QUEUE-NAME)
             INTO(TS-QUEUE-RECORD)
             ITEM(TS-ITEM-NUMBER)
             RESP(RESPONSE-CODE)
END-EXEC.
```

A READQ TS command that reads the next record

```
EXEC CICS
    READQ TS QUEUE(TS-QUEUE-NAME)
             INTO(TS-QUEUE-RECORD) NEXT
END-EXEC.
```

Description

- The READQ TS command retrieves a record from a temporary storage queue. If you specify the item number of the record to be read, that item is retrieved randomly. Otherwise, the next record in sequence is retrieved.

- If you specify an item number and a record with that number doesn't exist, the ITEMERR exceptional condition occurs. If the queue itself doesn't exist, the QIDERR condition occurs.

- Any task in a CICS system can affect the positioning of a sequential READQ TS command. If the queue has a unique name that includes the terminal-id, though, this shouldn't be a problem.

- If you need to insure that two or more tasks don't access the same queue at the same time, you can use the CICS ENQ command to reserve the queue exclusively. When you're done, you can use the CICS DEQ command to release the queue so other tasks can access it.

Figure 7-3   How to code the READQ TS command

How to code the DELETEQ TS command

Figure 7-4 gives the format of the DELETEQ TS command. You issue this command to delete a TS queue when you're finished processing it. If you don't, the queue remains indefinitely, wasting valuable disk or main storage space. Note that the DELETEQ TS command deletes an entire TS queue; there's no way to delete a single record. Since most queues contain just one record anyway, that shouldn't be a problem.

If you try to delete a queue that doesn't exist, the QIDERR condition is raised. As a result, you may want to code the RESP option to provide for this condition so your program doesn't abend. Even if you code this option, though, you can usually ignore the QIDERR condition if it occurs since you're trying to delete the queue anyway.

The syntax of the DELETEQ TS command

```
EXEC CICS
    DELETEQ TS {QUEUE | QNAME}(queue-name)
END-EXEC
```

Option	Description
QUEUE/ QNAME	Specifies the name of the temporary storage queue to be deleted. With QUEUE, the name can be 1 to 8 characters. With QNAME, it can be 1 to 16 characters. QNAME is supported by CICS TS version 1.3 and higher.

A DELETEQ TS command that deletes a temporary storage queue

```
EXEC CICS
    DELETEQ TS QUEUE(TS-QUEUE-NAME)
               RESP(RESPONSE-CODE)
END-EXEC.
```

Description

- The DELETEQ TS command deletes the temporary storage queue you specify. If the queue you name doesn't exist, the QIDERR exceptional condition occurs.

- If you don't delete a temporary storage queue when you're done with it, it remains in disk or main storage indefinitely.

- You can use the DELETEQ TS command only to delete an entire queue. You can't delete individual records from a queue.

Figure 7-4   How to code the DELETEQ TS command

A maintenance program that uses a temporary storage queue

Figure 7-5 presents the COBOL code for a customer maintenance program that uses a temporary storage queue instead of the communication area to store the current customer record between program executions. Because the specifications and design for this program are the same as for the maintenance program you saw in chapter 5, I won't present them again here. In addition, I'll only present the code that directly relates to using the temporary storage queue. The remaining code is identical to the code in chapter 5.

In the Working-Storage Section, notice that the customer record has been removed from the definition of the communication area. However, the customer number is still included in this area because it's used as a control field.

Working storage also includes an 01-level item that contains definitions for all the fields that will be used to process the temporary storage queue. TS-QUEUE-NAME provides the name of the queue. In this case, the first four bytes of the name will contain the terminal-id, and the second four bytes contain the trans-id for the transaction associated with the program (MNT3).

Next, TS-ITEM-NUMBER identifies the queue record to be processed. Because this queue will always contain just one record, this field is given an initial value of 1. Finally, the field named TS-CUSTOMER-RECORD will hold the record that's read from the queue, which will contain a copy of the data in the current customer record.

In procedure 0000, you can see the statement that retrieves the terminal-id from the Execute Interface Block and stores it in the terminal-id field of the queue name. Then, when the user starts the program for the first time, the program moves Low-Value to TS-CUSTOMER-RECORD and issues a WRITEQ TS command to write a blank record to the queue. Since the queue doesn't exist yet, this command creates it. Then, when the user ends the program by pressing PF3 or by pressing PF12 while the key map is displayed, the program issues a DELETEQ TS command to delete the queue (see page 2 of this listing).

In procedure 1200, you can see new statements that update the customer number field in the communication area. That way, other procedures that need access to the customer number don't have to read the TS queue to get it.

The rest of the shaded elements in this figure show how the program saves and retrieves the customer record in the temporary storage queue (see page 3). In procedure 1300, a WRITEQ TS command writes the current customer record to the queue, where it can be retrieved in the next execution of the program. This command includes the ITEM option with the REWRITE keyword so that the existing record will always be updated.

Procedures 3000 and 4000 both issue READQ TS commands to retrieve the saved customer record from the queue after they've read the customer record from the master file for update. Then, the master record is rewritten or deleted only if it's the same as the record that was saved in the queue.

A customer maintenance program that uses temporary storage   Page 1

```
IDENTIFICATION DIVISION.
*
PROGRAM-ID.  CUSTMNT3.
*
ENVIRONMENT DIVISION.
*
DATA DIVISION.
*
WORKING-STORAGE SECTION.
         .
         .
         .
01   COMMUNICATION-AREA.
*
     05  CA-CONTEXT-FLAG              PIC X.
         88  PROCESS-KEY-MAP                 VALUE '1'.
         88  PROCESS-ADD-CUSTOMER            VALUE '2'.
         88  PROCESS-CHANGE-CUSTOMER         VALUE '3'.
         88  PROCESS-DELETE-CUSTOMER         VALUE '4'.
     05  CA-CUSTOMER-NUMBER          PIC X(6).
*
01   TEMPORARY-STORAGE-FIELDS.
*
     05  TS-QUEUE-NAME.
         10  TS-TERMINAL-ID          PIC X(4).
         10  FILLER                  PIC X(4)    VALUE 'MNT3'.
     05  TS-ITEM-NUMBER              PIC S9(4)   COMP  VALUE +1.
     05  TS-CUSTOMER-RECORD.
         10  TS-CUSTOMER-NUMBER      PIC X(6).
         10  FILLER                  PIC X(112).
         .
         .
         .
LINKAGE SECTION.
*
01   DFHCOMMAREA                     PIC X(07).
*
PROCEDURE DIVISION.
*
0000-PROCESS-CUSTOMER-MAINT.
*
     IF EIBCALEN > ZERO
         MOVE DFHCOMMAREA TO COMMUNICATION-AREA
     END-IF.
*
     MOVE EIBTRMID TO TS-TERMINAL-ID.
*
     EVALUATE TRUE
         WHEN EIBCALEN = ZERO
             MOVE LOW-VALUE TO TS-CUSTOMER-RECORD
             EXEC CICS
                 WRITEQ TS QUEUE(TS-QUEUE-NAME)
                           FROM(TS-CUSTOMER-RECORD)
             END-EXEC
             MOVE LOW-VALUE TO MNTMAP1O
             SET SEND-ERASE TO TRUE
             MOVE -1 TO CUSTNO1L
             PERFORM 1500-SEND-KEY-MAP
             SET PROCESS-KEY-MAP TO TRUE
```

Figure 7-5   COBOL code for a maintenance program that uses temporary storage (part 1 of 3)

A customer maintenance program that uses temporary storage   Page 2

```
            WHEN EIBAID = DFHPF3
                EXEC CICS
                    DELETEQ TS QUEUE(TS-QUEUE-NAME)
                END-EXEC
                EXEC CICS
                    XCTL PROGRAM('INVMENU')
                END-EXEC
    *
            WHEN EIBAID = DFHPF12
                IF PROCESS-KEY-MAP
                    EXEC CICS
                        DELETEQ TS QUEUE(TS-QUEUE-NAME)
                    END-EXEC
                    EXEC CICS
                        XCTL PROGRAM('INVMENU')
                    END-EXEC
                ELSE
                .
                .


    1200-EDIT-KEY-DATA.
        .
        .
        IF VALID-DATA
            EVALUATE ACTIONI
                WHEN '1'
                    PERFORM 1300-READ-CUSTOMER-RECORD
                    IF RESPONSE-CODE = DFHRESP(NOTFND)
                        MOVE CM-CUSTOMER-NUMBER TO CA-CUSTOMER-NUMBER
                        MOVE ADD-INSTRUCTION TO INSTR2O
                        SET PROCESS-ADD-CUSTOMER TO TRUE
                        MOVE SPACE TO CUSTOMER-MASTER-RECORD
                    .
                    .

                WHEN '2'
                    PERFORM 1300-READ-CUSTOMER-RECORD
                    IF RESPONSE-CODE = DFHRESP(NORMAL)
                        MOVE CM-CUSTOMER-NUMBER TO CA-CUSTOMER-NUMBER
                        MOVE CHANGE-INSTRUCTION TO INSTR2O
                        SET PROCESS-CHANGE-CUSTOMER TO TRUE
                    .
                    .

                WHEN '3'
                    PERFORM 1300-READ-CUSTOMER-RECORD
                    IF RESPONSE-CODE = DFHRESP(NORMAL)
                        MOVE CM-CUSTOMER-NUMBER TO CA-CUSTOMER-NUMBER
                        MOVE DELETE-INSTRUCTION TO INSTR2O
                        SET PROCESS-DELETE-CUSTOMER TO TRUE
                        MOVE ATTR-PROT TO LNAMEA
                                         FN AMEA
                                         ADDRA
                                         CITYA
                                         STATEA
                                         ZIPCODEA
                    .
                    .
```

Figure 7-5   COBOL code for a maintenance program that uses temporary storage (part 2 of 3)

A customer maintenance program that uses temporary storage   Page 3

```
    1300-READ-CUSTOMER-RECORD.
*
        EXEC CICS
            READ FILE('CUSTMAS')
                 INTO(CUSTOMER-MASTER-RECORD)
                 RIDFLD(CUSTNO1I)
                 RESP(RESPONSE-CODE)
        END-EXEC.
        IF      RESPONSE-CODE NOT = DFHRESP(NORMAL)
            AND RESPONSE-CODE NOT = DFHRESP(NOTFND)
            PERFORM 9999-TERMINATE-PROGRAM
        END-IF.
        IF RESPONSE-CODE = DFHRESP(NORMAL)
            MOVE CUSTOMER-MASTER-RECORD TO TS-CUSTOMER-RECORD
            EXEC CICS
                WRITEQ TS QUEUE(TS-QUEUE-NAME)
                          FROM(TS-CUSTOMER-RECORD)
                          ITEM(TS-ITEM-NUMBER)
                          REWRITE
            END-EXEC
        END-IF.
            .
            .
    3000-PROCESS-CHANGE-CUSTOMER.
*
        PERFORM 2100-RECEIVE-DATA-MAP.
        MOVE CUSTNO2I TO CM-CUSTOMER-NUMBER.
        PERFORM 3100-READ-CUSTOMER-FOR-UPDATE.
        IF RESPONSE-CODE = DFHRESP(NORMAL)
            EXEC CICS
                READQ TS QUEUE(TS-QUEUE-NAME)
                         INTO(TS-CUSTOMER-RECORD)
                         ITEM(TS-ITEM-NUMBER)
            END-EXEC
            IF CUSTOMER-MASTER-RECORD = TS-CUSTOMER-RECORD
                PERFORM 3200-REWRITE-CUSTOMER-RECORD
            .
            .
    4000-PROCESS-DELETE-CUSTOMER.
*
        MOVE CA-CUSTOMER-NUMBER TO CM-CUSTOMER-NUMBER.
        PERFORM 3100-READ-CUSTOMER-FOR-UPDATE.
        IF RESPONSE-CODE = DFHRESP(NORMAL)
            EXEC CICS
                READQ TS QUEUE(TS-QUEUE-NAME)
                         INTO(TS-CUSTOMER-RECORD)
                         ITEM(TS-ITEM-NUMBER)
            END-EXEC
            IF CUSTOMER-MASTER-RECORD = TS-CUSTOMER-RECORD
                PERFORM 4100-DELETE-CUSTOMER-RECORD
            .
            .
```

Figure 7-5   COBOL code for a maintenance program that uses temporary storage (part 3 of 3)

Perspective

In most cases, you'll use the communication area to save data between executions of a pseudo-conversational program. If the amount of data you need to save is unusually large, though, you may want to store it in a temporary storage queue. Although additional disk access will be required to process the queue, resulting in slower processing, it will make better use of your system's resources by not tying up main memory.

You may also want to use temporary storage if you need to save a variable number of records between program executions. When you browse data in a DB2 table, for example, you can store all of the records related to a single browse operation in a temporary storage queue. If you want to learn more about browsing DB2 data in a CICS program, you can read chapter 17.

Terms

temporary storage
temporary storage queue
TS queue
record
item
item number
queue name
data-id
Temporary Storage Table (TST)
temporary storage file (DFHTEMP)

8

Additional CICS commands and programming techniques

This chapter builds on the programming basics you learned in the first two sections of this book. In particular, it presents the additional coding elements and techniques that you'll use in almost every program you write. You'll see many of these elements and techniques illustrated in the complete application that's presented in the next section of this book.

Terminal handling techniques

Among the most challenging aspects of learning CICS is mastering the techniques for interacting with the terminal user in an efficient way. How do you control the position of the cursor on the screen? How do you change the attributes of individual screen fields to highlight errors? What is the most efficient way to send data to the terminal? How do you edit numeric input data? In the topics that follow, I'll present the techniques you use to solve these basic problems.

How to position the cursor

Whenever you issue a SEND MAP command, you should make sure that the cursor is positioned properly. By default, CICS places the cursor in the top left corner of the screen. Then, the user must press the Tab key to move the cursor to the first data entry field. To save the user this keystroke, your program should place the cursor in the first data entry field. Beyond that, if your program detects an entry error, it should place the cursor in the field that's in error.

Figure 8-1 presents three techniques you can use to set the cursor position. First, if a map contains a single entry field, you can specify the IC option in the DFHMDF macro for that field. You saw this technique used in the customer inquiry map in chapter 2. For maps with more than one entry field, however, the IC technique isn't flexible enough. So you'll need to use one of the other two techniques: direct or symbolic cursor positioning.

To use *direct cursor positioning*, you include the CURSOR option on the SEND MAP command with a cursor position. Note that this cursor position is a displacement from the start of the screen, not a row/column address, so you have to calculate the value. Then, you can code the displacement directly in the CURSOR option, as shown in this figure. Or, you can move the value to a binary halfword field (PIC S9(4) COMP) that's specified in the CURSOR option.

Direct cursor positioning has two major drawbacks. First, cursor displacements are awkward to use. Second, and perhaps more important, direct cursor positioning ties your program to specific screen locations. So, if you change your mapset by moving a field from one screen location to another, you have to change your program as well.

Symbolic cursor positioning is much more flexible. With this technique, you move -1 to the corresponding length field in the symbolic map to tell CICS to move the cursor to that field. Then, you issue a SEND MAP command with the CURSOR option, but without a displacement value. You saw an example of this in the maintenance program in chapter 5. Note that if you move -1 to more than one length field, the cursor is positioned at the first field containing -1. So, when you edit data entry fields, it's common to move -1 to the length fields of all input fields that are invalid. That way, the cursor will be positioned at the start of the first field that's in error.

How to use the IC option in the DFHMDF macro for a field

```
CUSTNO    DFHMDF POS=(2,26),                                    X
                 LENGTH=6,                                      X
                 ATTRB=(NORM,UNPROT,IC),                        X
                 COLOR=TURQUOISE,                               X
                 INITIAL='_____'
```

- When you issue a SEND MAP command, CICS positions the cursor in the field defined with the IC (initial cursor) attribute. If you specify IC for more than one map field, CICS positions the cursor in the last one on the screen.

How to use direct cursor positioning

```
EXEC CICS
    SEND MAP('MNTMAP1')
         MAPSET('MNTSET1')
         FROM(MNTMAP1O)
         CURSOR(346)
END-EXEC.
```

- The CURSOR value specifies a screen position that represents a displacement from the start of the screen. For a 24x80 screen, it must be a number from 0 to 1919, where 0 is row 1/column 1 and 1919 is row 24/column 80. To calculate the displacement for a screen position, use this formula:

```
(Row-number - 1) x 80 + (Column-number - 1) = Displacement
```

How to use symbolic cursor positioning

```
MOVE -1 TO CUSTNO1L.

EXEC CICS
    SEND MAP('MNTMAP1')
         MAPSET('MNTSET1')
         FROM(MNTMAP1O)
         CURSOR
END-EXEC.
```

- When you issue the SEND MAP command with a CURSOR option that has no displacement value, CICS positions the cursor in the field whose length field (suffix L) in the symbolic map has a value of -1. If you move -1 to more than one length field, CICS positions the cursor in the first one on the screen.

Description

- *Symbolic cursor positioning* is the most flexible technique for positioning the cursor. Coding the IC option doesn't work well unless there's only one data entry field on the screen. And *direct cursor positioning* (1) forces you to work with displacement values and (2) ties the cursor position to specific screen locations.
- You can check the Execute Interface Block field EIBCPOSN if you need to know the position of the cursor when the user pressed an attention key. It contains the cursor displacement from the start of the screen.

Figure 8-1   How to position the cursor

It is also sometimes useful to know where the cursor was positioned when the user pressed an attention key. This information is made available to your program through the EIBCPOSN field in the Execute Interface Block. This field is a halfword binary item that contains the cursor displacement from the start of the screen. So, you'll have to do some simple calculations to interpret its value properly. Like EIBAID, EIBCPOSN is updated at the start of the task, so you don't have to issue a RECEIVE MAP command before using it.

How to modify field attributes

As you already know, the symbolic map definition for each screen field includes an attribute byte field. And if your BMS mapset includes DSATTS and MAPATTS parameters to specify extended color or highlighting, the symbolic map will also include fields to record these attributes. Before you issue a SEND MAP command, you can move a new value to any of these attribute fields so they will be applied to the data that's displayed on the screen.

You saw a good example of the use of this technique in the customer maintenance program in chapter 5. In that program, several of the fields in the data map are defined as unprotected so the user can enter data for an addition or a change. For a deletion, however, those fields should be protected since it doesn't make sense to let the user change them. So the program sets the attribute bytes for those fields to protected whenever it displays the map for a customer to be deleted.

You'll also want to change the attribute bytes for fields that contain invalid data to highlight those fields on the screen. But setting the attribute values isn't always enough. That's because there are three possible sources for field attributes: the symbolic map, the physical map, and the terminal itself. So the option you specify on the SEND MAP command also plays a part.

The table at the top of figure 8-2 summarizes where the attributes come from depending on the attribute field setting and the SEND MAP option. Basically, any time you issue a SEND MAP command with the MAPONLY option, the attributes for every screen field are set to those specified in the physical map; any attribute values in the symbolic map are ignored. On the other hand, if you move a value to an attribute field in the symbolic map and issue a SEND MAP command without the MAPONLY option, that value is used as the attribute setting for the field.

The only exception is when you move Low-Value to an attribute field. Then, if you code DATAONLY, the attributes currently on the screen will remain unchanged, since low values aren't sent to the terminal. If you don't code DATAONLY, the attributes specified in the physical map will be used.

One way to set an attribute field in the symbolic map is to move a literal value to it, as shown in the first Move statement in this figure. Here, the letter *Q* is the EBCDIC character for the bit combination that specifies the unprotected, numeric, and bright attributes. The only problem with this method is that you have to know the EBCDIC character for each attribute combination you need to use. And since not all attribute combinations have an EBCDIC equivalent, you can't code all attribute fields this way.

How screen attributes are modified

If an attribute field is	And this SEND MAP option is used	The screen attribute is
Set to anything other than Low-Value	MAPONLY DATAONLY None	Changed to physical map settings Changed to new symbolic map settings Changed to new symbolic map settings
Set to Low-Value	MAPONLY DATAONLY None	Changed to physical map settings Unchanged (the terminal settings remain in effect) Changed to physical map settings
Unchanged	MAPONLY DATAONLY None	Changed to physical map settings Unchanged (the terminal settings remain in effect) Changed to physical map settings

Data name suffixes for attribute fields in the symbolic map

Suffix	Usage	Example
A	A one-character field that contains the attribute byte for output operations. Occupies the same storage location as the F (flag) field.	CUSTNOA
C	A one-character field that contains the attribute for extended color. Generated only if DSATTS=COLOR is specified in the mapset.	MSGC
H	A one-character field that contains the attribute for extended highlighting. Generated only if DSATTS=HILIGHT is specified in the mapset.	INVNOH

Move statements that change the attributes of three fields

```
MOVE 'Q'          TO CUSTNOA.
MOVE ATTR-RED     TO MSGC.
MOVE ATTR-REVERSE TO INVNOH.
```

Description

- You can control a screen field's attributes by moving new hex values to its attribute fields in the symbolic map and issuing the SEND MAP command without the MAPONLY option.

- Some hex values have EBCDIC equivalents that you can use to set attributes. But most shops provide copy members with data names for common attribute combinations (see figure 8-3). Then, you simply move the appropriate data name to an attribute field.

- Low values are never sent to the screen. So if an attribute field is set to Low-Value, the screen attributes will remain unchanged when the DATAONLY option is used in the SEND MAP command. If it's not used, the physical map settings take effect.

- If the user clears a field on the screen, its flag field in the symbolic map (suffix F) is set to hex 80. Because this field occupies the same byte of storage as the attribute byte field (suffix A), you must set it to Low-Value or a valid attribute byte value before issuing a SEND MAP command or the results will be unpredictable.

- To reset screen attributes to their original values, move those values to the attribute fields in the symbolic map and issue a SEND MAP command with the DATAONLY option.

Figure 8-2   How to modify field attributes

To make it easier for you to modify attribute fields, most shops provide a copy member similar to the one in figure 8-3. As you can see, each attribute combination has a meaningful name. For example, the name for unprotected, numeric, and bright is ATTR-UNPROT-NUM-BRT. Then, to change an attribute, you simply move the correct value to the attribute field. For example,

```
MOVE ATTR-PROT TO CUSTNOA
```

changes the attribute byte for the customer number field to protected.

This copy member includes definitions for extended highlighting and color attribute values as well, making it just as easy to change those attributes. For example, if the user enters invalid data into the LNAME field, you can highlight the field with reverse video using use a Move statement like this one:

```
MOVE ATTR-REVERSE TO LNAMEH
```

Once you've changed an attribute value, you must be able to restore it to its original value. You can do this in several ways. One method is to send the map with the MAPONLY option, so the field attributes are restored from the physical map. However, since the labels and constant data in the physical map are sent as well, this is inefficient. Another method is to move Low-Value to the symbolic map and issue a SEND MAP command without the DATAONLY or MAPONLY option. This has the same inefficiency as the first method, however, so we don't recommend it.

The third technique is to move the original values to the attribute fields in the symbolic map and issue a SEND MAP command with the DATAONLY option. That way, the attribute fields in the symbolic map will be sent to the terminal. For efficiency reasons, this is usually the best technique.

Incidentally, there is a peculiar problem that often arises because of the way the symbolic map is structured. As you know, this map includes a flag field (suffix F) that indicates whether or not the user has cleared the field. If the user has not modified the field, the flag field contains hexadecimal 00 (Low-Value). However, if the user modified the field by erasing it, the flag field is set to hexadecimal 80.

Unfortunately, the flag field occupies the same storage position as the attribute byte field. So if the user clears a field, hex 80 will be placed in the attribute byte field when you issue a RECEIVE MAP command. If you then issue a SEND MAP command without replacing this hex 80 with Low-Value or a valid attribute byte, the results will be unpredictable. So be sure to move an attribute byte or Low-Value to each attribute field (or to the entire symbolic map) before you issue a SEND MAP command.

A typical copy member for attribute definitions

```
01   ATTRIBUTE-DEFINITIONS.
*STANDARD ATTRIBUTES*
     05   ATTR-UNPROT                    PIC X   VALUE ' '.
     05   ATTR-UNPROT-MDT                PIC X   VALUE X'C1'.
     05   ATTR-UNPROT-BRT                PIC X   VALUE X'C8'.
     05   ATTR-UNPROT-BRT-MDT            PIC X   VALUE X'C9'.
     05   ATTR-UNPROT-DARK               PIC X   VALUE X'4C'.
     05   ATTR-UNPROT-DARK-MDT           PIC X   VALUE X'4D'.
     05   ATTR-UNPROT-NUM                PIC X   VALUE X'50'.
     05   ATTR-UNPROT-NUM-MDT            PIC X   VALUE X'D1'.
     05   ATTR-UNPROT-NUM-BRT            PIC X   VALUE X'D8'.
     05   ATTR-UNPROT-NUM-BRT-MDT        PIC X   VALUE X'D9'.
     05   ATTR-UNPROT-NUM-DARK           PIC X   VALUE X'5C'.
     05   ATTR-UNPROT-NUM-DARK-MDT       PIC X   VALUE X'5D'.
     05   ATTR-PROT                      PIC X   VALUE X'60'.
     05   ATTR-PROT-MDT                  PIC X   VALUE X'61'.
     05   ATTR-PROT-BRT                  PIC X   VALUE X'E8'.
     05   ATTR-PROT-BRT-MDT              PIC X   VALUE X'E9'.
     05   ATTR-PROT-DARK                 PIC X   VALUE '%'.
     05   ATTR-PROT-DARK-MDT             PIC X   VALUE X'6D'.
     05   ATTR-PROT-SKIP                 PIC X   VALUE X'F0'.
     05   ATTR-PROT-SKIP-MDT             PIC X   VALUE X'F1'.
     05   ATTR-PROT-SKIP-BRT             PIC X   VALUE X'F8'.
     05   ATTR-PROT-SKIP-BRT-MDT         PIC X   VALUE X'F9'.
     05   ATTR-PROT-SKIP-DARK            PIC X   VALUE X'7C'.
     05   ATTR-PROT-SKIP-DARK-MDT        PIC X   VALUE X'7D'.
*EXTENDED HIGHLIGHTING*
     05   ATTR-NO-HIGHLIGHT              PIC X   VALUE X'00'.
     05   ATTR-BLINK                     PIC X   VALUE '1'.
     05   ATTR-REVERSE                   PIC X   VALUE '2'.
     05   ATTR-UNDERSCORE                PIC X   VALUE '4'.
*EXTENDED COLOR*
     05   ATTR-DEFAULT-COLOR             PIC X   VALUE X'00'.
     05   ATTR-BLUE                      PIC X   VALUE '1'.
     05   ATTR-RED                       PIC X   VALUE '2'.
     05   ATTR-PINK                      PIC X   VALUE '3'.
     05   ATTR-GREEN                     PIC X   VALUE '4'.
     05   ATTR-TURQUOISE                 PIC X   VALUE '5'.
     05   ATTR-YELLOW                    PIC X   VALUE '6'.
     05   ATTR-NEUTRAL                   PIC X   VALUE '7'.
```

Notes

- Attribute values can be given in hex codes or EBCDIC characters as shown in the copy member above.

- IBM also supplies a standard copy member, named DFHBMSCA, that defines many attribute settings. However, the names it uses are cryptic, it doesn't include some of the most commonly used attribute settings, and the definitions it does include are rarely used.

Figure 8-3   A typical copy member for attribute settings

How to optimize data transmission

Optimizing data transmission can have a measurable effect on efficiency in a CICS system...more so, in fact, than any technique other than pseudo-conversational programming. In general, you can optimize data transmission at two levels, as described in figure 8-4.

The first is to optimize data that is sent from your program to the terminal. For example, suppose a user running a data entry program enters data for 15 fields. When the user presses the Enter key, the data for all 15 fields is sent to the program and edited. If the program detects an error in one of the fields, is it necessary to send all 15 fields back to the terminal? Of course not. Instead, the program should send just the error message and the attributes necessary to highlight the field that's in error.

The techniques for minimizing data sent to the terminal are relatively straightforward. To start, you should use the DATAONLY option of the SEND MAP command whenever you send data using a map that's already on the screen. If your program uses only one map, that means you'll specify DATAONLY for all but the first SEND MAP command. If your program uses more than one map, however, you'll have to send both the physical and the symbolic map whenever the display changes from one map to another. But whenever you redisplay the same map (for example, to display an error message), you should specify DATAONLY. You'll see this technique used throughout the programs in this book.

In addition, you should move Low-Value to map fields that are already on the screen, since low values are never transmitted to the terminal. This is illustrated by the sample code in this figure, which was taken from the maintenance program in chapter 5. These statements are executed when the program detects an error in one of the two entry fields in the program's key map (CUSTNO1 and ACTION). Just before performing procedure 1500 to send the error message back to the terminal, the program moves Low-Value to these two fields and sets the send flag to SEND-DATAONLY-ALARM. That way, the data for these fields won't be sent back to the terminal, but the error message and attributes set by the edit procedure will.

The second level of optimization is to reduce the amount of data sent to your program when the user presses an attention key. For example, suppose the program detects an error in one of 15 fields and sends an error message back to the terminal. If the user then corrects the field in error and presses the Enter key again, how many of the fields are sent back to the program? Using the techniques presented in this book, all 15 are. That's because the modified data tags of all the fields remain unchanged from the last interaction. It's possible to eliminate this inefficiency by using the techniques summarized in this figure. But to be honest, these techniques are complicated and often not worth the effort. So unless your shop standards say otherwise, you should just concentrate on minimizing the amount of data that's sent from your program to the terminal.

How to minimize the data that's sent from your program to the terminal

- Use the DATAONLY option of the SEND MAP command whenever you send data using a map that's already on the screen.
- Move Low-Value to symbolic map fields that are already present on the screen and should remain unchanged.

Example

```
            .
            .
      MOVE LOW-VALUE TO CUSTNO1O
                       ACTIONO
      SET SEND-DATAONLY-ALARM TO TRUE
      PERFORM 1500-SEND-KEY-MAP
            .
            .
  1500-SEND-KEY-MAP.
*
      EVALUATE TRUE
            .
            .
      WHEN SEND-DATAONLY-ALARM
          EXEC CICS
              SEND MAP('MNTMAP1')
                   MAPSET('MNTSET1')
                   FROM(MNTMAP1O)
                   DATAONLY
                   ALARM
                   CURSOR
          END-EXEC
      END-EVALUATE.
```

How to minimize the data that's sent to your program when the user presses an attention key

1. Maintain a copy of all the fields on the screen in the communication area.
2. Specify the FRSET option on the SEND MAP command to turn off the modified data tags of all the unprotected fields. (If a field was changed before the last transmission, its MDT remains on so the same data can get transmitted again). If the user changes the field, the MDT will be turned back on, signifying that the new data should be transmitted.
3. When your program issues a RECEIVE MAP command, it must merge the new user entries with the fields saved in the communication area from the previous transmission.

Description

- Next to using pseudo-conversational programming, optimizing data transmission will probably improve overall performance in a CICS system more than any other efficiency technique.
- Minimizing the amount of data that's sent *from* your program to the terminal is fairly straightforward.
- Minimizing the amount of data that's sent *to* your program requires careful, complicated programming. In fact, most shops don't worry about it because the increased efficiency doesn't justify the programmer time needed.

Figure 8-4   How to optimize data transmission

How to identify data entry fields

If you follow the CUA guidelines that were summarized in chapter 4, you'll underline the data entry fields on a map. For terminals that support extended highlighting, you can do that by specifying HILIGHT=UNDERLINE in the DFHMDF macro for a field as shown in the first example in figure 8-5. You saw this technique in the customer maintenance program in chapter 5. The problem with it is that if the terminal doesn't support extended highlighting, the HILIGHT parameter will be ignored.

For terminals that don't support extended highlighting, you can simulate underlining by filling a field with underscores. Although the result is similar to the use of the underline attribute, it's different in that the underscores are a part of the field's contents. When the user types data into the field, the characters entered replace the underscores. Then, when the user presses the Enter key, any underscore characters remaining in the field are transmitted to the program as a part of the data.

To provide underscore characters, you should do the three things shown in the figure. First, you should fill all data entry fields with underscores using the INITIAL parameter of the DFHMDF macro. The exception is if the field won't always be treated as an entry field. In the customer maintenance program, for example, the customer fields that are displayed on the data map are protected for a delete operation, so they shouldn't contain underscores. But they should contain underscores for an add or change operation. In that case, the program will have to fill the fields with underscores when appropriate.

Second, after you issue a RECEIVE MAP command, you must remove any underscores from the data entry fields and replace them with spaces. The easiest way to do that is with an Inspect statement like the first one shown in this figure. Notice that this statement removes underscores from the entire symbolic map. Since the data entry fields are the only fields that will contain underscores, though, the result is the same as removing the underscores from each individual field.

Third, before you send the data back to the terminal, you need to replace any spaces with underscore characters so it will appear underlined on the screen. To do that, you can use another Inspect statement like the second one shown in this figure. Like the first Inspect statement, this statement replaces all spaces in the symbolic map with underscores.

If a program will be run both from terminals that support extended highlighting and terminals that don't, you typically underline data entry fields using underscore characters so the fields will be displayed properly on both types of terminals. If you prefer to, though, you can define the fields with the underline attribute and then use the ASSIGN command in your program to determine if the terminal where the program is running supports extended highlighting. Then, if it doesn't, you can execute the code necessary to add and remove underscores. Since you're not likely to do that, though, I won't present the ASSIGN command in this book. For an explanation of how this command works, please refer to our CICS desk reference book.

How to use extended highlighting to identify entry fields

```
CUSTNO    DFHMDF POS=(5,26),                                      X
                 LENGTH=6,                                        X
                 ATTRB=(NORM,UNPROT,IC),                          X
                 COLOR=TURQUOISE,                                 X
                 HILIGHT=UNDERLINE
```

How to use underscores to identify entry fields on terminals that don't support extended highlighting

How to initialize a field with underscores

```
CUSTNO    DFHMDF POS=(5,26),                                      X
                 LENGTH=6,                                        X
                 ATTRB=(NORM,UNPROT,IC),                          X
                 COLOR=TURQUOISE,                                 X
                 INITIAL='_____'
```

How to replace underscores with spaces after a RECEIVE MAP command

```
INSPECT INQMAP1I
    REPLACING ALL '_' BY SPACE.
```

How to replace spaces with underscores before a SEND MAP command

```
INSPECT INQMAP1I
    REPLACING ALL SPACE BY '_'.
```

Description

- IBM's CUA guidelines state that data entry fields should be clearly identified on the screen with underlines.

- If a terminal supports extending highlighting, entry fields can be identified with the underline attribute.

- If a terminal doesn't support extended highlighting, entry fields should be filled with underscores. The easiest way to do that is to code the INITIAL parameter on the DFHMDF macro for the field as shown above. If the field isn't always treated as a data entry field, however, you can omit this parameter. Then, the program will have to set the field value to underscores when necessary.

- Unlike underlining, underscores are part of a field's contents. So the COBOL program has to remove them from the field when it's processing the data and add them to the field before sending it back to the screen to be displayed.

Figure 8-5   How to identify entry fields

How to edit input data

One of the most important aspects of CICS programming—and one of the most detailed and tedious—is thoroughly editing data entered by the user. For each data entry field, you'll typically need one or more If statements to check for various entry errors. Then, if an error is detected, the program should respond by displaying an error message and highlighting the field in error with reverse video.

Figure 8-6 summarizes some common error conditions your programs should test for. It also gives a sample If statement for each test, except the test for valid numeric data. Because editing numeric data poses a special set of challenges, I'll discuss the requirements in the next topic.

Besides the conditions listed in this figure, certain fields have specific editing requirements. For example, you should test a state code field to be sure it contains a valid state code, and you should test a social security number to make sure the user entered nine digits. In addition, you'll need to test whether related data entry fields agree with one another. For example, you may want to make sure the zip code entered by the user is valid for the state entered.

For all but the simplest programs, you should isolate the editing function in its own procedure following the basic structure given in the figure. A procedure like this starts by resetting the extended highlighting attribute for all screen fields. Then, it uses nested If statements to thoroughly edit the entry fields, including doing any required cross-validation. Normally, it edits the fields from the bottom of the screen to the top. As a result, all of the invalid fields are highlighted, but the error message that's displayed relates to the first invalid field on the screen. The program should invoke a procedure like this after receiving map data, and it should continue processing the data only if the edit procedure detects no errors.

Because each edit condition requires five statements (an If and four Moves), and because a single field often requires multiple checks, edit procedures can easily be hundreds of lines long. But that's okay, as long as the code is straightforward. If the data being edited can be divided into logical groups, though, you may want to code each group in a separate procedure to keep the code more manageable. And, if an edit condition gets complex—requiring table or file lookups, for example—you should code it in a separate procedure to keep the code clear.

Incidentally, you can save a few lines by omitting the Move statement that sets VALID-DATA-SW to N from each If statement. Then, you can test for an error condition by adding code like this to the end of the editing procedure:

```
IF MSGO NOT = LOW-VALUE
    MOVE 'N' TO VALID-DATA-SW.
```

This works because when you issue a RECEIVE MAP command, CICS moves Low-Value to any field in the symbolic map that isn't entered by the user, including protected fields such as the message field. If the edit procedure detects an error, the program moves data into the message field. So a value other than Low-Value means the edit procedure detected an error.

Common field edits

Error condition	COBOL statements to test it
Field was not entered	IF CUSTNOL = ZERO
Field contains spaces	IF CUSTNOI = SPACE
Field is not numeric	(Call appropriate numeric editing routine)
Field is not positive	IF AMOUNTI NOT > ZERO
Field is zero	IF AMOUNTI = ZERO

The general structure of an edit procedure

```
MOVE ATTR-NO-HIGHLIGHT TO extended highlight field for all map fields.

IF error-condition-1 for field-1
    MOVE ATTR-REVERSE  TO extended highlight field for field-1
    MOVE -1            TO length field for field-1
    MOVE error-message TO message field
    MOVE 'N'           TO VALID-DATA-SW
ELSE IF error-condition-2 for field-1
    .

IF error-condition-1 for field-2
    .

IF tests for cross-validation conditions
    .
```

Sample editing code

```
MOVE ATTR-NO-HIGHLIGHT TO ZIPCODEH
                          STATEH.
IF      ZIPCODEI = SPACE
    OR ZIPCODEL = ZERO
    MOVE ATTR-REVERSE TO ZIPCODEH
    MOVE -1 TO ZIPCODEL
    MOVE 'You must enter a zip code.' TO MSG20
    MOVE 'N' TO VALID-DATA-SW
END-IF.
IF      STATEI = SPACE ...
    .
```

Description

- Most CICS programs have to edit data entered by the user to make sure that no fields are missing, that the entries consist of valid data, and that related fields (like state and zip code) have logically related values.

- If the editing is complicated, requiring table or file lookups for example, you can break it down into two or more procedures. In many cases, though, a single procedure is all you need.

- When an error is detected, the edit procedure should do four things: (1) highlight the field by modifying its attributes; (2) move -1 to the length field so the cursor will be placed under the field in error; (3) move an appropriate error message to the message field; and (4) set a switch to indicate that the data is invalid.

- It's common to edit data entry fields from the bottom of the screen to the top. That way, the error message the program displays relates to the first invalid field on the screen.

Figure 8-6   How to edit input data

How to edit numeric input

Editing numeric input data is a bit more challenging than editing alphanumeric input data. You might expect that specifying NUM in the ATTRB parameter of the DFHMDF macro insures that the user can enter only a valid number into a field. Unfortunately, that's not the case. The NUM option does two things. First, it forces the terminal into numeric shift, so the user can type only numbers, the decimal point, and hyphens. However, nothing prevents the user from inadvertently typing two decimal points, or some other invalid combination of numeric characters. Furthermore, the user can easily take the keyboard out of numeric shift and enter alphanumeric data.

Second, the NUM option causes BMS to right-justify data in the field and pad the field on the left with zeros as necessary. This is helpful, unless your program fills the field with underscore characters to mark its location on the screen. Suppose, for example, that the user types the number 123 into a five-byte field that's filled with underscores. In that case, the remaining two underscore characters are treated as part of the data, so right-justification has no effect. Although the user typed the three characters "123," CICS places the five-character value "123__" in the symbolic map input field.

CICS provides no support at all for decimal-aligned input. For example, if you assign a PICIN picture of 9(5)V99 to a field, the user must enter 10000 to obtain a value of 100.00. If the user enters 100, the value 1.00 will be placed in the field. And the user cannot use a decimal point to indicate the decimal position. For example, an entry of 49.95 is invalid.

Because of these problems, most shops have developed specialized routines for editing numeric input data. Typically, these routines are invoked with Call statements or are included in the program with Copy statements. They accept an unedited field as input and evaluate it byte by byte to determine if it contains a valid number. If so, they return an edited field in valid numeric format with an indication that the number is valid. These routines range from simple routines that just check for valid numbers to more complex routines that provide for commas and a decimal.

Figure 8-7 shows how an editing procedure might call a subprogram named NUMEDIT to do a numeric edit. Here, AMOUNT is the BMS map field to be edited. The first If statement in the editing procedure checks to see if the user entered any data by evaluating the length field, AMOUNTL. If so, NUMEDIT is called using AMOUNTI (the unedited data entered by the user), EDITED-AMOUNT (a working-storage field to hold the edited value that NUMEDIT will return), and VALID-AMOUNT-SW (the switch NUMEDIT will return to indicate whether the input was valid). Then, the next two If statements format error messages if the edited amount field is not numeric or not greater than zero.

An edit routine that calls a subprogram to do numeric editing

```
IF AMOUNTL = ZERO
    MOVE ATTR-REVERSE TO AMOUNTH
    MOVE -1 TO AMOUNTL
    MOVE 'You must enter an amount.' TO MSGO
    MOVE 'N' TO VALID-DATA-SW
ELSE
    CALL 'NUMEDIT' USING AMOUNTI
                        EDITED-AMOUNT
                        VALID-AMOUNT-SW
    IF NOT VALID-AMOUNT
        MOVE ATTR-REVERSE TO AMOUNTH
        MOVE -1 TO AMOUNTL
        MOVE 'Amount must be numeric.' TO MSGO
        MOVE 'N' TO VALID-DATA-SW
    ELSE
        IF EDITED-AMOUNT NOT > ZERO
            MOVE ATTR-REVERSE TO AMOUNTH
            MOVE -1 TO AMOUNTL
            MOVE 'Amount must be greater than zero.' TO MSGO
            MOVE 'N' TO VALID-DATA-SW
        END-IF
    END-IF
END-IF.
```

Description

- Numeric data entry errors are common. Even if a field has been defined with the NUM option, a user can enter more than one decimal point or take the keyboard out of numeric shift and enter alphanumeric data.

- CICS doesn't provide features for handling decimal-aligned input. Even if the PICIN picture for a field has an assumed decimal point, the user can't be sure where the decimal will be placed because it doesn't show up on the screen. In addition, if the user enters a value with a decimal point, it's considered invalid.

- Most shops have developed specialized subprograms to handle the complexities of editing numeric data. The fields that are passed to and from these subprograms generally include the input data itself, the edited data produced by the subprogram, and a switch indicating whether or not the subprogram found the data to be valid.

Figure 8-7   How to edit numeric input

Two subprograms that edit numeric data

To help you understand how typical editing routines work, I'll present two subprograms that will be used by the order entry program you'll see in chapter 13. The first one, named INTEDIT, is shown in figure 8-8. It accepts a five-byte alphanumeric field as input, and it returns a five-byte numeric field and a switch that indicates whether or not the input field contained a valid integer.

As you can see, it's a simple program that starts by replacing any leading spaces in the unedited number with zeros. Then, it determines the length of the number by counting all the characters up until the first space. (Remember that if the field was initially filled with underscores, they will have been replaced with spaces when the data was first received in the calling program.) Finally, it uses *reference modification* to determine whether that portion of the unedited number (before the first space) is numeric. If so, it moves that number to a formatted numeric field that's returned to the calling program.

The second editing subprogram, NUMEDIT, is shown in figure 8-9. This program checks a 10-digit alphanumeric entry that may contain a decimal point and returns a decimal-aligned edited number (PIC 9(7)V99) along with a validity switch. Note that although it checks for a decimal point, it doesn't check for commas or any other characters a user might enter into a numeric field. Even so, it's much more complex than the INTEDIT program.

NUMEDIT starts by locating the decimal point in the alphanumeric field that's passed to it. If the field contains a decimal point, it treats the characters on the left of the decimal point as the "integer part" and the numbers to the right of the decimal point as the "decimal part." Then, it checks characters one at a time to be sure they contain numeric data. If so, it moves the characters to working-storage fields named INTEGER-PART and DECIMAL-PART. To facilitate this, UNEDITED-NUMBER, INTEGER-PART, and DECIMAL-PART are all redefined as one-character tables. If the original field doesn't contain a decimal point—in other words, if it's an integer—all of the characters are moved into the INTEGER-PART field. In either case, the program ends by adding the INTEGER-PART and DECIMAL-PART fields together and storing the result in a formatted numeric field that's returned to the calling program.

The INTEDIT subprogram

```
IDENTIFICATION DIVISION.
*
PROGRAM-ID.  INTEDIT.
*
ENVIRONMENT DIVISION.
*
DATA DIVISION.
*
WORKING-STORAGE SECTION.
*
01  WORK-FIELDS.
*
    05  INTEGER-PART        PIC 9(05).
    05  INTEGER-LENGTH      PIC S9(03)  COMP-3.
*
LINKAGE SECTION.
*
01  UNEDITED-NUMBER         PIC X(05).
*
01  EDITED-NUMBER           PIC 9(05).
*
01  VALID-NUMBER-SW         PIC X(01).
    88  VALID-NUMBER            VALUE 'Y'.
*
PROCEDURE DIVISION USING  UNEDITED-NUMBER
                          EDITED-NUMBER
                          VALID-NUMBER-SW.
*
0000-EDIT-NUMBER.
*
    MOVE ZERO TO INTEGER-LENGTH.
    INSPECT UNEDITED-NUMBER
        REPLACING LEADING SPACE BY ZERO.
    INSPECT UNEDITED-NUMBER
        TALLYING INTEGER-LENGTH FOR CHARACTERS
            BEFORE INITIAL SPACE.
    IF UNEDITED-NUMBER(1:INTEGER-LENGTH) NUMERIC
        MOVE UNEDITED-NUMBER(1:INTEGER-LENGTH)
            TO EDITED-NUMBER
        MOVE 'Y' TO VALID-NUMBER-SW
    ELSE
        MOVE 'N' TO VALID-NUMBER-SW
    END-IF.
*
0000-EXIT.
*
    EXIT PROGRAM.
```

Description

- The INTEDIT subprogram checks whether a field contains a valid integer.

- *Reference modification* is used to check the individual characters in a field. The first value in parentheses after the field name specifies which character of the field to start with. It's followed by a colon and a second value that specifies the number of characters you want to work with.

Figure 8-8   The COBOL code for a subprogram that edits integer data

The NUMEDIT subprogram

```
            IDENTIFICATION DIVISION.
            PROGRAM-ID.  NUMEDIT.
       *
            ENVIRONMENT DIVISION.
       *
            DATA DIVISION.
       *
            WORKING-STORAGE SECTION.
       *
            01  WORK-FIELDS.
                05   INTEGER-PART        PIC 9(10).
                05   INTEGER-PART-X      REDEFINES    INTEGER-PART.
                    10   INTEGER-CHAR    PIC X(01)    OCCURS 10.
                05   DECIMAL-PART        PIC V9(10).
                05   DECIMAL-PART-X      REDEFINES    DECIMAL-PART.
                    10   DECIMAL-CHAR    PIC X(01)    OCCURS 10.
                05   DECIMAL-POS         PIC S9(03)   COMP-3.
                05   INTEGER-LENGTH      PIC S9(03)   COMP-3.
                05   INTEGER-SUB         PIC S9(03)   COMP-3.
                05   DECIMAL-SUB         PIC S9(03)   COMP-3.
                05   UNEDIT-SUB          PIC S9(03)   COMP-3.
       *
            LINKAGE SECTION.
       *
            01  UNEDITED-NUMBER.
                05   UNEDITED-CHAR       OCCURS 10    PIC X.
       *
            01  EDITED-NUMBER           PIC 9(07)V99.
       *
            01  VALID-NUMBER-SW         PIC X(01).
                88  VALID-NUMBER         VALUE 'Y'.
       *
            PROCEDURE DIVISION USING UNEDITED-NUMBER
                                     EDITED-NUMBER
                                     VALID-NUMBER-SW.
       *
            0000-EDIT-NUMBER.
       *
                MOVE 'Y' TO VALID-NUMBER-SW.
                MOVE ZERO TO INTEGER-PART
                             DECIMAL-PART
                             DECIMAL-POS.
                INSPECT UNEDITED-NUMBER
                    TALLYING DECIMAL-POS FOR CHARACTERS
                        BEFORE INITIAL '.'.
                IF DECIMAL-POS < 10
                    PERFORM 1000-EDIT-DECIMAL-NUMBER
                ELSE
                    PERFORM 2000-EDIT-INTEGER
                END-IF.
                IF VALID-NUMBER
                    COMPUTE EDITED-NUMBER = INTEGER-PART + DECIMAL-PART
                END-IF.
       *
            0000-EXIT.
       *
                EXIT PROGRAM.
```

Figure 8-9   The COBOL code for a subprogram that edits numeric decimal data (part 1 of 2)

The NUMEDIT subprogram   **Page 2**

```
     1000-EDIT-DECIMAL-NUMBER.
*

         MOVE 10 TO INTEGER-SUB.
         PERFORM 1100-EDIT-INTEGER-PART
             VARYING UNEDIT-SUB FROM DECIMAL-POS BY -1
                 UNTIL UNEDIT-SUB < 1.
         MOVE 1 TO DECIMAL-SUB.
         ADD 2 TO DECIMAL-POS.
         PERFORM 1200-EDIT-DECIMAL-PART
             VARYING UNEDIT-SUB FROM DECIMAL-POS BY 1
                 UNTIL UNEDIT-SUB > 10.
*
     1100-EDIT-INTEGER-PART.
*

         IF UNEDITED-CHAR(UNEDIT-SUB) NUMERIC
             MOVE UNEDITED-CHAR(UNEDIT-SUB)
                 TO INTEGER-CHAR(INTEGER-SUB)
             SUBTRACT 1 FROM INTEGER-SUB
         ELSE IF UNEDITED-CHAR(UNEDIT-SUB) NOT = SPACE
             MOVE 'N' TO VALID-NUMBER-SW
         END-IF.
*
     1200-EDIT-DECIMAL-PART.
*

         IF UNEDITED-CHAR(UNEDIT-SUB) NUMERIC
             MOVE UNEDITED-CHAR(UNEDIT-SUB)
                 TO DECIMAL-CHAR(DECIMAL-SUB)
             ADD 1 TO DECIMAL-SUB
         ELSE IF UNEDITED-CHAR(UNEDIT-SUB) NOT = SPACE
             MOVE 'N' TO VALID-NUMBER-SW
         END-IF.
*
     2000-EDIT-INTEGER.
*

         INSPECT UNEDITED-NUMBER
             REPLACING LEADING SPACE BY ZERO.
         MOVE ZERO TO INTEGER-LENGTH.
         INSPECT UNEDITED-NUMBER
             TALLYING INTEGER-LENGTH FOR CHARACTERS
                 BEFORE INITIAL SPACE.
         MOVE 10 TO INTEGER-SUB.
         PERFORM 1100-EDIT-INTEGER-PART
             VARYING UNEDIT-SUB FROM INTEGER-LENGTH BY -1
                 UNTIL UNEDIT-SUB < 1.
         MOVE ZERO TO DECIMAL-PART.
```

Description

- The NUMEDIT subprogram validates numeric input data that may contain a decimal point.

- This program uses subscripts and Perform Varying statements instead of reference modification to check the unedited number byte by byte.

Figure 8-9   The COBOL code for a subprogram that edits numeric decimal data (part 2 of 2)

How to use the SEND TEXT command

In many cases, you'll want to send a simple message to the terminal without having to create a BMS mapset. For example, when a program ends without transferring control to a menu program, you may want to display a brief message telling the user that the program has ended. To do that, you use the SEND TEXT command as shown in figure 8-10.

The code shown in this figure will display the message "Session ended." before the program ends. This message is stored in the working-storage field named TERMINATION-MESSAGE that's specified on the FROM option. When this command is issued, the message will be displayed at the top left of the screen. Because the ERASE option is specified, the entire screen will be cleared before the message is displayed. And, because the FREEKB option is specified, the keyboard will be unlocked so the user can enter another trans-id without having to press the Reset key first.

You can also use the SEND TEXT command to display a message at the terminal before control is transferred to another program. To do that, though, you have to end the program by issuing a RETURN command with the trans-id of the program to be invoked instead of an XCTL command. If you use XCTL, the message will just flash on the screen before the menu is displayed. If you use RETURN, though, CICS will wait for the user to press an attention key before it transfers control to the other program. You'll see this technique illustrated in the order entry program in chapter 13.

The syntax of the SEND TEXT command

```
EXEC CICS
    SEND TEXT FROM(data-name)
            [ERASE]
            [FREEKB]
END-EXEC
```

Option	Description
FROM	Specifies the name of the field containing the data to be displayed on the terminal.
ERASE	Indicates that the screen should be erased before the data is displayed.
FREEKB	Indicates that the terminal keyboard should be unlocked after the data is sent. If FREEKB is omitted, the user has to press the Reset key to unlock the keyboard.

A SEND TEXT command that displays a termination message

```
WORKING-STORAGE SECTION.
*
01  TERMINATION-MESSAGE    PIC X(14)    VALUE 'Session ended.'.
        .
        .
PROCEDURE DIVISION.
*
        .
        .
    EXEC CICS
        SEND TEXT FROM(TERMINATION-MESSAGE)
                  ERASE
                  FREEKB
    END-EXEC.
```

Description

- The SEND TEXT command makes it easy to display a brief message on the screen without having to create a BMS mapset.
- A SEND TEXT message is displayed starting at the top left corner of the screen. If you don't specify ERASE, the message overlays whatever is currently on the screen.

Figure 8-10   How to use the SEND TEXT command

How to handle unrecoverable errors

When CICS encounters an error situation from which it cannot recover, it raises an exceptional condition. In chapter 5, you learned how to code the RESP option on any CICS command to check on exceptional conditions and to handle them whenever possible. But an exceptional condition often signifies a serious error that should cause the program to abend. So most shops have standards for handling unrecoverable errors like these. Although these standards vary from shop to shop, it's common practice to provide a generic error handling program that can be invoked if an unrecoverable error is detected.

How to invoke a generalized error handling program

Figure 8-11 shows you how to invoke a simple error handling program. Note that this program, called SYSERR, is not intended to provide the type of error recovery that's necessary in a production environment. In fact, all it does is display an error message like the one shown in this figure and end by issuing a RETURN command without the TRANSID option. A more complete error-handling program might also write error information to an error log, reverse changes that were made to recoverable files, produce a dump, and abend the program. However, the simple example you'll see here is sufficient for illustrating the concept of performing a standard error processing routine when an unrecoverable error occurs.

The code in this figure includes a copy member named ERRPARM in the Working-Storage Section. ERRPARM defines an 01-level item named ERROR-PARAMETERS that will be passed to SYSERR. It contains four fields: two response codes (RESP and RESP2), the current trans-id, and the resource that was being used by the command that produced the error (such as a file or mapset). All four of these values can be obtained from Execute Interface Block fields (EIBRESP, EIBRESP2, EIBTRNID, and EIBRSRCE).

The Procedure Division code shows how to invoke SYSERR. Here, you can see that an If statement following a CICS command evaluates the response code. If the response is not normal, the program performs a procedure named 9999-TERMINATE-PROGRAM. This procedure simply moves fields from the Execute Interface Block to the Error-Parameters fields, then issues an XCTL command to transfer control to the SYSERR program. The Error-Parameters field is passed to SYSERR via the COMMAREA option.

The error message displayed by the error handling program

```
A serious error has occurred.  Please contact technical support.

EIBRESP  =          19
EIBRESP2 =           0
EIBTRNID = MNT1
EIBRSRCE = CUSTMAS
```

Code that invokes the error handling program

```
        WORKING-STORAGE SECTION.
        *
        COPY ERRPARM.
C       01  ERROR-PARAMETERS.
C       *
C           05  ERR-RESP       PIC S9(8)    COMP.
C           05  ERR-RESP2      PIC S9(8)    COMP.
C           05  ERR-TRNID      PIC X(4).
C           05  ERR-RSRCE      PIC X(8).
                .
                .
                .
        PROCEDURE DIVISION.
                .
                .
                .
            IF RESPONSE-CODE NOT = DFHRESP(NORMAL)
                PERFORM 9999-TERMINATE-PROGRAM.
                .
                .
                .
        9999-TERMINATE-PROGRAM.
        *
            MOVE EIBRESP  TO ERR-RESP.
            MOVE EIBRESP2 TO ERR-RESP2.
            MOVE EIBTRNID TO ERR-TRNID.
            MOVE EIBRSRCE TO ERR-RSRCE.
            EXEC CICS
                XCTL PROGRAM('SYSERR')
                     COMMAREA(ERROR-PARAMETERS)
            END-EXEC.
```

Description

- Most shops have standards for handling unrecoverable errors, and many provide a generic error handling program that can be invoked when an unrecoverable error is detected.

- In a production environment, an error handling program usually displays an error message to the user and does extensive processing, including writing detailed error information to an error log, reversing any changes that were made to recoverable files, and producing a storage dump. It may also cause the program to abend, or it may just end with a RETURN command.

- Any program that branches to the error handling program will probably be required to pass along information on its current status, including information that's available in the Execute Interface Block.

Figure 8-11   How to invoke a generalized error handling program

The COBOL code for a generalized error handling program

Figure 8-12 shows the source code for the SYSERR program. Most of it is devoted to defining the seven-line error message in the Working-Storage Section. In the Procedure Division, the program starts by moving DFHCOMMAREA to its working-storage copy of ERROR-PARAMETERS. Then, it moves fields individually to the appropriate error message fields. Next, it issues a SEND TEXT command to erase the screen, display the error message, and sound the alarm. Finally, it terminates the task by issuing a RETURN command without any options. Thus, to continue work, the user will have to clear the screen by pressing the Clear key, then type in a new trans-id.

The SYSERR program

```
IDENTIFICATION DIVISION.
PROGRAM-ID.  SYSERR.
*
ENVIRONMENT DIVISION.
*
DATA DIVISION.
*
WORKING-STORAGE SECTION.
*
01   ERROR-MESSAGE.
     05   ERROR-LINE-1.
          10   FILLER      PIC X(20)   VALUE 'A serious error has '.
          10   FILLER      PIC X(20)   VALUE 'occurred.  Please co'.
          10   FILLER      PIC X(20)   VALUE 'ntact technical supp'.
          10   FILLER      PIC X(19)   VALUE 'ort.               '.
     05   ERROR-LINE-2     PIC X(79)   VALUE SPACE.
     05   ERROR-LINE-3.
          10   FILLER      PIC X(11)   VALUE 'EIBRESP  = '.
          10   EM-RESP     PIC Z(08)9.
          10   FILLER      PIC X(59)   VALUE SPACE.
     05   ERROR-LINE-4.
          10   FILLER      PIC X(11)   VALUE 'EIBRESP2 = '.
          10   EM-RESP2    PIC Z(08)9.
          10   FILLER      PIC X(59)   VALUE SPACE.
     05   ERROR-LINE-5.
          10   FILLER      PIC X(11)   VALUE 'EIBTRNID = '.
          10   EM-TRNID    PIC X(04).
          10   FILLER      PIC X(64)   VALUE SPACE.
     05   ERROR-LINE-6.
          10   FILLER      PIC X(11)   VALUE 'EIBRSRCE = '.
          10   EM-RSRCE    PIC X(08).
          10   FILLER      PIC X(60)   VALUE SPACE.
     05   ERROR-LINE-7     PIC X(79)   VALUE SPACE.
*
COPY ERRPARM.
*
LINKAGE SECTION.
*
01   DFHCOMMAREA          PIC X(20).
*
PROCEDURE DIVISION.
*
0000-DISPLAY-ERROR-MESSAGE.
*
     MOVE DFHCOMMAREA TO ERROR-PARAMETERS.
     MOVE ERR-RESP   TO EM-RESP.
     MOVE ERR-RESP2 TO EM-RESP2.
     MOVE ERR-TRNID TO EM-TRNID.
     MOVE ERR-RSRCE TO EM-RSRCE.
     EXEC CICS
         SEND TEXT FROM(ERROR-MESSAGE)
                   ERASE
                   ALARM
                   FREEKB
     END-EXEC.
     EXEC CICS
          RETURN
     END-EXEC.
```

Figure 8-12   The COBOL code for a generalized error handling program

How to access data using the Linkage Section

You already know how to access two CICS storage areas that are outside your program's Working-Storage Section by using the Linkage Section: the communication area and the Execute Interface Block. Now, you'll learn how to use some of the EIB fields in greater depth. Then, you'll see how to access data in other CICS areas using the Linkage Section.

How to use fields in the Execute Interface Block

In chapter 2, you learned that the Execute Interface Block (EIB) is a CICS area that contains information related to the current task. Figure 8-13 lists all of the fields in the Execute Interface Block, along with their COBOL pictures and a brief description of each. The shaded fields are the ones you're likely to use in coding and debugging your programs. You learned how to use EIBCALEN and EIBAID in chapter 2, and I presented EIBCPOSN earlier in this chapter. Now, I'll explain how to use some of the other fields. For a complete explanation of these fields and their possible values, you can refer to the IBM manual *CICS Application Programming Reference*.

EIBDATE and EIBTIME contain the date and time your task was started. EIBDATE indicates what number day in the year it is and includes an identifier for the century. So December 31, 1999 is stored as 0099365 (the 365th day of 1999), and January 12, 2001 is stored as 0101012. EIBTIME reflects a 24-hour clock (where 2:00 p.m. is hour 14, for example). So midnight is stored as 0000000; one second before midnight is 0235959.

Although the date format is useful for date comparisons, it's inappropriate for display purposes. And two time values can only be compared if you're confident that both represent the same day. As a result, you'll often use the CICS FORMATTIME command to convert times and dates to and from various formats. You'll learn how to use the FORMATTIME command later in this chapter.

Several of the Execute Interface Block fields are particularly useful when debugging a CICS program. In fact, you saw four of them used in the SYSERR program: EIBRESP, EIBRESP2, EIBRSRCE, and EIBTRNID. You might also use EIBRCODE to get the CICS response code, or EIBFN to determine the last CICS command that was executed.

EIBTRNID is often used for purposes other than debugging, too. It contains the trans-id that started the current task, so one of its common uses is to determine how a program was started. For example, you might check this field to insure that a program is invoked only from a menu, not by entering the program's trans-id at a terminal. In that case, this field should contain the trans-id of the menu program.

The Execute Interface Block

Field name	COBOL Picture	Description
EIBAID	X(1)	Most recent AID character
EIBATT	X(1)	RU attach header flag
EIBCALEN	S9(4) COMP	Length of DFHCOMMAREA
EIBCOMPL	X(1)	RECEIVE command completion flag
EIBCONF	X(1)	APPC confirmation flag
EIBCPOSN	S9(4) COMP	Most recent cursor address, given as displacement value
EIBDATE	S9(7) COMP-3	Task start date in the format 0CYYDDD (day in year, where C identifies the century with 0 for the 1900s, 1 for the 2000s)
EIBDS	X(8)	Most recent data set name
EIBEOC	X(1)	RU end-of-chain flag
EIBERR	X(1)	APPC error flag
EIBERRCD	X(4)	APPC error code
EIBFMH	X(1)	FMH flag
EIBFN	X(2)	Most recent CICS command code
EIBFREE	X(1)	Free facility flag
EIBNODAT	X(1)	APPC no-data flag
EIBRCODE	X(6)	CICS response code
EIBRECV	X(1)	RECEIVE command more-data flag
EIBREQID	X(8)	Interval control request-id
EIBRESP	S9(8) COMP	Exceptional condition code
EIBRESP2	S9(8) COMP	Exceptional condition extended code
EIBRLDBK	X(1)	Rollback flag
EIBRSRCE	X(8)	Last resource (map name for a SEND MAP or RECEIVE MAP command, program name for a LINK or XCTL command, file name for a file control command, etc.)
EIBSIG	X(1)	SIGNAL flag
EIBSYNC	X(1)	Syncpoint flag
EIBSYNRB	X(1)	Syncpoint rollback flag
EIBTASKN	S9(7) COMP-3	Task number
EIBTIME	S9(7) COMP-3	Task starting time in the format 0HHMMSS (hours, minutes, seconds; assumes a 24-hour clock)
EIBTRMID	X(4)	Terminal-id
EIBTRNID	X(4)	Transaction-id

Description

- The Execute Interface Block is a CICS area that contains information related to the current task. Some of the fields in the EIB are initialized when the task is started, and others are updated each time certain CICS commands are executed.

- For a complete explanation of the fields in the EIB, you can refer to the IBM manual *CICS Application Programming Reference*.

Figure 8-13   How to use fields in the Execute Interface Block

The EIBTRMID field supplies the name of the terminal running the task. It isn't a physical device type like 3270-2, but rather a symbolic name like L131 assigned to a terminal in the Terminal Control Table (TCT). You might use this field for security purposes. For example, if you want to restrict a program to certain terminals, you can test EIBTRMID to make sure the terminal is eligible to run the task.

How to access CICS areas

Command-level CICS lets you access areas of storage that are owned by CICS rather than by your application program. Since these storage areas exist outside of your program's working storage, you must access them via the Linkage Section. When CICS loads and executes your program, it automatically provides *addressability* to the first two Linkage Section fields: DFHCOMMAREA and the Execute Interface Block. However, if you define any other fields in the Linkage Section, you must establish addressability to them yourself. If you don't, your program will abend with an addressing exception when you try to access the field.

To establish addressability, you use the ADDRESS command shown in figure 8-14. As you can see, this command lets you access three CICS areas: the *CWA* (*Common Work Area*), the *TWA* (*Transaction Work Area*), and the *TCTUA* (*Terminal Control Table User Area*). You'll hear and read about the last two areas, but they're largely holdovers from macro-level CICS and are seldom used in command-level programming. However, you may need to use the CWA in your programs.

The CWA is an area of storage that's available to all tasks in a CICS system. Typically, the CWA is used to store limited amounts of information that might be useful to many or all programs in an installation. For example, the CWA might contain fields for the current date in various formats (such as "10/12/2001" or "October 12, 2001") and the company name for use in report headings. The CWA might also contain fields such as the day of the week, the system start-up time, the time zone, the job name, and so on. The actual contents of the CWA vary from installation to installation.

To establish addressability to the CWA, you code the ADDRESS command with the CWA parameter as shown in this figure. On this parameter, you use the ADDRESS special register to give the address of the Linkage Section item you want to use for the CWA. In this example, the address of the Linkage Section field named COMMON-WORK-AREA is set to the address of the CWA.

The syntax of the ADDRESS command

```
EXEC CICS
    ADDRESS [CWA(pointer)]
            [TWA(pointer)]
            [TCTUA(pointer)]
END-EXEC
```

Option	Description
CWA	Establishes addressability to the Common Work Area, a user-defined storage area common to all tasks in a CICS system.
TWA	Establishes addressability to the Transaction Work Area, an area of storage assigned to the current task.
TCTUA	Establishes addressability to the Terminal Control Table User Area, an area of storage associated with the terminal.

Code that accesses the CWA

```
    LINKAGE SECTION.
*
    01  DFHCOMMAREA              PIC X.
*
    01  COMMON-WORK-AREA.
*
        05  CWA-CURRENT-DATE    PIC X(8).
        05  CWA-COMPANY-NAME    PIC X(30).
*
    PROCEDURE DIVISON.
*
    0000-PROCESS-CUSTOMER-INQUIRY.
*
        .
        .
        .
        EXEC CICS
            ADDRESS CWA(ADDRESS OF COMMON-WORK-AREA)
        END-EXEC.
        MOVE CWA-COMPANY-NAME TO COMPO.
```

Description

- You can use the Linkage Section to access areas of storage that are owned by CICS other than DFHCOMMAREA and the EIB. To do that, you must establish *addressability* to these areas using the CICS ADDRESS command.

- To set the address of a Linkage Section area to the address of the CICS area you want to access, you use the ADDRESS special register. If the area you specify doesn't exist, it's address is set to a null value.

- The ADDRESS command lets you access several CICS storage areas, but the CWA is the only one you'll use regularly. It stores information that's useful to many of the programs in an installation; the exact contents vary depending on the installation.

Figure 8-14   How to access CICS areas

How to format the date and time

As you just learned, you can obtain the current date and time from the EIBDATE and EIBTIME fields in the Execute Interface Block. (Actually, these fields contain the date and time that the task was started, not the current date and time, but that's usually what you want.) Although the date and time are stored in these fields in a format that's useful for some purposes, many applications require more control over the format of the date and time. For these applications, you can use the ASKTIME and FORMATTIME commands.

How to use the ASKTIME command

The ASKTIME command, shown in figure 8-15, retrieves an *absolute time* that represents the number of milliseconds that have elapsed since January 1, 1900. Then, the command uses this time to update the EIBDATE and EIBTIME fields. In addition, if you include the ABSTIME option on this command, the absolute time is stored in the field you specify. The command shown in this figure, for example, will store the absolute time in a field named ABSOLUTE-TIME.

Although you can use the absolute time value that's returned by the ASKTIME command directly, you'll usually want to convert it to a more useful format. To do that, you can use the FORMATTIME command.

The syntax of the ASKTIME command

```
EXEC CICS
    ASKTIME [ABSTIME(data-name)]
END-EXEC
```

Option	Description
ABSTIME	Specifies a 15-digit packed-decimal field (PIC S9(15) COMP-3) where CICS places an absolute time value representing the number of milliseconds that have elapsed since midnight, January 1, 1900.

Code that retrieves the absolute time

```
WORKING-STORAGE-SECTION.
    .
    .
    .
01  DATE-AND-TIME-FIELDS.
    05  ABSOLUTE-TIME     PIC S9(15) COMP-3.
    .
    .
PROCEDURE DIVISION.
    .
    .
    EXEC CICS
        ASKTIME ABSTIME(ABSOLUTE-TIME)
    END-EXEC.
    .
    .
```

Description

- The ASKTIME command retrieves the current date and time as an *absolute time*. For example, the absolute time for 2:24 p.m. on February 1, 2001 is +003190026294970.

- Each time this command is executed, the date and time in the EIBDATE and EIBTIME fields in the Execute Interface Block are updated. If you code the ABSTIME option, the date and time are also stored in the field you name.

- Although you can use the absolute time value directly, you're more likely to convert it to a more useful format using the FORMATTIME command.

Figure 8-15   How to use the ASKTIME command

How to use the FORMATTIME command

Figure 8-16 presents the syntax of the FORMATTIME command. As you can see, this command lets you format the date and time in a variety of ways. The first two date options, for example, let you format the date using the installation's default format. The difference between the two is that DATE returns a date with a two-digit year, and FULLDATE returns a date with a four-digit year. You can also format the date using a specific format like *mmddyyyy* or *yyyyddd*. The time, however, is available in only one format: *hhmmss*.

Before I go on, you should notice that all of the date formats shown in this figure, except for DATE, return a date with a four-digit year. These formats became available with release 4.1 of CICS/ESA to deal with the Year 2000 issue. If you don't need a four-digit year, however, you can still use the options that return two-digit years: MMDDYY, DDMMYY, YYMMDD, YYDDMM, and YYDDD.

If you want to separate the components of a date, you can include the DATESEP option. By default, this option will add a slash (/) between the month, day, and year fields, but you can specify any separator you want. You can also separate the components of a time by including the TIMESEP option. The default time separator is a colon (:).

The syntax of the FORMATTIME command

```
EXEC CICS
    FORMATTIME  ABSTIME(data-name)

                [DATE(data-name)]
                [FULLDATE(data-name)]
                [MMDDYYYY(data-name)]
                [DDMMYYYY(data-name)]
                [YYYYMMDD(data-name)]
                [YYYYDDMM(data-name)]
                [YYYYDDD(data-name)]
                [DATESEP[(data-name | literal)]]
                [DATEFORM(data-name)]

                [DAYCOUNT(data-name)]
                [DAYOFWEEK(data-name)]
                [DAYOFMONTH(data-name)]
                [MONTHOFYEAR(data-name)]
                [YEAR(data-name)]

                [TIME(data-name) [TIMESEP[(data-name | literal)]]]
    END-EXEC
```

Option	Description
ABSTIME	Specifies a 15-digit packed-decimal field (PIC S9(15) COMP-3) that contains the date to be formatted. This value is usually obtained with an ASKTIME command.
DATE	Specifies an eight-byte field where CICS places the date formatted according to the installation default.
FULLDATE	Specifies a ten-byte field where CICS places the date formatted according to the installation default, but with the year expanded to four digits.
MMDDYYYY	Specifies a ten-byte field where CICS places the month, day, and year in the form *mmddyyyy*.
DDMMYYYY	Specifies a ten-byte field where CICS places the day, month, and year in the form *ddmmyyyy*.
YYYYMMDD	Specifies a ten-byte field where CICS places the year, month, and day in the form *yyyymmdd*.
YYYYDDMM	Specifies a ten-byte field where CICS places the year, day, and month in the form *yyyyddmm*.
YYYYDDD	Specifies an eight-byte field where CICS places the year and day within the year in the form *yyyyddd*.
DATESEP	Specifies a single character value to be used as a separator between the month, day, and year components of a date value. If you omit DATESEP, no separator is used. If you specify DATESEP without a value, a slash (/) is used.
DATEFORM	Specifies a six-byte field where CICS returns YYMMDD, DDMMYY, or MMDDYY to indicate the installation's default date format.

Figure 8-16   How to use the FORMATTIME command (part 1 of 2)

To illustrate, suppose the current date is February 28, 2001, the current time is 4:35 p.m., and the default date format is *mmddyy*. Then, the first FORMATTIME command shown in part 2 of this figure would store the date "02/28/01" in the WS-DATE field and the time "16:35:00" in the WS-TIME field. And the second FORMATTIME command would store the date "28-02-2001" in the WS-FULL-DATE field.

You can also use the FORMATTIME command to retrieve the number of days represented by the absolute time (DAYCOUNT), the number of the day of the week (DAYOFWEEK), the number of the day of the month (DAYOFMONTH), the number of the month of the year (MONTHOFYEAR), or the four-digit year (YEAR). These formats can be useful in special situations. Note, however, that there isn't an option for retrieving the day of the year. If you need that information, you can use the YYYYDDD option to get it.

The syntax of the FORMATTIME command (continued)

Option	Description
DAYCOUNT	Specifies a binary fullword where CICS places the number of days that have passed since January 1, 1900. (January 1, 1900 is day 0.)
DAYOFWEEK	Specifies a binary fullword where CICS places a number that corresponds to the day of the week. Sunday is 0, Monday is 1, and so on.
DAYOFMONTH	Specifies a binary fullword where CICS places the day within the current month.
MONTHOFYEAR	Specifies a binary fullword where CICS places a number that corresponds to the current month. January is 1, February is 2, and so on.
YEAR	Specifies a binary fullword where CICS places the year expanded to four digits.
TIME	Specifies an eight-byte field where CICS places the time in the form *hhmmss*. The time is based on a 24-hour clock.
TIMESEP	Specifies a single character value to be used as a separator between the hours, minutes, and seconds components of a time value. If you omit TIMESEP, no separator is used. If you specify TIMESEP without a value, a colon (:) is used.

A FORMATTIME command that formats the date and time in the default format with the default separators

```
EXEC CICS
    FORMATTIME  ABSTIME(ABSOLUTE-TIME)
                DATE(WS-DATE)
                DATESEP
                TIME(WS-TIME)
                TIMESEP
END-EXEC.
```

A FORMATTIME command that formats the date in the format dd-mm-yyyy

```
EXEC CICS
    FORMATTIME  ABSTIME(ABSOLUTE-TIME)
                DDMMYYYY(WS-FULL-DATE)
                DATESEP('-')
END-EXEC.
```

Description

- The FORMATTIME command formats an absolute time with the specified format and places the date and time portions in the named fields.

- The date and time that are returned by the FORMATTIME command are always left justified in the named field, regardless of whether separator characters are included.

- Although they're not included in the syntax in this figure, you can also use the MMDDYY, DDMMYY, YYMMDD, YYDDMM, and YYDDD options to format a date with a two-digit year.

Figure 8-16   How to use the FORMATTIME command (part 2 of 2)

Perspective

Now that you've completed this chapter, you should have the skills you need to code most of the CICS programs you'll ever write. To make sure you understand how to apply these skills, though, the four chapters in the next section will present the system design for an invoicing application, along with the specifications, design, and code listings for three of the programs in that application. But first, the next chapter will show you how to debug abends that occur as you test your CICS programs.

Terms

direct cursor positioning
symbolic cursor positioning
reference modification
addressability
Common Work Area (CWA)
Transaction Work Area (TWA)
Terminal Control Table User Area (TCTUA)
absolute time

9

How to debug a CICS abend

When CICS encounters an error it can't recover from, it ends in an *abnormal termination*, or *abend*. To start, this chapter will describe the two most common types of abends and present the CICS abend codes for these and other types of abends. Then, you'll learn how to use an IBM-supplied debugging aid called the *Execution Diagnostics Facility*, or *EDF*, to determine the cause of an abend that occurs as you're testing your programs.

Although you can also use a storage dump to determine the cause of an abend, you're most likely to do that only after a program has been put into production. But even then, you may be able to use EDF to debug the program. Because of that, I won't present storage dumps in this chapter. For more information on using storage dumps, see our CICS desk reference book.

CICS abend codes

When a CICS program terminates abnormally, an *abnormal termination message* (or just *abend message*) like this is sent to the terminal:

`DFH006I TRANSACTION DFXX PROGRAM DFXXP00A  ABEND ASRA AT H400`

This message indicates that the program DFXXP00A started by transaction DFXX at terminal H400 ended with an *abend code* of ASRA. Almost always, it's the abend code that gives you the information you need to begin debugging your program. Fortunately, only a few of the over 300 possible abend codes occur regularly. And most of those fall into two categories: exceptional condition abends and program check abends.

Exceptional condition abends

As you know, when a CICS command encounters an unusual situation, it generates an exceptional condition. For example, if a READ command tries to read a record that doesn't exist, the NOTFND condition is raised. If an exceptional condition occurs when you don't code the RESP option for the command, the task is abnormally terminated. Then, CICS displays an abend code that identifies the exceptional condition that caused the abend.

The abend codes for these exceptional conditions are listed in figure 9-1. As you can see, all of them begin with the letters AEI or AEY. When you encounter one of these codes, you can refer to the list in this figure to see which condition was raised. In many cases, that will be enough to solve the problem. For example, if the abend code AEIS is encountered, it means that the program tried to access a file that isn't open. So all you have to do is check the status of each file accessed by the program to correct the problem.

Obviously, if you specify the RESP option on all of your CICS commands, you should never encounter AEI*x* or AEY*x* abends. In that case, your program's error processing routine should display a message that indicates which exceptional condition occurred.

Program check abends

When a program tries to perform an operation that isn't allowed by the hardware, a *program check* occurs. For example, if it tries to perform an arithmetic operation on non-numeric data, a *data exception* program check occurs. Figure 9-1 lists the fifteen different types of program checks that can occur on System/390-compatible machines. If you've developed COBOL batch programs, you're probably already familiar with some of these codes. Note that a program check always causes your program to abend with the code ASRA. As a result, ASRA is the abend code you'll probably see most often.

Exceptional condition abend codes

Code	Condition	Code	Condition	Code	Condition
AEIA	ERROR	AEIV	LENGERR	AEYL	FUNCERR
AEID	EOF	AEIW	QZERO	AEYM	UNEXPIN
AEIE	EIDS	AEIZ	ITEMERR	AEYN	NOPASSBKRD
AEIG	INBFMH	AEI0	PGMIDERR	AEYO	NOPASSBKWR
AEIH	ENDINPT	AEI1	TRANSIDERR	AEYP	SEQIDERR
AEII	NONVAL	AEI2	ENDDATA	AEYQ	SYSIDERR
AEIJ	NOSTART	AEI3	INVTSREQ	AEYR	ISINVREQ
AEIK	TERMIDERR	AEI8	TSIOERR	AEYT	ENVDEFERR
AEIL	DSIDERR	AEI9	MAPFAIL	AEYU	IGREQCD
AEIM	NOTFND	AEYA	INVERRTERM	AEYV	SESSERR
AEIN	DUPREC	AEYB	INVMPSZ	AEYY	NOTALLOC
AEIO	DUPKEY	AEYC	IGREQID	AEYZ	CBIDERR
AEIP	INVREQ	AEYE	INVLDC	AEY0	INVEXITREQ
AEIQ	IOERR	AEYG	JIDERR	AEY1	INVPARTNSET
AEIR	NOSPACE	AEYH	QIDERR	AEY2	INVPARTN
AEIS	NOTOPEN	AEYJ	DSSTAT	AEY3	PARTNFAIL
AEIT	ENDFILE	AEYK	SELNERR	AEY7	NOTAUTH
AEIU	ILLOGIC				

Types of program checks (ASRA abend code)

Operation exception	Specification exception	Decimal-divide exception
Privileged operation	Data exception	Exponent overflow
Execute exception	Fixed-point overflow	Exponent underflow
Protection exception	Fixed-point divide exception	Significance exception
Addressing exception	Decimal overflow	Floating-point divide exception

Description

- An *exceptional condition abend* occurs when a CICS command encounters an unusual situation, and the RESP option wasn't included on the command.
- A *program check abend* occurs when a program tries to perform an operation that isn't allowed by the hardware. This type of abend always results in an ASRA abend code.

Figure 9-1   Exceptional condition and program check abends

Other abend codes

Figure 9-2 lists some of the other abend codes you might encounter as you test your CICS programs. These abend codes represent errors other than program checks and exceptional conditions, so they're not covered by the ASRA, AEL*x* or AEY*x* codes. If you encounter one of these abends, the brief explanation in this figure should be enough to help you find the problem. If you need more information on any of these codes, though, or if you encounter an abend code that's not listed here, you can consult the IBM manual *CICS Messages and Codes*.

Other abend codes

Code	Explanation
ABMB	You used the absolute cursor positioning technique and supplied a cursor position that's beyond the limit of the output device.
ABM0	The specified map isn't in the mapset. The map name is misspelled either in the program or in the mapset, or the program specifies the wrong mapset.
AFCV	A request made against a file was unable to acquire a record-level lock. The wait time exceeded the maximum wait time allowed for that request.
AICA	The task exceeded the execution time limit for runaway tasks (the task was looping).
AKCS	The task was canceled because it was suspended for a period longer than the transaction's defined deadlock timeout period. Programming practices that lead to deadlock situations sometimes cause this, but it can also be caused by problems internal to CICS.
AKCT	The task was canceled because it was waiting for terminal input for a period longer than the transaction's defined terminal read timeout period. This happens when an operator starts a conversational program and then leaves the terminal unattended for a long period of time.
AKC3	The task was purged, probably as the result of a master terminal operator issuing the CEMT TASK PURGE command.
APCT	The program could not be found or is disabled.
ASRB	An operating system abend has occurred; CICS was able to abend the transaction and continue processing.
ATCH	The task was purged, probably as the result of a deadlock situation. The task may have been purged automatically when it exceeded the deadlock timeout, or it may have been purged by a master terminal operator issuing the CEMT TASK PURGE command.

Note

- IBM's *CICS Messages and Codes* manual documents more than 300 possible abend codes. If you encounter an abend code that's not listed here or in figure 9-1, you can consult that manual for an explanation.

Figure 9-2   Other CICS abend codes

How to use the Execution Diagnostics Facility

The *Execution Diagnostics Facility*, or *EDF*, is an online debugging tool that lets you trace the progress of a CICS program as it executes. When you use EDF to debug an abend, you'll need specific information from the program's compiler output. Before I show you how to use EDF, then, I'll show you some sample compiler output.

Compiler output used with EDF

Figure 9-3 presents compiler output for a program named DFXXP00A. This program produces various CICS abends depending on the PF key you press. The operation of this program is simple. On its first execution, it issues a SEND TEXT command that presents a menu that lets you select a particular type of abend. On subsequent executions, it issues another SEND TEXT command to acknowledge that it has received your abend request. Then, it evaluates EIBAID to determine which PF key you pressed and executes statements that will result in the selected abend. If you press PF1 to force a data exception abend, for example, the program moves invalid data to a numeric field, then uses the invalid data in a Multiply statement.

Obviously, this program is not typical of the CICS programs you'll develop on the job. Nevertheless, it serves as a good example to use when learning how to debug CICS programs.

By the way, the listing in this figure was produced by Release 2.1 of the IBM COBOL compiler for OS/390. Although the listings for other compilers may vary, they are similar enough that you should still be able to use the information that's presented here with those compilers as well.

The first 4 parts of this figure contain the source statement listing for the program. (Parts of this listing have been omitted since they just contain the definitions of areas like the DFHAID copy member and the Execute Interface Block.) Notice that because the CICS translator processed the source file before the compiler was run, the source listing includes many statements that were inserted by the translator.

Part 5 of this figure shows a portion of the *Data Division Map*, which you can generate by specifying the MAP compiler option. This map lists the characteristics of each data field that's defined in the program. You can use it to locate specific fields in working storage. In this figure, I've shaded the entry for PACKED-FIELD-2.

The main item you need to be concerned with in the Data Division Map is the *displacement* (or *offset*), found in the column labeled Hex-Displacement Blk. You use this value to locate a field in working storage. For PACKED-FIELD-2, the displacement is 005. You'll see how this value is used in the sample EDF session later in this chapter.

Compiler output for the abend tester program

Page 1

```
PP 5648-A25  IBM COBOL for OS/390 & VM  2.1.1                 DFXXP00A   Date 02/20/2001   Time 13:40:55   Page   3

LineID  PL SL  ---+--*A-1-B--+--2---+---3---+---4---+---5---+---6---+---7-|--+---8   Map and Cross Reference
000001         IDENTIFICATION DIVISION.
000002         *
000003         PROGRAM-ID.  DFXXP00A.
000004         *
000005         ENVIRONMENT DIVISION.
000006         *
000007         DATA DIVISION.
000008         *
000009         WORKING-STORAGE SECTION.
000010         *
000011         01  WORK-FIELDS.                                          BLW=0000+000             0CL10
000012         *
000013             05  PACKED-FIELD-1   PIC S9(07)V99  COMP-3.           BLW=0000+000,0000000     5P
000014             05  PACKED-FIELD-2   PIC S9(07)V99  COMP-3.           BLW=0000+005,0000005     5P
000015             05  ALPHA-FIELD-2    REDEFINES PACKED-FIELD-2         BLW=0000+005,0000005     5C
000016                                  PIC X(05).
000017         *
000018         01  I-O-AREA          PIC X(100)  VALUE LOW-VALUE.        BLW=0000+010             100C
000019         *
000021         01  START-UP-MESSAGE.                                     BLW=0000+078             0CL948
000022         *
000022             05  FILLER PIC X(30)  VALUE 'ABEND TESTER           .'  BLW=0000+078,0000000   30C
000023             05  FILLER PIC X(49)  VALUE SPACE.                    BLW=0000+096,000001E     49C
000024             05  FILLER PIC X(79)  VALUE SPACE.                    BLW=0000+0C7,000004F     79C
000025             05  FILLER PIC X(30)  VALUE 'Press a PF key to force one of'.  BLW=0000+116,000009E   30C
000026             05  FILLER PIC X(49)  VALUE ' the following abends:'.  BLW=0000+134,00000BC     49C
000027             05  FILLER PIC X(79)  VALUE SPACE.                    BLW=0000+165,00000ED     79C
000028             05  FILLER PIC X(30)  VALUE 'PF1 = ASRA (Data Exception)    '.  BLW=0000+1B4,000013C   30C
000029             05  FILLER PIC X(49)  VALUE SPACE.                    BLW=0000+1D2,000015A     49C
000030             05  FILLER PIC X(30)  VALUE 'PF2 = ASRA (Decimal Divide Exc'.  BLW=0000+203,000018B   30C
000031             05  FILLER PIC X(49)  VALUE 'eption)'.                BLW=0000+221,00001A9     49C
000032             05  FILLER PIC X(30)  VALUE 'PF3 = ASRA (Protection Excepti'.  BLW=0000+252,00001DA   30C
000033             05  FILLER PIC X(49)  VALUE 'on)'.                    BLW=0000+270,00001F8     49C
000034             05  FILLER PIC X(30)  VALUE 'PF4 = ABM0 (Missing Map)      '.  BLW=0000+2A1,0000229   30C
000035             05  FILLER PIC X(49)  VALUE SPACE.                    BLW=0000+2BF,0000247     49C
000036             05  FILLER PIC X(30)  VALUE 'PF5 = AEIO (PGMIDERR)'.  BLW=0000+2F0,0000278     30C
000037             05  FILLER PIC X(49)  VALUE SPACE.                    BLW=0000+30E,0000296     49C
000038             05  FILLER PIC X(30)  VALUE 'PF6 = AEIL (DSIDERR)'.   BLW=0000+33F,00002C7     30C
000039             05  FILLER PIC X(49)  VALUE SPACE.                    BLW=0000+35D,00002E5     49C
000040             05  FILLER PIC X(79)  VALUE SPACE.                    BLW=0000+38E,0000316     79C
000041             05  FILLER PIC X(30)  VALUE 'Or press Enter to exit without'.  BLW=0000+3DD,0000365   30C
000042             05  FILLER PIC X(49)  VALUE ' abending.'.             BLW=0000+3FB,0000383     49C
000043         *
000044         01  PROCESS-COMMAND-MESSAGE.                              BLW=0000+430             0CL49
000045             05  FILLER PIC X(49)  VALUE 'COMMAND ACCEPTED'.       BLW=0000+430,0000000     49C
000046         *
000047         01  TERMINATION-MESSAGE.                                  BLW=0000+468             0CL9
000048         *
000049             05  FILLER PIC X(09)  VALUE 'Good Bye.'.              BLW=0000+468,0000000     9C
```

Figure 9-3   Compiler output used with EDF (part 1 of 6)

Compiler output for the abend tester program   Page 2

```
PP 5648-A25 IBM COBOL for OS/390 & VM  2.1.1                DFXXP00A  Date 02/20/2001  Time 13:40:55   Page    4

LineID PL SL ---+--*-A-1-B--+---2---+---3---+---4---+---5---+---6---+---7-|-+---8    Map and Cross Reference
000050        *
000051         01  COMMUNICATION-AREA     PIC X(01).                          BLW=0000+478       1C
000052        *
000053         COPY DFHAID.
              .
000148         LINKAGE SECTION.
000149        *
000150         01  DFHEIBLK.                                                                      0CL85
000151         02  EIBTIME    COMP-3 PIC S9(7).                               BLL=0001+000       4P
000152         02  EIBDATE    COMP-3 PIC S9(7).                               BLL=0001+000,0000000 4P
000153         02  EIBTRNID   PIC X(4).                                       BLL=0001+004,0000004 4P
000154         02  EIBTASKN   COMP-3 PIC S9(7).                               BLL=0001+008,0000008 4C
000155         02  EIBTRMID   PIC X(4).                                       BLL=0001+00C,0000000C 4P
000156         02  DFHEIGDI   COMP PIC S9(4).                                 BLL=0001+010,0000010 4C
000157         02  EIBCPOSN   COMP PIC S9(4).                                 BLL=0001+014,0000014 2C
000158         02  EIBCALEN   COMP PIC S9(4).                                 BLL=0001+016,0000016 2C
000159         02  EIBAID     PIC X(1).                                       BLL=0001+018,0000018 2C
000160         02  EIBFN      PIC X(2).                                       BLL=0001+01A,000001A 1C
000161         02  EIBRCODE   PIC X(6).                                       BLL=0001+01B,000001B 2C
000162         02  EIBDS      PIC X(8).                                       BLL=0001+01D,000001D 6C
000163         02  EIBREQID   PIC X(8).                                       BLL=0001+023,0000023 8C
000164         02  EIBRSRCE   PIC X(8).                                       BLL=0001+02B,000002B 8C
                                                                              BLL=0001+033,0000033 8C
              .
000182         01  DFHCOMMAREA              PIC X(01).                        BLL=0002+000       1C
000183        *
000184         01  COMMON-WORK-AREA.                                                             0CL6
000185        *
000186         05  CWA-DATE                 PIC 9(06).                        BLL=0003+000       0CL6
000187        *                                                              BLL=0003+000,0000000 6C
000188         PROCEDURE DIVISION USING DFHEIBLK DFHCOMMAREA.
000189        *
000190         0000-FORCE-USER-ABEND.
000191        *
000192            IF EIBCALEN > ZERO
000193        *EXEC CICS
000194        *        SEND TEXT FROM(PROCESS-COMMAND-MESSAGE)
000195        *        ERASE
000196        *        FREEKB
000197        *END-EXEC
000198  1              MOVE '......B.......00068 '  TO DFHEIV0
000199  1              MOVE LENGTH OF PROCESS-COMMAND-MESSAGE TO DFHB0020
000200  1              CALL 'DFHEI1' USING DFHEIV0  DFHDUMMY
000201  1                 PROCESS-COMMAND-MESSAGE DFHB0020
000202  1
000203            END-IF.
000204        *
```

Figure 9-3   Compiler output used with EDF (part 2 of 6)

Compiler output for the abend tester program

Page 3

```
PP 5648-A25 IBM COBOL for OS/390 & VM  2.1.1                    DFXXP00A  Date 02/20/2001  Time 13:40:55  Page    7

LineID PL SL  ----+-*A-1-B--+----2----+----3----+----4----+----5----+----6----+----7-|--+----8 Map and Cross Reference
000205               EVALUATE TRUE
000206
000207                WHEN EIBCALEN = ZERO
000208          *EXEC CICS
000209          *        SEND TEXT FROM(START-UP-MESSAGE)
000210          *             ERASE
000211          *             FREEKB
000212          *END-EXEC
000213      1            MOVE '......B.......00078    ' TO DFHEIV0
000214      1            MOVE LENGTH OF START-UP-MESSAGE TO DFHB0020
000215      1            CALL 'DFHEI1' USING DFHEIV0  DFHDUMMY
000216      1            START-UP-MESSAGE DFHB0020
000217
000218
000219               WHEN EIBAID = DFHPF1
000220      1            MOVE SPACE TO ALPHA-FIELD-2
000221      1            MOVE 100  TO PACKED-FIELD-1
000222      1            MULTIPLY PACKED-FIELD-1 BY PACKED-FIELD-2
000223
000224               WHEN EIBAID = DFHPF2
000225      1            MOVE 100  TO PACKED-FIELD-1
000226      1            MOVE ZERO TO PACKED-FIELD-2
000227      1            DIVIDE PACKED-FIELD-2 INTO PACKED-FIELD-1
000228
000229               WHEN EIBAID = DFHPF3
000230      1            SET ADDRESS OF COMMON-WORK-AREA TO NULL
000231      1            MOVE ZERO TO CWA-DATE
000232
000233               WHEN EIBAID = DFHPF4
000234          *EXEC CICS
000235          *        SEND MAP('NOMAP1')
000236          *            MAPSET('NOSET1')
000237          *            FROM(I-O-AREA)
000238          *            ERASE
000239          *END-EXEC
000240      1            MOVE '..0.......S....00099    ' TO DFHEIV0
000241      1            MOVE 'NOMAP1' TO DFHC0070
000242      1            MOVE LENGTH OF I-O-AREA TO DFHB0020
000243      1            MOVE 'NOSET1' TO DFHC0071
000244      1            CALL 'DFHEI1' USING DFHEIV0  DFHC0070 DFHC0071 I-O-AREA
000245      1            DFHB0020 DFHC0071
000246
000247               WHEN EIBAID = DFHPF5
000248          *EXEC CICS
000249          *        XCTL PROGRAM('NOPGM1')
000250          *END-EXEC
```

Figure 9-3   Compiler output used with EDF (part 3 of 6)

Compiler output for the abend tester program

```
PP 5648-A25 IBM COBOL for OS/390 & VM  2.1.1                    DFXXP00A  Date 02/20/2001  Time 13:40:55   Page     8

LineID  PL SL  ----+--*A-1-B--+----2----+----3----+----4----+----5----+----6----+----7-|--+----8  Map and Cross Reference
000251   1                      MOVE '..Ø.....00107 ' TO DFHEIV0
000252   1                      MOVE 'NOPGM1' TO DFHC0080
000253   1                      CALL 'DFHEI1' USING DFHEIV0  DFHC0080
000254
000255                  WHEN EIBAID = DFHPF6
000256          *EXEC CICS
000257          *    READ DATASET('NOFILE')
000258          *        INTO(I-O-AREA)
000259          *        RIDFLD(ALPHA-FIELD-2)
000260          *END-EXEC
000261   1                      MOVE '..0....Ø.00112 ' TO DFHEIV0
000262   1                      MOVE 'NOFILE' TO DFHC0080
000263   1                      MOVE LENGTH OF I-O-AREA TO DFHB0020
000264   1                      CALL 'DFHEI1' USING DFHEIV0  DFHC0080 I-O-AREA
000265   1                      DFHB0020 ALPHA-FIELD-2
000266
000267                  WHEN EIBAID = DFHENTER OR DFHCLEAR
000268          *EXEC CICS
000269          *    SEND TEXT FROM(TERMINATION-MESSAGE)
000270          *        ERASE
000271          *        FREEKB
000272          *END-EXEC
000273   1                      MOVE '..-...B......00119 ' TO DFHEIV0
000274   1                      MOVE LENGTH OF TERMINATION-MESSAGE TO DFHB0020
000275   1                      CALL 'DFHEI1' USING DFHEIV0  DFHDUMMY
000276   1                      TERMINATION-MESSAGE DFHB0020
000277
000278          *EXEC CICS
000279          *    RETURN
000280          *END-EXEC
000281   1                      MOVE '........00124 ' TO DFHEIV0
000282   1                      CALL 'DFHEI1' USING DFHEIV0
000283
000284
000285                  END-EVALUATE.
000286
000287          *EXEC CICS
000288          *    RETURN TRANSID('DFXX')
000289          *        COMMAREA(COMMUNICATION-AREA)
000290          *END-EXEC.
000291   1                      MOVE '..\.....00130 ' TO DFHEIV0
000292   1                      MOVE 'DFXX' TO DFHC0040
000293   1                      MOVE LENGTH OF COMMUNICATION-AREA TO DFHB0020
000294   1                      CALL 'DFHEI1' USING DFHEIV0  DFHC0040 COMMUNICATION-AREA
000295   1                      DFHB0020.
000296
```

Figure 9-3   Compiler output used with EDF (part 4 of 6)

Compiler output for the abend tester program

Page 5

```
PP 5648-A25 IBM COBOL for OS/390 & VM  2.1.1          DFXXP00A  Date 02/20/2001  Time 13:40:55  Page  9

Data Division Map
Data Definition Attribute codes (rightmost column) have the following meanings:
   D = Object of OCCURS DEPENDING      G = GLOBAL                          S = Spanned file
   E = EXTERNAL                        O = Has OCCURS clause               U = Undefined format file
   F = Fixed-length file               OG= Group has own length definition  V = Variable-length file
   FB= Fixed-length blocked file      R = REDEFINES                       VB= Variable-length blocked file
```

Source LineID	Hierarchy and Data Name	Base Locator	Hex-Displacement Blk	Structure	Definition	Asmblr Data Definition	Data Type	Data Def Attributes
3	PROGRAM-ID DFXXP00A------							
11	1 WORK-FIELDS	BLW=0000	000	0 000	000	DS 0CL10	Group	
13	2 PACKED-FIELD-1 . . .	BLW=0000	000	0 000	000	DS 5P	Packed-Dec	
14	2 PACKED-FIELD-2 . . .	BLW=0000	005	0 000	005	DS 5P	Packed-Dec	R
15	2 ALPHA-FIELD-2 . . .	BLW=0000	005	0 000	005	DS 5C	Display	
18	1 I-O-AREA	BLW=0000	010	0 000	000	DS 100C	Display	
20	1 START-UP-MESSAGE . .	BLW=0000	078	0 000	000	DS 0CL948	Group	
22	2 FILLER	BLW=0000	078	0 000	000	DS 30C	Display	
23	2 FILLER	BLW=0000	096	0 000	01E	DS 49C	Display	
24	2 FILLER	BLW=0000	0C7	0 000	04F	DS 79C	Display	
25	2 FILLER	BLW=0000	116	0 000	09E	DS 30C	Display	
26	2 FILLER	BLW=0000	134	0 000	0BC	DS 49C	Display	
27	2 FILLER	BLW=0000	165	0 000	0ED	DS 79C	Display	
28	2 FILLER	BLW=0000	1B4	0 000	13C	DS 30C	Display	
29	2 FILLER	BLW=0000	1D2	0 000	15A	DS 49C	Display	
30	2 FILLER	BLW=0000	203	0 000	18B	DS 30C	Display	
31	2 FILLER	BLW=0000	221	0 000	1A9	DS 49C	Display	
32	2 FILLER	BLW=0000	252	0 000	1DA	DS 30C	Display	
33	2 FILLER	BLW=0000	270	0 000	1F8	DS 49C	Display	
34	2 FILLER	BLW=0000	2A1	0 000	229	DS 30C	Display	
35	2 FILLER	BLW=0000	2BF	0 000	247	DS 49C	Display	
36	2 FILLER	BLW=0000	2F0	0 000	278	DS 30C	Display	
37	2 FILLER	BLW=0000	30E	0 000	296	DS 49C	Display	
38	2 FILLER	BLW=0000	33F	0 000	2C7	DS 30C	Display	
39	2 FILLER	BLW=0000	35D	0 000	2E5	DS 49C	Display	
40	2 FILLER	BLW=0000	38E	0 000	316	DS 79C	Display	
41	2 FILLER	BLW=0000	3DD	0 000	365	DS 30C	Display	
42	2 FILLER	BLW=0000	3FB	0 000	383	DS 49C	Display	
44	1 PROCESS-COMMAND-MESSAGE .	BLW=0000	430	0 000	000	DS 0CL49	Group	
45	2 FILLER	BLW=0000	468	0 000	000	DS 49C	Display	
47	1 TERMINATION-MESSAGE .	BLW=0000	468	0 000	000	DS 0CL9	Group	
49	2 FILLER	BLW=0000	468	0 000	000	DS 9C	Display	
51	1 COMMUNICATION-AREA . .	BLW=0000	478	0 000	000	DS 1C	Display	
61	1 DFHAID	BLW=0000	480	0 000	000	DS 0CL36	Group	
62	2 DFHNULL	BLW=0000	480	0 000	000	DS 1C	Display	
63	2 DFHENTER	BLW=0000	481	0 000	001	DS 1C	Display	
64	2 DFHCLEAR	BLW=0000	482	0 000	002	DS 1C	Display	
65	2 DFHCLRP	BLW=0000	483	0 000	003	DS 1C	Display	
66	2 DFHPEN	BLW=0000	484	0 000	004	DS 1C	Display	
67	2 DFHOPID	BLW=0000	485	0 000	005	DS 1C	Display	

Figure 9-3   Compiler output used with EDF (part 5 of 6)

To find out which COBOL statement was executing when an abend occurred, you can consult the *Condensed Procedure Listing*, which you generate
by specifying the OFFSET compiler option. The Condensed Procedure Listing
for the DFXXP00A program is shown in the bottom portion of part 6 of this
figure.

For each executable statement in the Procedure Division, the Condensed
Procedure Listing shows three things: the line number where the statement
occurs, the verb name, and the statement's offset from the beginning of the
Procedure Division. The offset indicates the position of the first machine-
language instruction generated for the statement. For example, the shaded
portion in this listing indicates that the first instruction generated for line 222, a
Multiply statement, begins at offset 7B8 (hex). Again, you'll see how this
information is used in the sample EDF session I'll present in just a moment.

Compiler output for the abend tester program

Page 6

```
PP 5648-A25 IBM COBOL for OS/390 & VM  2.1.1          DFXXP00A   Date 02/20/2001   Time 13:40:55   Page   13

CONSTANT GLOBAL TABLE BEGINS AT LOCATION 000130 FOR 0002E9 BYTES
LITERAL POOL MAP FOR LITERALS IN THE CGT:

00013C (LIT+0)    FFFFFFFC 00001000 00000000 00090064 03B40031 D6994097 9985A2A2            |................Or press|
00015C (LIT+32)   40C595A3 859940A6 964085A7 89A340A6 89A38896 A4A3D7C6 F6407E40 C1C5C9D3   | Enter to exit withoutPF6 = AEIL|
00017C (LIT+64)   404DC4E2 C9C4C5D9 D95D4040 40404040 40404040 D7C6F540 7E40C1C5 C9D6404D   | (DSIDERR)          PF5 = AEIO (|
00019C (LIT+96)   D7C7D4C9 C4C5D9D9 5D404040 40404040 4040D7C6 F4407E40 C1C2D4F0 404DD489   |PGMIDERR)          PF4 = ABM0 (Mi|
0001BC (LIT+128)  A2A28995 8740D481 975D4040 A7838597 A389D7C6 F3407E40 C1E2D9C1 D79996A3   |ssing Map)      ....PF3 = ASRA (Prot|
0001DC (LIT+160)  8583A389 969540C5 A7838597 A3898940 7E40C1E2 D9C14D84 404DC485 83899481   |ection ExceptiPF2 = ASRA (Decima|
0001FC (LIT+192)  9340C489 A5898485 40C5A783 D7C6F140 7E40C1E2 D9C14D84 40C5A783 40A39640   |l Divide ExcPF1 = ASRA (Data Exc|
00021C (LIT+224)  8597A389 969500A8 4040D785 85A2A240 8140D7C6 409285A8 40A39640 86969983   |eption)     Press a PF key to forc|
00023C (LIT+256)  85409695 85409686 C1C2C5D5 C440E3C5 E2E3C5D9 40404040 40404040 40404040   |e one ofABEND TESTER|
00025C (LIT+288)  40404040 40401806 60000700 C2000008 22040000 20F0F0F1 F1F94040 401804F0   |    .---.B.......00119     ..0|
00027C (LIT+320)  0007F000 000005E2 04000020 06600007 00C20000 18066000 07000200 00082204   |    ....S...00099   .--..B....|
00029C (LIT+352)  000020F0 F0F0F7F8 40404018 D3C540C4 C6C8C5C9 E3C1C240 F4F1F04B 40869693   |  ..00078   .--..B.....00068|
0002BC (LIT+384)  4040D3C4 40E3C1C2 D3C540C4 C6C8C5C9 E3C1C240 F4F1F04B 40A38885 40869693   |  LD TABLE DFHEITAB 410. the fol|
0002DC (LIT+416)  9396A689 95874081 82859584 A27A0E08 E0000700 010000F0 F0F1F3F0 4040400E   |lowing abends:     ....00130   .|
0002FC (LIT+448)  08000007 00E04080 00070000 0602F000 07000080 00F0F0F1 F1F24040 F1F24040   |    .......00124   ..0...00112|
00031C (LIT+480)  400E0480 00070000 F1F0F740 4040C3D6 D4D4C1D5 C440C1C3 C3C5D7E3            |    .......00107  COMMAND ACCEPT|
00033C (LIT+512)  C5C44081 82859584 8995874B 40C2A885 4BD5D6C6 C9D3C540 40D5D6D7            |ED abending.Good Bye.NOFILE  NOP|
00035C (LIT+544)  C7D4F140 40C4C6E7 E7D7F0F0 C1404040 40404040 D6E4E8E2 40C9C7E9            |GM1 DFXXP00A    SYSOUT  IGZ|
00037C (LIT+576)  E2D9E3C3 C4D5D6E2 C5E3F140 D5D6D4C1 D7F14085 97A38596 955D0000 10000C00   |SRTCDNOSET1 NOMAP1 eption)......|
00039C (LIT+608)  00000000 00012800 00000100 00000000 00000080 00000040 00000000            |................................|
0003BC (LIT+640)  00000000 00000000 00000000 00000000 00000040 00000000 00000040            |................................|
0003DC (LIT+672)  00000000 00000000 00000000 00000000 25C00001 C0000808 00002C02            |................................|
0003FC (LIT+704)  31400000 000040C0 08080000 00014000 2C023102 C0000808 00002C02 31         |...|
```

```
LINE #  HEXLOC  VERB              LINE #  HEXLOC  VERB              LINE #  HEXLOC  VERB
000192  0006C4  IF                000198  0006D4  MOVE              000199  0006E4  MOVE
000200  0006EA  CALL              000205  00072C  EVALUATE          000207  00072C  WHEN
000213  00073E  MOVE              000214  00074E  MOVE              000215  000754  CALL
000219  00079A  WHEN              000220  0007AC  MOVE              000221  0007B2  MOVE
000222  0007B8  MULTIPLY          000224  0007D4  WHEN              000225  0007E6  MOVE
000226  0007BC  MOVE              000227  0007F2  DIVIDE            000229  00080E  WHEN
000230  000820  SET               000231  00082A  MOVE             000233  000834  WHEN
000240  000846  MOVE              000241  000856  MOVE             000242  00085C  MOVE
000243  000862  MOVE              000244  000868  CALL             000247  0008B6  WHEN
000251  0008C8  MOVE              000252  0008D8  MOVE             000253  0008DE  CALL
000255  000914  WHEN              000261  000926  MOVE             000262  000936  MOVE
000263  00093C  MOVE              000264  000942  CALL             000267  000990  WHEN
000273  0009AC  MOVE              000274  0009BC  MOVE             000275  0009C2  CALL
000281  000A04  MOVE              000282  000A14  MOVE             000291  000A3A  MOVE
000292  000A4A  MOVE              000293  000A50  MOVE             000294  000A56  CALL
```

Figure 9-3   Compiler output used with EDF (part 6 of 6)

Three ways to use EDF

You can use EDF in one of three ways, as summarized by the examples in figure 9-4. As you can see, the command you issue to start EDF determines how you're using it. And the message that's displayed when EDF starts reflects this use.

First, you can use EDF in *single-screen mode* to debug a program running at your own terminal. To do that, you just enter the transaction identifier CEDF as shown in the first example in this figure. After CICS responds with a message indicating that EDF is on, you can type the trans-id of the program you want to debug to start its execution. Then, your terminal will alternate between screens displayed by your program and screens displayed by EDF. The terminal session I'll describe in a moment uses EDF in single-screen mode.

You can also use EDF in *dual-screen mode*. In this mode, you run EDF at one terminal and the program you're debugging at another. For example, you could use the second command shown in this figure to debug a program that's running at a terminal named H400. You're most likely to use this technique to test a program at a different type of terminal than the one you're using for program development. You may also use this technique to let a user interact with the program as you debug it at another terminal.

Finally, you can start EDF by typing the CEDX command as shown in the third example in this figure. In this case, you must include the trans-id that starts the program you want to debug. Then, you can debug that program regardless of the terminal where it's executing. This technique is most useful for non-terminal transactions. For example, you could use it to test the business logic portion of a program whose presentation logic runs outside the CICS environment. You'll learn more about this type of program in chapters 20 and 21.

How to use EDF to debug a program running at the same terminal

The command to start EDF

```
CEDF
```

The message that's displayed on the screen when EDF starts

```
THIS TERMINAL: EDF MODE ON
```

How to use EDF to debug a program running at another terminal

The command to start EDF at a terminal named H400

```
CEDF H400,ON
```

The message that's displayed on the screen when EDF starts

```
TERMINAL H400: EDF MODE ON
```

How to use EDF to debug a specific program running at any terminal

The command to start EDF for the program started with trans-id MNTB

```
CEDX MNTB,ON
```

The message that's displayed on the screen when EDF starts

```
TRANSACTION MNTB: EDF ON
```

Description

- In *single-screen mode*, you run EDF and the program you want to debug at the same terminal. This is the technique you'll use most often.

- In *dual-screen mode*, you run EDF at one terminal and the program you want to debug at the terminal you name when you start EDF. You may want to use this technique to test a program at different types of terminals.

- You can also use EDF to debug a program running at any terminal that's started by the trans-id you specify when you start EDF. You can use this technique to test a program that's not started from a terminal, such as a business logic program whose presentation logic runs outside the CICS environment.

Figure 9-4   Three ways to use EDF

A sample session that uses EDF

Now that you know how to start EDF, I'll illustrate how it works by presenting a series of screens from a sample terminal session. During this session, I'll run the DFXXP00A program you saw earlier to generate a data exception abend. Then, I'll show you how to use the compiler listing in conjunction with EDF to determine the cause of the abend.

Once you've started EDF and the program you want to debug, but before the first instruction of the program is executed, EDF displays a program initiation screen like the first one shown in figure 9-5. This screen shows the contents of some of the fields in the Execute Interface Block for the DFXXP00A program. Notice that the value of EIBCALEN is zero, indicating that no communication area was passed to the program. Also notice that a variety of PF keys are available. Since the function of most of these keys is self-explanatory, I won't describe them here.

As your program executes, EDF intercepts all CICS commands and displays two screens: one before and one after the execution of the command. For example, when I pressed the Enter key from screen 1, the DFXXP00A program began execution and continued until it reached the SEND TEXT command. Then, EDF took over and displayed a screen like the one in screen 2. As you can see, EDF shows you the command and all of its options along with their values. In addition, it shows you the command's line number from the translator listing (*not* the compiler listing).

To execute the CICS command, I pressed the Enter key. In this case, since the SEND TEXT command displays output at the terminal, its contents are displayed at the terminal as shown in screen 3 in part 2 of this figure. (Note that this screen will only appear if you're using the CEDF transaction with single-screen mode.) Then, to continue with the debugging session, I pressed the Enter key again. When I did, EDF displayed the command completion screen shown in screen 4. This screen shows the results of the SEND TEXT command. In this case, you can see by the entry in the RESPONSE field that the command completed normally. If an exceptional condition had been raised by the command, though, the condition name would have been displayed in this field.

To continue the execution of the program, I pressed the Enter key. Then, the program continued until it encountered the next CICS command: RETURN. At that point, screen 5 (in part 3) was displayed indicating that this command was about to be executed. To execute the command, I pressed the Enter key.

Before the program was terminated, EDF displayed the program termination screen shown in screen 6 of this figure. This screen indicates that the program is about to end. To end the program, I pressed the Enter key.

Screen 1

To start EDF in single-screen mode, enter CEDF. Then, enter the trans-id of the program you want to debug. EDF displays the program initiation screen, which shows information from the Execute Interface Block.

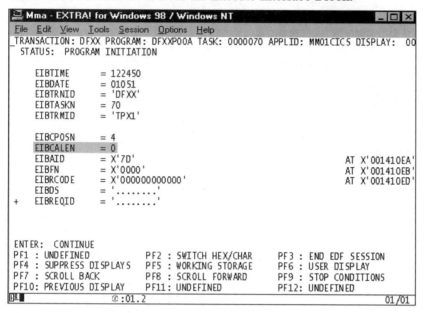

Screen 2

To begin program execution, press the Enter key. Before the first CICS command is issued, EDF displays the command (in this case, SEND TEXT) along with its options and their values.

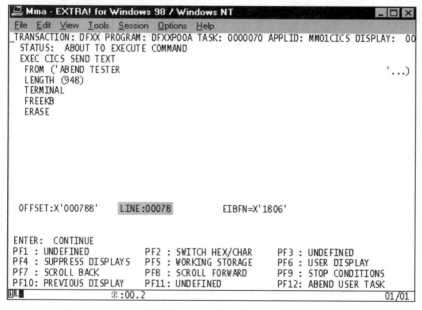

Figure 9-5   A sample session that uses EDF (part 1 of 6)

Screen 3

To execute the SEND TEXT command, press the Enter key. In this case, because the command produces terminal output, the output is displayed on the screen.

Screen 4

To continue program execution after the terminal output is displayed, press the Enter key. EDF will display the completion status of the command. In this case, the command completed normally.

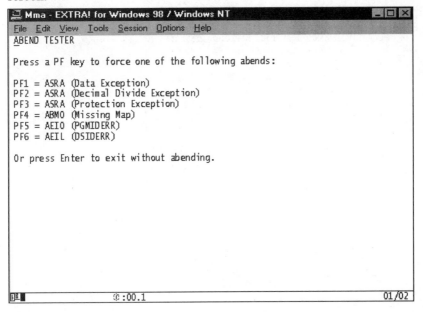

Figure 9-5   A sample session that uses EDF (part 2 of 6)

Screen 5

Press the Enter key to continue program execution. The program will continue until it encounters the next CICS command, in this case, RETURN.

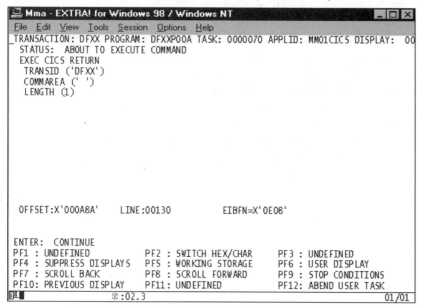

```
Mma - EXTRA! for Windows 98 / Windows NT                    _ □ ×
File  Edit  View  Tools  Session  Options  Help
TRANSACTION: DFXX PROGRAM: DFXXP00A TASK: 0000070 APPLID: MM01CICS DISPLAY:  00
 STATUS:  ABOUT TO EXECUTE COMMAND
 EXEC CICS RETURN
  TRANSID ('DFXX')
  COMMAREA (' ')
  LENGTH (1)




  OFFSET:X'000A8A'    LINE:00130          EIBFN=X'0E08'


ENTER:  CONTINUE
PF1 : UNDEFINED          PF2 : SWITCH HEX/CHAR     PF3 : UNDEFINED
PF4 : SUPPRESS DISPLAYS  PF5 : WORKING STORAGE     PF6 : USER DISPLAY
PF7 : SCROLL BACK        PF8 : SCROLL FORWARD      PF9 : STOP CONDITIONS
PF10: PREVIOUS DISPLAY   PF11: UNDEFINED           PF12: ABEND USER TASK
                    ©:02.3                              01/01
```

Screen 6

To execute the RETURN command, press the Enter key. Before the program ends, EDF displays its program termination screen.

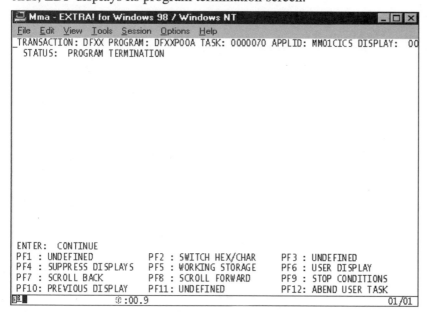

```
Mma - EXTRA! for Windows 98 / Windows NT                    _ □ ×
File  Edit  View  Tools  Session  Options  Help
TRANSACTION: DFXX PROGRAM: DFXXP00A TASK: 0000070 APPLID: MM01CICS DISPLAY:  00
 STATUS:  PROGRAM TERMINATION









ENTER:  CONTINUE
PF1 : UNDEFINED          PF2 : SWITCH HEX/CHAR     PF3 : UNDEFINED
PF4 : SUPPRESS DISPLAYS  PF5 : WORKING STORAGE     PF6 : USER DISPLAY
PF7 : SCROLL BACK        PF8 : SCROLL FORWARD      PF9 : STOP CONDITIONS
PF10: PREVIOUS DISPLAY   PF11: UNDEFINED           PF12: ABEND USER TASK
                    ©:00.9                              01/01
```

Figure 9-5   A sample session that uses EDF (part 3 of 6)

Next, EDF displayed the task termination screen shown in screen 7. Notice the REPLY field on this screen. If I had wanted to end the EDF session at this point, I could have entered NO in this field and then pressed the Enter key. Because I wanted to continue the EDF session, though, I accepted the default of YES.

When I pressed the Enter key from the task termination screen, the current user screen (screen 3 in the figure) was displayed again. Then, I pressed the PF1 key to restart the program. Note that if the screen had required any data entry, I could have entered the data before pressing an attention key.

When the program restarted, EDF displayed the program initiation screen again as shown in screen 8 of this figure. This time, you can see that EIBCALEN contains a value of one, indicating that a communication area was passed to the program. You can also see that EIBAID contains a value of F1, the attention key that was used to restart the program.

Screen 7

To end the program, press the Enter key. Then, EDF displays the task termination screen. To continue the EDF session after the task terminates, press the Enter key with the REPLY field at its default value of YES.

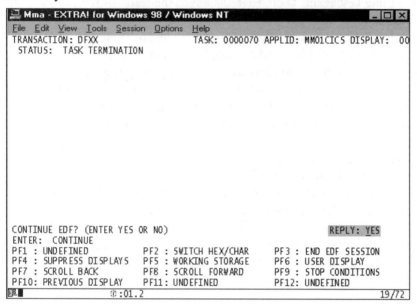

Screen 8

When the task terminates, the user screen (screen 3) is displayed again. Then, you can type data into any entry fields (in this case, there aren't any) and press the appropriate attention key to restart the program. EDF responds by displaying the program initiation screen again.

```
Mma - EXTRA! for Windows 98 / Windows NT                         _ □ ×
 File  Edit  View  Tools  Session  Options  Help
TRANSACTION: DFXX PROGRAM: DFXXP00A TASK: 0000077 APPLID: MM01CIC5 DISPLAY: 00
  STATUS:  PROGRAM INITIATION
      COMMAREA    = ' '
      EIBTIME     = 123124
      EIBDATE     = 01051
      EIBTRNID    = 'DFXX'
      EIBTASKN    = 77
      EIBTRMID    = 'TPX1'

      EIBCPOSN    = 1
      EIBCALEN    = 1
      EIBAID      = X'F1'                          AT X'001410EA'
      EIBFN       = X'0000'                        AT X'001410EB'
      EIBRCODE    = X'000000000000'                AT X'001410ED'
      EIBDS       = '........'
 +    EIBREQID    = '........'


 ENTER:  CONTINUE
 PF1 : UNDEFINED        PF2 : SWITCH HEX/CHAR   PF3 : END EDF SESSION
 PF4 : SUPPRESS DISPLAYS  PF5 : WORKING STORAGE   PF6 : USER DISPLAY
 PF7 : SCROLL BACK      PF8 : SCROLL FORWARD    PF9 : STOP CONDITIONS
 PF10: PREVIOUS DISPLAY  PF11: UNDEFINED         PF12: UNDEFINED
                      ℗:01.2                              01/01
```

Figure 9-5   A sample session that uses EDF (part 4 of 6)

When I pressed the Enter key, the program executed until it reached the first CICS command. In this case, the command is a SEND TEXT command that displays a simple message as indicated in screen 9 of this figure. To execute this command, I pressed the Enter key. When CICS displayed the message on the screen, I pressed the Enter key again. Then, EDF displayed the result of the SEND TEXT command.

To continue program execution, I pressed the Enter key again. Then, the program detected the use of the PF1 key and executed statements that resulted in a data exception abend. Screen 10 shows the results displayed by EDF. Here, you can see that an ASRA abend has occurred. The offset of the instruction that caused the abend is 7BE (hex), and the type of interrupt is data exception. In other words, the instruction at offset 7BE tried to perform an arithmetic operation with non-numeric data.

To find the COBOL statement that caused the abend, I looked in the Condensed Procedure Listing for the statement with an offset closest to the offset in the EDF screen, but not exceeding it. In part 6 of figure 9-3, the shaded Multiply statement has an offset of 7B8, less than the offset on the EDF screen (7BE). Since the offset of the next statement (the When clause at offset 7D4) is greater than 7BE, I concluded that the abend occurred during the execution of the Multiply statement in line 222 of the program. This statement is highlighted in part 3 of figure 9-3.

Screen 9

Press the Enter key to begin program execution. EDF displays the first CICS command to be executed (SEND TEXT). Press the Enter key to execute the command, and press it again when the SEND TEXT message is displayed on the screen.

```
┌─ Mma - EXTRA! for Windows 98 / Windows NT ─────────────── _ □ ✕ ─┐
│ File  Edit  View  Tools  Session  Options  Help                   │
│_TRANSACTION: DFXX PROGRAM: DFXXP00A TASK: 0000077 APPLID: MM01CICS DISPLAY: 00│
│  STATUS:  ABOUT TO EXECUTE COMMAND                                 │
│  EXEC CICS SEND TEXT                                               │
│    FROM ('COMMAND ACCEPTED                            ')           │
│    LENGTH (49)                                                     │
│    TERMINAL                                                        │
│    FREEKB                                                          │
│    ERASE                                                           │
│                                                                    │
│                                                                    │
│                                                                    │
│                                                                    │
│                                                                    │
│   OFFSET:X'00071E'    LINE:00068        EIBFN=X'1806'              │
│                                                                    │
│ ENTER:  CONTINUE                                                   │
│ PF1 : UNDEFINED          PF2 : SWITCH HEX/CHAR    PF3 : UNDEFINED  │
│ PF4 : SUPPRESS DISPLAYS  PF5 : WORKING STORAGE    PF6 : USER DISPLAY│
│ PF7 : SCROLL BACK        PF8 : SCROLL FORWARD     PF9 : STOP CONDITIONS│
│ PF10: PREVIOUS DISPLAY   PF11: UNDEFINED          PF12: ABEND USER TASK│
│▯▯▮             ⓦ:01.8                                       01/01  │
└────────────────────────────────────────────────────────────────┘
```

Screen 10

When the results of the SEND TEXT command are displayed, press the Enter key to continue program execution. When the program abends, EDF displays a screen that indicates the abend code, the offset of the instruction that caused the abend, and the type of interrupt.

```
┌─ Mma - EXTRA! for Windows 98 / Windows NT ─────────────── _ □ ✕ ─┐
│ File  Edit  View  Tools  Session  Options  Help                   │
│_TRANSACTION: DFXX PROGRAM: DFXXP00A TASK: 0000077 APPLID: MM01CICS DISPLAY: 00│
│  STATUS:  AN ABEND HAS OCCURRED                                    │
│      COMMAREA      = ' '                                           │
│      EIBTIME       = 123124                                        │
│      EIBDATE       = 01051                                         │
│      EIBTRNID      = 'DFXX'                                        │
│      EIBTASKN      = 77                                            │
│      EIBTRMID      = 'TPX1'                                        │
│                                                                    │
│      EIBCPOSN      = 1                                             │
│      EIBCALEN      = 1                                             │
│      EIBAID        = X'F1'                          AT X'001410EA' │
│      EIBFN         = X'1806'  SEND                  AT X'001410EB' │
│      EIBRCODE      = X'000000000000'               AT X'001410ED'  │
│      EIBDS         = '........'                                    │
│  +   EIBREQID      = '........'                                    │
│  OFFSET:X'0007BE'                INTERRUPT: DATA EXCEPTION         │
│  ABEND :   ASRA                  PSW: X'078D2000 896007E4 00060007'│
│                                                                    │
│ ENTER:  CONTINUE                                                   │
│ PF1 : UNDEFINED          PF2 : SWITCH HEX/CHAR    PF3 : END EDF SESSION│
│ PF4 : SUPPRESS DISPLAYS  PF5 : WORKING STORAGE    PF6 : USER DISPLAY│
│ PF7 : SCROLL BACK        PF8 : SCROLL FORWARD     PF9 : STOP CONDITIONS│
│ PF10: PREVIOUS DISPLAY   PF11: UNDEFINED          PF12: REGISTERS AT ABEND│
│▯▯▮             ⓦ:47.6                                       01/01  │
└────────────────────────────────────────────────────────────────┘
```

Figure 9-5   A sample session that uses EDF (part 5 of 6)

By examining the Multiply statement, I concluded that either PACKED-FIELD-1 or PACKED-FIELD-2 contains invalid data. To find out which, I pressed PF5 to display the contents of working storage. The result is shown in screen 11 of this figure.

Notice in this display that working-storage data is presented in columns: (1) the address of the data in hex; (2) the displacement (or offset) of each line of data in hex; (3) 16 bytes of working-storage data in hex (in four columns of four bytes each); and (4) the same 16 bytes of data in character format. To find PACKED-FIELD-2 in the display, I determined the field's displacement from the beginning of working storage using the Data Division Map in the compiler output (part 5 of figure 9-3). In this case, the offset is 005.

Next, I scanned the offset column on the EDF screen looking for the value that's closest to, but not greater than, that offset. (You can use the PF8 key to scroll forward in the display if you need to.) In this case, the field begins in the first line, since that line begins with offset zero and the next line begins with offset ten. Finally, I counted over five bytes to determine that the field contains spaces (hex 4040404040). Since this is not valid numeric data, I concluded that it was the cause of the abend. Looking at the source listing, of course, you can see that just before the Multiply statement, a Move statement moved spaces to ALPHA-FIELD-2, which occupies the same storage location as PACKED-FIELD-2.

After I determined the cause of the abend, I pressed the Enter key to return to the abend screen. Then, I pressed the Enter key again, and EDF displayed the task termination screen shown in screen 12. Because I wanted to terminate EDF at this point, I entered NO into the REPLY field on this screen. Then, when I pressed the Enter key, EDF was terminated.

Screen 11

To display the contents of working storage, press PF5. Then, locate the fields whose values you want to look up using information in the compiler listing.

```
 Mma - EXTRA! for Windows 98 / Windows NT                    _ □ ✕
 File  Edit  View  Tools  Session  Options  Help
 TRANSACTION: DFXX PROGRAM: DFXXPOOA TASK: 0000077 APPLID: MM01CIC5 DISPLAY: 00
   ADDRESS: 08D04660                    WORKING STORAGE
 08D04660   000000   00001000 0C404040 40400000 00000000    .....     ......
 08D04670   000010   00000000 00000000 00000000 00000000    ...............
 08D04680   000020   00000000 00000000 00000000 00000000    ...............
 08D04690   000030   00000000 00000000 00000000 00000000    ...............
 08D046A0   000040   00000000 00000000 00000000 00000000    ...............
 08D046B0   000050   00000000 00000000 00000000 00000000    ...............
 08D046C0   000060   00000000 00000000 00000000 00000000    ...............
 08D046D0   000070   00000000 40404040 C1C2C5D5 C440E3C5    ....     ABEND TE
 08D046E0   000080   E2E3C5D9 40404040 40404040 40404040    STER
 08D046F0   000090   40404040 40404040 40404040 40404040
 08D04700   0000A0   40404040 40404040 40404040 40404040
 08D04710   0000B0   40404040 40404040 40404040 40404040
 08D04720   0000C0   40404040 40404040 40404040 40404040
 08D04730   0000D0   40404040 40404040 40404040 40404040
 08D04740   0000E0   40404040 40404040 40404040 40404040
 08D04750   0000F0   40404040 40404040 40404040 40404040

 ENTER:  CURRENT DISPLAY
 PF1 : UNDEFINED           PF2 : BROWSE TEMP STORAGE PF3 : UNDEFINED
 PF4 : EIB DISPLAY         PF5 : INVOKE CECI         PF6 : USER DISPLAY
 PF7 : SCROLL BACK HALF    PF8 : SCROLL FORWARD HALF PF9 : UNDEFINED
 PF10: SCROLL BACK FULL    PF11: SCROLL FORWARD FULL PF12: REMEMBER DISPLAY
 🖵■              ☺:01.6                                          02/12
```

Screen 12

When you're done, press the Enter key to return to the abend screen, and press Enter again to display the task termination screen. This time, type NO in the REPLY field, then press the Enter key to end the EDF session.

```
 Mma - EXTRA! for Windows 98 / Windows NT                    _ □ ✕
 File  Edit  View  Tools  Session  Options  Help
 TRANSACTION: DFXX            TASK: 0000077 APPLID: MM01CIC5 DISPLAY: 00
   STATUS:  ABNORMAL TASK TERMINATION

       EIBTIME     = 123124
       EIBDATE     = 01051
       EIBTRNID    = 'DFXX'
       EIBTASKN    = 77
       EIBTRMID    = 'TPX1'

       EIBCPOSN    = 1
       EIBCALEN    = 1
       EIBAID      = X'F1'                         AT X'001410EA'
       EIBFN       = X'1806'  SEND                 AT X'001410EB'
       EIBRCODE    = X'000000000000'               AT X'001410ED'
       EIBDS       = '........'
 +     EIBREQID    = '........'
                                 INTERRUPT: DATA EXCEPTION
   ABEND :    ASRA                 PSW: X'078D2000 896007E4 00060007'
 CONTINUE EDF? (ENTER YES OR NO)                        REPLY: no _
 ENTER:  CONTINUE
 PF1 : UNDEFINED           PF2 : SWITCH HEX/CHAR   PF3 : END EDF SESSION
 PF4 : SUPPRESS DISPLAYS   PF5 : WORKING STORAGE   PF6 : USER DISPLAY
 PF7 : SCROLL BACK         PF8 : SCROLL FORWARD    PF9 : STOP CONDITIONS
 PF10: PREVIOUS DISPLAY    PF11: UNDEFINED         PF12: UNDEFINED
 🖵■              ☺:00.9                                          19/75
```

Figure 9-5   A sample session that uses EDF (part 6 of 6)

Perspective

As you can imagine, EDF is a powerful debugging tool. However, it has a built-in limitation: It traces only the execution of CICS commands. In other words, COBOL statements are not traced. Since there may be many COBOL statements between two CICS commands, it can sometimes be hard to isolate a bug. Because of this limitation, third-party source debuggers such as Intertest are often used in addition to (or instead of) EDF.

Terms

abnormal termination
abend
abnormal termination message
abend message
abend code
program check
data exception
Execution Diagnostics Facility (EDF)
Data Division Map
displacement
offset
Condensed Procedure Listing
EDF single-screen mode
EDF dual-screen mode

Section 4

A complete CICS application

Now that you've learned the essential skills for developing CICS programs, you're ready to see a complete CICS application. The first chapter in this section presents an overview of that application that describes the programs and files it uses. Then, the remaining chapters present three of the programs from this application. Once you understand these programs, you can use them as models for many of the programs you write.

10

A systems overview

This chapter presents a brief overview of an invoicing application. This application includes the customer inquiry program you saw in chapter 2 and an enhanced version of the customer maintenance program you saw in chapter 5. In addition, it includes a menu program that lets the user select the program to be executed and an order entry program that lets the user enter orders.

The system design for the sample application

Figure 10-1 is a *data flow diagram* (or *DFD*) for the sample application. A DFD identifies the relationships between data and user interactions to give you a clearer idea of what the programs in a system will need to do. Even if you don't know how to create data flow diagrams yourself, I think you'll find that this one gives you a good overview of the invoicing application.

The key program in this application is the order entry program. It accepts orders from the user and writes them to an invoice file using three other files for reference information: products, customers, and invoice control. (The invoice control file is used to record the next invoice number that should be used.) The customer maintenance program lets users add, change, and delete records in the customer master file. You saw a simplified version of this program in chapter 5. The customer inquiry program lets users display information about customers, as you saw in chapter 2.

Since this application has been simplified to make it easier to understand, many critical functions have been omitted. For example, the application doesn't print the invoices, post sales to accounts receivable, or update the inventory status in the product file. These and other functions would certainly be provided in a production application.

The sample application *does* include a menu program that invokes the three programs shown in the data flow diagram. The menu program itself isn't part of the DFD because its only purpose is to let the user control the execution of the other programs; it doesn't process any data.

A data flow diagram for the sample application

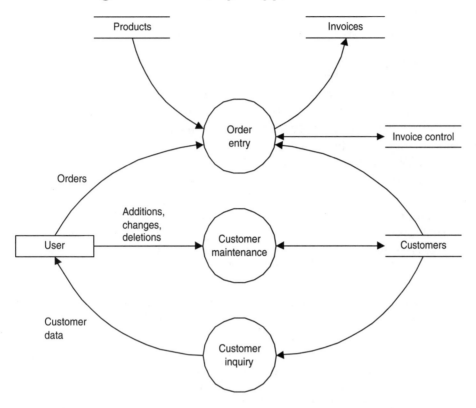

Description

- The sample application consists of four CICS programs—an order entry program, a customer maintenance program, a customer inquiry program, and a menu program—and four files—a customer file, an invoice file, an invoice control file, and a product file.

- The order entry program accepts orders from the user and writes them to an invoice file using the products, customers, and invoice control files for reference.

- The customer maintenance program lets the user add new customers and change or delete existing customers.

- The inquiry program lets the user display information about specific customers.

- The menu program lets the user execute any of the other three programs. Because it doesn't process any data, it's not shown in the diagram above.

How to interpret the data flow diagram

- The *data flow diagram* (or *DFD*) shows the relationships between programs (or *processes*), indicated by circles, and files (or *data stores*), indicated by parallel lines.

- The link between a process and a data store, called a *data flow*, is indicated by an arrow.

Figure 10-1   The system design for the sample application

Program control for the sample application

Figure 10-2 illustrates the flow of control for all of the programs in the invoicing application. At the highest level, of course, CICS is the program in control. Then, the three application programs shown in figure 10-1, along with the menu program that invokes them, are all at the next level. Notice that because the program control for the maintenance and inquiry programs is the same, these programs are represented as a single box in this chart. Also notice that because other versions of the inquiry and maintenance programs are presented elsewhere in this book, they're named CUSTINQ1 and CUSTMNT2 here.

The sample application starts when the user enters the trans-id MENU at the terminal. That causes CICS to invoke the menu program (INVMENU). When the user makes a selection, the menu program issues an XCTL command to transfer control to the order entry program (ORDRENT), the maintenance program, or the inquiry program. Then, because each of these programs is pseudo-conversational, they must return control to CICS and restart when the user presses an attention key. The technique that's used to do that is the same one you've seen throughout this book: Each program issues a RETURN command with its own trans-id.

These programs return control to the menu program in one of two ways. The maintenance and inquiry programs each issue an XCTL command that specifies PROGRAM('INVMENU'). In contrast, the order entry program issues a RETURN command with TRANSID('MENU') specified. That's because the order entry program displays a termination message before returning to the menu, but the maintenance and inquiry programs do not. The RETURN command waits for a user entry before proceeding, so the user has time to read the termination message. In contrast, an XCTL command would transfer control to INVMENU immediately after displaying the message. The effect would be that the message would just flash across the screen, so the user wouldn't get a chance to look at it.

Once control returns to the menu program, the user can invoke another program or end the application. To end the application, the menu program issues a RETURN command with no trans-id to return control to CICS.

At the next level of control is a subprogram called GETINV. This subprogram retrieves the next sequential invoice number from the invoice control file. ORDRENT invokes GETINV by issuing a LINK command, and GETINV returns to ORDRENT with a RETURN command.

How the application uses program control commands

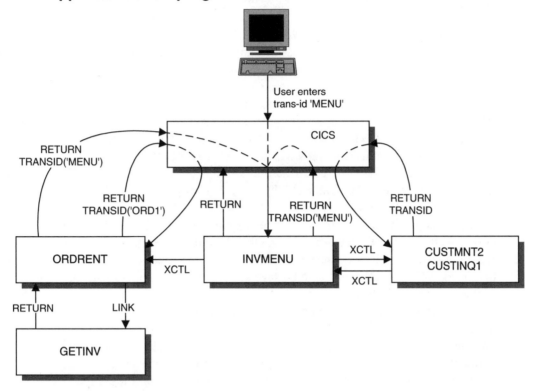

Description

- At the highest level, CICS is the program in control. Four application programs are at the next level: the order entry program (ORDRENT), the menu program (INVMENU), the maintenance program (CUSTMNT2), and the inquiry program (CUSTINQ1).

- When the user enters the trans-id MENU at the terminal, it invokes the INVMENU program. INVMENU uses XCTL commands to transfer control to any of the other three programs.

- The maintenance and inquiry programs return to the menu using an XCTL command.

- The order entry program returns control to the menu using a RETURN command with TRANSID('MENU') specified. That way, the menu program isn't started until the user presses an attention key, which means they will see the termination message that the order entry program displays before it ends.

- The order entry program executes a subprogram named GETINV to obtain the next sequential invoice number for the invoice file. Control is passed to and from GETINV using the LINK and RETURN commands.

- To provide for pseudo-conversational programming, each program except for GETINV issues RETURN commands specifying their own trans-id. This passes control back to CICS so it can restart the program directly when the user presses an attention key, without going through the menu.

Figure 10-2   Program control for the sample application

Resources for the sample application

For an application like this to work, the CICS system must have definitions for the application's resources: files, programs, mapsets, and transactions. In most installations, systems programmers create these definitions when new programs are developed or change them when existing programs are modified. To do that, they can use an online facility called *Resource Definition Online*, or *RDO*. With RDO, the systems programmer runs a special CICS transaction (*CEDA*) to define CICS resources interactively using full-screen panels. These definitions are stored in a file known as the *CSD (CICS System Definition) file* and can then be installed as CICS system tables like the Program Control Table (PCT), Processing Program Table (PPT), and File Control Table (FCT) you learned about earlier in this book.

Systems programmers can also define resources using a cataloged procedure named *DFHCSDUP*. Unlike RDO, DFHCSDUP can be run while the CICS region is active, and it can be used to define several resources at once. The job that invokes DFHCSDUP can also be saved or printed to provide documentation of the resource definitions.

As an application programmer, it's not your responsibility to create or modify the resource definitions. However, you may need to provide information on your applications to the systems programmers who handle this. And you definitely need to know what resources your applications are using.

Figure 10-3 summarizes the files, programs, mapsets, and transactions that are part of the sample invoicing application. All of this material is self-explanatory, with the exception of the operations that are allowed for each file. Read, add, delete, and update indicate that you can issue the CICS READ, WRITE, DELETE, and REWRITE commands for the file as described in chapter 5. Browse lets you access a file sequentially. You'll learn how to use the browse commands in chapter 14.

The files in the sample application

File name	Description	Operations allowed	Record format
CUSTMAS	Customer master file	Read, Add, Delete, Update, Browse	Fixed-length Key-sequenced
PRODUCT	Product master file	Read, Add, Delete, Update, Browse	Fixed-length Key-sequenced
INVOICE	Invoice file	Read, Add, Delete, Update, Browse	Fixed-length Key-sequenced
INVCTL	Invoice control file	Read, Add, Delete, Update, Browse	Fixed-length Key-sequenced

The trans-ids, programs, and mapsets in the sample application

Trans-id	Program	Mapset	Function
MENU	INVMENU	MENSET1	Display menu
INQ1	CUSTINQ1	INQSET1	Display customer information
MNT2	CUSTMNT2	MNTSET2	Maintain customer records
ORD1	ORDRENT	ORDSET1	Enter orders
	GETINV		Retrieve the next invoice number

Description

* The resources that are needed by a CICS application can be defined using an online facility called *Resource Definition Online* (*RDO*) or a cataloged procedure named *DFHCSDUP*.

* Systems programmers are typically responsible for defining resources, but you may need to provide them with information on the resources used in the application you're developing. This information may or may not be included in the program specifications.

Figure 10-3   The resources used in the sample application

Files for the sample application

Figure 10-4 shows the copy members for the four files used by the sample application. Note that the record layouts presented here are less complicated than they would be in a production system. For example, the customer file might contain sales history data, and the invoice file might contain shipping information as well as freight and sales tax charges. Still, the simplified record formats shown in this figure are adequate for the programs in the invoicing application.

All four of these files are implemented as VSAM key-sequenced files. As is usually the case, the first field in each file identifies the primary key for the file. So the primary key for the customer file is the customer number field, and the primary key for the product file is the product code field.

In addition to the primary keys, these files could also be defined with alternate indexes that enforce the relationships among the files. For example, the customer number field might be an alternate index in the invoice file. You'll learn more about working with alternate indexes in chapter 15.

The copy member for the CUSTMAS file

```
01   CUSTOMER-MASTER-RECORD.
*
     05   CM-CUSTOMER-NUMBER          PIC X(6).
     05   CM-FIRST-NAME              PIC X(20).
     05   CM-LAST-NAME               PIC X(30).
     05   CM-ADDRESS                 PIC X(30).
     05   CM-CITY                    PIC X(20).
     05   CM-STATE                   PIC X(2).
     05   CM-ZIP-CODE                PIC X(10).
*
```

The copy member for the PRODUCT file

```
01   PRODUCT-MASTER-RECORD.
*
     05   PRM-PRODUCT-CODE           PIC X(10).
     05   PRM-PRODUCT-DESCRIPTION    PIC X(20).
     05   PRM-UNIT-PRICE             PIC S9(7)V99    COMP-3.
     05   PRM-QUANTITY-ON-HAND       PIC S9(7)       COMP-3.
*
```

The copy member for the INVOICE file

```
01   INVOICE-RECORD.
*
     05   INV-INVOICE-NUMBER         PIC 9(6).
     05   INV-INVOICE-DATE           PIC 9(8).
     05   INV-CUSTOMER-NUMBER        PIC X(6).
     05   INV-PO-NUMBER              PIC X(10).
     05   INV-LINE-ITEM              OCCURS 10.
          10   INV-PRODUCT-CODE      PIC X(10).
          10   INV-QUANTITY          PIC S9(7)       COMP-3.
          10   INV-UNIT-PRICE        PIC S9(7)V99    COMP-3.
          10   INV-AMOUNT            PIC S9(7)V99    COMP-3.
     05   INV-INVOICE-TOTAL          PIC S9(7)V99    COMP-3.
*
```

The copy member for the INVCTL file

```
01   INVCTL-RECORD.
*
     05   INVCTL-RECORD-KEY          PIC X.
     05   INVCTL-NEXT-INVOICE-NUMBER PIC 9(6).
*
```

Note

- All of the files are defined as VSAM key-sequenced files, and the first field in each record layout identifies the primary key for the file.

Figure 10-4   Copy members for the files in the sample application

Perspective

Now that you've been introduced to the sample application, you're ready to study three model programs from it. In the next three chapters, then, you'll see the designs and the complete program listings for the menu program, the enhanced customer maintenance program, and the order entry program. Since the inquiry program from this application was presented in chapter 2, I won't repeat it in this section. If you ever need to write an inquiry program, though, you can use the one in chapter 2 as a model.

Because the programs in this application combine many CICS and COBOL elements that are new to you, you may need to review them more than once to understand them completely. As you review these programs, here are some suggestions that you may find helpful. First, study each program using its event/response chart as a guide. In other words, read through the program once for each input event to see how the program responds to the event. Second, if possible, run the program using whatever debugger is available to you. That way, you can trace the execution of the program and observe the results of each COBOL statement or CICS command. Finally, design and develop your own CICS programs using one or more of these model programs as a guide. By experimenting with the CICS commands and the related COBOL statements, you'll rapidly come to understand how they work.

Terms

data flow diagram (DFD)
process
data store
data flow
Resource Definition Online (RDO)
CEDA transaction
CICS System Definition (CSD) file
DFHCSDUP procedure

The menu program

This chapter presents the master menu program for the invoicing application. Because its main function is to transfer control to another program, it works somewhat differently than most of the pseudo-conversational programs you'll write. Even so, you shouldn't have any trouble understanding the design or code for this program.

The specifications for the menu program

Figure 11-1 gives the specifications for the master menu program. As you can see, when the user has selected one of the other three programs in the invoicing application (by entering 1, 2, or 3 for the action code), the menu program issues an XCTL command to load and execute the correct program. If the user presses the PF3 or PF12 key, the program displays a message and terminates without invoking another program.

The program overview for the menu program

Program	INVMENU: Invoice menu program
Trans-id	MENU
Overview	Displays a menu and lets the user select which program to run: customer inquiry, customer maintenance, or order entry.
Input/output specifications	MENMAP1 Menu map
Processing specifications	1. The menu program is invoked when the user enters the trans-id MENU, when another program transfers control to it via an XCTL command with no communication area, or when another program transfers control to it via a RETURN command with the MENU trans-id. The program should respond by displaying the menu map.
	2. On the menu map, the user enters an action code. If the action code is valid (1, 2, or 3), the program should XCTL to the inquiry program, the maintenance program, or the order entry program. If the action code is not valid, the program should display an error message.
	3. If the user presses PF3 or PF12, the program should display the message "Session ended" and terminate by issuing a RETURN command without a trans-id.

The screen layout for the menu program

Map name _____ MENMAP1 _____   **Date** _____ 03/07/2001 _____

Program name _____ INVMENU _____   **Designer** Doug Lowe

```
 1 MENMAP1              Master Menu                                                XXXX
 2
 3 Select an action.    Then press Enter.
 4
 5 Action . . . . X  1. Display customer information
 6                   2. Maintain customer information
 7                   3. Enter orders
 8
...
23 XXXXXXXXXXXXXXXXXXXXXXXXXXXXXXXXXXXXXXXXXXXXXXXXXXXXXXXXXXXXXXXXXXXXXXXXXXXXXXXXX
24 F3=Exit     F12=Cancel                                                             X
```

Figure 11-1   The specifications for the menu program

The design for the menu program

Figure 11-2 shows an event/response chart for the menu program. If you study this chart for a moment, you'll see that every possible input event is accounted for. The one that requires the most handling is when the user presses the Enter key. Then, the program checks the action code and transfers control to the requested program. If the user doesn't enter a valid action code, the program simply displays an error message.

This figure also presents the structure chart for the menu program. Notice the three modules subordinate to module 0000. Module 1000 responds to the Enter key; module 2000 displays a termination message when the user presses PF3 or PF12; and module 1400 handles the responses to other input events (such as "Start the program"). Module 1000, in turn, has subordinates to receive the action code that the user entered, check it for validity, and issue an XCTL command to invoke the appropriate program if it's valid. If it isn't valid, module 1400 sends the menu map to the screen to display an error message.

An event/response chart for the menu program

Event	Response
Start the program	Display the menu map.
PF3 or PF12	Display a termination message and end.
Enter key	If the action code is 1, XCTL to the inquiry program.
	If the action code is 2, XCTL to the maintenance program.
	If the action code is 3, XCTL to the order entry program.
	Otherwise, display an error message.
Clear key	Redisplay the menu map.
Any PA key	Ignore the key.
Any other key	Display an appropriate error message.

The structure chart for the menu program

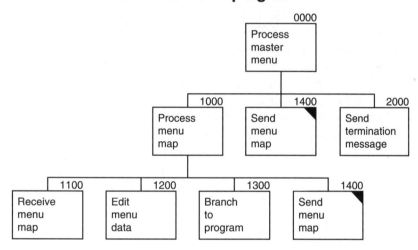

Description

- When the user presses the Enter key, the program must evaluate the action code entered by the user to determine which program to transfer control to.

- Module 1000 controls the processing for responding to the Enter key. Its subordinates receive the menu map (1100), edit the action code (1200), and branch to the selected program if the action code is valid (1300). If the action code is invalid, module 1000 redisplays the menu map with an error message (1400).

- Before the program ends, module 2000 is performed to display a message on the screen indicating that the session has ended.

Figure 11-2   The event/response chart and structure chart for the menu program

The BMS mapset and symbolic map for the menu program

Figure 11-3 presents the mapset listing for the menu program. Note that the DSATTS and MAPATTS parameters are coded on the DFHMSD macro, both specifying extended color and highlighting. As a result, fields that control those attributes will be generated in the symbolic map for each named field in the mapset.

Also notice that the ACTION field is defined with the IC attribute. That way, the cursor will be positioned in this field every time the map is displayed. Since this is the only entry field on the map, using IC is the easiest way to position the cursor.

Finally, notice that the constant field that follows the ACTION field is defined with the ASKIP attribute. This field ends the ACTION field and causes the cursor to skip to the next entry field. In this case, though, there isn't another entry field. So the cursor stays on the ACTION field.

Figure 11-4 presents the symbolic map BMS generated from this mapset. Here, you can see the effect of the DSATTS and MAPATTS parameters. Each field in the input map has a two-byte Filler field between its attribute byte field (suffix A) and its input data field (suffix I). Then, in the output map, these Filler fields are redefined as two single-byte attribute fields: one for extended color (suffix C) and one for extended highlighting (suffix H). In a moment, you'll see how the ACTIONH field is used to control the display of the action code on the screen.

The code for the BMS mapset   **Page 1**

```
          PRINT NOGEN
MENSET1   DFHMSD TYPE=&SYSPARM,                                    X
                 LANG=COBOL,                                       X
                 MODE=INOUT,                                       X
                 TERM=3270-2,                                      X
                 CTRL=FREEKB,                                      X
                 STORAGE=AUTO,                                     X
                 DSATTS=(COLOR,HILIGHT),                           X
                 MAPATTS=(COLOR,HILIGHT),                          X
                 TIOAPFX=YES
****************************************************************************
MENMAP1   DFHMDI SIZE=(24,80),                                     X
                 LINE=1,                                           X
                 COLUMN=1
****************************************************************************
          DFHMDF POS=(1,1),                                        X
                 LENGTH=7,                                         X
                 ATTRB=(NORM,PROT),                                X
                 COLOR=BLUE,                                       X
                 INITIAL='MENMAP1'
          DFHMDF POS=(1,20),                                       X
                 LENGTH=11,                                        X
                 ATTRB=(NORM,PROT),                                X
                 COLOR=GREEN,                                      X
                 INITIAL='Master Menu'
TRANID    DFHMDF POS=(1,76),                                       X
                 LENGTH=4,                                         X
                 ATTRB=(NORM,PROT),                                X
                 COLOR=BLUE,                                       X
                 INITIAL='XXXX'
****************************************************************************
          DFHMDF POS=(3,1),                                        X
                 LENGTH=36,                                        X
                 ATTRB=(NORM,PROT),                                X
                 COLOR=NEUTRAL,                                    X
                 INITIAL='Select an action.   Then press Enter.'
          DFHMDF POS=(5,1),                                        X
                 LENGTH=14,                                        X
                 ATTRB=(NORM,PROT),                                X
                 COLOR=GREEN,                                      X
                 INITIAL='Action . . . .'
ACTION    DFHMDF POS=(5,16),                                       X
                 LENGTH=1,                                         X
                 ATTRB=(NORM,NUM,IC),                              X
                 COLOR=TURQUOISE,                                  X
                 INITIAL='_'
          DFHMDF POS=(5,18),                                       X
                 LENGTH=32,                                        X
                 ATTRB=(NORM,ASKIP),                               X
                 COLOR=NEUTRAL,                                    X
                 INITIAL='1.  Display customer information'
          DFHMDF POS=(6,18),                                       X
                 LENGTH=33,                                        X
                 ATTRB=(NORM,PROT),                                X
                 COLOR=NEUTRAL,                                    X
                 INITIAL='2.  Maintain customer information'
```

Figure 11-3   The BMS mapset for the menu program (part 1 of 2)

The code for the BMS mapset   Page 2

```
           DFHMDF POS=(7,18),                                          X
                  LENGTH=16,                                           X
                  ATTRB=(NORM,PROT),                                   X
                  COLOR=NEUTRAL,                                       X
                  INITIAL='3.  Enter orders'
*********************************************************************
MESSAGE    DFHMDF POS=(23,1),                                          X
                  LENGTH=79,                                           X
                  ATTRB=(BRT,PROT),                                    X
                  COLOR=YELLOW
           DFHMDF POS=(24,1),                                          X
                  LENGTH=20,                                           X
                  ATTRB=(NORM,PROT),                                   X
                  COLOR=BLUE,                                          X
                  INITIAL='F3=Exit    F12=Cancel'
DUMMY      DFHMDF POS=(24,79),                                         X
                  LENGTH=1,                                            X
                  ATTRB=(DRK,PROT,FSET),                               X
                  INITIAL=' '
*********************************************************************
           DFHMSD TYPE=FINAL
           END
```

Figure 11-3   The BMS mapset for the menu program (part 2 of 2)

The code for the symbolic map

```
01 MENMAP1I.
    03 FILLER                       PIC X(12).
    03 TRANIDL                      PIC S9(4) COMP.
    03 TRANIDF                      PIC X.
    03 FILLER REDEFINES TRANIDF.
        05 TRANIDA                  PIC X.
    03 FILLER                       PIC X(2).
    03 TRANIDI                      PIC X(4).
    03 ACTIONL                      PIC S9(4) COMP.
    03 ACTIONF                      PIC X.
    03 FILLER REDEFINES ACTIONF.
        05 ACTIONA                  PIC X.
    03 FILLER                       PIC X(2).
    03 ACTIONI                      PIC X(1).
    03 MESSAGEL                     PIC S9(4) COMP.
    03 MESSAGEF                     PIC X.
    03 FILLER REDEFINES MESSAGEF.
        05 MESSAGEA                 PIC X.
    03 FILLER                       PIC X(2).
    03 MESSAGEI                     PIC X(79).
    03 DUMMYL                       PIC S9(4) COMP.
    03 DUMMYF                       PIC X.
    03 FILLER REDEFINES DUMMYF.
        05 DUMMYA                   PIC X.
    03 FILLER                       PIC X(2).
    03 DUMMYI                       PIC X(1).
01 MENMAP1O REDEFINES MENMAP1I.
    03 FILLER                       PIC X(12).
    03 FILLER                       PIC X(3).
    03 TRANIDC                      PIC X.
    03 TRANIDH                      PIC X.
    03 TRANIDO                      PIC X(4).
    03 FILLER                       PIC X(3).
    03 ACTIONC                      PIC X.
    03 ACTIONH                      PIC X.
    03 ACTIONO                      PIC X(1).
    03 FILLER                       PIC X(3).
    03 MESSAGEC                     PIC X.
    03 MESSAGEH                     PIC X.
    03 MESSAGEO                     PIC X(79).
    03 FILLER                       PIC X(3).
    03 DUMMYC                       PIC X.
    03 DUMMYH                       PIC X.
    03 DUMMYO                       PIC X(1).
```

Figure 11-4   The symbolic map for the menu program

The COBOL code for the menu program

Figure 11-5 presents the source code for the master menu program. As in the other programs you've seen in this book, a switch is defined in the Working-Storage Section to indicate if the data entered by the user is valid (VALID-DATA-SW), and a flag is defined to control the SEND MAP command that's executed by the general-purpose send module (SEND-FLAG). The termination message that's displayed when the program ends is also defined in working storage.

The one working-storage field that might confuse you is PROGRAM-TABLE. This is a simple table that defines the names of the three programs the menu program can invoke. These names are redefined by the field named PROGRAM-NAME, which occurs 3 times. The Program-Name field is used along with a subscript in the PROGRAM option of the XCTL command to transfer control to the appropriate program. The subscript value will be the number the user enters for the action code, which is stored in the working-storage field named ACTION-SUB.

Like the inquiry program you saw in chapter 2, the menu program doesn't need to pass data forward to the next execution of the program. Because of that, the communication area is just one byte long. This byte will be used to determine when the program is executed for the first time in a pseudo-conversational session.

The last three items in the Working-Storage Section are Copy statements. The first copies MENSET1, the symbolic map for the menu screen. The second includes the DFHAID copy member you've seen in the other programs in this book. And the third copies the code for the ATTR copy member, which contains the attribute byte definitions you saw in figure 8-3.

The menu program   **Page 1**

```
        IDENTIFICATION   DIVISION.
        *
        PROGRAM-ID.   INVMENU.
        *
        ENVIRONMENT DIVISION.
        *
        DATA DIVISION.
        *
        WORKING-STORAGE SECTION.
        *
        01   SWITCHES.
        *
             05   VALID-DATA-SW          PIC X(01) VALUE 'Y'.
                  88   VALID-DATA                   VALUE 'Y'.
        *
        01   FLAGS.
        *
             05   SEND-FLAG              PIC X(01).
                  88   SEND-ERASE                   VALUE '1'.
                  88   SEND-DATAONLY                VALUE '2'.
                  88   SEND-DATAONLY-ALARM          VALUE '3'.
        *
        01   PROGRAM-TABLE.
        *
             05   PROGRAM-LIST.
                  10   PROGRAM-1         PIC X(08) VALUE 'CUSTINQ1'.
                  10   PROGRAM-2         PIC X(08) VALUE 'CUSTMNT2'.
                  10   PROGRAM-3         PIC X(08) VALUE 'ORDRENT '.
             05   PROGRAM-NAME           REDEFINES PROGRAM-LIST
                                         OCCURS 3 TIMES
                                         PIC X(08).
        *
        01   SUBSCRIPTS.
        *
             05   ACTION-SUB            PIC 9(01).
        *
        01   END-OF-SESSION-MESSAGE     PIC X(13) VALUE 'Session ended'.
        *
        01   RESPONSE-CODE              PIC S9(08) COMP.
        *
        01   COMMUNICATION-AREA         PIC X(01).
        *
        COPY MENSET1.
        *
        COPY DFHAID.
        *
        COPY ATTR.
        *
        LINKAGE SECTION.
        *
        01   DFHCOMMAREA                PIC X(01).
        *
```

Figure 11-5   The COBOL code for the menu program (part 1 of 3)

In the Procedure Division, procedure 0000 contains an Evaluate statement to manage the program's event processing. Notice that if the user presses PF3 or PF12 to end the program, procedure 2000 is performed to send the termination message before the program is terminated. If the user presses the Enter key, however, procedure 1000 is performed to process the menu map. As you'll see in a moment, this procedure transfers control to another program if the action code the user entered is valid. In that case, control never returns to module 0000, and the RETURN command that follows the Evaluate statement is never performed. This is different from the way that most pseudo-conversational programs work.

Procedure 1000 starts by performing procedure 1100 to receive the menu map and procedure 1200 to edit the action code field. Then, if the action code is valid, it's moved to the Action-Sub field and procedure 1300 is performed to invoke the selected program. If the action code is invalid, or if an error occurs in procedure 1300 so that control isn't transferred to another program, procedure 1000 continues by performing procedure 1400 to redisplay the map with an error message.

The menu program   **Page 2**

```
    PROCEDURE DIVISION.
*
 0000-PROCESS-MASTER-MENU.
*
    EVALUATE TRUE
*
        WHEN EIBCALEN = ZERO
            MOVE LOW-VALUE TO MENMAP1O
            SET SEND-ERASE TO TRUE
            PERFORM 1400-SEND-MENU-MAP
*
        WHEN EIBAID = DFHCLEAR
            MOVE LOW-VALUE TO MENMAP1O
            SET SEND-ERASE TO TRUE
            PERFORM 1400-SEND-MENU-MAP
*
        WHEN EIBAID = DFHPA1 OR DFHPA2 OR DFHPA3
            CONTINUE
*
        WHEN EIBAID = DFHPF3 OR DFHPF12
            PERFORM 2000-SEND-TERMINATION-MESSAGE
            EXEC CICS
                RETURN
            END-EXEC
*
        WHEN EIBAID = DFHENTER
            PERFORM 1000-PROCESS-MENU-MAP
*
        WHEN OTHER
            MOVE 'Invalid key pressed.' TO MESSAGEO
            SET SEND-DATAONLY-ALARM TO TRUE
            PERFORM 1400-SEND-MENU-MAP
*
    END-EVALUATE.
*
    EXEC CICS
        RETURN TRANSID('MENU')
                COMMAREA(COMMUNICATION-AREA)
    END-EXEC.
*
 1000-PROCESS-MENU-MAP.
*
    PERFORM 1100-RECEIVE-MENU-MAP.
    PERFORM 1200-EDIT-MENU-DATA.
    IF VALID-DATA
        MOVE ACTIONI TO ACTION-SUB
        PERFORM 1300-BRANCH-TO-PROGRAM
    END-IF.
    SET SEND-DATAONLY-ALARM TO TRUE.
    PERFORM 1400-SEND-MENU-MAP.
*
 1100-RECEIVE-MENU-MAP.
*
    EXEC CICS
        RECEIVE MAP('MENMAP1')
                MAPSET('MENSET1')
                INTO(MENMAP1I)
    END-EXEC.
```

Figure 11-5   The COBOL code for the menu program (part 2 of 3)

Notice in module 1200 that if the action code is invalid, the ATTR-REVERSE attribute is moved to the ACTIONH field in the symbolic map (the field that contains the highlight attribute for the ACTION field). This adheres to the CUA standards for highlighting errors, and it's the reason that the DSATTS and MAPATTS parameters were included in the BMS mapset.

In procedure 1300, you can see the XCTL command that transfers control to the program indicated by the user. On the PROGRAM option, the program is specified by the Program-Name field, subscripted by the Action-Sub field. If you look back at the definition of Program-Name, you see that if Action-Sub is 1, this command will invoke CUSTINQ1; if it's 2, it will invoke CUSTMNT2; and if it's 3, it will invoke ORDRENT.

Now, notice the Move statement that follows the XCTL command. In most cases, this statement will never be executed because control will have been transferred to another program. If an exceptional condition occurs when the XCTL command is executed, however, the RESP option that's coded on this command will cause the program to continue. Then, the Move statement moves an appropriate error message to MESSAGEO, and that message is displayed when control returns to module 1000.

From the point of view of structured programming, you might object to placing the XCTL command in procedure 1300. After all, one of the basic premises of structured programming is that every procedure should have one entry point and one exit point. So shouldn't the XCTL command be placed in procedure 0000, thus maintaining the structural integrity of the program?

I don't think so. If you place the XCTL command in procedure 0000, you'll have to create a switch that procedure 1000 sets to tell procedure 0000 whether or not it should issue the XCTL command. Then, you'll have to provide for exceptional conditions in procedure 0000, adding code that formats and displays an error message right after the XCTL command. In short, procedure 0000 becomes overly complicated and its primary purpose of responding to events is obscured. So in this case, it's best to compromise strict adherence to the rules of structured programming for the sake of program clarity and simplicity.

The menu program   **Page 3**

```
    1200-EDIT-MENU-DATA.
*
        IF ACTIONI NOT = '1' AND '2' AND '3'
            MOVE ATTR-REVERSE TO ACTIONH
            MOVE 'You must enter 1, 2, or 3.' TO MESSAGEO
            MOVE 'N' TO VALID-DATA-SW
        END-IF.
*
    1300-BRANCH-TO-PROGRAM.
*
        EXEC CICS
            XCTL PROGRAM(PROGRAM-NAME(ACTION-SUB))
            RESP(RESPONSE-CODE)
        END-EXEC.
*
        MOVE 'That program is not available.' TO MESSAGEO.
*
    1400-SEND-MENU-MAP.
*
        MOVE 'MENU' TO TRANIDO.
        EVALUATE TRUE
            WHEN SEND-ERASE
                EXEC CICS
                    SEND MAP('MENMAP1')
                        MAPSET('MENSET1')
                        FROM(MENMAP1O)
                        ERASE
                END-EXEC
            WHEN SEND-DATAONLY
                EXEC CICS
                    SEND MAP('MENMAP1')
                        MAPSET('MENSET1')
                        FROM(MENMAP1O)
                        DATAONLY
                END-EXEC
            WHEN SEND-DATAONLY-ALARM
                EXEC CICS
                    SEND MAP('MENMAP1')
                        MAPSET('MENSET1')
                        FROM(MENMAP1O)
                        DATAONLY
                        ALARM
                END-EXEC
        END-EVALUATE.
*
    2000-SEND-TERMINATION-MESSAGE.
*
        EXEC CICS
            SEND TEXT FROM(END-OF-SESSION-MESSAGE)
                        ERASE
                        FREEKB
        END-EXEC.
```

Figure 11-5   The COBOL code for the menu program (part 3 of 3)

Perspective

Although the menu program presented in this chapter provides for only three selections, it can be easily adapted to provide for additional selections. To do that, you just increase the size of the program table by adding an entry for each additional program and then update the Occurs clause to indicate the number of entries. In addition, you need to modify the edit module so it provides for all of the valid selections. Of course, you need to update the BMS mapset too, so it lists all of the selections. With just these three changes, though, you can implement a menu that provides for as many selections as you need.

12

The maintenance program

In section 2 of this book, you saw the mapset, design, and code for a maintenance program that lets the user add, change, and delete records in a customer master file. The program in this chapter is an enhanced version of that program that incorporates the data editing and error processing techniques you learned about in chapter 8. Since you're already familiar with the basic operation of this program, this chapter focuses mostly on those enhancements.

The specifications for the maintenance program

Figure 12-1 presents the specifications for the customer maintenance program. In part 1, the program overview indicates that this program should edit the entry fields for an add or change operation to be sure that the user entered data in all of them. In addition, the program should terminate by calling the SYSERR program you saw in chapter 8 if an unrecoverable error occurs. Other than that, the specifications are the same as those for the maintenance program presented in chapter 3.

The program overview for the customer maintenance program

Program	CUSTMNT2: Customer maintenance program
Trans-id	MNT2
Overview	Maintains customer information in the customer master file by allowing the user to enter new customers, change existing customers, or delete existing customers.
Input/output specifications	CUSTMAS Customer master file MNTMAP1 Customer maintenance key map MNTMAP2 Customer maintenance data map
Processing specifications	1. Control is transferred to this program via XCTL from the menu program INVMENU with no communication area. The user can also start the program by entering the trans-id MNT2. In either case, the program should respond by displaying the key map.
	2. On the key map, the user enters a customer number and selects a processing action (Add, Change, or Delete). Both the action field and the customer number field must be entered. If the user selects Add, the customer number entered must not exist in the file. For Change or Delete, the customer number must exist in the file. If a valid combination isn't entered, an error message should be displayed.
	3. If the user enters a valid combination of action and customer number, the program displays the customer maintenance data map. For an add operation, the user can then enter the customer information. For a change operation, the user can change any of the existing information. For a delete operation, all fields should be set to protected so the user can't enter changes. To complete any of these operations, the user must press the Enter key.
	4. For an add or change, edit the fields to make sure they aren't blank.
	5. If the user presses PF3 from either the key map or the data map, return to the menu program INVMENU by issuing an XCTL command. If the user presses PF12 from the key map, return to the menu program. However, if the user presses PF12 from the data map, redisplay the key map without completing the current operation.
	6. For a change or delete operation, maintain an image of the customer record in the communication area between program executions. If the record is changed in any way between program executions, notify the user and do not complete the operation.
	7. If an unrecoverable error occurs, terminate the program by invoking the SYSERR subprogram with an XCTL command.

Figure 12-1   The specifications for the customer maintenance program (part 1 of 2)

In part 2 of this figure, you can see the screen layouts for the two maps used by this program. These screen layouts are identical to the ones you saw in chapter 4. The program uses the first one to let the user enter a customer number and an action code. Then, the program displays the second screen to let the user add, change, or delete the selected customer.

The screen layout for the customer maintenance key map

Map name MNTMAP1	**Date** 03/12/2001
Program name CUSTMNT2	**Designer** Doug Lowe

```
MNTMAP1                 Customer Maintenance                                    XXXX

Type a customer number.    Then select an action and press Enter.

Customer number. .  . . XXXXXX

Action . . . . . . . . X  1.  Add a new customer
                          2.  Change an existing customer
                          3.  Delete an existing customer












XXXXXXXXXXXXXXXXXXXXXXXXXXXXXXXXXXXXXXXXXXXXXXXXXXXXXXXXXXXXXXXXXXXXXXXXXXXXXXXXX
F3=Exit      F12=Cancel                                                           X
```

The screen layout for the customer maintenance data map

Map name MNTMAP2	**Date** 03/12/2001
Program name CUSTMNT2	**Designer** Doug Lowe

```
MNTMAP2                 Customer Maintenance                                    XXXX

XXXXXXXXXXXXXXXXXXXXXXXXXXXXXXXXXXXXXXXXXXXXXXXXXXXXXXXXXXXXXXXXXXXXXXXXXXXXXXXXXXX

Customer number. .  . . : XXXXXX

Last name. .  . . . . XXXXXXXXXXXXXXXXXXXXXXXXXXX
First name . .  . . . XXXXXXXXXXXXXXXXXXXX
Address. .  . . . . . XXXXXXXXXXXXXXXXXXXXXXXXXXXX
City . .  . . . . . . XXXXXXXXXXXXXXXXXXX
State. .  . . . . . . XX
Zip Code. .  . . . . XXXXXXXXXX












XXXXXXXXXXXXXXXXXXXXXXXXXXXXXXXXXXXXXXXXXXXXXXXXXXXXXXXXXXXXXXXXXXXXXXXXXXXXXXXXX
F3=Exit      F12=Cancel                                                           X
```

Figure 12-1   The specifications for the customer maintenance program (part 2 of 2)

An event/response chart for the maintenance program

Figure 12-2 presents an event/response chart for the customer maintenance program. Because I explained this chart in chapter 3, I won't review it in detail here. The only real change has to do with editing the input data. As you can see, if the user presses the Enter key when the "Add customer" or "Change customer" context is current, the program responds by editing the data before adding or changing the record. If the data isn't valid, the program issues an error message, but the context is unchanged.

An event/response chart for the customer maintenance program

Event	Context	Response	New context
Start the program	n/a	Display the key map.	Get key
PF3	All	Transfer control to the menu program.	n/a
PF12	Get key	Transfer control to the menu program.	n/a
	Add customer Change customer Delete customer	Cancel the operation and display the key map.	Get key
Enter key	Get key	Edit input data. If valid display data map else display an error message.	Add customer, Change customer, or Delete customer Get key
	Add customer	Edit input data. If valid add customer record display key map else display an error message.	Get key Add customer
	Change customer	Edit input data. If valid change customer record display key map else display an error message.	Get key Change customer
	Delete customer	Delete the customer record. Display the key map.	Get key
Clear	Get key	Redisplay the key map without any data.	Unchanged
	Add, Change, or Delete customer	Redisplay the data map with unprotected data erased.	Unchanged
Any PA key	All	Ignore the key.	Unchanged
Any other key	All	Display an appropriate error message.	Unchanged

Description

- The customer maintenance program must manage four event contexts. Whenever the key map is displayed on the screen, the "Get key" context is current. Whenever the data map is displayed, the context is "Add customer," "Change customer," or "Delete customer," depending on the action the user requested on the key map.

Figure 12-2   An event/response chart for the customer maintenance program

The structure chart for the maintenance program

Figure 12-3 shows the structure chart for the enhanced version of the customer maintenance program. It includes one new module, module 2200, that wasn't in the structure chart in chapter 3. This module edits the entry fields, making sure that each contains data (not just spaces or zeros). As a result, it's subordinate to both module 2000, the control module for adding new customers, and module 3000, the control module for changing existing records. Module 1400 is also added as a subordinate to modules 2000 and 3000. This module is called if an error is detected in any of the entry fields.

You may remember that this program includes another module that's not shown in the structure chart. It's module 9999-TERMINATE-PROGRAM, and it's subordinate to every I/O module that's coded with the RESP option. In this version of the maintenance program, it executes SYSERR, the subprogram presented in chapter 8 that handles serious errors. Although you can include the 9999 module and SYSERR on the structure chart, they tend to clutter rather than clarify the design since they're subordinate to so many modules. Because of that, they've been omitted from the structure charts for all the programs in this book.

The structure chart for the customer maintenance program

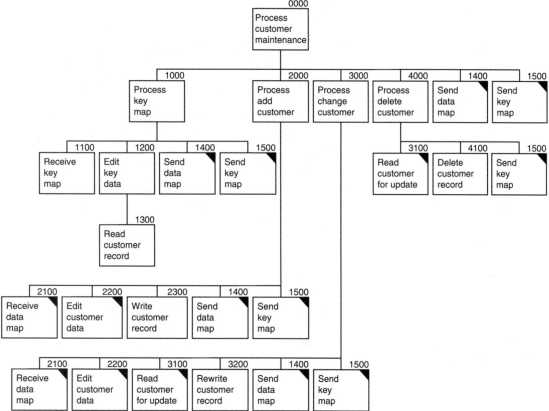

Description

- Modules 1000, 2000, 3000, and 4000 perform the processing for the four contexts that can be current when the user presses the Enter key.

- Module 1000 is called when the key map is displayed. This module receives the key map (1100) and edits its data (1200), including reading the customer record (1300). If the data is valid, the data map is displayed (1400). Otherwise, the key map is redisplayed with an error message (1500).

- Module 2000 is called when the data map is displayed for an add operation. This module receives the data map (2100) and edits the customer data (2200). If the data is valid, it writes the customer record (2300) and displays the key map (1500) with a completion message. Otherwise, the data map is redisplayed with an error message (1400).

- Module 3000 is called when the data map is displayed for a change operation. It works like module 2000, except it reads the customer record for update (3100) and then re-writes it (3200).

- Module 4000 is called when the data map is displayed for a delete operation. It reads the customer record for update (3100), deletes the customer record (4100), and then displays the key map with either a completion message or an error message.

Figure 12-3   The structure chart for the customer maintenance program

The BMS mapset and symbolic map for the maintenance program

Figure 12-4 presents the BMS mapset for the customer maintenance program. If you compare this to the mapset for the maintenance program in chapter 4, you'll notice just two differences. First, the DSATTS and MAPATTS parameters are coded on the DFHMSD macro, both specifying extended color and highlighting. Second, the data entry fields aren't defined with the underline attribute. Instead, the data entry fields in MNTMAP1 are defined with INITIAL parameters that give them a starting value of underscores. In contrast, the data entry fields in MNTMAP2 aren't defined with underlining at all. That's because these fields should have a starting value of underscores only when the user is adding a record. For a change operation, the customer data should be displayed with underscores only in the positions that don't contain data. And for a delete operation, the customer data should be displayed without underscores since the user can't enter data into these fields. Because of that, the program code will control the display of underscores for these fields.

Figure 12-5 (on pages 337 to 339) shows the BMS-generated symbolic map for this mapset. Here, you can see the effect of the DSATTS and MAPATTS parameters: extended color and highlighting fields in the output area for each data field. In a minute, you'll see how these fields are used to control the display of information in the key and data maps.

The code for the BMS mapset   **Page 1**

```
          PRINT NOGEN
MNTSET2   DFHMSD TYPE=&SYSPARM,                                      X
                 LANG=COBOL,                                         X
                 MODE=INOUT,                                         X
                 TERM=3270-2,                                        X
                 CTRL=FREEKB,                                        X
                 STORAGE=AUTO,                                       X
                 DSATTS=(COLOR,HILIGHT),                             X
                 MAPATTS=(COLOR,HILIGHT),                            X
                 TIOAPFX=YES
**********************************************************************
MNTMAP1   DFHMDI SIZE=(24,80),                                      X
                 LINE=1,                                            X
                 COLUMN=1
**********************************************************************
          DFHMDF POS=(1,1),                                         X
                 LENGTH=7,                                          X
                 ATTRB=(NORM,PROT),                                 X
                 COLOR=BLUE,                                        X
                 INITIAL='MNTMAP1'
          DFHMDF POS=(1,20),                                        X
                 LENGTH=20,                                         X
                 ATTRB=(NORM,PROT),                                 X
                 COLOR=GREEN,                                       X
                 INITIAL='Customer Maintenance'
TRANID1   DFHMDF POS=(1,76),                                        X
                 LENGTH=4,                                          X
                 ATTRB=(NORM,PROT),                                 X
                 COLOR=BLUE,                                        X
                 INITIAL='XXXX'
**********************************************************************
          DFHMDF POS=(3,1),                                         X
                 LENGTH=63,                                         X
                 ATTRB=(NORM,PROT),                                 X
                 COLOR=NEUTRAL,                                     X
                 INITIAL='Type a customer number.  Then select an action X
                 and press Enter.'
          DFHMDF POS=(5,1),                                         X
                 LENGTH=24,                                         X
                 ATTRB=(NORM,PROT),                                 X
                 COLOR=GREEN,                                       X
                 INITIAL='Customer number. . . . .'
CUSTNO1   DFHMDF POS=(5,26),                                        X
                 LENGTH=6,                                          X
                 ATTRB=(NORM,UNPROT,FSET),                          X
                 COLOR=TURQUOISE,                                   X
                 INITIAL='_____'
          DFHMDF POS=(5,33),                                        X
                 LENGTH=1,                                          X
                 ATTRB=ASKIP
          DFHMDF POS=(7,1),                                         X
                 LENGTH=24,                                         X
                 ATTRB=(NORM,PROT),                                 X
                 COLOR=GREEN,                                       X
                 INITIAL='Action . . . . . . . . . .'
```

Figure 12-4   The BMS mapset for the customer maintenance program (part 1 of 4)

The code for the BMS mapset

```
ACTION     DFHMDF POS=(7,26),                                     X
                  LENGTH=1,                                       X
                  ATTRB=(NORM,NUM,FSET),                          X
                  COLOR=TURQUOISE,                                X
                  INITIAL='_'
           DFHMDF POS=(7,28),                                     X
                  LENGTH=21,                                      X
                  ATTRB=(NORM,ASKIP),                             X
                  COLOR=NEUTRAL,                                  X
                  INITIAL='1. Add a new customer'
           DFHMDF POS=(8,28),                                     X
                  LENGTH=30,                                      X
                  ATTRB=(NORM,ASKIP),                             X
                  COLOR=NEUTRAL,                                  X
                  INITIAL='2. Change an existing customer'
           DFHMDF POS=(9,28),                                     X
                  LENGTH=21,                                      X
                  ATTRB=(NORM,ASKIP),                             X
                  COLOR=NEUTRAL,                                  X
                  INITIAL='3. Delete an existing customer'
MSG1       DFHMDF POS=(23,1),                                     X
                  LENGTH=79,                                      X
                  ATTRB=(BRT,PROT),                               X
                  COLOR=YELLOW
           DFHMDF POS=(24,1),                                     X
                  LENGTH=20,                                      X
                  ATTRB=(NORM,PROT),                              X
                  COLOR=BLUE,                                     X
                  INITIAL='F3=Exit    F12=Cancel'
DUMMY1     DFHMDF POS=(24,79),                                    X
                  LENGTH=1,                                       X
                  ATTRB=(DRK,PROT,FSET),                          X
                  INITIAL=' '
***********************************************************************
MNTMAP2    DFHMDI SIZE=(24,80),                                   X
                  LINE=1,                                         X
                  COLUMN=1
***********************************************************************
           DFHMDF POS=(1,1),                                      X
                  LENGTH=7,                                       X
                  ATTRB=(NORM,PROT),                              X
                  COLOR=BLUE,                                     X
                  INITIAL='MNTMAP2'
           DFHMDF POS=(1,20),                                     X
                  LENGTH=20,                                      X
                  ATTRB=(NORM,PROT),                              X
                  COLOR=GREEN,                                    X
                  INITIAL='Customer Maintenance'
TRANID2    DFHMDF POS=(1,76),                                     X
                  LENGTH=4,                                       X
                  ATTRB=(NORM,PROT),                              X
                  COLOR=BLUE,                                     X
                  INITIAL='XXXX'
***********************************************************************
INSTR2     DFHMDF POS=(3,1),                                      X
                  LENGTH=79,                                      X
                  ATTRB=(NORM,PROT),                              X
                  COLOR=NEUTRAL
```

Figure 12-4   The BMS mapset for the customer maintenance program (part 2 of 4)

The code for the BMS mapset

```
           DFHMDF POS=(5,1),                                    X
                  LENGTH=24,                                    X
                  ATTRB=(NORM,PROT),                            X
                  COLOR=GREEN,                                  X
                  INITIAL='Customer number. . . . :'
CUSTNO2    DFHMDF POS=(5,26),                                   X
                  LENGTH=6,                                     X
                  ATTRB=(NORM,PROT,FSET),                       X
                  COLOR=TURQUOISE
*********************************************************************
           DFHMDF POS=(7,1),                                    X
                  LENGTH=24,                                    X
                  ATTRB=(NORM,PROT),                            X
                  COLOR=GREEN,                                  X
                  INITIAL='Last name. . . . . . . .'
LNAME      DFHMDF POS=(7,26),                                   X
                  LENGTH=30,                                    X
                  ATTRB=(NORM,UNPROT,FSET),                     X
                  COLOR=TURQUOISE
           DFHMDF POS=(7,57),                                   X
                  LENGTH=1,                                     X
                  ATTRB=ASKIP
*********************************************************************
           DFHMDF POS=(8,1),                                    X
                  LENGTH=24,                                    X
                  ATTRB=(NORM,PROT),                            X
                  COLOR=GREEN,                                  X
                  INITIAL='First name . . . . . . .'
FNAME      DFHMDF POS=(8,26),                                   X
                  LENGTH=20,                                    X
                  ATTRB=(NORM,UNPROT,FSET),                     X
                  COLOR=TURQUOISE
           DFHMDF POS=(8,47),                                   X
                  LENGTH=1,                                     X
                  ATTRB=ASKIP
*********************************************************************
           DFHMDF POS=(9,1),                                    X
                  LENGTH=24,                                    X
                  ATTRB=(NORM,PROT),                            X
                  COLOR=GREEN,                                  X
                  INITIAL='Address. . . . . . . . .'
ADDR       DFHMDF POS=(9,26),                                   X
                  LENGTH=30,                                    X
                  ATTRB=(NORM,UNPROT,FSET),                     X
                  COLOR=TURQUOISE
           DFHMDF POS=(9,57),                                   X
                  LENGTH=1,                                     X
                  ATTRB=ASKIP
*********************************************************************
           DFHMDF POS=(10,1),                                   X
                  LENGTH=24,                                    X
                  ATTRB=(NORM,PROT),                            X
                  COLOR=GREEN,                                  X
                  INITIAL='City . . . . . . . . . .'
CITY       DFHMDF POS=(10,26),                                  X
                  LENGTH=20,                                    X
                  ATTRB=(NORM,UNPROT,FSET),                     X
                  COLOR=TURQUOISE
```

Figure 12-4   The BMS mapset for the customer maintenance program (part 3 of 4)

The code for the BMS mapset   **Page 4**

```
          DFHMDF POS=(10,47),                                          X
                 LENGTH=1,                                             X
                 ATTRB=ASKIP
***********************************************************************
          DFHMDF POS=(11,1),                                           X
                 LENGTH=24,                                            X
                 ATTRB=(NORM,PROT),                                    X
                 COLOR=GREEN,                                          X
                 INITIAL='State. . . . . . . . . .'
STATE     DFHMDF POS=(11,26),                                          X
                 LENGTH=2,                                             X
                 ATTRB=(NORM,UNPROT,FSET),                             X
                 COLOR=TURQUOISE
          DFHMDF POS=(11,29),                                          X
                 LENGTH=1,                                             X
                 ATTRB=ASKIP
***********************************************************************
          DFHMDF POS=(12,1),                                           X
                 LENGTH=24,                                            X
                 ATTRB=(NORM,PROT),                                    X
                 COLOR=GREEN,                                          X
                 INITIAL='Zip Code . . . . . . . .'
ZIPCODE   DFHMDF POS=(12,26),                                          X
                 LENGTH=10,                                            X
                 ATTRB=(NORM,UNPROT,FSET),                             X
                 COLOR=TURQUOISE
          DFHMDF POS=(12,37),                                          X
                 LENGTH=1,                                             X
                 ATTRB=ASKIP
***********************************************************************
MSG2      DFHMDF POS=(23,1),                                           X
                 LENGTH=79,                                            X
                 ATTRB=(BRT,PROT),                                     X
                 COLOR=YELLOW
          DFHMDF POS=(24,1),                                           X
                 LENGTH=20,                                            X
                 ATTRB=(NORM,PROT),                                    X
                 COLOR=BLUE,                                           X
                 INITIAL='F3=Exit    F12=Cancel'
DUMMY2    DFHMDF POS=(24,79),                                          X
                 LENGTH=1,                                             X
                 ATTRB=(DRK,PROT,FSET),                                X
                 INITIAL=' '
***********************************************************************
          DFHMSD TYPE=FINAL
          END
```

Figure 12-4   The BMS mapset for the customer maintenance program (part 4 of 4)

The code for the symbolic map   **Page 1**

```
01 MNTMAP1I.
    03 FILLER                       PIC X(12).
    03 TRANID1L                     PIC S9(4) COMP.
    03 TRANID1F                     PIC X.
    03 FILLER REDEFINES TRANID1F.
        05 TRANID1A                 PIC X.
    03 FILLER                       PIC X(2).
    03 TRANID1I                     PIC X(4).
    03 CUSTNO1L                     PIC S9(4) COMP.
    03 CUSTNO1F                     PIC X.
    03 FILLER REDEFINES CUSTNO1F.
        05 CUSTNO1A                 PIC X.
    03 FILLER                       PIC X(2).
    03 CUSTNO1I                     PIC X(6).
    03 ACTIONL                      PIC S9(4) COMP.
    03 ACTIONF                      PIC X.
    03 FILLER REDEFINES ACTIONF.
        05 ACTIONA                  PIC X.
    03 FILLER                       PIC X(2).
    03 ACTIONI                      PIC X(1).
    03 MSG1L                        PIC S9(4) COMP.
    03 MSG1F                        PIC X.
    03 FILLER REDEFINES MSG1F.
        05 MSG1A                    PIC X.
    03 FILLER                       PIC X(2).
    03 MSG1I                        PIC X(79).
    03 DUMMY1L                      PIC S9(4) COMP.
    03 DUMMY1F                      PIC X.
    03 FILLER REDEFINES DUMMY1F.
        05 DUMMY1A                  PIC X.
    03 FILLER                       PIC X(2).
    03 DUMMY1I                      PIC X(1).
01 MNTMAP1O REDEFINES MNTMAP1I.
    03 FILLER                       PIC X(12).
    03 FILLER                       PIC X(3).
    03 TRANID1C                     PIC X.
    03 TRANID1H                     PIC X.
    03 TRANID1O                     PIC X(4).
    03 FILLER                       PIC X(3).
    03 CUSTNO1C                     PIC X.
    03 CUSTNO1H                     PIC X.
    03 CUSTNO1O                     PIC X(6).
    03 FILLER                       PIC X(3).
    03 ACTIONC                      PIC X.
    03 ACTIONH                      PIC X.
    03 ACTIONO                      PIC X(1).
    03 FILLER                       PIC X(3).
    03 MSG1C                        PIC X.
    03 MSG1H                        PIC X.
    03 MSG1O                        PIC X(79).
    03 FILLER                       PIC X(3).
    03 DUMMY1C                      PIC X.
    03 DUMMY1H                      PIC X.
    03 DUMMY1O                      PIC X(1).
```

Figure 12-5   The symbolic map for the customer maintenance program (part 1 of 3)

The code for the symbolic map

```
01 MNTMAP2I.
    03 FILLER                       PIC X(12).
    03 TRANID2L                     PIC S9(4) COMP.
    03 TRANID2F                     PIC X.
    03 FILLER REDEFINES TRANID2F.
        05 TRANID2A                 PIC X.
    03 FILLER                       PIC X(2).
    03 TRANID2I                     PIC X(4).
    03 INSTR2L                      PIC S9(4) COMP.
    03 INSTR2F                      PIC X.
    03 FILLER REDEFINES INSTR2F.
        05 INSTR2A                  PIC X.
    03 FILLER                       PIC X(2).
    03 INSTR2I                      PIC X(79).
    03 CUSTNO2L                     PIC S9(4) COMP.
    03 CUSTNO2F                     PIC X.
    03 FILLER REDEFINES CUSTNO2F.
        05 CUSTNO2A                 PIC X.
    03 FILLER                       PIC X(2).
    03 CUSTNO2I                     PIC X(6).
    03 LNAMEL                       PIC S9(4) COMP.
    03 LNAMEF                       PIC X.
    03 FILLER REDEFINES LNAMEF.
        05 LNAMEA                   PIC X.
    03 FILLER                       PIC X(2).
    03 LNAMEI                       PIC X(30).
    03 FNAMEL                       PIC S9(4) COMP.
    03 FNAMEF                       PIC X.
    03 FILLER REDEFINES FNAMEF.
        05 FNAMEA                   PIC X.
    03 FILLER                       PIC X(2).
    03 FNAMEI                       PIC X(20).
    03 ADDRL                        PIC S9(4) COMP.
    03 ADDRF                        PIC X.
    03 FILLER REDEFINES ADDRF.
        05 ADDRA                    PIC X.
    03 FILLER                       PIC X(2).
    03 ADDRI                        PIC X(30).
    03 CITYL                        PIC S9(4) COMP.
    03 CITYF                        PIC X.
    03 FILLER REDEFINES CITYF.
        05 CITYA                    PIC X.
    03 FILLER                       PIC X(2).
    03 CITYI                        PIC X(20).
    03 STATEL                       PIC S9(4) COMP.
    03 STATEF                       PIC X.
    03 FILLER REDEFINES STATEF.
        05 STATEA                   PIC X.
    03 FILLER                       PIC X(2).
    03 STATEI                       PIC X(2).
    03 ZIPCODEL                     PIC S9(4) COMP.
    03 ZIPCODEF                     PIC X.
    03 FILLER REDEFINES ZIPCODEF.
        05 ZIPCODEA                 PIC X.
    03 FILLER                       PIC X(2).
    03 ZIPCODEI                     PIC X(10).
```

Figure 12-5   The symbolic map for the customer maintenance program (part 2 of 3)

The code for the symbolic map

```
    03  MSG2L                       PIC S9(4) COMP.
    03  MSG2F                       PIC X.
    03  FILLER REDEFINES MSG2F.
        05  MSG2A                       PIC X.
    03  FILLER                      PIC X(2).
    03  MSG2I                       PIC X(79).
    03  DUMMY2L                     PIC S9(4) COMP.
    03  DUMMY2F                     PIC X.
    03  FILLER REDEFINES DUMMY2F.
        05  DUMMY2A                     PIC X.
    03  FILLER                      PIC X(2).
    03  DUMMY2I                     PIC X(1).
01  MNTMAP2O REDEFINES MNTMAP2I.
    03  FILLER                      PIC X(12).
    03  FILLER                      PIC X(3).
    03  TRANID2C                    PIC X.
    03  TRANID2H                    PIC X.
    03  TRANID2O                    PIC X(4).
    03  FILLER                      PIC X(3).
    03  INSTR2C                     PIC X.
    03  INSTR2H                     PIC X.
    03  INSTR2O                     PIC X(79).
    03  FILLER                      PIC X(3).
    03  CUSTNO2C                    PIC X.
    03  CUSTNO2H                    PIC X.
    03  CUSTNO2O                    PIC X(6).
    03  FILLER                      PIC X(3).
    03  LNAMEC                      PIC X.
    03  LNAMEH                      PIC X.
    03  LNAMEO                      PIC X(30).
    03  FILLER                      PIC X(3).
    03  FNAMEC                      PIC X.
    03  FNAMEH                      PIC X.
    03  FNAMEO                      PIC X(20).
    03  FILLER                      PIC X(3).
    03  ADDRC                       PIC X.
    03  ADDRH                       PIC X.
    03  ADDRO                       PIC X(30).
    03  FILLER                      PIC X(3).
    03  CITYC                       PIC X.
    03  CITYH                       PIC X.
    03  CITYO                       PIC X(20).
    03  FILLER                      PIC X(3).
    03  STATEC                      PIC X.
    03  STATEH                      PIC X.
    03  STATEO                      PIC X(2).
    03  FILLER                      PIC X(3).
    03  ZIPCODEC                    PIC X.
    03  ZIPCODEH                    PIC X.
    03  ZIPCODEO                    PIC X(10).
    03  FILLER                      PIC X(3).
    03  MSG2C                       PIC X.
    03  MSG2H                       PIC X.
    03  MSG2O                       PIC X(79).
    03  FILLER                      PIC X(3).
    03  DUMMY2C                     PIC X.
    03  DUMMY2H                     PIC X.
    03  DUMMY2O                     PIC X(1).
```

Figure 12-5   The symbolic map for the customer maintenance program (part 3 of 3)

The COBOL code for the maintenance program

Figure 12-6 shows the source listing for the maintenance program. Because it's similar to the program you saw in chapter 5, I'll focus mainly on the differences here.

In the Working-Storage Section, you can see a Copy statement for the ERRPARM copy member you saw chapter 8. As described in that chapter, this program will use this copy member to pass EIB values to the error handling subprogram, SYSERR.

In the Procedure Division, the procedures that process the key map (1000, 1100, and 1200) contain new code for manipulating the screen display. First, notice the Inspect statements in procedures 1000 and 1100 (on pages 3 and 4 of the listing). The Inspect statement in procedure 1100 removes underscores from the data in the key map that was retrieved by the preceding RECEIVE MAP command. That way, procedure 1200 can edit these fields properly. Then, the Inspect statement in procedure 1000 replaces any spaces in the customer record fields with underscores before the data is sent to the terminal.

Also notice the Move statement at the beginning of procedure 1200 that turns off the highlight attributes of the two entry fields in the key map. If the editing statements that follow find the customer number or action field to contain invalid data, the highlight attribute for that field is then set to reverse video. In addition, the length field is set to -1, and an appropriate error message is moved to the message field. As a result, when the screen is displayed, all the fields that contain errors will be highlighted, and the cursor will appear in the first of those fields. And because the fields are edited in reverse order, the error message that's displayed will refer to the first field in error.

The customer maintenance program

```
       IDENTIFICATION DIVISION.
       PROGRAM-ID.  CUSTMNT2.
      *
       ENVIRONMENT DIVISION.
      *
       DATA DIVISION.
      *
       WORKING-STORAGE SECTION.
      *
       01  SWITCHES.
           05  VALID-DATA-SW              PIC X(01) VALUE 'Y'.
               88  VALID-DATA                       VALUE 'Y'.
      *
       01  FLAGS.
           05  SEND-FLAG                  PIC X(01).
               88  SEND-ERASE                       VALUE '1'.
               88  SEND-ERASE-ALARM                 VALUE '2'.
               88  SEND-DATAONLY                    VALUE '3'.
               88  SEND-DATAONLY-ALARM              VALUE '4'.
      *
       01  WORK-FIELDS.
           05  RESPONSE-CODE              PIC S9(08) COMP.
      *
       01  USER-INSTRUCTIONS.
           05  ADD-INSTRUCTION            PIC X(79) VALUE
               'Type information for new customer.  Then Press Enter.'.
           05  CHANGE-INSTRUCTION         PIC X(79) VALUE
               'Type changes.  Then press Enter.'.
           05  DELETE-INSTRUCTION         PIC X(79) VALUE
               'Press Enter to delete this customer or press F12 to canc
      -        'el.'.
      *
       01  COMMUNICATION-AREA.
           05  CA-CONTEXT-FLAG            PIC X(01).
               88  PROCESS-KEY-MAP                  VALUE '1'.
               88  PROCESS-ADD-CUSTOMER             VALUE '2'.
               88  PROCESS-CHANGE-CUSTOMER          VALUE '3'.
               88  PROCESS-DELETE-CUSTOMER          VALUE '4'.
           05  CA-CUSTOMER-RECORD.
               10  CA-CUSTOMER-NUMBER     PIC X(06).
               10  FILLER                 PIC X(112).
      *
       COPY CUSTMAS.
      *
       COPY MNTSET2.
      *
       COPY DFHAID.
      *
       COPY ATTR.
      *
       COPY ERRPARM.
      *
       LINKAGE SECTION.
      *
       01  DFHCOMMAREA                    PIC X(119).
      *
```

Figure 12-6   The COBOL code for the customer maintenance program (part 1 of 10)

The customer maintenance program   **Page 2**

```
PROCEDURE DIVISION.
*
0000-PROCESS-CUSTOMER-MAINT.
*
    IF EIBCALEN > ZERO
        MOVE DFHCOMMAREA TO COMMUNICATION-AREA
    END-IF.
*
    EVALUATE TRUE
        WHEN EIBCALEN = ZERO
            MOVE LOW-VALUE TO MNTMAP1O
            MOVE -1 TO CUSTNO1L
            SET SEND-ERASE TO TRUE
            PERFORM 1500-SEND-KEY-MAP
            SET PROCESS-KEY-MAP TO TRUE
*
        WHEN EIBAID = DFHPF3
            EXEC CICS
                XCTL PROGRAM('INVMENU')
            END-EXEC
*
        WHEN EIBAID = DFHPF12
            IF PROCESS-KEY-MAP
                EXEC CICS
                    XCTL PROGRAM('INVMENU')
                END-EXEC
            ELSE
                MOVE LOW-VALUE TO MNTMAP1O
                MOVE -1 TO CUSTNO1L
                SET SEND-ERASE TO TRUE
                PERFORM 1500-SEND-KEY-MAP
                SET PROCESS-KEY-MAP TO TRUE
            END-IF
*
        WHEN EIBAID = DFHCLEAR
            IF PROCESS-KEY-MAP
                MOVE LOW-VALUE TO MNTMAP1O
                MOVE -1 TO CUSTNO1L
                SET SEND-ERASE TO TRUE
                PERFORM 1500-SEND-KEY-MAP
            ELSE
                MOVE LOW-VALUE TO MNTMAP2O
                MOVE CA-CUSTOMER-NUMBER TO CUSTNO2O
                EVALUATE TRUE
                    WHEN PROCESS-ADD-CUSTOMER
                        MOVE ADD-INSTRUCTION    TO INSTR2O
                    WHEN PROCESS-CHANGE-CUSTOMER
                        MOVE CHANGE-INSTRUCTION TO INSTR2O
                    WHEN PROCESS-DELETE-CUSTOMER
                        MOVE DELETE-INSTRUCTION TO INSTR2O
                END-EVALUATE
                MOVE -1 TO LNAMEL
                SET SEND-ERASE TO TRUE
                PERFORM 1400-SEND-DATA-MAP
            END-IF
*
        WHEN EIBAID = DFHPA1 OR DFHPA2 OR DFHPA3
            CONTINUE
```

Figure 12-6   The COBOL code for the customer maintenance program (part 2 of 10)

The customer maintenance program   **Page 3**

```
                    WHEN EIBAID = DFHENTER
                        EVALUATE TRUE
                            WHEN PROCESS-KEY-MAP
                                PERFORM 1000-PROCESS-KEY-MAP
                            WHEN PROCESS-ADD-CUSTOMER
                                PERFORM 2000-PROCESS-ADD-CUSTOMER
                            WHEN PROCESS-CHANGE-CUSTOMER
                                PERFORM 3000-PROCESS-CHANGE-CUSTOMER
                            WHEN PROCESS-DELETE-CUSTOMER
                                PERFORM 4000-PROCESS-DELETE-CUSTOMER
                        END-EVALUATE
*
                    WHEN OTHER
                        IF PROCESS-KEY-MAP
                            MOVE LOW-VALUE TO MNTMAP1O
                            MOVE 'That key is unassigned.' TO MSG1O
                            MOVE -1 TO CUSTNO1L
                            SET SEND-DATAONLY-ALARM TO TRUE
                            PERFORM 1500-SEND-KEY-MAP
                        ELSE
                            MOVE LOW-VALUE TO MNTMAP2O
                            MOVE 'That key is unassigned.' TO MSG2O
                            MOVE -1 TO LNAMEL
                            SET SEND-DATAONLY-ALARM TO TRUE
                            PERFORM 1400-SEND-DATA-MAP
                        END-IF
                END-EVALUATE.
*
            EXEC CICS
                RETURN TRANSID('MNT2')
                        COMMAREA(COMMUNICATION-AREA)
            END-EXEC.
*
        1000-PROCESS-KEY-MAP.
*
            PERFORM 1100-RECEIVE-KEY-MAP.
            PERFORM 1200-EDIT-KEY-DATA.
            IF VALID-DATA
                IF NOT PROCESS-DELETE-CUSTOMER
                    INSPECT CUSTOMER-MASTER-RECORD
                        REPLACING ALL SPACE BY '_'
                END-IF
                MOVE CUSTNO1I      TO CUSTNO2O
                MOVE CM-LAST-NAME  TO LNAMEO
                MOVE CM-FIRST-NAME TO FNAMEO
                MOVE CM-ADDRESS    TO ADDRO
                MOVE CM-CITY       TO CITYO
                MOVE CM-STATE      TO STATEO
                MOVE CM-ZIP-CODE   TO ZIPCODEO
                MOVE -1 TO LNAMEL
                SET SEND-ERASE TO TRUE
                PERFORM 1400-SEND-DATA-MAP
            ELSE
                MOVE LOW-VALUE TO CUSTNO1O
                                  ACTIONO
                SET SEND-DATAONLY-ALARM TO TRUE
                PERFORM 1500-SEND-KEY-MAP
            END-IF.
```

Figure 12-6   The COBOL code for the customer maintenance program (part 3 of 10)

The customer maintenance program

```
     1100-RECEIVE-KEY-MAP.
*
     EXEC CICS
         RECEIVE MAP('MNTMAP1')
                 MAPSET('MNTSET2')
                 INTO(MNTMAP1I)
     END-EXEC.
     INSPECT MNTMAP1I
         REPLACING ALL '_' BY SPACE.
*
 1200-EDIT-KEY-DATA.
*
     MOVE ATTR-NO-HIGHLIGHT TO ACTIONH
                               CUSTNO1H.
*
     IF ACTIONI NOT = '1' AND '2' AND '3'
         MOVE ATTR-REVERSE TO ACTIONH
         MOVE -1 TO ACTIONL
         MOVE 'Action must be 1, 2, or 3.' TO MSG1O
         MOVE 'N' TO VALID-DATA-SW
     END-IF.
     IF       CUSTNO1L = ZERO
          OR CUSTNO1I = SPACE
         MOVE ATTR-REVERSE TO CUSTNO1H
         MOVE -1 TO CUSTNO1L
         MOVE 'You must enter a customer number.' TO MSG1O
         MOVE 'N' TO VALID-DATA-SW
     END-IF.
*
     IF VALID-DATA
         MOVE LOW-VALUE TO MNTMAP2O
         EVALUATE ACTIONI
             WHEN '1'
                 PERFORM 1300-READ-CUSTOMER-RECORD
                 IF RESPONSE-CODE = DFHRESP(NOTFND)
                     MOVE ADD-INSTRUCTION TO INSTR2O
                     SET PROCESS-ADD-CUSTOMER TO TRUE
                     MOVE SPACE TO CUSTOMER-MASTER-RECORD
                 ELSE
                     IF RESPONSE-CODE = DFHRESP(NORMAL)
                         MOVE 'That customer already exists.'
                             TO MSG1O
                         MOVE 'N' TO VALID-DATA-SW
                     END-IF
                 END-IF
             WHEN '2'
                 PERFORM 1300-READ-CUSTOMER-RECORD
                 IF RESPONSE-CODE = DFHRESP(NORMAL)
                     MOVE CUSTOMER-MASTER-RECORD TO
                         CA-CUSTOMER-RECORD
                     MOVE CHANGE-INSTRUCTION TO INSTR2O
                     SET PROCESS-CHANGE-CUSTOMER TO TRUE
                 ELSE
                     IF RESPONSE-CODE = DFHRESP(NOTFND)
                         MOVE 'That customer does not exist.' TO
                             MSG1O
                         MOVE 'N' TO VALID-DATA-SW
                     END-IF
                 END-IF
```

Figure 12-6   The COBOL code for the customer maintenance program (part 4 of 10)

The customer maintenance program   Page 5

```
              WHEN '3'
                  PERFORM 1300-READ-CUSTOMER-RECORD
                  IF RESPONSE-CODE = DFHRESP(NORMAL)
                      MOVE CUSTOMER-MASTER-RECORD TO
                          CA-CUSTOMER-RECORD
                      MOVE DELETE-INSTRUCTION TO INSTR2O
                      SET PROCESS-DELETE-CUSTOMER TO TRUE
                      MOVE ATTR-PROT TO LNAMEA
                                        FNAMEA
                                        ADDRA
                                        CITYA
                                        STATEA
                                        ZIPCODEA
                  ELSE
                      IF RESPONSE-CODE = DFHRESP(NOTFND)
                          MOVE 'That customer does not exist.' TO
                              MSG1O
                          MOVE 'N' TO VALID-DATA-SW
                      END-IF
                  END-IF
          END-EVALUATE.
*
 1300-READ-CUSTOMER-RECORD.
*
     EXEC CICS
         READ FILE('CUSTMAS')
              INTO(CUSTOMER-MASTER-RECORD)
              RIDFLD(CUSTNO1I)
              RESP(RESPONSE-CODE)
     END-EXEC.
     IF      RESPONSE-CODE NOT = DFHRESP(NORMAL)
         AND RESPONSE-CODE NOT = DFHRESP(NOTFND)
         PERFORM 9999-TERMINATE-PROGRAM
     END-IF.
*
 1400-SEND-DATA-MAP.
*
     MOVE 'MNT2' TO TRANID2O.
*
     EVALUATE TRUE
         WHEN SEND-ERASE
             EXEC CICS
                 SEND MAP('MNTMAP2')
                      MAPSET('MNTSET2')
                      FROM(MNTMAP2O)
                      ERASE
                      CURSOR
             END-EXEC
         WHEN SEND-DATAONLY-ALARM
             EXEC CICS
                 SEND MAP('MNTMAP2')
                      MAPSET('MNTSET2')
                      FROM(MNTMAP2O)
                      DATAONLY
                      ALARM
                      CURSOR
             END-EXEC
     END-EVALUATE.
```

Figure 12-6   The COBOL code for the customer maintenance program (part 5 of 10)

Procedure 2000 is invoked to add a customer to the customer file. It begins by performing procedure 2100 to receive the data map. Like procedure 1100, procedure 2100 (on page 7 of the listing) ends with an Inspect statement to remove any underscores that are in any of the data map's input fields.

Then, procedure 2000 performs procedure 2200 to edit the customer data. Although module 2200 is long, it's not complicated since the only editing requirement for this program is that every field must be entered. The code tests the fields starting at the bottom of the screen, following the basic editing pattern: If a field is in error, its highlight attribute is set to reverse video, its length field is set to -1, an error message is moved to the message field, and a validity switch is set to N.

If the data is valid, the program calls procedure 2300 to write a record to the customer file. Otherwise, it moves low values to the output data fields so they're not sent to the terminal again, sets Send-Dataonly-Alarm to True, and calls module 1400 to send the data map so the user can correct the invalid entries.

Procedure 3000 (on page 9 of the listing) controls changes to customer records and is much like procedure 2000. It too performs procedure 2100 to receive the data map, then procedure 2200 to edit the data. However, instead of invoking procedure 2300 to write the record, it invokes procedure 3100 to read the record for update and procedure 3200 to rewrite the record if it hasn't already been updated or deleted by another user.

The only other procedure that's changed in this version of the maintenance program is 9999-TERMINATE-PROGRAM (on page 10). This procedure sets the values of the fields in the ERRPARM copy member, and then invokes the SYSERR subprogram and passes it those fields. As you learned in chapter 8, SYSERR displays an error message using the passed fields and then ends the task by issuing a RETURN command without any options.

The customer maintenance program   **Page 6**

```
    1500-SEND-KEY-MAP.
*
    MOVE 'MNT2' TO TRANID1O.
*
    EVALUATE TRUE
        WHEN SEND-ERASE
            EXEC CICS
                SEND MAP('MNTMAP1')
                     MAPSET('MNTSET2')
                     FROM(MNTMAP1O)
                     ERASE
                     CURSOR
            END-EXEC
        WHEN SEND-ERASE-ALARM
            EXEC CICS
                SEND MAP('MNTMAP1')
                     MAPSET('MNTSET2')
                     FROM(MNTMAP1O)
                     ERASE
                     ALARM
                     CURSOR
            END-EXEC
        WHEN SEND-DATAONLY-ALARM
            EXEC CICS
                SEND MAP('MNTMAP1')
                     MAPSET('MNTSET2')
                     FROM(MNTMAP1O)
                     DATAONLY
                     ALARM
                     CURSOR
            END-EXEC
    END-EVALUATE.
*
 2000-PROCESS-ADD-CUSTOMER.
*
    PERFORM 2100-RECEIVE-DATA-MAP.
    PERFORM 2200-EDIT-CUSTOMER-DATA.
    IF VALID-DATA
        PERFORM 2300-WRITE-CUSTOMER-RECORD
        IF RESPONSE-CODE = DFHRESP(NORMAL)
            MOVE 'Customer record added.' TO MSG1O
            SET SEND-ERASE TO TRUE
        ELSE
            IF RESPONSE-CODE = DFHRESP(DUPREC)
                MOVE 'Another user has added a record with that c
-                    'ustomer number.' TO MSG1O
                SET SEND-ERASE-ALARM TO TRUE
            END-IF
        END-IF
        MOVE -1 TO CUSTNO1L
        PERFORM 1500-SEND-KEY-MAP
        SET PROCESS-KEY-MAP TO TRUE
```

Figure 12-6   The COBOL code for the customer maintenance program (part 6 of 10)

The customer maintenance program

```
            ELSE
                MOVE LOW-VALUE TO LNAMEO
                                 FNAMEO
                                 ADDRO
                                 CITYO
                                 STATEO
                                 ZIPCODEO
                SET SEND-DATAONLY-ALARM TO TRUE
                PERFORM 1400-SEND-DATA-MAP
            END-IF.
*
    2100-RECEIVE-DATA-MAP.
*
        EXEC CICS
            RECEIVE MAP('MNTMAP2')
                    MAPSET('MNTSET2')
                    INTO(MNTMAP2I)
        END-EXEC.
        INSPECT MNTMAP2I
            REPLACING ALL '_' BY SPACE.
*
    2200-EDIT-CUSTOMER-DATA.
*
        MOVE ATTR-NO-HIGHLIGHT TO ZIPCODEH
                                  STATEH
                                  CITYH
                                  ADDRH
                                  FNAMEH
                                  LNAMEH.
*
        IF      ZIPCODEI = SPACE
            OR ZIPCODEL = ZERO
            MOVE ATTR-REVERSE TO ZIPCODEH
            MOVE -1 TO ZIPCODEL
            MOVE 'You must enter a zip code.' TO MSG2O
            MOVE 'N' TO VALID-DATA-SW
        END-IF.
*
        IF      STATEI = SPACE
            OR STATEL = ZERO
            MOVE ATTR-REVERSE TO STATEH
            MOVE -1 TO STATEL
            MOVE 'You must enter a state.' TO MSG2O
            MOVE 'N' TO VALID-DATA-SW
        END-IF.
*
        IF      CITYI = SPACE
            OR CITYL = ZERO
            MOVE ATTR-REVERSE TO CITYH
            MOVE -1 TO CITYL
            MOVE 'You must enter a city.' TO MSG2O
            MOVE 'N' TO VALID-DATA-SW
        END-IF.
*
```

Figure 12-6   The COBOL code for the customer maintenance program (part 7 of 10)

The customer maintenance program   **Page 8**

```
        IF       ADDRI = SPACE
             OR ADDRL = ZERO
           MOVE ATTR-REVERSE TO ADDRH
           MOVE -1 TO ADDRL
           MOVE 'You must enter an address.' TO MSG2O
           MOVE 'N' TO VALID-DATA-SW
        END-IF.
*
        IF       FNAMEI = SPACE
             OR FNAMEL = ZERO
           MOVE ATTR-REVERSE TO FNAMEH
           MOVE -1 TO FNAMEL
           MOVE 'You must enter a first name.' TO MSG2O
           MOVE 'N' TO VALID-DATA-SW
        END-IF.
*
        IF       LNAMEI = SPACE
             OR LNAMEL = ZERO
           MOVE ATTR-REVERSE TO LNAMEH
           MOVE -1 TO LNAMEL
           MOVE 'You must enter a last name.' TO MSG2O
           MOVE 'N' TO VALID-DATA-SW
        END-IF.
*
    2300-WRITE-CUSTOMER-RECORD.
*
        MOVE CUSTNO2I TO CM-CUSTOMER-NUMBER.
        MOVE LNAMEI    TO CM-LAST-NAME.
        MOVE FNAMEI    TO CM-FIRST-NAME.
        MOVE ADDRI     TO CM-ADDRESS.
        MOVE CITYI     TO CM-CITY.
        MOVE STATEI    TO CM-STATE.
        MOVE ZIPCODEI TO CM-ZIP-CODE.
        EXEC CICS
            WRITE FILE('CUSTMAS')
                  FROM(CUSTOMER-MASTER-RECORD)
                  RIDFLD(CM-CUSTOMER-NUMBER)
                  RESP(RESPONSE-CODE)
        END-EXEC.
        IF       RESPONSE-CODE NOT = DFHRESP(NORMAL)
             AND RESPONSE-CODE NOT = DFHRESP(DUPREC)
           PERFORM 9999-TERMINATE-PROGRAM
        END-IF.
*
```

Figure 12-6   The COBOL code for the customer maintenance program (part 8 of 10)

The customer maintenance program   **Page 9**

```
    3000-PROCESS-CHANGE-CUSTOMER.
*
    PERFORM 2100-RECEIVE-DATA-MAP.
    PERFORM 2200-EDIT-CUSTOMER-DATA.
    IF VALID-DATA
        MOVE CUSTNO2I TO CM-CUSTOMER-NUMBER
        PERFORM 3100-READ-CUSTOMER-FOR-UPDATE
        IF RESPONSE-CODE = DFHRESP(NORMAL)
            IF CUSTOMER-MASTER-RECORD = CA-CUSTOMER-RECORD
                PERFORM 3200-REWRITE-CUSTOMER-RECORD
                MOVE 'Customer record updated.' TO MSG1O
                SET SEND-ERASE TO TRUE
            ELSE
                MOVE 'Another user has updated the record.  Try a
-                   'gain.' TO MSG1O
                SET SEND-ERASE-ALARM TO TRUE
            END-IF
        ELSE
            IF RESPONSE-CODE = DFHRESP(NOTFND)
                MOVE 'Another user has deleted the record.' TO
                    MSG1O
                SET SEND-ERASE-ALARM TO TRUE
            END-IF
        END-IF
        MOVE -1 TO CUSTNO1L
        PERFORM 1500-SEND-KEY-MAP
        SET PROCESS-KEY-MAP TO TRUE
    ELSE
        MOVE LOW-VALUE TO LNAMEO
                         FNAMEO
                         ADDRO
                         CITYO
                         STATEO
                         ZIPCODEO
        SET SEND-DATAONLY-ALARM TO TRUE
        PERFORM 1400-SEND-DATA-MAP
    END-IF.
*
    3100-READ-CUSTOMER-FOR-UPDATE.
*
    EXEC CICS
        READ FILE('CUSTMAS')
             INTO(CUSTOMER-MASTER-RECORD)
             RIDFLD(CM-CUSTOMER-NUMBER)
             UPDATE
             RESP(RESPONSE-CODE)
    END-EXEC.
    IF    RESPONSE-CODE NOT = DFHRESP(NORMAL)
        AND RESPONSE-CODE NOT = DFHRESP(NOTFND)
        PERFORM 9999-TERMINATE-PROGRAM
    END-IF.
*
    3200-REWRITE-CUSTOMER-RECORD.
*
    MOVE LNAMEI    TO CM-LAST-NAME.
    MOVE FNAMEI    TO CM-FIRST-NAME.
    MOVE ADDRI     TO CM-ADDRESS.
```

Figure 12-6   The COBOL code for the customer maintenance program (part 9 of 10)

The customer maintenance program   **Page 10**

```
        MOVE CITYI    TO CM-CITY.
        MOVE STATEI   TO CM-STATE.
        MOVE ZIPCODEI TO CM-ZIP-CODE.
        EXEC CICS
            REWRITE FILE('CUSTMAS')
                    FROM(CUSTOMER-MASTER-RECORD)
                    RESP(RESPONSE-CODE)
        END-EXEC.
        IF RESPONSE-CODE NOT = DFHRESP(NORMAL)
            PERFORM 9999-TERMINATE-PROGRAM
        END-IF.
*
    4000-PROCESS-DELETE-CUSTOMER.
*
        MOVE CA-CUSTOMER-NUMBER TO CM-CUSTOMER-NUMBER.
        PERFORM 3100-READ-CUSTOMER-FOR-UPDATE.
        IF RESPONSE-CODE = DFHRESP(NORMAL)
            IF CUSTOMER-MASTER-RECORD = CA-CUSTOMER-RECORD
                PERFORM 4100-DELETE-CUSTOMER-RECORD
                MOVE 'Customer deleted.' TO MSG10
                SET SEND-ERASE TO TRUE
            ELSE
                MOVE 'Another user has updated the record.  Try again
                    '.' TO MSG10
                SET SEND-ERASE-ALARM TO TRUE
            END-IF
        ELSE
            IF RESPONSE-CODE = DFHRESP(NOTFND)
                MOVE 'Another user has deleted the record.' TO
                    MSG10
                SET SEND-ERASE-ALARM TO TRUE
            END-IF
        END-IF.
        MOVE -1 TO CUSTNO1L.
        PERFORM 1500-SEND-KEY-MAP.
        SET PROCESS-KEY-MAP TO TRUE.
*
    4100-DELETE-CUSTOMER-RECORD.
*
        EXEC CICS
            DELETE FILE('CUSTMAS')
                   RESP(RESPONSE-CODE)
        END-EXEC.
        IF  RESPONSE-CODE NOT = DFHRESP(NORMAL)
            PERFORM 9999-TERMINATE-PROGRAM
        END-IF.
*
    9999-TERMINATE-PROGRAM.
*
        MOVE EIBRESP   TO ERR-RESP.
        MOVE EIBRESP2 TO ERR-RESP2.
        MOVE EIBTRNID TO ERR-TRNID.
        MOVE EIBRSRCE TO ERR-RSRCE.
        EXEC CICS
            XCTL PROGRAM('SYSERR')
                 COMMAREA(ERROR-PARAMETERS)
        END-EXEC.
```

Figure 12-6   The COBOL code for the customer maintenance program (part 10 of 10)

Perspective

As you might guess, there are other ways to implement a maintenance program like the one presented in this chapter. For example, the key map could accept just a customer number. Then, if the user enters a customer number that doesn't exist, the program could assume that a customer is to be added to the file. If the user enters a number that does exist, however, the program could display the data for that customer and let the user delete the record by pressing a PF key or update it by typing changes and pressing the Enter key. Alternatively, you could develop separate programs to add, change, and delete customers. Regardless of how the maintenance function is implemented, though, the program presented here illustrates the basic requirements of any file maintenance program.

13

The order entry program

This chapter presents the order entry program, the most complex one in the invoicing application. It implements several techniques that you won't see anywhere else in this book. In particular, this program handles numeric input data, it uses the ASKTIME and FORMATTIME commands to get the current date for invoices, and it uses a programmer-generated symbolic map. In addition, the editing requirements for this program are complex, as is the code for changing the attributes for the fields in the map used by this program. Because of that, you'll want to study this program carefully.

The specifications for the order entry program

Figure 13-1 presents the specifications for the order entry program. Simply put, this program accepts orders from the user and writes them to the invoice file, a VSAM indexed file keyed by invoice number. The data for each order consists of a customer number, an optional purchase order number, and up to 10 line items. Each line item must include a product code and a quantity. In addition, the user can enter a net price for a line item to override the unit price stored in the product record.

After the user enters the data for an order, the program edits it. If the program detects no entry errors, it redisplays the order data, along with information from the customer and product files, so the user can sight-verify the order. To post the order, the user presses the Enter key. Alternatively, the user can press PF4 to make corrections to the order before posting it. Or, the user can press PF12 to cancel the order altogether. When the user exits the order entry program, the program displays a message showing how many orders were entered before it returns to the menu.

The editing requirements for this program are more demanding than for the programs you've seen so far. To begin, the customer number must be in the customer file, and any product codes entered must be in the product file. In addition, any quantity and net price fields entered must be valid numbers.

Beyond these requirements, the program has a number of cross-validation editing requirements. For example, if the user enters a product code, a quantity must also be entered, and vice versa. The net price field is optional, but if the user enters it, a product code must also be entered. Finally, the user must enter at least one line item.

The program overview for the order entry program

Program	ORDRENT: Order entry program
Trans-id	ORD1
Overview	Writes orders to an invoice file based on data entered by the user.
Input/output	INVOICE Invoice file CUSTMAS Customer master file PRODUCT Product (inventory) file ORDMAP1 Order entry map

Processing specifications

1. Control is transferred to this program via XCTL from the menu program INVMENU with no communication area. The user can also start the program by entering the trans-id ORD1. In either case, the program should respond by displaying the order entry map.

2. On the order entry map, the user enters a customer number, a PO number, and data for up to 10 line items. The program edits the data according to the rules listed in step 3. If the data is valid, the program redisplays the map with all fields protected. Then, the user can post the order by pressing the Enter key or make additional changes by pressing PF4. If the user presses PF4, the program should unprotect the entry fields and let the user enter changes. If the user presses PF12, the program should cancel the order and redisplay the entry screen with blank fields. The user ends the program by pressing PF3.

3. Order data should be edited according to the following rules:

Customer number	Must be in the customer file
Product code	Must be in the product file
Quantity	Must be a valid integer (use the INTEDIT subprogram)
Net price	Must be a valid decimal number (use the NUMEDIT subprogram)

   In addition, the following cross-validation requirements must be checked:

   a. If the user enters a product code, a quantity for that line item is required;

   b. The user cannot enter a quantity or net price on a line without a product code;

   c. The user must enter at least one line item.

4. If the user does not enter a net price, use the list price from the appropriate product record.

5. To obtain the invoice number, invoke the GETINV program with a LINK command.

6. Use the ASKTIME and FORMATTIME commands to get the current date for the invoices and format it as MMDDYYYY.

7. When the user exits the program, display the total number of orders entered before returning to the menu.

8. If an unrecoverable error occurs, terminate the program by invoking the SYSERR subprogram with an XCTL command.

Figure 13-1   The specifications for the order entry program (part 1 of 2)

Although this program could be implemented with two maps, I decided to use the same map for the entry screen and the verify screen. Because of that, this program makes several formatting changes depending on which screen it displays.

First, to display the verify screen, the program sets the attribute bytes of each entry field to protected so the user can't make changes. Then, if the user wants to modify the order, the program restores the attribute bytes to unprotected before the entry screen is redisplayed. Second, the program displays the quantity fields on the verify screen with leading zeros suppressed (picture ZZZZ9) and the net price fields with both zero suppression and decimal point insertion (picture ZZZZZZ9.99). Finally, the program adjusts the function key assignments shown in line 24 depending on which screen is being displayed. That's why that area is filled with X's in the screen layout instead of a constant value as in all the other programs you've seen so far.

The screen layout for the order entry program

Map name	ORDMAP1	Date	03/19/2001
Program name	ORDRENT	Designer	Doug Lowe

```
ORDMAP1              Order Entry                                                          XXXX

XXXXXXXXXXXXXXXXXXXXXXXXXXXXXXXXXXXXXXXXXXXXXXXXXXXXXXXXXXXXXXXXXXXXXXXXXXXXXXXXXX

Customer number  .  .  .  XXXXXX         Customer: XXXXXXXXXXXXXXXXXXXXXXXXXXXXXX
P.O.  number     .  .  .  .  XXXXXXXXXX             XXXXXXXXXXXXXXXXXXXXXXXX
                                                   XXXXXXXXXXXXXXXXXXXXXXXXXXXXX
                                                   XXXXXXXXXXXXXXXXXXXX  XX  XXXXXXXXXX

Prod code        Qty   Description              List          Net            Amount
XXXXXXXXXXX  XXXXX   XXXXXXXXXXXXXXXXXXXXX  Z,ZZZ,ZZ9.99  XXXXXXXXXX  Z,ZZZ,ZZ9.99
XXXXXXXXXXX  XXXXX   XXXXXXXXXXXXXXXXXXXXX  Z,ZZZ,ZZ9.99  XXXXXXXXXX  Z,ZZZ,ZZ9.99
XXXXXXXXXXX  XXXXX   XXXXXXXXXXXXXXXXXXXXX  Z,ZZZ,ZZ9.99  XXXXXXXXXX  Z,ZZZ,ZZ9.99
XXXXXXXXXXX  XXXXX   XXXXXXXXXXXXXXXXXXXXX  Z,ZZZ,ZZ9.99  XXXXXXXXXX  Z,ZZZ,ZZ9.99
XXXXXXXXXXX  XXXXX   XXXXXXXXXXXXXXXXXXXXX  Z,ZZZ,ZZ9.99  XXXXXXXXXX  Z,ZZZ,ZZ9.99
XXXXXXXXXXX  XXXXX   XXXXXXXXXXXXXXXXXXXXX  Z,ZZZ,ZZ9.99  XXXXXXXXXX  Z,ZZZ,ZZ9.99
XXXXXXXXXXX  XXXXX   XXXXXXXXXXXXXXXXXXXXX  Z,ZZZ,ZZ9.99  XXXXXXXXXX  Z,ZZZ,ZZ9.99
XXXXXXXXXXX  XXXXX   XXXXXXXXXXXXXXXXXXXXX  Z,ZZZ,ZZ9.99  XXXXXXXXXX  Z,ZZZ,ZZ9.99
XXXXXXXXXXX  XXXXX   XXXXXXXXXXXXXXXXXXXXX  Z,ZZZ,ZZ9.99  XXXXXXXXXX  Z,ZZZ,ZZ9.99
XXXXXXXXXXX  XXXXX   XXXXXXXXXXXXXXXXXXXXX  Z,ZZZ,ZZ9.99  XXXXXXXXXX  Z,ZZZ,ZZ9.99

                                       Invoice total:        Z,ZZZ,ZZ9.99
XXXXXXXXXXXXXXXXXXXXXXXXXXXXXXXXXXXXXXXXXXXXXXXXXXXXXXXXXXXXXXXXXXXXXXXXXXXXXXXXXX
XXXXXXXXXXXXXXXXXXXXXXXXXXXXXXXXXXXXXXXXXXXXX                                    X
```

Description

- The order entry program lets the user enter orders for up to 10 line items. The user can also enter a net price for any line item to override the list price. Once the user entries have been edited, the screen is redisplayed with additional information from the customer and product files so the user can accept the order or make changes to it.

- The same screen layout is used for both the entry and verify screens. The data entry fields are protected when they're displayed in the verify screen.

- Two of the data entry fields, quantity and net price, must contain numeric data, so they're displayed in a numeric edited format on the verify screen.

- The function key values that are shown in line 24 of each screen are determined by the program.

Figure 13-1   The specifications for the order entry program (part 2 of 2)

An event/response chart for the order entry program

Figure 13-2 shows the event/response chart used in the design of this program. As you can see, it identifies two event contexts that correspond to the entry and verify operations of the program. The program's responses to three of the input events (PF12, Enter, and PF4) depend on which of these contexts is current. If the user presses PF12 when the context is "Process entry," the program returns to the menu; on the other hand, if the context is "Process verify," the program cancels the current order and redisplays the entry screen.

If the user presses Enter when the context is "Process entry," the program edits the input data. If the data is valid, the program sets the attribute bytes of the entry fields to protected and displays the verify screen with a message asking the user to confirm the order. Then, it changes the context to "Process verify." If the data is invalid, the program simply displays an error message without changing the context. If the user presses Enter when the context is "Process verify," the program posts the order, redisplays the entry screen, and changes the context to "Process entry."

If the user presses PF4 when the context is "Process entry," the program displays an "invalid key pressed" message, since PF4 has no meaning when the entry screen is displayed. But if the user presses PF4 when the context is "Process verify," the program redisplays the entry screen with the data entry fields unprotected and changes the context to "Process entry." That way, the user can make changes to the order data.

An event/response chart for the order entry program

Event	Context	Response	New context
Start the program	n/a	Display the order map.	Process entry
PF3	All	Transfer control to the menu program.	n/a
PF12	Process entry	Transfer control to the menu program.	n/a
	Process verify	Cancel the order and redisplay the order map with entry fields unprotected.	Process entry

Enter key	Process entry	Edit input data.
		If valid
		   protect all fields
		   display confirmation message.
		If not valid
		   display error message.
			Process verify
			
			Process entry

	Process verify	Get the invoice number. Write the invoice record. Redisplay the order map with entry fields unprotected.	Process entry
PF4	Process entry	Display an "invalid key pressed" message.	Unchanged
	Process verify	Redisplay the order map with entry fields unprotected.	Process entry
Clear key	All	Redisplay the map.	Process entry
Any PA key	All	Ignore the key.	Unchanged
Any other key	All	Display an appropriate error message.	Unchanged

Description

- The order map that's used by this program can be processed in one of two contexts: "Process entry" and "Process verify." The "Process entry" context indicates that the user is entering or modifying an order, and the "Process verify" context indicates that the user is confirming an order.

- The program's responses to three of the input events—PF12, Enter, and PF4— depend on the event context that's current.

Figure 13-2   An event/response chart for the order entry program

The structure chart for the order entry program

Figure 13-3 shows the structure chart for this program. Modules 1000 and 2000 handle the program's response to the Enter key for the two contexts. The other program responses will be handled directly by module 0000.

Module 1000 is called when the user presses the Enter key after entering order data. It first calls module 1100 to receive the order data, then it calls module 1200 to edit the data. If module 1200 indicates that the data is valid, module 1000 then calls module 1300 to format an invoice record, which will be passed forward to the next program execution via the communication area. Then, it calls module 1400 to display the order map with the entry fields protected so the user can verify the data.

Because the editing requirements of this program are complex, module 1200 has several subordinates. First, module 1210 reads a record from the customer file using the customer number entered by the user. Then, module 1220 is performed repeatedly to edit each line item. This module, in turn, calls module 1230 to read a record from the product file using the product code entered by the user. And it calls two subprograms, NUMEDIT and INTEDIT, to edit the numeric values.

As in previous programs, this program uses a single send module (1400) to handle several variations of the SEND MAP command. However, the send module for this program has the added responsibility of setting the attribute bytes for each entry field, so it calls two subordinate modules. Module 1410 moves protected attributes to these fields before they're displayed on the verify screen. And module 1420 restores these attributes to their original unprotected status before the entry screen is redisplayed for modification.

Module 2000 is called when the user confirms an order by pressing the Enter key while the verify screen is displayed. Its operation is straightforward. Because the invoice record to be written was formatted by module 1300 and passed to this execution in the communication area, module 2000 doesn't need to receive data from the map. Instead, it invokes the GETINV subprogram to obtain the invoice number for the invoice record, then performs module 2100 to write the invoice record. Finally, it performs module 1400 to send a fresh entry map so the user can enter another order.

The structure chart for the order entry program

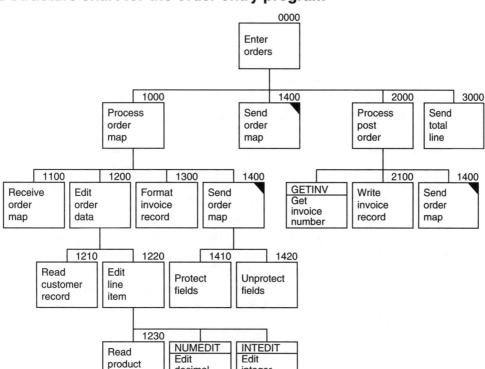

Description

- Modules 1000 and 2000 handle the program's response to the Enter key for the two contexts of the program.

- Module 1000 is executed when the user presses the Enter key after entering an order. It receives the order data (1100) and then edits it (1200). If the data is valid, it formats an invoice record (1300) and then displays the order map with all the fields protected (1400). If the data is invalid, it redisplays the order map with an error message.

- The edit module (1200) calls module 1210 to read the appropriate customer record and module 1220 to edit the line items. Module 1220, in turn, calls module 1230 to read the product record for each line item and the NUMEDIT and INTEDIT subprograms to edit the numeric values.

- In addition to issuing the appropriate SEND MAP command, module 1400 calls module 1410 to protect the entry fields when the map is displayed for verification and module 1420 to unprotect the entry fields when the map is displayed for modification.

- When the user confirms an order by pressing the Enter key from the verify screen, module 2000 executes the GETINV subprogram to obtain the next invoice number, writes the order to the invoice file (2100), and sends a fresh entry map so the user can enter another order (1400).

- When the user ends the program, module 3000 displays the number of invoices entered.

Figure 13-3   The structure chart for the order entry program

The BMS mapset for the order entry program

Figure 13-4 shows a portion of the BMS mapset for this program. Since the coding for the line items is repetitious, only the first one is included here. (It starts near the bottom of page 2 of the listing.) The coding for the second through tenth line items is similar, but the field names are different (for example, PCODE2 instead of PCODE1) and the POS parameters are different.

Most of the coding in this mapset is similar to what you've seen before, so you shouldn't have any trouble understanding it. But I want you to notice a couple of things. First, the definition of the NET1 field (on page 3 of the listing) includes the NUM attribute so the user can enter only numbers, decimal points, and hyphens into it. Because the PICIN parameter isn't coded, though, the program will treat the input data as alphanumeric. Then, once it's been edited and found to be valid, the PICOUT parameter will cause it to display with zero suppression and a decimal point. Normally, the NUM option also causes the data to be right-justified as it's entered on the screen. But since the INITIAL parameter fills the NET1 field with underscores, right-justification will have no effect.

Note, too, the FKEY field near the end of the mapset. This is the 40-byte area that's used to display the function key assignments in line 24 of the screen. The program will move the appropriate literal into this field depending on whether the entry or verify screen is being displayed.

The code for the BMS mapset   **Page 1**

```
           PRINT NOGEN
ORDSET1    DFHMSD TYPE=&SYSPARM,                                      X
                  LANG=COBOL,                                         X
                  MODE=INOUT,                                         X
                  TERM=3270-2,                                        X
                  CTRL=FREEKB,                                        X
                  STORAGE=AUTO,                                       X
                  DSATTS=(COLOR,HILIGHT),                             X
                  MAPATTS=(COLOR,HILIGHT),                            X
                  TIOAPFX=YES
***********************************************************************
ORDMAP1    DFHMDI SIZE=(24,80),                                      X
                  LINE=1,                                            X
                  COLUMN=1
***********************************************************************
           DFHMDF POS=(1,1),                                         X
                  LENGTH=7,                                          X
                  ATTRB=(NORM,PROT),                                 X
                  COLOR=BLUE,                                        X
                  INITIAL='ORDMAP1'
           DFHMDF POS=(1,20),                                        X
                  LENGTH=11,                                         X
                  ATTRB=(NORM,PROT),                                 X
                  COLOR=GREEN,                                       X
                  INITIAL='Order Entry'
TRANID     DFHMDF POS=(1,76),                                        X
                  LENGTH=4,                                          X
                  ATTRB=(NORM,PROT),                                 X
                  COLOR=BLUE,                                        X
                  INITIAL='XXXX'
***********************************************************************
INSTR      DFHMDF POS=(3,1),                                         X
                  LENGTH=79,                                         X
                  ATTRB=(NORM,PROT),                                 X
                  COLOR=NEUTRAL
           DFHMDF POS=(5,1),                                         X
                  LENGTH=21,                                         X
                  ATTRB=(NORM,PROT),                                 X
                  COLOR=GREEN,                                       X
                  INITIAL='Customer number . . . .'
CUSTNO     DFHMDF POS=(5,23),                                        X
                  LENGTH=6,                                          X
                  ATTRB=(NORM,UNPROT),                               X
                  COLOR=TURQUOISE,                                   X
                  INITIAL='_____'
           DFHMDF POS=(5,30),                                        X
                  LENGTH=1,                                          X
                  ATTRB=ASKIP
           DFHMDF POS=(5,36),                                        X
                  LENGTH=9,                                          X
                  ATTRB=(NORM,PROT),                                 X
                  COLOR=GREEN,                                       X
                  INITIAL='Customer:'
LNAME      DFHMDF POS=(5,46),                                        X
                  LENGTH=30,                                         X
                  ATTRB=(NORM,PROT),                                 X
                  COLOR=TURQUOISE
```

Figure 13-4   The BMS mapset for the order entry program (part 1 of 3)

The code for the BMS mapset   **Page 2**

```
             DFHMDF POS=(6,1),                                    X
                    LENGTH=21,                                    X
                    ATTRB=(NORM,PROT),                            X
                    COLOR=GREEN,                                  X
                    INITIAL='P.O. number . . . . .'
PO           DFHMDF POS=(6,23),                                   X
                    LENGTH=10,                                    X
                    ATTRB=(NORM,UNPROT),                          X
                    COLOR=TURQUOISE,                              X
                    INITIAL='_____'
             DFHMDF POS=(6,34),                                   X
                    LENGTH=1,                                     X
                    ATTRB=ASKIP
FNAME        DFHMDF POS=(6,46),                                   X
                    LENGTH=20,                                    X
                    ATTRB=(NORM,PROT),                            X
                    COLOR=TURQUOISE
ADDR         DFHMDF POS=(7,46),                                   X
                    LENGTH=30,                                    X
                    ATTRB=(NORM,PROT),                            X
                    COLOR=TURQUOISE
CITY         DFHMDF POS=(8,46),                                   X
                    LENGTH=20,                                    X
                    ATTRB=(NORM,PROT),                            X
                    COLOR=TURQUOISE
STATE        DFHMDF POS=(8,67),                                   X
                    LENGTH=2,                                     X
                    ATTRB=(NORM,PROT),                            X
                    COLOR=TURQUOISE
ZIPCODE      DFHMDF POS=(8,70),                                   X
                    LENGTH=10,                                    X
                    ATTRB=(NORM,PROT),                            X
                    COLOR=TURQUOISE
             DFHMDF POS=(10,1),                                   X
                    LENGTH=30,                                    X
                    ATTRB=(NORM,PROT),                            X
                    COLOR=BLUE,                                   X
                    INITIAL='Prod code     Qty  Description'
             DFHMDF POS=(10,49),                                  X
                    LENGTH=29,                                    X
                    ATTRB=(NORM,PROT),                            X
                    COLOR=BLUE,                                   X
                    INITIAL='List          Net      Amount'
*********************************************************************
*            LINE PCODE 1                                          *
*********************************************************************
PCODE1       DFHMDF POS=(11,1),                                   X
                    LENGTH=10,                                    X
                    ATTRB=(NORM,UNPROT),                          X
                    COLOR=TURQUOISE,                              X
                    INITIAL='_____'
             DFHMDF POS=(11,12),                                  X
                    LENGTH=1,                                     X
                    ATTRB=ASKIP
QTY1         DFHMDF POS=(11,13),                                  X
                    LENGTH=5,                                     X
                    ATTRB=(NORM,NUM),                             X
                    COLOR=TURQUOISE,                              X
                    INITIAL='_____'
```

Figure 13-4   The BMS mapset for the order entry program (part 2 of 3)

The code for the BMS mapset   **Page 3**

```
              DFHMDF POS=(11,19),                                    X
                     LENGTH=1,                                       X
                     ATTRB=ASKIP
DESC1         DFHMDF POS=(11,20),                                    X
                     LENGTH=20,                                      X
                     ATTRB=(NORM,PROT),                              X
                     COLOR=TURQUOISE
LIST1         DFHMDF POS=(11,41),                                    X
                     LENGTH=12,                                      X
                     ATTRB=(NORM,PROT),                              X
                     COLOR=TURQUOISE,                                X
                     PICOUT='Z,ZZZ,ZZ9.99'
NET1          DFHMDF POS=(11,55),                                    X
                     LENGTH=10,                                      X
                     ATTRB=(NORM,NUM),                               X
                     COLOR=TURQUOISE,                                X
                     PICOUT='ZZZZZZ9.99',                            X
                     INITIAL='_____'
AMT1          DFHMDF POS=(11,66),                                    X
                     LENGTH=12,                                      X
                     ATTRB=(NORM,PROT),                              X
                     COLOR=TURQUOISE,                                X
                     PICOUT='Z,ZZZ,ZZ9.99'
**********************************************************************
  .
  .          ┌──────────────────────────────────────────────────────┐
  .          │  The BMS macro instructions that define line items 2  │
             │  through 10 are similar to those that define line item 1. │
             └──────────────────────────────────────────────────────┘

**********************************************************************
              DFHMDF POS=(22,44),                                    X
                     LENGTH=14,                                      X
                     ATTRB=(NORM,PROT),                              X
                     COLOR=GREEN,                                    X
                     INITIAL='Invoice total:'
TOTAL         DFHMDF POS=(22,66),                                    X
                     LENGTH=12,                                      X
                     ATTRB=(NORM,PROT),                              X
                     COLOR=TURQUOISE,                                X
                     PICOUT='Z,ZZZ,ZZ9.99'
**********************************************************************
MSG           DFHMDF POS=(23,1),                                     X
                     LENGTH=79,                                      X
                     ATTRB=(BRT,PROT),                               X
                     COLOR=YELLOW
FKEY          DFHMDF POS=(24,1),                                     X
                     LENGTH=40,                                      X
                     ATTRB=(NORM,PROT),                              X
                     COLOR=BLUE
DUMMY         DFHMDF POS=(24,79),                                    X
                     LENGTH=1,                                       X
                     ATTRB=(DRK,PROT,FSET),                          X
                     INITIAL=' '
**********************************************************************
              DFHMSD TYPE=FINAL
              END
```

Figure 13-4   The BMS mapset for the order entry program (part 3 of 3)

The programmer-generated symbolic map for the order entry program

For this program, I chose to discard the symbolic map BMS generated and create my own instead. That way, I could use an Occurs clause to process the line item data efficiently, as shown in figure 13-5 (page 2 contains the Occurs clause).

Whenever you create your own symbolic map like this, it must have the same structure as the BMS-generated symbolic map. So, following the 12-byte filler item, there are five COBOL fields for each map field: a length field, an attribute field, an extended color attribute field, an extended highlighting attribute field, and the data field itself.

Notice the definition of the QTY field:

```
10   ORD-D-QTY               PIC ZZZZ9
                             BLANK WHEN ZERO.
10   ORD-D-QTY-ALPHA         REDEFINES ORD-D-QTY
                             PIC X(05).
```

This redefinition of a numeric edited field as an alphanumeric field simulates the effect of coding PICOUT in the DFHMDF macro. Then, the program can edit the input data using the alphanumeric field, and it can display the output data using the numeric field so it will be displayed right-justified with leading zeros suppressed. The NET field is defined in a similar manner.

I hope you can appreciate the need to create your own symbolic map in this type of situation. BMS provides no convenient way to group these repeating line items, so it generates separate fields for each. As a result, the symbolic map BMS generated for this mapset is 12 pages long, and the COBOL code that would be required to handle this mapset would be cumbersome. Remember, though, that if you create your own symbolic map, you must remember to change it when you change the mapset it's based on so the two are consistent. For that reason, I don't recommend creating your own symbolic maps unless there's a clear advantage to doing so.

The code for the symbolic map   **Page 1**

```
01  ORDMAP1.
*
    05   FILLER              PIC X(12).
*
    05   ORD-L-TRANID        PIC S9(04)  COMP.
    05   ORD-A-TRANID        PIC X(01).
    05   ORD-C-TRANID        PIC X(01).
    05   ORD-H-TRANID        PIC X(01).
    05   ORD-D-TRANID        PIC X(04).
*
    05   ORD-L-INSTR         PIC S9(04)  COMP.
    05   ORD-A-INSTR         PIC X(01).
    05   ORD-C-INSTR         PIC X(01).
    05   ORD-H-INSTR         PIC X(01).
    05   ORD-D-INSTR         PIC X(79).
*
    05   ORD-L-CUSTNO        PIC S9(04)  COMP.
    05   ORD-A-CUSTNO        PIC X(01).
    05   ORD-C-CUSTNO        PIC X(01).
    05   ORD-H-CUSTNO        PIC X(01).
    05   ORD-D-CUSTNO        PIC X(06).
*
    05   ORD-L-LNAME         PIC S9(04)  COMP.
    05   ORD-A-LNAME         PIC X(01).
    05   ORD-C-LNAME         PIC X(01).
    05   ORD-H-LNAME         PIC X(01).
    05   ORD-D-LNAME         PIC X(30).
*
    05   ORD-L-PO            PIC S9(04)  COMP.
    05   ORD-A-PO            PIC X(01).
    05   ORD-C-PO            PIC X(01).
    05   ORD-H-PO            PIC X(01).
    05   ORD-D-PO            PIC X(10).
*
    05   ORD-L-FNAME         PIC S9(04)  COMP.
    05   ORD-A-FNAME         PIC X(01).
    05   ORD-C-FNAME         PIC X(01).
    05   ORD-H-FNAME         PIC X(01).
    05   ORD-D-FNAME         PIC X(20).
*
    05   ORD-L-ADDR          PIC S9(04)  COMP.
    05   ORD-A-ADDR          PIC X(01).
    05   ORD-C-ADDR          PIC X(01).
    05   ORD-H-ADDR          PIC X(01).
    05   ORD-D-ADDR          PIC X(30).
*
    05   ORD-L-CITY          PIC S9(04)  COMP.
    05   ORD-A-CITY          PIC X(01).
    05   ORD-C-CITY          PIC X(01).
    05   ORD-H-CITY          PIC X(01).
    05   ORD-D-CITY          PIC X(20).
*
    05   ORD-L-STATE         PIC S9(04)  COMP.
    05   ORD-A-STATE         PIC X(01).
    05   ORD-C-STATE         PIC X(01).
    05   ORD-H-STATE         PIC X(01).
    05   ORD-D-STATE         PIC X(02).
*
```

Figure 13-5   The programmer-generated symbolic map for the order entry program (part 1 of 3)

The code for the symbolic map   **Page 2**

```
     05   ORD-L-ZIPCODE            PIC S9(04)   COMP.
     05   ORD-A-ZIPCODE            PIC X(01).
     05   ORD-C-ZIPCODE            PIC X(01).
     05   ORD-H-ZIPCODE            PIC X(01).
     05   ORD-D-ZIPCODE            PIC X(10).
*
     05   ORD-LINE-ITEM            OCCURS 10 TIMES.
*
          10   ORD-L-PCODE         PIC S9(04)   COMP.
          10   ORD-A-PCODE         PIC X(01).
          10   ORD-C-PCODE         PIC X(01).
          10   ORD-H-PCODE         PIC X(01).
          10   ORD-D-PCODE         PIC X(10).
*
          10   ORD-L-QTY           PIC S9(04)   COMP.
          10   ORD-A-QTY           PIC X(01).
          10   ORD-C-QTY           PIC X(01).
          10   ORD-H-QTY           PIC X(01).
          10   ORD-D-QTY           PIC ZZZZ9
                                   BLANK WHEN ZERO.
          10   ORD-D-QTY-ALPHA     REDEFINES ORD-D-QTY
                                   PIC X(05).
*
          10   ORD-L-DESC          PIC S9(04)   COMP.
          10   ORD-A-DESC          PIC X(01).
          10   ORD-C-DESC          PIC X(01).
          10   ORD-H-DESC          PIC X(01).
          10   ORD-D-DESC          PIC X(20).
*
          10   ORD-L-LIST          PIC S9(04)   COMP.
          10   ORD-A-LIST          PIC X(01).
          10   ORD-C-LIST          PIC X(01).
          10   ORD-H-LIST          PIC X(01).
          10   ORD-D-LIST          PIC Z,ZZZ,ZZ9.99
                                   BLANK WHEN ZERO.
*
          10   ORD-L-NET           PIC S9(04)   COMP.
          10   ORD-A-NET           PIC X(01).
          10   ORD-C-NET           PIC X(01).
          10   ORD-H-NET           PIC X(01).
          10   ORD-D-NET           PIC ZZZZZZ9.99
                                   BLANK WHEN ZERO.
          10   ORD-D-NET-ALPHA     REDEFINES ORD-D-NET
                                   PIC X(10).
*
          10   ORD-L-AMOUNT        PIC S9(04)   COMP.
          10   ORD-A-AMOUNT        PIC X(01).
          10   ORD-C-AMOUNT        PIC X(01).
          10   ORD-H-AMOUNT        PIC X(01).
          10   ORD-D-AMOUNT        PIC Z,ZZZ,ZZ9.99
                                   BLANK WHEN ZERO.
*
     05   ORD-L-TOTAL              PIC S9(04)   COMP.
     05   ORD-A-TOTAL              PIC X(01).
     05   ORD-C-TOTAL              PIC X(01).
     05   ORD-H-TOTAL              PIC X(01).
     05   ORD-D-TOTAL              PIC Z,ZZZ,ZZ9.99
                                   BLANK WHEN ZERO.
```

Figure 13-5   The programmer-generated symbolic map for the order entry program (part 2 of 3)

The code for the symbolic map   **Page 3**

```
*
      05    ORD-L-MESSAGE              PIC  S9(04)   COMP.
      05    ORD-A-MESSAGE              PIC  X(01).
      05    ORD-C-MESSAGE              PIC  X(01).
      05    ORD-H-MESSAGE              PIC  X(01).
      05    ORD-D-MESSAGE              PIC  X(79).
*
      05    ORD-L-FKEY                 PIC  S9(04)   COMP.
      05    ORD-A-FKEY                 PIC  X(01).
      05    ORD-C-FKEY                 PIC  X(01).
      05    ORD-H-FKEY                 PIC  X(01).
      05    ORD-D-FKEY                 PIC  X(40).
*
      05    ORD-L-DUMMY                PIC  S9(04)   COMP.
      05    ORD-A-DUMMY                PIC  X(01).
      05    ORD-C-DUMMY                PIC  X(01).
      05    ORD-H-DUMMY                PIC  X(01).
      05    ORD-D-DUMMY                PIC  X(01).
*
```

Figure 13-5   The programmer-generated symbolic map for the order entry program (part 3 of 3)

The COBOL code for the order entry program

Figure 13-6 shows the source listing for the order entry program. Before I describe the Procedure Division code for this program, I want you to notice several things in the Data Division.

The Data Division

First, notice the second flag that's defined in the Working-Storage Section (FIELD-PROTECTION-FLAG). This flag will be used to tell the send procedure how to set the protection attributes for the data entry fields. When the program needs to display the verify screen, it sets the Protect-Fields condition to True before calling the send procedure. And when the program needs to redisplay the entry screen so the user can modify an order, it sets the Unprotect-Fields condition to True. When the program needs to redisplay the entry screen for a new order, though, this flag isn't set. That's because the send procedure issues a SEND command without the DATAONLY option in that case. As a result, the physical map will be sent to the terminal, which means the attributes will be reset to their original values.

Second, notice the work field named ABSOLUTE-TIME. This field will be used to store the value that's returned by the ASKTIME command. The FORMATTIME command will then convert this value to a more usable format that can be stored in the date field of each invoice record.

Third, notice the fields in the communication area. As usual, this area contains a field named CA-CONTEXT-FLAG that keeps track of the program's current context. In addition, it contains a field named CA-TOTAL-ORDERS. The order entry program uses this field to keep a count of the number of orders entered by the user. The communication area also contains a complete copy of the invoice record. Then, that record can be passed from the program execution that formats the invoice record to the execution that writes it to the invoice file.

The last group in the communication area, CA-FIELDS-ENTERED, contains a switch for each data entry field in the order map. When the program detects that the user has entered data into a field, the corresponding switch is set. As you'll see, these switches are used in several places throughout the program.

Finally, notice the copy members at the end of the Working-Storage Section. The first four contain the record descriptions for the files used by this program. (If you want to review these descriptions, you can refer back to figure 10-4 in chapter 10.) The fifth one is for the symbolic map used by this program. And the other three are for copy members you've seen throughout this book.

Procedure 0000: Enter orders

As in the other sample programs you've seen, procedure 0000 contains an Evaluate statement that manages the program's event processing. Although this Evaluate statement is long, each of its When clauses is manageable. The best way to understand this program is to study the Evaluate statement one When clause at a time, making sure you understand how the program responds to each input event.

The order entry program   **Page 1**

```
        IDENTIFICATION DIVISION.
       *
        PROGRAM-ID.  ORDRENT.
       *
        ENVIRONMENT DIVISION.
       *
        DATA DIVISION.
       *
        WORKING-STORAGE SECTION.
       *
        01   SWITCHES.
             05   VALID-DATA-SW              PIC X(01)    VALUE 'Y'.
                  88  VALID-DATA                          VALUE 'Y'.
             05   CUSTOMER-FOUND-SW          PIC X(01)    VALUE 'Y'.
                  88  CUSTOMER-FOUND                      VALUE 'Y'.
             05   PRODUCT-FOUND-SW           PIC X(01)    VALUE 'Y'.
                  88  PRODUCT-FOUND                       VALUE 'Y'.
             05   VALID-QUANTITY-SW          PIC X(01)    VALUE 'Y'.
                  88  VALID-QUANTITY                      VALUE 'Y'.
             05   VALID-NET-SW               PIC X(01)    VALUE 'Y'.
                  88  VALID-NET                           VALUE 'Y'.
       *
        01   FLAGS.
             05   SEND-FLAG                  PIC X(01).
                  88  SEND-ERASE                          VALUE '1'.
                  88  SEND-DATAONLY                       VALUE '2'.
                  88  SEND-DATAONLY-ALARM                 VALUE '3'.
             05   FIELD-PROTECTION-FLAG      PIC X(01).
                  88  PROTECT-FIELDS                      VALUE '1'.
                  88  UNPROTECT-FIELDS                    VALUE '2'.
       *
        01   WORK-FIELDS.
             05   ITEM-SUB           PIC S9(03)  COMP-3  VALUE ZERO.
             05   LINE-ITEM-COUNT    PIC S9(03)  COMP-3  VALUE ZERO.
             05   NET-NUMERIC        PIC 9(07)V99.
             05   QTY-NUMERIC        PIC 9(05).
             05   ABSOLUTE-TIME      PIC S9(15)  COMP-3.
       *
        01   RESPONSE-CODE                   PIC S9(08)  COMP.
       *
        01   COMMUNICATION-AREA.
             05   CA-CONTEXT-FLAG            PIC X(01).
                  88  PROCESS-ENTRY                       VALUE '1'.
                  88  PROCESS-VERIFY                      VALUE '2'.
             05   CA-TOTAL-ORDERS            PIC S9(03)  COMP-3.
             05   CA-INVOICE-RECORD          PIC X(318).
             05   CA-FIELDS-ENTERED.
                  10  CA-PO-ENTERED-SW       PIC X(01).
                      88  CA-PO-ENTERED                   VALUE 'Y'.
                  10  CA-LINE-ITEM           OCCURS 10.
                      15  CA-PCODE-ENTERED-SW  PIC X(01).
                          88  CA-PCODE-ENTERED            VALUE 'Y'.
                      15  CA-QTY-ENTERED-SW    PIC X(01).
                          88  CA-QTY-ENTERED              VALUE 'Y'.
                      15  CA-NET-ENTERED-SW    PIC X(01).
                          88  CA-NET-ENTERED             VALUE 'Y'.
```

Figure 13-6   The COBOL code for the order entry program (part 1 of 12)

The order entry program Page 2

```
01   TOTAL-LINE.
     05   TL-TOTAL-ORDERS    PIC ZZ9.
     05   FILLER             PIC X(20) VALUE ' Orders entered.  Pr'.
     05   FILLER             PIC X(20) VALUE 'ess Enter to continu'.
     05   FILLER             PIC X(02) VALUE 'e.'.
*
 COPY INVOICE.
*
 COPY CUSTMAS.
*
 COPY PRODUCT.
*
 COPY INVCTL.
*
 COPY ORDSET1.
*
 COPY DFHAID.
*
 COPY ATTR.
*
 COPY ERRPARM.
*
 LINKAGE SECTION.
*
 01   DFHCOMMAREA          PIC X(352).
*
 PROCEDURE DIVISION.
*
 0000-ENTER-ORDERS.
*
     IF EIBCALEN > ZERO
         MOVE DFHCOMMAREA TO COMMUNICATION-AREA
     END-IF.
*
     EVALUATE TRUE
*
         WHEN EIBCALEN = ZERO
             MOVE LOW-VALUE TO ORDMAP1
             MOVE LOW-VALUE TO COMMUNICATION-AREA
             MOVE ZERO       TO CA-TOTAL-ORDERS
             MOVE 'Type order details.  Then press Enter.'
                 TO ORD-D-INSTR
             MOVE 'F3=Exit    F12=Cancel' TO ORD-D-FKEY
             MOVE -1 TO ORD-L-CUSTNO
             SET SEND-ERASE TO TRUE
             PERFORM 1400-SEND-ORDER-MAP
             SET PROCESS-ENTRY TO TRUE
*
```

Figure 13-6   The COBOL code for the order entry program (part 2 of 12)

The order entry program   **Page 3**

```
            WHEN EIBAID = DFHCLEAR
                MOVE LOW-VALUE TO ORDMAP1
                MOVE LOW-VALUE TO CA-INVOICE-RECORD
                                  CA-FIELDS-ENTERED
                MOVE 'Type order details.  Then press Enter.'
                    TO ORD-D-INSTR
                MOVE 'F3=Exit    F12=Cancel' TO ORD-D-FKEY
                MOVE -1 TO ORD-L-CUSTNO
                SET SEND-ERASE TO TRUE
                PERFORM 1400-SEND-ORDER-MAP
                SET PROCESS-ENTRY TO TRUE
        *
            WHEN EIBAID = DFHPA1 OR DFHPA2 OR DFHPA3
                CONTINUE
        *
            WHEN EIBAID = DFHPF3
                PERFORM 3000-SEND-TOTAL-LINE
                EXEC CICS
                    RETURN TRANSID('MENU')
                END-EXEC
        *
            WHEN EIBAID = DFHPF12
                IF PROCESS-VERIFY
                    MOVE LOW-VALUE TO ORDMAP1
                    MOVE LOW-VALUE TO CA-INVOICE-RECORD
                                      CA-FIELDS-ENTERED
                    MOVE 'Type order details.  Then press Enter.'
                        TO ORD-D-INSTR
                    MOVE 'F3=Exit    F12=Cancel' TO ORD-D-FKEY
                    MOVE -1 TO ORD-L-CUSTNO
                    SET SEND-ERASE TO TRUE
                    PERFORM 1400-SEND-ORDER-MAP
                    SET PROCESS-ENTRY TO TRUE
                ELSE
                    IF PROCESS-ENTRY
                        PERFORM 3000-SEND-TOTAL-LINE
                        EXEC CICS
                            RETURN TRANSID('MENU')
                        END-EXEC
                    END-IF
                END-IF
        *
            WHEN EIBAID = DFHENTER
                IF PROCESS-ENTRY
                    PERFORM 1000-PROCESS-ORDER-MAP
                ELSE
                    IF PROCESS-VERIFY
                        PERFORM 2000-PROCESS-POST-ORDER
                        SET PROCESS-ENTRY TO TRUE
                    END-IF
                END-IF
        *
```

Figure 13-6   The COBOL code for the order entry program (part 3 of 12)

Probably the most important When clauses in this Evaluate statement are the ones that handle the Enter key and the PF4 key. The When clause that handles the Enter key simply invokes procedure 1000 or 2000 depending on the context. If the context is "Process verify," the When clause sets the context to "Process entry" after invoking procedure 2000. If the context is "Process entry," however, the When clause doesn't set the context after invoking procedure 1000. Instead, procedure 1000 sets the new context depending on whether the user entered valid data.

The When clause that handles PF4 also checks the context. If the context is "Process verify," it sets up the order map so the user can modify the order, including setting Unprotect-Fields and Send-Dataonly to True. Then, it displays the map and sets the new context to "Process entry." If the context is "Process entry," the program treats PF4 as an error and displays an appropriate message.

Procedure 1000: Process order map

Procedure 1000 is straightforward. It performs procedures 1100 and 1200 to receive and edit the order data. If the data is valid, it performs procedures 1300 and 1400 to format the invoice record and display the verify map. If the data is invalid, however, it performs procedure 1400 to display an error message.

Notice how procedure 1000 formats the instructions and function key area and sets the flags that control procedure 1400's operation. Also notice that if the data is valid, procedure 1000 sets the context to "Process verify." If the data isn't valid, it leaves the context unchanged.

Procedure 1200: Edit order data

Procedure 1200 and its subordinates edit the order data. It starts by performing procedure 1220 repeatedly to edit each line item. Notice that the Perform statement varies the subscript backwards, from 10 to 1 by -1. That way, the line items will be edited from the bottom up. As a result, the error message in ORD-D-MESSAGE (if any) will reflect the error closest to the top of the screen.

Among other things, procedure 1220 counts the line items entered by the user so procedure 1200 can check to make sure that at least one line item has been entered. Then, procedure 1200 checks whether the purchase order field has been entered. Since this field is optional, no error message is formatted if it hasn't been entered. This edit is done only to set CA-PO-ENTERED-SW, which will be used elsewhere in the program.

Next, procedure 1200 edits the customer number field. First, it checks to make sure the field was entered. If it was, it performs procedure 1210 to read the record from the customer file. Then, if the record is found, it moves the customer's name and address to the appropriate map fields. Otherwise, it formats an error message and moves spaces to the map fields.

Procedure 1220, which is invoked once for each line item, is the most complex procedure in the program. It starts by checking whether the user entered a product code, quantity, and net price for the line item, setting the communication area switches accordingly. Then, it performs various edits against the net price and quantity fields, including calling the NUMEDIT and INTEDIT subprograms you saw in chapter 8, to make sure these fields contain valid numbers.

The order entry program   **Page 4**

```
            WHEN EIBAID = DFHPF4
                IF PROCESS-VERIFY
                    MOVE LOW-VALUE TO ORDMAP1
                    MOVE 'Type corrections.  Then press Enter.'
                        TO ORD-D-INSTR
                    MOVE 'F3=Exit    F12=Cancel' TO ORD-D-FKEY
                    MOVE -1 TO ORD-L-CUSTNO
                    SET UNPROTECT-FIELDS TO TRUE
                    SET SEND-DATAONLY TO TRUE
                    PERFORM 1400-SEND-ORDER-MAP
                    SET PROCESS-ENTRY TO TRUE
                ELSE
                    IF PROCESS-ENTRY
                        MOVE LOW-VALUE TO ORDMAP1
                        MOVE 'Invalid key pressed.' TO ORD-D-MESSAGE
                        MOVE -1 TO ORD-L-CUSTNO
                        SET SEND-DATAONLY-ALARM TO TRUE
                        PERFORM 1400-SEND-ORDER-MAP
                    END-IF
                END-IF
*
            WHEN OTHER
                MOVE LOW-VALUE TO ORDMAP1
                MOVE 'Invalid key pressed.' TO ORD-D-MESSAGE
                MOVE -1 TO ORD-L-CUSTNO
                SET SEND-DATAONLY-ALARM TO TRUE
                PERFORM 1400-SEND-ORDER-MAP
*
        END-EVALUATE.
*
        EXEC CICS
            RETURN TRANSID('ORD1')
                    COMMAREA(COMMUNICATION-AREA)
        END-EXEC.
*
     1000-PROCESS-ORDER-MAP.
*
        PERFORM 1100-RECEIVE-ORDER-MAP.
        PERFORM 1200-EDIT-ORDER-DATA.
*
        IF VALID-DATA
            PERFORM 1300-FORMAT-INVOICE-RECORD
            MOVE 'Press Enter to post this order.  Or press F4 to ent
-             'er corrections.' TO ORD-D-INSTR
            MOVE 'F3=Exit    F4=Change    F12=Cancel' TO ORD-D-FKEY
            MOVE SPACE TO ORD-D-MESSAGE
            SET SEND-DATAONLY TO TRUE
            SET PROTECT-FIELDS TO TRUE
            PERFORM 1400-SEND-ORDER-MAP
            SET PROCESS-VERIFY TO TRUE
        ELSE
            MOVE 'Type corrections.  Then press Enter.'
                TO ORD-D-INSTR
            MOVE 'F3=Exit    F12=Cancel' TO ORD-D-FKEY
            SET SEND-DATAONLY-ALARM TO TRUE
            PERFORM 1400-SEND-ORDER-MAP
        END-IF.
*
```

Figure 13-6   The COBOL code for the order entry program (part 4 of 12)

The order entry program   **Page 5**

```
      1100-RECEIVE-ORDER-MAP.
*
          EXEC CICS
              RECEIVE MAP('ORDMAP1')
                      MAPSET('ORDSET1')
                      INTO(ORDMAP1)
          END-EXEC.
*
          INSPECT ORDMAP1
              REPLACING ALL '_' BY SPACE.
*
      1200-EDIT-ORDER-DATA.
*
          MOVE ATTR-NO-HIGHLIGHT TO ORD-H-CUSTNO
                                    ORD-H-PO.
          MOVE ZERO TO LINE-ITEM-COUNT
                       INV-INVOICE-TOTAL.
*
          PERFORM 1220-EDIT-LINE-ITEM
              VARYING ITEM-SUB FROM 10 BY -1
                UNTIL ITEM-SUB < 1.
*
          MOVE INV-INVOICE-TOTAL TO ORD-D-TOTAL.
          IF        LINE-ITEM-COUNT = ZERO
              AND VALID-DATA
              MOVE ATTR-REVERSE TO ORD-H-PCODE(1)
              MOVE -1 TO ORD-L-PCODE(1)
              MOVE 'You must enter at least one line item.'
                  TO ORD-D-MESSAGE
              MOVE 'N' TO VALID-DATA-SW
          END-IF.
*
          IF        ORD-L-PO = ZERO
              OR ORD-D-PO = SPACE
              MOVE 'N' TO CA-PO-ENTERED-SW
          ELSE
              MOVE 'Y' TO CA-PO-ENTERED-SW
          END-IF.
*
          IF        ORD-L-CUSTNO = ZERO
              OR ORD-D-CUSTNO = SPACE
              MOVE ATTR-REVERSE TO ORD-H-CUSTNO
              MOVE -1 TO ORD-L-CUSTNO
              MOVE 'You must enter a customer number.'
                  TO ORD-D-MESSAGE
              MOVE 'N' TO VALID-DATA-SW
          ELSE
              PERFORM 1210-READ-CUSTOMER-RECORD
              IF CUSTOMER-FOUND
                  MOVE CM-LAST-NAME   TO ORD-D-LNAME
                  MOVE CM-FIRST-NAME  TO ORD-D-FNAME
                  MOVE CM-ADDRESS     TO ORD-D-ADDR
                  MOVE CM-CITY        TO ORD-D-CITY
                  MOVE CM-STATE       TO ORD-D-STATE
                  MOVE CM-ZIP-CODE    TO ORD-D-ZIPCODE
```

Figure 13-6   The COBOL code for the order entry program (part 5 of 12)

The order entry program   **Page 6**

```
            ELSE
                MOVE SPACE TO ORD-D-LNAME
                             ORD-D-FNAME
                             ORD-D-ADDR
                             ORD-D-CITY
                             ORD-D-STATE
                             ORD-D-ZIPCODE
                MOVE ATTR-REVERSE TO ORD-H-CUSTNO
                MOVE -1 TO ORD-L-CUSTNO
                MOVE 'That customer does not exist.'
                    TO ORD-D-MESSAGE
                MOVE 'N' TO VALID-DATA-SW
            END-IF
        END-IF.
*
        IF VALID-DATA
            MOVE -1 TO ORD-L-CUSTNO
        END-IF.
*
 1210-READ-CUSTOMER-RECORD.
*
        EXEC CICS
            READ FILE('CUSTMAS')
                 INTO(CUSTOMER-MASTER-RECORD)
                 RIDFLD(ORD-D-CUSTNO)
                 RESP(RESPONSE-CODE)
        END-EXEC.
*
        IF RESPONSE-CODE = DFHRESP(NORMAL)
            MOVE 'Y' TO CUSTOMER-FOUND-SW
        ELSE
            IF RESPONSE-CODE = DFHRESP(NOTFND)
                MOVE 'N' TO CUSTOMER-FOUND-SW
            ELSE
                PERFORM 9999-TERMINATE-PROGRAM
            END-IF
        END-IF.
*
 1220-EDIT-LINE-ITEM.
*
        MOVE ATTR-NO-HIGHLIGHT TO ORD-H-PCODE(ITEM-SUB)
                                  ORD-H-QTY(ITEM-SUB)
                                  ORD-H-NET(ITEM-SUB).
        MOVE 'N' TO PRODUCT-FOUND-SW.
        MOVE 'N' TO VALID-QUANTITY-SW.
*
        IF          ORD-L-PCODE(ITEM-SUB) > ZERO
            AND ORD-D-PCODE(ITEM-SUB) NOT = SPACE
            MOVE 'Y' TO CA-PCODE-ENTERED-SW(ITEM-SUB)
        ELSE
            MOVE 'N' TO CA-PCODE-ENTERED-SW(ITEM-SUB)
        END-IF.
*
        IF          ORD-L-QTY(ITEM-SUB) > ZERO
            AND ORD-D-QTY-ALPHA(ITEM-SUB) NOT = SPACE
            MOVE 'Y' TO CA-QTY-ENTERED-SW(ITEM-SUB)
        ELSE
            MOVE 'N' TO CA-QTY-ENTERED-SW(ITEM-SUB)
        END-IF.
```

Figure 13-6   The COBOL code for the order entry program (part 6 of 12)

Next, procedure 1220 edits the product code (if one was entered) by calling procedure 1230 to read a record from the product file. If a record with that product code is found, the product description and unit price from that record are moved to the appropriate map fields. Finally, if the product record is found and both the quantity and net price fields contain valid numbers, the computations necessary to extend the line item and update the invoice total are performed. Note that even the Multiply and Add statements involve editing: If a size error occurs for either, an error message is displayed and the data is considered invalid.

Procedure 1300: Format invoice record

Procedure 1300 is relatively straightforward. However, I want you to notice three things. First, it uses the ASKTIME command to get the current date and time, and it uses the FORMATTIME command to format the date and store it in the invoice date field in the invoice record. (Since the invoice date field is only eight bytes long, the last two characters of the ten-byte date that's returned by FORMATTTIME will be truncated. Since separator characters aren't included in the date format, though, those last two characters will contain spaces.)

Second, it uses an inline Perform statement to format each line item. Third, it uses the CA-PCODE-ENTERED switch to determine whether or not the user entered data for a line item. If so, it moves data from the symbolic map to the corresponding invoice record line item. Note that it isn't necessary to move data to the Inv-Amount field here, because that field was set by the Multiply statement in procedure 1220. If the user didn't enter data for a line item, this procedure moves space to the product code field and zero to the quantity, unit price, and amount fields.

Finally, once the invoice is formatted, it's moved to the communication area. That way, if the user accepts the order from the verify screen, the invoice record will be available to the next program execution so it can be written to the invoice file.

The order entry program   **Page 7**

```
        IF          ORD-L-NET(ITEM-SUB) > ZERO
            AND ORD-D-NET-ALPHA(ITEM-SUB) NOT = SPACE
          MOVE 'Y' TO CA-NET-ENTERED-SW(ITEM-SUB)
        ELSE
          MOVE 'N' TO CA-NET-ENTERED-SW(ITEM-SUB)
        END-IF.
*
        IF             CA-NET-ENTERED(ITEM-SUB)
            AND NOT CA-PCODE-ENTERED(ITEM-SUB)
          MOVE ATTR-REVERSE TO ORD-H-PCODE(ITEM-SUB)
          MOVE -1 TO ORD-L-PCODE(ITEM-SUB)
          MOVE 'You cannot enter a net price without a product code
-         '.' TO ORD-D-MESSAGE
          MOVE 'N' TO VALID-DATA-SW
        END-IF.
*
        IF CA-NET-ENTERED(ITEM-SUB)
          CALL 'NUMEDIT' USING ORD-D-NET-ALPHA(ITEM-SUB)
                               NET-NUMERIC
                               VALID-NET-SW
          IF VALID-NET
            MOVE NET-NUMERIC TO ORD-D-NET(ITEM-SUB)
          ELSE
            MOVE ATTR-REVERSE TO ORD-H-NET(ITEM-SUB)
            MOVE -1 TO ORD-L-NET(ITEM-SUB)
            MOVE 'Net price must be numeric.' TO ORD-D-MESSAGE
            MOVE 'N' TO VALID-DATA-SW
            MOVE 'N' TO VALID-QUANTITY-SW
          END-IF
        END-IF.
*
        IF             CA-QTY-ENTERED(ITEM-SUB)
            AND NOT CA-PCODE-ENTERED(ITEM-SUB)
          MOVE ATTR-REVERSE TO ORD-H-PCODE(ITEM-SUB)
          MOVE -1 TO ORD-L-PCODE(ITEM-SUB)
          MOVE 'You cannot enter a quantity without a product code.
            ' ' TO ORD-D-MESSAGE
          MOVE 'N' TO VALID-DATA-SW
        END-IF.
*
        IF CA-QTY-ENTERED(ITEM-SUB)
          CALL 'INTEDIT' USING ORD-D-QTY-ALPHA(ITEM-SUB)
                               QTY-NUMERIC
                               VALID-QUANTITY-SW
          IF VALID-QUANTITY
            IF QTY-NUMERIC > ZERO
                MOVE QTY-NUMERIC TO ORD-D-QTY(ITEM-SUB)
            ELSE
                MOVE ATTR-REVERSE TO ORD-H-QTY(ITEM-SUB)
                MOVE -1 TO ORD-L-QTY(ITEM-SUB)
                MOVE 'Quantity must be greater than zero.'
                    TO ORD-D-MESSAGE
                MOVE 'N' TO VALID-DATA-SW
                MOVE 'N' TO VALID-QUANTITY-SW
            END-IF
```

Figure 13-6   The COBOL code for the order entry program (part 7 of 12)

The order entry program

```
        ELSE
            MOVE ATTR-REVERSE TO ORD-H-QTY(ITEM-SUB)
            MOVE -1 TO ORD-L-QTY(ITEM-SUB)
            MOVE 'Quantity must be numeric.' TO ORD-D-MESSAGE
            MOVE 'N' TO VALID-DATA-SW
            MOVE 'N' TO VALID-QUANTITY-SW
        END-IF
    END-IF.
*
    IF           CA-PCODE-ENTERED(ITEM-SUB)
        AND NOT CA-QTY-ENTERED(ITEM-SUB)
        MOVE ATTR-REVERSE TO ORD-H-QTY(ITEM-SUB)
        MOVE -1 TO ORD-L-QTY(ITEM-SUB)
        MOVE 'You must enter a quantity.' TO ORD-D-MESSAGE
        MOVE 'N' TO VALID-DATA-SW
    END-IF.
*
    IF NOT CA-PCODE-ENTERED(ITEM-SUB)
        MOVE SPACE TO ORD-D-DESC(ITEM-SUB)
        MOVE ZERO  TO ORD-D-LIST(ITEM-SUB)
                      ORD-D-AMOUNT(ITEM-SUB)
    ELSE
        ADD 1 TO LINE-ITEM-COUNT
        PERFORM 1230-READ-PRODUCT-RECORD
        IF PRODUCT-FOUND
            MOVE PRM-PRODUCT-DESCRIPTION
                              TO ORD-D-DESC(ITEM-SUB)
            MOVE PRM-UNIT-PRICE TO ORD-D-LIST(ITEM-SUB)
            IF NOT CA-NET-ENTERED(ITEM-SUB)
                MOVE PRM-UNIT-PRICE TO ORD-D-NET(ITEM-SUB)
                                       NET-NUMERIC
            END-IF
            IF VALID-QUANTITY AND VALID-NET
                MULTIPLY NET-NUMERIC BY QTY-NUMERIC
                    GIVING ORD-D-AMOUNT(ITEM-SUB)
                           INV-AMOUNT(ITEM-SUB)
                    ON SIZE ERROR
                        MOVE ATTR-REVERSE TO ORD-H-QTY(ITEM-SUB)
                        MOVE -1 TO ORD-L-QTY(ITEM-SUB)
                        MOVE 'Line item amount is too large.'
                            TO ORD-D-MESSAGE
                        MOVE 'N' TO VALID-DATA-SW
                        MOVE ZERO TO ORD-D-AMOUNT(ITEM-SUB)
                                     INV-AMOUNT(ITEM-SUB)
                END-MULTIPLY
                ADD INV-AMOUNT(ITEM-SUB) TO INV-INVOICE-TOTAL
                    ON SIZE ERROR
                        MOVE ATTR-REVERSE TO ORD-H-QTY(ITEM-SUB)
                        MOVE -1 TO ORD-L-QTY(ITEM-SUB)
                        MOVE 'Invoice total is too large.'
                            TO ORD-D-MESSAGE
                        MOVE 'N' TO VALID-DATA-SW
                        MOVE ZERO TO INV-INVOICE-TOTAL
                END-ADD
            END-IF
```

Figure 13-6   The COBOL code for the order entry program (part 8 of 12)

The order entry program   **Page 9**

```
            ELSE
                MOVE SPACE TO ORD-D-DESC(ITEM-SUB)
                MOVE ZERO  TO ORD-D-LIST(ITEM-SUB)
                             ORD-D-AMOUNT(ITEM-SUB)
                MOVE ATTR-REVERSE TO ORD-H-PCODE(ITEM-SUB)
                MOVE -1    TO ORD-L-PCODE(ITEM-SUB)
                MOVE 'That product does not exist.'
                             TO ORD-D-MESSAGE
                MOVE 'N'   TO VALID-DATA-SW
            END-IF
        END-IF.
*
 1230-READ-PRODUCT-RECORD.
*
        EXEC CICS
            READ FILE('PRODUCT')
                INTO(PRODUCT-MASTER-RECORD)
                RIDFLD(ORD-D-PCODE(ITEM-SUB))
                RESP(RESPONSE-CODE)
        END-EXEC.
*
        IF RESPONSE-CODE = DFHRESP(NORMAL)
            MOVE 'Y' TO PRODUCT-FOUND-SW
        ELSE
            IF RESPONSE-CODE = DFHRESP(NOTFND)
                MOVE 'N' TO PRODUCT-FOUND-SW
            ELSE
                PERFORM 9999-TERMINATE-PROGRAM
            END-IF
        END-IF.
*
 1300-FORMAT-INVOICE-RECORD.
*
        EXEC CICS
            ASKTIME ABSTIME(ABSOLUTE-TIME)
        END-EXEC.
        EXEC CICS
            FORMATTIME ABSTIME(ABSOLUTE-TIME)
            MMDDYYYY(INV-INVOICE-DATE)
        END-EXEC.
        MOVE ORD-D-CUSTNO TO INV-CUSTOMER-NUMBER.
        MOVE ORD-D-PO     TO INV-PO-NUMBER.
        PERFORM VARYING ITEM-SUB FROM 1 BY 1
                UNTIL ITEM-SUB > 10
            IF CA-PCODE-ENTERED(ITEM-SUB)
                MOVE ORD-D-PCODE(ITEM-SUB)
                        TO INV-PRODUCT-CODE(ITEM-SUB)
                MOVE ORD-D-QTY(ITEM-SUB)
                        TO INV-QUANTITY(ITEM-SUB)
                MOVE ORD-D-NET(ITEM-SUB)
                        TO INV-UNIT-PRICE(ITEM-SUB)
            ELSE
                MOVE SPACE TO INV-PRODUCT-CODE(ITEM-SUB)
                MOVE ZERO  TO INV-QUANTITY(ITEM-SUB)
                             INV-UNIT-PRICE(ITEM-SUB)
                             INV-AMOUNT(ITEM-SUB)
            END-IF
        END-PERFORM.
        MOVE INVOICE-RECORD TO CA-INVOICE-RECORD.
```

Figure 13-6   The COBOL code for the order entry program (part 9 of 12)

Procedure 1400: Send order map

Procedure 1400 is also straightforward, but I want to point out a few details in its subordinate procedures. To set up the verify screen, this procedure performs procedure 1410. This procedure moves a protected attribute to the attribute field of each unprotected field on the map so the user can't change the data in those fields. Notice that the actual attribute byte value it moves to each attribute field depends on whether the user has entered data for the field. If the user has entered data, the procedure moves ATTR-PROT to the attribute field. But if the user has not entered data for the field, the procedure moves ATTR-PROT-DARK to the attribute field. As a result, not only will the field be protected, but its contents will be hidden. I used this technique so that the underscores in those fields won't appear on the screen. (Although, the Inspect statement in procedure 1100 removes the underscores from all the fields in the symbolic map after the data is received from the terminal, only the fields that contain data are sent back to the terminal. Because of that, the underscores in the empty fields remain on the screen.)

Procedure 1420 is performed when the user presses PF4 from the verify screen to modify an order. In that case, the attributes for the entry fields need to be reset to unprotected so the user can make the necessary changes. Although you might expect that this procedure could simply move ATTR-UNPROT to each attribute byte field, that's not the case.

The order entry program expects each field entered by the operator to be transmitted to the program whenever the user presses the Enter key. But when the program moved ATTR-PROT to the attribute bytes of these fields in procedure 1410, it overwrote the modified data tags for these fields. So, procedure 1420 must move ATTR-UNPROT to each field that wasn't entered by the user, and ATTR-UNPROT-MDT to each field that was. That way, the modified data tags will be restored, and all of the entered fields will be sent to the program. Like procedure 1410, procedure 1420 uses the switches in CA-FIELDS-ENTERED to determine which fields were entered and which were not.

Note that if a screen is to be displayed for a new order, the Send-Protection-Flag will not be set at all, so neither procedure 1410 nor 1420 will be performed. Instead, the Send-Erase condition will cause the screen to be displayed using the physical map, so the protection attributes will be reset to their original values.

Procedure 2000: Process post order

Because procedure 1200 and its subordinates thoroughly edit the order data and procedure 1300 formats the invoice record and saves it in the communication area, procedure 2000 is simple. First, it invokes the GETINV subprogram with a LINK command to retrieve an invoice number from the invoice control file. GETINV returns the invoice number via its communication area, so the LINK command simply specifies INV-INVOICE-NUMBER in its COMMAREA option. Then, procedure 2000 performs procedure 2100 to write the invoice record to the invoice file. Finally, it performs procedure 1400 to display the order map. But first, it sets the Send-Erase condition to True so that procedure 1400 doesn't have to worry about resetting the protected attribute bytes that were set by procedure 1410. Instead, the attribute bytes will be reset to the values specified in the physical map.

The order entry program   Page 10

```
      1400-SEND-ORDER-MAP.
*
          MOVE 'ORD1' TO ORD-D-TRANID.
*
          IF PROTECT-FIELDS
              PERFORM 1410-PROTECT-FIELDS
          ELSE
              IF UNPROTECT-FIELDS
                  PERFORM 1420-UNPROTECT-FIELDS
              END-IF
          END-IF.
*
          EVALUATE TRUE
              WHEN SEND-ERASE
                  EXEC CICS
                      SEND MAP('ORDMAP1')
                          MAPSET('ORDSET1')
                          FROM(ORDMAP1)
                          CURSOR
                          ERASE
                  END-EXEC
              WHEN SEND-DATAONLY
                  EXEC CICS
                      SEND MAP('ORDMAP1')
                          MAPSET('ORDSET1')
                          FROM(ORDMAP1)
                          CURSOR
                          DATAONLY
                  END-EXEC
              WHEN SEND-DATAONLY-ALARM
                  EXEC CICS
                      SEND MAP('ORDMAP1')
                          MAPSET('ORDSET1')
                          FROM(ORDMAP1)
                          CURSOR
                          DATAONLY
                          ALARM
                  END-EXEC
          END-EVALUATE.
*
      1410-PROTECT-FIELDS.
*
          MOVE ATTR-PROT TO ORD-A-CUSTNO.
          IF CA-PO-ENTERED
              MOVE ATTR-PROT TO ORD-A-PO
          ELSE
              MOVE ATTR-PROT-DARK TO ORD-A-PO
          END-IF.
*
```

Figure 13-6   The COBOL code for the order entry program (part 10 of 12)

```
          PERFORM VARYING ITEM-SUB FROM 1 BY 1
                  UNTIL ITEM-SUB > 10
              IF CA-PCODE-ENTERED(ITEM-SUB)
                  MOVE ATTR-PROT TO ORD-A-PCODE(ITEM-SUB)
              ELSE
                  MOVE ATTR-PROT-DARK TO ORD-A-PCODE(ITEM-SUB)
              END-IF
              IF CA-QTY-ENTERED(ITEM-SUB)
                  MOVE ATTR-PROT TO ORD-A-QTY(ITEM-SUB)
              ELSE
                  MOVE ATTR-PROT-DARK TO ORD-A-QTY(ITEM-SUB)
              END-IF
              IF        CA-NET-ENTERED(ITEM-SUB)
                     OR CA-PCODE-ENTERED(ITEM-SUB)
                  MOVE ATTR-PROT TO ORD-A-NET(ITEM-SUB)
              ELSE
                  MOVE ATTR-PROT-DARK TO ORD-A-NET(ITEM-SUB)
              END-IF
          END-PERFORM.
 *
      1420-UNPROTECT-FIELDS.
 *
          MOVE ATTR-UNPROT-MDT TO ORD-A-CUSTNO.
          IF CA-PO-ENTERED
              MOVE ATTR-UNPROT-MDT TO ORD-A-PO
          ELSE
              MOVE ATTR-UNPROT       TO ORD-A-PO
          END-IF.
 *
          MOVE ATTR-TURQUOISE TO ORD-C-CUSTNO
                                 ORD-C-PO.
 *
          PERFORM VARYING ITEM-SUB FROM 1 BY 1
                  UNTIL ITEM-SUB > 10
              IF CA-PCODE-ENTERED(ITEM-SUB)
                  MOVE ATTR-UNPROT-MDT TO ORD-A-PCODE(ITEM-SUB)
              ELSE
                  MOVE ATTR-UNPROT       TO ORD-A-PCODE(ITEM-SUB)
              END-IF
              IF CA-QTY-ENTERED(ITEM-SUB)
                  MOVE ATTR-UNPROT-MDT TO ORD-A-QTY(ITEM-SUB)
              ELSE
                  MOVE ATTR-UNPROT       TO ORD-A-QTY(ITEM-SUB)
              END-IF
              IF CA-NET-ENTERED(ITEM-SUB)
                  MOVE ATTR-UNPROT-MDT TO ORD-A-NET(ITEM-SUB)
              ELSE
                  MOVE ATTR-UNPROT       TO ORD-A-NET(ITEM-SUB)
              END-IF
              MOVE ATTR-TURQUOISE TO ORD-C-PCODE(ITEM-SUB)
                                     ORD-C-QTY(ITEM-SUB)
                                     ORD-C-NET(ITEM-SUB)
          END-PERFORM.
 *
```

Figure 13-6   The COBOL code for the order entry program (part 11 of 12)

The order entry program   **Page 12**

```
2000-PROCESS-POST-ORDER.
*
    MOVE CA-INVOICE-RECORD TO INVOICE-RECORD.
*
    EXEC CICS
        LINK PROGRAM('GETINV')
             COMMAREA(INV-INVOICE-NUMBER)
    END-EXEC.
*
    PERFORM 2100-WRITE-INVOICE-RECORD.
    ADD 1 TO CA-TOTAL-ORDERS.
    MOVE 'Type order details.  Then press Enter.'
        TO ORD-D-INSTR.
    MOVE 'Order posted.' TO ORD-D-MESSAGE.
    MOVE 'F3=Exit    F12=Cancel' TO ORD-D-FKEY.
    MOVE -1 TO ORD-L-CUSTNO.
    SET SEND-ERASE TO TRUE.
    PERFORM 1400-SEND-ORDER-MAP.
*
2100-WRITE-INVOICE-RECORD.
*
    EXEC CICS
        WRITE FILE('INVOICE')
              FROM(INVOICE-RECORD)
              RIDFLD(INV-INVOICE-NUMBER)
    END-EXEC.
*
3000-SEND-TOTAL-LINE.
*
    MOVE CA-TOTAL-ORDERS TO TL-TOTAL-ORDERS.
*
    EXEC CICS
        SEND TEXT FROM(TOTAL-LINE)
                  ERASE
                  FREEKB
    END-EXEC.
*
9999-TERMINATE-PROGRAM.
*
    MOVE EIBRESP  TO ERR-RESP.
    MOVE EIBRESP2 TO ERR-RESP2.
    MOVE EIBTRNID TO ERR-TRNID.
    MOVE EIBRSRCE TO ERR-RSRCE.
*
    EXEC CICS
        XCTL PROGRAM('SYSERR')
             COMMAREA(ERROR-PARAMETERS)
    END-EXEC.
```

Figure 13-6   The COBOL code for the order entry program (part 12 of 12)

The COBOL code for the GETINV subprogram

Figure 13-7 shows the source listing for the GETINV subprogram. As you can see, this program simply reads the only record in the invoice control file (which has a key value of zero), moves the next invoice number to the communication area, adds 1 to the next invoice number in the invoice control record, and rewrites the record. By using this subprogram, the order entry program produces invoices with unique ascending invoice numbers, even if many users are entering orders at once.

By the way, the GETINV program is invoked using a LINK command because it's only executed once during a single execution of the order entry program. So there's no advantage to use the Call statement. In contrast, the NUMEDIT and INTEDIT subprograms may be called multiple times during a single execution, so it's more efficient to invoke them using the Call statement.

The GETINV subprogram

```
IDENTIFICATION DIVISION.
*
PROGRAM-ID.   GETINV.
*
ENVIRONMENT DIVISION.
*
DATA DIVISION.
*
WORKING-STORAGE SECTION.
*
COPY INVCTL.
*
LINKAGE SECTION.
*
01  DFHCOMMAREA    PIC 9(06).
*
PROCEDURE DIVISION.
*
0000-GET-INVOICE-NUMBER.
*
    MOVE ZERO TO INVCTL-RECORD-KEY.
    EXEC CICS
        READ FILE('INVCTL')
             INTO(INVCTL-RECORD)
             RIDFLD(INVCTL-RECORD-KEY)
             UPDATE
    END-EXEC.
    MOVE INVCTL-NEXT-INVOICE-NUMBER TO DFHCOMMAREA.
    ADD 1 TO INVCTL-NEXT-INVOICE-NUMBER.
    EXEC CICS
        REWRITE FILE('INVCTL')
                FROM(INVCTL-RECORD)
    END-EXEC.
    EXEC CICS
        RETURN
    END-EXEC.
```

Figure 13-7   The COBOL code for the GETINV subprogram

Perspective

If you understand all of the code used by the order entry program presented in this chapter, you're well on your way to developing CICS applications of professional quality. If you don't understand every aspect of this program, though, don't worry. CICS is complicated, and this program requires you to keep track of a lot of details. As you apply what you've learned to your own programs, your understanding will improve.

Section 5

CICS for file and database processing

Up to this point, you've learned how to use the basic file control commands to process VSAM files randomly. Now, in the chapters in this section, you'll learn how to use advanced file handling features as well as features for working with DB2 databases. In chapter 14, you'll learn how to process files sequentially using browse commands. In chapter 15, you'll learn how to process VSAM files using alternate indexes. In chapter 16, you'll learn how to use other file handling features, including generic keys and the MASSINSERT command. And in chapter 17, you'll learn how to write CICS programs that access data in a DB2 database.

Because chapter 15 assumes that you understand the browse commands presented in chapter 14, you should read those two chapters in sequence. Likewise, you should read chapter 14 before reading the topic on generic keys in chapter 16. Other than that, you can read the chapters in any sequence you like.

14

How to process files sequentially

Most online applications process files using the random file processing elements you've learned so far. Still, some online applications need to access files sequentially. Under CICS, this is called *browsing*. So in this chapter, you'll learn how to use the CICS *browse commands*.

How to use the browse commands

In the topics that follow, you'll learn how to use the five commands for browsing a file: STARTBR, READNEXT, READPREV, ENDBR, and RESETBR. You can use these commands to process all three types of VSAM files: key-sequenced data sets (KSDS), relative record data sets (RRDS), and entry-sequenced data sets (ESDS). Sequential processing of a KSDS is usually based on the file's key values. For an RRDS, sequential processing uses relative record numbers. And for an ESDS, it uses relative byte addresses.

How to code the STARTBR command

The STARTBR command, shown in figure 14-1, initiates a browse operation and identifies the location within the file where the browse begins. The STARTBR command doesn't retrieve a record from the file itself. Instead, it just establishes a position in the file so subsequent READNEXT or READPREV commands can retrieve records.

You can think of a STARTBR command like a standard COBOL Start statement—its function is similar. The main difference is that a STARTBR command is *always* required when you want to browse a file, even if you want to begin with the first record in the file. In contrast, standard COBOL requires a Start statement only when you want to begin sequential retrieval at a point other than the first record in the file.

In its simplest form, you code the STARTBR command like this:

```
EXEC CICS
    STARTBR FILE('CUSTMAS')
            RIDFLD(CM-CUSTOMER-NUMBER)
            RESP(RESPONSE-CODE)
END-EXEC.
```

This command initiates a browse operation for the KSDS named CUSTMAS. The browse begins at the record identified by the value of CM-CUSTOMER-NUMBER. For example, if CM-CUSTOMER-NUMBER is 10000, the browse begins at the record whose key is 10000. If there's no record with that key, processing starts with the first record whose key is greater than 10000, since the GTEQ option is the default.

If there's no record in the KSDS whose key is greater than or equal to the value in the RIDFLD field, the RESP field will indicate that the NOTFND condition was raised. You should always provide for this possibility by coding the RESP option and testing its value following the STARTBR command.

Note that if you're processing an RRDS instead of a KSDS, the value of the RIDFLD field is a relative record number within the file, and you must specify the RRN option. For an ESDS, the RIDFLD is a relative byte address, and you must code the RBA option. (You can also use an RBA to access a KSDS, but you'll probably never do that.)

The syntax of the STARTBR command

```
EXEC CICS
    STARTBR  FILE(filename)
             RIDFLD(data-name)
             [RRN | RBA]
             [GTEQ | EQUAL]
             [GENERIC]
             [KEYLENGTH(data-name | literal)]
END-EXEC
```

Option	Description
FILE	Specifies the file name from the File Control Table.
RIDFLD	For a KSDS, specifies the name of the field that contains the key of the record where the browse operation will start. If RRN or RBA is specified, this field is interpreted as a relative record number or a relative byte address.
RRN	Indicates that the RIDFLD value is a relative record number for an RRDS. In this case, the RIDFLD is a binary fullword.
RBA	Indicates that the RIDFLD option should be interpreted as a relative byte address for an ESDS or KSDS. In this case, the RIDFLD is a binary fullword.
GTEQ	Indicates that the browse operation will start at the first record whose key is greater than or equal to the value in RIDFLD (this is the default).
EQUAL	Indicates that the browse operation will start at the record whose key is equal to the value in RIDFLD.
GENERIC	Indicates that only a part of the key in the RIDFLD field should be used. Positioning is established at the first record with a key whose leftmost character positions, as specified by the KEYLENGTH option, match the RIDFLD field. Valid only for a KSDS.
KEYLENGTH	Specifies a binary halfword or literal value that indicates the length of the key, which must be less than the file's defined key length. Used with the GENERIC option.

Description

- The STARTBR command initiates the browse and identifies a starting location within the file, but doesn't retrieve a record from the file. This command is required if you want to browse a file, even if you're starting with the first record in the file.

- The GTEQ/EQUAL option determines whether the browse should start with the record whose key is greater than or equal to the RIDFLD value, or whether it must be an equal relationship. If a matching record isn't found, the NOTFND condition is raised.

Figure 14-1   How to code the STARTBR command

The last two options you can code on the STARTBR command, GENERIC and KEYLENGTH, let you specify a RIDFLD key whose length is less than the full length of the key defined for the file. You'll learn how these two options work in chapter 16.

How to control the STARTBR position

You can start processing with the first record in a KSDS by moving Low-Value to the RIDFLD field before you issue the STARTBR command. That way, processing begins at the first record whose key is greater than or equal to hexadecimal zeros—and that's always the first record in the file. If a KSDS has a numeric key, though, you must move Zero rather than Low-Value to the key field to start a browse at the first record. That's because the COBOL compiler won't let you move Low-Value to a numeric field.

The first example in figure 14-2 shows the coding for a STARTBR procedure like this. First, the file's RIDFLD field is set to Low-Value to position the file at its first record. After the STARTBR command executes, an If statement checks the response code. If the NOTFND condition occurs, INVOICE-EOF-SW is set to indicate that the end of the file has been reached. If a more serious error occurs, the program performs procedure 9999 to terminate the program.

To start a browse at the beginning of an ESDS instead of a KSDS, you move Zero to the RIDFLD field and include the RBA option. That way, the browse starts at the record whose relative byte address is zero—the first record in the file. To browse an RRDS from the beginning, you move 1 to the RIDFLD field and include the RRN option. Then, the browse starts at the record with relative record number 1—again, the first record in the file.

To start a browse at a specific record that *must* exist in the file, you code the EQUAL option on the STARTBR command as shown in the second example in this figure. To illustrate, suppose CM-CUSTOMER-NUMBER contains 10000. Then, processing will start *only* with record 10000. If there's no record in the file with that key value, the NOTFND condition will be raised.

In some cases, you might want to start processing with the last record in a KSDS. If the RIDFLD field for the browse is alphanumeric, you can do that by moving High-Value (hexadecimal FFs) to that field. Issuing the STARTBR command when the RIDFLD field contains High-Value is a special case—it doesn't cause the NOTFND condition to be raised, as you might expect. Instead, it establishes the position in the file at the last record.

If the RIDFIELD is numeric, you might think that you could move all 9's to it to start the browse at the end of the file. Unfortunately, this will cause the NOTFND condition to be raised if there isn't a record in the file with that key. Since you can't move High-Value to a numeric field, though, you have to redefine the RIDFLD as alphanumeric and then move High-Value to it.

A STARTBR procedure that starts a browse at the beginning of the file

```
1000-START-INVOICE-BROWSE.
*
    MOVE LOW-VALUE TO STARTBR-KEY.
    EXEC CICS
        STARTBR FILE('INVOICE')
                RIDFLD(STARTBR-KEY)
                RESP(RESPONSE-CODE)
    END-EXEC.
    IF RESPONSE-CODE = DFHRESP(NOTFND)
        MOVE 'Y' TO INVOICE-EOF-SW
    ELSE
        IF RESPONSE-CODE NOT = DFHRESP(NORMAL)
            PERFORM 9999-TERMINATE-PROGRAM
        END-IF
    END-IF.
```

A STARTBR procedure that starts a browse at a specific record

```
2100-START-CUSTOMER-BROWSE.
*
    EXEC CICS
        STARTBR FILE('CUSTMAS')
                RIDFLD(CM-CUSTOMER-NUMBER)
                EQUAL
                RESP(RESPONSE-CODE)
    END-EXEC.
    EVALUATE RESPONSE-CODE
        WHEN DFHRESP(NORMAL)
            MOVE 'Y' TO CUSTOMER-FOUND-SW
        WHEN DFHRESP(NOTFND)
            MOVE 'N' TO CUSTOMER-FOUND-SW
        WHEN OTHER
            PERFORM 9999-TERMINATE-PROGRAM
    END-EVALUATE.
```

Description

- To start a browse at the beginning of a KSDS, move Low-Value to the RIDFLD field if it's alphanumeric. If it's numeric, move Zero to it. For an ESDS, move Zero to this field. And for an RRDS, move 1.

- To start a browse at the end of a file, move High-Value to the RIDFLD field. For a KSDS, if this field is numeric, you must redefine it as alphanumeric and then move High-Value to it (moving all 9's to a numeric RIDFLD field won't work because it raises the NOTFND condition).

- To start a browse at a specific record, code the EQUAL option on the STARTBR command. This tells CICS to start the browse with the record whose key value is equal to the value in the RIDFLD field.

- Because the NOTFND condition will occur if no records are found that meet the GTEQ/EQUAL test, you should code the RESP option on the STARTBR command and then test for this condition.

Figure 14-2   How to control the STARTBR position

How to code the READNEXT and READPREV commands

After you've used the STARTBR command to initiate a browse operation, you can retrieve records sequentially using the READNEXT or READPREV command. As their names imply, READNEXT retrieves the next record in a file, and READPREV reads the previous record in a file. The formats of these two commands are shown in figure 14-3.

Each time you issue a READNEXT command, the next record in the file identified by the FILE option is retrieved and stored in the INTO field. When there are no more records in the file, the ENDFILE condition is raised. So you'll want to test the response code field immediately after the READNEXT command.

The data name you specify on the RIDFLD option is usually the same as the one you specified on the STARTBR command, although it doesn't have to be. When the READNEXT command is executed, it updates this field to indicate the key, RRN, or RBA value of the record it retrieved. In most cases, you won't need to worry about the value in this field or how it's used by the browse operation. If you want to reposition the browse so that the next record to be read is not the next record in sequence, though, you can do that by changing the value of this field. Then, if the EQUAL option was specified on the STARTBR command, the record with the value you specify is retrieved. Otherwise, the next record whose key value is greater than or equal to the RIDFLD value is retrieved. (If that record doesn't exist, the NOTFND condition is raised.) Note that for this to work, the value you specify in the RIDFLD field must be greater than its current value. In other words, you can't reposition a browse to a record that's located before the current record using this technique.

To retrieve records sequentially from an RRDS, you code RRN on the READNEXT command. Similarly, to retrieve records sequentially from an ESDS, you specify RBA. If you omit both RRN and RBA, CICS assumes you're processing a KSDS.

The READPREV command is similar to the READNEXT command, except that it retrieves records in reverse order. In other words, it lets you read a file backwards, from the current position toward the beginning of the file. When a READPREV command tries to retrieve a record that would be beyond the beginning of the file, the ENDFILE condition is raised. You should provide for it just as you do for the READNEXT command.

The READPREV command has two peculiarities you should know about. First, if you issue a READPREV command following a READNEXT command, the same record is retrieved twice. For example, suppose a file contains three records with keys 1000, 1001, and 1002, and you issue a READNEXT command that retrieves record 1001. If you then issue a READPREV command, it too retrieves record 1001. To retrieve record 1000, you must issue *two* READPREV commands: the first retrieves record 1001, the second record 1000. The opposite is true as well: If you issue a READNEXT command following a READPREV command, the same record is retrieved.

The syntax of the READNEXT and READPREV commands

```
EXEC CICS
    {READNEXT | READPREV}  FILE(filename)
                           INTO(data-name)
                           RIDFLD(data-name)
                           [RRN | RBA]
                           [KEYLENGTH(data-name | literal)]
END-EXEC
```

Option	Description
FILE	Specifies the file name from the File Control Table.
INTO	Specifies the area that will contain the record being read.
RIDFLD	Specifies the name of the field that identifies the record. After the completion of the READNEXT or READPREV command, this field contains the key, RRN, or RBA of the record that was read.
RRN	Indicates that the RIDFLD value is a relative record number for an RRDS.
RBA	Indicates that the RIDFLD value is a relative byte address for an ESDS or KSDS.
KEYLENGTH	Specifies a binary halfword or literal value that indicates the length of the key, which must be less than the file's defined key length. Usually used with the GENERIC option of the STARTBR or RESETBR command.

Description

- The READNEXT and READPREV commands let you read a file in sequence, forwards or backwards. The ENDFILE condition is raised when there are no more records in the specified direction.

- If you code a READPREV following a READNEXT, the same record is retrieved twice. To retrieve the previous record, you must code *two* READPREV commands in a row. Likewise, when READNEXT follows READPREV, you have to code two READNEXT commands to retrieve the next record.

- If you issue a READPREV command after issuing a STARTBR command that specifies anything other than High-Value for the RIDFLD field, the NOTFND condition will occur. To avoid this problem, you can issue a READNEXT command followed by two READPREV commands.

- You can change the position of a browse operation by changing the value of the RIDFLD field before you issue a READNEXT or READPREV command. Then, the record with the key you specify is retrieved. You can also use the RESETBR command to reposition a browse (see figure 14-6).

- You can't use a READPREV command with a STARTBR command that includes the GENERIC option.

Figure 14-3   How to code the READNEXT and READPREV commands

The second peculiarity of READPREV has to do with issuing the command immediately after a STARTBR command. If the value of the RIDFLD field for the STARTBR command is set to High-Value, positioning the browse at the end of the file, it's safe to issue a READPREV command. If the browse isn't positioned at the end of the file, though, a READPREV command will cause the NOTFND condition to be raised, even if the GTEQ option is in effect. As a rule, then, you shouldn't code a READPREV command right after a STARTBR command unless the RIDFLD field in the STARTBR contains High-Value.

So how can you retrieve the previous record when you don't want to start at the end of the file? You must issue four commands: STARTBR, READNEXT, READPREV, and READPREV. The STARTBR command positions the file to the record you specify. Then, the READNEXT command retrieves the record. Next, the READPREV command changes the direction of the browse. But since it retrieves the same record as the READNEXT command, another READPREV command is required to read the previous record. You'll see an example of this in the customer inquiry program that's presented later in this chapter, so don't worry if it seems confusing.

A typical READNEXT procedure

Figure 14-4 shows the coding for a typical READNEXT procedure. It's executed once for each record in an invoice file, retrieving the records in invoice-number sequence. After the READNEXT command is executed, an If statement checks the response code. If the ENDFILE condition is raised, it sets an EOF switch that's used in the higher-level procedures to control processing. If a serious error occurs, it performs a procedure that will end the program.

The code for a typical READPREV procedure is similar. Remember, though, that if the browse doesn't start at the end of the file, you can't code a READPREV command immediately following the STARTBR command. Instead, you must follow the STARTBR command with a READNEXT command followed by two READPREV commands.

A typical READNEXT procedure

```
        .
        .
    PERFORM 1000-START-INVOICE-BROWSE.
    PERFORM 2000-PROCESS-INVOICE-RECORD
        UNTIL INVOICE-EOF.
        .
        .
*
 2000-PROCESS-INVOICE-RECORD.
*
    PERFORM 2100-READ-NEXT-INVOICE.
    IF NOT INVOICE-EOF
        .
        .
 2100-READ-NEXT-INVOICE.
*
    EXEC CICS
        READNEXT FILE('INVOICE')
                 INTO(INVOICE-RECORD)
                 RIDFLD(INV-INVOICE-NUMBER)
                 RESP(RESPONSE-CODE)
    END-EXEC.
    IF RESPONSE-CODE = DFHRESP(ENDFILE)
        MOVE 'Y' TO INVOICE-EOF-SW
    ELSE
        IF RESPONSE-CODE NOT = DFHRESP(NORMAL)
            PERFORM 9999-TERMINATE-PROGRAM
        END-IF
    END-IF.
```

Description

- After a STARTBR command has been executed, the READNEXT command reads the next record in sequence.

- Because the ENDFILE condition occurs when you reach the end (READNEXT) or beginning (READPREV) of the file, you should include the RESP option on READNEXT and READPREV commands and then test for this condition. See figure 14-7 for other exceptional conditions that can occur as a result of these commands.

- You can replace the READNEXT command with READPREV in the procedure above as long as the STARTBR command positions the file at its end. If it doesn't, you must issue the READNEXT command followed by two READPREV commands to read the previous record.

Figure 14-4   A typical READNEXT procedure

How to code the ENDBR command

Figure 14-5 gives the format of the ENDBR command, which is used to terminate a browse operation. Although a browse is terminated automatically when the task ends, it's a good practice to end a browse explicitly. That's because as long as the browse is active, additional VSAM resources are allocated to the task. So if your program does extensive processing after it completes a browse operation (or if it's possible the program will evolve over time to include more extensive processing), issuing an ENDBR command makes better use of your system's resources. What's more, you can't perform certain I/O operations on a file that's involved in a browse operation. In particular, you can't update the file by issuing WRITE, REWRITE, or DELETE commands. As a result, I recommend you use ENDBR to end all of your browse operations.

The syntax of the ENDBR command

```
EXEC CICS
    ENDBR FILE(filename)
END-EXEC
```

Option	Description
FILE	Specifies the file name from the File Control Table.

A typical ENDBR command

```
EXEC CICS
    ENDBR FILE('INVOICE')
END-EXEC.
```

Description

- The ENDBR command terminates a browse operation and releases the VSAM resources that were allocated to the browse.

- You should code the ENDBR command as soon as you're done browsing a file. This will improve the overall efficiency of the system, and it will remove the restrictions on issuing file control commands that are in place when a browse is active.

Figure 14-5   How to code the ENDBR command

How to code the RESETBR command

If you need to restart a browse operation at a new position in a file, you can change the RIDFLD value before issuing a READNEXT command as described earlier in this chapter. This is the most efficient technique if the record you want to skip to is close to the current record. Because you usually won't know if the records are close together, though, I don't recommend this technique. Instead, you should use the RESETBR command shown in figure 14-6.

As you can see, the options of the RESETBR command are identical to those of the STARTBR command. So if you understand how to code the STARTBR command, you won't have any trouble with RESETBR.

By the way, you can also restart a browse by issuing an ENDBR command followed by a STARTBR command. That's inefficient, though, because the ENDBR command causes the VSAM resources that are allocated to the browse to be released. Then, the subsequent STARTBR command must reallocate them. In contrast, the RESETBR command doesn't release VSAM resources, so they don't need to be reallocated.

The syntax of the RESETBR command

```
EXEC CICS
    RESETBR  FILE(filename)
             RIDFLD(data-name)
             [RRN | RBA]
             [GTEQ | EQUAL]
             [GENERIC]
             [KEYLENGTH(data-name | literal)]
END-EXEC
```

Option	Description
FILE	Specifies the file name from the File Control Table.
RIDFLD	For a KSDS, specifies the name of the field that contains the key of the record where the browse operation will restart. If RRN or RBA is specified, this field is interpreted as a relative record number or a relative byte address.
RRN	Indicates that the RIDFLD value is a relative record number for an RRDS. In this case, the RIDFLD is a binary fullword.
RBA	Indicates that the RIDFLD option should be interpreted as a relative byte address for an ESDS or KSDS. In this case, the RIDFLD is a binary fullword.
GTEQ	Indicates that the browse operation will be repositioned at the first record whose key is greater than or equal to the value in RIDFLD (this is the default).
EQUAL	Indicates that the browse operation will be repositioned at the record whose key is equal to the value in RIDFLD.
GENERIC	Indicates that only a part of the key in the RIDFLD field should be used. Positioning is established at the first record with a key whose leftmost character positions, as specified by the KEYLENGTH option, match the RIDFLD field. Valid only for a KSDS file.
KEYLENGTH	Specifies a binary halfword or literal value that indicates the length of the key, which must be less than the file's defined key length. Used with the GENERIC option.

A RESETBR command that restarts the browse at a specific record

```
EXEC CICS
    RESETBR FILE('CUSTMAS')
            RIDFLD(CM-CUSTOMER-NUMBER)
            EQUAL
            RESP(RESPONSE-CODE)
END-EXEC.
```

Description

- The RESETBR command is similar to the STARTBR command. It lets you restart a browse operation at a new position in a file.
- If no record is found that matches the GTEQ/EQUAL condition you specify, the NOTFND condition is raised.

Figure 14-6   How to code the RESETBR command

Browse exceptional conditions

Besides the NOTFND and ENDFILE conditions I've already mentioned, a number of other exceptional conditions might be raised during a browse operation. These conditions are summarized in figure 14-7. Most of them are caused by programming errors or CICS problems, so there's usually no need to provide for them in production programs. Still, you should find out your shop's standards for handling these conditions and follow them.

Browse exceptional conditions

Condition	Cause
FILENOTFOUND	The file isn't defined in the FCT.
ENDFILE	There are no more records to be read.
ILLOGIC	A VSAM error has occurred.
INVREQ	The browse request is invalid. Usually, this is because you didn't issue a successful STARTBR command before a READNEXT or READPREV command.
IOERR	An I/O error has occurred.
NOTFND	The record specified in a browse command doesn't exist.
NOTOPEN	The file isn't open.

Description

- Besides ENDFILE and NOTFND, most browse exceptional conditions are caused by programming errors that you'll find and correct during testing or by CICS problems that your production programs won't have to handle.

Figure 14-7   Exceptional conditions that may be raised by the browse commands

Two sample applications that do sequential processing

To show you how the browse commands work together, the topics that follow present two programs that do sequential processing. The first one summarizes the data in an invoice file. The second one is a variation of the inquiry program you saw in chapter 2 that lets the user display customer records.

An invoice summary program

Figure 14-8 gives the specifications for a simple, non-interactive program that browses a file of invoice records and displays information summarized from the file. As you can see in the screen layout in part 2, the summary display shows the number of invoices in the file, the first and last invoice numbers, and the sum of the total values of all the invoices in the file.

Because the invoice summary program doesn't interact with a user, it's conversational rather than pseudo-conversational. As a result, its structure is more like what you'd expect for a batch COBOL report-preparation program than for a CICS program. This is illustrated by the structure chart shown in this figure. Here, you can see that module 0000 calls module 1000 to start the browse. Then, it calls module 2000 repeatedly to read records sequentially from the invoice file. When the end of the file has been reached, module 0000 calls module 3000 to end the browse and module 4000 to send the summary display to the terminal.

Figure 14-9 (on pages 409 and 410) gives the mapset listing for this program. It's unusual in that the DFHMSD macro is coded with the MODE=OUT parameter. Although I could have coded MODE=INOUT as in the other maps in this book, that's not necessary because the map doesn't accept any input. Keep in mind, though, that this program isn't typical of CICS programs. Most require user input and are pseudo-conversational rather than conversational.

The code for the symbolic map (on page 411) illustrates the result of coding MODE=OUT. Here, the copy member consists of a single 01-level item that defines the output map. Notice that the three-byte FILLER field you usually see before each named field in an output map has been broken down into two fields: a two-byte FILLER field and a one-byte attribute field (suffix A). As a result, you can still manipulate the standard attributes for all the output fields.

The program overview for the invoice summary program

Program	INVSUM1: Invoice summary
Trans-id	SUM1
Overview	Reads the records in the invoice file and displays a summary screen showing a count of the invoices, the beginning and ending invoice numbers, and the sum of the invoice total fields.
Input/output specifications	SUMMAP1 Invoice summary map INVOICE Invoice file
Processing specifications	1. Control is transferred to this program via XCTL from a menu program with no communication area. The user can also start the program by entering the trans-id SUM1. 2. Process the invoice records using CICS browse commands, then display the summary map and terminate with a RETURN command. The TRANSID on this command should specify that the MENU transaction is invoked when the user presses the Enter key (or any other attention key). 3. If an unrecoverable error occurs, terminate the program by invoking the SYSERR subprogram with an XCTL command.

Figure 14-8   The specifications and design for the invoice summary program (part 1 of 2)

The screen layout for the invoice summary program

Map name	SUMMAP1	Date	03/29/2001
Program name	INVSUM1	Designer	Doug Lowe

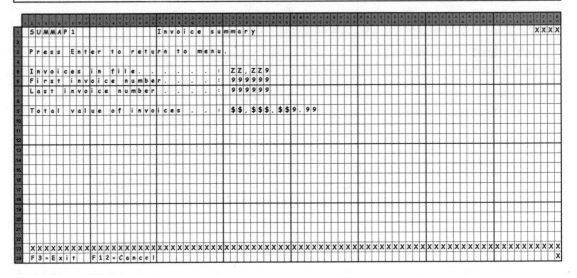

```
SUMMAP1                  Invoice summary                                                    XXXX

Press Enter to return to menu.

Invoices in file. . . . . :  ZZ,ZZ9
First invoice number. . . :  999999
Last invoice number . . . :  999999

Total value of invoices . :  $$,$$$,$$9.99
```

```
XXXXXXXXXXXXXXXXXXXXXXXXXXXXXXXXXXXXXXXXXXXXXXXXXXXXXXXXXXXXXXXXXXXXXXXXXXXXXX
F3=Exit    F12=Cancel                                                        X
```

The structure chart

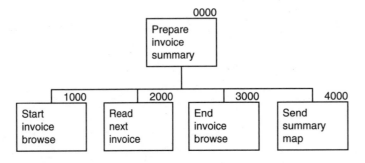

Description

- This simple, non-interactive program browses a file of invoice records and displays information summarized from the file.
- Because it's not interactive, this program is conversational rather than pseudo-conversational.

Figure 14-8   The specifications and design for the invoice summary program (part 2 of 2)

The code for the BMS mapset   **Page 1**

```
          PRINT NOGEN
SUMSET1   DFHMSD TYPE=&SYSPARM,                                     X
                 LANG=COBOL,                                        X
                 MODE=OUT,                                          X
                 TERM=3270-2,                                       X
                 CTRL=FREEKB,                                       X
                 STORAGE=AUTO,                                      X
                 TIOAPFX=YES
*********************************************************************
SUMMAP1   DFHMDI SIZE=(24,80),                                     X
                 LINE=1,                                            X
                 COLUMN=1
*********************************************************************
          DFHMDF POS=(1,1),                                        X
                 LENGTH=8,                                          X
                 ATTRB=(NORM,PROT),                                 X
                 COLOR=BLUE,                                        X
                 INITIAL='SUMMAP1'
          DFHMDF POS=(1,20),                                       X
                 LENGTH=15,                                         X
                 ATTRB=(NORM,PROT),                                 X
                 COLOR=GREEN,                                       X
                 INITIAL='Invoice summary'
TRANID    DFHMDF POS=(1,76),                                       X
                 LENGTH=4,                                          X
                 ATTRB=(NORM,PROT),                                 X
                 COLOR=BLUE,                                        X
                 INITIAL='XXXX'
*********************************************************************
          DFHMDF POS=(3,1),                                        X
                 LENGTH=29,                                         X
                 ATTRB=(NORM,PROT),                                 X
                 COLOR=NEUTRAL,                                     X
                 INITIAL='Press Enter to return to menu.'
          DFHMDF POS=(5,1),                                        X
                 LENGTH=29,                                         X
                 ATTRB=(NORM,PROT),                                 X
                 COLOR=GREEN,                                       X
                 INITIAL='Invoices in file. . . . . . :'
COUNT     DFHMDF POS=(5,31),                                       X
                 LENGTH=6,                                          X
                 ATTRB=(NORM,PROT),                                 X
                 COLOR=TURQUOISE,                                   X
                 PICOUT='ZZ,ZZ9'
          DFHMDF POS=(6,1),                                        X
                 LENGTH=29,                                         X
                 ATTRB=(NORM,PROT),                                 X
                 COLOR=GREEN,                                       X
                 INITIAL='First invoice number. . . . :'
```

Figure 14-9   The BMS mapset for the invoice summary program (part 1 of 2)

The code for the BMS mapset

```
FIRST     DFHMDF POS=(6,31),                                              X
                 LENGTH=6,                                                X
                 COLOR=TURQUOISE,                                         X
                 ATTRB=(NORM,PROT),                                       X
                 PICOUT='999999'
          DFHMDF POS=(7,1),                                               X
                 LENGTH=29,                                               X
                 ATTRB=(NORM,PROT),                                       X
                 COLOR=GREEN,                                             X
                 INITIAL='Last invoice number . . . . :'
LAST      DFHMDF POS=(7,31),                                              X
                 LENGTH=6,                                                X
                 COLOR=TURQUOISE,                                         X
                 ATTRB=(NORM,PROT),                                       X
                 PICOUT='999999'
          DFHMDF POS=(9,1),                                               X
                 LENGTH=29,                                               X
                 ATTRB=(NORM,PROT),                                       X
                 COLOR=GREEN,                                             X
                 INITIAL='Total value of invoices . . :'
TOTAL     DFHMDF POS=(9,31),                                              X
                 LENGTH=13,                                               X
                 COLOR=TURQUOISE,                                         X
                 ATTRB=(NORM,PROT),                                       X
                 PICOUT='$$,$$$,$$9.99'
**************************************************************************
MESSAGE   DFHMDF POS=(23,1),                                             X
                 LENGTH=79,                                               X
                 ATTRB=(BRT,PROT),                                        X
                 COLOR=YELLOW
          DFHMDF POS=(24,1),                                             X
                 LENGTH=19,                                               X
                 ATTRB=(NORM,PROT),                                       X
                 COLOR=BLUE,                                              X
                 INITIAL='F3=Exit   F12=Cancel'
DUMMY     DFHMDF POS=(24,79),                                            X
                 LENGTH=1,                                                X
                 ATTRB=(DRK,PROT,FSET),                                   X
                 INITIAL=' '
**************************************************************************
          DFHMSD TYPE=FINAL
          END
```

Figure 14-9   The BMS mapset for the invoice summary program (part 2 of 2)

The code for the symbolic map

```
01  SUMMAP1O.
        03  FILLER                      PIC X(12).
        03  FILLER                      PIC X(2).
        03  TRANIDA                     PIC X.
        03  TRANIDO                     PIC X(4).
        03  FILLER                      PIC X(2).
        03  COUNTA                      PIC X.
        03  COUNTO                      PIC ZZ,ZZ9.
        03  FILLER                      PIC X(2).
        03  FIRSTA                      PIC X.
        03  FIRSTO                      PIC 999999.
        03  FILLER                      PIC X(2).
        03  LASTA                       PIC X.
        03  LASTO                       PIC 999999.
        03  FILLER                      PIC X(2).
        03  TOTALA                      PIC X.
        03  TOTALO                      PIC $$,$$$,$$9.99.
        03  FILLER                      PIC X(2).
        03  MESSAGEA                    PIC X.
        03  MESSAGEO                    PIC X(79).
        03  FILLER                      PIC X(2).
        03  DUMMYA                      PIC X.
        03  DUMMYO                      PIC X(1).
```

Description

- Because MODE=OUT is coded on the DFHMSD macro for this map, only an output area is generated in the symbolic map.

- Unlike the output area of a symbolic map that's generated when MODE=INOUT is coded, a field is included for the attribute byte for each output field in the map so the program can change the field attributes.

Figure 14-10   The symbolic map for the invoice summary program

The COBOL code for the invoice summary program

Figure 14-11 gives the complete source listing for this program. Procedure 0000 controls the execution of procedures 1000, 2000, 3000, and 4000, just as the structure chart shows. After procedure 4000 sends the summary map to the terminal, a RETURN command terminates the program. When the operator presses an attention key after looking at the summary display, the MENU transaction is started because its trans-id is specified on the RETURN command.

In procedure 1000, the value of the key field for the invoice file, INV-INVOICE-NUMBER, is set to zero. Then, the STARTBR command names this field in the RIDFLD option. That way, the command will position the file at the first record.

Once the STARTBR command has been executed, the program checks the response code. If it's anything other than NOTFND or NORMAL, the program performs procedure 9999 to terminate the program. Like the programs you saw in section 4 of this book, this procedure passes control and diagnostic information to the generalized error handling program named SYSERR.

If the STARTBR command returns a NOTFND condition, procedure 1000 moves Y to INVOICE-EOF-SW. If you look again at procedure 0000, you'll see that procedure 2000 is performed until INVOICE-EOF, so records are read until the end of the file is reached. But since a COBOL Perform Until test is done before the specified paragraph is performed, procedure 2000 isn't performed at all if the NOTFND condition is raised on the STARTBR command. As a result, this program works properly even if the invoice file is empty: The invoice count and total value fields will contain zero, and the first and last invoice number fields will be blank.

The invoice summary program   **Page 1**

```
IDENTIFICATION DIVISION.
*
PROGRAM-ID. INVSUM1.
*
ENVIRONMENT DIVISION.
*
DATA DIVISION.
*
WORKING-STORAGE SECTION.
*
01  SWITCHES.
*
    05  INVOICE-EOF-SW          PIC X(01)      VALUE 'N'.
        88  INVOICE-EOF                        VALUE 'Y'.
    05  FIRST-RECORD-SW         PIC X(01)      VALUE 'Y'.
        88  FIRST-RECORD                       VALUE 'Y'.
*
01  WORK-FIELDS.
*
    05  INVOICE-COUNT           PIC S9(05)     COMP-3  VALUE ZERO.
    05  INVOICE-TOTAL           PIC S9(07)V99  COMP-3  VALUE ZERO.
*
01  RESPONSE-CODE              PIC S9(08)     COMP.
*
COPY SUMSET1.
COPY INVOICE.
COPY ERRPARM.
*
PROCEDURE DIVISION.
*
0000-PREPARE-INVOICE-SUMMARY.
*
    MOVE LOW-VALUE TO SUMMAP1O.
    PERFORM 1000-START-INVOICE-BROWSE.
    PERFORM 2000-READ-NEXT-INVOICE
        UNTIL INVOICE-EOF.
    PERFORM 3000-END-INVOICE-BROWSE.
    PERFORM 4000-SEND-SUMMARY-MAP.
*
    EXEC CICS
        RETURN TRANSID('MENU')
    END-EXEC.
*
1000-START-INVOICE-BROWSE.
*
    MOVE 0 TO INV-INVOICE-NUMBER.
*
    EXEC CICS
        STARTBR FILE('INVOICE')
                RIDFLD(INV-INVOICE-NUMBER)
                RESP(RESPONSE-CODE)
    END-EXEC.
    IF RESPONSE-CODE = DFHRESP(NOTFND)
        MOVE 'Y' TO INVOICE-EOF-SW
    ELSE
        IF RESPONSE-CODE NOT = DFHRESP(NORMAL)
            PERFORM 9999-TERMINATE-PROGRAM
        END-IF
    END-IF.
```

Figure 14-11   The COBOL code for the invoice summary program (part 1 of 2)

Procedure 2000 starts by issuing a READNEXT command to read the next record in the invoice file. Then, it checks the response code from this command to determine if it completed normally. If it did, the invoice number in the record that was just retrieved is moved to the LASTO field in the symbolic map (in case this is the last invoice in the file). Then, the invoice total fields are updated. In addition, if the record that was read is the first record in the file, the invoice number is moved to the FIRSTO field in the map.

If the READNEXT command raises the ENDFILE condition indicating that there are no more records in the file, the procedure sets the EOF switch to Y. Then, procedure 0000 will perform procedure 3000 to end the browse and procedure 4000 to display the invoice summary. If any other exceptional condition occurs, procedure 2000 performs procedure 9999 to terminate the program.

The invoice summary program

Page 2

```
2000-READ-NEXT-INVOICE.
*
    EXEC CICS
        READNEXT FILE('INVOICE')
                 INTO(INVOICE-RECORD)
                 RIDFLD(INV-INVOICE-NUMBER)
                 RESP(RESPONSE-CODE)
    END-EXEC.
    EVALUATE RESPONSE-CODE
        WHEN DFHRESP(NORMAL)
            MOVE INV-INVOICE-NUMBER TO LASTO
            ADD 1 TO INVOICE-COUNT
            ADD INV-INVOICE-TOTAL TO INVOICE-TOTAL
            IF FIRST-RECORD
                MOVE INV-INVOICE-NUMBER TO FIRSTO
                MOVE 'N' TO FIRST-RECORD-SW
            END-IF
        WHEN DFHRESP(ENDFILE)
            MOVE 'Y' TO INVOICE-EOF-SW
        WHEN OTHER
            PERFORM 9999-TERMINATE-PROGRAM
    END-EVALUATE.
*
 3000-END-INVOICE-BROWSE.
*
    EXEC CICS
        ENDBR FILE('INVOICE')
              RESP(RESPONSE-CODE)
    END-EXEC.
    IF RESPONSE-CODE NOT = DFHRESP(NORMAL)
        PERFORM 9999-TERMINATE-PROGRAM
    END-IF.
*
 4000-SEND-SUMMARY-MAP.
*
    MOVE 'SUM1'         TO TRANIDO.
    MOVE INVOICE-COUNT TO COUNTO.
    MOVE INVOICE-TOTAL TO TOTALO.
*
    EXEC CICS
        SEND MAP('SUMMAP1')
             MAPSET('SUMSET1')
             FROM(SUMMAP1O)
             ERASE
    END-EXEC.
*
 9999-TERMINATE-PROGRAM.
*
    MOVE EIBRESP  TO ERR-RESP.
    MOVE EIBRESP2 TO ERR-RESP2.
    MOVE EIBTRNID TO ERR-TRNID.
    MOVE EIBRSRCE TO ERR-RSRCE.
*
    EXEC CICS
        XCTL PROGRAM('SYSERR')
             COMMAREA(ERROR-PARAMETERS)
    END-EXEC.
```

Figure 14-11   The COBOL code for the invoice summary program (part 2 of 2)

A customer inquiry program

Figure 14-12 presents the specifications for a customer inquiry program that lets a terminal user display records from a customer file. As you can see, various attention keys indicate which record is displayed. To display a specific customer record, the user types a customer number and presses the Enter key. To display the first record in the file, the user presses PF5. To display the last record, the user presses PF6. And to display the previous customer or the next customer, the user presses PF7 or PF8.

Because this is a pseudo-conversational program, each execution that requires a browse must start a new browse operation. To keep track of the customer record that's currently displayed, the program stores the customer number in the communication area between program executions. Then, if the user requests the next or previous customer, the program can use the customer number in the communication area to position the browse at the appropriate record. You'll see how that works in a moment.

Figure 14-13 shows an event/response chart for the inquiry program. It lists the series of commands that will be executed in response to each attention key. For example, if the user invokes the program by pressing PF5, the program responds by starting a browse at the beginning of the file, reading the first record, ending the browse, and displaying the record at the terminal. And if the user invokes the program by pressing PF6, the program starts the browse at the end of the file, reads the last record, ends the browse, and displays the record at the terminal.

Notice that the processing for displaying the previous or next customer is more complicated than for displaying the first or last customer. That's because the STARTBR command will position the browse at the customer record that's currently displayed. So the READNEXT command that follows will read that record. Then, to display the previous customer, the program must issue two READPREV commands as described earlier in this chapter. And to display the next customer, it must issue another READNEXT command.

The program overview for the customer inquiry program

Program	CUSTINQ2: Customer inquiry
Trans-id	INQ2
Overview	Displays records from the customer file, allowing the user to scroll forwards or backwards using PF keys.
Input/output specifications	INQMAP2 Customer inquiry map CUSTMAS Customer master file
Processing specifications	1. Control is transferred to this program via XCTL from the menu program INVMENU with no communication area. The user can also start the program by entering the trans-id INQ2. In either case, the program should respond by displaying the customer inquiry map.

2. The user selects a customer record display by pressing an attention key, as follows:

Enter	Display the customer indicated by the entry in the customer number field.
PF5	Display the first customer in the file.
PF6	Display the last customer in the file.
PF7	Display the previous customer.
PF8	Display the next customer.

The program then reads and displays the appropriate customer record.

3. Use the pseudo-conversational programming technique. To restart the browse at the correct record during the next program execution, save the key of the customer currently displayed in the communication area.

4. If the user presses PF3 or PF12, return to the menu program INVMENU by issuing an XCTL command.

5. If an unrecoverable error occurs, terminate the program by invoking the SYSERR subprogram with an XCTL command.

Description

- This program lets users display customer records. The user can enter a customer number to display a specific record or use the PF keys to display the first record in the file, the last record in the file, the previous record, or the next record.

- This is a pseudo-conversational program, so each execution that performs a browse requires one STARTBR command, one or more READNEXT or READPREV commands, and an ENDBR command. Between executions, the program keeps track of the position in the customer file by storing the customer number in the communication area.

Figure 14-12   The specifications for the customer inquiry program (part 1 of 2)

The screen layout for the customer inquiry program

Map name	INQMAP2	Date	04/03/2001
Program name	CUSTINQ2	Designer	Doug Lowe

```
INQMAP2              Customer Inquiry                                      XXXX

To start a new browse, type a customer number.   Then press Enter.

Customer number. . . . .  XXXXXX

Name and address . . . :  XXXXXXXXXXXXXXXXXXXXXXXXXXXXXX
                          XXXXXXXXXXXXXXXXXXXX
                          XXXXXXXXXXXXXXXXXXXXXXXXXXXX
                          XXXXXXXXXXXXXXXXX  XX  XXXXXXXXX




XXXXXXXXXXXXXXXXXXXXXXXXXXXXXXXXXXXXXXXXXXXXXXXXXXXXXXXXXXXXXXXXXXXXXXXXXXXXXXXXXX
F3=Exit    F5=First    F6=Last    F7=Prev    F8=Next    F12=Cancel              X
```

Figure 14-12   The specifications for the customer inquiry program (part 2 of 2)

An event/response chart for the customer inquiry program

Event	Response
Start the program	Display the inquiry map.
PF3 or PF12	Transfer control to the menu program.
Enter key	Read and display the customer record for the customer number entered by the user using this sequence of commands: RECEIVE MAP READ SEND MAP
PF5	Read and display the first record in the file using this sequence of commands: STARTBR RIDFLD(low-values) READNEXT ENDBR SEND MAP
PF6	Read and display the last record in the file using this sequence of commands: STARTBR RIDFLD(high-values) READPREV ENDBR SEND MAP
PF7	Read and display the previous record using this sequence of commands: STARTBR RIDFLD(commarea key) READNEXT READPREV READPREV ENDBR SEND MAP
PF8	Read and display the next record using this sequence of commands: STARTBR RIDFLD(commarea key) READNEXT READNEXT ENDBR SEND MAP
Clear key	Redisplay the current map without any data.
Any PA key	Ignore the key.
Any other key	Display an error message.

Figure 14-13   An event/response chart for the customer inquiry program

Figure 14-14 gives the structure chart for this program. Although module 0000 is the main control module, the key to understanding this program's sequential processing lies in modules 2000, 3000, 4000, and 5000. These are the modules that retrieve the first, last, previous, and next record based on the user's input. Notice that these modules do not invoke a module to receive map input. Modules 2000 and 3000 don't need to get data from the terminal because they know they're dealing with the first and last records in the file. And modules 4000 and 5000 don't need data from the terminal because they can get the current customer number from the communication area and then use that value to retrieve the previous or next customer number. So the only module that invokes the receive map module is module 1000. This module must read and display a random record based on the customer number entered by the user.

Figures 14-15 (on pages 422 and 423) and 14-16 (on pages 424 and 425) present the BMS mapset and symbolic map listings for this program. They're similar to the listings for the customer inquiry program presented in chapter 2, so you shouldn't have any trouble understanding them.

The structure chart for the customer inquiry program

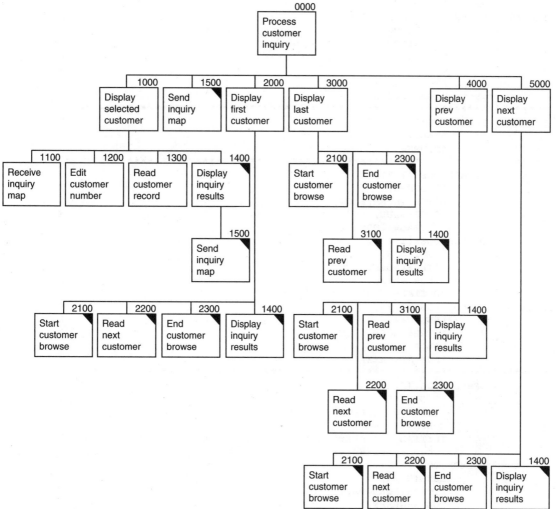

Description

- Module 0000 controls the retrieval of customer information based on the user's input.

- Module 1000 retrieves data for a specific customer. It calls subordinates to receive the inquiry map, edit the customer number, read the customer file to look for a matching record, and display the customer record if it's found.

- Modules 2000, 3000, 4000, and 5000 process the file sequentially to retrieve the first, last, previous, and next record. These modules all have the same basic structure. They call subordinates to start the browse, read the next or previous customer, and display the customer record.

- Because modules 2000 and 3000 start a browse at the beginning or end of the file and modules 4000 and 5000 get the starting customer number from the communication area, they don't have to receive the customer number from the inquiry map.

Figure 14-14   The structure chart for the customer inquiry program

The code for the BMS mapset

```
          PRINT NOGEN
INQSET2   DFHMSD TYPE=&SYSPARM,                                          X
                 LANG=COBOL,                                             X
                 MODE=INOUT,                                             X
                 TERM=3270-2,                                            X
                 CTRL=FREEKB,                                            X
                 STORAGE=AUTO,                                           X
                 TIOAPFX=YES
*********************************************************************
INQMAP2   DFHMDI SIZE=(24,80),                                          X
                 LINE=1,                                                 X
                 COLUMN=1
*********************************************************************
          DFHMDF POS=(1,1),                                             X
                 LENGTH=8,                                              X
                 ATTRB=(NORM,PROT),                                     X
                 COLOR=BLUE,                                            X
                 INITIAL='INQMAP2'
          DFHMDF POS=(1,20),                                           X
                 LENGTH=16,                                             X
                 ATTRB=(NORM,PROT),                                     X
                 COLOR=GREEN,                                           X
                 INITIAL='Customer Inquiry'
TRANID    DFHMDF POS=(1,76),                                           X
                 LENGTH=4,                                              X
                 ATTRB=(NORM,PROT),                                     X
                 COLOR=BLUE,                                            X
                 INITIAL='XXXX'
*********************************************************************
          DFHMDF POS=(3,1),                                            X
                 LENGTH=65,                                             X
                 ATTRB=(NORM,PROT),                                     X
                 COLOR=NEUTRAL,                                         X
                 INITIAL='To start a new browse, type a customer number. X
                   Then press Enter.'
          DFHMDF POS=(5,1),                                            X
                 LENGTH=24,                                             X
                 ATTRB=(NORM,PROT),                                     X
                 COLOR=GREEN,                                           X
                 INITIAL='Customer number. . . . .'
CUSTNO    DFHMDF POS=(5,26),                                           X
                 LENGTH=6,                                              X
                 ATTRB=(NORM,UNPROT),                                   X
                 COLOR=TURQUOISE,                                       X
                 INITIAL='_____'
          DFHMDF POS=(5,33),                                           X
                 LENGTH=1,                                              X
                 ATTRB=ASKIP
*********************************************************************
          DFHMDF POS=(7,1),                                            X
                 LENGTH=24,                                             X
                 ATTRB=(NORM,PROT),                                     X
                 COLOR=GREEN,                                            X
                 INITIAL='Name and address . . . :'
LNAME     DFHMDF POS=(7,26),                                           X
                 LENGTH=30,                                              X
                 COLOR=TURQUOISE,                                        X
                 ATTRB=(NORM,PROT)
```

Figure 14-15   The BMS mapset for the customer inquiry program (part 1 of 2)

The code for the BMS mapset   **Page 2**

```
FNAME      DFHMDF POS=(8,26),                                           X
                  LENGTH=20,                                            X
                  COLOR=TURQUOISE,                                      X
                  ATTRB=(NORM,PROT)
ADDR       DFHMDF POS=(9,26),                                           X
                  LENGTH=30,                                            X
                  COLOR=TURQUOISE,                                      X
                  ATTRB=(NORM,PROT)
CITY       DFHMDF POS=(10,26),                                          X
                  LENGTH=20,                                            X
                  COLOR=TURQUOISE,                                      X
                  ATTRB=(NORM,PROT)
STATE      DFHMDF POS=(10,47),                                          X
                  LENGTH=2,                                             X
                  COLOR=TURQUOISE,                                      X
                  ATTRB=(NORM,PROT)
ZIPCODE    DFHMDF POS=(10,50),                                          X
                  LENGTH=10,                                            X
                  COLOR=TURQUOISE,                                      X
                  ATTRB=(NORM,PROT)
**********************************************************************
MESSAGE    DFHMDF POS=(23,1),                                           X
                  LENGTH=79,                                            X
                  ATTRB=(BRT,PROT),                                     X
                  COLOR=YELLOW
           DFHMDF POS=(24,1),                                           X
                  LENGTH=35,                                            X
                  ATTRB=(NORM,PROT),                                    X
                  COLOR=BLUE,                                           X
                  INITIAL='F3=Exit   F5=First   F6=Last   F7=Prev'
           DFHMDF POS=(24,38),                                          X
                  LENGTH=19,                                            X
                  ATTRB=(NORM,PROT),                                    X
                  COLOR=BLUE,                                           X
                  INITIAL='F8=Next   F12=Cancel'
DUMMY      DFHMDF POS=(24,79),                                          X
                  LENGTH=1,                                             X
                  ATTRB=(DRK,PROT,FSET),                                X
                  INITIAL=' '
**********************************************************************
           DFHMSD TYPE=FINAL
           END
```

Figure 14-15   The BMS mapset for the customer inquiry program (part 2 of 2)

The code for the symbolic map

```
01 INQMAP2I.
    03 FILLER                      PIC X(12).
    03 TRANIDL                     PIC S9(4) COMP.
    03 TRANIDF                     PIC X.
    03 FILLER REDEFINES TRANIDF.
        05 TRANIDA                     PIC X.
    03 TRANIDI                     PIC X(4).
    03 CUSTNOL                     PIC S9(4) COMP.
    03 CUSTNOF                     PIC X.
    03 FILLER REDEFINES CUSTNOF.
        05 CUSTNOA                     PIC X.
    03 CUSTNOI                     PIC X(6).
    03 LNAMEL                      PIC S9(4) COMP.
    03 LNAMEF                      PIC X.
    03 FILLER REDEFINES LNAMEF.
        05 LNAMEA                      PIC X.
    03 LNAMEI                      PIC X(30).
    03 FNAMEL                      PIC S9(4) COMP.
    03 FNAMEF                      PIC X.
    03 FILLER REDEFINES FNAMEF.
        05 FNAMEA                      PIC X.
    03 FNAMEI                      PIC X(20).
    03 ADDRL                       PIC S9(4) COMP.
    03 ADDRF                       PIC X.
    03 FILLER REDEFINES ADDRF.
        05 ADDRA                       PIC X.
    03 ADDRI                       PIC X(30).
    03 CITYL                       PIC S9(4) COMP.
    03 CITYF                       PIC X.
    03 FILLER REDEFINES CITYF.
        05 CITYA                       PIC X.
    03 CITYI                       PIC X(20).
    03 STATEL                      PIC S9(4) COMP.
    03 STATEF                      PIC X.
    03 FILLER REDEFINES STATEF.
        05 STATEA                      PIC X.
    03 STATEI                      PIC X(2).
    03 ZIPCODEL                    PIC S9(4) COMP.
    03 ZIPCODEF                    PIC X.
    03 FILLER REDEFINES ZIPCODEF.
        05 ZIPCODEA                    PIC X.
    03 ZIPCODEI                    PIC X(10).
    03 MESSAGEL                    PIC S9(4) COMP.
    03 MESSAGEF                    PIC X.
    03 FILLER REDEFINES MESSAGEF.
        05 MESSAGEA                    PIC X.
    03 MESSAGEI                    PIC X(79).
    03 DUMMYL                      PIC S9(4) COMP.
    03 DUMMYF                      PIC X.
    03 FILLER REDEFINES DUMMYF.
        05 DUMMYA                       PIC X.
    03 DUMMYI                      PIC X(1).
```

Figure 14-16   The symbolic map for the customer inquiry program (part 1 of 2)

The code for the symbolic map   **Page 2**

```
01 INQMAP2O REDEFINES INQMAP2I.
   03 FILLER                    PIC X(12).
   03 FILLER                    PIC X(3).
   03 TRANIDO                   PIC X(4).
   03 FILLER                    PIC X(3).
   03 CUSTNOO                   PIC X(6).
   03 FILLER                    PIC X(3).
   03 LNAMEO                    PIC X(30).
   03 FILLER                    PIC X(3).
   03 FNAMEO                    PIC X(20).
   03 FILLER                    PIC X(3).
   03 ADDRO                     PIC X(30).
   03 FILLER                    PIC X(3).
   03 CITYO                     PIC X(20).
   03 FILLER                    PIC X(3).
   03 STATEO                    PIC X(2).
   03 FILLER                    PIC X(3).
   03 ZIPCODEO                  PIC X(10).
   03 FILLER                    PIC X(3).
   03 MESSAGEO                  PIC X(79).
   03 FILLER                    PIC X(3).
   03 DUMMYO                    PIC X(1).
```

Figure 14-16   The symbolic map for the customer inquiry program (part 2 of 2)

The COBOL code for the customer inquiry program

Figure 14-17 gives the complete source listing for the customer inquiry program. In the Data Division, you should notice a couple of differences from the inquiry program in chapter 2. First, a switch named CUSTOMER-FOUND-SW has been added. Its value is set based on the response code in the various READ procedures and the STARTBR procedure. Second, a flag named DISPLAY-FLAG has been added to control the information that's displayed on the screen. Third, the ERRPARM copy member has been added for use with the SYSERR subprogram. And fourth, the communication area is now a 6-byte field that passes the current customer number from one program execution to another.

The customer inquiry program   **Page 1**

```
      IDENTIFICATION DIVISION.
      *
      PROGRAM-ID.  CUSTINQ2.
      *
      ENVIRONMENT DIVISION.
      *
      DATA DIVISION.
      *
      WORKING-STORAGE SECTION.
      *
      01   SWITCHES.
      *
           05   VALID-DATA-SW            PIC X(01)  VALUE 'Y'.
                88   VALID-DATA                     VALUE 'Y'.
           05   CUSTOMER-FOUND-SW        PIC X(01)  VALUE 'Y'.
                88   CUSTOMER-FOUND                 VALUE 'Y'.
      *
      01   FLAGS.
      *
           05   DISPLAY-FLAG             PIC X(01).
                88   DISPLAY-NEW-CUSTOMER           VALUE '1'.
                88   DISPLAY-SPACES                 VALUE '2'.
                88   DISPLAY-LOW-VALUES             VALUE '3'.
           05   SEND-FLAG                PIC X(01).
                88   SEND-ERASE                     VALUE '1'.
                88   SEND-DATAONLY                  VALUE '2'.
                88   SEND-DATAONLY-ALARM            VALUE '3'.
      *
      01   COMMUNICATION-AREA.
      *
           05   CA-CUSTOMER-NUMBER       PIC X(06).
      *
      01   RESPONSE-CODE                 PIC S9(08) COMP.
      *
      COPY CUSTMAS.
      *
      COPY INQSET2.
      *
      COPY DFHAID.
      *
      COPY ERRPARM.
      *
      LINKAGE SECTION.
      *
      01   DFHCOMMAREA                   PIC X(06).
      *
```

Figure 14-17   The COBOL code for the customer inquiry program (part 1 of 7)

Procedure 0000 handles the pseudo-conversational processing requirements just as you've seen in previous programs. Because this program uses more attention keys than the other programs you've seen, though, the Evaluate statement must also provide for these keys. In particular, if the user presses PF5, PF6, PF7, or PF8, the program responds by performing procedure 2000, 3000, 4000, or 5000 to start a browse operation and retrieve and display the appropriate record.

Procedure 1000 is executed when the user requests a specific customer record by pressing the Enter key. It performs procedure 1100 to receive the inquiry map, then it performs procedure 1200 to edit the customer number to be sure that the user entered a value. Next, it performs procedure 1300 to read the customer record and procedure 1400 to display the inquiry results. It also records the customer number in the communication area so it can be passed to the next program execution.

Procedure 1400 is coded so that it can be called from various places in the inquiry program to format and display the result of each inquiry. Notice how it uses DISPLAY-FLAG to determine how to display the inquiry result. The first of DISPLAY-FLAG's three possible settings, Display-New-Customer, is used to display data for a successful inquiry. In that case, the procedure moves data from the customer record to the output map, then it performs procedure 1500 to send the map.

Display-Spaces is used when an inquiry for a specific customer number, the first customer, or the last customer is unsuccessful. In that case, procedure 1400 moves spaces to the data fields in the output map so that the data that was previously displayed on the screen will be erased. Then, it performs procedure 1500 to send the map.

Display-Low-Values is used when an inquiry for the previous or next customer is unsuccessful. In that case, procedure 1400 performs procedure 1500 without changing the contents of the symbolic map. Since Low-Value is moved to the map elsewhere in the program (see procedures 4000 and 5000), the data currently displayed on the screen will be unchanged.

Display-Low-Values is also used when the user presses the Enter key without entering a customer number. In this case, though, Low-Value is not moved to the map. Since no data was sent to the program, though, no data will be sent back to the terminal.

The customer inquiry program   **Page 2**

```
      PROCEDURE DIVISION.
*
      0000-PROCESS-CUSTOMER-INQUIRY.
*
          IF EIBCALEN > ZERO
              MOVE DFHCOMMAREA TO COMMUNICATION-AREA
          END-IF.
*
          EVALUATE TRUE
*
              WHEN EIBCALEN = ZERO
                  MOVE LOW-VALUE TO CA-CUSTOMER-NUMBER
                  MOVE LOW-VALUE TO INQMAP2O
                  SET SEND-ERASE TO TRUE
                  PERFORM 1500-SEND-INQUIRY-MAP
*
              WHEN EIBAID = DFHCLEAR
                  MOVE LOW-VALUE TO CA-CUSTOMER-NUMBER
                  MOVE LOW-VALUE TO INQMAP2O
                  SET SEND-ERASE TO TRUE
                  PERFORM 1500-SEND-INQUIRY-MAP
*
              WHEN EIBAID = DFHPA1 OR DFHPA2 OR DFHPA3
                  CONTINUE
*
              WHEN EIBAID = DFHPF3 OR DFHPF12
                  EXEC CICS
                      XCTL PROGRAM('INVMENU')
                  END-EXEC
*
              WHEN EIBAID = DFHENTER
                  PERFORM 1000-DISPLAY-SELECTED-CUSTOMER
*
              WHEN EIBAID = DFHPF5
                  PERFORM 2000-DISPLAY-FIRST-CUSTOMER
*
              WHEN EIBAID = DFHPF6
                  PERFORM 3000-DISPLAY-LAST-CUSTOMER
*
              WHEN EIBAID = DFHPF7
                  PERFORM 4000-DISPLAY-PREV-CUSTOMER
*
              WHEN EIBAID = DFHPF8
                  PERFORM 5000-DISPLAY-NEXT-CUSTOMER
*
              WHEN OTHER
                  MOVE LOW-VALUE TO INQMAP2O
                  MOVE 'Invalid key pressed.' TO MESSAGEO
                  SET SEND-DATAONLY-ALARM TO TRUE
                  PERFORM 1500-SEND-INQUIRY-MAP
*
          END-EVALUATE.
*
          EXEC CICS
              RETURN TRANSID('INQ2')
                      COMMAREA(COMMUNICATION-AREA)
          END-EXEC.
*
```

Figure 14-17   The COBOL code for the customer inquiry program (part 2 of 7)

The customer inquiry program

```
     1000-DISPLAY-SELECTED-CUSTOMER.
*
         PERFORM 1100-RECEIVE-INQUIRY-MAP.
         PERFORM 1200-EDIT-CUSTOMER-NUMBER.
         IF VALID-DATA
             PERFORM 1300-READ-CUSTOMER-RECORD
             IF CUSTOMER-FOUND
                 SET DISPLAY-NEW-CUSTOMER TO TRUE
                 PERFORM 1400-DISPLAY-INQUIRY-RESULTS
                 MOVE CM-CUSTOMER-NUMBER TO CA-CUSTOMER-NUMBER
             ELSE
                 SET DISPLAY-SPACES TO TRUE
                 PERFORM 1400-DISPLAY-INQUIRY-RESULTS
             END-IF
         ELSE
             SET DISPLAY-LOW-VALUES TO TRUE
             PERFORM 1400-DISPLAY-INQUIRY-RESULTS
         END-IF.
*
     1100-RECEIVE-INQUIRY-MAP.
*
         EXEC CICS
             RECEIVE MAP('INQMAP2')
                     MAPSET('INQSET2')
                     INTO(INQMAP2I)
         END-EXEC.
*
         INSPECT INQMAP2I
             REPLACING ALL '_' BY SPACE.
*
     1200-EDIT-CUSTOMER-NUMBER.
*
         IF      CUSTNOL = ZERO
             OR CUSTNOI = SPACE
             MOVE 'N' TO VALID-DATA-SW
             MOVE 'You must enter a customer number.' TO MESSAGEO
         END-IF.
*
     1300-READ-CUSTOMER-RECORD.
*
         EXEC CICS
             READ FILE('CUSTMAS')
                  INTO(CUSTOMER-MASTER-RECORD)
                  RIDFLD(CUSTNOI)
                  RESP(RESPONSE-CODE)
         END-EXEC.
*
         IF RESPONSE-CODE = DFHRESP(NOTFND)
             MOVE 'N' TO CUSTOMER-FOUND-SW
             MOVE 'That customer does not exist.' TO MESSAGEO
         ELSE
             IF RESPONSE-CODE NOT = DFHRESP(NORMAL)
                 PERFORM 9999-TERMINATE-PROGRAM
             END-IF
         END-IF.
*
```

Figure 14-17   The COBOL code for the customer inquiry program (part 3 of 7)

The customer inquiry program   **Page 4**

```
      1400-DISPLAY-INQUIRY-RESULTS.
*
          IF DISPLAY-NEW-CUSTOMER
              MOVE CM-CUSTOMER-NUMBER TO CUSTNOO
              MOVE CM-LAST-NAME        TO LNAMEO
              MOVE CM-FIRST-NAME       TO FNAMEO
              MOVE CM-ADDRESS          TO ADDRO
              MOVE CM-CITY             TO CITYO
              MOVE CM-STATE            TO STATEO
              MOVE CM-ZIP-CODE         TO ZIPCODEO
              MOVE SPACE               TO MESSAGEO
              SET SEND-DATAONLY        TO TRUE
          ELSE
              IF DISPLAY-SPACES
                  MOVE LOW-VALUE TO CUSTNOO
                  MOVE SPACE      TO LNAMEO
                                     FNAMEO
                                     ADDRO
                                     CITYO
                                     STATEO
                                     ZIPCODEO
                  SET SEND-DATAONLY-ALARM TO TRUE
              ELSE
                  IF DISPLAY-LOW-VALUES
                      SET SEND-DATAONLY-ALARM TO TRUE
                  END-IF
              END-IF
          END-IF.
*
          PERFORM 1500-SEND-INQUIRY-MAP.
*
      1500-SEND-INQUIRY-MAP.
*
          MOVE 'INQ2' TO TRANIDO.
*
          EVALUATE TRUE
              WHEN SEND-ERASE
                  EXEC CICS
                      SEND MAP('INQMAP2')
                           MAPSET('INQSET2')
                           FROM(INQMAP2O)
                           ERASE
                  END-EXEC
              WHEN SEND-DATAONLY
                  EXEC CICS
                      SEND MAP('INQMAP2')
                           MAPSET('INQSET2')
                           FROM(INQMAP2O)
                           DATAONLY
                  END-EXEC
              WHEN SEND-DATAONLY-ALARM
                  EXEC CICS
                      SEND MAP('INQMAP2')
                           MAPSET('INQSET2')
                           FROM(INQMAP2O)
                           DATAONLY
                           ALARM
                  END-EXEC
          END-EVALUATE.
```

Figure 14-17   The COBOL code for the customer inquiry program (part 4 of 7)

Procedure 2000 is executed when the user presses PF5 to display the first record in the file. It starts by moving Low-Value to the key field and the output map. Then, it performs procedure 2100 to start a browse operation. If the STARTBR command is successful, procedure 2000 performs procedure 2200 to read the first record in the file with a READNEXT command. Then, it performs procedure 2300 to end the browse and procedure 1400 to display the new customer data.

Notice that procedure 2100 can be called from anywhere in the program to start a browse at any location in the file. To accomplish that, the RIDFLD value isn't set in this procedure. Instead the higher-level procedures (2000, 3000, 4000, and 5000) set CM-CUSTOMER-NUMBER to an appropriate value depending on which attention key the user pressed.

Procedure 3000 displays the last record in the file. It's similar to procedure 2000, but begins by moving High-Value to the customer number so that the browse operation will begin at the end of the file. Then, after it performs module 2100 to start the browse, it invokes procedure 3100, which issues a READPREV command instead of a READNEXT command. Finally, it performs procedure 1400 to display the new customer data.

Procedure 4000 displays the previous record in sequence by calling procedures to (1) issue a STARTBR command, (2) issue a READNEXT command, (3) issue a READPREV command to retrieve the same record retrieved in step 2, and (4) issue another READPREV command to retrieve the previous record. Notice how it uses the customer number from the communication area to establish the position for the browse. Notice also that if the beginning of the file has been reached, it performs procedure 1400 with Display-Low-Values set to True. This means that the previous customer data will remain on the screen, since the map was set to Low-Value at the beginning of the procedure.

Procedure 5000 displays the next record in sequence by calling procedures to issue a STARTBR command followed by two READNEXT commands—the first to read the record at the STARTBR position and the second to read the next record. It too uses the customer number stored in the communication area to establish position in the customer file. And again, if the READNEXT command finds that there aren't any more records in the file, Display-Low-Values is set to True so that the previous record display will remain intact.

The customer inquiry program   **Page 5**

```
*
 2000-DISPLAY-FIRST-CUSTOMER.
*
     MOVE LOW-VALUE TO CM-CUSTOMER-NUMBER
                      INQMAP2O.
     PERFORM 2100-START-CUSTOMER-BROWSE.
     IF CUSTOMER-FOUND
         PERFORM 2200-READ-NEXT-CUSTOMER
     END-IF.
     PERFORM 2300-END-CUSTOMER-BROWSE.
     IF CUSTOMER-FOUND
         SET DISPLAY-NEW-CUSTOMER TO TRUE
         PERFORM 1400-DISPLAY-INQUIRY-RESULTS
         MOVE CM-CUSTOMER-NUMBER TO CA-CUSTOMER-NUMBER
     ELSE
         SET DISPLAY-SPACES TO TRUE
         PERFORM 1400-DISPLAY-INQUIRY-RESULTS
     END-IF.
*
 2100-START-CUSTOMER-BROWSE.
*
     EXEC CICS
         STARTBR FILE('CUSTMAS')
                 RIDFLD(CM-CUSTOMER-NUMBER)
                 RESP(RESPONSE-CODE)
     END-EXEC.
     IF RESPONSE-CODE = DFHRESP(NORMAL)
         MOVE 'Y' TO CUSTOMER-FOUND-SW
         MOVE SPACE TO MESSAGEO
     ELSE
         IF RESPONSE-CODE = DFHRESP(NOTFND)
             MOVE 'N' TO CUSTOMER-FOUND-SW
             MOVE 'There are no customers in the file.'
                 TO MESSAGEO
         ELSE
             PERFORM 9999-TERMINATE-PROGRAM
         END-IF
     END-IF.
*
 2200-READ-NEXT-CUSTOMER.
*
     EXEC CICS
         READNEXT FILE('CUSTMAS')
                  INTO(CUSTOMER-MASTER-RECORD)
                  RIDFLD(CM-CUSTOMER-NUMBER)
                  RESP(RESPONSE-CODE)
     END-EXEC.
     EVALUATE RESPONSE-CODE
         WHEN DFHRESP(NORMAL)
             MOVE 'Y' TO CUSTOMER-FOUND-SW
         WHEN DFHRESP(ENDFILE)
             MOVE 'N' TO CUSTOMER-FOUND-SW
             MOVE 'There are no more records in the file.'
                 TO MESSAGEO
         WHEN OTHER
             PERFORM 9999-TERMINATE-PROGRAM
     END-EVALUATE.
*
```

Figure 14-17   The COBOL code for the customer inquiry program (part 5 of 7)

The customer inquiry program

```
    2300-END-CUSTOMER-BROWSE.
*
    EXEC CICS
        ENDBR FILE('CUSTMAS')
              RESP(RESPONSE-CODE)
    END-EXEC.
    IF RESPONSE-CODE NOT = DFHRESP(NORMAL)
        PERFORM 9999-TERMINATE-PROGRAM
    END-IF.
*
 3000-DISPLAY-LAST-CUSTOMER.
*
    MOVE HIGH-VALUE TO CM-CUSTOMER-NUMBER.
    MOVE LOW-VALUE   TO INQMAP2O.
    PERFORM 2100-START-CUSTOMER-BROWSE.
    IF CUSTOMER-FOUND
        PERFORM 3100-READ-PREV-CUSTOMER
    END-IF.
    PERFORM 2300-END-CUSTOMER-BROWSE.
    IF CUSTOMER-FOUND
        SET DISPLAY-NEW-CUSTOMER TO TRUE
        PERFORM 1400-DISPLAY-INQUIRY-RESULTS
        MOVE CM-CUSTOMER-NUMBER TO CA-CUSTOMER-NUMBER
    ELSE
        SET DISPLAY-SPACES TO TRUE
        PERFORM 1400-DISPLAY-INQUIRY-RESULTS
    END-IF.
*
 3100-READ-PREV-CUSTOMER.
*
    EXEC CICS
        READPREV FILE('CUSTMAS')
                 INTO(CUSTOMER-MASTER-RECORD)
                 RIDFLD(CM-CUSTOMER-NUMBER)
                 RESP(RESPONSE-CODE)
    END-EXEC.
    EVALUATE RESPONSE-CODE
        WHEN DFHRESP(NORMAL)
            MOVE 'Y' TO CUSTOMER-FOUND-SW
        WHEN DFHRESP(ENDFILE)
            MOVE 'N' TO CUSTOMER-FOUND-SW
            MOVE 'There are no more records in the file.'
                TO MESSAGEO
        WHEN OTHER
            PERFORM 9999-TERMINATE-PROGRAM
    END-EVALUATE.
*
```

Figure 14-17   The COBOL code for the customer inquiry program (part 6 of 7)

The customer inquiry program

```
 4000-DISPLAY-PREV-CUSTOMER.
*
     MOVE CA-CUSTOMER-NUMBER TO CM-CUSTOMER-NUMBER.
     MOVE LOW-VALUE            TO INQMAP2O.
     PERFORM 2100-START-CUSTOMER-BROWSE.
     IF CUSTOMER-FOUND
         PERFORM 2200-READ-NEXT-CUSTOMER
         PERFORM 3100-READ-PREV-CUSTOMER
         PERFORM 3100-READ-PREV-CUSTOMER
     END-IF.
     PERFORM 2300-END-CUSTOMER-BROWSE.
     IF CUSTOMER-FOUND
         SET DISPLAY-NEW-CUSTOMER TO TRUE
         PERFORM 1400-DISPLAY-INQUIRY-RESULTS
         MOVE CM-CUSTOMER-NUMBER TO CA-CUSTOMER-NUMBER
     ELSE
         SET DISPLAY-LOW-VALUES TO TRUE
         PERFORM 1400-DISPLAY-INQUIRY-RESULTS
     END-IF.
*
 5000-DISPLAY-NEXT-CUSTOMER.
*
     MOVE CA-CUSTOMER-NUMBER TO CM-CUSTOMER-NUMBER.
     MOVE LOW-VALUE            TO INQMAP2O.
     PERFORM 2100-START-CUSTOMER-BROWSE.
     IF CUSTOMER-FOUND
         PERFORM 2200-READ-NEXT-CUSTOMER
         PERFORM 2200-READ-NEXT-CUSTOMER
     END-IF.
     PERFORM 2300-END-CUSTOMER-BROWSE.
     IF CUSTOMER-FOUND
         SET DISPLAY-NEW-CUSTOMER TO TRUE
         PERFORM 1400-DISPLAY-INQUIRY-RESULTS
         MOVE CM-CUSTOMER-NUMBER TO CA-CUSTOMER-NUMBER
     ELSE
         SET DISPLAY-LOW-VALUES TO TRUE
         PERFORM 1400-DISPLAY-INQUIRY-RESULTS
     END-IF.
*
 9999-TERMINATE-PROGRAM.
*
     MOVE EIBRESP  TO ERR-RESP.
     MOVE EIBRESP2 TO ERR-RESP2.
     MOVE EIBTRNID TO ERR-TRNID.
     MOVE EIBRSRCE TO ERR-RSRCE.
*
     EXEC CICS
         XCTL PROGRAM('SYSERR')
              COMMAREA(ERROR-PARAMETERS)
     END-EXEC.
```

Figure 14-17   The COBOL code for the customer inquiry program (part 7 of 7)

Perspective

In a production environment, it's not uncommon to find inquiry programs like the one in this chapter that let users access records in a variety of ways. So although you probably won't use the browse commands every day, there are times when you'll need them to process files sequentially. You'll also use them occasionally to process VSAM key-sequenced files by their alternate indexes, as you'll see in the next chapter.

Terms

browsing
browse commands

15

How to use VSAM alternate indexes

In the last chapter, you learned how to read the records in a VSAM key-sequenced file sequentially by the file's primary key. In some cases, though, you'll need to access records in a sequence other than that specified by the primary key. To do that, you use an alternate index.

In this chapter, you'll learn how to use the browse commands presented in the last chapter to process VSAM files using alternate indexes. Keep in mind, though, that before you can use an alternate index, it must be defined using the VSAM utility program called IDCAMS, or AMS. But because defining and maintaining alternate indexes is usually the job of systems programmers, you shouldn't need to worry about that.

Alternate indexing concepts

Before you see how to use the browse commands to process alternate indexes, you need to understand how alternate indexes are implemented by VSAM. That's what you'll learn in the topics that follow.

How alternate indexes work

A VSAM *alternate index* lets you access the records of a key-sequenced file in a sequence other than that provided by the file's *primary key* (or *base key*). To understand how alternate indexes work, take a look at the example at the top of figure 15-1. Here, the *base cluster* (the file over which an alternate index exists) is a KSDS containing employee records. Each record in the base cluster contains three fields: employee number, social security number, and department number. The primary key for the base cluster is employee number. As a result, you can access the base cluster sequentially by employee number using the browse commands you learned in chapter 14. Or, you can read any record directly if you know the record's employee number.

In addition to the primary key, the employee file has an alternate index for the social security number. As you can see, this alternate index relates each *alternate key* value to a primary key value. So, as the shading indicates, when you tell VSAM to retrieve the record for the employee whose social security number is 565-37-5511, VSAM searches the alternate index, retrieves the primary key (1008), and uses that value to locate the correct record in the base cluster. Because the alternate index is maintained in alternate key sequence, you can use it to process the employee file in social security number sequence.

In the first example in this figure, each alternate key is associated with a single primary key and, therefore, a single record. This type of alternate key is called a *unique key*. In contrast, the second example in this figure illustrates an alternate index with *non-unique*, or *duplicate*, *keys*. Here, the alternate key is the department number, which can be related to one or more employee records.

To see how duplicate keys work, consider the alternate index record for department number 101. Here, four employee numbers are specified: 1004, 1011, 1019, and 1023. When you use browse commands to process this alternate index sequentially, all four of these employee records are retrieved in primary key sequence.

When you process duplicate keys sequentially, you need to know how to determine whether there are additional records with the same key. To do that, you use the DUPKEY exceptional condition. This condition is raised whenever you issue a READ, READNEXT, or READPREV command and at least one *more* record—*not* counting the one currently being read—exists with the same alternate key value. If there are no more records with the same alternate key value, CICS returns the NORMAL condition instead. In the program later in this chapter, you'll see how to use the DUPKEY condition to control the processing of duplicate keys.

An alternate index with unique keys

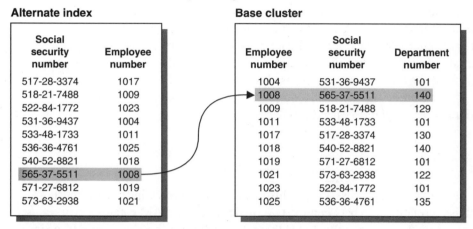

An alternate index with duplicate keys

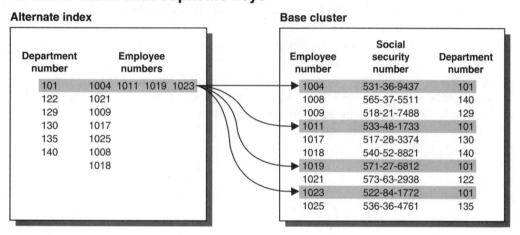

Description

- A VSAM key-sequenced file can have one or more *alternate indexes*. The entries in an alternate index relate an *alternate key* in each record to the record's *primary key* (or *base key*). These entries are maintained in alternate key sequence. The file over which an alternate index is built is called a *base cluster*.

- When you access a base cluster by an alternate index, VSAM looks up the alternate key in the index to find the record's primary key, then accesses the correct record using that key.

- An alternate index can contain *unique keys* that each point to a single record in the base cluster or *duplicate* (*non-unique*) *keys* that each point to one or more records.

- To access all the records with the same duplicate key in a file, you retrieve them sequentially using browse commands (random access retrieves just the first record).

- When using duplicate keys, the DUPKEY exceptional condition is raised during a read operation if there is at least one more record in the base cluster with the same alternate key.

Figure 15-1   How alternate indexes work

Although this chapter shows you how to use alternate indexes to access records sequentially, you should realize that you can also retrieve records randomly using an alternate index. When you do that, however, keep in mind that if the alternate index has duplicate keys, only the first record with an alternate key value is retrieved. Because that's not usually what you want, you won't learn how to use random access in this chapter. After reviewing the sample program in this chapter, though, you shouldn't have any trouble using random access if you ever need to.

How to use paths

Before you can process a base cluster using an alternate index, you must establish a relationship between the two by defining a VSAM catalog entry called a *path*. Figure 15-2 illustrates this relationship for the alternate indexes in figure 15-1. Here, two alternate indexes (SSNAIX and DEPAIX) are defined for a single base cluster (EMPMAST). Each alternate index is related to the base cluster through a path (SSNPATH and DEPPATH).

To process a base cluster through an alternate index, you actually process the path. So, as you'll see in the program example later in this chapter, you specify a path name rather than a file name in the FILE option of the file control commands. Otherwise, the CICS commands you code to process a file are the same whether you're using an alternate index or not.

The relationships among alternate indexes, paths, and a base cluster

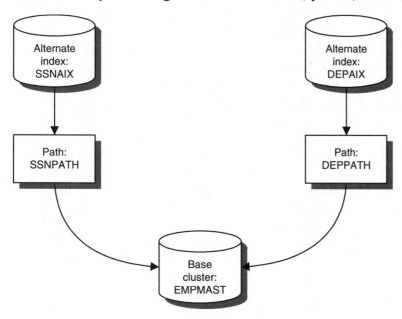

Description

- A *path* establishes the relationship between an alternate index and its base cluster. A path is a VSAM catalog entry that's defined by using the VSAM utility, *Access Method Services* (also known as *AMS* or *IDCAMS*).

- When you process a file by an alternate index, you specify the appropriate path name—*not* the file name—in the FILE option of the file control commands.

Figure 15-2   How a path relates an alternate index to its base cluster

How alternate indexes are updated

Figure 15-3 illustrates how an alternate index can be updated when a record is added to a base cluster. In this case, a record for employee 1013 has been added to the employee file you saw in figure 15-1. As the shading indicates, a new entry has also been added to the social security number alternate index, and the entry for department 101 has been extended in the department number alternate index to include the new record. This process of updating an alternate index is called *upgrading*.

Although you'd probably expect the changes made to a base cluster to be reflected immediately in any associated alternate indexes, that's not usually the case. Instead, only indexes that are defined as *upgradable* are updated. Because upgrading alternate indexes requires a considerable amount of overhead, most alternate indexes are not upgradable. In that case, the alternate indexes must be recreated on a regular basis so they contain up-to-date entries.

From a coding standpoint, you don't need to worry about whether or not an alternate index is upgradable. You should realize, however, that if an alternate index is not upgradable, changes made to the base cluster won't be reflected in the alternate index until the alternate index is recreated. And that means that a program that uses the alternate index may not return all of the records in the base cluster with a given alternate key.

Although upgradable indexes are updated as changes are made to the base cluster, they may also need to be recreated on a regular basis. That's because when a new primary key is added to an alternate index with duplicate keys, it's added to the end of the existing primary keys for the appropriate entry. In this figure, for example, the primary key for employee 1013 was added after the entry for employee 1023 in the department number alternate index—not between the entries for employees 1011 and 1019. Because of that, if you processed the employee file sequentially using the department number alternate index, the records for department 101 would not be retrieved in employee number sequence.

A base cluster and its alternate indexes after a record is added

Base cluster

Employee number	Social security number	Department number
1004	531-36-9437	101
1008	565-37-5511	140
1009	518-21-7488	129
1011	533-48-1733	101
1013	552-57-2735	101
1017	517-28-3374	130
1018	540-52-8821	140
1019	571-27-6812	101
1021	573-63-2938	122
1023	522-84-1772	101
1025	536-36-4761	135

Upgrade set

Alternate index
(social security number)

Social security number	Employee number
517-28-3374	1017
518-21-7488	1009
522-84-1772	1023
531-36-9437	1004
533-48-1733	1011
536-36-4761	1025
540-52-8821	1018
552-57-2735	1013
565-37-5511	1008
571-27-6812	1019
573-63-2938	1021

Alternate index
(department number)

Department number	Employee numbers
101	1004 1011 1019 1023 1013
122	1021
129	1009
130	1017
135	1025
140	1008 1018

Description

- An *upgrade set* consists of all of the upgradable alternate indexes for a single base cluster. An *upgradable index* is one that's updated whenever changes are made to the base cluster.

- For efficiency reasons, most alternate indexes are not upgradable. In that case, changes that are made to the base cluster aren't reflected in the alternate index until the alternate index is recreated.

- When an upgradable alternate index with duplicate keys is updated as the result of a record being added to the base cluster, the primary key for the record is added to the end of the existing primary keys in the alternate index entry. To return the keys to primary key sequence, the alternate index must be recreated.

Figure 15-3   How alternate indexes are updated

An enhanced customer inquiry program

Now that you understand how alternate indexes are implemented, you're ready to learn how to write programs that process files using an alternate index. To illustrate, the topics that follow present an enhanced version of the customer inquiry program that you saw in the last chapter. Because you're already familiar with the basic operation of this program, I'll focus only on the differences here.

The specifications for the enhanced customer inquiry program

Figure 15-4 gives the specifications for the enhanced customer inquiry program. In the program overview, you can see that this program lets you browse through a file of customer records just as the program in chapter 14 did. In addition to displaying customer information, though, it also displays information for up to ten invoices for each customer. To do that, it uses an alternate index that provides for retrieving the records in the invoice file by customer number. The program accesses this alternate index through a path named INVPATH.

The program overview for the enhanced customer inquiry program

Program	CUSTINQ3: Customer inquiry
Trans-id	INQ3
Overview	Displays records from the customer and invoice files, allowing the user to scroll forwards or backwards using PF keys.
Input/output specifications	INQMAP3 Customer inquiry map CUSTMAS Customer master file INVPATH Customer number path to the invoice file

Processing specifications

1. Control is transferred to this program via XCTL from the menu program INVMENU with no communication area. The user can also start the program by entering the trans-id INQ3. In either case, the program should respond by displaying the customer inquiry map.

2. The user selects a customer record display by pressing an attention key, as follows:

Enter	Display the customer indicated by the entry in the customer number field.
PF5	Display the first customer in the file.
PF6	Display the last customer in the file.
PF7	Display the previous customer.
PF8	Display the next customer.

   The program then reads and displays the appropriate customer record.

3. For each customer record selected, display the first 10 invoice records from the invoice file. Use the INVPATH path to access the invoice records via the customer number alternate index.

4. Use the pseudo-conversational programming technique. To restart the browse at the correct record during the next program execution, save the key of the customer currently displayed in the communication area.

5. If the user presses PF3 or PF12, return to the menu program INVMENU by issuing an XCTL command.

6. If an unrecoverable error occurs, terminate the program by invoking the SYSERR subprogram with an XCTL command.

Figure 15-4   The specifications for the enhanced customer inquiry program (part 1 of 2)

Part 2 of this figure shows the copy member for the invoice file and the screen layout for the program. In the copy member, you can see the field that will be used to access the records in the invoice file: INV-CUSTOMER-NUMBER. And in the screen layout, you can see the format of the invoice information this program will display.

Before I go on, I want to point out that an actual production program like this would provide for displaying more invoices than will fit on one screen. Although that's a reasonable requirement, it makes the program's logic more complicated without illustrating any additional CICS elements related to alternate indexing. So, to help you focus on the coding requirements for alternate indexes, this program displays a maximum of ten invoices for each customer—that's just enough to fit on one screen.

The INVOICE copy member

```
01  INVOICE-RECORD.
*
    05  INV-INVOICE-NUMBER          PIC 9(06).
    05  INV-INVOICE-DATE            PIC X(08).
    05  INV-CUSTOMER-NUMBER         PIC X(06).
    05  INV-PO-NUMBER               PIC X(10).
    05  INV-LINE-ITEM               OCCURS 10.
        10  INV-PRODUCT-CODE        PIC X(10).
        10  INV-QUANTITY            PIC S9(07)      COMP-3.
        10  INV-UNIT-PRICE          PIC S9(07)V99   COMP-3.
        10  INV-AMOUNT              PIC S9(07)V99   COMP-3.
    05  INV-INVOICE-TOTAL           PIC S9(07)V99   COMP-3.
*
```

The screen layout for the enhanced customer inquiry program

Map name	INQMAP3	Date	04/09/2001
Program name	CUSTINQ3	Designer	Doug Lowe

Description

- This program displays the name and address for the customer requested by the user, along with up to 10 invoices for that customer.

- To retrieve the invoice records for a customer, the program uses the customer number alternate index for the invoice file. This alternate index is associated with the invoice file through the path named INVPATH.

Figure 15-4   The specifications for the enhanced customer inquiry program (part 2 of 2)

The design for the enhanced customer inquiry program

The top part of figure 15-5 presents the event/response chart for the enhanced customer inquiry program. As you can see, it provides for the same events as the inquiry program in chapter 14. The difference is that whenever a customer record is displayed, the related invoices for that customer are displayed as well.

The bottom part of this figure presents the structure chart for this program. Again, it's similar to the structure chart for the inquiry program in chapter 14. In fact, the only difference is that it includes four new modules (1410, 1420, 1430, and 1440) to handle the invoice display. Module 1410 is invoked by module 1400 to start a browse operation on the invoice file at the appropriate customer number. Then, module 1400 invokes module 1420 to format each invoice line. Module 1420, in turn, invokes module 1430 to read the invoice records for the current customer. Finally, module 1400 invokes module 1440 to end the browse operation.

An event/response chart for the enhanced customer inquiry program

Event	Response
Start the program	Display the inquiry map.
PF3 or PF12	Transfer control to the menu program.
Enter key	Read and display the customer and related invoice records indicated by the customer number entered by the user.
PF5	Read and display the first customer record and related invoice records.
PF6	Read and display the last customer record and related invoice records.
PF7	Read and display the previous customer record and related invoice records.
PF8	Read and display the next customer record and related invoice records.
Clear key	Redisplay the current map.
Any PA key	Ignore the key.
Any other key	Display an error message.

The structure chart for the program

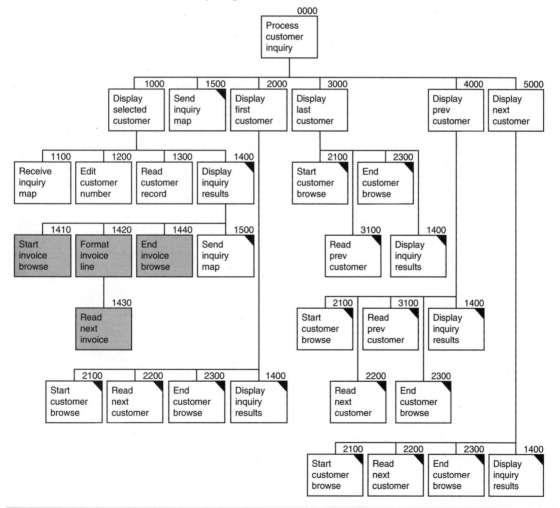

Figure 15-5   The event/response chart and structure chart for the enhanced customer inquiry program

The BMS mapset for the enhanced customer inquiry program

Figure 15-6 presents part of the BMS mapset for this program. Except for the map name that's displayed in the first line of the screen, the rest of the code is identical to the code in the mapset for the inquiry program in chapter 14. So you can refer back to that chapter if you need to.

In the middle of this listing, you can see the definition for the invoice area of the screen. As indicated by the screen layout, this definition starts with a constant that contains the column headings for the invoice data. That heading is followed by the definitions of each of the ten invoice lines. Notice that each of these lines is defined as a single 44-byte field. That way, if a customer has fewer than ten invoices, the program can simply move spaces to the appropriate fields so that nothing is displayed in those lines. For this to work, the program must format the invoice lines in the Working-Storage Section before they're moved to the appropriate screen fields.

The code for the BMS mapset

```
         PRINT NOGEN
INQSET3  DFHMSD TYPE=&SYSPARM,                                           X
                LANG=COBOL,                                             X
                MODE=INOUT,                                             X
                TERM=3270-2,                                            X
                CTRL=FREEKB,                                            X
                STORAGE=AUTO,                                           X
                TIOAPFX=YES
*********************************************************************
INQMAP3  DFHMDI SIZE=(24,80),                                           X
                LINE=1,                                                 X
                COLUMN=1
*********************************************************************

             .

             .
         DFHMDF POS=(12,1),                                             X
                LENGTH=45,                                             X
                COLOR=GREEN,                                           X
                ATTRB=(NORM,PROT),                                     X
                INITIAL='Invoice  PO Number    Date              Total'
INV1     DFHMDF POS=(13,2),                                             X
                LENGTH=44,                                             X
                COLOR=TURQUOISE,                                       X
                ATTRB=(NORM,PROT)
INV2     DFHMDF POS=(14,2),                                             X
                LENGTH=44,                                             X
                COLOR=TURQUOISE,                                       X
                ATTRB=(NORM,PROT)
INV3     DFHMDF POS=(15,2),                                             X
                LENGTH=44,                                             X
                COLOR=TURQUOISE,                                       X
                ATTRB=(NORM,PROT)
INV4     DFHMDF POS=(16,2),                                             X
                LENGTH=44,                                             X
                COLOR=TURQUOISE,                                       X
                ATTRB=(NORM,PROT)
INV5     DFHMDF POS=(17,2),                                             X
                LENGTH=44,                                             X
                COLOR=TURQUOISE,                                       X
                ATTRB=(NORM,PROT)

             .

             .
INV10    DFHMDF POS=(22,2),                                             X
                LENGTH=44,                                             X
                COLOR=TURQUOISE,                                       X
                ATTRB=(NORM,PROT)
*********************************************************************

             .

             .
         DFHMSD TYPE=FINAL
         END
```

Figure 15-6   The BMS mapset for the enhanced customer inquiry program

The programmer-generated symbolic map for the enhanced customer inquiry program

To make it easier to manipulate the invoice fields in the COBOL program, I created my own symbolic map, shown in figure 15-7. Here, I used an Occurs clause to define the invoice lines so I could process them in my COBOL code using subscripts. Without a programmer-generated symbolic map like this, you would have to code for each invoice line separately in your program...a tedious task, to say the least.

The code for the programmer-generated symbolic map

```
01  CUSTOMER-INQUIRY-MAP.
*
    05   FILLER                  PIC X(12).
*
    05   CIM-L-TRANID            PIC S9(04)  COMP.
    05   CIM-A-TRANID            PIC X(01).
    05   CIM-D-TRANID            PIC X(04).
*
    05   CIM-L-CUSTNO            PIC S9(04)  COMP.
    05   CIM-A-CUSTNO            PIC X(01).
    05   CIM-D-CUSTNO            PIC X(06).
*
    05   CIM-L-LNAME             PIC S9(04)  COMP.
    05   CIM-A-LNAME             PIC X(01).
    05   CIM-D-LNAME             PIC X(30).
*
    05   CIM-L-FNAME             PIC S9(04)  COMP.
    05   CIM-A-FNAME             PIC X(01).
    05   CIM-D-FNAME             PIC X(20).
*
    05   CIM-L-ADDR              PIC S9(04)  COMP.
    05   CIM-A-ADDR              PIC X(01).
    05   CIM-D-ADDR              PIC X(30).
*
    05   CIM-L-CITY              PIC S9(04)  COMP.
    05   CIM-A-CITY              PIC X(01).
    05   CIM-D-CITY              PIC X(20).
*
    05   CIM-L-STATE             PIC S9(04)  COMP.
    05   CIM-A-STATE             PIC X(01).
    05   CIM-D-STATE             PIC X(02).
*
    05   CIM-L-ZIPCODE           PIC S9(04)  COMP.
    05   CIM-A-ZIPCODE           PIC X(01).
    05   CIM-D-ZIPCODE           PIC X(10).
*
    05   CIM-INVOICE-LINE        OCCURS 10 TIMES.
*
        10   CIM-L-INVOICE-LINE  PIC S9(04)  COMP.
        10   CIM-A-INVOICE-LINE  PIC X(01).
        10   CIM-D-INVOICE-LINE  PIC X(44).
*
    05   CIM-L-MESSAGE           PIC S9(04)  COMP.
    05   CIM-A-MESSAGE           PIC X(01).
    05   CIM-D-MESSAGE           PIC X(79).
*
    05   CIM-L-DUMMY             PIC S9(04)  COMP.
    05   CIM-A-DUMMY             PIC X(01).
    05   CIM-D-DUMMY             PIC X(01).
*
```

Figure 15-7   The programmer-generated symbolic map for the enhanced customer inquiry program

The COBOL code for the enhanced customer inquiry program

Figure 15-8 shows the code that was added to the inquiry program to display the customer invoices. On page 1 of this listing, you can see the fields that were added to the Working-Storage Section. To start, a switch named MORE-INVOICES-SW was added to monitor whether there are any more invoices for a specified customer. In addition, a subscript named INVOICE-SUB was added to handle the ten invoice lines. Next, a group item named INVOICE-LINE was added that will contain the formatted information for each invoice. Finally, a Copy statement for the INVOICE copy member was added so the record description it contains will be included in the program.

A customer inquiry program that uses an alternate index   Page 1

```
       IDENTIFICATION DIVISION.
*
       PROGRAM-ID.  CUSTINQ3.
*
       ENVIRONMENT DIVISION.
*
       DATA DIVISION.
*
       WORKING-STORAGE SECTION.
*
       01  SWITCHES.
*
           05  VALID-DATA-SW           PIC X(01)   VALUE 'Y'.
               88  VALID-DATA                      VALUE 'Y'.
           05  CUSTOMER-FOUND-SW       PIC X(01)   VALUE 'Y'.
               88  CUSTOMER-FOUND                  VALUE 'Y'.
           05  MORE-INVOICES-SW        PIC X(01)   VALUE 'Y'.
               88  MORE-INVOICES                   VALUE 'Y'.

           .
           .
       01  WORK-FIELDS.
*
           05  INVOICE-SUB             PIC S9(04)  COMP.
*
       01  INVOICE-LINE.
*
           05  IL-INVOICE-NUMBER       PIC 9(06).
           05  FILLER                  PIC X(02)   VALUE SPACE.
           05  IL-PO-NUMBER            PIC X(10).
           05  FILLER                  PIC X(02)   VALUE SPACE.
           05  IL-INVOICE-DATE         PIC Z9/99/9999.
           05  FILLER                  PIC X(02)   VALUE SPACE.
           05  IL-INVOICE-TOTAL        PIC Z,ZZZ,ZZ9.99.
           .
           .
       COPY CUSTMAS.
       COPY INVOICE.
       COPY INQSET3.
       COPY DFHAID.
       COPY ERRPARM.
           .
           .
```

Figure 15-8   The COBOL code for the enhanced customer inquiry program (part 1 of 3)

On page 2 of this listing, you can see the code for the procedure that formats and displays the results of each inquiry (1400). You may recall from chapter 14 that before this procedure is performed, the program sets DISPLAY-FLAG to indicate how the procedure should operate. If it's set to Display-New-Customer, this procedure moves data from the customer record to the output map and performs procedure 1500 to send the map. If it's set to Display-Spaces, this procedure moves spaces to the data fields in the output map before it performs procedure 1500. And if it's set to Display-Low-Values, this procedure performs procedure 1500 without moving any data to the output map.

For this version of the inquiry program, the function of procedure 1400 has been enhanced to format the invoice lines on the screen. Now, if Display-Spaces is set to True, the inline Perform Varying statement near the end of the procedure moves space to all ten invoice lines. In contrast, if Display-New-Customer is set to True, more extensive processing is done to display the invoice data for a customer.

To display the invoices for a customer, procedure 1400 starts by performing procedure 1410 to start a browse operation. On the STARTBR command, you can see that the FILE parameter specifies INVPATH, the name of the path for the customer number alternate index for the invoice file. As a result, the browse operation will use the file's alternate key, not its primary key. Then, the RIDFLD option names the field that will contain the alternate key value. In this case, that field is the primary key field in the customer record: CM-CUSTOMER-NUMBER. That makes good sense since the program is retrieving all of the invoice records that relate to a particular customer record.

The STARTBR command also includes the EQUAL option. That way, if the invoice file doesn't contain any records for a customer, the NOTFND condition will be raised. In that case, the program moves N to MORE-INVOICES-SW. As you'll see in moment, this switch is used by procedure 1420 to determine how each invoice line is formatted.

If the STARTBR command doesn't raise a serious error, procedure 1400 continues by performing procedure 1420 once for each of the ten invoice lines. To do that, it varies INVOICE-SUB from one to ten so that each of the ten invoice lines on the screen is formatted. When it's done, procedure 1400 performs procedure 1440 to end the browse operation.

A customer inquiry program that uses an alternate index   **Page 2**

```
        PROCEDURE DIVISION.
            .
            .
        1400-DISPLAY-INQUIRY-RESULTS.
      *
            EVALUATE TRUE
                WHEN DISPLAY-NEW-CUSTOMER
                    MOVE CM-CUSTOMER-NUMBER TO CIM-D-CUSTNO
                    MOVE CM-LAST-NAME         TO CIM-D-LNAME
                    MOVE CM-FIRST-NAME        TO CIM-D-FNAME
                    MOVE CM-ADDRESS           TO CIM-D-ADDR
                    MOVE CM-CITY              TO CIM-D-CITY
                    MOVE CM-STATE             TO CIM-D-STATE
                    MOVE CM-ZIP-CODE          TO CIM-D-ZIPCODE
                    MOVE SPACE                TO CIM-D-MESSAGE
                    PERFORM 1410-START-INVOICE-BROWSE
                    PERFORM 1420-FORMAT-INVOICE-LINE
                        VARYING INVOICE-SUB FROM 1 BY 1
                        UNTIL INVOICE-SUB > 10
                    PERFORM 1440-END-INVOICE-BROWSE
                    SET SEND-DATAONLY TO TRUE
                WHEN DISPLAY-SPACES
                    MOVE LOW-VALUE TO CIM-D-CUSTNO
                    MOVE SPACE        TO CIM-D-LNAME
                                         CIM-D-FNAME
                                         CIM-D-ADDR
                                         CIM-D-CITY
                                         CIM-D-STATE
                                         CIM-D-ZIPCODE
                    PERFORM VARYING INVOICE-SUB FROM 1 BY 1
                            UNTIL INVOICE-SUB > 10
                        MOVE SPACE TO CIM-D-INVOICE-LINE(INVOICE-SUB)
                    END-PERFORM
                    SET SEND-DATAONLY-ALARM TO TRUE
                WHEN DISPLAY-LOW-VALUES
                    SET SEND-DATAONLY-ALARM TO TRUE
            END-EVALUATE.
            PERFORM 1500-SEND-INQUIRY-MAP.
      *
        1410-START-INVOICE-BROWSE.
      *
            EXEC CICS
                STARTBR FILE('INVPATH')
                        RIDFLD(CM-CUSTOMER-NUMBER)
                        EQUAL
                        RESP(RESPONSE-CODE)
            END-EXEC.
            IF RESPONSE-CODE = DFHRESP(NOTFND)
                MOVE 'N' TO MORE-INVOICES-SW
            ELSE
                IF RESPONSE-CODE NOT = DFHRESP(NORMAL)
                    PERFORM 9999-TERMINATE-PROGRAM
                END-IF
            END-IF.
```

Figure 15-8   The COBOL code for the enhanced customer inquiry program (part 2 of 3)

Procedure 1420 starts by testing the More-Invoices switch to determine if the invoice file contains additional invoices for the customer. If it does, this procedure performs procedure 1430 to read the next invoice record. Then, it moves data from the invoice record to the INVOICE-LINE fields in working storage. Finally, it uses INVOICE-SUB to move INVOICE-LINE to the appropriate field in the symbolic map. On the other hand, if there are no more invoice records to be read, procedure 1420 simply moves space to the appropriate map field so that any invoice data from the previous inquiry will be erased. (This probably isn't the most efficient way to erase existing invoice data on the screen, but it's sufficient for this example.)

In procedure 1430, you can see that, like the STARTBR command, the READNEXT command names the path to the alternate index on the FILE option and the primary key field from the customer file on the RIDFLD option. This procedure also illustrates the one significant variation for processing files using an alternate index: handling the DUPKEY condition. As I mentioned earlier, the DUPKEY condition is raised whenever you issue a READ, READNEXT, or READPREV command and at least one more record—not counting the one currently being read—exists with the same alternate key value.

To illustrate, suppose the program is reading invoice records for customer 10000. If the file contains just one invoice record for this customer, the DUPKEY condition is never raised. That's because when the program reads the first invoice record, there aren't any additional invoice records with the same alternate key. If the file contains two invoices for customer 10000, DUPKEY is raised when the program reads the first record since there's one more record with the same key. But when the program reads the second (and last) record, DUPKEY isn't raised. If the file contains three invoices for the customer, DUPKEY is raised for the first two but not for the third, and so on. In short, the DUPKEY condition is not raised when you read the last record with a given alternate key value.

Look now to see how procedure 1430 deals with the DUPKEY condition. To start, if a response code other than NORMAL or DUPKEY is raised, this procedure performs procedure 9999 to terminate the program. Otherwise, if the response code is NORMAL, it means the READNEXT command has read the last invoice record for a given customer. In that case, the More-Invoices switch is turned off. If the response code is DUPKEY, though, this switch is left on so the READNEXT command will be issued again on the next iteration of procedure 1420.

A customer inquiry program that uses an alternate index   Page 3

```
1420-FORMAT-INVOICE-LINE.
*
    IF MORE-INVOICES
        PERFORM 1430-READ-NEXT-INVOICE
        MOVE INV-INVOICE-NUMBER TO IL-INVOICE-NUMBER
        MOVE INV-PO-NUMBER        TO IL-PO-NUMBER
        MOVE INV-INVOICE-DATE     TO IL-INVOICE-DATE
        MOVE INV-INVOICE-TOTAL    TO IL-INVOICE-TOTAL
        MOVE INVOICE-LINE TO CIM-D-INVOICE-LINE(INVOICE-SUB)
    ELSE
        MOVE SPACE TO CIM-D-INVOICE-LINE(INVOICE-SUB)
    END-IF.
*
1430-READ-NEXT-INVOICE.
*
    EXEC CICS
        READNEXT FILE('INVPATH')
                 RIDFLD(CM-CUSTOMER-NUMBER)
                 INTO(INVOICE-RECORD)
                 RESP(RESPONSE-CODE)
    END-EXEC.
*
    IF RESPONSE-CODE = DFHRESP(NORMAL)
        MOVE 'N' TO MORE-INVOICES-SW
    ELSE
        IF RESPONSE-CODE NOT = DFHRESP(DUPKEY)
            PERFORM 9999-TERMINATE-PROGRAM
        END-IF
    END-IF.
*
1440-END-INVOICE-BROWSE.
*
    EXEC CICS
        ENDBR FILE('INVPATH')
              RESP(RESPONSE-CODE)
    END-EXEC.
    IF RESPONSE-CODE NOT = DFHRESP(NORMAL)
        PERFORM 9999-TERMINATE-PROGRAM
    END-IF.
*
        .
        .
```

Figure 15-8   The COBOL code for the enhanced customer inquiry program (part 3 of 3)

Perspective

As you can imagine, alternate indexes introduce considerable overhead into the processing of VSAM files. Depending on factors such as how many alternate indexes are associated with the file and how many of those alternate indexes are upgradable, a single WRITE command for a file with alternate indexes can cause dozens of physical I/O operations. And that can result in considerable performance degradation, especially if many users are updating the same file at once. As a result, alternate indexes—particularly upgradable alternate indexes—are used only when their advantages outweigh their disadvantages.

Terms

alternate index
primary key
base key
base cluster
alternate key
unique key
non-unique key
duplicate key
path
Access Method Services (AMS)
IDCAMS
upgrading
upgradable index
upgrade set

16

How to use other file processing features

In this chapter, you'll learn about a variety of CICS file handling features that you can use for special purposes. Although you probably won't use these features often, you'll want to know about them so you can use them in the appropriate situations.

How to use generic keys

A *generic key* is a portion of a primary or alternate key that's used to identify records in a key-sequenced file. For example, consider the record description for an inventory parts file shown at the top of figure 16-1. This file is indexed by a ten-byte key that's made up of a vendor number and an item number. In this case, you could use a generic key to access records based on vendor number alone. Because a generic key must start at the beginning of the full key, though, you couldn't use the item number as a generic key.

How to use generic keys to start a browse operation

In chapter 14, you saw the complete syntax of the browse commands. If you need to refresh your memory on how these commands work, you can refer back to that chapter. In this topic, I'll describe just the two options provided by those commands for working with generic keys.

To start a browse operation using a generic key, you include the GENERIC and KEYLENGTH options on a STARTBR or RESETBR command. The GENERIC option tells CICS to treat the key that's specified in the RIDFLD option as a generic key, and the KEYLENGTH option provides the length of the generic key. Note that although only part of a file's key is used when you specify GENERIC, the RIDFLD field must still be large enough to hold the record's entire key.

The two procedures shown in figure 16-1 illustrate the difference between using the GTEQ option on the STARTBR command and using a generic key. Both procedures are designed to start a browse operation at the first inventory parts record for a particular vendor. To do that using the GTEQ option, the first procedure moves a vendor number to the vendor number portion of the key and moves low-values to the item number portion. Then, when the STARTBR command is issued, the browse will be positioned at the first record for the specified vendor. The exception is if the file doesn't contain any records for that vendor. Then, the browse will be positioned at the first record for the next vendor in sequence. To determine whether or not a record for the specified vendor was found, the program must read the first record.

In contrast, you can code a STARTBR command with the GENERIC option so that if a record isn't found for the specified vendor, the NOTFND condition is raised. To do that, you code the EQUAL option along with the GENERIC and KEYLENGTH options as illustrated in the second example. Here, because only the vendor number is used to locate a record, the NOTFND condition is raised if a record for that vendor isn't found.

Although you might think that you could obtain the same result by using the EQUAL option in the first procedure, you can't. Because the item number portion of the key is set to low-values before the STARTBR operation, and because the file would never contain a record that has an item number with low-values, coding the EQUAL option would always result in a NOTFND condition.

The record description for an inventory parts file

```
01   INVENTORY-PARTS-RECORD.
*
     05  IP-RECORD-KEY.
         10  IP-VENDOR-NUMBER    PIC X(4).
         10  IP-ITEM-NUMBER      PIC X(6).
     05  IP-INVENTORY-DATA.
     .
     .
```

A procedure that starts a browse on the vendor number without a generic key

```
2100-START-INVENTORY-BROWSE.
*
     MOVE VENDNOI    TO IP-VENDOR-NUMBER.
     MOVE LOW-VALUE TO IP-ITEM-NUMBER.
     EXEC CICS
         STARTBR FILE('INVPART')
                 RIDFLD(IP-RECORD-KEY)
                 GTEQ
                 RESP(RESPONSE-CODE)
     END-EXEC.
*
```

A procedure that starts a browse on the vendor number with a generic key

```
2100-START-INVENTORY-BROWSE.
*
     MOVE VENDNOI TO IP-VENDOR-NUMBER.
     EXEC CICS
         STARTBR FILE('INVPART')
                 RIDFLD(IP-RECORD-KEY)
                 GENERIC
                 KEYLENGTH(4)
                 EQUAL
                 RESP(RESPONSE-CODE)
     END-EXEC.
*
```

Description

- A *generic key* lets you locate a record in a KSDS using only part of its primary or alternate key. A generic key always begins with the first byte of the primary or alternate key.
- To use generic keys with the STARTBR or RESETBR command, you include the GENERIC and KEYLENGTH options, and you specify the name of the field that contains the full key in the RIDFLD option.
- The value you specify on the KEYLENGTH option must be a numeric literal or a binary halfword, and it must be greater than zero. If the length is not less than the length of the RIDFLD field, the INVREQ condition is raised.
- If you use a generic key on a STARTBR or RESETBR command, you can use the KEYLENGTH option on succeeding READNEXT commands to change the length of the generic key.

Figure 16-1   How to use generic keys to start a browse operation

How to use generic keys with the READ command

When you use a generic key with the READ command, CICS retrieves the first record with the key you specify. Because you're not likely to want to retrieve just the first record with a generic key, though, you probably won't use this form of the READ command often. Instead, you'll use the STARTBR command to start a browse operation at the first record with the generic key. Then, you'll use READNEXT commands to retrieve all of the records with that key. Nonetheless, you should understand how to use generic keys with the READ command in case the need ever arises.

Figure 16-2 presents the syntax of the READ command you use to retrieve a record based on a generic key. If you compare this syntax with the basic syntax of the READ command presented back in chapter 5, you'll notice three differences. First, you can't code the RRN and RBA options when you use generic keys. That's because you can only use generic keys with key-sequenced files that are retrieved by a primary or alternate key. Second, you code the GENERIC and KEYLENGTH options to identify the generic key just as you do for the STARTBR command. And third, you can code the EQUAL or GTEQ option to indicate whether only a record with the generic key you specify can be retrieved, or whether the next record in sequence is retrieved if a record with the generic key doesn't exist.

The example in this figure illustrates how you can use the READ command with a generic key. This procedure uses a generic key that consists of a vendor number to retrieve a record from the inventory parts file you saw in figure 16-1. To start, it moves a value to the vendor number portion of the key field. Then, it issues a READ command with the GENERIC, KEYLENGTH, and EQUAL options. That way, the first record with the specified vendor number will be retrieved. If the file doesn't contain any records for that vendor, though, the NOTFND condition is raised.

The syntax of the READ command for use with generic keys

```
EXEC CICS
    READ   FILE(filename)
           INTO(data-name)
           RIDFLD(data-name)
           GENERIC
           KEYLENGTH(data-name | literal)
           [GTEQ | EQUAL]
           [UPDATE]
END-EXEC
```

Option	Description
FILE	Specifies the name of the file that contains the record to be read. This name must be defined in the File Control Table.
INTO	Specifies the name of the data area where the input record is placed.
RIDFLD	Specifies the name of the field that contains the key of the record to be read.
GENERIC	Indicates that only a part of the key in the RIDFLD field should be used. The key consists of the number of bytes indicated by the KEYLENGTH option, starting with the first byte of the RIDFLD field.
KEYLENGTH	Specifies a binary halfword or literal value that indicates the length of the key, which must be less than the file's defined key length. Used with the GENERIC option.
GTEQ	Indicates that the first record with a generic key that's greater than or equal to the key specified by the RIDFLD and KEYLENGTH options will be retrieved.
EQUAL	Indicates that the first record with a generic key that's equal to the key specified by the RIDFLD and KEYLENGTH options will be retrieved.
UPDATE	Indicates that you intend to update the record with a subsequent REWRITE or DELETE command.

A read procedure that uses a generic key

```
3200-READ-FIRST-INVENTORY-RECORD.
*
    MOVE VENDNOI TO IP-VENDOR-NUMBER.
    EXEC CICS
        READ FILE('INVPART')
             INTO(INVENTORY-PARTS-RECORD)
             RIDFLD(IP-RECORD-KEY)
             GENERIC
             KEYLENGTH(4)
             EQUAL
             RESP(RESPONSE-CODE)
    END-EXEC.
```

Description

- To use generic keys with the READ command, you include the GENERIC and KEYLENGTH options, along with the RIDFLD option that identifies the field that contains the full key value. You can also code the GTEQ/EQUAL option to indicate what record will be read.

- The READ command reads only the first record with the specified generic key, and it doesn't establish position for subsequent reads. So you'll seldom use it in this format.

Figure 16-2   How to use generic keys with the READ command

How to use generic keys with the DELETE command

Figure 16-3 presents the syntax of the DELETE command you can use to delete records based on a generic key. Like the other commands for working with generic keys, you code the GENERIC and KEYLENGTH options on the DELETE command to identify the generic key. Then, if you code the EQUAL option, all of the records with the specified key value will be deleted. In the procedure shown in this figure, for example, all of the inventory part records for the specified vendor will be deleted. You can also code the GTEQ option to delete all of the records with key values equal to or greater than a specified value, but you're not likely to do that. Whether you use EQUAL or GTEQ, though, you should be careful when you use this command because it can delete a large number of records.

The DELETE command in this figure also includes the NUMREC option. You can use this option with generic keys when you want to know how many records were deleted by the operation.

The syntax of the DELETE command for use with generic keys

```
EXEC CICS
    DELETE FILE(filename)
           RIDFLD(data-name)
           GENERIC
           KEYLENGTH(data-name | literal)
           [GTEQ | EQUAL]
           [NUMREC(data-name)]
END-EXEC
```

Option	Description
FILE	Specifies the name of the file that contains the record to be deleted. This name must be defined in the File Control Table.
RIDFLD	Specifies the name of the field that contains the key of the record to be deleted.
GENERIC	Indicates that only a part of the key in the RIDFLD field should be used. The key consists of the number of bytes indicated by the KEYLENGTH option, starting with the first byte of the RIDFLD field.
KEYLENGTH	Specifies a binary halfword or literal value that indicates the length of the key, which must be less than the file's defined key length. Used with the GENERIC option.
GTEQ	Indicates that all of the records with a generic key that's greater than or equal to the key specified by the RIDFLD and KEYLENGTH options will be deleted.
EQUAL	Indicates that all of the records with a generic key that's equal to the key specified by the RIDFLD and KEYLENGTH options will be deleted.
NUMREC	Specifies the name of a binary halfword field that will contain a count of the records that were deleted.

A delete procedure that uses a generic key

```
    4200-DELETE-INVENTORY-RECORD.
*
        MOVE VENDNOI TO IP-VENDOR-NUMBER.
        EXEC CICS
            DELETE FILE('INVPART')
                   RIDFLD(IP-RECORD-KEY)
                   GENERIC
                   KEYLENGTH(4)
                   EQUAL
                   NUMREC(WS-DELETE-COUNT)
                   RESP(RESPONSE-CODE)
        END-EXEC.
```

Description

- To use generic keys with the DELETE command, you code the GENERIC and KEYLENGTH options along with the RIDFLD option that identifies the field that contains the full key value.

- If you code the EQUAL option on the DELETE command or let it default, all of the records with the specified generic key will be deleted. If you code the GTEQ option, all of the records with generic keys equal to or greater than the specified generic key will be deleted.

Figure 16-3   How to use generic keys with the DELETE command

How to use the MASSINSERT option of the WRITE command

If a program adds more than one record in sequence at the same point in a VSAM key-sequenced file, you may want to use the MASSINSERT option of the WRITE command to make the operation more efficient. To understand how this option works, you need to know that VSAM stores records in blocks called *control intervals*. Whenever you write a record to a control interval that's full, a *control interval split* occurs. Normally, VSAM does a control interval split by moving half of the records in the control interval to another control interval. Then, it inserts the new record.

When you use the MASSINSERT option, VSAM changes the way it splits control intervals. Rather than split the control interval in half, it splits it at the point of insertion. That leaves free space after the inserted record, so subsequent records can be inserted without unnecessary control interval splits.

Figure 16-4 shows a portion of a program that uses a MASSINSERT operation to write records to a file named CUSTINV. This file includes three types of records: customers, invoices, and line items. For each customer record, the file may contain one or more invoice records. And for each invoice record, the file may contain one or more line item records. The file's primary key is arranged so that the line item records follow their related invoice record, and invoice records follow their related customer record. Because of that, when the records for a new invoice are written to this file, they're inserted after the related customer record and any existing invoice and line item records for that customer.

In this example, notice that the WRITE command that adds an invoice record and the WRITE command that adds a line item record both contain the MASSINSERT option. The MASSINSERT operation begins when the program issues its first WRITE command with this option. Then, any subsequent WRITE commands you want to include in the MASSINSERT operation must also contain the MASSINSERT option. If they don't, the results will be unpredictable.

To end a MASSINSERT operation, you can issue an UNLOCK command as shown in this example. If you don't, the operation ends when the task ends. I recommend you always end a MASSINSERT operation explicitly, though, so that the control intervals involved in the operation and the VSAM resources necessary to process the operation are released. Note that if you don't issue an UNLOCK command to end the operation, you won't be able to issue any other file control commands against the file.

Code that includes a MASSINSERT operation

```
        .
        .
        .
      PERFORM 3200-WRITE-INVOICE-RECORD.
      PERFORM 3300-WRITE-LINE-ITEM-RECORD
          VARYING LINE-ITEM-SUB FROM 1 BY 1
          UNTIL LINE-ITEM-SUB > LINE-ITEM-COUNT.
      EXEC CICS
          UNLOCK FILE('CUSTINV')
      END-EXEC.
        .
        .
 3200-WRITE-INVOICE-RECORD.
*
      EXEC CICS
          WRITE FILE('CUSTINV')
              FROM(INVOICE-RECORD)
              RIDFLD(INV-RECORD-KEY)
              MASSINSERT
              RESP(RESPONSE-CODE)
      END-EXEC.
      IF RESPONSE-CODE NOT = DFHRESP(NORMAL)
          PERFORM 9999-TERMINATE-PROGRAM
      END-IF.
*
 3300-WRITE-LINE-ITEM-RECORD.
*
      MOVE LINE-ITEM-DATA(LINE-ITEM-SUB) TO LINE-ITEM-RECORD.
      EXEC CICS
          WRITE FILE('CUSTINV')
              FROM(LINE-ITEM-RECORD)
              RIDFLD(LI-RECORD-KEY)
              MASSINSERT
              RESP(RESPONSE-CODE)
      END-EXEC.
      IF RESPONSE-CODE NOT = DFHRESP(NORMAL)
          PERFORM 9999-TERMINATE-PROGRAM
      END-IF.
```

Description

- When a write operation adds a record to a block of VSAM records, or *control interval*, that's full, a *control interval split* occurs. Then, VSAM moves half of the records to a new control interval.

- If you code the MASSINSERT option on the WRITE command, VSAM splits the control interval at the point of insertion rather than in the middle. That way, if additional records are written in ascending key sequence at the same point in the file, the need for subsequent control interval splits will be reduced.

- All the WRITE commands involved in a MASSINSERT operation must include the MASSINSERT option.

- Before you can issue additional file control commands for a file involved in a MASSINSERT operation, you must end the operation. To do that, you issue an UNLOCK command.

Figure 16-4   How to use the MASSINSERT option of the WRITE command

How to use the TOKEN option of the file control commands

Normally, a CICS program that updates the records in a file performs a single update each time the program is executed in a pseudo-conversational session. However, you may occasionally need to update two or more records in the same file during the same execution of a program. In addition, if those records are related, you may need to read each one for update before rewriting any of them. To do that, you can use the TOKEN option as shown in figure 16-5.

Before I describe the TOKEN option, you should realize that if you issue a READ for UPDATE command without this option, any previous record that may have been held for update is released. When you use the TOKEN option with the READ command, though, CICS holds the record you specify and returns a unique value, called a *token*, that identifies the held record. This record is held until the program issues a subsequent REWRITE, DELETE, or UNLOCK command that includes the TOKEN option with the same value. Because of that, you can hold two or more records for update at the same time.

The example in this figure illustrates how tokens work. Here, two related customer records are updated concurrently. For this to work, each READ command includes a TOKEN option that names a different field that will contain the token for the record that's retrieved. Then, the REWRITE commands that follow include TOKEN options that name those same fields. Notice in this example that the records aren't rewritten in the same sequence they were read. Because a token identifies a specific record, the records can be updated in any sequence. Also notice that the READ commands don't include the UPDATE option. That's because when you code the TOKEN option, UPDATE is assumed.

Code that uses the TOKEN option to update two records concurrently

```
            WORKING-STORAGE SECTION.
                .
                .
                .
        01  WORK-FIELDS.
            05  TOKEN-1     PIC S9(8) COMP.
            05  TOKEN-2     PIC S9(8) COMP.
                .
                .
                .
        3100-UPDATE-ASSOCIATED-RECORDS.
        *
            EXEC CICS
                READ FILE('CUSTMAS')
                     INTO(CUSTOMER-MASTER-RECORD-1)
                     RIDFLD(CUST1I)
                     TOKEN(TOKEN-1)
                     RESP(RESPONSE-CODE)
            END-EXEC.
                .
                .
            EXEC CICS
                READ FILE('CUSTMAS')
                     INTO(CUSTOMER-MASTER-RECORD-2)
                     RIDFLD(CUST2I)
                     TOKEN(TOKEN-2)
                     RESP(RESPONSE-CODE)
            END-EXEC.
                .
                .
            EXEC CICS
                REWRITE FILE('CUSTMAS')
                     FROM(CUSTOMER-MASTER-RECORD-2)
                     TOKEN(TOKEN-2)
                     RESP(RESPONSE-CODE)
            END-EXEC.
                .
                .
            EXEC CICS
                REWRITE FILE('CUSTMAS')
                     FROM(CUSTOMER-MASTER-RECORD-1)
                     TOKEN(TOKEN-1)
                     RESP(RESPONSE-CODE)
            END-EXEC.
```

Token 1

Token 2

Description

- The TOKEN option lets you perform concurrent updates on two or more records in the same file within the same task. The field it names must be defined as a binary fullword.

- When you issue a READ command with the TOKEN option, CICS places a unique value in the TOKEN field. Then, you can use this field in a subsequent REWRITE, DELETE, or UNLOCK command to identify the record you want to operate on.

- When you issue a REWRITE, DELETE, or UNLOCK command with the TOKEN option, the specified record, which was held for update by a previous READ command, is released.

- If you include the TOKEN option on a READ command, UPDATE is implied, so you can omit this option.

Figure 16-5   How to use the TOKEN option of the file control commands

How to use shared data tables

CICS uses *shared data tables* to dramatically improve the performance of files that are accessed frequently. As illustrated in figure 16-6, a shared data table is a virtual storage copy of a VSAM key-sequenced file. When CICS starts up, it copies records from the VSAM file (called the *source data set*) into the data table. Then, whenever an application program performs an I/O operation against the file, CICS uses the data in the data table instead of accessing the file on disk. The result, as you can imagine, is much faster file access.

Before I go on, you should know that the use of data tables is transparent to an application program. In other words, they don't affect how you code your CICS file control commands. Instead, whether or not a file is accessed from disk or from virtual storage as a data table depends on how the systems programmer sets up the resource definition for the file. Because you may hear about data tables and the terms related to using them, though, you'll want to know what they are.

One of the features of a shared data table is that it can be accessed by more than one CICS system. That's because the shared data table is stored in a *data space* that's separate from the *address spaces* where the CICS regions are executing. (Unlike an address space, which can contain programs as well as data files, a data space can contain only data files.) The only restriction is that each CICS region that accesses the table must be run under the same OS/390 system.

What happens when an application program updates data in a shared data table by writing, rewriting, or deleting records? That depends on whether the data table is defined as a CICS-maintained table or a user-maintained table. For a *CICS-maintained table* (or *CMT*), CICS automatically updates records in the source data set. Note, however, that your application program doesn't have to wait until the disk update has completed before it can continue. Instead, control returns to your application program as soon as the update has been reflected in the data table.

In contrast, CICS does *not* automatically update the source data set when a *user-maintained table* (or *UMT*) is updated. Instead, you must provide a program that periodically updates the source data set. Because of this complexity, UMTs are typically used only for read-only files.

If you're working on a *sysplex* (a network of OS/390 systems), you can also use *Coupling Facility Data Tables* (*CFDTs*). In contrast to other types of data tables, CFDTs can be shared across OS/390 systems in the sysplex. Like UMTs, though, the source data set for a CFDT isn't updated when the data table is updated. So CFDTs are typically used with read-only files.

A shared data table in CICS storage

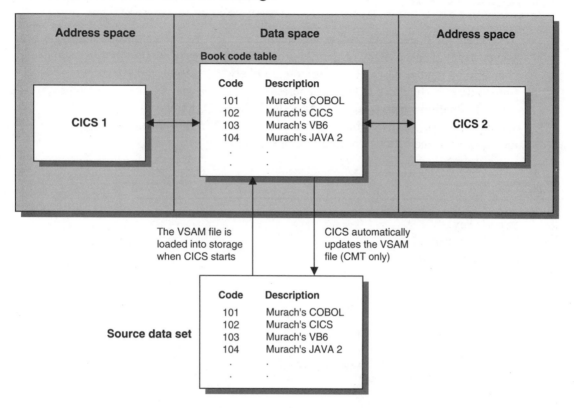

Description

- A *shared data table* is a virtual storage copy of a VSAM KSDS. These data tables can be accessed by multiple CICS regions running within the same OS/390 system.

- Shared data tables improve performance by providing faster access to frequently used files.

- Data tables are loaded from VSAM *source data sets* into a CICS *data space* when CICS is started. From that point on, the CICS file control commands access the records in the shared data tables as if they were in traditional disk files.

- When a *CICS-maintained table* (*CMT*) is used, the VSAM source data set is automatically updated whenever any changes are made to the records in virtual storage.

- When a *user-maintained table* (*UMT*) is used, the VSAM source data set is not automatically updated. So it's up to the programmer to provide a way of updating the source file. Because of that, UMTs are typically used for read-only files.

- *Coupling Facility Data Tables* (*CFDTs*) work in much the same way as UMTs. The difference is that the data in CFDTs can be shared across OS/390 systems that are part of the same *sysplex*.

Figure 16-6   How to use shared data tables

Perspective

Except for shared data tables, which don't require any special programming, you probably won't use any of the file processing features presented in this chapter on a regular basis. However, you are likely to use generic keys from time to time, particularly in browse operations. And you may occasionally come across a situation where using the MASSINSERT or TOKEN option makes sense. If you do, you'll be able to use the information in this chapter to implement practical and efficient programming solutions.

Terms

generic key
control interval
control interval split
token
shared data table
source data set
data space
address space
CICS-maintained table (CMT)
user-maintained table (UMT)
sysplex
Coupling Facility Data Table (CFDT)

17

How to work with DB2 databases

Although most CICS programs process VSAM files, it's becoming more and more common for CICS programs to process data stored in databases instead. In particular, more and more programs are processing data in IBM's relational database management system, DB2. So this chapter will teach you the CICS considerations for processing data stored by DB2.

Because DB2 is a complicated subject, this chapter won't try to teach you DB2. Instead, it assumes that you already know how to write DB2 programs in COBOL. In particular, it assumes that you know how to code SQL statements to process DB2 tables, including cursor-controlled result tables.

Even if you don't have DB2 experience, you may want to read this chapter. Although you probably won't understand some of the techniques and coding details, it will give you an idea of what's involved in developing CICS/DB2 programs and the challenges that presents. Then, if you want to learn more about DB2, you can get our book, *DB2 for the COBOL Programmer, Part 1*.

CICS/DB2 concepts

Although this chapter assumes that you already know how to develop DB2 programs, you should understand how CICS and DB2 work together before you develop your first CICS/DB2 program. In addition, you'll want to know about some special requirements for preparing CICS/DB2 programs for execution. That's what you'll learn in the topics that follow.

How CICS and DB2 work together

Like CICS, *DB2*, which stands for *Database 2*, executes as a subsystem within the operating system environment. To request a DB2 function, a CICS program issues a statement written in the *Structured Query Language*, or *SQL*. SQL provides a variety of statements, but the ones you'll use most often in an application program are SELECT, to select specific data from one or more DB2 tables; INSERT, to add new rows to a table; UPDATE, to change existing rows; and DELETE to delete existing rows.

When CICS receives the SQL statement, it passes the statement on to the DB2 subsystem for processing. When it's done, DB2 returns the result to CICS, which passes it along to the program that issued the request. At the least, that means that the program receives a DB2 status code value that reports the success or failure of the statement. If the program issued a SELECT statement, though, it also means that the program receives the DB2 data specified by that statement.

To manage its communications with DB2, CICS uses special interface modules called the *CICS/DB2 attachment facility*. As illustrated in figure 17-1, these modules are loaded into storage along with the other CICS modules. Then, when a CICS program issues a SQL statement, the attachment facility establishes a connection with DB2 called a *thread*. Once the connection is made, the attachment facility uses it to pass the SQL statement, and any subsequent SQL statements issued by the program, to DB2. Then, after DB2 performs the requested function, it passes the result back to CICS through the attachment facility.

Keep in mind that the communication between CICS and DB2 is transparent to you. As an application programmer, all you have to do is include the appropriate SQL statements in your program. On the other hand, to define the connection between your program and DB2, the systems programmer must include an entry in the CICS *Resource Control Table* (*RCT*). This entry includes the trans-id of the transaction that starts the program, the name of the DB2 application plan for the program, the DB2 authorizations for CICS transactions, and the number of threads that will be available to connect CICS and DB2.

How CICS communicates with DB2

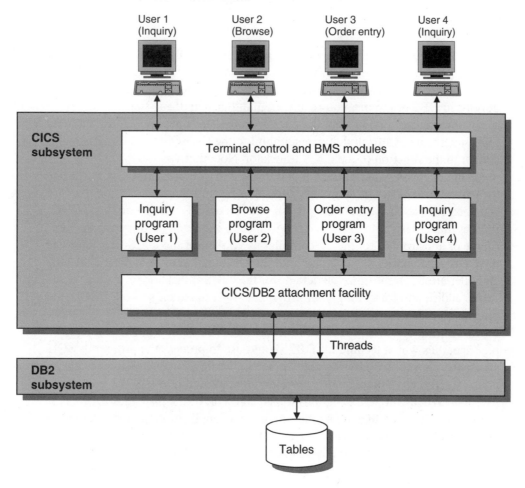

Description

- When DB2 is used with CICS, DB2 interface modules are loaded into storage along with the CICS modules. These modules make up the *CICS/DB2 attachment facility.*

- To access DB2 data, a CICS program issues SQL statements. Then, CICS sends a request to the attachment facility to establish a connection to DB2 called a *thread.*

- Once a connection is established with DB2, the attachment facility uses it to pass the SQL statement to DB2 and the results of the SQL statement back to the program.

- CICS systems programmers are responsible for defining the connection between a program's CICS transaction and DB2 with an entry in the CICS *Resource Control Table (RCT).*

Figure 17-1   How CICS and DB2 work together

How to prepare a CICS/DB2 program for execution

Figure 17-2 shows the steps for preparing a CICS/DB2 program for execution. As you can see, the process includes all the steps required for any CICS program, along with two additional steps: precompilation and binding. If you've developed DB2 programs, you're already familiar with these steps.

In the precompilation step, the *DB2 precompiler* converts the program's SQL statements to a form that's meaningful to the COBOL compiler. This is similar to the function of the CICS translator. Note that you must run the precompiler *before* you run the CICS translator. If you don't, the CICS translator will return a series of diagnostic messages because it doesn't recognize SQL statements. In contrast, the DB2 precompiler recognizes CICS commands and ignores them. Also note that you need to specify the same delimiter character (quote or apostrophe) for the precompiler as you do for the CICS translator and the COBOL compiler. (The defaults for the DB2 precompiler and the COBOL compiler are different from the default for the CICS translator.)

In addition to translating your program's SQL statements into COBOL, the precompiler also creates a *database request module*, or *DBRM*. DB2 uses the DBRM during the *bind* procedure to create an *application plan*. The application plan specifies which techniques DB2 should use to process the program's SQL statements most efficiently. As you can see in the figure, you can bind a program directly into a plan, but it's more efficient to bind it to a *package* and then to a plan. When you bind programs to packages, all of the packages in one or more *collections* can then be bound into a single application plan. Regardless of the technique you use, information about the application plan (and the package, if there is one) is stored in the DB2 catalog, and the actual plan (and package) are stored in the DB2 directory. Both the catalog and the directory are required to execute a CICS/DB2 program.

When you link-edit a CICS/DB2 program, you must be sure to include a module called DSNCLI. This module provides the interface to the CICS/DB2 attachment facility. If your shop uses a cataloged procedure for CICS/DB2 program development, it almost certainly includes this module.

How to prepare a CICS/DB2 program for execution

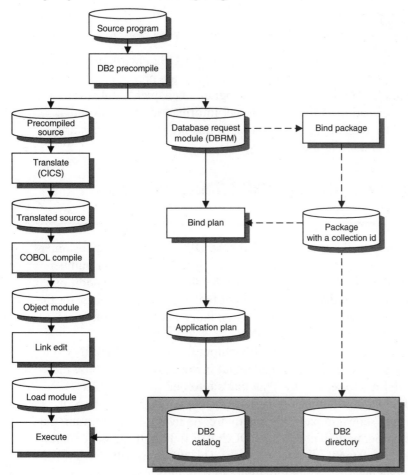

Description

- Before you translate a CICS/DB2 program, you must convert the DB2 statements into a form that the COBOL compiler can interpret using the *DB2 precompiler*.

- The *database request module*, or *DBRM*, that's created by the precompiler is used to create an *application plan* in a process called *binding*. During this process, DB2 checks all the DB2 functions used in the program and selects the most efficient way to implement them.

- Information about the application plan is stored in the *DB2 catalog*, and the actual plan is stored in the *DB2 directory*. If the application plan is created from the *packages* in one or more *collections*, information about the package is also stored in the DB2 catalog, and the actual package is stored in the DB2 directory.

- The link-edit step that creates the load module for a CICS/DB2 program must include the DSNCLI module, which provides the interface to the CICS/DB2 attachment facility.

- The load module and the DB2 catalog and directory are all required to execute the program.

Figure 17-2   How to prepare a CICS/DB2 program for execution

The DB2 version of the customer inquiry program

Now that you have some background on the CICS/DB2 environment, you're ready to see a complete CICS/DB2 program. The program presented here is a DB2 version of the CICS customer inquiry program in chapter 2, enhanced to display invoice information as well as customer information. Because you should already understand the basic operation of this program, I'll focus primarily on the DB2 programming implications.

The specifications for the CICS/DB2 inquiry program

Figure 17-3 presents the specifications for the DB2 version of the customer inquiry program. Like the program in chapter 2, it accepts a customer number from the user and then displays the information for that customer. In addition, this version of the program displays up to ten of the most recent invoices for the customer. The customer and invoice information that's displayed is retrieved from two DB2 tables, named CUST and INV.

Part 2 of this figure shows the DCLGEN output for the CUST and INV tables. As you know, you can include this output in your program and use the host variables it defines to receive the data that's returned from a SELECT statement. In addition, you'll typically include the copy member for the SQL communication area shown in part 3 of this figure. As in any DB2 program, the customer inquiry program will check the SQLCODE field in this area to make sure that each SQL statement executes properly. This program will also use the ERRPARM copy member shown in this figure to pass information to the SYSERR program when an unrecoverable error occurs.

By the way, if you've read chapter 15, you'll realize that this program is very similar to the one presented there. However, it doesn't provide PF keys for displaying the first, last, previous, or next customer. As you'll learn later in this chapter, browsing DB2 data in a CICS program causes some programming complications. So I've kept this program fairly simple to make it easier to focus on the DB2 considerations.

The program overview for the CICS/DB2 inquiry program

Program	DB2INQ1
Trans-id	DIN1
Overview	Displays data from a selected row in the customer table, along with detail information for the first ten invoices for that customer.
Input/output specifications	DB2MAP1 Customer inquiry map CUST Customer table INV Invoice table
Processing specifications	1. Control is transferred to this program via XCTL from the menu program INVMENU with no communication area. The user can also start the program by entering the trans-id DIN1. In either case, the program should respond by displaying the customer inquiry map. 2. When the user enters a customer number, select the corresponding row from the customer table. 3. If the requested customer row is selected successfully, retrieve the invoice data for that customer from the invoice table and display data from the ten most recent invoices. 4. If the user presses PF3 or PF12, return to the menu program INVMENU by issuing an XCTL command. 5. If an unrecoverable error occurs, terminate the program by invoking the SYSERR subprogram with an XCTL command.

The screen layout for the program

Map name   DB2MAP1   Date   04/16/2001

Program name   DB2INQ1   Designer   Doug Lowe

```
DB2MAP1                    Customer Inquiry                                          XXXX

Type a customer number.    Then press Enter.

Customer number. . . . .  XXXXXX

Name and address . . . :  XXXXXXXXXXXXXXXXXXXXXXXXXXXXXX
                          XXXXXXXXXXXXXXXXXXXX
                          XXXXXXXXXXXXXXXXXXXXXXXXXXXXXX
                          XXXXXXXXXXXXXXXXXX  XX  XXXXXXXXXX

Invoice   PO Number      Date            Total
999999    XXXXXXXXXX     XXXXXXXXXX     Z,ZZZ,ZZ9.99
999999    XXXXXXXXXX     XXXXXXXXXX     Z,ZZZ,ZZ9.99
999999    XXXXXXXXXX     XXXXXXXXXX     Z,ZZZ,ZZ9.99
999999    XXXXXXXXXX     XXXXXXXXXX     Z,ZZZ,ZZ9.99
999999    XXXXXXXXXX     XXXXXXXXXX     Z,ZZZ,ZZ9.99
999999    XXXXXXXXXX     XXXXXXXXXX     Z,ZZZ,ZZ9.99
999999    XXXXXXXXXX     XXXXXXXXXX     Z,ZZZ,ZZ9.99
999999    XXXXXXXXXX     XXXXXXXXXX     Z,ZZZ,ZZ9.99
999999    XXXXXXXXXX     XXXXXXXXXX     Z,ZZZ,ZZ9.99
999999    XXXXXXXXXX     XXXXXXXXXX     Z,ZZZ,ZZ9.99
XXXXXXXXXXXXXXXXXXXXXXXXXXXXXXXXXXXXXXXXXXXXXXXXXXXXXXXXXXXXXXXXXXXXXXXXXXXXXXXXX
F3=Exit    F12=Cancel                                                                  X
```

Figure 17-3   The specifications for the CICS/DB2 inquiry program (part 1 of 3)

The DCLGEN copy member for the customer table (CUST)

```
****************************************************************
* DCLGEN TABLE(MMADBV.CUST)                                    *
*         LIBRARY(MMA002.DCLGENS.COBOL(CUST))                  *
*         ACTION(REPLACE)                                      *
*         STRUCTURE(CUSTOMER-ROW)                              *
*         APOST                                                *
* ... IS THE DCLGEN COMMAND THAT MADE THE FOLLOWING STATEMENTS *
****************************************************************
      EXEC SQL DECLARE MMADBV.CUST TABLE
       ( CUSTNO                    CHAR (6) NOT NULL,
         FNAME                     CHAR (20) NOT NULL,
         LNAME                     CHAR (30) NOT NULL,
         ADDR                      CHAR (30) NOT NULL,
         CITY                      CHAR (20) NOT NULL,
         STATE                     CHAR (2) NOT NULL,
         ZIPCODE                   CHAR (10) NOT NULL
       ) END-EXEC.
****************************************************************
* COBOL DECLARATION FOR TABLE MMADBV.CUST                      *
****************************************************************
 01   CUSTOMER-ROW.
      10 CUSTNO              PIC X(6).
      10 FNAME               PIC X(20).
      10 LNAME               PIC X(30).
      10 ADDR                PIC X(30).
      10 CITY                PIC X(20).
      10 STATE               PIC X(2).
      10 ZIPCODE             PIC X(10).
****************************************************************
* THE NUMBER OF COLUMNS DESCRIBED BY THIS DECLARATION IS 7     *
****************************************************************
```

The DCLGEN copy member for the invoice table (INV)

```
****************************************************************
* DCLGEN TABLE(MMADBV.INV)                                     *
*         LIBRARY(MMA002.DCLGENS.COBOL(INV))                   *
*         ACTION(REPLACE)                                      *
*         STRUCTURE(INVOICE-ROW)                               *
*         APOST                                                *
* ... IS THE DCLGEN COMMAND THAT MADE THE FOLLOWING STATEMENTS *
****************************************************************
      EXEC SQL DECLARE MMADBV.INV TABLE
       ( INVCUST                   CHAR (6) NOT NULL,
         INVNO                     CHAR (6) NOT NULL,
         INVDATE                   DATE NOT NULL,
         INVSUBT                   DECIMAL (9, 2) NOT NULL
         INVSHIP                   DECIMAL (7, 2) NOT NULL,
         INVTAX                    DECIMAL (7, 2) NOT NULL,
         INVTOTAL                  DECIMAL (9, 2) NOT NULL,
         INVPO                     CHAR (10) NOT NULL
       ) END-EXEC.
****************************************************************
* COBOL DECLARATION FOR TABLE MMADBV.INV                       *
****************************************************************
 01   INVOICE-ROW.
      10 INVCUST             PIC X(6).
      10 INVNO               PIC X(6).
      10 INVDATE             PIC X(10).
      10 INVSUBT             PIC S9999999V99 USAGE COMP-3.
      10 INVSHIP             PIC S99999V99 USAGE COMP-3.
      10 INVTAX              PIC S99999V99 USAGE COMP-3.
      10 INVTOTAL            PIC S9999999V99 USAGE COMP-3.
      10 INVPO               PIC X(10).
****************************************************************
* THE NUMBER OF COLUMNS DESCRIBED BY THIS DECLARATION IS 8     *
****************************************************************
```

Figure 17-3   The specifications for the CICS/DB2 inquiry program (part 2 of 3)

The copy member for the SQL communication area (SQLCA)

```
01 SQLCA.
    05 SQLCAID    PIC X(8).
    05 SQLCABC    PIC S9(4) COMP-4.
    05 SQLCODE    PIC S9(4) COMP-4.
    05 SQLERRM.
        49 SQLERRML PIC S9(4) COMP-4.
        49 SQLERRMC PIC X(70).
    05 SQLERRP    PIC X(8).
    05 SQLERRD    OCCURS 6 TIMES
                  PIC S9(9) COMP-4.
    05 SQLWARN.
        10 SQLWARN0 PIC X.
        10 SQLWARN1 PIC X.
        10 SQLWARN2 PIC X.
        10 SQLWARN3 PIC X.
        10 SQLWARN4 PIC X.
        10 SQLWARN5 PIC X.
        10 SQLWARN6 PIC X.
        10 SQLWARN7 PIC X.
    05 SQLEXT     PIC X(8).
```

The ERRPARM copy member

```
*
 01   ERROR-PARAMETERS.
*
     05   ERR-RESP    PIC S9(8)    COMP.
     05   ERR-RESP2   PIC S9(8)    COMP.
     05   ERR-TRNID   PIC X(4).
     05   ERR-RSRCE   PIC X(4).
```

Figure 17-3   The specifications for the CICS/DB2 inquiry program (part 3 of 3)

The design for the CICS/DB2 inquiry program

Figure 17-4 presents the event/response chart and structure chart for the CICS/DB2 inquiry program. The top levels of the structure chart are similar to those for the inquiry program in chapter 2. Module 1000 starts by receiving the inquiry map (module 1100) and editing the customer number (module 1200). Instead of reading the customer record, though, module 1300 issues a SQL SELECT statement to select the customer row from the customer table. Then, module 1400 displays the results of the query.

Module 1400 and its subordinates control the invoice display in this version of the inquiry program. Module 1400 starts by calling module 1410 to open the invoice cursor and create the cursor-controlled result table that contains the invoices for the specified customer. Then, it calls module 1420 repeatedly to format the ten invoice lines. This module, in turn, calls module 1430 to retrieve a row from the cursor-controlled result table. When all of the invoices have been formatted, module 1400 calls module 1440 to close the invoice cursor and module 1500 to display the inquiry map.

The BMS mapset and symbolic map for the CICS/DB2 inquiry program

Figure 17-5 presents the part of the BMS mapset that differs from the mapset for the inquiry program in chapter 2. As you can see, the bulk of this code defines the invoice area in the inquiry screen. The definition starts with a constant that gives the column headings for the invoice data. That heading is followed by the definitions of each of the ten invoice lines. Notice that each of these lines is defined as a single 44-byte field. That way, if a customer has fewer than ten invoices, the program can simply move spaces to the appropriate fields so that nothing is displayed in those lines. For this to work, the program must format the invoice lines in the Working-Storage Section before they're moved to the appropriate screen fields.

To make it easier to manipulate the invoice fields in the COBOL program, I created my own symbolic map, shown in figure 17-6. Here, an Occurs clause defines the invoice lines so they can be processed in the COBOL code using subscripts. Without a programmer-generated symbolic map like this, you would have to code for each invoice line separately in your program.

An event/response chart for the CICS/DB2 inquiry program

Event	Response
Start the program	Display the customer inquiry map.
PF3 or PF12	Transfer control to the menu program.
Enter	Select and display the customer row and the ten most recent invoice rows for the customer number entered by the user.
Clear	Redisplay the customer inquiry map.
PA1, PA2, or PA3	Ignore the key.
Any other key	Display an appropriate error message.

The structure chart for the program

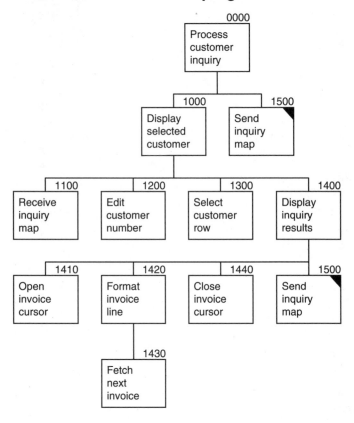

Figure 17-4   The design for the CICS/DB2 inquiry program

The code for the BMS mapset

```
        PRINT NOGEN
DB2SET1 DFHMSD TYPE=&SYSPARM,                                             X
               LANG=COBOL,                                               X
               MODE=INOUT,                                               X
               TERM=3270-2,                                              X
               CTRL=FREEKB,                                              X
               STORAGE=AUTO,                                             X
               TIOAPFX=YES
*********************************************************************************
DB2MAP1 DFHMDI SIZE=(24,80),                                             X
               LINE=1,                                                   X
               COLUMN=1
*********************************************************************************
        DFHMDF POS=(1,1),                                                X
               LENGTH=8,                                                 X
               ATTRB=(NORM,PROT),                                        X
               COLOR=BLUE,                                               X
               INITIAL='DB2MAP1'
               .
               .
        DFHMDF POS=(12,1),                                               X
               LENGTH=45,                                                X
               COLOR=GREEN,                                              X
               ATTRB=(NORM,PROT),                                        X
               INITIAL='Invoice  PO Number    Date            Total'
INV1    DFHMDF POS=(13,2),                                               X
               LENGTH=44,                                                X
               COLOR=TURQUOISE,                                          X
               ATTRB=(NORM,PROT)
INV2    DFHMDF POS=(14,2),                                               X
               LENGTH=44,                                                X
               COLOR=TURQUOISE,                                          X
               ATTRB=(NORM,PROT)
INV3    DFHMDF POS=(15,2),                                               X
               LENGTH=44,                                                X
               COLOR=TURQUOISE,                                          X
               ATTRB=(NORM,PROT)
INV4    DFHMDF POS=(16,2),                                               X
               LENGTH=44,                                                X
               COLOR=TURQUOISE,                                          X
               ATTRB=(NORM,PROT)
INV5    DFHMDF POS=(17,2),                                               X
               LENGTH=44,                                                X
               COLOR=TURQUOISE,                                          X
               ATTRB=(NORM,PROT)
               .
               .
INV10   DFHMDF POS=(22,2),                                               X
               LENGTH=44,                                                X
               COLOR=TURQUOISE,                                          X
               ATTRB=(NORM,PROT)
*********************************************************************************
               .
               .
        DFHMSD TYPE=FINAL
        END
```

Figure 17-5   The BMS mapset for the CICS/DB2 inquiry program

The code for the programmer-generated symbolic map

```
01  CUSTOMER-INQUIRY-MAP.
*
    05  FILLER                   PIC X(12).
*
    05  CIM-L-TRANID             PIC S9(04)  COMP.
    05  CIM-A-TRANID             PIC X(01).
    05  CIM-D-TRANID             PIC X(04).
*
    05  CIM-L-CUSTNO             PIC S9(04)  COMP.
    05  CIM-A-CUSTNO             PIC X(01).
    05  CIM-D-CUSTNO             PIC X(06).
*
    05  CIM-L-LNAME              PIC S9(04)  COMP.
    05  CIM-A-LNAME              PIC X(01).
    05  CIM-D-LNAME              PIC X(30).
*
    05  CIM-L-FNAME              PIC S9(04)  COMP.
    05  CIM-A-FNAME              PIC X(01).
    05  CIM-D-FNAME              PIC X(20).
*
    05  CIM-L-ADDR               PIC S9(04)  COMP.
    05  CIM-A-ADDR               PIC X(01).
    05  CIM-D-ADDR               PIC X(30).
*
    05  CIM-L-CITY               PIC S9(04)  COMP.
    05  CIM-A-CITY               PIC X(01).
    05  CIM-D-CITY               PIC X(20).
*
    05  CIM-L-STATE              PIC S9(04)  COMP.
    05  CIM-A-STATE              PIC X(01).
    05  CIM-D-STATE              PIC X(02).
*
    05  CIM-L-ZIPCODE            PIC S9(04)  COMP.
    05  CIM-A-ZIPCODE            PIC X(01).
    05  CIM-D-ZIPCODE            PIC X(10).
*
    05  CIM-INVOICE-LINE         OCCURS 10 TIMES.
*
        10  CIM-L-INVOICE-LINE   PIC S9(04)  COMP.
        10  CIM-A-INVOICE-LINE   PIC X(01).
        10  CIM-D-INVOICE-LINE   PIC X(44).
*
    05  CIM-L-MESSAGE            PIC S9(04)  COMP.
    05  CIM-A-MESSAGE            PIC X(01).
    05  CIM-D-MESSAGE            PIC X(79).
*
    05  CIM-L-DUMMY              PIC S9(04)  COMP.
    05  CIM-A-DUMMY              PIC X(01).
    05  CIM-D-DUMMY              PIC X(01).
*
```

Figure 17-6   The programmer-generated symbolic map for the CICS/DB2 inquiry program

The COBOL code for the CICS/DB2 inquiry program

Figure 17-7 presents the COBOL source code for the DB2 version of the customer inquiry program. For the most part, I'll concentrate on the DB2 aspects of this code. But note that several items have been added to the Working-Storage Section to handle the display of customer invoices: MORE-INVOICES-SW to determine whether a customer still has more invoices to be displayed; INVOICE-SUB to provide the subscript for the invoice lines defined in the symbolic map; and INVOICE-LINE to format each invoice line before it's moved to the appropriate line in the symbolic map. In addition, CUSTOMER-FOUND-SW and DISPLAY-FLAG have been added to control the screen formatting depending on whether a customer record is found for the specified customer number.

On page 2 of this listing, you can see that the last four items in the Working-Storage Section are SQL statements. The first two are INCLUDE statements for the DCLGEN output for the CUST and INV tables. The third is an INCLUDE statement for the SQLCA copy member. And the last is a SQL DECLARE CURSOR statement. This statement defines the cursor-controlled result table named CUSTINV that will be created for the customer invoices.

As you can see, the SELECT statement within the DECLARE CURSOR statement indicates that four columns will be retrieved from the invoice table. (The third column specification uses the CHAR function to format the date according in the pattern MM/DD/YYYY.) The WHERE clause indicates that only the rows for the customer number in the CIM-D-CUSTNO field (the number entered by the user in the inquiry map) will be returned. And the ORDER BY clause indicates that those rows will be sorted in descending sequence by the first column (INVNO) so the most recent invoices will be displayed first.

The CICS/DB2 inquiry program   **Page 1**

```
     IDENTIFICATION DIVISION.
*
     PROGRAM-ID.  DB2INQ1.
*
     ENVIRONMENT DIVISION.
*
     DATA DIVISION.
*
     WORKING-STORAGE SECTION.
*
     01   SWITCHES.
*
          05   VALID-DATA-SW        PIC X(01)      VALUE 'Y'.
               88   VALID-DATA                     VALUE 'Y'.
          05   CUSTOMER-FOUND-SW     PIC X(01)      VALUE 'Y'.
               88   CUSTOMER-FOUND                 VALUE 'Y'.
          05   MORE-INVOICES-SW     PIC X(01)      VALUE 'Y'.
               88   MORE-INVOICES                  VALUE 'Y'.
*
     01   FLAGS.
*
          05   DISPLAY-FLAG         PIC X(01).
               88   DISPLAY-NEW-CUSTOMER           VALUE '1'.
               88   DISPLAY-SPACES                 VALUE '2'.
               88   DISPLAY-LOW-VALUES             VALUE '3'.
          05   SEND-FLAG            PIC X(01).
               88   SEND-ERASE                     VALUE '1'.
               88   SEND-DATAONLY                  VALUE '2'.
               88   SEND-DATAONLY-ALARM            VALUE '3'.
*
     01   WORK-FIELDS.
*
          05   INVOICE-SUB          PIC S9(04)     COMP.
*
     01   INVOICE-LINE.
*
          05   IL-INVOICE-NUMBER    PIC X(06).
          05   FILLER               PIC X(02)      VALUE SPACE.
          05   IL-PO-NUMBER         PIC X(10).
          05   FILLER               PIC X(02)      VALUE SPACE.
          05   IL-INVOICE-DATE      PIC X(10).
          05   FILLER               PIC X(02)      VALUE SPACE.
          05   IL-INVOICE-TOTAL     PIC Z,ZZZ,ZZ9.99.
*
     01   COMMUNICATION-AREA        PIC X(01).
*
     COPY DB2SET1.
*
     COPY DFHAID.
*
     COPY ERRPARM.
*
```

Figure 17-7   The COBOL code for the CICS/DB2 inquiry program (part 1 of 6)

The CICS/DB2 inquiry program

```
    EXEC SQL
        INCLUDE CUST
    END-EXEC.
*
    EXEC SQL
        INCLUDE INV
    END-EXEC.
*
    EXEC SQL
        INCLUDE SQLCA
    END-EXEC.
*
    EXEC SQL
        DECLARE CUSTINV CURSOR FOR
            SELECT INVNO, INVPO, CHAR(INVDATE,USA), INVTOTAL
                FROM MMADBV.INV
                WHERE INVCUST = :CIM-D-CUSTNO
                ORDER BY 1 DESC
    END-EXEC.
*
 LINKAGE SECTION.
*
 01  DFHCOMMAREA               PIC X(01).
*
 PROCEDURE DIVISION.
*
 0000-PROCESS-CUSTOMER-INQUIRY.
*
     EVALUATE TRUE
*
         WHEN EIBCALEN = ZERO
             MOVE LOW-VALUE TO CUSTOMER-INQUIRY-MAP
             MOVE 'DIN1' TO CIM-D-TRANID
             SET SEND-ERASE TO TRUE
             PERFORM 1500-SEND-INQUIRY-MAP
*
         WHEN EIBAID = DFHCLEAR
             MOVE LOW-VALUE TO CUSTOMER-INQUIRY-MAP
             MOVE 'DIN1' TO CIM-D-TRANID
             SET SEND-ERASE TO TRUE
             PERFORM 1500-SEND-INQUIRY-MAP
*
         WHEN EIBAID = DFHPA1 OR DFHPA2 OR DFHPA3
             CONTINUE
*
         WHEN EIBAID = DFHPF3 OR DFHPF12
             EXEC CICS
                 XCTL PROGRAM('INVMENU')
             END-EXEC
*
         WHEN EIBAID = DFHENTER
             PERFORM 1000-DISPLAY-SELECTED-CUSTOMER
*
```

Figure 17-7   The COBOL code for the CICS/DB2 inquiry program (part 2 of 6)

The CICS/DB2 inquiry program   Page 3

```
                WHEN OTHER
                    MOVE LOW-VALUE TO CUSTOMER-INQUIRY-MAP
                    MOVE 'Invalid key pressed.' TO CIM-D-MESSAGE
                    SET SEND-DATAONLY-ALARM TO TRUE
                    PERFORM 1500-SEND-INQUIRY-MAP
     *
         END-EVALUATE.
     *
         EXEC CICS
             RETURN TRANSID('DIN1')
                     COMMAREA(COMMUNICATION-AREA)
         END-EXEC.
     *
      1000-DISPLAY-SELECTED-CUSTOMER.
     *
         PERFORM 1100-RECEIVE-INQUIRY-MAP.
         PERFORM 1200-EDIT-CUSTOMER-NUMBER.
         IF VALID-DATA
             PERFORM 1300-SELECT-CUSTOMER-ROW
             IF CUSTOMER-FOUND
                 SET DISPLAY-NEW-CUSTOMER TO TRUE
                 PERFORM 1400-DISPLAY-INQUIRY-RESULTS
             ELSE
                 SET DISPLAY-SPACES TO TRUE
                 PERFORM 1400-DISPLAY-INQUIRY-RESULTS
             END-IF
         ELSE
             SET DISPLAY-LOW-VALUES TO TRUE
             PERFORM 1400-DISPLAY-INQUIRY-RESULTS
         END-IF.
     *
      1100-RECEIVE-INQUIRY-MAP.
     *
         EXEC CICS
             RECEIVE MAP('DB2MAP1')
                     MAPSET('DB2SET1')
                     INTO(CUSTOMER-INQUIRY-MAP)
         END-EXEC.
     *
         INSPECT CUSTOMER-INQUIRY-MAP
             REPLACING ALL '_' BY SPACE.
     *
      1200-EDIT-CUSTOMER-NUMBER.
     *
         IF       CIM-L-CUSTNO = ZERO
             OR CIM-D-CUSTNO = SPACE
             MOVE 'N' TO VALID-DATA-SW
             MOVE 'You must enter a customer number.'
                 TO CIM-D-MESSAGE
         END-IF.
     *
```

Figure 17-7   The COBOL code for the CICS/DB2 inquiry program (part 3 of 6)

In the Procedure Division, after the program receives and edits the customer number entered by the user, procedure 1300 issues a SELECT statement to retrieve data for the customer from the CUST table. The row that's returned will include all of the columns in the CUST table, except for CUSTNO. (Since the customer number is available from the symbolic map, it doesn't need to be retrieved from the customer table.) These columns will be placed in fields in the symbolic map rather than in fields in the DCLGEN structure for the CUST table. If the DCLGEN fields had been used, the program would then have had to move the data into the symbolic map fields. So it saved some coding to move data directly into the map fields. Note that since the DCLGEN fields aren't used by this program, the DCLGEN output could have been omitted altogether. However, I recommend that you always include this output for documentation.

After it executes the SELECT statement, procedure 1300 tests the value of the SQLCODE field to be sure the statement completed successfully. If the customer row wasn't found (SQLCODE = 100), it moves N to CUSTOMER-FOUND-SW and an error message to the error field in the symbolic map (CIM-D-MESSAGE). If a more serious error occurred, it performs procedure 9999 to end the program.

If the SELECT statement in procedure 1300 successfully retrieves a customer row, the program performs procedure 1400 to display the inquiry results with the Display-New-Customer condition set to True. Then, this procedure starts by performing procedure 1410 (on page 5 of this listing). This procedure issues a SQL OPEN statement to generate a cursor-controlled result table with invoice rows for the current customer. Next, procedure 1400 performs procedure 1420 ten times to build the invoice detail lines for the display. This procedure retrieves a row from the result table by performing procedure 1430, then moves the invoice line formatted by that procedure into the appropriate invoice line in the symbolic map. Or, if no more rows are available, it just moves space to the invoice line.

Procedure 1430 issues a SQL FETCH statement that names the cursor for the INV table (CUSTINV) and the host variables in the DCLGEN output for that table where the returned data will be stored. Then, it evaluates SQLCODE to determine if the FETCH statement was successful. If it was, the contents of the host variables are moved into corresponding fields in the invoice line in working storage. If no more rows are available, though, it simply moves N to MORE-INVOICES-SW so procedure 1430 won't be performed again. And if a more serious error is encountered, it performs procedure 9999 to end the program.

After procedure 1400 prepares the ten invoice detail lines, it performs procedure 1440. This procedure issues a SQL CLOSE statement to release the cursor-controlled result table. If this statement returns any SQLCODE value other than zero, the program performs procedure 9999 to end the program.

The CICS/DB2 inquiry program   **Page 4**

```
1300-SELECT-CUSTOMER-ROW.
*
    EXEC SQL
        SELECT       FNAME,          LNAME,
                     ADDR,           CITY,
                     STATE,          ZIPCODE
              INTO :CIM-D-FNAME,  :CIM-D-LNAME,
                   :CIM-D-ADDR,   :CIM-D-CITY,
                   :CIM-D-STATE,  :CIM-D-ZIPCODE
              FROM MMADBV.CUST
              WHERE CUSTNO = :CIM-D-CUSTNO
    END-EXEC.
*
    IF SQLCODE = 100
        MOVE 'N' TO CUSTOMER-FOUND-SW
        MOVE 'That customer does not exist.' TO CIM-D-MESSAGE
    ELSE
        IF SQLCODE NOT = 0
            PERFORM 9999-TERMINATE-PROGRAM
        END-IF
    END-IF.
*
 1400-DISPLAY-INQUIRY-RESULTS.
*
    EVALUATE TRUE
        WHEN DISPLAY-NEW-CUSTOMER
            PERFORM 1410-OPEN-INVOICE-CURSOR
            PERFORM 1420-FORMAT-INVOICE-LINE
                VARYING INVOICE-SUB FROM 1 BY 1
                UNTIL INVOICE-SUB > 10
            PERFORM 1440-CLOSE-INVOICE-CURSOR
            MOVE SPACE        TO CIM-D-MESSAGE
            SET SEND-DATAONLY TO TRUE
        WHEN DISPLAY-SPACES
            MOVE LOW-VALUE TO CIM-D-CUSTNO
            MOVE SPACE        TO CIM-D-LNAME
                                 CIM-D-FNAME
                                 CIM-D-ADDR
                                 CIM-D-CITY
                                 CIM-D-STATE
                                 CIM-D-ZIPCODE
            PERFORM VARYING INVOICE-SUB FROM 1 BY 1
                    UNTIL INVOICE-SUB > 10
                MOVE SPACE TO CIM-D-INVOICE-LINE(INVOICE-SUB)
            END-PERFORM
            SET SEND-DATAONLY-ALARM TO TRUE
        WHEN DISPLAY-LOW-VALUES
            SET SEND-DATAONLY-ALARM TO TRUE
    END-EVALUATE.

    PERFORM 1500-SEND-INQUIRY-MAP.
*
```

Figure 17-7   The COBOL code for the CICS/DB2 inquiry program (part 4 of 6)

The CICS/DB2 inquiry program

```
1410-OPEN-INVOICE-CURSOR.
*
     EXEC SQL
         OPEN CUSTINV
     END-EXEC.
*
     IF SQLCODE NOT = 0
         PERFORM 9999-TERMINATE-PROGRAM
     END-IF.
*
 1420-FORMAT-INVOICE-LINE.
*
     IF MORE-INVOICES
         PERFORM 1430-FETCH-NEXT-INVOICE
         IF MORE-INVOICES
             MOVE INVOICE-LINE TO CIM-D-INVOICE-LINE(INVOICE-SUB)
         ELSE
             MOVE SPACE TO CIM-D-INVOICE-LINE(INVOICE-SUB)
         END-IF
     ELSE
         MOVE SPACE TO CIM-D-INVOICE-LINE(INVOICE-SUB)
     END-IF.
*
1430-FETCH-NEXT-INVOICE.
*
     EXEC SQL
         FETCH CUSTINV
             INTO :INVNO, :INVPO, :INVDATE, :INVTOTAL
     END-EXEC.
*
     EVALUATE SQLCODE
         WHEN 0
             MOVE INVNO     TO IL-INVOICE-NUMBER
             MOVE INVPO     TO IL-PO-NUMBER
             MOVE INVDATE   TO IL-INVOICE-DATE
             MOVE INVTOTAL  TO IL-INVOICE-TOTAL
         WHEN 100
             MOVE 'N' TO MORE-INVOICES-SW
         WHEN OTHER
             PERFORM 9999-TERMINATE-PROGRAM
     END-EVALUATE.
*
1440-CLOSE-INVOICE-CURSOR.
*
     EXEC SQL
         CLOSE CUSTINV
     END-EXEC.
*
     IF SQLCODE NOT = 0
         PERFORM 9999-TERMINATE-PROGRAM
     END-IF.
*
```

Figure 17-7   The COBOL code for the CICS/DB2 inquiry program (part 5 of 6)

The CICS/DB2 inquiry program   **Page 6**

```
      1500-SEND-INQUIRY-MAP.
  *
      EVALUATE TRUE
          WHEN SEND-ERASE
              EXEC CICS
                  SEND MAP('DB2MAP1')
                       MAPSET('DB2SET1')
                       FROM(CUSTOMER-INQUIRY-MAP)
                       ERASE
              END-EXEC
          WHEN SEND-DATAONLY
              EXEC CICS
                  SEND MAP('DB2MAP1')
                       MAPSET('DB2SET1')
                       FROM(CUSTOMER-INQUIRY-MAP)
                       DATAONLY
              END-EXEC
          WHEN SEND-DATAONLY-ALARM
              EXEC CICS
                  SEND MAP('DB2MAP1')
                       MAPSET('DB2SET1')
                       FROM(CUSTOMER-INQUIRY-MAP)
                       DATAONLY
                       ALARM
              END-EXEC
      END-EVALUATE.
  *
   9999-TERMINATE-PROGRAM.
  *
      MOVE EIBRESP   TO ERR-RESP.
      MOVE EIBRESP2  TO ERR-RESP2.
      MOVE EIBTRNID  TO ERR-TRNID.
      MOVE EIBRSRCE  TO ERR-RSRCE.
  *
      EXEC CICS
          XCTL PROGRAM('SYSERR')
               COMMAREA(ERROR-PARAMETERS)
      END-EXEC.
```

Figure 17-7   The COBOL code for the CICS/DB2 inquiry program (part 6 of 6)

CICS/DB2 programming considerations

In the topics that follow, you'll learn about some additional considerations for developing CICS/DB2 programs. I recommend you use this information as a guide for developing all your CICS/DB2 programs. If you do, you can be sure that you're developing the most efficient programs possible.

Programming strategies for browsing DB2 data

As I mentioned earlier in this chapter, browsing DB2 data (that is, accessing DB2 rows sequentially) in a CICS program can cause programming complications. The problem stems from the fact that DB2 and CICS were designed with different objectives in mind. DB2 was designed to provide the most flexible retrieval of information, while CICS was designed to allow the most efficient execution of online transactions.

These design objectives come into conflict when you browse DB2 data under CICS. That's because when a pseudo-conversational CICS program ends, DB2 drops any result tables it was using. Then, when the program restarts, it must somehow recreate the result tables and reestablish the previous positions within them. Unfortunately, there's no easy way to do that. In fact, the conflict between the operating modes of CICS and DB2 is so severe that some shops prohibit CICS/DB2 browse programs altogether or strictly limit their use. If a result table contains a modest numbers of rows, however, browsing with a CICS program may be reasonable if you adopt an appropriate programming strategy.

Figure 17-8 lists three such strategies. The first is to code the program using the conversational method. This method requires so much overhead, though, it's rarely used. The second method is to recreate the result table each time the CICS program executes and to keep track of the table position between executions. Although this method provides the best initial performance for each inquiry, it doesn't provide good performance for subsequent scrolling requests. In contrast, if you use the third method, the query is done only once. Then, the results are saved in a DB2 work table or outside DB2 in a VSAM file or in CICS temporary storage. This results in a longer waiting time for the initial query as the program creates the result table and copies it to some other location. But it offers faster response for subsequent browsing because DB2 doesn't have to process the complete base table each time.

Additional CICS/DB2 programming considerations

Figure 17-8 also lists some additional programming considerations for developing CICS/DB2 programs. To start, regardless of the strategy you use to browse DB2 data, you can reduce the impact of DB2 browse operations by following two general guidelines. First, you should minimize the number of rows DB2 includes in the result tables it produces. That means that if you know

Programming strategies for CICS/DB2 browse programs

Strategy 1: Do a single query and browse in a conversational style

- Because a conversational program runs continuously, you don't have to recreate the result table or reestablish the correct position within it.

- This strategy is most appropriate when the DB2 costs for doing browse operations in a pseudo-conversational program are excessive and the application is critical. But because long browse operations implemented this way tie up resources in both the CICS and DB2 subsystems, this strategy is unusual.

Strategy 2: Do a separate query for each execution of the program

- To implement this strategy, the program needs to store values between executions to indicate the current table position. Then, the next time the program is executed, that data can be used to determine which rows to retrieve, format, and display.

- This strategy may be acceptable if the number of rows to be browsed is small. It is most efficient from the CICS perspective, but imposes a burden on DB2.

Strategy 3: Do a single query and save the results in a temporary area between pseudo-conversational executions

- One approach is to perform a DB2 mass insert at the beginning of the browse operation to create a DB2 work table that contains only the rows to be browsed. Then, each execution of the program can create a cursor-controlled result table from the work table instead of the base table. This improves program efficiency, but requires extra overhead in terms of disk space and processor time.

- Another approach is to create a cursor-controlled result table at the beginning of the browse operation, and write its contents to a VSAM file. Then, you can use CICS's browse commands to retrieve the data for the display. This approach is more efficient in terms of processor time, but may be unacceptable for performance reasons.

- A final approach is to write the contents of a cursor-controlled result table created at the beginning of the browse operation to CICS temporary storage. This is a simple and straightforward approach.

Other programming considerations

- To reduce the burden imposed by *any* DB2 browse operation, you should minimize the number of rows included in the result table and display as much data as you can on each screen.

- To make your programs small and quick, you should minimize the number of different SQL statements you use, code the simplest statements you can, and minimize the number of tables you process.

- You may be able to improve performance by grouping SQL statements close together and deferring them to near the end of the program's execution.

- CICS/DB2 programs should commit their work often to reduce the amount of data in a unit of work, make the data available to other programs sooner, and release threads.

Figure 17-8   CICS/DB2 programming considerations

the limiting key values for the rows you want to select, you should specify them in the WHERE clause of the DECLARE CURSOR statement. Second, you should display as much data on each screen as you can. If you do, you'll reduce the number of screen interactions required for a browse program.

It also makes sense to minimize the number of different SQL statements you use, to code the simplest statements you can, and to minimize the number of different tables you process in any CICS/DB2 program. That keeps the program small and makes execution as quick as possible, a necessity for online transaction-processing programs.

You may also be able to improve the performance of a CICS/DB2 program by grouping SQL statements as closely as you can and deferring them to near the end of the execution of a program. That can reduce the amount of time a program controls a thread, since the CICS/DB2 attachment facility doesn't create a thread for a transaction until the program makes its first DB2 request.

Just as with programs that process DB2 data in batch or under TSO, CICS/DB2 programs should commit their work often. That reduces the amount of data DB2 has to maintain during a unit of work, and it makes the data available to other programs sooner. In addition, under CICS, committing a unit of work causes threads to be released and made available to other users. You'll learn more about units of work and how to commit them in chapter 18.

Perspective

DB2 programming is a complicated subject. Because of that, this chapter didn't attempt to teach you how to code DB2 programs. Instead, it focused on the implications of accessing DB2 data from CICS programs. Now, if you already know how to write DB2 programs, you should be able to apply those skills in a CICS environment. On the other hand, if this is your first exposure to DB2, you'll need some additional training before you can develop CICS/DB2 programs. To get that training, we recommend our book, *DB2 for the COBOL Programmer, Part 1*.

Terms

DB2 (Database 2)	database request module (DBRM)
Structured Query Language (SQL)	bind
CICS/DB2 attachment facility	application plan
thread	package
Resource Control Table (RCT)	collection
DB2 precompiler	

Section 6

Advanced CICS features and skills

The chapters in this section present a variety of CICS features you might need to use on occasion. In chapter 18, you'll learn about some of the CICS control features that aren't presented elsewhere in this book. In chapter 19, you'll learn how to use the CICS intercommunication features that let two or more CICS systems work together. In chapter 20, you'll learn about a new trend for designing CICS programs. And in chapter 21, you'll learn about using CICS to implement Web applications. Because Web applications require the use of the intercommunication features presented in chapter 19 and the design techniques presented in chapter 20, you'll want to be sure to read these chapters before you read chapter 21. Finally, in chapter 22, you'll learn about some of the CICS features that you won't use as you develop new programs but that you might see as you maintain existing programs.

18

How to use other CICS control features

So far in this book, you've learned how to use the services provided by CICS for program control, terminal control, file control, and temporary storage control. Now, in this chapter, you'll learn about some of the services related to the other CICS control facilities. As you read this chapter, keep in mind that you won't need to use these services in most of the CICS programs you write. In fact, your shop may have strict standards regarding the use of most of them. But it's good to know about them so you can use them in accordance with your shop standards if you ever need to.

How to use interval control

CICS *interval control* provides a variety of time-related features. You learned about the ASKTIME and FORMATTIME commands in chapter 8. Now, you'll learn about the interval control commands that let you perform functions related to tasks. But first, you'll learn about the CICS facility that lets you start and schedule tasks: automatic time-ordered transaction initiation.

How automatic time-ordered transaction initiation works

Automatic time-ordered transaction initiation, or *time-ordered ATI*, is a CICS facility lets you start a new task by issuing a START command from a program. To use time-ordered ATI, you need to understand the difference between starting a task and using the program control commands (LINK or XCTL) to invoke a program.

As a multitasking system, CICS can process more than one task at a time. As a result, a task initiated by a START command can execute simultaneously with the task that issued the START command. In other words, the *starting task* can run at the same time as the *started task*. In contrast, programs invoked by LINK and XCTL commands run one at a time as part of a single task.

To illustrate, consider how you might use program control and interval control commands in a menu-driven application that includes a data entry program that requires user interaction and a report preparation program that doesn't. When a user selects the data entry program, the menu program should issue an XCTL command to transfer control directly to that program. If the user selects the report preparation program, though, the menu program should issue a START command to start the program as a separate task. Then, control returns to the menu program, and the user can continue other work while the report is being prepared.

Figure 18-1 shows how interval control schedules a task and how a scheduled task is started. The most important thing to notice here is that when a START command is issued, interval control creates a special data area called an *interval control element*, or *ICE*, that contains information about the task to be started. Then, a CICS program called *interval control expiration analysis* uses that information to determine when the task is started. In the next topic, you'll see how you can code the START command to specify when a task should start. In any case, keep in mind that once a task issues a START command, it continues execution without regard for the status of the started task. In other words, the started task is independent of the starting task.

Also notice that the starting task can pass data to the started task. If it does, interval control invokes temporary storage control to store the data in a temporary storage file named DFHTEMP. Then, when the task is started, it can retrieve the data from this file.

How a task is scheduled

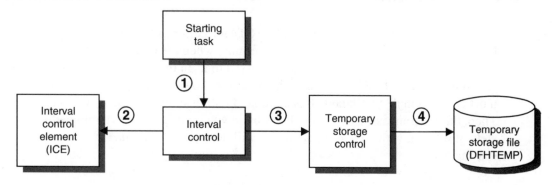

1. A user task issues a START command that's processed by interval control.

2. Interval control creates an ICE that indicates the trans-id, expiration time, and terminal-id for the task to be started.

3. If data is passed to the started task, interval control invokes temporary storage control to save that data.

4. Temporary storage control saves the data in the temporary storage file.

How a scheduled task is started

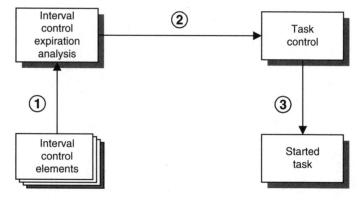

1. Interval control expiration analysis compares the current time of day with the expiration time of each ICE.

2. For each expired ICE, expiration analysis invokes task control.

3. Task control starts a task.

Description

*   *Automatic time-ordered transaction initiation*, or *time-ordered ATI*, lets you start a new task from another task by issuing a START command.

*   The *interval control element*, or *ICE*, is a special data area that's used to store information about the task to be started.

*   *Interval control expiration analysis* is a CICS program that periodically examines all interval control elements to determine when they've expired.

Figure 18-1   How automatic time-ordered transaction initiation works

How to code the START command

Figure 18-2 presents the format of the START command. As you can see, it has a variety of options you can use to determine when the task is started, where it will run, and what information will be passed to it. In the next topic, you'll see some sample START commands that illustrate how to use these options. In most cases, though, you'll code this command with just the TRANSID option. Then, the program associated with the trans-id you specify will be run immediately, it will run without a terminal, and it will not receive any data from the starting task.

The syntax of the START command

```
EXEC CICS
     START     TRANSID(trans-id)
               ⎡⎡INTERVAL(hhmmss)                                      ⎤⎤
               ⎢⎢TIME(hhmmss)                                          ⎥⎥
               ⎢⎨AFTER [HOURS(hh)] [MINUTES(mins)] [SECONDS(secs)]     ⎬⎥
               ⎢⎣AT    [HOURS(hh)] [MINUTES(mins)] [SECONDS(secs)]     ⎦⎥
               ⎢ [TERMID(term-id)]                                     ⎥
               ⎢ [FROM(data-name)]                                     ⎥
               ⎢ [RTERMID(term-id)]                                    ⎥
               ⎢ [RTRANSID(trans-id)]                                  ⎥
               ⎢ [QUEUE(queue-name)]                                   ⎥
               ⎣ [REQID(request-id)]                                   ⎦
     END-EXEC
```

Option	Description
TRANSID	Specifies the transaction-identifier that will be used to start the task.
INTERVAL	Specifies an interval that CICS will add to the current time to determine when the task should start. If a data name is specified, it must name a four-byte signed packed-decimal field.
TIME	Specifies the time when the task should start. If the time is more than 18 hours after the current time, it's considered to have expired already. If a data name is specified, it must name a four-byte signed packed-decimal field.
AFTER	Indicates that the task should start after the interval specified in the HOURS, MINUTES, and SECONDS options.
AT	Indicates that the task should start at the time specified in the HOURS, MINUTES, and SECONDS options.
HOURS	Must be a number between 0 and 99. If a data name is specified, it must name a binary fullword.
MINUTES	If HOURS or SECONDS is also coded, must be a number between 0 and 59. Other-wise, can be a number between 0 and 5999 (one minute less than 100 hours). If a data name is specified, it must name a binary fullword.
SECONDS	If HOURS or MINUTES is also coded, must be a number between 0 and 59. Other-wise, can be a number between 0 and 359,999 (one second less than 100 hours). If a data name is specified, it must name a binary fullword.
TERMID	Specifies the name of a terminal where the task will run. If omitted, the task will run without a terminal.
FROM	Specifies the name of a field whose value is passed to the started task.
RTERMID	Specifies a four-byte terminal-id that's passed to the started task.
RTRANSID	Specifies a four-byte trans-id that's passed to the started task.
QUEUE	Specifies an eight-byte temporary storage queue name that's passed to the started task.
REQID	Specifies an eight-byte value that identifies the START command so the started task can be canceled with a CANCEL command. If omitted, CICS generates a request-id and returns it in EIBREQID.

Description

- The START command starts a task at a scheduled time and, optionally, passes data to the started task.

Figure 18-2   How to code the START command

Typical START commands

Figure 18-3 presents some typical START commands that use a variety of options. The first example shows the START command I described in the previous topic. Because it doesn't include any of the options for scheduling the task, the task will run immediately.

If a task requires terminal I/O, you'll need to include the TERMID option on the START command as shown in the second example. In this case, the terminal is a printer named L86P. Although a started task can also send I/O to a terminal screen, that's unlikely.

The next four examples show different ways to schedule a task for execution at a later time. To do that, they specify an *expiration time* that determines when the task should begin executing. In example 3, the TIME option is used to specify the expiration time in hours, minutes, and seconds. In this case, the task will expire at 5:00 p.m. (hour 17 on a 24-hour clock). Note that you can't use the TIME option to specify an expiration time that's more than 18 hours from the current time. If you do, interval control assumes that the time you specify has already expired, and the task is started immediately.

Example 4 shows how to use the INTERVAL option to specify an expiration time. When you use this option, the hours, minutes, and seconds you specify are added to the current time to determine the expiration time. In this example, the task will be started 15 minutes from the current time.

Examples 5 and 6 show you how to use the AT and AFTER options to specify an expiration time. These options work like the TIME and INTERVAL options, but the hours, minutes, and seconds are stored as binary fullwords rather that packed-decimal fields. Example 5 sets the expiration time to 10:45 a.m., and example 6 sets the expiration time to a minute-and-a-half after the current time.

To pass data to the started task, you include the FROM option as shown in example 7. In this case, the value of the field named ITEM-NUMBER will be passed to the task. You can also pass specific types of data to the started task using the RTRANSID, RTERMID, and QUEUE options. In the next topic, you'll see how to retrieve the data that's passed to the started task.

The last option you can code on a START command is REQID. You can use the value you specify on this option to identify the START request. Then, if you need to, you can use this value on a CANCEL command to cancel the task. Because you'll use the REQID option only if the program needs to provide for canceling a started task, I'll show you a START command with this option in the topic that presents the CANCEL command.

1: A command that schedules a task for immediate execution

```
EXEC CICS
    START TRANSID('LST1')
END-EXEC.
```

2: A command that attaches the task to a terminal

```
EXEC CICS
    START TRANSID('LST1')
          TERMID('L86P')
END-EXEC.
```

3: A command that uses the TIME option to specify an expiration time

```
EXEC CICS
    START TRANSID('LST1')
          TIME('170000')
END-EXEC.
```

4: A command that uses the INTERVAL option to specify an expiration time

```
EXEC CICS
    START TRANSID('LST1')
          INTERVAL(001500)
END-EXEC.
```

5: A command that uses the AT option to specify an expiration time

```
EXEC CICS
    START TRANSID('LST1')
          AT HOURS(10) MINUTES(45)
END-EXEC.
```

6: A command that uses the AFTER option to specify an expiration time

```
EXEC CICS
    START TRANSID('LST1')
          AFTER MINUTES(1) SECONDS(30)
END-EXEC.
```

7: A command that passes data to the started task

```
EXEC CICS
    START TRANSID('LST1')
          FROM(ITEM-NUMBER)
END-EXEC.
```

Description

- You should include the TERMID option whenever the started task does terminal I/O. In most cases, this option will specify a printer.
- The hours that you specify on the TIME and AT options are based on a 24-hour clock.
- The AT and AFTER options were added for compatibility with the C language, which doesn't support the packed-decimal data type required by the TIME and INTERVAL options.
- Data that's passed to the started task is stored in a record in temporary storage. Then, the started task can use a RETRIEVE command to retrieve the data in that record.

Figure 18-3   Typical START commands

How to code the RETRIEVE command

To retrieve data passed to it by the starting task, the started task must issue a RETRIEVE command as illustrated in figure 18-4. Then, interval control invokes temporary storage control, which retrieves the correct record from the temporary storage file and returns it to the started task. That record is then placed in the field that's named on the INTO option. Note that the RETRIEVE command doesn't have to identify the temporary storage queue that contains the record. Interval control takes care of that.

The example in this figure shows a RETRIEVE command that retrieves the data passed to the program by the last START command in figure 18-3. In this case, the retrieved data is placed in a field named ITEM-NUMBER. (Although the name of this field is the same as the field named in the START command, it doesn't have to be.) Because CICS will raise the NOTFND condition if a RETRIEVE command is issued and no data was sent to the started task, the RESP option is also included. Of course, if the START command includes the RTRANSID, RTERMID, or QUEUE options, the RETRIEVE command should include them as well.

In most cases, you won't pass data to a started task. Even if you do, you'll usually pass just a single record. If you need to pass two or more records to a started task, though, you can do that by executing the START command once for each record. Then, if the same expiration time and terminal-id are specified on each command, all of the START requests will be fulfilled by a single execution of the task. Once the task is started, it can retrieve the records passed by the START commands by issuing RETRIEVE commands repeatedly. Each command will retrieve one record until there's no more data to be retrieved. CICS indicates that no more records are available by raising the ENDDATA condition. So you'll want to be sure to check for this condition after the RETRIEVE command executes if you use this technique.

The syntax of the RETRIEVE command

```
EXEC CICS
    RETRIEVE  INTO(data-name)
              [RTRANSID(data-name)]
              [RTERMID(data-name)]
              [QUEUE(data-name)]
END-EXEC
```

Option	Description
INTO	Specifies the name of the field where the data sent via the FROM option of the START command will be placed.
RTRANSID	Specifies the name of a four-byte field where the data sent via the RTRANSID option of the START command will be placed.
RTERMID	Specifies the name of a four-byte field where the data sent via the RTERMID option of the START command will be placed.
QUEUE	Specifies the name of an eight-byte field where the data sent via the QUEUE option of the START command will be placed.

A RETRIEVE command that retrieves data from the starting task

```
EXEC CICS
    RETRIEVE  INTO(ITEM-NUMBER)
              RESP(RESPONSE-CODE)
END-EXEC.
```

Description

- The RETRIEVE command is coded in a program that was started by another task to retrieve data sent to it by that task. That data is retrieved from temporary storage, where it was placed by the START command.

- Interval control keeps track of where the data to be passed to various tasks is stored and insures that it's coordinated with the current interval control elements. As a result, a started task doesn't have to identify the temporary storage queue that contains the data it's retrieving.

- If a program issues a RETRIEVE command and no data was passed to it, the NOTFND condition is raised.

- If two or more START commands that pass data to the started task are issued for the same task with the same expiration time and the task is attached to a terminal, a single execution of the task can fulfill all the pending START requests. To do that, the started task issues a RETRIEVE command repeatedly until the ENDDATA condition is raised.

Figure 18-4   How to code the RETRIEVE command

How to code the CANCEL command

Occasionally, you may need to cancel a task that you scheduled using a START command. To do that, you use the CANCEL command shown in figure 18-5. Note that you can use this command only for a task that is still waiting to be executed. You can't cancel a task that has already started.

The only option you need to code on this command, REQID, identifies the START request you want to cancel. If you coded the REQID option on the START command, you'll code the same value on the CANCEL command. This is illustrated in the first example in this figure.

If you don't code the REQID option on the START command, you can use the value in the EIBREQID field to identify the command to be canceled. This is illustrated in the second example in this figure. Notice that the value in the EIBREQID field is saved in another field immediately following the START command. That way, if the program issues another CICS command that updates the EIBREQID field before it issues the CANCEL command, this value won't be lost.

Quite frankly, it's uncommon to cancel a task once you've scheduled it. In most cases, you'll schedule a task for immediate execution, so it can't be canceled. Even if the task is scheduled for future execution, though, the only reason you might cancel it is if a serious error condition occurs in the starting task. But even then, you're not likely to need to cancel it since its operation is independent of the starting task.

The syntax of the CANCEL command

```
EXEC CICS
    CANCEL REQID(request-id)
END-EXEC
```

Option	Description
REQID	Specifies an eight-byte value that identifies the START command to be canceled.

How to cancel a task with a program-assigned request-id

The START command

```
EXEC CICS
    START TRANSID('LST1')
          INTERVAL(010000)
          REQID('TRANDEP1')
END-EXEC.
```

The CANCEL command

```
EXEC CICS
    CANCEL REQID('TRANDEP1')
END-EXEC.
```

How to cancel a task with a CICS-assigned request-id

The START command

```
EXEC CICS
    START TRANSID('LST1')
          INTERVAL(010000)
END-EXEC.
MOVE EIBREQID TO REQUEST-ID.
```

The CANCEL command

```
EXEC CICS
    CANCEL REQID(REQUEST-ID)
END-EXEC.
```

Description

- The CANCEL command cancels a task you scheduled with the START command. It removes the interval control element created by the START command, along with any data to be passed to the started task.
- You can't issue the CANCEL command to cancel a task after it has started.
- If a request-id isn't specified on the START command, you can use the value in the EIBREQID field in the Execute Interface Block to identify the task. You must move this value to a working-storage field after you issue the START command and before you issue another command since other commands update the EIBREQID field.
- In most cases, you'll issue the CANCEL command from the same task that issued the START command, but that's not required.

Figure 18-5   How to code the CANCEL command

How to use task control

Task control refers to the CICS functions that manage the execution of tasks. One of the major components of task control is the *dispatcher*, which keeps track of all current tasks and decides which of several waiting tasks should be given control of the processor. Although task dispatching is mostly an automatic function, task control provides two facilities an application program can use to influence the dispatcher's operation: (1) the SUSPEND command and (2) the ENQ and DEQ commands.

How to code the SUSPEND command

Normally, an application program gives up control whenever it issues a CICS command. For example, when your program issues a READ command, it gives up control while CICS fulfills the read request. In the meantime, the dispatcher gives control to another task. In this way, many tasks can be operating at once. Only one of them is actually executing, though; the rest are either waiting for an I/O operation to complete, or just waiting for their turn to execute.

It's important to note that whenever a program gains control, it continues to execute until it issues a CICS command. For most applications, that's not a long time. If an application requires a long stretch of CPU processing without an intervening CICS command, though, it can cause two problems. First, it can degrade the performance of other tasks in the system because it monopolizes CPU time. And second, it might exceed the CICS limit for how long a task can run without returning control to CICS.

To avoid both of these problems, you use the SUSPEND command shown in figure 18-6. Its only function is to temporarily return control to CICS so another program can gain control. Because this command has no options, you always code it just as shown.

How to code the ENQ and DEQ commands

The ENQ and DEQ commands, also shown in figure 18-6, provide a general queuing facility that's similar to the UPDATE option of the READ command. They let you ensure that two or more tasks don't access a non-sharable *resource* (like a printer terminal) at the same time. That's called *single-threading* because only one task at a time can access the resource. Any other tasks that try to access that resource must wait their turn.

You use the ENQ command to single-thread a resource, or *enqueue* it. Once you enqueue a resource, any other tasks that try to enqueue the same resource are suspended until you issue a DEQ command to release, or *dequeue*, the resource.

The syntax of the SUSPEND command

```
EXEC CICS
    SUSPEND
END-EXEC
```

The syntax of the ENQ and DEQ commands

```
EXEC CICS
    {ENQ | DEQ}  RESOURCE(data-name)
END-EXEC
```

Option	Description
RESOURCE	Specifies the name of the field that contains the name of the resource to be enqueued or dequeued. The field can be from 1 to 255 bytes in length.

A typical ENQ command

```
EXEC CICS
    ENQ RESOURCE(DESTINATION-ID)
END-EXEC.
```

A typical DEQ command

```
EXEC CICS
    DEQ RESOURCE(DESTINATION-ID)
END-EXEC.
```

Description

- The SUSPEND command temporarily suspends the execution of a task and returns control to CICS so other tasks can execute. When a task is suspended, it's placed at the end of the list of tasks waiting to gain control and the task at the head of the list takes over.

- The ENQ and DEQ commands ensure that two or more tasks don't access a non-sharable *resource* at the same time. In most cases, a resource is a printer terminal, a temporary storage queue, or an area of main storage, such as a table.

- The ENQ command enqueues a resource so that other tasks can't access it. When you're done with the resource, you issue the DEQ command to release it.

- CICS doesn't provide a mechanism for relating resource names to actual CICS facilities. Because of that, every program that enqueues a resource must use the same name for it, and every program that processes the resource must enqueue it. So be sure to follow your shop's naming conventions and standards for coding the task control commands.

Figure 18-6   How to code the task control commands

How to use storage control

In most cases, you acquire the main storage a program requires by defining fields in the Working-Storage Section. You can also access areas of storage owned by CICS using the Linkage Section as described in chapter 8. To access other areas of storage, though, you have to use the *storage control* facilities provided by the GETMAIN and FREEMAIN commands. Although you'll rarely, if ever, need these commands, you should know about them in case you do.

How to code the GETMAIN command

The format of the GETMAIN command is shown in figure 18-7. You use this command to allocate the amount of main storage specified on the FLENGTH option. Then, the SET option establishes addressability to that area by assigning its address to a field defined in the Linkage Section of the program. The command shown in this figure, for example, allocates 2048 bytes of storage and assigns the address of that storage to a field named PRODUCT-RECORD.

The command shown in this figure also includes the INITIMG option. You use this option to initialize the acquired area of storage. In this case, it's initialized to Low-Value.

By default, the storage amount you specify on the FLENGTH option is allocated from above the 16MB line, which is usually what you want. If you need to, though, you can allocate storage from below the 16MB line by including the BELOW option. You'll need to do that if the program will run in 24-bit mode, which isn't likely.

The syntax of the GETMAIN command

```
EXEC CICS
    GETMAIN  SET(pointer)
             FLENGTH(data-name | literal) [BELOW]
             [INITIMG(data-name)]
END-EXEC
```

Option	Description
SET	Establishes addressability to the acquired storage area by assigning the address of that area to the Linkage Section field you name.
FLENGTH	Specifies the number of bytes of main storage to acquire using a binary fullword.
BELOW	Specifies that storage is to be acquired from below the 16MB line.
INITIMG	Specifies the name of a one-byte field that's used to initialize the storage acquired. If omitted, the storage is not initialized.

Code that uses the GETMAIN command

```
WORKING-STORAGE SECTION.
    .
    .
    05  INITIAL-VALUE    PIC X    VALUE LOW-VALUE.
    .
    .
LINKAGE SECTION.
    .
    .
01  PRODUCT-RECORD.
    .
    .
PROCEDURE DIVISION.
    .
    .
    EXEC CICS
        GETMAIN SET(ADDRESS OF PRODUCT-RECORD)
                FLENGTH(2048)
                INITIMG(INITIAL-VALUE)
    END-EXEC.
    .
    .
```

Description

- The GETMAIN command allocates a specified amount of main storage and returns the address of that storage. If you specify the INITIMG option, it also initializes the storage to the value of the field you specify.

- By default, the amount of storage you specify on the FLENGTH option is allocated from above the 16MB line. To allocate storage from below the 16MB line, you must include the BELOW option.

- CICS always allocates space from main storage on doubleword boundaries. If you request less than a doubleword or less than a multiple of a doubleword, CICS rounds the length up to the nearest doubleword multiple.

Figure 18-7   How to code the GETMAIN command

How to code the FREEMAIN command

Normally, any storage acquired for your task—whether by a GETMAIN command or any other means—is released automatically when your task ends. Even so, I recommend you release storage you acquire with the GETMAIN command as soon as your program is done with it. To do that, you use the FREEMAIN command shown in figure 18-8.

To identify the area of storage to be released, you can code either the DATA or DATAPOINTER option. The two examples in this figure illustrate the difference between these two options. As you can see, if you use the DATA option, you just name the field in the Linkage Section that's used to access the area of storage. But if you use the DATAPOINTER option, you specify the actual address of the storage area using the ADDRESS special register.

The syntax of the FREEMAIN command

```
EXEC CICS
    FREEMAIN { DATA(data-name)
             { DATAPOINTER(pointer) }
END-EXEC
```

Option	Description
DATA	Specifies the name of the Linkage Section field for the storage to be released.
DATAPOINTER	Specifies the address of the storage to be released.

A FREEMAIN command that uses the DATA option

```
EXEC CICS
    FREEMAIN DATA(PRODUCT-RECORD)
END-EXEC.
```

A FREEMAIN command that uses the DATAPOINTER option

```
EXEC CICS
    FREEMAIN DATAPOINTER(ADDRESS OF PRODUCT-RECORD)
END-EXEC.
```

Description

* The FREEMAIN command releases an area of storage that was acquired by the GETMAIN command. You can refer to that area of storage using the name of the Linkage Section field used to access that area or the address of the storage area.
* If you don't issue the FREEMAIN command, the storage is released when the task ends. For efficiency, though, you should always code the FREEMAIN command.

Figure 18-8   How to code the FREEMAIN command

How to use recovery processing

When a task or CICS itself abends, the files and other resources that were in the process of being updated can be left in an inconsistent state. When that happens, the best thing to do is to reverse all of the changes made by the transaction so it can be run again. That's the purpose of the CICS recovery facility that you'll learn about in the topics that follow.

How updates are logged

For CICS to reverse the changes made by a task when the task or CICS abends, it must keep track of those changes. To do that, it logs the changes to two separate logs: the system log and the dynamic log. The *system log* keeps track of changes made throughout the CICS system, while the *dynamic log* keeps track of changes for just a single task. As you might guess, each CICS task has its own dynamic log.

Figure 18-9 illustrates how logging works for a program that updates files. In this case, each time the program invokes file control to update a file, file control invokes *journal control* to log the change to the system and dynamic logs. Similar processing is done for other types of resources, such as temporary storage queues. Keep in mind, though, that CICS only logs changes made to *protected resources*, which are resources whose definitions provide for automatic recovery.

The recovery information that's stored in both the system log and the dynamic log consists of *before-images* of each protected resource that's added, changed, or deleted. In other words, journal control stores an exact image of each record as it existed before each update occurred. If an abend occurs, the CICS recovery facility can then restore the resource to its previous condition. This type of recovery is called *backward recovery*.

An optional CICS product called *CICS VSAM Recovery* (or *CICSVR*) can be used to implement *forward recovery*. With forward recovery, CICS keeps *after-images* of records in VSAM files that are updated. Then, if the file becomes so damaged that backward recovery isn't possible, CICSVR can apply the after-images to a recent backup copy of the file.

How file updates are logged

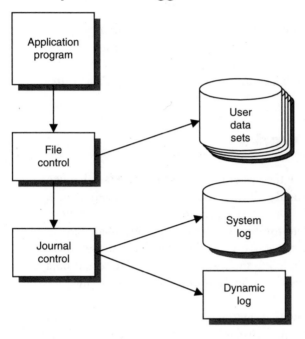

Description

- As a task executes, any changes it makes to protected resources are logged so the changes can be reversed if the task or CICS abends. A *protected resource* is a resource whose definition provides for automatic recovery.

- Each time an application program invokes file control to update a protected file, file control invokes *journal control* to log the change. Logging for other protected resources is similar.

- CICS records recovery information in both the system log and the dynamic log. The *system log* maintains recovery data for an entire system on either disk or tape. The *dynamic log* maintains recovery data for a single task in main storage.

- If a task ends abnormally, the data in the dynamic log is used to restore protected resources. If a task ends normally, its dynamic log is deleted.

- CICS uses *backward recovery* to restore a resource to its previous condition if an abend occurs. To do that, it maintains a *before-image* of each record in a protected resource that's added, changed, or deleted.

Figure 18-9   How updates are logged to the system log and the dynamic log

How dynamic transaction backout works

Figure 18-10 illustrates what happens when a transaction terminates abnormally. In that case, the *dynamic backout program* processes the before-images in the dynamic log to reverse the changes recorded in that log. When this process, called *dynamic transaction backout*, or *DTB*, is complete, it's as if the transaction was never started.

How emergency restart works

Figure 18-10 also illustrates how the system log is used to reverse changes when CICS itself terminates abnormally. In this case, CICS is restarted using a procedure called *emergency restart*. During this procedure, *recovery control* reads the system log backwards, determining which updates were made by *in-flight tasks*—that is, tasks that were active when the uncontrolled shutdown occurred. These updates are then copied to the *restart data set*. The restart data set, in turn, is processed by the *transaction backout program* to restore the protected resources.

Before I go on, you should know that, by default, the CICS recovery facility treats all of the changes made by a single execution of a task as a *logical unit of work*, or *LUW*. That means that when the transaction or the CICS system abends, the backout programs reverse all of the updates made by the transaction as a unit. In some cases, though, that's not necessary.

For example, consider a non-interactive program that reads invoice records stored in a sequential file and updates corresponding records in other files. If the program abends after processing 100 invoice records, DTB reverses the updates for all 100 records, even though that's probably not necessary: Just the updates for the invoice that was being processed when the abend occurred need to be reversed. In that case, you can use the SYNCPOINT command to limit the scope of an LUW.

How dynamic transaction backout works

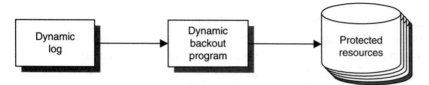

How emergency restart works

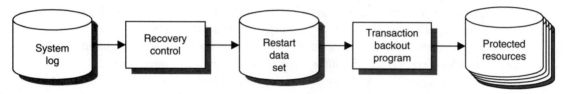

Description

- When a transaction terminates abnormally, CICS invokes the *dynamic backout program* to perform *dynamic transaction backout* (or *DTB*). DTB uses the before-images in the dynamic log to reverse any changes the transaction made to protected resources.

- When CICS terminates abnormally, a procedure called *emergency restart* must be used to restart CICS. During emergency restart, recovery control uses the system log to determine which tasks, called *in-flight tasks*, were active when CICS terminated.

- Each update that was made by an in-flight task is copied to the *restart data set*, which is then processed by the *transaction backout program*. This program works like the dynamic backout program, except that it can reverse changes made by many tasks.

- A collection of updating activity that's treated as a single unit during dynamic transaction backout or emergency restart is called a *logical unit of work*, or *LUW*. Normally, an LUW corresponds to a single task execution. To limit the scope of an LUW, you can use the SYNCPOINT command.

Figure 18-10   How dynamic transaction backout and emergency restart work

How to code the SYNCPOINT command

Figure 18-11 shows the format of the SYNCPOINT command. This command tells CICS that all of the updates made to protected resources so far are final and shouldn't be backed out even if an abend occurs. In other words, the SYNCPOINT command ends the current logical unit of work and begins a new one. Note that the conclusion of an LUW is called a *syncpoint*. That's true whether it's caused by the end of the task or by an explicit SYNCPOINT command.

This figure also shows a typical use of the SYNCPOINT command. This code is from a program that reads a file of invoice transaction records and updates related records in a customer file, an accounts receivable file, and an inventory file. Here, procedure 0000 invokes procedure 1000 once for each record in the invoice file. After invoking procedure 1100 to read the invoice record, procedure 1000 invokes procedure 1200 to update the master files. Then, it issues a SYNCPOINT command to finalize all of the updates related to a single invoice. In this case, the updates related to each invoice are treated as a single logical unit of work.

If an error occurs during the processing of a logical unit of work, you can use the ROLLBACK option of the SYNCPOINT command to reverse any changes that were already made during the LUW. If, for example, an error occurs while procedure 1400 in this figure is updating the accounts receivable file, you can use the SYNCPOINT command with the ROLLBACK option to reverse the changes that were already made to the customer file. As you might guess, the SYNCPOINT ROLLBACK command is often used in an abend exit.

The syntax of the SYNCPOINT command

```
EXEC CICS
    SYNCPOINT [ROLLBACK]
END-EXEC
```

Option	Description
ROLLBACK	Indicates that updates logged since the last SYNCPOINT command (or the beginning of the task) should be reversed.

A typical use of the SYNCPOINT command

```
*
 0000-POST-INVOICE-TRANSACTIONS.
*
     .
     .
     PERFORM 1000-POST-INVOICE-TRANSACTION
         UNTIL INVOICE-EOF.
     .
     .
*
 1000-POST-INVOICE-TRANSACTION.
*
     PERFORM 1100-READ-INVOICE-TRANSACTION.
     IF NOT INVOICE-EOF
         PERFORM 1200-UPDATE-MASTER-FILES
         EXEC CICS
             SYNCPOINT
         END-EXEC.
     .
     .
*
 1200-UPDATE-MASTER-FILES
*
     .
     .
     PERFORM 1300-UPDATE-CUSTOMER-FILE.
     .
     .
     PERFORM 1400-UPDATE-AR-FILE.
     .
     .
     PERFORM 1500-UPDATE-INVENTORY-FILE.
     .
     .
```

Description

- The SYNCPOINT command ends a logical unit of work and causes a *syncpoint* to occur. A syncpoint finalizes the updates to protected resources so they aren't backed out if an abend occurs.
- If you omit the SYNCPOINT command, a syncpoint occurs when the task ends.
- You can use the ROLLBACK option of the SYNCPOINT command to reverse any changes made to that point in a logical unit of work.

Figure 18-11 How to code the SYNCPOINT command

Perspective

In chapter 1 of this book, you learned about the management services CICS makes available to application programs. If you review the list shown in figure 1-10, you'll see that you've now learned about most of those features. Because you're not likely to use the other control features, I won't present them in this book. If you'd like to learn more about the commands that are provided by these features, though, I recommend our CICS desk reference book. It includes the complete syntax and description of all the CICS commands.

Terms

interval control	journal control
automatic time-ordered transaction initiation	protected resource
	before-image
time-ordered ATI	backward recovery
starting task	CICS VSAM Recovery (CICSVR)
started task	
interval control element (ICE)	forward recovery
interval control expiration analysis	after-image
	dynamic backout program
expiration time	dynamic transaction backout (DTB)
task control	
dispatcher	emergency restart
resource	recovery control
single-threading	in-flight task
enqueue	restart data set
dequeue	transaction backout program
storage control	logical unit of work (LUW)
system log	syncpoint
dynamic log	

19

How to use CICS intercommunication features

CICS provides a variety of *intercommunication* features that let two or more systems work together. That means a program running on one system can access resources owned by CICS on another system, provided the two systems are properly connected. This chapter presents an overview of the concepts and terms you need to know to use the CICS intercommunication features. It also explains the programming considerations for some of the most popular features.

Intercommunication concepts

CICS provides two basic mechanisms to support intercommunication: Multi-Region Operation and Intersystem Communication. *Multi-Region Operation*, or *MRO*, lets two or more CICS systems within the same host processor communicate with each other. In contrast, *Intersystem Communication*, or *ISC*, is designed to let systems on separate processors communicate with each other. Note that with ISC, only the system that receives the request for CICS resources needs to be a CICS system. The system that issues the request can be a non-CICS system.

How Multi-Region Operation works

The systems programmer who sets up MRO can specify one of two mechanisms for transmitting data between MRO systems. The first uses a special *InterRegion Communication* (*IRC*) access method that's unique to CICS. It depends on supervisor calls that let the InterRegion Communication modules operate in supervisor state while they exchange data between CICS regions (the supervisor is the part of a control program that coordinates resources and processor operations). The second mechanism uses *Cross-Memory Services* to exchange data directly between address spaces without the overhead of a supervisor call.

Figure 19-1 shows a typical use of MRO in a production CICS environment. Here, three CICS systems are running on a single host processor. All of the terminals are owned by a CICS system called the *Terminal Owning Region*, or *TOR*. All of the application programs are owned by the *Application Owning Region*, or *AOR*. And all of the files are owned by the *File Owning Region*, or *FOR*. This common MRO configuration is completely transparent to the application programs. In other words, an application program running in the AOR is unaware that it's accessing a terminal that's owned by the TOR and files that are owned by the FOR.

At this point, you may be wondering why you'd want terminals, applications, and files to be owned by separate CICS systems. The answer is simple: If one of the systems goes down, it doesn't affect the other systems. So, for example, if the AOR goes down, any files that may have been open in the FOR are unaffected.

A system that uses Multi-Region Operation

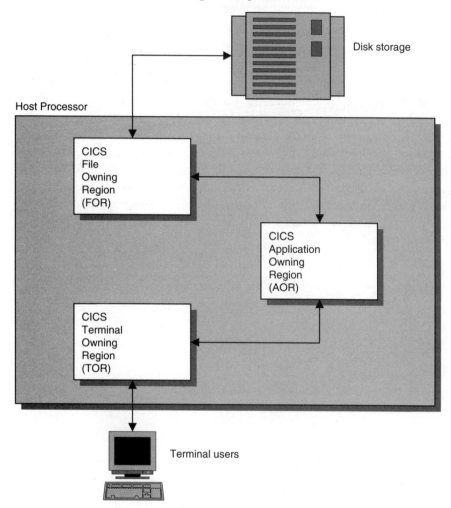

Description

- You use *MRO* (*Multi-Region Operation*) to connect CICS systems running on the same processor. Each system runs independently in its own address space. That way, if one system goes down, the others aren't affected.

- A typical MRO configuration includes a *Terminal Owning Region* (*TOR*) that owns all the terminals, an *Application Owning Region* (*AOR*) that owns all the applications, and a *File Owning Region* (*FOR*) that owns all the files.

- MRO can use a special *InterRegion Communication* (*IRC*) access method or *Cross-Memory Services* to transmit data between systems. Cross-Memory Services exchange data directly between systems. With InterRegion Communication access method, supervisor calls are used to exchange data.

Figure 19-1   How Multi-Region Operation works

How Intersystem Communication works

In the past, Intersystem Communication was used strictly for connecting two CICS systems. This type of connection is illustrated in figure 19-2. Here, a CICS system running on a local mainframe processor is communicating with a CICS system running on a remote mainframe processor. To do that, the systems use *SNA* (*Systems Network Architecture*) and the *APPC* (*Advanced Program-to-Program Communication*) protocols provided by VTAM.

Notice that the two systems in this example are using different versions of CICS. In addition, they're running under two different operating systems. As the list in this figure indicates, ISC can be used to connect a variety of CICS systems. It can also be used to connect a CICS system with a non-CICS system, such as Windows NT or Windows 2000. For this to work, the appropriate CICS software must be installed on the non-CICS system. You'll learn more about that later in this chapter.

Two mainframe systems that use Intersystem Communication

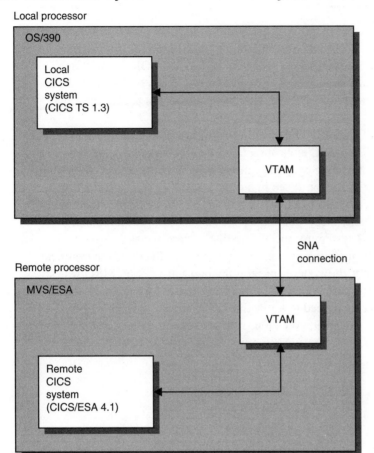

CICS systems that can communicate using ISC

CICS Transaction Server versions 1.1, 1.2, 1.3, and 2.1
CICS/ESA versions 3 thru 4
CICS/MVS version 2
CICS/VSE version 2

CICS/400
CICS on Open Systems
CICS for OS/2
CICS for Windows NT/2000

Description

- You use *ISC* (*Intersystem Communication*) to connect CICS systems running on different processors. The two systems are connected by *SNA* (*Systems Network Architecture*) using an *Advanced Program-to-Program Communication* (*APPC*) protocol. The APPC protocol is typically provided by VTAM.
- The systems participating in ISC don't have to be the same CICS version and don't have to be running under the same operating system.

Figure 19-2   How Intersystem Communication works

A typical MRO/ISC environment

Figure 19-3 presents a typical system configuration that uses both MRO and ISC. Here, three host processors—one in San Diego, one in Houston, and one in Boston—each use MRO to run separate TORs, AORs, and FORs. In addition, the AORs in Houston and Boston are connected by ISC links to the FOR in San Diego. As a result, transactions run in Boston or Houston can access files that reside in San Diego.

Notice the name of each CICS system in this figure (they're enclosed in parentheses). In an MRO or ISC environment, every CICS system must have a unique name so that other CICS systems can identify it. This name is called the *system identifier* or *sysid*. As you'll see in a moment, the systems programmers use these names in the table entries that are required to implement intercommunication. In addition, many CICS commands let you access a resource that's owned by another CICS system by specifying that system's sysid.

Frankly, the details of setting up and maintaining an MRO/ISC environment are complex. Fortunately, the systems programmers usually set up MRO/ISC so that it is completely transparent to application programs. So as an application programmer, you don't even need to know that MRO or ISC is in use. From a practical point of view, however, you should have a general understanding of your installation's MRO/ISC configuration, including each system's sysid.

Systems that use MRO and ISC

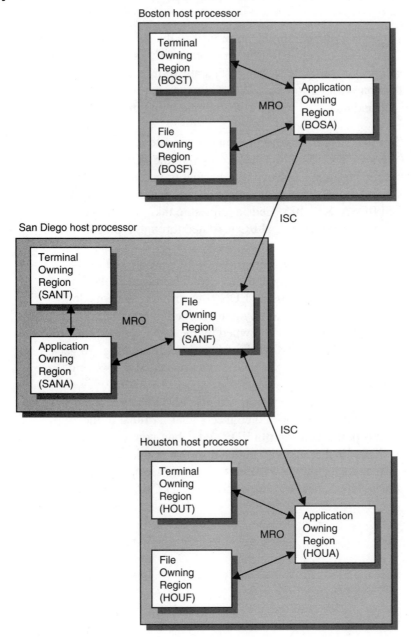

Description

- A CICS system participating in an MRO environment can use ISC to communicate with a CICS system on another processor
- Each CICS system in an MRO or ISC environment must have a unique one- to four-character name, called a *system identifier* or *sysid*, that can be used to identify the system.

Figure 19-3   A typical MRO/ISC environment

How transaction routing works

Transaction routing is a intercommunication facility that lets a terminal owned by one CICS system run a transaction on another CICS system. Transaction routing is what makes it possible to set up separate Terminal Owning Regions and Application Owning Regions. When transaction routing is used, the terminal is owned and managed by the TOR, but the transactions are executed by the AOR.

Figure 19-4 illustrates how transaction routing works. Here, you can see that when a user enters the trans-id INQ1 at a terminal in the TOR named BOST, CICS checks the Program Control Table for that transaction. In this case, the entry indicates that the transaction is a remote transaction that should be run on the system named BOSA. So CICS sends a request to that system to run the INQ1 transaction. As it executes, terminal I/O is routed through BOST back to the originating terminal.

From an application programming point of view, transaction routing is completely transparent. The only time you even need to be aware of its use is when you debug a remote transaction using EDF. (Because test systems don't usually use MRO, you'll need to do that only in a production environment.) Because EDF requires your terminal to be owned by the same system that owns the program you're debugging, it won't work with transaction routing. To get around this limitation, IBM supplies a special transaction called the *routing transaction*, or *CRTE*.

The two commands in this figure show how to use CRTE. The first command, CRTE, starts the routing session and connects your terminal to the specified system. At this point, you can run EDF and debug your program. When you're done, you issue the second command shown in this figure, CANCEL, to disconnect your terminal and end the routing session. Note that for this to work, your terminal must be defined to the other CICS system as a remote terminal.

How a transaction is routed to another system

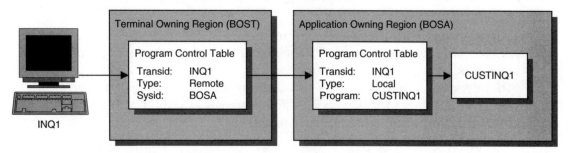

How to debug a remote program using EDF

A command that connects your terminal to a remote system for debugging

`CRTE SYSID=BOSA`

A command that cancels a remote connection

`CANCEL`

Description

- *Transaction routing* lets a terminal owned by one CICS system run a transaction on another CICS system.

- The Terminal Owning Region that will initiate the transaction must define the transaction in its Program Control Table (PCT) as a remote transaction, and it must name the Application Owning region where it will run.

- The Application Owning Region that will run the transaction must define the transaction in its Program Control Table as a local transaction, and it must identify the program to be executed.

- When a user enters the trans-id for the transaction at a terminal in the TOR, the system locates the transaction in the PCT and passes it to the specified remote system. The remote system locates the transaction in its PCT, and then executes the specified program. Any terminal I/O done by the program is routed back to the terminal in the TOR.

- To debug a remote program using EDF, you must first connect your terminal to the remote system using the *routing transaction*, or *CRTE*. For that to work, your terminal must be defined to the other CICS system as a remote terminal.

- After you start a routing session, you can use EDF as usual (see chapter 9). When you're finished, you use the CANCEL command to end the routing session.

Figure 19-4   How transaction routing works

How function shipping works

Function shipping lets a CICS program running at one CICS system access a resource that's owned by another CICS system. For example, a transaction running in the AOR on one system can use function shipping to access a VSAM file in the FOR on another system. Note that CICS supports function shipping for resources besides VSAM files, such as temporary storage queues and DL/I (IMS) databases. (DB2 has its own distributed processing features.)

How a function is shipped to another system

Figure 19-5 illustrates how a function is shipped to another system. Here, a program named CUSTINQ1 is running in an AOR named BOSA. When the program issues a READ command for the file named CUSTMAS, CICS locates the entry for that file in the File Control Table. This entry indicates that the file is stored on the remote system named BOSF, so CICS ships the request to that system. (Notice that the FCT entry for a remote VSAM KSDS must also indicate the record length and key length of the records in the file.) The remote system then locates the file in its File Control Table, reads the record, and ships it back to BOSA.

This figure also shows a typical COBOL paragraph you might use to read a record from the remote CUSTMAS file. As you can see, the READ command doesn't indicate that the file is remote. As a result, the fact that function shipping is used here is nearly transparent to the program. I say *nearly* transparent because although the use of function shipping doesn't affect the way you code CICS commands, it may affect the exceptional condition testing that follows each command. In this figure, for example, you can see that the code includes a test for the SYSIDERR condition. This condition occurs whenever the connection to the remote CICS system can't be made. This can happen because of an incorrect sysid, but in a production system, it's more likely to happen because of a failure in the communications link or in the remote CICS system.

When you use function shipping, CICS considers the processing done on the local and remote systems to be a single logical unit of work. It does this by coordinating syncpoints across the systems, and if a failure occurs, by backing out updates made on the local and remote systems together. Unfortunately, there is a slight chance that a failure might occur while CICS is attempting to coordinate syncpoints. When that happens, CICS can't guarantee that data on the local and remote systems is coordinated. The likelihood of that happening is very small, however. (If you aren't familiar with syncpoints and logical units of work, please see chapter 18.)

Function shipping for most other resources works much the same as it does for VSAM files. If the systems programmer creates the appropriate table entries, the function shipping is transparent to the application programmer, except for the possibility of the SYSIDERR condition occurring. For DL/I, function shipping is set up by the database administrator, so you code the application program as if it were accessing a local database.

How a function is shipped to another system

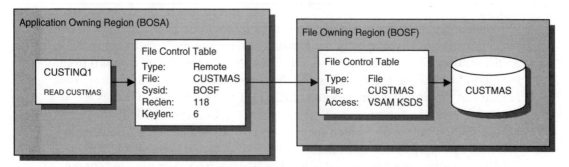

A read module that uses function shipping

```
2100-READ-CUSTOMER-RECORD.
*
    EXEC CICS
        READ FILE('CUSTMAS')
            INTO(CUSTOMER-MASTER-RECORD)
            RIDFLD(CM-CUSTOMER-NUMBER)
            RESP(RESPONSE-CODE)
    END-EXEC.
    EVALUATE RESPONSE-CODE
        WHEN DFHRESP(NORMAL)
            MOVE 'Y' TO CUSTOMER-FOUND-SW
        WHEN DFHRESP(NOTFND)
            MOVE 'N' TO CUSTOMER-FOUND-SW
            MOVE 'That customer does not exist.' TO MSG0
        WHEN DFHRESP(SYSIDERR)
            MOVE 'N' TO CUSTOMER-FOUND-SW
            MOVE 'The remote system is not available. Try again later.'
                TO MSG0
        WHEN OTHER
            PERFORM 9999-TERMINATE-PROGRAM
    END-EVALUATE.
```

Description

- *Function shipping* lets a CICS program running at one CICS system access a resource that's owned by another CICS system. CICS supports function shipping for resources like VSAM files, temporary storage queues, and DL/I databases.

- The Application Owning Region where the application will run must define the resource in its File Control Table (FCT) as a remote resource, and it must name the system where the resource resides. For a KSDS, it must also give the record length and key length.

- The File Owning Region where the resource resides defines the resource as a local file.

- When a program in the AOR issues a request for the file, it's shipped to the remote system specified in the FCT, where the requested function is performed. If the request retrieves data, the data is shipped back to the application in the AOR.

Figure 19-5   How function shipping works

How to use the SYSID option

Although you probably shouldn't use it, you should be aware that many CICS commands let you specify the location of a remote resource by using the SYSID option, shown in figure 19-6. For example, you could read a record from the CUSTMAS file at SANF by issuing the command shown in this figure. Notice that this command includes the LENGTH and KEYLENGTH options. That's because when you use the SYSID option, CICS doesn't look up the local FCT definition for the file, which specifies the record and key length values. So you have to supply those values in the command. In fact, when you specify SYSID on a file control command, a local FCT entry isn't even required for the file.

Before you use the SYSID option, you should consider what will happen if the location of the file changes. If you specify the location in the SYSID option, you'll have to change and recompile each program that accesses the file. If you specify the location in the FCT entry instead, all you'll have to do is change the FCT. Because of that, you'll probably never use the SYSID option.

The syntax of the SYSID option

```
SYSID(system-name)
```

Commands that support the SYSID option

File control	Transient data control	Temporary storage control
DELETE	DELETEQ TD	DELETEQ TS
ENDBR	READQ TD	READQ TS
READ	WRITEQ TD	WRITEQ TS
READNEXT		
READPREV	**Interval control**	**Program control**
RESETBR	START	LINK
STARTBR	CANCEL	
UNLOCK		
WRITE		

A READ command that uses the SYSID option

```
EXEC CICS
    READ FILE('CUSTMAS')
         INTO(CUSTOMER-MASTER-RECORD)
         RIDFLD(CM-CUSTOMER-NUMBER)
         SYSID('SANF')
         LENGTH(CUSTMAS-LENGTH)
         KEYLENGTH(6)
         RESP(RESPONSE-CODE)
END-EXEC.
```

Description

- Instead of defining a remote resource in the File Control Table, you can identify the system that owns the resource in a file control command using the SYSID option. This option specifies the one- to four-character name of the remote system.

- When you use the SYSID option on a file control command for a KSDS, you must include the LENGTH and KEYLENGTH options.

- If the remote location may change, you'll want to use an FCT entry instead of the SYSID option. That way, you can change the location in the FCT instead of in every file control command that accesses the remote system.

Figure 19-6   How to use the SYSID option

How to use Distributed Program Link

In chapter 5, you learned how to use the LINK command to transfer control to a program at the next logical level. With *Distributed Program Link*, or *DPL*, you can issue a LINK command that invokes a program on another CICS system.

Distributed Program Link provides an easy way to implement *client/server applications*. In this type of application, the client program requests that the server program perform some type of processing. In chapter 20, for example, you'll learn how to design programs whose presentation logic (the logic that controls how the program interacts with the user) is coded separately from the business logic (the logic that performs all the business operations, including file handling). Then, the presentation logic links to the business logic whenever it requires a business function. In that case, the presentation logic program is the client, and the business logic program is the server.

For DPL to work, you should realize that the server program cannot issue any terminal I/O requests. That's because the server program isn't connected to a terminal; the client program is. So only the client program can request terminal I/O.

How DPL reduces network transmissions

One common reason for using DPL is to reduce network traffic by avoiding a long sequence of function shipping requests. For example, suppose an application program running in Boston (BOSA) needs to update five records in San Diego (SANF). Figure 19-7 compares how this could be done using function shipping and Distributed Program Link. With function shipping, each file control command requires two network transmissions: one to ship the function request to the remote system, the other to return the results. Since each update operation requires two CICS commands (a READ UPDATE command followed by a REWRITE command), the five updates will require 20 network transmissions.

With DPL, an application program that updates the five records can be placed on the SANA system. Then, when the program running at BOSA needs to update the five records, it can use a distributed LINK command to invoke the update program at SANA, passing the data for the updates via the communication area. The result would be two network transmissions rather than 20, resulting in a tenfold reduction of network traffic. Of course, the application program running at SANA would still have to function ship the I/O requests to SANF. But that communication would occur at dramatically faster MRO speeds, so it isn't much of a concern.

Network transmissions for a program that uses function shipping

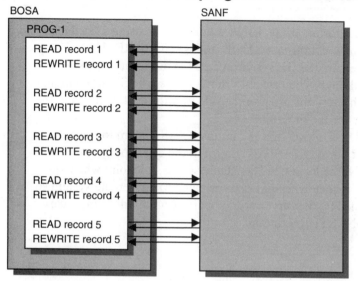

Network transmissions for a program that uses Distributed Program Link

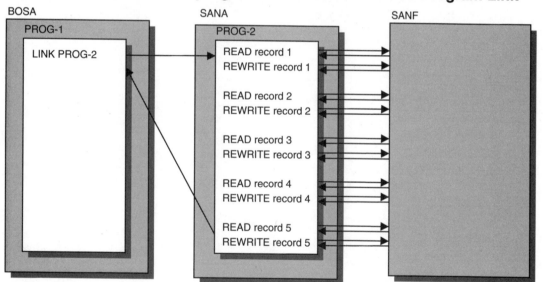

Description

- *Distributed Program Link*, or *DPL*, lets a program running in one CICS system issue a LINK command that invokes a program in another CICS system.

- DPL provides an easy way to implement *client/server applications*. In that case, the program that issues the LINK command is called the *client*, and the program it links to is called the *server*.

- DPL can reduce network traffic by avoiding a long sequence of function shipping requests.

Figure 19-7   How Distributed Program Link reduces network transmissions

How to code the LINK command

Figure 19-8 shows the format of the LINK command for using Distributed Program Link. The two new options are SYSID and SYNCONRETURN. You use SYSID to specify the name of the system where the program resides. As with function shipping, though, you probably shouldn't use the SYSID option. Instead, you should let the systems programmer identify the system name in the local system's PPT entry for the program.

The SYNCONRETURN option tells the remote CICS system to issue a syncpoint when the server program returns control to the client program. If you omit SYNCONRETURN, the local CICS system issues a syncpoint when the client program ends. Then, that syncpoint is propagated to the remote system so that any updates performed by the server program are committed. In most cases, you'll omit the SYNCONRETURN option.

The syntax of the LINK command for use with DPL

```
EXEC CICS
    LINK  PROGRAM(program-name)
          [SYSID(system-name)]
          [COMMAREA(data-name | literal)]
          [DATALENGTH(data-name | literal)]
          [SYNCONRETURN]
END-EXEC
```

Option	Description
PROGRAM	Specifies the one- to eight-character name of the program to be invoked. The name must be defined in the Processing Program Table on the system identified by the SYSID option.
SYSID	Specifies the one- to four-character name of the system where the program resides.
COMMAREA	Specifies the name of the data area that's passed to the invoked program as a communication area.
DATALENGTH	Specifies a binary halfword or numeric literal that indicates the length of the data to be sent from the area specified in the COMMAREA option. The value may be less than the total length of this area.
SYNCONRETURN	Indicates that the server program should perform a syncpoint when it returns control to the client program. If omitted, the syncpoint is taken when the client program ends.

A LINK command that includes the SYSID option

```
EXEC CICS
    LINK PROGRAM('PROG-2')
         SYSID('SANA')
         COMMAREA(PROG-2-DATA)
END-EXEC.
```

Description

- If you omit the SYSID option, the program you name on the PROGRAM option must be defined as a remote program in the Processing Program Table of the local system.
- If all of the updates made by an application are done by the server program, you might gain a performance benefit by including the SYNCONRETURN option. Otherwise, you should omit this option.

Figure 19-8   How to code the LINK command for use with DPL

Other intercommunication features

Although transaction routing, function shipping, and Distributed Program Link are the intercommunication features you'll use most often, CICS provides some additional features you'll want to know about. You'll learn about some of those features in the remaining topics of this chapter.

How to use asynchronous processing

Asynchronous processing is the term IBM uses to describe a distributed START command. If you've read chapter 18, you know that the START command lets you invoke a transaction that's run as a separate task. When you use asynchronous processing, you issue a START command that includes the SYSID option or that identifies a transaction whose Processing Program Table entry specifies a remote system. The START command shown in figure 19-9, for example, will start the LST1 transaction on the SANA system. When this command is issued, the local system sends the request to the remote system, where the transaction is scheduled for execution.

How to use Distributed Transaction Processing

Distributed Transaction Processing, or *DTP*, lets one program, called the *front end*, initiate a *conversation* with another program, called the *back end*. (The terms *front end* and *back end* are synonymous with *client* and *server*.) DTP is implemented using APPC. Because of that, a CICS program that uses DTP can communicate with any other program that follows the APPC standard, regardless of the language it's written in. For example, you might create a CICS back-end program that communicates with a front-end program written in standard COBOL running on an AS/400.

Figure 19-9 lists the most important CICS commands used for DTP. This should give you an idea of the complexity involved in programming with DTP. For more information, you can refer to the IBM manual entitled *CICS Distributed Transaction Programming Guide*.

Although DTP lets you create distributed applications with complicated conversations, most DTP applications have relatively simple conversations: The front end starts the back end and requests some work; the back end does the work and sends the results; and the front end terminates the conversation. Because of that, you're usually better off implementing this type of application using Distributed Program Link. Then, you don't have to worry about any of the commands in this figure. Instead, you just code a LINK command and pass data between the programs using the communication area.

How to use asynchronous processing

Description

- *Asynchronous processing* refers to a START command that starts a transaction on a remote system.

- To implement asynchronous processing, you issue a START command with a SYSID option that identifies the system where the transaction will be run. Alternatively, you can name a transaction on the TRANSID option of the START command whose Processing Program Table entry names the remote system.

- When you perform asynchronous processing, you can use all of the START command options you learned about in chapter 18. That means you can schedule a task for later execution, and you can pass data to the started task.

A START command that includes the SYSID option

```
EXEC CICS
    START TRANSID('LST1')
          SYSID('SANA')
          INTERVAL(001500)
END-EXEC.
```

How to use Distributed Transaction Processing

CICS commands used for Distributed Transaction Processing

Command	Description
ALLOCATE	Issued by the front-end program to establish a session with the back-end system.
CONNECT PROCESS	Issued by the front-end program to initiate the back-end program.
SEND	Sends data.
WAIT CONVID	Forces accumulated buffer data to be transmitted.
RECEIVE	Receives data.
CONVERSE	Combines the operation of a SEND, WAIT CONVID, and RECEIVE command.
FREE	Releases the session so it can be used by another application.

Description

- *Distributed Transaction Processing*, or *DTP*, lets two or more programs running on different systems communicate with each other in a *conversation*.

- The program that initiates a conversation is called the *front end*. The other program involved in the conversation is called the *back end*.

- DTP is implemented using the APPC protocol. One of the biggest advantages of DTP is that only the back-end program needs to be a CICS program. The front-end program can be written in any language that follows the APPC standards.

Figure 19-9   How to use asynchronous processing and Distributed Transaction Processing

How to use the external CICS interface

The *external CICS interface*, or *EXCI*, provides a way for a non-CICS program, such as a batch program, running in an MVS address space to execute a CICS program. The diagram at the top of figure 19-10 illustrates the easiest way to do that. Here, a batch program uses DPL with a special form of the CICS LINK command to invoke a CICS program. Notice that, like the LINK command you issue from a CICS program, you can include the COMMAREA option on a LINK command issued from a batch program to pass data to the CICS program's communication area.

Although the program that issues the LINK command isn't a CICS program, it must be processed by the CICS translator so that the LINK command can be converted to COBOL before the program is compiled. When you translate the program, note that you must specify the EXCI translator option. That way, CICS will translate the LINK command into the appropriate Call statements.

When you use the LINK command in a non-CICS program, you use the syntax shown in this figure. The two options you haven't seen before are APPLID and RETCODE. (You can refer back to figure 19-8 if you want to see a description of the other options.) You use the APPLID option to name the CICS region where the program will run, and you use the RETCODE option to name a field where EXCI will place return information about the success or failure of the command. Notice that the field you name on the RETCODE option should be divided into five fullword areas. You're already familiar with the information that's placed in the first three areas: RESP, RESP2, and ABCODE. In addition, if the CICS region issued a message during the execution of the CICS program, the MSGLEN area will contain the length of that message and the MSGPTR area will contain a pointer to that message.

The example in this figure shows a LINK command that uses the APPLID and RETCODE options. This command will invoke a program named PROG-2 in a CICS region named MM01CICS. It will pass data in the field named PROG-2-DATA to that program's communication area, and EXCI will place return code information in a field named EXCI-RETURN-AREA.

If the non-CICS program issues a single DPL request or issues DPL requests infrequently, using the LINK command is an efficient way to implement the requests. If the program issues two or more requests, however, or issues requests frequently, you may want to use another interface, called the *EXCI CALL interface*. This interface consists of six commands that let you allocate and open one or more sessions within a CICS region, issue DPL requests to that region, and then close and deallocate the sessions. Although this interface can be more efficient, it's also more difficult to program and therefore more prone to errors. Because of the complexity of this interface, I won't describe it in detail here. For more information, you can refer to the IBM manual, *CICS External Interfaces Guide*.

A batch program that invokes a CICS program using a LINK command

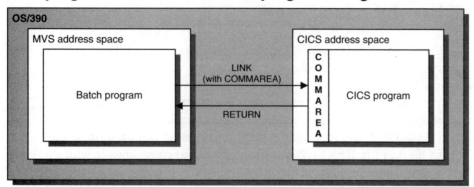

The syntax of the LINK command for use in a batch program

```
EXEC CICS
    LINK  PROGRAM(program-name)
          [COMMAREA(data-name | literal)]
          [DATALENGTH(data-name | literal)]
          [APPLID(applid-name)]
          [RETCODE(data-name)]
          [SYNCONRETURN]
END-EXEC
```

Option	Description
APPLID	Specifies the application-id that VTAM uses to identify the CICS region where the program specified in the PROGRAM option resides.
RETCODE	Specifies the name of a 20-byte data area where EXCI places return code information. The area is formatted into five fullword fields: RESP, RESP2, ABCODE, MSGLEN, and MSGPTR.

A typical LINK command issued from a batch program

```
EXEC CICS
    LINK PROGRAM('PROG-2')
         APPLID('MM01CICS')
         COMMAREA(PROG-2-DATA)
         RETCODE(EXCI-RETURN-AREA)
END-EXEC.
```

Description

- The *external CICS interface*, or *EXCI*, lets a non-CICS program running in an MVS address space invoke a CICS program and pass data to it via its communication area.
- To invoke a CICS program, the non-CICS program can use the EXCI CALL interface or a special form of the CICS LINK command.
- The EXCI CALL interface consists of six commands that let you control sessions with a CICS system and issue DPL requests on those sessions. It's most appropriate for non-CICS programs that issue more than one DPL request.
- The LINK command incorporates all of the functions of the EXCI CALL and is most appropriate for programs that issue a single DPL request. Programs that use the LINK command must be translated with the EXCI translator option before they're compiled.

Figure 19-10 How to use the External CICS Interface

How the External Call Interface and the External Presentation Interface work

The CICS intercommunication features presented so far in this chapter let programs running in two CICS regions communicate with each other. (The exception is EXCI, which lets a non-CICS program communicate with a CICS region on the same processor.) However, CICS also provides two facilities that let a client application running on another platform (including Windows NT, Windows 2000, OS/2, and AIX) and written in a different language (including C, C++, COBOL, PL/I, REXX, Visual Basic, and Java) communicate with a CICS program. These facilities are provided by *CICS client software* that comes with CICS and must be installed on the client machine. This software receives requests from the client program and then sends those requests on to CICS in a form it will recognize. Conversely, if CICS passes data back to the client, the CICS client software converts that data to a form that the client program will recognize.

Figure 19-11 presents the two interfaces you can use to request CICS services from a client program. The first one, called the *External Call Interface*, or *ECI*, lets a client program invoke a CICS program by issuing an ECI call. In this example, the client program is running on a Windows 2000 machine. When the client program issues an ECI call to invoke a CICS program, that call is intercepted by the CICS client software. Then, the client software sends the request on to CICS, and the CICS program is executed. When the program completes, control is returned to the client program through the CICS client software.

When a program issues an ECI call, it can pass a variety of information to CICS. That information can include a user-id and password for accessing the CICS region, the name of the CICS program to be invoked, and data that will be passed to the communication area of the CICS program. Then, the CICS program is invoked just as if another CICS program had issued a LINK command. Keep in mind that when you use ECI, though, the CICS program can't perform any terminal I/O. Instead, it usually performs some type of file handling or other business logic.

The second interface a client program can use to communicate with CICS is the *External Presentation Interface*, or *EPI*. Unlike ECI, a CICS program you invoke with EPI *can* perform terminal I/O. In fact, the main function of EPI is to send and receive 3270 data from a CICS program. Instead of displaying the data it receives in 3270 format, though, the client program can display it in a *graphical user interface* (*GUI*) like the one shown in this figure. In this case, the interface was developed in Visual Basic. Note that the CICS program processes 3270 data that's sent to it just as if it had been entered at a terminal. Because of that, you can use EPI with legacy programs that are designed to interact only with 3270 display terminals.

A non-CICS program that uses an ECI call to invoke a CICS program

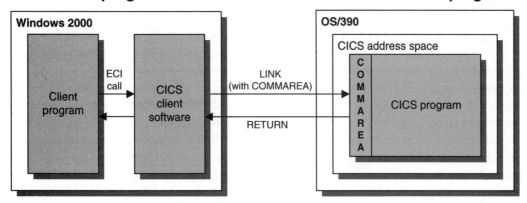

A non-CICS program that uses EPI calls to process a 3270-based CICS application

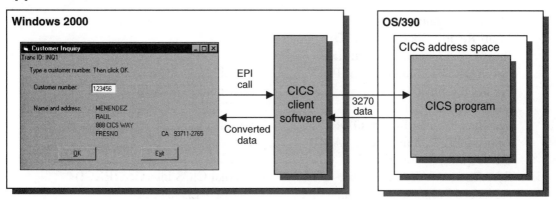

Description

- The *External Call Interface*, or *ECI*, is an *application programming interface (API)* that lets a non-CICS program (the client) invoke a CICS program (the server). The CICS program must not issue any terminal I/O requests.

- In addition to the name of the program to be invoked, the client program can pass data to CICS that will be stored in the communication area of the invoked program. In effect, the CICS program is invoked just as if a CICS LINK command had been issued.

- The *External Presentation Interface*, or *EPI*, is an application programming interface that lets a non-CICS program (the client) pass data back and forth between a CICS program (the server) as if it were a 3270 display terminal. The data can then be incorporated into a client application and presented to the user in a *graphical user interface (GUI)*.

- To use either ECI or EPI, *CICS client software* that comes with CICS must be installed on the client. This software intercepts the ECI and EPI calls and converts them to a form CICS recognizes. It also converts data sent back to the client by CICS to a form the client program recognizes.

Figure 19-11   How the External Call Interface and the External Presentation Interface work

Perspective

Just a few years ago, CICS intercommunication was considered exotic. Today, however, more and more applications are being developed using these features. One of the reasons for this is that CICS now runs in a variety of operating system environments, and those systems need to be able to communicate with each other. Another reason is that more and more programs are being written in languages like Visual Basic and Java that run on platforms like Windows or as Web applications in a Web browser. And it makes sense for those programs to work in conjunction with CICS programs to perform the function that CICS does best: process transactions. In the future, then, I expect to see the CICS intercommunication features being used more and more often.

Terms

CICS intercommunication
Multi-Region Operation (MRO)
Intersystem Communication (ISC)
InterRegion Communication (IRC)
   access method
Cross-Memory Services
Terminal Owning Region (TOR)
Application Owning Region (AOR)
File Owning Region (FOR)
Systems Network Architecture (SNA)
Advanced Program-to-Program
   Communication (APPC)
system identifier
sysid
transaction routing
routing transaction (CRTE)
function shipping
Distributed Program Link (DPL)

client/server application
server
client
asynchronous processing
Distributed Transaction Processing
   (DTP)
conversation
front end
back end
external CICS interface (EXCI)
EXCI CALL interface
CICS client software
External Call Interface (ECI)
application programming interface
   (API)
External Presentation Interface (EPI)
graphical user interface (GUI)

20

How to design, code, and test a modular CICS program

Traditionally, CICS programs were written so that a single source program performed all of the required functions. Those are the types of programs you've seen so far in this book. Today, however, it's more and more common to divide a program into two program modules: one that performs all of the functions for interacting with the user, and one that performs all of the business operations. That way, the two programs can run on different systems in a distributed environment. In addition, the programs can be written in different languages, and they can run on different platforms. In this chapter, you'll learn how to design, code, and test programs that use this modular design technique.

Program design considerations

Before you can design a modular program, you need to understand the concept behind this design technique. The easiest way to explain this concept is to compare it to the traditional design concept. That's what I'll do in the next two topics. Then, I'll explain how you can separate the logic of a program into two program modules.

Traditional program design techniques

The diagram in figure 20-1 illustrates how a program works using traditional program design. As you can see, both the *presentation logic*—the logic that handles the program's interaction with the user—and the *business logic*—the logic that handles the processing of the data that's received from the user—are contained in a single program module. The module works in conjunction with BMS and CICS terminal control to interact with the user at a terminal. And it works in conjunction with CICS file control to access data on disk.

The biggest advantage of this design is that, because all of the code is contained in a single module, it's easy to implement. The biggest disadvantage is that it is inflexible. Because the entire program runs under the control of CICS, it can use only commands and statements that CICS recognizes. In contrast, if you separate the presentation logic from the business logic, the business logic can still be written to run under CICS, but the presentation logic can be written in another language to run in another environment.

Traditional program design

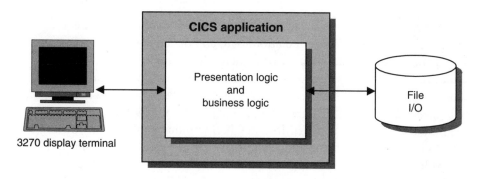

Description

- Traditional CICS programs consist of a single program module that handles both the interaction with the user at a terminal (the *presentation logic*) and the processing of data (the *business logic*).

- Both the presentation logic and the business logic are implemented using COBOL in conjunction with CICS commands, and the user interface is implemented using BMS.

- Although programs designed using this technique are easy to implement, they are inflexible because they run entirely under the control of CICS.

Figure 20-1   Traditional program design techniques

Modular program design techniques

The diagram in figure 20-2 illustrates how modular CICS programs are being designed. Here, the 3270 presentation logic and the business logic are coded in separate modules that interact with each other. Notice that only the module that contains the presentation logic can interact with the user, and only the module that contains the business logic can access data.

The biggest advantage of this design technique is that you don't have to implement the user interface using BMS and CICS terminal control, and you don't have to implement the presentation logic in COBOL and CICS. Instead, you can develop an alternate user interface that handles all the presentation logic and terminal I/O using modern languages and tools like Visual Basic and Java. That's ideal for a client/server environment where the clients are PCs and the server is an OS/390 system. In that case, a tool like Visual Basic can be used to develop a more robust and user-friendly interface than can be developed in CICS, and it can be done more quickly and easily. This design technique is also critical to the development of Web-based applications, since the presentation logic for these applications can't be implemented in CICS.

But even shops that are still developing programs entirely in COBOL and CICS can benefit from modular program design. For example, programs that will run in a distributed environment like the ones described in chapter 19 can be designed so that the presentation logic will run on one CICS system, and the business logic will run on another. In addition, modular design can be used to prepare for client/server or Web-based applications in the future. That way, when the time comes, the presentation logic can be rewritten in the appropriate language, while the business logic can continue to run without change.

Unfortunately, separating the presentation and business logic can complicate the code that's required to implement a program. You'll have a better idea of why that is when you see the code for the customer maintenance program that's written using this technique later in this chapter. For now, just realize that the interface that allows the two modules to interact with each other is critical. For a program whose presentation logic and business logic are both written using COBOL and CICS, that interface is implemented using a LINK command in the presentation logic program that invokes the business logic program and passes data to it through the communication area. If the presentation logic is written in another language, however, additional facilities are required to implement the interface. You learned about some of those facilities in chapter 19, and you'll learn about others in chapter 21. Even with this complication, though, I believe that you should code the presentation and business logic in separate modules for all new CICS programs you develop because of the added flexibility it gives you.

Modular program design

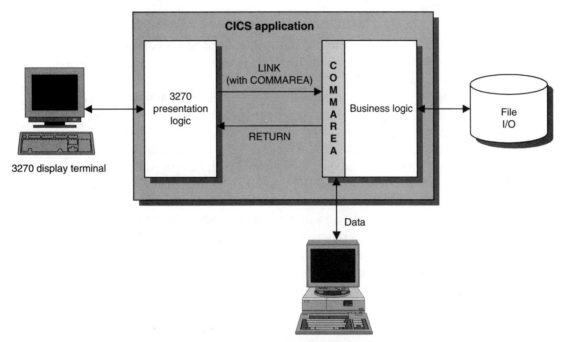

Figure 20-2   Modular program design techniques

Description

- Modular CICS programs separate the presentation logic from the business logic. That way, the presentation logic can be implemented using something other than COBOL and CICS, and the user interface can be implemented using something other than BMS.

- With this technique, only the presentation logic can perform terminal I/O, and only the business logic can perform file I/O.

- Because the business logic is independent of the presentation logic, it can be used with presentation logic that's written in any language and that can run on any platform, as long as the appropriate interface is provided between the two.

- The interface for a program whose presentation and business logic are both developed using COBOL and CICS is implemented using a LINK command and the communication area. If the presentation logic is developed using another language, more sophisticated facilities are required.

- The technique of separating the presentation and business logic facilitates the development of client/server applications and is critical to the development of Web-based applications.

Figure 20-2   Modular program design techniques

How to identify the presentation logic and the business logic

One of the tricks of separating the presentation and business logic is deciding what code goes in what program. To help you with that, figure 20-3 presents some guidelines you can follow.

To start, the presentation logic should always include the high-level logic for the program. That makes sense if you remember that a pseudo-conversational program performs functions based on user actions, and only the module that contains the presentation logic can interact with the user. Because the presentation logic drives the execution of the program, this program can be referred to as the *driver program*. If this program is written in CICS, it's the program that CICS will start when the user presses an attention key at the terminal, and it's the program that will end after it sends information to the terminal. That means that this program must also maintain the required information in the communication area between program executions.

In addition to controlling the execution of the program and interacting with the user, the presentation logic should handle any basic editing of the data the user enters. For example, it might check to be sure that a field that should contain a quantity is numeric or that a date entered by the user contains a valid month, day, and year. If it determines that the data should be processed further, it can then link to the business logic to perform that processing.

The business logic can do additional editing based on business rules, like checking that the date entered for an invoice isn't in the future or that a zip code is valid for the associated state. The business logic should also perform all calculations and handle all file I/O. It's also responsible for maintaining data integrity. That means it must ensure that two users can't update the same data at the same time, and that related updates are committed or rolled back as necessary. In short, the business logic should handle all processing that isn't directly related to interacting with the user.

Processing typically done by presentation logic

- Because CICS programs are driven by user events, the presentation logic should contain the high-level logic for the program. The presentation logic can be referred to as the *driver program* since it drives the execution of the program.

- The presentation logic must determine what processing is done based on user input and the context in which it's received.

- The presentation logic should handle all screen interactions with the user.

- The presentation logic should handle preliminary editing of the input that's entered by the user. That includes making sure that required entries are made, that entries are numeric when required, and that a valid key has been pressed.

- The presentation logic should link to the business logic whenever business processing is required.

- The presentation logic should maintain a copy of any data it requires between executions in a pseudo-conversational session. It should also maintain a copy of any data that's required by the business logic between its executions.

Processing typically done by business logic

- The processing done by the business logic should be based on information sent to it by the presentation logic.

- The business logic should handle all file processing.

- The business logic should ensure that data integrity is maintained.

- The business logic should handle all editing of data that depends on business rules. That includes checking that a value falls within a particular range, making sure that a record with a corresponding key value does or does not exist, and making sure that related fields agree with one another.

- The business logic should perform all calculations.

Note

- The presentation logic should *never* include any file I/O statements, and the business logic should *never* include any terminal I/O statements.

Figure 20-3   How to identify the presentation logic and the business logic

How to design a modular CICS program

In the topics that follow, you'll learn how to design a modular CICS program. Because the main purpose of this book is to teach you CICS, I'll assume that you're developing both the presentation logic and the business logic using COBOL and CICS and that the presentation logic will run on a 3270 display. If the presentation logic will be developed in another language or run on another platform, though, you'll want to get complete specifications on how that program will work and what information it will pass to the business logic program. Then, you can use that information to design the business logic program.

You use many of the same techniques to design a modular CICS program that you use to design a traditional program. To start, you develop an event/response chart that identifies each event that can trigger the execution of the driver program (the presentation logic), the context in which each of those events can occur, and the program's response to each event. Then, you can use the event/response chart to plan the modules for the program using a structure chart or another design tool. The biggest difference is that because the logic is separated into two programs, you have to create two structure charts: one for the presentation logic portion of the program, and one for the business logic portion.

In the topics that follow, you'll see the event/response chart and structure charts for a customer maintenance program that's implemented using the modular design technique. This is the same program you saw in chapter 12. To give you an idea how this program works when implemented with separate presentation and business logic, I'll start by presenting an overview for the program.

The program overview for the customer maintenance program

Figure 20-4 presents the program overview for the customer maintenance program. In many ways, it's the same as the overview for the program in chapter 12. Notice, however, that this overview is for two programs: CSTMNTP, which contains the presentation logic for the program; and CSTMNTB, which contains the business logic. Also notice that, when appropriate, the processing specifications indicate when CSTMNTP (the driver program) should link to CSTMNTB. In step 2, for example, CSTMNTP should link to CSTMNTB if the user enters a customer number and action code. Then, CUSTMNTB should read the customer record to be sure that the combination of customer number and action code is valid.

Note that although the business logic program in this case is executed via a LINK command from the presentation logic, the two programs are written as independent modules. That means that the business logic program could be executed by a program written in another language running on another platform. The only requirement is that an interface must be provided to receive requests from the presentation logic program and convert them to requests that CICS recognizes.

The program overview for the customer maintenance program

Program	CSTMNTP: Customer maintenance program (presentation logic)
	CSTMNTB: Customer maintenance program (business logic)
Trans-id	CMNT
Overview	Lets the user enter new customer records, change existing customer records, or delete existing customer records.
Input/output specifications	CUSTMAS Customer master file
	CMNTMP1 Customer maintenance key map
	CMNTMP2 Customer maintenance data map

Processing specifications

1. Control is transferred to the presentation logic portion of this program (CSTMNTP) via XCTL from the menu program INVMENU with no communication area. The user can also start the program by entering the trans-id CMNT. In either case, the program should respond by displaying the key map.

2. On the key map, the user enters a customer number and selects a processing action (Add, Change, or Delete). Both the action field and the customer number field must be entered. If they are, the program should link to CSTMNTB to make sure the customer doesn't exist for an add operation, but does exist for a change or delete operation. If a valid combination of customer number and action isn't entered, an error message should be displayed.

3. Display the data map. For an add operation, the user can then enter the customer information. For a change operation, the user can change any of the existing information. For a delete operation, all fields should be set to protected so the user can't enter changes. To complete any of these operations, the user must press the Enter key.

4. For an add or change, edit the fields to make sure they aren't blank, then link to CUSTMNTB and write or rewrite the record; for a delete, link to CUSTMNTB and delete the record.

5. If the user presses PF3 from either the key map or the data map, return to the menu program INVMENU by issuing an XCTL command. If the user presses PF12 from the key map, return to the menu program. However, if the user presses PF12 from the data map, redisplay the key map without completing the current operation.

6. For a change or delete operation, maintain an image of the customer record in the communication area between program executions. If the record is changed in any way between program executions, notify the user and do not complete the operation.

7. If an unrecoverable error occurs, terminate the program from CSTMNTP by invoking the SYSERR subprogram.

Figure 20-4   The program overview for the customer maintenance program

How to create an event/response chart

Figure 20-5 presents the event/response chart for the customer maintenance program . If you compare this chart to the event/response chart for the maintenance program in chapter 12, you'll see that they're identical. That's because even though the logic is separated into two programs, the program still processes the same events within the same contexts and responds in the same manner.

If you understand the concept of modular program design, you shouldn't have any trouble figuring out whether the presentation logic or the business logic should implement the responses shown in the event/response chart in this figure. If you want to, though, you can use some type of notation to make this clear. For example, you could include the characters *(P)* after each portion of a response that will be handled by the presentation logic and the characters *(B)* after each portion that will be handled by the business logic. After you gain some experience using the new design technique, though, I think you'll find that this isn't necessary.

An event/response chart for the customer maintenance program

Event	Context	Response	New context
Start the program	n/a	Display the key map.	Get key
PF3	All	Transfer control to the menu program.	n/a
PF12	Get key	Transfer control to the menu program.	n/a
	Add customer Change customer Delete customer	Cancel the operation and display the key map.	Get key

Enter key	Get key	Edit input data.
		If valid
		    display data map
		
		else
		    display an error message.
			Add customer,
			Change customer, or
			Delete customer
			
			Get key

	Add customer	Edit input data.
		If valid
		    add customer record
		    display key map
		else
		    display an error message.
			Get key
			
			Add customer

	Change customer	Edit input data.
		If valid
		    change customer record
		    display key map
		else
		    display an error message.
			Get key
			
			Change customer

	Delete customer	Delete the customer record. Display the key map.	Get key
Clear	Get key	Redisplay the key map without any data.	Unchanged
	Add, Change, or Delete customer	Redisplay the data map with unprotected data erased.	Unchanged
Any PA key	All	Ignore the key.	Unchanged
Any other key	All	Display an appropriate error message.	Unchanged

Description

- You create an event/response chart for a modular CICS program using the same techniques you use for traditional programs: by identifying the events and event contexts and then planning the program's response to each one.
- If you want to, you can include information in the event/response chart that indicates which program (presentation logic or business logic) does what processing. If you design the program using the guidelines in figure 20-3, though, that's usually not necessary.

Figure 20-5   An event/response chart for the customer maintenance program

How to create a structure chart for the presentation logic

To create a structure chart for the presentation logic of a program, you use the same basic techniques that were presented in chapter 3. To start, you draw a box that represents the entire program and that will manage the event processing for the program. Then, you decide which portions of the event processing should be implemented as separate modules, and you draw one box for each subordinate to the top-level module.

For example, the first two levels of the structure chart for the presentation logic of the customer maintenance program are shown at the top of figure 20-6. Notice that these two levels are identical to those shown in the structure chart for the traditional implementation of the customer maintenance program that was presented in chapter 3. Although that's usually the case, you may occasionally need to add modules for other functions. That's because in addition to the guidelines presented in chapter 3 for determining what modules to include at the second level of a structure chart, you should follow one more guideline for designing the presentation logic. That is, you should include a module for any function that links to the business logic program.

After you complete the second level of the structure chart, you can continue by breaking each module down into its component functions. For example, the second chart shown in this figure is for the process-key-map leg of the customer maintenance program. Notice that after the process-key-map module calls modules to retrieve the key map and edit the key data, it calls a module to get the customer record. This module, in turn, calls another module to process the customer record. This is a generalized module that invokes the business logic program, and its name reflects the function of that program. By including this code in a separate module, it can be called from anywhere in the program. To indicate that this module invokes the business logic program, you should include a module subordinate to it that identifies that program as shown in this figure. Of course, this leg also includes the send-key-map and send-data-map modules to display the key and data maps when appropriate.

The first two levels of the structure chart for the presentation logic of the customer maintenance program

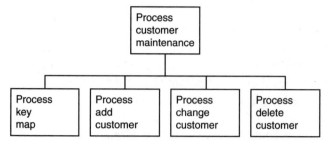

The process-key-map leg of the customer maintenance program

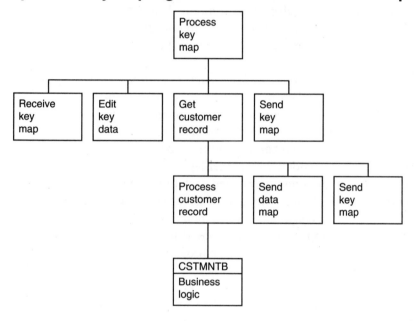

Description

- The second level of the structure chart for the presentation logic of a modular program should include the modules required to respond to the event contexts of the program. Any function that requires linking to the business logic should be coded in its own module.

- The lower levels of the structure chart should include only the modules for processing the program's terminal I/O.

- Include a generalized processing module that handles the link to the business logic program. This module can then be called from any module that requires one of the functions of the business logic program.

- Also include a module that identifies the business logic program. This program can be identified like any other linked program: with a stripe at the top of the module that gives the name of the program.

Figure 20-6   How to create the structure chart for the presentation logic

The complete structure chart for the presentation logic

Figure 20-7 presents the complete structure chart for the presentation logic of the customer maintenance program. Like the structure chart for the traditional program presented in chapter 3, the send modules for the key map and the data map have been added to the second level of this structure chart. Just as in that program, these modules will be used to respond to events other than the user pressing the Enter key.

This structure chart also includes some new modules. I've already described the purpose of the get-customer-record module (1300) and the process-customer-record module (1400) in the process-key-map leg. As you can see, the process-customer-record module is also called from the three legs that add, change, and delete a customer since these functions require processing that's done by the business logic program. (Remember, this is the module that actually invokes the business logic program.)

Before module 1400 is called for an add or change operation, module 2300 is called to set the customer data. This module will move the customer information in the data map to the customer record in the communication area so it can be passed to the business logic program for processing. Because the delete function needs only the customer number to perform its processing, module 2300 isn't included in the process-delete-customer leg.

Although the business logic program is called each time module 1400 is executed, you'll notice that the business logic module is shown only once in this structure chart. As explained in chapter 3, it's common practice to include the modules subordinate to a common module just once. If it helps you identify the functions that require the use of the business logic program, though, by all means include this module wherever it's appropriate.

The complete structure chart for the presentation logic

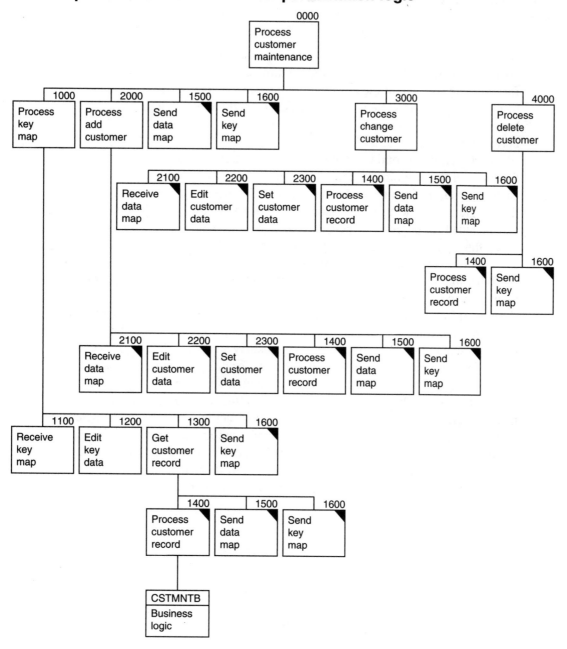

Note

- Because the module that invokes the business logic is a common module (a module that appears more than once in the structure chart), its subordinate (the business logic program itself) needs to be included only once. If it helps you design the business logic program, though, you can repeat it wherever necessary.

Figure 20-7   The complete structure chart for the presentation logic of the customer maintenance program

How to create a structure chart for the business logic

Once you complete the structure chart for the presentation logic, you can create the chart for the business logic. Figure 20-8 presents the structure chart for the business logic of the customer maintenance program. Notice that the top-level module has the same name as the generalized module that invokes the business logic in the chart for the presentation logic. That makes the link between the two programs clear.

To design the second level of this structure chart, you identify the main functions of the program. Usually, you can do that by including one module for each occurrence of the generalized module in the presentation logic that invokes this program. For the customer maintenance program, for example, one module was included for processing the customer key, along with one module for each of the three operations the user can request: add, change, and delete.

Subordinate to each of these modules, you include the file I/O modules and any other modules that are required to perform the operation. For the customer maintenance program, the only other module that's required is the one that sets the error information when an unrecoverable error occurs. Since the business logic program can't perform any terminal I/O, this information must be returned to the presentation logic program so it can display an appropriate error message and end the program. As you'll see in the code for this program, it uses the SYSERR subprogram you saw in chapter 8 to do that.

As you review this structure chart, keep in mind that the customer maintenance program is relatively simple, so the main function of the business logic is to perform the required file I/O. However, more complex programs would require additional modules to edit data, perform calculations, and maintain the integrity of the data in the files being processed. In short, a business logic program should include any processing that's not directly related to terminal I/O.

The complete structure chart for the business logic of the customer maintenance program

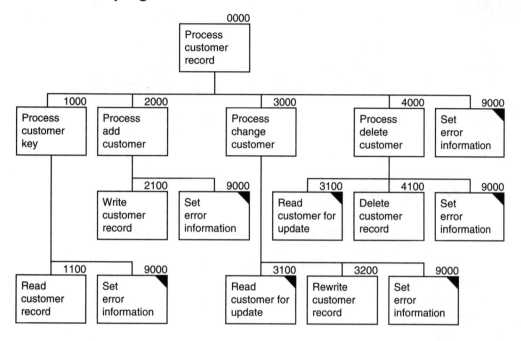

Description

- The top-level module of the business logic program should represent the function indicated by the module in the presentation logic program that links to the business logic. In fact, we recommend you use the same name for both modules.

- The modules at the second level should represent the main functions of the business logic. In most cases, these functions will be directly related to the event processing identified by the modules at the second level of the presentation logic.

- The lower levels of the structure chart should include the modules needed to implement the functions at the second level. This should include any required file I/O modules, but no terminal I/O modules.

Figure 20-8   How to create the structure chart for the business logic

How to code and test a modular CICS program

Some special considerations apply to the coding and testing of a program with separate presentation and business logic. To start, you need to determine what information will be passed between the two programs so you can include it in the communication area. Next, you need to learn how to code the high-level logic of the business logic program. Finally, you need to learn the best techniques for coding and testing both programs. That's what you'll learn in the topics that follow.

How to code the communication area

Figure 20-9 presents the communication area for the customer maintenance program. If you compare this with the communication area in the maintenance program presented in chapter 12, you'll notice several new fields. These fields contain information established in the presentation logic that the business logic needs to perform its functions, along with information established in the business logic that the presentation logic needs.

Each program you develop will have different requirements for the communication area. Most programs, however, will require fields like the last three 05-level fields shown in this figure. The first one, CA-RETURN-CONDITION, is a flag that will indicate the result of the processing done by the business logic. In this case, the three possible results are that the processing completed successfully (Process-OK), the processing caused an error that can be handled by the program (Process-Error), and the processing caused a severe error that the program can't recover from (Process-Severe-Error). The presentation logic can then use this flag to determine what processing to do next.

If a recoverable error is encountered, the business logic typically returns a message that describes the error. It may also return a message to indicate that the processing completed successfully. The CA-RETURN-MESSAGE field will hold these messages. If the program can't recover from the error, however, error information is typically returned. In this example, the error will be processed using the SYSERR program, so the business logic returns the fields that are required by that program in the fields subordinate to CA-ERROR-PARAMETERS.

In addition to these fields, the communication area for this program also includes a flag that indicates the action that was requested by the user on the key map (add, change, or delete). This flag is used by the business logic to determine whether or not a customer record should exist for the selected customer. If the user selects an add operation, for example, the customer record should not already exist. For a change or delete operation, however, it should.

Although you might think that you could use the context flag for that purpose, you can't. That's because this flag isn't set to add, change, or delete until it's determined that the user entries in the key map are valid. But it's the procedure that checks the key map entries for validity that needs to know what operation was requested.

The communication area for the customer maintenance program

```
01   COMMUNICATION-AREA.
*
     05   CA-CONTEXT-FLAG                 PIC X(01).
          88   PROCESS-KEY-MAP                        VALUE '1'.
          88   PROCESS-ADD-CUSTOMER                   VALUE '2'.
          88   PROCESS-CHANGE-CUSTOMER                VALUE '3'.
          88   PROCESS-DELETE-CUSTOMER                VALUE '4'.
     05   CA-ACTION-FLAG                  PIC X(01).
          88   ADD-REQUEST                            VALUE '1'.
          88   CHANGE-REQUEST                         VALUE '2'.
          88   DELETE-REQUEST                         VALUE '3'.
     05   CA-CUSTOMER-RECORD.
          10   CA-CUSTOMER-NUMBER         PIC X(06).
          10   CA-FIRST-NAME              PIC X(20).
          10   CA-LAST-NAME               PIC X(30).
          10   CA-ADDRESS                 PIC X(30).
          10   CA-CITY                    PIC X(20).
          10   CA-STATE                   PIC X(02).
          10   CA-ZIP-CODE                PIC X(10).
     05   CA-SAVE-CUSTOMER-MASTER         PIC X(118).
     05   CA-RETURN-CONDITION             PIC X(01).
          88   PROCESS-OK                             VALUE '1'.
          88   PROCESS-ERROR                          VALUE '2'.
          88   PROCESS-SEVERE-ERROR                   VALUE '3'.
     05   CA-RETURN-MESSAGE               PIC X(79).
     05   CA-ERROR-PARAMETERS.
          10   CA-ERR-RESP                PIC S9(08)  COMP.
          10   CA-ERR-RESP2               PIC S9(08)  COMP.
          10   CA-ERR-RSRCE               PIC X(08).
```

Description

- In addition to the data that's maintained in the communication area for any pseudo-conversational program, the communication area for a program with separate business and presentation logic should include data that's passed between the two programs.

- Sometimes, a flag is needed to indicate the action that has been requested by the user. Then, the business logic program can use that flag to determine what processing it needs to do. In other cases, the context flag can be used for that purpose.

- A flag should also be included to indicate whether or not the business processing completed successfully. Then, the presentation logic program can use that flag to determine how it proceeds.

- If the business logic encounters an error it can recover from, it should pass an appropriate error message back to the presentation logic so the message can be displayed at the terminal. To do that, the communication area must include a field to hold the error message.

- If the business logic encounters an error that it can't recover from, it should pass information about that error back to the presentation logic so it can process the error and end the program. To do that, the communication area must include fields to hold the error information.

Figure 20-9   How to code the communication area

You'll also notice that all of the fields in the customer master record are named in the communication area. (In chapter 12, only the customer number field was named explicitly. The others were included in a Filler item.) That's because the presentation logic will need to refer to each of these fields individually when it formats the data map. It can't use the data from the actual record because that record isn't defined in the presentation logic.

Finally, the communication area includes a field that will contain a second copy of the customer master record (CA-SAVE-CUSTOMER-MASTER). This field will hold the original contents of the record for a change or delete operation. Then, before the record is changed or deleted, the business logic can check to be sure that the record hasn't been changed by another user. In contrast, the CA-CUSTOMER-RECORD field will contain the new customer information for an add operation or the modified information for a change operation.

How to code the top-level module of the business logic program

Unlike a presentation logic program, whose top-level module must respond to user events, the top-level module of a business logic program must respond to information passed to it from the presentation logic program. In most cases, though, the response is still based on the context in which the entry was made. In figure 20-10, for example, you can see the code in the top-level module for the customer maintenance program. Here, an Evaluate statement is used to determine the program's response based on the current context. As you might expect, each When clause checks for one context and then performs one of the functions identified by the modules in the second level of the structure chart.

You should also notice the code at the beginning of this procedure. It tests if the length of the data that was passed to the program through the communication area is equal to the length of DFHCOMMAREA. If it isn't, that indicates one of two errors. Either the program was invoked directly from CICS, in which case no communication area was passed to it, or a problem exists with the interface between the presentation logic and the business logic. Because the business logic program isn't typically defined in the Program Control Table with a trans-id, it's not likely for the first error to occur. In either case, though, the program sets up the error processing and then returns control to the presentation logic program.

If the data in the communication area is the correct length, the program moves it to the communication area that's defined in working storage. Then, it continues by performing the appropriate processing based on the context. When that processing is complete, the program issues a RETURN command to return control to the presentation logic program. Before it does that, though, it moves the data from the communication area in working storage back into DFHCOMMAREA. That way, any changes made by the business logic will be reflected in the presentation logic.

The code for the top-level module of the business logic program

```
0000-PROCESS-CUSTOMER-RECORD.
*
    IF EIBCALEN NOT = LENGTH OF DFHCOMMAREA
        SET PROCESS-SEVERE-ERROR TO TRUE
        PERFORM 9000-SET-ERROR-INFO
    ELSE
        MOVE DFHCOMMAREA TO COMMUNICATION-AREA
        EVALUATE TRUE
            WHEN PROCESS-KEY-MAP
                PERFORM 1000-PROCESS-CUSTOMER-KEY
            WHEN PROCESS-ADD-CUSTOMER
                PERFORM 2000-PROCESS-ADD-CUSTOMER
            WHEN PROCESS-CHANGE-CUSTOMER
                PERFORM 3000-PROCESS-CHANGE-CUSTOMER
            WHEN PROCESS-DELETE-CUSTOMER
                PERFORM 4000-PROCESS-DELETE-CUSTOMER
        END-EVALUATE
    END-IF.
*
    MOVE COMMUNICATION-AREA TO DFHCOMMAREA.
    EXEC CICS
        RETURN
    END-EXEC.
```

Description

- The top-level module of the business logic program should start by checking that the length of the data that's passed to it is the same as the length of its communication area. If it's not, it should set up the appropriate error processing. If it is, it should move DFHCOMMAREA to the communication area that's defined in working storage.

- The main logic of a business logic program can be coded in an Evaluate statement, just like the main logic of other pseudo-conversational programs. In this case, though, the logic is based on the context flag that's passed to the program through its communication area. It doesn't need to deal with user events.

- After the program does its processing, it should move the communication area in working storage to DFHCOMMAREA so that this data is then available to the presentation logic program. Then, it should issue a RETURN command to return control to the presentation logic program.

Figure 20-10   How to code the top-level module of the business logic program

How to test the program

As recommended in chapter 6, the best way to test a CICS program is to code and test in phases using top-down coding and testing. When you code the presentation and business logic in separate programs, however, you have the added burden of making sure that the two programs work together. If both programs are developed using COBOL and CICS and run on the same platform, that process is straightforward. You start by testing the code in the presentation logic. Then, you test the interface between the presentation logic and the business logic. Finally, you test the code in the business logic.

If the presentation logic is written in a different language or runs on another platform, however, you may have to test the business logic without the benefit of that program. To do that, you'll probably have to write a simple CICS program that passes test data through the communication area to the business logic just as if it had been entered at a terminal. As you can imagine, that can be time-consuming, but it's usually necessary.

Figure 20-11 presents a sample test plan for the customer maintenance program. As you can see, the first five phases test the code in the presentation logic, starting with the most critical modules. To do that, phases 2 through 5 must simulate the retrieval of data. Then, phase 6 tests that the interface between the two programs works as planned. At this point, the simulation of the data retrieval can be moved to the business logic. Finally, phases 7 through 10 test that the data processing done by the business logic works correctly.

When you develop a business logic program, you want to be sure that the program doesn't contain any terminal I/O commands and doesn't invoke any programs that do. That's particularly true if the presentation logic is written in a different language or runs in a different environment or on a different system. That's because the terminal I/O will be processed by the CICS system where the business logic is executing, not on the system where the presentation logic is executing. And that means that the user will never see it.

To be sure that the business logic doesn't perform any terminal I/O, you can set the program to *DPL (Distributed Program Link) mode* before you test it. (In case you haven't read chapter 19, you should know that DPL is an intercommunication feature of CICS that lets a program running in one CICS system issue a LINK command that invokes a program in another CICS system.) While in DPL mode, an error will occur if the program tries to issue a terminal I/O command. To set a program in DPL mode, you use the CEMT SET PROGRAM command with the DPLSUBSET option as shown in the figure.

A test plan for the customer maintenance program

Phase	Modules	Test
1	0000, 1000, 1100, 1200, and 1600 (presentation)	Enter all valid and invalid key map entries to test that they're processed properly and the key map is displayed properly
2	1500 (presentation)	Enter valid key map entries to test that the data map is displayed properly (simulate data retrieval)
3	2000, 2100, and 2200 (presentation)	Enter valid key map and data map entries for an add operation to test that the data in the data map is retrieved and edited properly (simulate data retrieval)
4	3000 (presentation)	Same as above, but for a change operation
5	4000 (presentation)	Same as above, but for a delete operation
6	1300 and 1400 (presentation) 0000 and 1000 (business)	Enter valid key map entries to test that they're processed properly by the business logic (simulate data retrieval in business logic)
7	1100 (business)	Enter valid and invalid key map entries to test that they're edited properly and that the correct customer record is retrieved
8	2000 and 2100 (business)	Enter valid key map and data map entries for an add operation to test that the new record is written properly
9	3000, 3100, and 3200 (business)	Enter valid key map and data map entries for a change operation to test that the record is rewritten properly
10	4000 and 4100 (business)	Enter valid key map and data map entries for a delete operation to test that the record is deleted

Description

- When you use top-down coding and testing for a program with separate presentation and business logic, you should code and test the presentation logic first, then the interface between the presentation logic and the business logic, then the business logic.

- Before you can test the program, both the presentation logic and business logic programs must be defined in the Processing Program Table (PPT). However, only the presentation logic program needs to be defined in the Program Control Table (PCT) since the business logic program can't be started with a trans-id.

- To be sure that the business logic doesn't contain any terminal I/O commands, you should set it to *DPL mode*. In this mode, the program won't be allowed to issue any CICS commands that attempt to access a terminal. To set a program to this mode, you use a CEMT command like this:

```
CEMT SET PROGRAM(CUSTMNTB) DPLSUBSET
```

- If the presentation logic is written in a different language or runs on another platform, you may have to develop a CICS program you can use to pass data to the business logic program so you can test it.

Figure 20-11   How to test a modular CICS program

The customer maintenance program

Now that you understand the basic techniques for designing, coding, and testing a modular CICS program, you're ready to see the complete customer maintenance program. Because the BMS mapset and symbolic map are almost identical to the ones shown in chapter 12, I won't present them again here. The only differences are the map and mapset names. The mapset is named CMNTSET, and the key map and data map are named CMNTMP1 and CMNTMP2. You can refer back to chapter 12 if you want to see the details of these maps.

The COBOL code for the presentation logic

Figure 20-12 presents the code for the presentation logic of the customer maintenance program. The code in the Data Division is similar to that in the maintenance program in chapter 12. The differences are that it doesn't include a response code field or the copy member for the customer master file since all the file I/O is done by the business logic, and it includes an expanded communication area as described in figure 20-9.

On pages 2 and 3 of the program listing, you can see the code for the top-level module. Because this code processes the user events and event contexts, it's almost identical to the code you saw in chapter 12. The only differences are the names that are used to refer to the output areas of the symbolic maps and the trans-id that's used in the RETURN command that ends the program.

The presentation logic of the customer maintenance program   Page 1

```
        IDENTIFICATION DIVISION.
        PROGRAM-ID.  CSTMNTP.
*
        ENVIRONMENT DIVISION.
*
        DATA DIVISION.
*
        WORKING-STORAGE SECTION.
*
        01    SWITCHES.
              05    VALID-DATA-SW              PIC X(01)    VALUE 'Y'.
                    88    VALID-DATA                        VALUE 'Y'.
*
        01    FLAGS.
              05    SEND-FLAG                  PIC X(01).
                    88    SEND-ERASE                        VALUE '1'.
                    88    SEND-ERASE-ALARM                  VALUE '2'.
                    88    SEND-DATAONLY                     VALUE '3'.
                    88    SEND-DATAONLY-ALARM               VALUE '4'.
*
        01    USER-INSTRUCTIONS.
              05    ADD-INSTRUCTION            PIC X(79)    VALUE
                    'Type information for new customer.  Then Press Enter.'.
              05    CHANGE-INSTRUCTION         PIC X(79)    VALUE
                    'Type changes.  Then press Enter.'.
              05    DELETE-INSTRUCTION         PIC X(79)    VALUE
                    'Press Enter to delete this customer or press F12 to canc
    -         'el.'.
*
        01    COMMUNICATION-AREA.
              05    CA-CONTEXT-FLAG            PIC X(01).
                    88    PROCESS-KEY-MAP                   VALUE '1'.
                    88    PROCESS-ADD-CUSTOMER              VALUE '2'.
                    88    PROCESS-CHANGE-CUSTOMER           VALUE '3'.
                    88    PROCESS-DELETE-CUSTOMER           VALUE '4'.
              05    CA-ACTION-FLAG             PIC X(01).
                    88    ADD-REQUEST                       VALUE '1'.
                    88    CHANGE-REQUEST                    VALUE '2'.
                    88    DELETE-REQUEST                    VALUE '3'.
              05    CA-CUSTOMER-RECORD.
                    10    CA-CUSTOMER-NUMBER    PIC X(06).
                    10    CA-FIRST-NAME         PIC X(20).
                    10    CA-LAST-NAME          PIC X(30).
                    10    CA-ADDRESS            PIC X(30).
                    10    CA-CITY               PIC X(20).
                    10    CA-STATE              PIC X(02).
                    10    CA-ZIP-CODE           PIC X(10).
              05    CA-SAVE-CUSTOMER-MASTER     PIC X(118).
              05    CA-RETURN-CONDITION         PIC X(01).
                    88    PROCESS-OK                        VALUE '1'.
                    88    PROCESS-ERROR                     VALUE '2'.
                    88    PROCESS-SEVERE-ERROR              VALUE '3'.
              05    CA-RETURN-MESSAGE           PIC X(79).
              05    CA-ERROR-PARAMETERS.
                    10    CA-ERR-RESP           PIC S9(08)   COMP.
                    10    CA-ERR-RESP2          PIC S9(08)   COMP.
                    10    CA-ERR-RSRCE          PIC X(08).
```

Figure 20-12   The COBOL code for the presentation logic of the program (part 1 of 9)

The presentation logic of the customer maintenance program   Page 2

```
*
 COPY CMNTSET.
*
 COPY DFHAID.
*
 COPY ATTR.
*
 COPY ERRPARM.
*
 LINKAGE SECTION.
*
 01  DFHCOMMAREA                          PIC X(334).
*
 PROCEDURE DIVISION.
*
 0000-PROCESS-CUSTOMER-MAINT.
*
     IF EIBCALEN > ZERO
         MOVE DFHCOMMAREA TO COMMUNICATION-AREA
     END-IF.
*
     EVALUATE TRUE
*
         WHEN EIBCALEN = ZERO
             MOVE LOW-VALUE TO CMNTMP1O
             MOVE -1 TO CUSTNO1L
             SET SEND-ERASE TO TRUE
             PERFORM 1600-SEND-KEY-MAP
             SET PROCESS-KEY-MAP TO TRUE
*
         WHEN EIBAID = DFHPF3
             EXEC CICS
                 XCTL PROGRAM('INVMENU')
             END-EXEC
*
         WHEN EIBAID = DFHPF12
             IF PROCESS-KEY-MAP
                 EXEC CICS
                     XCTL PROGRAM('INVMENU')
                 END-EXEC
             ELSE
                 MOVE LOW-VALUE TO CMNTMP1O
                 MOVE -1 TO CUSTNO1L
                 SET SEND-ERASE TO TRUE
                 PERFORM 1600-SEND-KEY-MAP
                 SET PROCESS-KEY-MAP TO TRUE
             END-IF
*
```

Figure 20-12   The COBOL code for the presentation logic of the program (part 2 of 9)

The presentation logic of the customer maintenance program   Page 3

```
            WHEN EIBAID = DFHCLEAR
                IF PROCESS-KEY-MAP
                    MOVE LOW-VALUE TO CMNTMP1O
                    MOVE -1 TO CUSTNO1L
                    SET SEND-ERASE TO TRUE
                    PERFORM 1600-SEND-KEY-MAP
                ELSE
                    MOVE LOW-VALUE TO CMNTMP2O
                    MOVE CA-CUSTOMER-NUMBER TO CUSTNO2O
                    EVALUATE TRUE
                        WHEN PROCESS-ADD-CUSTOMER
                            MOVE ADD-INSTRUCTION    TO INSTR2O
                        WHEN PROCESS-CHANGE-CUSTOMER
                            MOVE CHANGE-INSTRUCTION TO INSTR2O
                        WHEN PROCESS-DELETE-CUSTOMER
                            MOVE DELETE-INSTRUCTION TO INSTR2O
                    END-EVALUATE
                    MOVE -1 TO LNAMEL
                    SET SEND-ERASE TO TRUE
                    PERFORM 1500-SEND-DATA-MAP
                END-IF
*
            WHEN EIBAID = DFHPA1 OR DFHPA2 OR DFHPA3
                CONTINUE
*
            WHEN EIBAID = DFHENTER
                EVALUATE TRUE
                    WHEN PROCESS-KEY-MAP
                        PERFORM 1000-PROCESS-KEY-MAP
                    WHEN PROCESS-ADD-CUSTOMER
                        PERFORM 2000-PROCESS-ADD-CUSTOMER
                    WHEN PROCESS-CHANGE-CUSTOMER
                        PERFORM 3000-PROCESS-CHANGE-CUSTOMER
                    WHEN PROCESS-DELETE-CUSTOMER
                        PERFORM 4000-PROCESS-DELETE-CUSTOMER
                END-EVALUATE
*
            WHEN OTHER
                IF PROCESS-KEY-MAP
                    MOVE LOW-VALUE TO CMNTMP1O
                    MOVE 'That key is unassigned.' TO MSG1O
                    MOVE -1 TO CUSTNO1L
                    SET SEND-DATAONLY-ALARM TO TRUE
                    PERFORM 1600-SEND-KEY-MAP
                ELSE
                    MOVE LOW-VALUE TO CMNTMP2O
                    MOVE 'That key is unassigned.' TO MSG2O
                    MOVE -1 TO LNAMEL
                    SET SEND-DATAONLY-ALARM TO TRUE
                    PERFORM 1500-SEND-DATA-MAP
                END-IF
*
        END-EVALUATE.
*
        EXEC CICS
            RETURN TRANSID('CMNT')
                   COMMAREA(COMMUNICATION-AREA)
        END-EXEC.
```

Figure 20-12   The COBOL code for the presentation logic of the program (part 3 of 9)

Procedure 1000 on page 4 of this listing performs the processing for the key map. It starts by clearing the customer record in the communication area. Then, it performs procedure 1100 to receive the key map and procedure 1200 to edit the key map data. If the user entered a customer number and a valid action code, it continues by performing procedure 1300 to get the customer record. Otherwise, it sends the key map back to the screen to display an error message.

Procedures 1300 and 1400 on pages 5 and 6 of this listing contain the critical code for this program. Procedure 1300 starts by moving the customer number and action code entered by the user to the communication area so they will be available to the business logic program. Then, it performs procedure 1400 to link to this program.

Procedure 1400 starts by issuing a LINK command to invoke the business logic program (CSTMNTB). As you'll see in a moment, when the context flag that's passed in the communication area is set to Process-Key-Map, CSTMNTB checks the customer master file to determine whether the user entered an acceptable combination of customer number and action code. Then, it sets the return condition flag in the communication area to an appropriate value: Process-OK if the key data is acceptable; Process-Error if there's problem; and Process-Severe-Error if the READ command returned a condition code that indicates a severe error. It also formats an error message in the return message field if the key data is invalid. Then, it returns control to procedure 1400 in the presentation logic program.

Procedure 1400 continues by checking the return condition flag for the Process-Severe-Error condition. If it's True, procedure 9999 is performed to terminate the program. Otherwise, it moves the return message field to the key map. (If CSTMNTB didn't detect any errors in the key fields, this field will contain spaces.)

After the processing in procedure 1400 is complete, procedure 1300 continues by checking the value of the return condition flag. If the value is Process-OK, this procedure sets the data map fields and context flag as appropriate, and then performs procedure 1500 to display the data map. Otherwise, it performs procedure 1600 to redisplay the key map with the error message.

The presentation logic of the customer maintenance program   Page 4

```
*
 1000-PROCESS-KEY-MAP.
*
     MOVE LOW-VALUE TO CA-CUSTOMER-RECORD.
     PERFORM 1100-RECEIVE-KEY-MAP.
     PERFORM 1200-EDIT-KEY-DATA.
     IF VALID-DATA
         PERFORM 1300-GET-CUSTOMER-RECORD
     ELSE
         MOVE LOW-VALUE TO CUSTNO1O
                          ACTIONO
         SET SEND-DATAONLY-ALARM TO TRUE
         PERFORM 1600-SEND-KEY-MAP
     END-IF.
*
 1100-RECEIVE-KEY-MAP.
*
     EXEC CICS
         RECEIVE MAP('CMNTMP1')
                 MAPSET('CMNTSET')
                 INTO(CMNTMP1I)
     END-EXEC.
     INSPECT CMNTMP1I
         REPLACING ALL '_' BY SPACE.
*
 1200-EDIT-KEY-DATA.
*
     MOVE ATTR-NO-HIGHLIGHT TO ACTIONH
                             CUSTNO1H.

     IF ACTIONI NOT = '1' AND '2' AND '3'
         MOVE ATTR-REVERSE TO ACTIONH
         MOVE -1 TO ACTIONL
         MOVE 'Action must be 1, 2, or 3.' TO MSG1O
         MOVE 'N' TO VALID-DATA-SW
     END-IF.
*
     IF    CUSTNO1L = ZERO
        OR CUSTNO1I = SPACE
         MOVE ATTR-REVERSE TO CUSTNO1H
         MOVE -1 TO CUSTNO1L
         MOVE 'You must enter a customer number.' TO MSG1O
         MOVE 'N' TO VALID-DATA-SW
     END-IF.
*
```

Figure 20-12   The COBOL code for the presentation logic of the program (part 4 of 9)

The presentation logic of the customer maintenance program   **Page 5**

```
    1300-GET-CUSTOMER-RECORD.
*
        MOVE CUSTNO1I TO CA-CUSTOMER-NUMBER.
        MOVE ACTIONI  TO CA-ACTION-FLAG.
        PERFORM 1400-PROCESS-CUSTOMER-RECORD.
        IF PROCESS-OK
            EVALUATE ACTIONI
                WHEN '1'
                    MOVE ADD-INSTRUCTION TO INSTR2O
                    SET PROCESS-ADD-CUSTOMER TO TRUE
                WHEN '2'
                    MOVE CHANGE-INSTRUCTION TO INSTR2O
                    SET PROCESS-CHANGE-CUSTOMER TO TRUE
                WHEN '3'
                    MOVE DELETE-INSTRUCTION TO INSTR2O
                    SET PROCESS-DELETE-CUSTOMER TO TRUE
                    MOVE ATTR-PROT TO LNAMEA
                                      FNAMEA
                                      ADDRA
                                      CITYA
                                      STATEA
                                      ZIPCODEA
            END-EVALUATE
            IF NOT PROCESS-DELETE-CUSTOMER
                INSPECT CA-CUSTOMER-RECORD
                    REPLACING ALL SPACE BY '_'
            END-IF
            MOVE CUSTNO1I       TO CUSTNO2O
            MOVE CA-LAST-NAME   TO LNAMEO
            MOVE CA-FIRST-NAME  TO FNAMEO
            MOVE CA-ADDRESS     TO ADDRO
            MOVE CA-CITY        TO CITYO
            MOVE CA-STATE       TO STATEO
            MOVE CA-ZIP-CODE    TO ZIPCODEO
            MOVE -1             TO LNAMEL
            SET SEND-ERASE TO TRUE
            PERFORM 1500-SEND-DATA-MAP
        ELSE
            MOVE LOW-VALUE TO CUSTNO1O
                              ACTIONO
            SET SEND-DATAONLY-ALARM TO TRUE
            MOVE -1 TO CUSTNO1L
            PERFORM 1600-SEND-KEY-MAP
        END-IF.
*
```

Figure 20-12   The COBOL code for the presentation logic of the program (part 5 of 9)

The presentation logic of the customer maintenance program   Page 6

```
 1400-PROCESS-CUSTOMER-RECORD.
*
     EXEC CICS
         LINK PROGRAM('CSTMNTB')
         COMMAREA(COMMUNICATION-AREA)
     END-EXEC.
*
     IF PROCESS-SEVERE-ERROR
         PERFORM 9999-TERMINATE-PROGRAM
     ELSE
         MOVE CA-RETURN-MESSAGE TO MSG10
     END-IF.
*
 1500-SEND-DATA-MAP.
*
     MOVE 'CMNT' TO TRANID20.
     EVALUATE TRUE
         WHEN SEND-ERASE
             EXEC CICS
                 SEND MAP('CMNTMP2')
                      MAPSET('CMNTSET')
                      FROM(CMNTMP20)
                      ERASE
                      CURSOR
             END-EXEC
         WHEN SEND-DATAONLY-ALARM
             EXEC CICS
                 SEND MAP('CMNTMP2')
                      MAPSET('CMNTSET')
                      FROM(CMNTMP20)
                      DATAONLY
                      ALARM
                      CURSOR
             END-EXEC
     END-EVALUATE.
*
 1600-SEND-KEY-MAP.
*
     MOVE 'CMNT' TO TRANID10.
     EVALUATE TRUE
         WHEN SEND-ERASE
             EXEC CICS
                 SEND MAP('CMNTMP1')
                      MAPSET('CMNTSET')
                      FROM(CMNTMP10)
                      ERASE
                      CURSOR
             END-EXEC
         WHEN SEND-ERASE-ALARM
             EXEC CICS
                 SEND MAP('CMNTMP1')
                      MAPSET('CMNTSET')
                      FROM(CMNTMP10)
                      ERASE
                      ALARM
                      CURSOR
             END-EXEC
```

Figure 20-12   The COBOL code for the presentation logic of the program (part 6 of 9)

Procedure 2000 on page 7 contains the code for an add operation. It starts by receiving the data map and editing the customer data. Notice that this edit procedure checks only that the user entered data into each field, which is acceptable for a presentation logic program. If the program did more complete checking, though—for example, if it checked that the zip code was valid for the state code—that checking would be done by the business logic program.

If the customer data is valid, the program performs procedure 2300 to move this data to the communication area so it's available to the business logic program. Then, it performs procedure 1400 to link to that program. This time, because the context is Process-Add-Customer, the business logic program writes the new customer to the file, checks that the WRITE command executed properly, and sets the return condition flag and the return message field accordingly.

When the business logic program completes, procedure 1400 checks the return condition flag for a severe error and performs procedure 9999 to end the program if a severe error occurred. Otherwise, it moves the return message field from the communication area to the message field in the key map. If the operation completed successfully, this field will contain a completion message. But if the business logic program detected that another user had already added a record with the specified customer number, an error message is returned in this field.

Unless a severe error occurred in the business logic program, procedure 2000 continues by performing procedure 1600 to display the key map. But first, it sets the value of the send flag depending on the result of the processing done by the business logic program. If the business logic program detected an error, this flag is set to Send-Erase-Alarm so the alarm is sounded when the error message is displayed. Otherwise, it's set to Send-Erase. Note, too, that if the customer data is not valid, the business logic program is never invoked. Instead, the data map is redisplayed with an error message.

Procedure 3000 (on page 9) processes a change operation. Note that it's identical to the procedure that processes an add operation (2000). The difference is in the processing that's done by the business logic. Although I could have coded the add and change operations as a single procedure, I chose to code them separately since they perform two distinct functions.

Procedure 4000 processes a delete operation. It simply performs procedure 1400 to link to the business logic, then sends the key map to display a completion message if the processing completed successfully or an error message if an error occurred.

The last procedure, 9999, terminates the program whenever a severe error occurs in the business logic that the program can't recover from. Like the maintenance program in chapter 12, this procedure executes the SYSERR subprogram to display an error message and end the program. In this case, though, most of the information that's displayed comes from the Execute Interface Block of the business logic program, since that's where the error occurred. This information is passed back to the presentation logic program through the error fields in the communication area. These fields are then moved to the appropriate fields in the ERRPARM copy member. The exception is the trans-id field, which must be obtained from the EIB of the presentation logic program since the business logic program isn't started with a trans-id.

The presentation logic of the customer maintenance program   Page 7

```
                WHEN  SEND-DATAONLY-ALARM
                    EXEC CICS
                        SEND MAP('CMNTMP1')
                            MAPSET('CMNTSET')
                            FROM(CMNTMP1O)
                            DATAONLY
                            ALARM
                            CURSOR
                    END-EXEC
            END-EVALUATE.
    *
      2000-PROCESS-ADD-CUSTOMER.
    *
            PERFORM 2100-RECEIVE-DATA-MAP.
            PERFORM 2200-EDIT-CUSTOMER-DATA.
            IF VALID-DATA
                PERFORM 2300-SET-CUSTOMER-DATA
                PERFORM 1400-PROCESS-CUSTOMER-RECORD
                IF PROCESS-OK
                    SET SEND-ERASE TO TRUE
                ELSE
                    SET SEND-ERASE-ALARM TO TRUE
                END-IF
                MOVE -1 TO CUSTNO1L
                PERFORM 1600-SEND-KEY-MAP
                SET PROCESS-KEY-MAP TO TRUE
            ELSE
                MOVE LOW-VALUE TO LNAMEO
                                  FNAMEO
                                  ADDRO
                                  CITYO
                                  STATEO
                                  ZIPCODEO
                SET SEND-DATAONLY-ALARM TO TRUE
                PERFORM 1500-SEND-DATA-MAP
            END-IF.
    *
      2100-RECEIVE-DATA-MAP.
    *
            EXEC CICS
                RECEIVE MAP('CMNTMP2')
                        MAPSET('CMNTSET')
                        INTO(CMNTMP2I)
            END-EXEC.
            INSPECT CMNTMP2I
                REPLACING ALL '_' BY SPACE.
    *
      2200-EDIT-CUSTOMER-DATA.
    *
            MOVE ATTR-NO-HIGHLIGHT TO ZIPCODEH
                                      STATEH
                                      CITYH
                                      ADDRH
                                      FNAMEH
                                      LNAMEH.
    *
```

Figure 20-12   The COBOL code for the presentation logic of the program (part 7 of 9)

The presentation logic of the customer maintenance program   Page 8

```
        IF    ZIPCODEI = SPACE
           OR ZIPCODEL = ZERO
             MOVE ATTR-REVERSE TO ZIPCODEH
             MOVE -1 TO ZIPCODEL
             MOVE 'You must enter a zip code.' TO MSG2O
             MOVE 'N' TO VALID-DATA-SW
        END-IF.
    *
        IF    STATEI = SPACE
           OR STATEL = ZERO
             MOVE ATTR-REVERSE TO STATEH
             MOVE -1 TO STATEL
             MOVE 'You must enter a state.' TO MSG2O
             MOVE 'N' TO VALID-DATA-SW
        END-IF.
    *
        IF    CITYI = SPACE
           OR CITYL = ZERO
             MOVE ATTR-REVERSE TO CITYH
             MOVE -1 TO CITYL
             MOVE 'You must enter a city.' TO MSG2O
             MOVE 'N' TO VALID-DATA-SW
        END-IF.
    *
        IF    ADDRI = SPACE
           OR ADDRL = ZERO
             MOVE ATTR-REVERSE TO ADDRH
             MOVE -1 TO ADDRL
             MOVE 'You must enter an address.' TO MSG2O
             MOVE 'N' TO VALID-DATA-SW
        END-IF.
    *
        IF    FNAMEI = SPACE
           OR FNAMEL = ZERO
             MOVE ATTR-REVERSE TO FNAMEH
             MOVE -1 TO FNAMEL
             MOVE 'You must enter a first name.' TO MSG2O
             MOVE 'N' TO VALID-DATA-SW
        END-IF.
    *
        IF    LNAMEI = SPACE
           OR LNAMEL = ZERO
             MOVE ATTR-REVERSE TO LNAMEH
             MOVE -1 TO LNAMEL
             MOVE 'You must enter a last name.' TO MSG2O
             MOVE 'N' TO VALID-DATA-SW
        END-IF.
    *
     2300-SET-CUSTOMER-DATA.
    *
        MOVE CUSTNO2I TO CA-CUSTOMER-NUMBER.
        MOVE LNAMEI   TO CA-LAST-NAME.
        MOVE FNAMEI   TO CA-FIRST-NAME.
        MOVE ADDRI    TO CA-ADDRESS.
        MOVE CITYI    TO CA-CITY.
        MOVE STATEI   TO CA-STATE.
        MOVE ZIPCODEI TO CA-ZIP-CODE.
    *
```

Figure 20-12   The COBOL code for the presentation logic of the program (part 8 of 9)

The presentation logic of the customer maintenance program   Page 9

```
3000-PROCESS-CHANGE-CUSTOMER.
*
    PERFORM 2100-RECEIVE-DATA-MAP.
    PERFORM 2200-EDIT-CUSTOMER-DATA.
    IF VALID-DATA
        PERFORM 2300-SET-CUSTOMER-DATA
        PERFORM 1400-PROCESS-CUSTOMER-RECORD
        IF PROCESS-OK
            SET SEND-ERASE TO TRUE
        ELSE
            SET SEND-ERASE-ALARM TO TRUE
        END-IF
        MOVE -1 TO CUSTNO1L
        PERFORM 1600-SEND-KEY-MAP
        SET PROCESS-KEY-MAP TO TRUE
    ELSE
        MOVE LOW-VALUE TO LNAMEO
                          FNAMEO
                          ADDRO
                          CITYO
                          STATEO
                          ZIPCODEO
        SET SEND-DATAONLY-ALARM TO TRUE
        PERFORM 1500-SEND-DATA-MAP
    END-IF.
*
 4000-PROCESS-DELETE-CUSTOMER.
*
    PERFORM 1400-PROCESS-CUSTOMER-RECORD.
    IF PROCESS-OK
        SET SEND-ERASE TO TRUE
    ELSE
        SET SEND-ERASE-ALARM TO TRUE
    END-IF.
    MOVE -1 TO CUSTNO1L.
    PERFORM 1600-SEND-KEY-MAP.
    SET PROCESS-KEY-MAP TO TRUE.
*
 9999-TERMINATE-PROGRAM.
*
    MOVE CA-ERR-RESP  TO ERR-RESP.
    MOVE CA-ERR-RESP2 TO ERR-RESP2.
    MOVE EIBTRNID     TO ERR-TRNID.
    MOVE CA-ERR-RSRCE TO ERR-RSRCE.
*
    EXEC CICS
        XCTL PROGRAM('SYSERR')
             COMMAREA(ERROR-PARAMETERS)
    END-EXEC.
```

Figure 20-12   The COBOL code for the presentation logic of the program (part 9 of 9)

The COBOL code for the business logic

Figure 20-13 presents the business logic for the maintenance program. As you can see on the first page of this listing, a response-code field is defined in the Working-Storage Section of this program for use with the file I/O commands. In addition, working storage includes a definition of the communication area and the customer master record.

The business logic of the customer maintenance program   Page 1

```
      IDENTIFICATION DIVISION.
*
      PROGRAM-ID.   CSTMNTB.
*
      ENVIRONMENT DIVISION.
*
      DATA DIVISION.
*
      WORKING-STORAGE SECTION.
*
      01  WORK-FIELDS.
*
          05   RESPONSE-CODE                 PIC S9(08)  COMP.
*
      01  COMMUNICATION-AREA.
*
          05   CA-CONTEXT-FLAG               PIC X(01).
               88   PROCESS-KEY-MAP                       VALUE '1'.
               88   PROCESS-ADD-CUSTOMER                  VALUE '2'.
               88   PROCESS-CHANGE-CUSTOMER               VALUE '3'.
               88   PROCESS-DELETE-CUSTOMER               VALUE '4'.
          05   CA-ACTION-FLAG                PIC X(01).
               88   ADD-REQUEST                           VALUE '1'.
               88   CHANGE-REQUEST                        VALUE '2'.
               88   DELETE-REQUEST                        VALUE '3'.
          05   CA-CUSTOMER-RECORD.
               10   CA-CUSTOMER-NUMBER       PIC X(06).
               10   CA-FIRST-NAME            PIC X(20).
               10   CA-LAST-NAME             PIC X(30).
               10   CA-ADDRESS               PIC X(30).
               10   CA-CITY                  PIC X(20).
               10   CA-STATE                 PIC X(02).
               10   CA-ZIP-CODE              PIC X(10).
          05   CA-SAVE-CUSTOMER-MASTER       PIC X(118).
          05   CA-RETURN-CONDITION           PIC X(01).
               88   PROCESS-OK                            VALUE '1'.
               88   PROCESS-ERROR                         VALUE '2'.
               88   PROCESS-SEVERE-ERROR                  VALUE '3'.
          05   CA-RETURN-MESSAGE             PIC X(79).
          05   CA-ERROR-PARAMETERS.
               10   CA-ERR-RESP              PIC S9(08)  COMP.
               10   CA-ERR-RESP2             PIC S9(08)  COMP.
               10   CA-ERR-RSRCE             PIC X(08).
*
      COPY CUSTMAS.
*
      LINKAGE SECTION.
*
      01  DFHCOMMAREA                        PIC X(334).
*
```

Figure 20-13   The COBOL code for the business logic of the program (part 1 of 5)

The main function of procedure 0000 is to determine the processing to be done based on the context flag that was passed through the communication area. Since I described this processing earlier in this chapter, I won't dwell on it here.

If the context flag indicates that the key map is being processed, procedure 1000 is performed. This procedure performs procedure 1100 to read the customer record and then evaluates the response code. If the response code is normal indicating that the customer record was found, the response depends on the action the user requested. This action is passed to the business logic in the CA-ACTION-FLAG field of the communication area. If this flag indicates an add request, procedure 1000 sets the Process-Error condition in the communication area to True and moves an error message to the CA-RETURN-MESSAGE field in the communication area. When this program returns control to the presentation logic program, this information is passed back to that program for processing. If the action flag indicates a change or delete request, the Process-OK condition is set to True, the customer record is moved to both customer areas in the communication area, and space is moved to the return message field.

If the customer record wasn't found and the user requested an add operation, procedure 1000 sets the Process-OK condition to True. Otherwise, it sets the Process-Error condition to True and moves an error message to the return message field. Finally, if the response code is anything other than normal or not-found, the Process-Severe-Error condition is set to True and procedure 9000 is performed to set the values of the error fields. This procedure simply moves fields from the EIB to the communication area so they can be passed back to the presentation logic.

The business logic of the customer maintenance program   Page 2

```
      PROCEDURE DIVISION.
 *
  0000-PROCESS-CUSTOMER-RECORD.
 *
      IF EIBCALEN NOT = LENGTH OF DFHCOMMAREA
          SET PROCESS-SEVERE-ERROR TO TRUE
          PERFORM 9000-SET-ERROR-INFO
      ELSE
          MOVE DFHCOMMAREA TO COMMUNICATION-AREA
          EVALUATE TRUE
              WHEN PROCESS-KEY-MAP
                  PERFORM 1000-PROCESS-CUSTOMER-KEY
              WHEN PROCESS-ADD-CUSTOMER
                  PERFORM 2000-PROCESS-ADD-CUSTOMER
              WHEN PROCESS-CHANGE-CUSTOMER
                  PERFORM 3000-PROCESS-CHANGE-CUSTOMER
              WHEN PROCESS-DELETE-CUSTOMER
                  PERFORM 4000-PROCESS-DELETE-CUSTOMER
          END-EVALUATE
      END-IF.
 *
      MOVE COMMUNICATION-AREA TO DFHCOMMAREA.
      EXEC CICS
          RETURN
      END-EXEC.
 *
  1000-PROCESS-CUSTOMER-KEY.
 *
      PERFORM 1100-READ-CUSTOMER-RECORD.
      EVALUATE RESPONSE-CODE
          WHEN DFHRESP(NORMAL)
              IF ADD-REQUEST
                  SET PROCESS-ERROR TO TRUE
                  MOVE 'That customer already exists.' TO
                      CA-RETURN-MESSAGE
              ELSE
                  SET PROCESS-OK TO TRUE
                  MOVE CUSTOMER-MASTER-RECORD TO CA-CUSTOMER-RECORD
                  MOVE CUSTOMER-MASTER-RECORD TO
                      CA-SAVE-CUSTOMER-MASTER
                  MOVE SPACE TO CA-RETURN-MESSAGE
              END-IF
          WHEN DFHRESP(NOTFND)
              IF ADD-REQUEST
                  SET PROCESS-OK TO TRUE
              ELSE
                  SET PROCESS-ERROR TO TRUE
                  MOVE 'That customer does not exist.' TO
                      CA-RETURN-MESSAGE
              END-IF
          WHEN OTHER
              SET PROCESS-SEVERE-ERROR TO TRUE
              PERFORM 9000-SET-ERROR-INFO
      END-EVALUATE.
 *
```

Figure 20-13   The COBOL code for the business logic of the program (part 2 of 5)

Procedure 2000 is performed to process an add operation. This procedure starts by moving the customer record in the communication area to the customer record in working storage and then performing procedure 2100 to write the record to the customer master file. If the write operation is successful, the procedure then sets the Process-OK condition to True and moves an appropriate message to the return message field. If a record is found with the same customer number, though, the Process-Error condition is set to True and an error message is moved to the return message field. Finally, if any other error occurred, the Process-Severe-Error condition is set to True and procedure 9000 is performed to set the error fields.

Procedures 3000 (on page 4 of this listing) and 4000 (on page 5) for changing and deleting a customer perform similar processing. The biggest difference is that before a record is rewritten or deleted, the record is read for update and then checked to be sure it hasn't changed since it was first read. To do that, the program compares the record just read to CA-SAVE-CUSTOMER-MASTER in the communication area. If they're the same, processing continues. Otherwise, the Process-Error condition is set to True and an error message is moved to the return message field.

The business logic of the customer maintenance program   Page 3

```
 1100-READ-CUSTOMER-RECORD.
*
     EXEC CICS
         READ FILE('CUSTMAS')
             INTO(CUSTOMER-MASTER-RECORD)
             RIDFLD(CA-CUSTOMER-NUMBER)
             RESP(RESPONSE-CODE)
     END-EXEC.
*
 2000-PROCESS-ADD-CUSTOMER.
*
     MOVE CA-CUSTOMER-RECORD TO CUSTOMER-MASTER-RECORD.
     PERFORM 2100-WRITE-CUSTOMER-RECORD.
     EVALUATE RESPONSE-CODE
         WHEN DFHRESP(NORMAL)
             SET PROCESS-OK TO TRUE
             MOVE 'Customer record added.' TO CA-RETURN-MESSAGE
         WHEN DFHRESP(DUPREC)
             SET PROCESS-ERROR TO TRUE
             MOVE 'Another user has added a record with that custo
-                'mer number.' TO CA-RETURN-MESSAGE
         WHEN OTHER
             SET PROCESS-SEVERE-ERROR TO TRUE
             PERFORM 9000-SET-ERROR-INFO
     END-EVALUATE.
*
 2100-WRITE-CUSTOMER-RECORD.
*
     EXEC CICS
         WRITE FILE('CUSTMAS')
             FROM(CUSTOMER-MASTER-RECORD)
             RIDFLD(CM-CUSTOMER-NUMBER)
             RESP(RESPONSE-CODE)
     END-EXEC.
*
```

Figure 20-13   The COBOL code for the business logic of the program (part 3 of 5)

The business logic of the customer maintenance program   Page 4

```
 3000-PROCESS-CHANGE-CUSTOMER.
*
     PERFORM 3100-READ-CUSTOMER-FOR-UPDATE.
     EVALUATE RESPONSE-CODE
         WHEN DFHRESP(NORMAL)
             IF CUSTOMER-MASTER-RECORD = CA-SAVE-CUSTOMER-MASTER
                 MOVE CA-CUSTOMER-RECORD TO
                     CUSTOMER-MASTER-RECORD
                 PERFORM 3200-REWRITE-CUSTOMER-RECORD
                 IF RESPONSE-CODE NOT = DFHRESP(NORMAL)
                     SET PROCESS-SEVERE-ERROR TO TRUE
                     PERFORM 9000-SET-ERROR-INFO
                 ELSE
                     SET PROCESS-OK TO TRUE
                     MOVE 'Customer record updated.' TO
                         CA-RETURN-MESSAGE
                 END-IF
             ELSE
                 SET PROCESS-ERROR TO TRUE
                 MOVE 'Another user has updated the record. Try ag
-                    'ain.' TO CA-RETURN-MESSAGE
             END-IF
         WHEN DFHRESP(NOTFND)
             SET PROCESS-ERROR TO TRUE
             MOVE 'Another user has deleted the record.'
                 TO CA-RETURN-MESSAGE
         WHEN OTHER
             SET PROCESS-SEVERE-ERROR TO TRUE
             PERFORM 9000-SET-ERROR-INFO
     END-EVALUATE.
*
 3100-READ-CUSTOMER-FOR-UPDATE.
*
     EXEC CICS
         READ FILE('CUSTMAS')
             INTO(CUSTOMER-MASTER-RECORD)
             RIDFLD(CA-CUSTOMER-NUMBER)
             UPDATE
             RESP(RESPONSE-CODE)
     END-EXEC.
*
 3200-REWRITE-CUSTOMER-RECORD.
*
     EXEC CICS
         REWRITE FILE('CUSTMAS')
             FROM(CUSTOMER-MASTER-RECORD)
             RESP(RESPONSE-CODE)
     END-EXEC.
*
```

Figure 20-13   The COBOL code for the business logic of the program (part 4 of 5)

The business logic of the customer maintenance program   Page 5

```
    4000-PROCESS-DELETE-CUSTOMER.
*
        PERFORM 3100-READ-CUSTOMER-FOR-UPDATE.
        EVALUATE RESPONSE-CODE
            WHEN DFHRESP(NORMAL)
                IF CUSTOMER-MASTER-RECORD = CA-SAVE-CUSTOMER-MASTER
                    PERFORM 4100-DELETE-CUSTOMER-RECORD
                    IF RESPONSE-CODE NOT = DFHRESP(NORMAL)
                        SET PROCESS-SEVERE-ERROR TO TRUE
                        PERFORM 9000-SET-ERROR-INFO
                    ELSE
                        SET PROCESS-OK TO TRUE
                        MOVE 'Customer record deleted.' TO
                            CA-RETURN-MESSAGE
                    END-IF
                ELSE
                    SET PROCESS-ERROR TO TRUE
                    MOVE 'Another user has updated the record.  Try a
-                       'gain.' TO CA-RETURN-MESSAGE
                END-IF
            WHEN DFHRESP(NOTFND)
                SET PROCESS-ERROR TO TRUE
                MOVE 'Another user has deleted the record.'
                    TO CA-RETURN-MESSAGE
            WHEN OTHER
                SET PROCESS-SEVERE-ERROR TO TRUE
                PERFORM 9000-SET-ERROR-INFO
        END-EVALUATE.
*
    4100-DELETE-CUSTOMER-RECORD.
*
        EXEC CICS
            DELETE FILE('CUSTMAS')
                   RESP(RESPONSE-CODE)
        END-EXEC.
*
    9000-SET-ERROR-INFO.
*
        MOVE EIBRESP  TO CA-ERR-RESP.
        MOVE EIBRESP2 TO CA-ERR-RESP2.
        MOVE EIBRSRCE TO CA-ERR-RSRCE.
```

Figure 20-13   The COBOL code for the business logic of the program (part 5 of 5)

Perspective

After reviewing the program presented in this chapter, I think you'll agree that the modular design technique adds an extra level of complexity when compared with traditional techniques. That's why I didn't design all the programs in this book using this technique. That would have made it much more difficult to fulfill the main purpose of this book, which is to teach you CICS. If you understand the concepts and techniques presented in this chapter, though, you should be able to apply them to any program you develop.

Terms

presentation logic
business logic
driver program
Distributed Program Link (DPL) mode

21

Introduction to CICS Web programming

In chapter 19, you learned about the CICS intercommunication features that let a non-CICS program running on another platform communicate with a CICS program. And in chapter 20, you learned how to design a modular CICS program to separate the business logic from the presentation logic so that the two can be written in different languages and run on different platforms. Now, this chapter will show you how you can use those features and techniques to access CICS applications from the Web.

CICS and the Internet

Before you learn about the various techniques for accessing CICS programs from a Web application, you should know the benefits of doing that. You should also know how a client machine that displays the user interface for a Web application is connected over the Internet to the server machine where the CICS program resides. That's what you'll learn in the next two topics.

The benefits of using CICS with Web-based applications

Figure 21-1 lists three benefits of using CICS to implement Web-based applications. Even more so than standard CICS applications, Web-based applications must be able to support large numbers of users and handle large volumes of transactions. Because of that, CICS is a good choice for implementing the back-end processing for these applications.

Just as important is the fact that a large number of business applications are already written in CICS. And those applications can be Web-enabled—in some cases without any changes to the source code—much more quickly than they can be rewritten in another language. So it makes sense to preserve the time and money that's been invested in these proven applications.

How to connect to CICS through the Internet

One of the advantages of Web-enabling CICS applications is that anyone who has access to the Internet can access those applications. To do that, the *Web browser* running on the client machine sends requests to the server using *HTTP* (*Hypertext Transfer Protocol*). Then, the server interprets the HTTP requests and invokes the appropriate CICS program in response. When the program's processing is complete, any data returned by the program is converted to *HTML* (*Hypertext Markup Language*) and sent back to the browser. The browser then processes the HTML and formats and displays the information it contains in the Web browser.

Notice in the illustration in figure 21-1 that the client machine can connect directly to a mainframe that acts as a Web server, or it can connect to the mainframe through an intermediate server such as a PC server. One advantage of using an intermediate server is that it lets you regulate the amount of traffic that's sent to the mainframe. On the other hand, a direct connection to the mainframe is simpler because it eliminates the complexities of managing the intermediate server. In either case, the server must provide software that interprets and processes the HTTP requests sent from the client machines.

The benefits of using CICS with Web-based applications

- Web-based applications require the processing of large numbers of transactions, and CICS is capable of processing billions of transactions per day.

- Web-based applications can be accessed by a large number of users at the same time, and CICS can handle those users while insuring the integrity of the data being processed.

- A large number of mission-critical business applications are already written in CICS. These applications can be Web-enabled quicker and at much less cost than they can be rewritten in another language.

Two ways to connect a client machine to a mainframe through the Internet

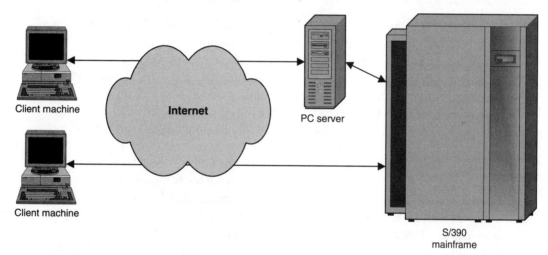

Description

- An Internet user can access a CICS application running on an S/390 mainframe directly or through an intermediate server such as a PC server. The protocol that's used to provide the communication between the machines is *TCP/IP* (*Telecommunications Protocol/Internet Protocol*).

- To access the Internet, a *Web browser* is run on the client machine. The main job of the browser is to process pages written in *HTML* (*Hypertext Markup Language*). The browser communicates with the mainframe or intermediate server using *HTTP* (*Hypertext Transfer Protocol*).

- The mainframe or intermediate server must provide Web server software that interprets the HTTP requests sent from the user's Web browser and translates them into a form that CICS recognizes.

Figure 21-1   CICS and the Internet

How to access CICS programs from a Web browser

When an HTTP request is sent from a Web browser to a server, the server must be able to interpret the request and perform the requested processing. If the request includes invoking a CICS program, the server must also be able to convert the request to a form CICS recognizes. CICS provides three techniques you can use to handle these functions.

Three techniques for accessing CICS programs

Figure 21-2 illustrates three techniques for accessing CICS programs from a Web browser. Notice that the first two techniques both use a facility called the *CICS Transaction Gateway*. The difference between the two is that with the first technique, the CICS Transaction Gateway is running on the mainframe under OS/390. With the second technique, it's running on an intermediate server. You'll see how these two techniques differ in just a minute. In either case, though, it's the CICS Transaction Gateway that communicates with the CICS server.

Notice that with both of these techniques, the CICS Transaction Gateway runs under the control of the Web server software. This is the software that provides the basic services for interpreting and processing HTTP requests. In contrast, with the third technique, a facility called *CICS Web Support* (*CWS*) provides services that allow CICS itself to function as a Web server. (Although CWS doesn't provide all the features of other Web servers, it does provide all the features that are needed to Web-enable CICS programs.) You'll learn more about CICS Web Support and the CICS Transaction Gateway in the remainder of this chapter.

How a Web server running under OS/390 accesses CICS programs

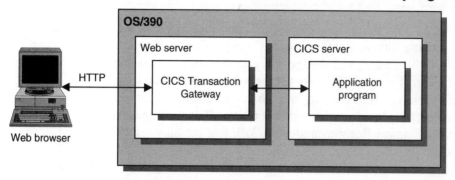

How a Web server running on a separate system accesses CICS programs

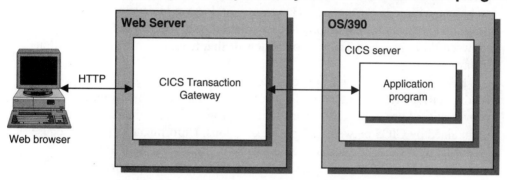

How CICS provides for Web support on its own

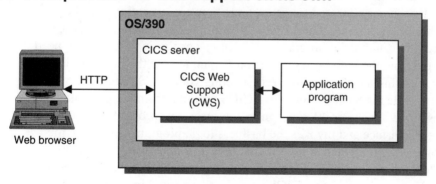

Description

- The services needed to access CICS applications from a Web browser can be provided by the *CICS Transaction Gateway* or by *CICS Web Support* (*CWS*).
- The CICS Transaction Gateway runs under the control of a Web server on either the same OS/390 system as CICS or on a separate server platform.
- CICS Web Support provides the services needed for CICS to function as a Web server on its own.

Figure 21-2   Three techniques for accessing CICS programs from a Web browser

How the CICS Transaction Gateway works

Figure 21-3 illustrates how the CICS Transaction Gateway works. Notice that you can use this facility to invoke a CICS program that contains 3270 terminal I/O. To do that, you use the *External Presentation Interface* (*EPI*). As you learned in chapter 19, EPI lets you pass 3270 data to and from a CICS program. Then, the front-end program processes that data so it can be displayed in a graphical user interface. Note that because EPI isn't supported by the CICS Transaction Gateway that runs under OS/390, you can only use EPI from an intermediate server.

When you use EPI with the CICS Transaction Gateway, it's not necessary to modify the source code for the CICS program or separate the program into presentation logic and business logic modules. That means you can use this technique with legacy programs. However, you do have to develop the front-end program that provides the graphical user interface that's displayed in the Web browser. With the CICS Transaction Gateway, that front-end program is written in Java.

Keep in mind if you use this technique that the CICS program ends by issuing a RETURN command with a trans-id, just like any other pseudo-conversational program. That means that the program's communication area is maintained by CICS between program executions. Unfortunately, that can cause a conflict with the user interface that's displayed in the Web browser.

The problem is that unlike CICS, the Internet is a *stateless environment*. So a user who displays a page at a Web browser expects to be able to walk away from it and return minutes or hours later and continue with it. But CICS may not maintain the resources allocated to the program between executions for the same length of time. Instead, when a specified time out is reached, it releases the resources allocated to the program. And that means the application will need to be restarted from the Web browser. So you'll want to take this into consideration when choosing a technique for Web-enabling your CICS programs.

If you separate the business logic in a CICS program from the presentation logic as described in chapter 20, you can then write a Java program that provides the user interface and invokes the business logic program. To invoke the business logic program, you can use the *External Call Interface* (*ECI*) or the *external CICS interface* (*EXCI*). Like EPI, you learned about these facilities in chapter 19. They let you link to a CICS program that's running on the same system (EXCI) or a separate system (ECI). Remember that when you use these facilities, the CICS program must *not* contain terminal I/O commands.

As you can see in this figure, the Java program that provides the user interface for either a 3270 program or a business logic program communicates with that program through the CICS Transaction Gateway. To do that, it uses the *classes* that are defined in the Java *class library*. These classes provide the programming interface for the gateway. The Java program uses them to invoke services provided by the *Java gateway application*. It's the gateway application that actually communicates with CICS.

An overview of the CICS Transaction Gateway

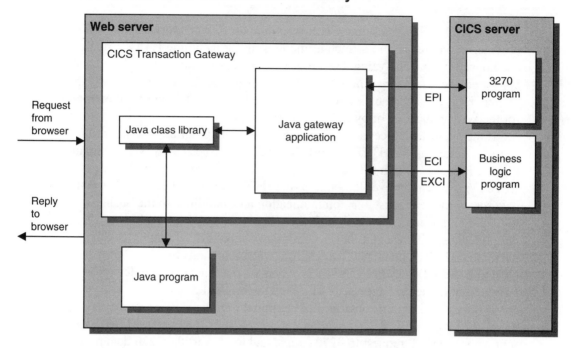

Description

- The CICS Transaction Gateway includes a *Java gateway application*, which provides services for communicating with CICS programs, and a Java *class library*, which provides the programming interface for using the gateway application services.

- A Java program provides the graphical user interface for a CICS program. The Java program communicates with the CICS application through the CICS Transaction Gateway.

- If a CICS program contains only business logic, the CICS Transaction Gateway can invoke that program using either *ECI* (the *External Call Interface*) or *EXCI* (the *external CICS interface*). EXCI is used when the CICS Transaction Gateway is running on the same OS/390 system as the CICS program, and ECI is used when it's running on a separate system.

- If the CICS Transaction Gateway is running on a separate system, you can use *EPI* (the *External Presentation Interface*) to communicate with a CICS program that includes 3270 terminal I/O. EPI lets the CICS Transaction Gateway pass 3270 data back and forth to the CICS program as if it were a 3270 display terminal.

- For more information on EPI, ECI, and EXCI, please refer to chapter 19.

Figure 21-3   How the CICS Transaction Gateway works

How CICS Web Support works

Figure 21-4 illustrates how CICS Web Support (CWS) works. This facility provides basic Web services, such as monitoring for incoming HTTP requests and converting and analyzing those requests. Once the request is analyzed and converted, the *alias transaction* is invoked. This transaction determines whether the request is processed by a CICS program that contains the presentation logic for the Web application or by the *3270 Bridge exit*.

If the request is processed by a presentation logic program, that program starts by retrieving the HTTP request. To do that, it issues CICS Web commands like WEB READ, which extracts the HTTP header information, and WEB RECEIVE, which retrieves the body of the HTTP request. Then, it converts the data sent with the request to a communication area and links to the business logic program using a standard CICS LINK command. When the business logic program ends, the presentation logic program converts the communication area data into an HTML document using CICS Web commands like DOCUMENT CREATE and DOCUMENT INSERT. When the document is complete, it's passed back to the Web browser that issued the original request.

If the CICS program contains 3270 terminal I/O, the HTTP request is processed by the 3270 Bridge exit. Its main purpose is to translate HTML data sent with the HTTP request to 3270 format and to convert the 3270 data returned by the CICS program back into HTML. The 3270 Bridge exit also invokes the CICS program using the trans-id that's passed as part of the HTTP request.

You can use the 3270 Bridge exit to execute CICS programs without changing their source code or separating the presentation logic from the business logic. In addition, you don't have to write a separate program to implement the user interface as you do with the CICS Transaction Gateway. Because of that, this is the easiest way to Web-enable an existing CICS program. However, the 3270 Bridge exit has its limitations, as you'll see in the next figure.

The 3270 Bridge exit also has the same conflict with the Internet as using EPI with the CICS Transaction Gateway does. That is, the resources allocated to the program between pseudo-conversational executions may be released while the user interface is still displayed in the Web browser. That means the user may have to restart the program if it's left sitting idle for too long. So you'll want to be sure that this is acceptable before you decide to use the 3270 Bridge exit.

Although it's not illustrated in this figure, you can also use CICS Web Support to invoke a single CICS program that contains both business logic and the Web presentation logic for an application. However, I recommend that you always separate the presentation logic from the business logic. That way, the same business logic can also be accessed through systems that use the CICS Transaction Gateway. In addition, separating the logic gives you the flexibility of implementing the presentation logic in another language later on without changing the business logic program.

An overview of CICS Web Support

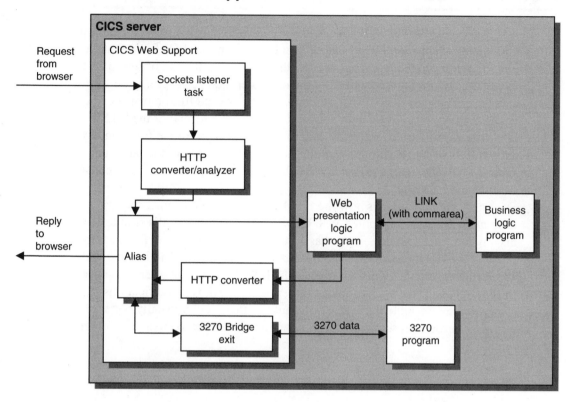

Description

- CICS Web Support eliminates the need for Web server software by providing services for intercepting HTTP requests, converting and analyzing the requests, and sending the result of the requests back to the Web browser.

- The *sockets listener task* monitors for incoming HTTP requests. When one is received, it's converted from ASCII to EBCDIC and its contents are analyzed. Then, the *alias transaction* determines how the request is processed.

- If the HTTP request is for a CICS program that contains only business logic, the alias invokes the program that contains the Web presentation logic for the application. This program uses CICS Web commands to retrieve and interpret the request. Then, it can convert any data sent with the request to a communication area and invoke the business logic program.

- The Web presentation logic program formats the data sent back to it from the business logic program into an HTML document, again using Web commands. Then, the document is converted to ASCII and sent back to the Web browser that issued the request.

- If the HTTP request is for a CICS program that contains 3270 terminal I/O, the alias passes it to the *3270 Bridge exit*, which invokes the program and handles the translation of the 3270 data. See figure 21-5 for more information on the 3270 Bridge exit.

Figure 21-4   How CICS Web Support works

How the CICS 3270 Bridge exit works

You can use the 3270 Bridge exit of CICS Web Support to Web-enable a CICS program that uses BMS mapsets and 3270 terminal I/O. To do that, you include macros in the BMS mapset like those shown at the top of figure 21-5. These macros are for the mapset for the customer inquiry program you saw in chapter 2. They cause an HTML document to be created for the mapset when it's assembled. In addition, they let you customize the format of the HTML page that's displayed. For example, the macros shown here make the function key assignments available through buttons; add a title and logo to the page; and suppress the display of the first and last lines of the map (the ones that contain the title and PF keys).

This figure also shows how the HTML page for the customer inquiry program will be displayed in a Web browser. As you can see, it's similar to the display produced by BMS, but it has a more graphical interface. Even so, the graphics are rudimentary when compared with those you'll find in most Web applications. Although you can modify the HTML document after it's generated so the page looks the way you want it to, you'll lose those modifications if you change and reassemble the mapset. Because of that, you're usually better off writing your own presentation logic program if you want to create a customized interface.

BMS macros for creating HTML documents

```
MACRO
DFHMSX
DFHMDX MAPSET=*,MAP=*,ENTER='Enter',RESET=NO,           X
       CLEAR='Clear',PF3='Exit',PF12='Cancel',           X
       TITLE='Customer Inquiry',                          X
       BGCOLOR=WHITE,                                      X
       MASTHEAD=www.murach.com/images/murachlogo.gif
DFHMDX MAPSET=INQSET1,MAP=INQMAP1,SUPPRESS=((1,*),(24,*))
MEND
```

The customer inquiry screen displayed in a Web browser

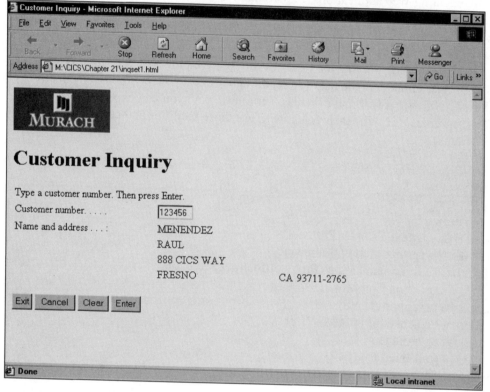

Description

- The 3270 Bridge exit lets CICS programs that perform 3270 terminal I/O run on a Web browser with no source code changes. The main function of the 3270 Bridge exit is to translate HTML data to 3270 data, and vice versa.

- Before you can use the 3270 Bridge exit with a program, you must modify the BMS mapset for the program to include macros like those shown above. When you reassemble the mapset, these macros cause an HTML version of the mapset to be produced. The 3270 Bridge exit uses this mapset to perform the necessary translation.

- The BMS macros for creating HTML documents were introduced with CICS TS 1.3 and provide for some basic formatting of HTML pages.

Figure 21-5   How the 3270 Bridge exit works

Perspective

Now that you've completed this chapter, you should have a basic idea of the different techniques that are used to Web-enable CICS programs. As you can see, IBM is committed to providing the tools required to keep both old and new CICS applications running on the Internet. So this is certain to be a part of CICS application programming in the years to come.

Keep in mind, though, that there's a lot more you need to know about using the CICS Transaction Gateway and CICS Web Support before you can start implementing Web applications. In particular, if your shop is using CICS Web Support, you need to know about the Web commands CICS provides. And if your shop is using the CICS Transaction Gateway, you need to know about the services provided by the Java class library and the Java gateway application.

Keep in mind, too, that the facilities for Web-enabling CICS programs are still in their infancy. In the near future, though, I expect to see improvements to these facilities that will make them easier to use. And you can expect to see books from us that will teach you how to use these facilities and code Java programs.

Terms

Web browser
HTTP (Hypertext Transfer Protocol)
HTML (Hypertext Markup Language)
TCP/IP (Telecommunications Protocol/Internet Protocol)
CICS Transaction Gateway
CICS Web Support (CWS)
External Presentation Interface (EPI)
stateless environment
External Call Interface (ECI)
External CICS interface (EXCI)
class library
class
Java gateway application
alias transaction
3270 Bridge exit
sockets listener task

22

What else a maintenance programmer needs to know

If you're assigned the task of maintaining existing CICS programs, you may come across some coding conventions that you haven't seen in the programs in this book. That's particularly true if the programs are *legacy programs* that were written to run under older compilers (typically, the OS/VS COBOL compiler). In this chapter, you'll learn about the most common coding conventions used in legacy programs. That will make it easier for you to maintain programs that use these conventions.

How to use the HANDLE AID command

In chapter 2, you learned how to use the EIBAID field in the Execute Interface Block to determine what attention key the user pressed to start a program. However, CICS provides another technique you can use to detect attention keys. To implement this technique, you use the HANDLE AID command. Although I don't recommend you use this command, you may come across it in programs written by other programmers. So you'll want to understand how it works.

How to code the HANDLE AID command

Figure 22-1 shows the format of the HANDLE AID command. This command names one or more attention keys and the procedure that should be executed when each attention key is detected. Note that the HANDLE AID command itself doesn't detect the use of the AID key; it's the RECEIVE MAP command that does that. As a result, the HANDLE AID command is always used along with a RECEIVE MAP command. In effect, the HANDLE AID command sets up the processing to be done if the RECEIVE MAP command detects the use of an AID key.

For example, consider the first HANDLE AID command shown in this figure. It specifies that the program should pass control to the procedure named 1100-PF3 if the user presses PF3 and to the procedure named 1100-CLEAR if the user presses the Clear key. If the user presses any other key, no special action will be taken.

If you want a program to perform some generic processing when a key other than the ones identified in the HANDLE AID command is pressed, you can include the ANYKEY option on this command. This option is illustrated in the second example in this figure. Here, if any key other than PF3 or Clear is pressed, the program will pass control to the procedure named 1100-ANYKEY. Note, however, that the ANYKEY option doesn't provide for the Enter key. To handle this key, you have to include ENTER as one of the options. Usually, though, you won't do any special processing for the Enter key (the basic processing in the program will handle it), so you won't code it on the HANDLE AID command.

This example also illustrates what happens when you specify an attention key without a procedure name. In this case, if the user presses the Clear key, no special action is taken. That's true even if the ANYKEY option is included.

You should realize that the actions specified by the HANDLE AID command remain in effect until another HANDLE AID command is issued. Keep in mind, though, that this command is used in conjunction with a RECEIVE MAP command, and a pseudo-conversational program issues a single RECEIVE MAP during any execution of the program. Because of that, you don't have to worry about coding conflicting HANDLE AID commands. Instead, you just code one HANDLE AID command for each RECEIVE MAP command.

The syntax of the HANDLE AID command

```
EXEC CICS
    HANDLE AID
        option[(procedure-name)]...
END-EXEC
```

Option	Description
option	The name of the attention key to be handled.
procedure-name	The name of the procedure that control is passed to when the attention key is detected. If omitted, the attention key is ignored.

Common options

Option	Description
PA1-PA3	Program attention keys
PF1-PF24	Program function keys
ENTER	The Enter key
CLEAR	The Clear key
ANYKEY	Any attention key not previously specified in a HANDLE AID command, except the Enter key

A HANDLE AID command that handles two AID keys

```
EXEC CICS
    HANDLE AID PF3(1100-PF3)
            CLEAR(1100-CLEAR)
END-EXEC.
```

A HANDLE AID command that handles all AID keys except Enter

```
EXEC CICS
    HANDLE AID PF3(1100-PF3)
            ANYKEY(1100-ANYKEY)
            CLEAR
END-EXEC.
```

Description

- The HANDLE AID command tells your program what to do when the user presses an attention key. It can specify the processing to be done for up to 16 attention keys. To handle more than 16 attention keys, code two or more HANDLE AID commands.

- The attention key the user pressed is detected when the RECEIVE MAP command is issued. Because of that, the program must issue a RECEIVE MAP command even if it doesn't need to receive any input data from the terminal.

- If the procedure name is omitted for an attention key, no action is taken when the specified key is detected. That's true even if the ANYKEY option is specified.

Figure 22-1   How to code the HANDLE AID command

A RECEIVE MAP procedure that uses the HANDLE AID command

To help you understand how the HANDLE AID and RECEIVE MAP commands work together, figure 22-2 presents a typical RECEIVE MAP procedure that uses the HANDLE AID command. Here, the HANDLE AID command sets up attention key processing for PF3, PF12, the Clear key, and any other key besides Enter. Then, the RECEIVE MAP command that follows receives the map and detects the use of AID keys.

Notice that the entire procedure is coded as a section. Then, each procedure named by the HANDLE AID command is coded as a paragraph within that section. In addition, a final paragraph that includes just the Exit statement is included in the section. After the other paragraphs complete their processing, they branch to the exit paragraph with a Go To statement. (The 1100-ANYKEY paragraph doesn't include a Go To statement because control will automatically fall through to the exit paragraph.)

If you've never seen sections used in a COBOL program before, this may seem strange to you. But this structure provides the easiest way to implement AID key detection when you use the HANDLE AID command. Then, you use a Perform statement to perform the entire section, which includes all of the procedures named in the HANDLE AID command. And when the Exit statement in that section is executed, control returns to the statement that follows the Perform statement.

Besides using sections and Go To statements, the HANDLE AID command forces you to issue a RECEIVE MAP command just to detect the use of an attention key. That means you have to use this command even if the map you're receiving doesn't contain any data that the program will use. In contrast, when you use EIBAID to detect attention keys, you use the RECEIVE MAP command only if you need to retrieve data from the screen.

A RECEIVE MAP procedure that uses HANDLE AID

```
1100-RECEIVE-INQUIRY-MAP SECTION.
*
    EXEC CICS
        HANDLE AID PF3(1100-PF3)
                   PF12(1100-PF3)
                   CLEAR(1100-CLEAR)
                   ANYKEY(1100-ANYKEY)
    END-EXEC.
*
    EXEC CICS
        RECEIVE MAP('INQMAP1')
                MAPSET('INQSET1')
                INTO(INQMAP1I)
    END-EXEC.
    GO TO 1100-EXIT.
*
 1100-PF3.
*
    MOVE 'Y' TO END-SESSION-SW.
    GO TO 1100-EXIT.
*
 1100-CLEAR.
*
    MOVE 'Y' TO CLEAR-KEY-SW.
    GO TO 1100-EXIT.
*
 1100-ANYKEY.
*
    MOVE 'Invalid key pressed.' TO MSGO.
    MOVE 'N' TO VALID-DATA-SW.
*
 1100-EXIT.
*
    EXIT.
*
```

Description

- Programs that use HANDLE AID are typically coded in sections. Then, the HANDLE AID command and the corresponding RECEIVE MAP command are coded in the main paragraph of that section, and a Perform statement is used to perform the section.

- Each procedure named in the HANDLE AID command is coded as a separate paragraph within the section. In addition, a final exit paragraph is included to provide an exit point for the section.

- Each paragraph within the RECEIVE MAP section ends with a Go To statement that branches to the exit paragraph. The exception is the last paragraph before the exit paragraph, in which case control falls through to the exit paragraph.

Figure 22-2   A RECEIVE MAP procedure that uses the HANDLE AID command

How to use the HANDLE CONDITION command

Throughout this book, you've seen how to use response code checking to detect and handle exceptional conditions that can result from a CICS command. However, you can also handle exceptional conditions using the HANDLE CONDITION command. Because response code checking is easier to use, you probably won't see the HANDLE CONDITION command in newer programs. But you may see it in older programs that you're asked to maintain.

How to code the HANDLE CONDITION command

Figure 22-3 presents the syntax of the HANDLE CONDITION command. Like the HANDLE AID command, this command sets up processing to be done as a result of a subsequent command. In this case, HANDLE CONDITION names the exceptional conditions that require special processing and the procedures that should be executed in response to those conditions.

The first example in this figure illustrates how this works. Here, if a subsequent command completes with a DUPREC condition, procedure 3100-DUPREC is executed. Similarly, if a command completes with the NOSPACE condition, procedure 3100-NOSPACE is executed. And if a command completes with the NOTOPEN condition, procedure 3100-NOTOPEN is executed. If any other condition occurs, though, no special action is taken.

If you want to provide for any condition not explicitly named on the HANDLE CONDITION command, you can code the special ERROR condition as illustrated in the second example. In this case, if any exceptional condition other than DUPREC and NOTOPEN occurs, the procedure named 3100-ERROR will be executed.

You can also nullify the effect of one or more actions that are specified on a HANDLE CONDITION command. To do that, you issue another HANDLE CONDITION command that names the conditions you want to nullify without a procedure name. This is illustrated in the third example in this figure. Here, if the NOSPACE condition was specified on a previous HANDLE CONDITION command, this command will override the action specified by the previous command. As a result, no special action will be taken for this condition.

The syntax of the HANDLE CONDITION command

```
EXEC CICS
    HANDLE CONDITION condition-name[(procedure-name)]...
END-EXEC
```

Option	Description
condition-name	The name of a CICS exceptional condition to be handled. The special condition name ERROR traps all exceptional conditions not otherwise listed.
procedure-name	The name of the procedure that control is transferred to when the specified condition occurs. If omitted, the HANDLE CONDITION action previously specified for that condition is canceled.

A HANDLE CONDITION command that handles three conditions

```
EXEC CICS
    HANDLE CONDITION DUPREC(3100-DUPREC)
                     NOSPACE(3100-NOSPACE)
                     NOTOPEN(3100-NOTOPEN)
END-EXEC.
```

A HANDLE CONDITION command that handles all exceptional conditions

```
EXEC CICS
    HANDLE CONDITION DUPREC(3100-DUPREC)
                     NOTOPEN(3100-NOTOPEN)
                     ERROR(3100-ERROR)
END-EXEC.
```

A HANDLE CONDITION command that nullifies the effect of a previous HANDLE CONDITION action

```
EXEC CICS
    HANDLE CONDITION NOSPACE
END-EXEC.
```

Description

- The HANDLE condition command tells your program what to do when an exceptional condition occurs as the result of any subsequent CICS command.
- You can specify up to 16 conditions in a single HANDLE CONDITION command. To handle more than 16 conditions, code two or more HANDLE CONDITION commands.
- If both HANDLE AID and HANDLE CONDITION commands are in effect when you issue a RECEIVE MAP command, the HANDLE AID command takes precedence.

Figure 22-3   How to code the HANDLE CONDITION command

A READ procedure that uses the HANDLE CONDITION command

Figure 22-4 shows how a HANDLE CONDITION command is typically used. Here, this command is paired with a READ command in a procedure that reads a record from a customer master file. Because several paragraphs and Go To statements are required to code this procedure, it's implemented as a section. That way, the program can issue a Perform statement to perform the entire section. Then, when the processing done by the section is complete, the Exit statement at the end of the section will return control to the statement that follows the Perform statement.

In this example, the HANDLE CONDITION command specifies that if the NOTFND condition is raised, the program should pass control to the paragraph named 2100-NOTFND. This paragraph simply sets RECORD-FOUND-SW to N, then branches to the paragraph named 2100-RESET. This paragraph contains another HANDLE CONDITION command that deactivates the condition handling established by the first HANDLE CONDITION command. That way, it won't affect the handling of conditions that may occur as a result of CICS commands issued elsewhere in the program.

After the HANDLE CONDITION command in the reset paragraph is executed, control falls through to the last paragraph in the section, which contains the Exit statement. Although you might think that you could code this statement at the end of the reset paragraph, you can't. That's because older COBOL compilers required that the Exit statement be coded in a paragraph by itself.

Similar processing occurs if any error other than NOTFND occurs. In this case, the ERROR condition in the HANDLE CONDITION command indicates that the program should branch to the paragraph named 2100-ERROR. This paragraph sets RECORD-FOUND-SW to N and UNRECOVERABLE-ERROR-SW to Y. Then, control falls through to the reset and exit paragraphs.

Of course, if the READ command results in a NORMAL condition, neither of the procedures specified in the HANDLE CONDITION command are executed. Instead, the Move statement that follows the READ command sets RECORD-FOUND-SW to Y, and the Go To statement that follows branches to the reset paragraph.

A READ procedure that uses HANDLE CONDITION

```
2100-READ-CUSTOMER-RECORD SECTION.
*
    EXEC CICS
        HANDLE CONDITION NOTFND(2100-NOTFND)
                         ERROR(2100-ERROR)
    END-EXEC.
*
    EXEC CICS
        READ DATASET('CUSTMAS')
             INTO(CUSTOMER-MASTER-RECORD)
             RIDFLD(CM-CUSTOMER-NUMBER)
    END-EXEC.
    MOVE 'Y' TO RECORD-FOUND-SW.
    GO TO 2100-RESET.
*
 2100-NOTFND.
*
    MOVE 'N' TO RECORD-FOUND-SW.
    GO TO 2100-RESET.
*
 2100-ERROR.
*
    MOVE 'N' TO RECORD-FOUND-SW.
    MOVE 'Y' TO UNRECOVERABLE-ERROR-SW.
*
 2100-RESET.
*
    EXEC CICS
        HANDLE CONDITION NOTFND
                         ERROR
    END-EXEC.
*
 2100-EXIT.
*
    EXIT.
```

Description

- Programs that use HANDLE CONDITION are typically coded in sections. Then, the HANDLE CONDITION command and the corresponding CICS command are coded in the main paragraph of that section, and a Perform statement is used to perform the section.

- Each procedure named in the HANDLE CONDITION command is coded as a separate paragraph within the section. In addition, a final exit paragraph is included to provide an exit point for the section.

- A section that uses HANDLE CONDITION typically includes a paragraph that nullifies the actions set by that command. That way, the actions are in effect only for the commands issued within that section. The other paragraphs can branch to this paragraph (or, if it's omitted, the exit paragraph) with a Go To statement when necessary.

Figure 22-4   A READ procedure that uses the HANDLE CONDITION command

How to access Linkage Section data using BLL cells

In chapter 8, you learned how to use the ADDRESS command to establish addressability to an area of storage owned by CICS like the CWA. To do that, you use the ADDRESS special register to assign the address to an area in the Linkage Section of the program. Because this special register only became available with the VS COBOL II compiler, though, any programs written to run under OS/VS COBOL couldn't use it. Instead, they had to use a convention called *Base Locator for Linkage*, or *BLL*. Figure 22-5 illustrates this convention.

To use this convention, you must define an 01-level item in the Linkage Section following DFHCOMMAREA. In this example, I named this item BLL-CELLS. Each field in BLL-CELLS is a pointer that stores the address of a Linkage Section field. The first pointer points to the BLL-CELLS item itself. Then, each subsequent pointer points to an 01-level item that follows in the Linkage Section. In this figure, for example, the pointer named BLL-CWA is used to establish addressability to the Linkage Section field named COMMON-WORK-AREA. Note that if two or more 01-level items are named in the Linkage Section, the BLL pointers must be defined in the same order as those items.

Before you can use the BLL pointers to address a field in the Linkage Section, you must load the pointers with the correct addresses. To do that, you use the ADDRESS command as shown in this figure. This command simply loads the address of the named area into the specified BLL cell. For example, the command shown here loads the address of the CWA into the pointer named BLL-CWA.

Notice in this example that the ADDRESS command is followed by a Service Reload statement. This statement is a compiler directive that's necessary because of the optimizing features of the OS/VS COBOL compiler. It ensures that addressability is established and should be coded any time your program changes the contents of a BLL cell. In this case, after the Service Reload statement is issued, the program can refer to the fields in the CWA by the names defined in the Linkage Section.

Code that accesses the CWA using BLL cells

```
LINKAGE SECTION.
*
01   DFHCOMMAREA              PIC X.
*
01   BLL-CELLS.
*
     05   FILLER              PIC S9(8)   COMP.
     05   BLL-CWA             PIC S9(8)   COMP.
*
01   COMMON-WORK-AREA.
*
     05   CWA-CURRENT-DATE    PIC X(8).
     05   CWA-COMPANY-NAME    PIC X(30).
*
PROCEDURE DIVISION.
*
000-PROCESS-CUSTOMER-INQUIRY.
*

     .
     .
     EXEC CICS
         ADDRESS CWA(BLL-CWA)
     END-EXEC.
     SERVICE RELOAD BLL-CWA.
     MOVE CWA-COMPANY-NAME TO COMPO.
     .
     .
```

Description

- To establish addressability to a field in the Linkage Section using the OS/VS COBOL compiler, you must use a convention called *Base Locator for Linkage*, or *BLL*.

- To use the BLL convention, you define an 01-level item in the Linkage Section following DFHCOMMAREA. Then, each field in this group item is a pointer (defined as PIC S9(8) COMP) that will store the address of the Linkage Section fields that follow. (The first pointer points to the BLL group item itself.)

- To load the address of a Linkage Section field into a pointer field, you use the ADDRESS command. This command must be followed by a Service Reload statement that names the pointer field.

- Service Reload is a compiler directive that's required by the OS/VS COBOL compiler any time a BLL cell is changed.

Figure 22-5   How to access Linkage Section data using BLL cells

How to use the LENGTH option

Although it's not shown in the syntax of the CICS commands presented in this book, many of these commands can be coded with the LENGTH option. This option was required on some commands in programs written to run under the OS/VS COBOL compiler. If a program added or updated records in a file that contained variable-length records, for example, the LENGTH option had to be included on the WRITE or REWRITE command to indicate the length of the record to be written. Similarly, this option had to be coded on LINK, XCTL, and RETURN commands that included the COMMAREA option to indicate the length of that area.

Figure 22-6 lists all of the commands presented in this book that can be coded with the LENGTH option. Since VS COBOL II and later compilers don't require that you code this option, you'll usually omit it. However, you may still see it in older programs.

The syntax of the LENGTH option

```
LENGTH(data-name)
```

Common commands that provide for the LENGTH option

Program control	File control	Interval control
LINK	READ	START
XCTL	WRITE	RETRIEVE
RETURN	REWRITE	

Terminal control	Task control	Temporary storage control
SEND TEXT	ENQ	READQ TS
	DEQ	WRITEQ TS

A READ command that uses the LENGTH option

```
EXEC CICS
    READ FILE('INVOICE')
        INTO(INVOICE-RECORD)
        LENGTH(INVOICE-RECORD-LENGTH)
        RIDFLD(INVOICE-NUMBER)
        RESP(RESPONSE-CODE)
END-EXEC.
```

Description

- The LENGTH option specifies the name of a binary halfword field that contains the length of the data to be processed. This option is required on many of the CICS commands when they're used under OS/VS COBOL. But it's optional, and typically omitted, under newer compilers.

- The LENGTH option is required on the READ, WRITE, and REWRITE commands only when the file being processed contains variable-length records or when the SYSID option is used to identify the remote system where the file resides as described in chapter 19.

- Before you issue the READ command, you should set the field named on the LENGTH option to the length of the INTO field. When the record is read, the LENGTH field is set to the actual length of the record.

- Before you issue the WRITE or REWRITE command, you must set the LENGTH field to the length of the record being written.

- The LENGTH option is required on the LINK, XCTL, and RETURN commands only if the COMMAREA option is included.

- The LENGTH option is required on the START command only if the FROM option is included.

Figure 22-6   How to use the LENGTH option

Perspective

As I've said throughout this chapter, the coding conventions presented here aren't typically used for new program development. So you'll probably come across them only if you're maintaining existing programs. In that case, you need to understand how these conventions work. Keep in mind, though, that even if you're asked to maintain programs that use these conventions, you shouldn't attempt to replace them with newer conventions (unless, of course, you're specifically asked to do that). Instead, you should just focus on the maintenance task at hand and get it done as quickly and efficiently as possible.

Terms

legacy program
Base Locator for Linkage (BLL)

Index

F

Y

The CICS Programmer's Desk Reference

Second Edition   **Doug Lowe**

Ever feel buried by IBM manuals?

It seems like you need stacks of them, close at hand, if you want to be an effective CICS programmer. Because frankly, there's just too much you have to know to do your job well; you can't keep it all in your head.

That's why Doug Lowe decided to write *The CICS Programmer's Desk Reference*. In it, he's collected all the information you need to have at your fingertips, and organized it into 12 sections that make it easy for you to find what you're looking for. So there are sections on:

- BMS macro instructions—their formats (with an explanation of each parameter) and coding examples
- CICS commands—their syntax (with an explanation of each parameter), coding examples, and suggestions on how and when to use each one most effectively
- MVS and DOS/VSE JCL for CICS applications
- AMS commands for handling VSAM files
- details for MVS users on how to use ISPF
- complete model programs, including specs, design, and code

- a summary of CICS program design techniques that lead to simple, maintainable, and efficient programs
- guidelines for testing and debugging your CICS applications
- and more!

So clear the IBM manuals off your terminal table. Let the *Desk Reference* be your everyday guide to CICS instead.

CICS Desk Reference, 12 sections, 507 pages, **$49.50**
ISBN 0-911625-68-2

Note: The *Desk Reference* has not yet been revised to the latest versions of CICS (it covers up through CICS 3.3). However, because CICS has been a mature product for so long, most of the material is still current. So although there are a few commands and some command options that aren't included, this is still a valuable reference that will save any CICS/COBOL programmer many hours of research (we wouldn't keep it in our product line otherwise).

DB2 for the COBOL Programmer

Part 1 / Second Edition   **Curtis Garvin and Steve Eckols**

If you're looking for a practical DB2 book that focuses on application programming, this is the book for you. Written from the programmer's point of view, it will quickly teach you what you need to know to access and process DB2 data in your COBOL programs using embedded SQL. You'll learn:

- what DB2 is and how it works, so you'll have the background you need to program more easily and logically

- how to design and code application programs that retrieve and update DB2 data

- how to use joins and unions to combine data from two or more tables into a single table (that includes recent enhancements like outer joins and the explicit syntax for inner joins that simplify your coding)

- how to use column functions and scalar functions to save COBOL coding

- how to code subqueries whenever one SQL statement depends on the results of another

- how to handle the complications caused by variable-length data and null values in DB2 tables

- how to use error handling techniques and ROLLBACK to protect DB2 data

- why program efficiency is vital under DB2...and how to use the locking features right so you don't tie up the whole system

- how to use SPUFI and QMF to create the test tables you need to debug your programs

- how to develop DB2 programs interactively (using DB2I, a TSO facility) or in batch

So if you want to learn how to write DB2 application programs, get a copy of this book today!

DB2, Part 1, 15 chapters, 431 pages, **$45.00**
ISBN 1-890774-02-2

DB2 for the COBOL Programmer

Part 2 / Second Edition   **Curtis Garvin and Anne Prince**

Once you've mastered the basics of DB2 programming, there's still plenty to learn. So this book teaches you all the advanced DB2 features that a senior programmer or programmer/analyst needs to know...and shows you when to use each one. You'll learn:

- how data sharing works on the parallel sysplex and other System/390 configurations

- advanced locking concepts that let you understand how locking and data sharing affect each other and what impact that has on program efficiency

- how to use dynamic SQL

- how to work with distributed DB2 data

- how to execute stored procedures that move SQL code off of the client and onto the database server to reduce network overhead

- how to use DB2 from CICS programs

- what you need to know about database administration to set up a quality assurance environment

- and more!

So don't wait to expand your DB2 skills. Get a copy of this book TODAY.

DB2, Part 2, 13 chapters, 395 pages, **$45.00**
ISBN 1-890774-03-0

 www.murach.com • Toll-free 1-800-221-5528 (Weekdays, 8-5 Pacific Time) • Fax 1-559-440-0963

For mainframe programmers

Murach's Structured COBOL with CD ROM	$62.50
Micro Focus Personal COBOL (compiler and Animator on CD ROM)	50.00
Murach's CICS for the COBOL Programmer	$54.00
The CICS Programmer's Desk Reference (Second Edition)	49.50
DB2 for the COBOL Programmer, Part 1 (Second Edition)	$45.00
DB2 for the COBOL Programmer, Part 2 (Second Edition)	45.00
MVS JCL (Second Edition)	$49.50
MVS TSO, Part 1 (Second Edition)	42.50
MVS TSO, Part 2 (Second Edition)	42.50

For desktop developers

Murach's Visual Basic 6	$45.00
Client/Server Programming: Access 97	40.00

Coming soon

Murach's Beginning Java 2	Scheduled for September 2001

*Prices and availability are subject to change. Please visit our web site or call for current information.

Our unlimited guarantee...when you order directly from us

You must be satisfied with our books. If they aren't better than any other programming books you've ever used...both for training and reference....you can send them back for a full refund. No questions asked!

Your opinions count

If you have any comments on this book, I'm eager to get them. Thanks for your feedback!

To comment by

E-mail: murachbooks@murach.com
Web: www.murach.com
Postal mail: Mike Murach & Associates, Inc.
2560 West Shaw Lane, Suite 101
Fresno, California 93711-2765

To order now,

Call toll-free
1-800-221-5528
(Weekdays, 8 am to 5 pm Pacific Time)

Fax: 1-559-440-0963

Web: www.murach.com

Mike Murach & Associates, Inc.
Practical computer books since 1974